Residential Design Using Autodesk® Revit® 2027

Daniel John Stine

SDC
PUBLICATIONS

SDC Publications
P.O. Box 1334
Mission, KS 66222
913-262-2664
www.SDCpublications.com
Publisher: Stephen Schroff

Examination Copies
Books received as examination copies are for review purposes only and may not be made available for student use. Resale of examination copies is prohibited.

Electronic Files
Any electronic files associated with this book are licensed to the original user only. These files may not be transferred to any other party.

Trademarks
Autodesk®, **AutoCAD®**, **Maya®, mental ray®, Revit®, 3ds Max®** are registered trademarks or trademarks of Autodesk, Inc., and/or its subsidiaries and/or affiliates in the USA and/or other countries. All other trademarks are trademarks of their respective holders.

Disclaimer
The author and publisher of this book have used their best efforts in preparing this book. These efforts include the development, research and testing of the material presented. The author and publisher shall not be liable in any event for incidental or consequential damages with, or arising out of, the furnishing, performance, or use of the material.

ISBN-13: 978-1-63057-798-8
ISBN-10: 1-63057-798-7

Printed and bound in the United States of America.

FOREWORD

To the Student:

This book has been written with the assumption that the reader has no prior experience using Autodesk® Revit®. The intent of this book is to provide students with a well-rounded understanding of architectural tools and techniques for use in both school and industry.

The book consists of a series of tutorials that primarily focus on developing a single project. When you finish the book, you will have learned how to document and model all of the major architectural aspects of a residential project. This includes floor plans, interior and exterior elevations, wall and building sections, 2D details, door and room finish schedules, and organizing drawings on sheets for printing.

The exclusive **online content** contains several videos that supplement the book. Studying these videos along with the book will help the reader to better understand Autodesk Revit features. The book and videos will also help you prepare for the Autodesk Revit Architecture Certification Exam; see Appendix A for more information.

Errata:
Please check the publisher's website from time to time for any errors or typos found in this book after it went to the printer. Simply browse to www.SDCpublications.com, and then navigate to the page for this book. Click the **View/Submit errata** link in the upper right corner of the page. If you find an error, please submit it so we can correct it in the next edition.

You may contact the publisher with comments or suggestions at service@SDCpublications.com.
Please do not email with Revit questions unless they relate to a problem with this book.

To the Instructor:

This book was designed for the architectural student using *Autodesk Revit 2027*. Throughout the book, the student develops a single-family residence. The drawings start with floor plans and progress to photo-realistic renderings.

Throughout the book, many Autodesk Revit *architectural* tools and techniques are covered while creating the house BIM. Also, in a way that is applicable to the current exercise, industry standards and conventions are discussed. Access to the internet is required for some exercises.

Each chapter concludes with a self-exam and review questions. The answers to the self-exam questions are provided, but the answers to the review questions are not (they can only be found in the Instructor's Guide available from the publisher).

Since its initial release in 2005, this book has been updated each year to reflect the latest version of Autodesk Revit. The printed text has always been available for the fall term.

An Instructor's Resource Guide is available for this book. It contains:

- Answers to the questions at the end of each chapter
- Example images of each exercise to be turned in (can be used to grade students' work)
- Outline of tools and topics to be covered in each lesson's lecture
- Suggestions for additional student work (for each lesson)
- Author's direct contact information

See Appendix A for an introduction to the **Autodesk Certification Exam** and available *study guide* and *practice exam software*, prepared by Daniel John Stine, from SDC Publications.

About the Author:
Daniel John Stine, AIA, CSI, CDT, IES, WELL AP, is a distinguished Wisconsin-registered architect with over two decades of professional experience, currently serving as the Director of Design Technology at Lake Flato Architects, a leading architecture firm based in San Antonio, Texas. Dan is an active member of the national AIA Technology in Architectural Practice Leadership Group (TAP LG) and the AIA AI Task Force, where his expertise helps advance the industry in the adoption and use of technology.

Dan's remarkable contributions to the field include pioneering the integration of Building Information Modeling (BIM) for lighting analysis with ElumTools, early-stage energy modeling using Autodesk Insight, and immersive experiences through virtual reality (VR) and augmented reality (AR) technologies with platforms like HTC Vive, Oculus Rift, Fuzor, Enscape, and Microsoft HoloLens 2. He has also co-developed the Electrical Productivity Pack for Revit, a tool that enhances electrical design efficiency, marketed by ATG under the CTC Software brand. His innovative work has caught the attention of industry giants Dell and Autodesk, leading to feature videos that showcase his impactful contributions to architecture and design technology.

Dan is an esteemed speaker who has shared his insights on BIM, design technology, and sustainable design at prestigious international forums across the USA, Mexico, Canada, Europe, Asia, and Australia, including Autodesk University, RTC/BILT, and various AIA national and state conferences. His engagement with the global architectural community led to a special invitation from Autodesk to collaborate on future Revit features at their largest R&D facility in Shanghai, China, in 2017.

Dedicated to educating the next generation of architects, Dan is an adjunct professor at North Dakota State University, where he mentors graduate students in architecture. His academic contributions span lectures and workshops at universities across the United States, fostering growth and innovation in both architecture and interior design education. Dan's affiliations with professional organizations such as the American Institute of Architects, the Construction Specifications Institute, the Illuminating Engineering Society, and the Autodesk Developer Network underscore his commitment to excellence and innovation in the architectural field. Through his teaching and pioneering work, Dan continues to shape the future of architectural design and technology.

Dan writes about design on his blog, BIM Chapters, and in his textbooks published by SDC Publications:

- *Residential Design Using Autodesk Revit 2027*
- *Commercial Design Using Autodesk Revit 2027*
- *Design Integration Using Autodesk Revit 2027 (Architecture, Structure and MEP)*
- *Interior Design Using Autodesk Revit 2027 (with co-author Aaron Hansen)*
- *Autodesk Revit 2021 Architectural Command Reference*
- *Residential Design Using AutoCAD 2027*
- *Commercial Design Using AutoCAD 2023*
- *Chapters in Architectural Drawing (with co-author Steven H. McNeill, AIA, LEED AP)*
- *Interior Design Using Hand Sketching, SketchUp and Photoshop (also with Steven H. McNeill)*
- *SketchUp 2024 for Interior Designers (with co-author Maria Delgado, PhD)*

You may contact the publisher with comments or suggestions at **service@SDCpublications.com**

BIM Chapters (Author's Blog):
http://bimchapters.blogspot.com

LinkedIn
https://www.linkedin.com/in/danstinemn

Certification Study Guides

The author of this book has also prepared the following certification study guides for students to use to achieve successful results on certification exams, which can make the difference when trying to secure that dream job!

- *Microsoft Office Specialist Excel Associate 365/2019 Exam Preparation*
- *Microsoft Office Specialist Word Associate 365/2019 Introduction & Exam Preparation*
- *Microsoft Office Specialist PowerPoint Associate 365/2019 Introduction & Exam Preparation*
- *Autodesk Revit for Architecture Certified User Exam Preparation (Revit 2027 Edition)*
- *Autodesk AutoCAD Certified User Study Guide (2025 Edition)*

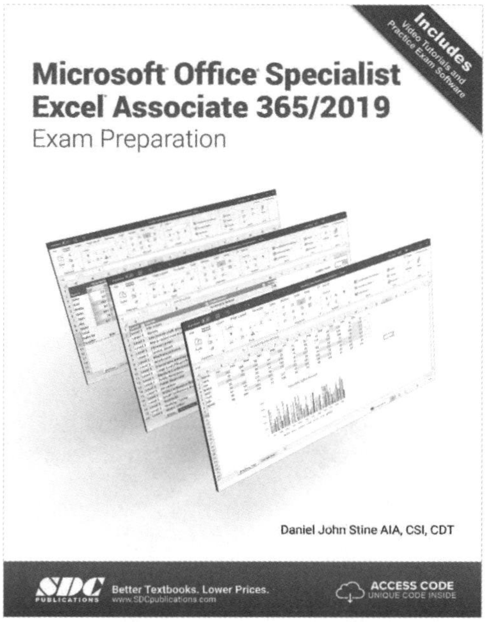

Notes:

TABLE OF CONTENTS

Exclusive Online Content: Bonus Chapters

Instructions for download on inside front cover of book

Bonus Videos

This book comes with several short videos, approximately 3-5 minutes each, that can be watched in order as you work through the book. The full index of video titles is on the next page.

These videos are supplementary and not required to complete the exercises in this book. Rather, the videos are intended to cover many fundamental Revit topics in a different context, helping the reader better understand this important material.

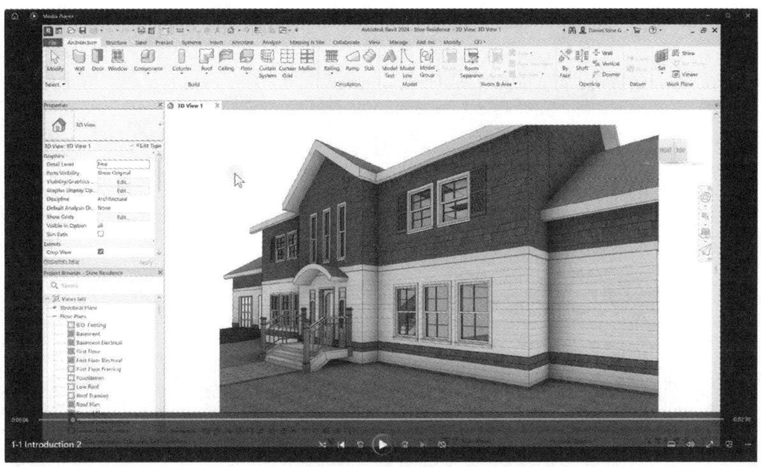

Bonus Videos Index:

Lesson 1
Getting Started with Autodesk Revit:

This chapter will introduce you to Autodesk® Revit®. You will study the User Interface and learn how to open and exit a project, and adjust the drawing view on the screen. It is recommended that you spend an ample amount of time learning this material, as it will greatly enhance your ability to progress smoothly through subsequent chapters.

Exercise 1-1:
What is Revit?

What is Autodesk Revit used for?

Autodesk Revit (Architecture, Structure, and MEP) is the world's first fully parametric building design software. This revolutionary software, for the first time, truly takes architectural computer-aided design beyond simply being a high-tech pencil. Revit is a product of Autodesk, makers of AutoCAD, Civil 3D, Forma, Inventor, 3DS Max, Maya, and many other popular design programs.

Revit can be thought of as the foundation of a larger process called **Building Information Modeling** (BIM). The BIM process revolves around a virtual, information-rich 3D model. In this model, all major building elements are represented and include information such as manufacturer, model, cost, phase, and more. Once a model has been developed in Revit, third-party add-ins and applications can be used to further leverage the data. Some examples are Facilities Management, Analysis (e.g., energy, wind, structural, and lighting), Construction Sequencing, Cost Estimating, Code Compliance, and much more!

Revit can be an invaluable tool to designers when leveraged to its full potential. The iterative design process can be implemented using specialized Revit features, such as *Phasing* and *Design Options*. Material selections can be developed and attached to various elements in the model, allowing a single change to switch the wood from oak to maple throughout the project. The power of (live) schedules may be used to accurately determine quantities and document various parameters contained within content (this is the "I" in BIM, which stands for Information). Finally, the three-dimensional nature of a Revit-based model allows the designer to present compelling visualizations, including still images and animations. These graphics help to more clearly communicate the design intent to clients and stakeholders. This book will cover many of these tools and techniques to **assist** in the creative process.

What is a parametric building modeler?

Revit is a program designed from the ground up to be a parametric architectural design platform. The term parametric describes a process by which an element is modified, and an adjacent element(s) is automatically modified to maintain a previously established relationship. For example, if a wall is moved, perpendicular walls will lengthen or shorten to remain attached to the related wall. Additionally, elements attached to the wall will move, such as wall cabinets, doors, windows, and air grilles.

Revit stands for **Rev**ise **I**ns**t**antly; a change made in one view is automatically updated in all other views, schedules, and sheets. For example, if you move a door in an interior elevation view, the floor plan will automatically update. Or, if you delete a door, it will be deleted from all other views and schedules.

A major goal of Revit is to eliminate many of the repetitive and mundane tasks traditionally associated with CAD programs, allowing more time for design, coordination, and visualization. For example, all sheet numbers, elevation tags, and reference bubbles are automatically updated when they are changed anywhere in the project. Therefore, it is difficult to find a mis-referenced detail tag.

The best way to understand how a parametric model works is to describe the Revit project file. A single Revit file contains your entire building project. Even though you mostly draw in 2D views, you are actually drawing in 3D. In fact, the entire building project is a 3D model. From this 3D model, Revit generates (live) 2D elevations, 2D sections, and perspective views. Therefore, when you delete a door in an elevation view, you are actually deleting it from the 3D model from which all 2D views are generated and automatically updated.

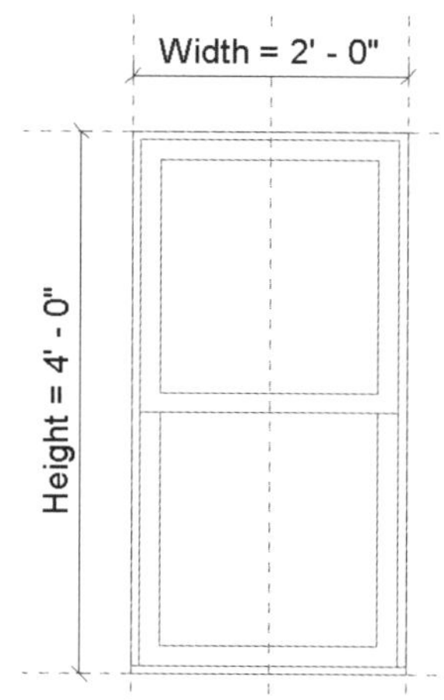

Window model size controlled by parameters *Width* and *Height*

Another way in which Revit is a parametric building modeler is that **parameters** can be used to control the size and shape of geometry. For example, a window model can have two *parameters* that control the window's size. Thus, from a window's properties, it is possible to control the size of the window without using any of Revit's modify tools, such as *Scale* or *Move*. Furthermore, the *parameter* settings (i.e., width and height in this example) can be saved within the window model (called a *Family*). You could have the 2′ x 4′ settings saved as "Type A" and the 2′ x 6′ as "Type B." Each saved list of values is called a *Type* within the *Family*. Thus, this one double-hung window *Family* could represent an unlimited number of rectangular window sizes! You will learn more about this later in the book.

What Disciplines does Revit Support?

Revit supports **Architecture, Interior Design, Structure**, and **MEP** (Mechanical, Electrical, and Plumbing). You can download the free trial from autodesk.com. Students may download a free, renewable 1-year version of Revit and other Autodesk products at www.autodesk.com/education.

Revit is not meant to support professional site design. Civil engineers and surveyors use tools such as Autodesk AutoCAD Civil 3D for accurate site grading, road and parking lot design, and related documentation.

Now is as good a time as any to make sure the reader understands that Revit is not, and has never been, backward compatible. This means there is no *Save As* option to revert to a previous version of Revit. Also, an older version of Revit cannot open a file, project, or family saved in a newer format. So, make sure you consider what version your school or employer is currently standardized on before upgrading any projects or content. Revit will automatically upgrade an older format when opened in a newer version of the software. This is a one-time process that can take several minutes.

Revit model of an existing building, with architecture, structural, mechanical, plumbing and electrical all modeled.
Image courteous of LHB, Inc. *www.LHBcorp.com*

3D model of lunchroom created in *Interior Design Using Autodesk Revit by Stine*

Download Autodesk Content

Content originally provided with Revit, such as doors, windows, toilets, etc., is no longer downloaded to your hard drive during the software installation. Instead, the content is downloaded as needed from the **Insert → Load Autodesk Family** tool. An internet connection will be required to place content. Optionally, all content may be downloaded, see: https://autode.sk/30EJYkX

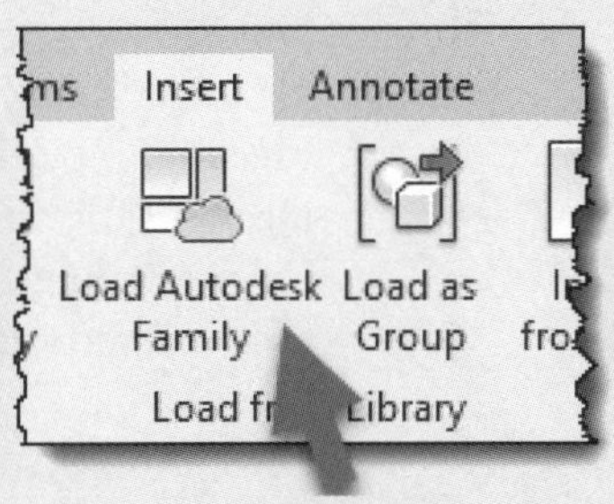

Lobby rendering from *Interior Design Using Autodesk Revit*

Why use Revit?

Many people ask, "Why use Revit versus other programs?" The answer can certainly vary depending on the situation and particular needs of an individual or organization.

Generally speaking, this is why most companies use Revit:

- Many designers and drafters are using Revit to streamline repetitive drafting tasks and focus more on designing and detailing a project.
- Revit is a widely used program and offers many features for designing buildings. Revit is constantly being developed, and Autodesk provides incremental upgrades and patches regularly; Revit 2027 was released about a year after the previous version.
- Multiple firms can collaborate and coordinate closely in Revit. The models can also be hosted in the cloud, via Autodesk Forma (previously BIM 360).
- Revit was designed specifically for architectural design and includes features like:
    - *Autodesk Renderer* Photo Realistic Rendering
    - Phasing: model changes over time
    - Design Options: model changes during the same time period
    - Live schedules
    - Cloud Rendering via *Autodesk cloud services*
    - Conceptual Energy Analysis via *Autodesk cloud services*
    - Daylighting Analysis via *Autodesk cloud services*

A few basic Revit concepts

The following is a brief overview of the basic organization of Revit as a software application. You should not get too hung up on these concepts and terms, as they will make more sense as you work through the tutorials in this book. This discussion is simply laying the groundwork, so you have a general frame of reference on how Revit works.

The Revit platform has three fundamental types of elements:

- Model Elements
- Datum Elements
- View-Specific Elements

Model Elements

Think of *Model Elements* as things you can put your hands on once the building has been constructed. They are typically 3D but can sometimes be 2D. There are two types of *Model Elements*:

- **Host Elements**: walls, floors, slabs, roofs, ceilings.

- **Model Components**: Stairs, Doors, Furniture, Casework, Beams, Columns, Pipes, Ducts, Light Fixtures, Model Lines, etc.

    - Some *Model Components* require a host before they can be placed within a project. For example, a window can only be placed in a host, which could be a wall, roof, or floor, depending on how the element was created. If the host is deleted, all hosted or dependent elements are automatically deleted.

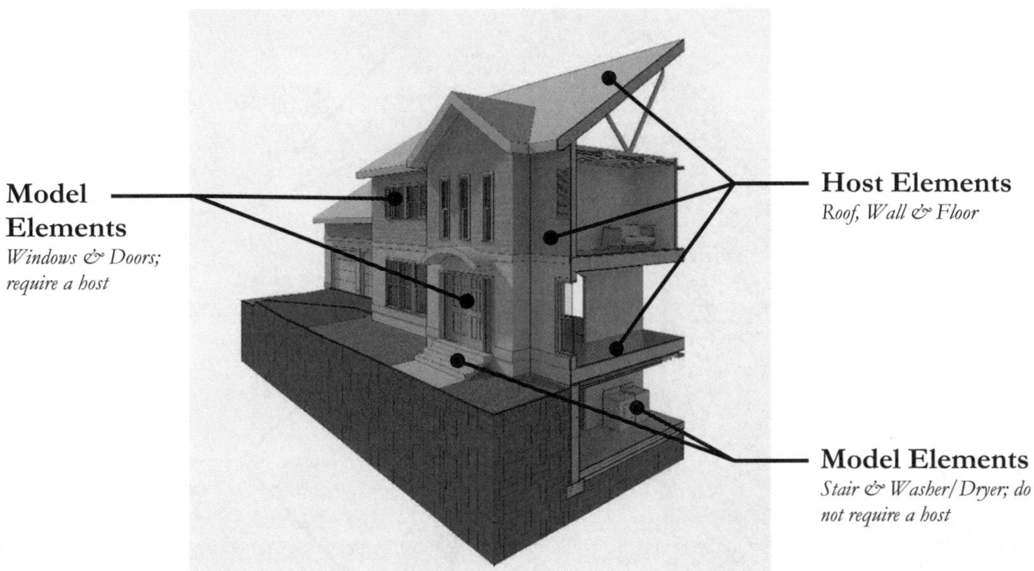

Datum Elements

Datum Elements are reference planes within the building that graphically and parametrically define the location of various elements within the model. These are the three types of *Datum Elements,* all of which define 3D planes:

- **Grids**
  - Typically laid out in a plan view to locate structural elements such as columns and beams, as well as walls. Grids show up in plan, elevation, and section views. Moving a grid in one view moves it in all other views, as it is the same element. (See the next page for an example of a grid in plan view.)

- **Levels**
  - Used to define vertical relationships, mainly surfaces that you walk on. They only show up in elevation, section, and 3D views. Most elements are placed relative to a *Level*; when the *Level* is moved, those elements move with it (e.g., doors, windows, casework, ceilings).

- **Reference Planes**
  - These are similar to grids in that they show up in plan, elevation, or sections. They do not have reference bubbles at the end like grids. Revit breaks many tasks down into simple 2D tasks, which result in 3D geometry. *Reference Planes* are used to define 2D surfaces on which to work within the 3D model. They can be placed in any view, horizontally, vertically, or at an angle.

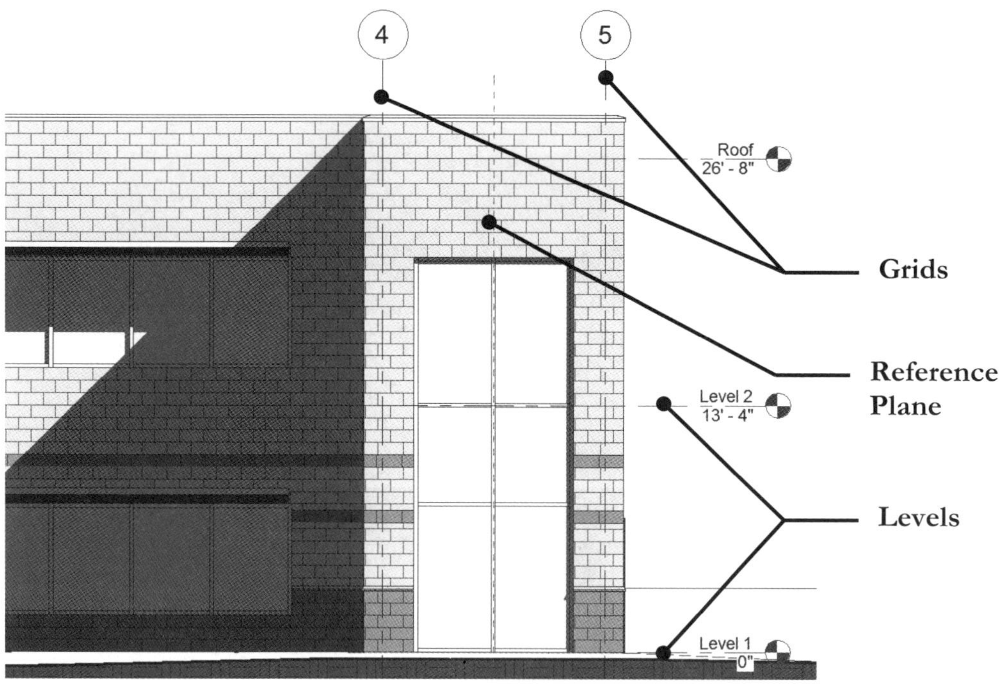

View-Specific Elements

As the name implies, the items about to be discussed only show up in the specific view in which they are created. For example, notes and dimensions added to the architectural floor plans will not appear in the structural floor plans. These elements are all 2D and primarily serve as communication tools to accurately document the building for construction or presentations.

- **Annotation elements** (text, tags, symbols, dimensions)
  - Size automatically set and changed based on selected view scale
- **Details** (detail lines, filled regions, 2D detail components)

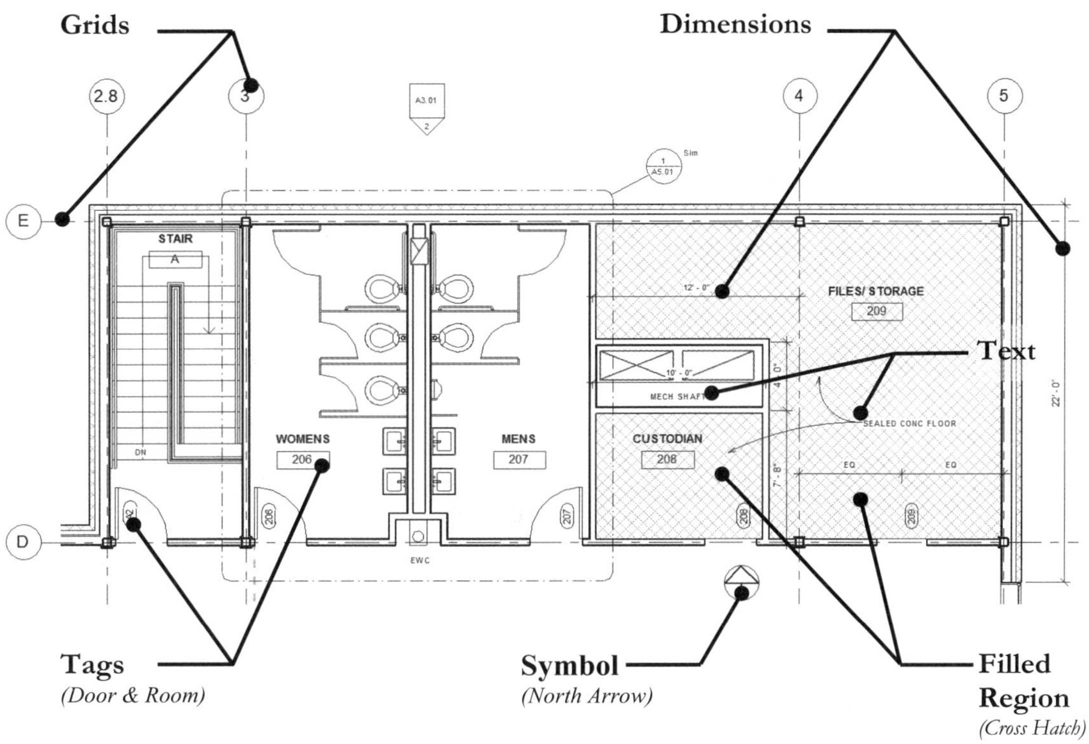

> **File Types (and extensions):**
> Revit has four primary file types that you will work with as a Revit user. Each file type, as with any Microsoft Windows-based program, has a specific three-letter file name extension; that is, after the name of the file on your hard drive, you will see a period and three letters:
>
> | | |
> |---|---|
> | .RVT | Revit project files; the file most used (also for backup files) |
> | .RFA | Revit family file; loadable content for your project |
> | .RTE | Revit template; a project starter file with office standards preset |
> | .RFT | Revit family template; a family starter file with parameters |

The Revit platform has three fundamental ways in which to work with the elements (for display and manipulation):

- Views
- Schedules
- Sheets

The following is a cursory overview of the main ideas you need to know. This is not an exhaustive study on views, schedules, and sheets.

Views

Views, accessible from the *Project Browser*, are where most work is done in Revit. Think of views as slices through the building, both horizontal (plans) and vertical (elevations and sections).

- **Plans**
    - A *Plan View* is a horizontal slice through the building. You can specify the location of the **cut plane**, which determines if certain windows show up or how much of the stair is seen. A few examples are architectural floor plan, reflected ceiling plan, site plan, structural framing plan, HVAC floor plan, electrical floor plan, lighting [ceiling] plan, etc. The images below show this concept; the image on the left is the 3D BIM. The middle image shows the portion of the building above the cut plane removed. Finally, the last image on the right shows the plan view in which you work and place on a sheet.

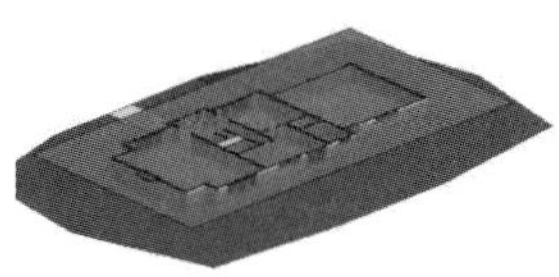
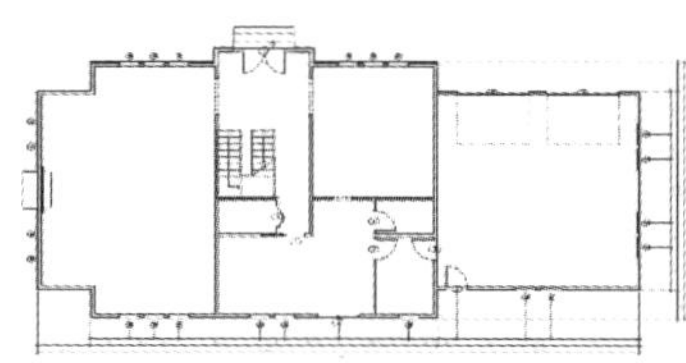

- **Elevations**
    - An "exterior" elevation is a vertical slice, but where the slice lies outside the floor plan, as in the middle image below. Each elevation created is listed in the *Project Browser*. The image on the right is an example of a South exterior elevation view, which is a "live" view of the 3D model. If you select a window here and delete it, the floor plans will update instantly.

- Similarly, an "interior" elevation is a vertical slice, but inside the building. This interior view is cropped at the perimeter of a given room.

- **Sections**
  - Similar to elevations, sections are also vertical slices. However, these slices cut through the building. A section view can be cropped down to become a wall section or even look just like an elevation. The images below show the slice, the portion of the building in the foreground removed, and then the actual view created by the slice. A setting exists for each section view to control how far into that view you can see. The example on the right is "seeing" deep enough to show the doors on the interior walls.

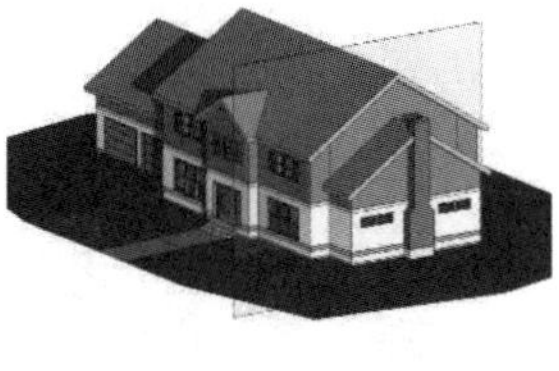

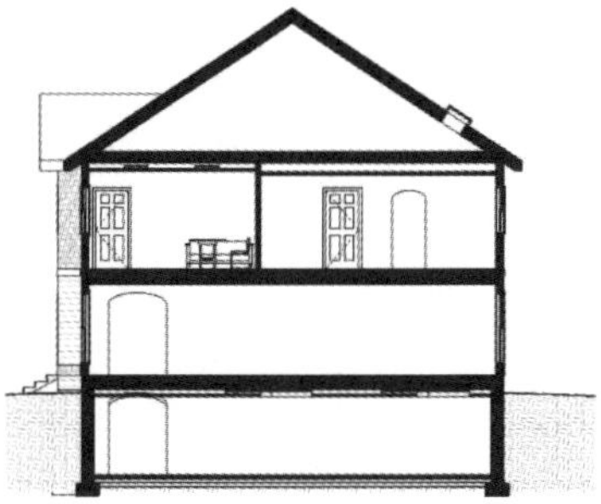

- **3D and Camera**
  - In addition to the traditional "flattened" 2D views that you will typically work in, you are able to see your designs more naturally via 3D and Camera views. A 3D view is simply an orthogonal view of the project viewed from the exterior. A Camera view is a perspective view; cameras can be created both inside and outside of the building. Like the 2D views, these 3D/Camera views can be placed on a sheet for printing and presenting. Revit provides a number of tools to help explore the 3D view, such as Section Box, Steering Wheel, Temporary Hide and Isolate, and Render.

    The image on the left is a 3D view in "shade mode" with shadows enabled. The image on the right is a camera view set up inside the building; the view is set to "hidden line" rather than shaded, and the camera is at eye level.

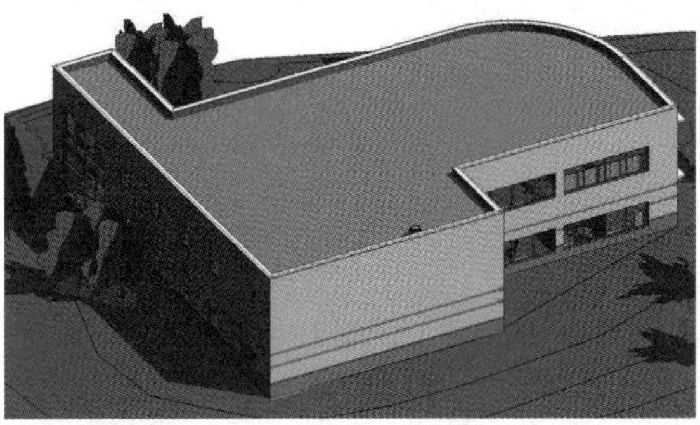
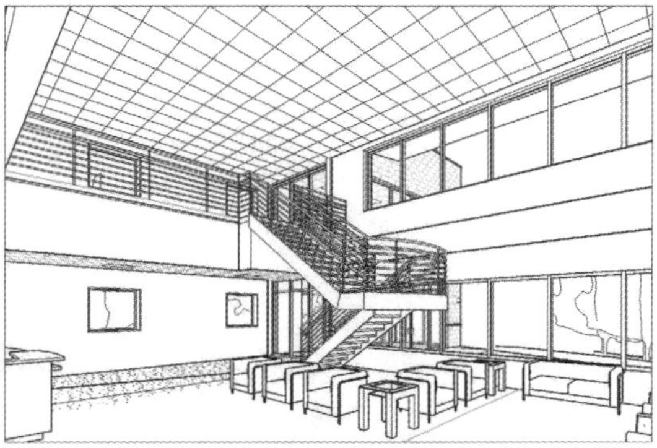

Schedules

Schedules are lists of information generated from content placed or modeled within the project. A schedule can be created, such as the door schedule shown below, that lists selected data for each door in the project. Revit allows you to work directly in the schedule views. Any change in a schedule view is applied directly to the element being scheduled. Again, if a door were deleted from this schedule, it would be instantly removed from the project.

DOOR AND FRAME SCHEDULE													
DOOR	DOOR				FRAME		DETAIL				FIRE	HDWR	
NUMBER	WIDTH	HEIGHT	MATL	TYPE	MATL	TYPE	HEAD	JAMB	SILL	GLAZING	RATING	GROUP	
1000A	3' - 8"	7' - 2"	WD		HM		11/A8.01	11/A8.01					
1046	3' - 0"	7' - 2"	WD	D10	HM	F10	11/A8.01	11/A8.01 SIM				34	
1047A	6' - 0"	7' - 10"	ALUM	D15	ALUM	SF4	6/A8.01	6/A8.01	1/A8.01 SIM	1" INSUL		2	CARD READER N. LEAF
1047B	8' - 0"	7' - 2"	WD	D10	HM	F13	12/A8.01	11/A8.01 SIM			60 MIN	85	MAG HOLD OPENS
1050	3' - 0"	7' - 2"	WD	D10	HM	F21	8/A8.01	11/A8.01		1/4" TEMP		33	
1051	3' - 0"	7' - 2"	WD	D10	HM	F21	8/A8.01	11/A8.01		1/4" TEMP		33	
1052	3' - 0"	7' - 2"	WD	D10	HM	F21	8/A8.01	11/A8.01		1/4" TEMP		33	
1053	3' - 0"	7' - 2"	WD	D10	HM	F21	8/A8.01	11/A8.01		1/4" TEMP		33	
1054A	3' - 0"	7' - 2"	WD	D10	HM	F10	8/A8.01	11/A8.01		1/4" TEMP	-	34	
1054B	3' - 0"	7' - 2"	WD	D10	HM	F21	8/A8.01	11/A8.01		1/4" TEMP	-	33	
1055	3' - 0"	7' - 2"	WD	D10	HM	F21	8/A8.01	11/A8.01		1/4" TEMP	-	33	
1056A	3' - 0"	7' - 2"	WD	D10	HM	F10	9/A8.01	9/A8.01			20 MIN	33	
1056B	3' - 0"	7' - 2"	WD	D10	HM	F10	11/A8.01	11/A8.01			20 MIN	34	
1056C	3' - 0"	7' - 2"	WD	D10	HM	F10	20/A8.01	20/A8.01			20 MIN	33	
1057A	3' - 0"	7' - 2"	WD	D10	HM	F10	8/A8.01	11/A8.01			20 MIN	34	
1057B	3' - 0"	7' - 2"	WD	D10	HM	F30	9/A8.01	9/A8.01		1/4" TEMP	20 MIN	33	
1058A	3' - 0"	7' - 2"	WD	D10	HM	F10	9/A8.01	9/A8.01			-	33	

Sheets

You can think of sheets as the pieces of paper on which your views and schedules will be printed. Views and schedules are placed on sheets and then arranged. Once a view has been placed on a sheet, its reference bubble is automatically filled out, and that view cannot be placed on any other sheet. The setting for each view, called "view scale," controls the size of the drawing on each sheet; it also controls the size of text and dimensions.

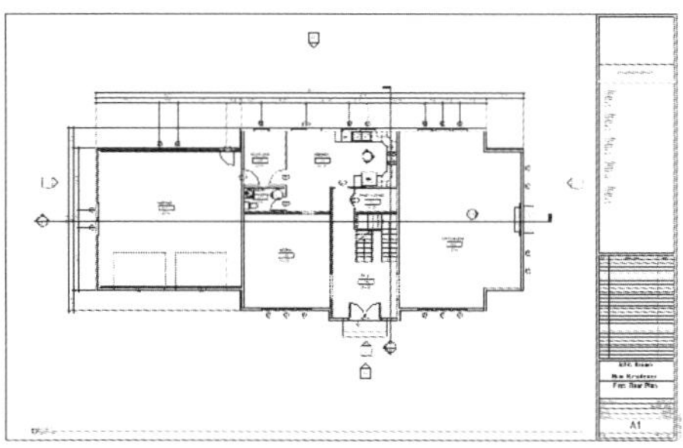

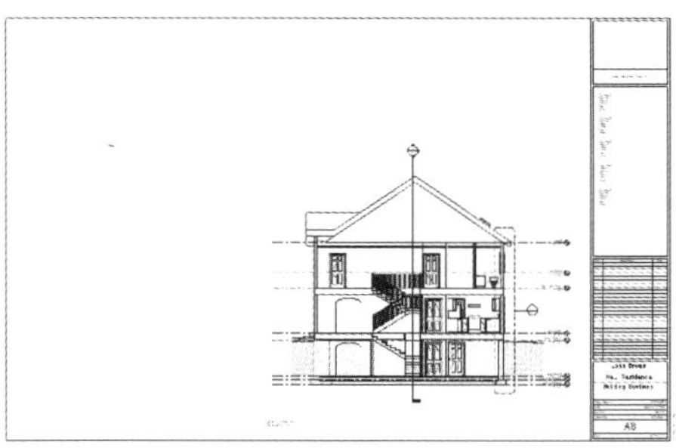

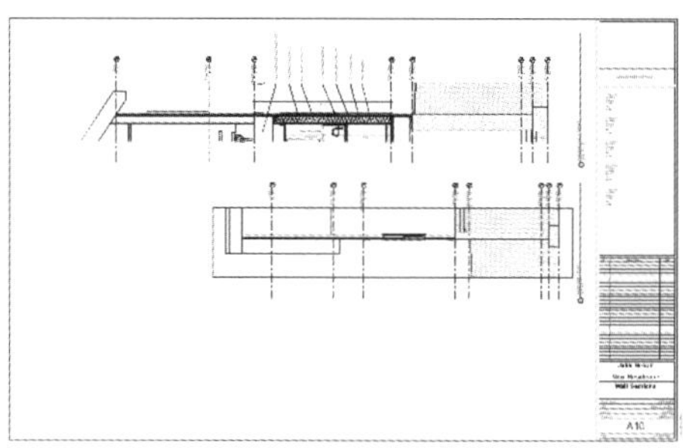

Exercise 1-2:
Overview of the Revit User Interface

Revit is a powerful and sophisticated program. Because of its robust feature set, it has a measurable learning curve, though its intuitive design makes it easier to learn than other CAD-based programs. However, like most things, when broken down into smaller pieces, we can easily learn to harness the power of Revit. That is the goal of this book.

This section will walk through the different aspects of the User Interface (UI). As with any program, understanding the user interface is key to using its features.

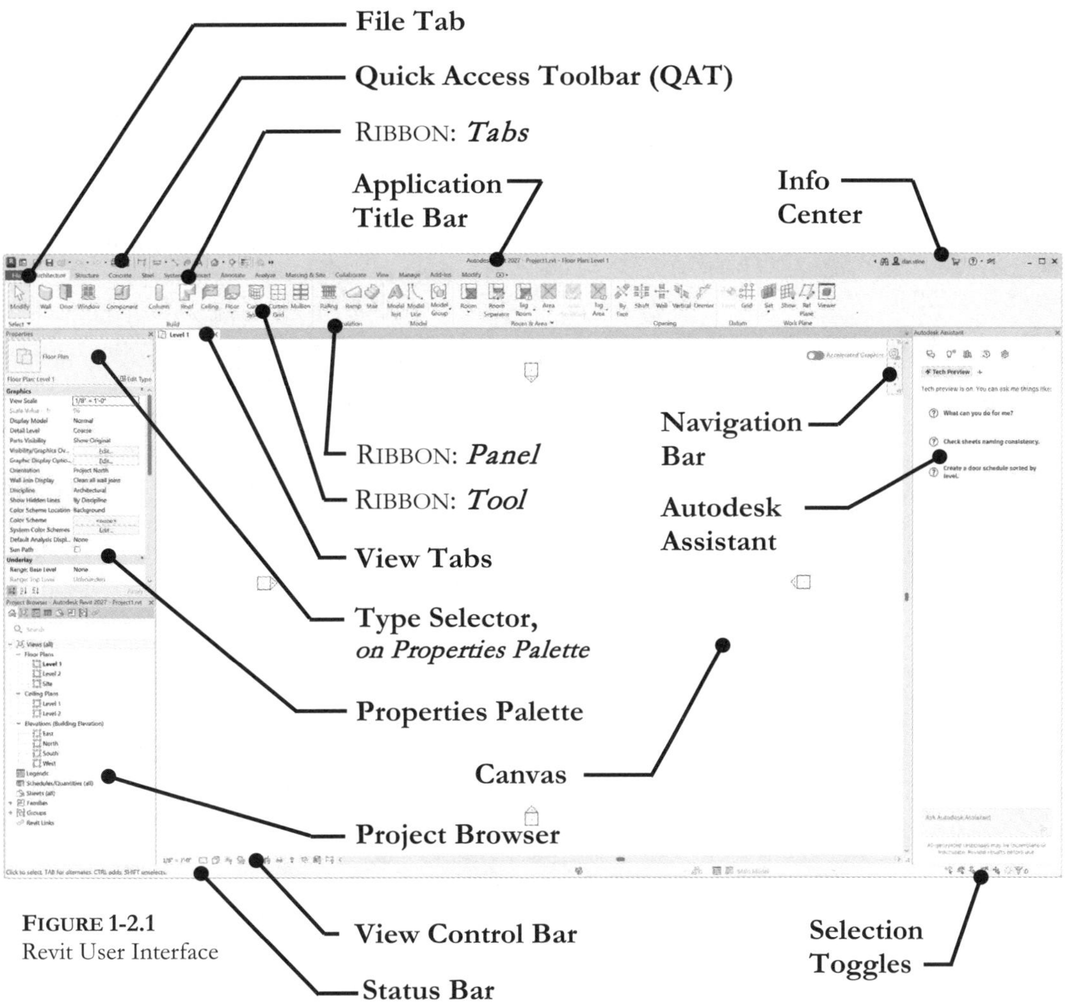

FIGURE 1-2.1
Revit User Interface

The Revit User Interface

TIP: See the online videos on the User Interface.

Application Title Bar

In addition to the *Quick Access Toolbar* and *Info Center*, which are covered in the next few sections, you are also presented with the product name, version, and the current file & view name in the center. As previously noted, the version is important as you do not want to upgrade unless you have coordinated with other staff and/or consultants; everyone must be using the same version of Revit.

File Tab

Access to *File* tools such as *Save*, *Plot*, *Export*, and *Print* (both hardcopy and electronic printing). You also have access to tools that control the Revit application as a whole, not just the current project, such as *Options* (see the end of this section for more on *Options*).

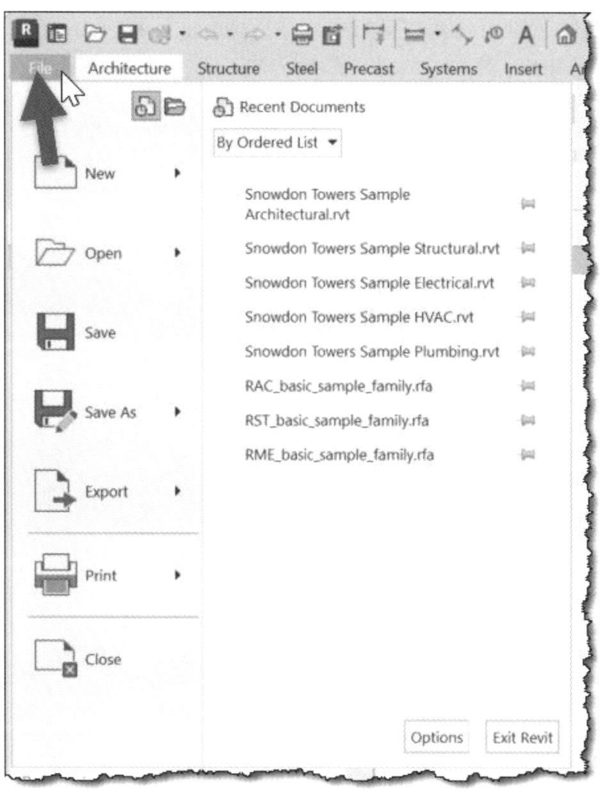

Recent and Open Documents:

These two icons (from the *File tab*) toggle the entire area on the right to show either the recent documents you have been in (icon on the left) or a list of the documents you currently have open.

In the *Recent Documents* list, you click a listed document to open it. This saves time as you do not have to click *Open* → *Project* and browse for the document (*Document* and *Project* mean the same thing here). Finally, clicking the "Pin" icon keeps that project from dropping off the list as additional projects are opened.

In the *Open Documents* list, the "active" project you are working in is listed first; clicking another project switches you to that open project.

The list on the left, in the *File Tab* shown on the previous page, represents three different types of buttons: *button, drop-down button,* and *split button.* Save and Close are simply **buttons**. Save-As and Export are **drop-down buttons** that reveal a group of related tools. If you click or hover your cursor over one of these buttons, you will get a list of tools on the right. Finally, **split buttons** have two actions depending on which part of the button you click on; hovering over the button reveals the two parts (see the bottom image to the right). The main area is the most used tool; the arrow reveals additional related options.

Button

Drop-down Button

Split Button

Quick Access Toolbar

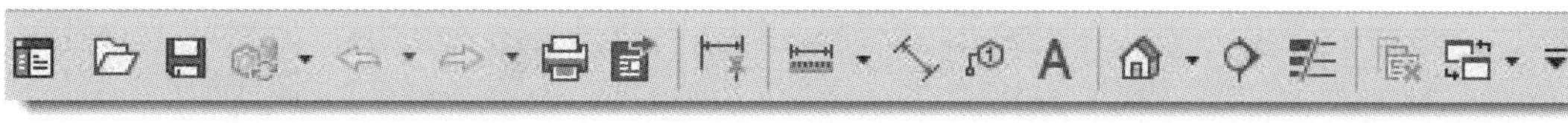

Referred to as *QAT* in this book, this single toolbar provides access to often used tools (Home, *Open*, *Save*, *Undo*, *Redo*, *Measure*, *Tag*, etc.). It is always visible regardless of what part of the *Ribbon* is active.

The *QAT* can be positioned above or below the *Ribbon,* and any command from the *Ribbon* can be added to it; simply right-click any tool on the *Ribbon* and select *Add to Quick Access Toolbar.* Moving the *QAT* below the *Ribbon* gives you much more room to add your favorite commands from the *Ribbon.* Clicking the larger down-arrow to the far right reveals a list of common tools that can be toggled on and off.

The first icon returns to the Home screen shown when Revit first opens. Some icons on the QAT have a down arrow on the right, which, when clicked, reveals a list of related tools. In the case of *Undo* and *Redo*, you can undo (or redo) several actions at once.

Ribbon – Architecture Tab

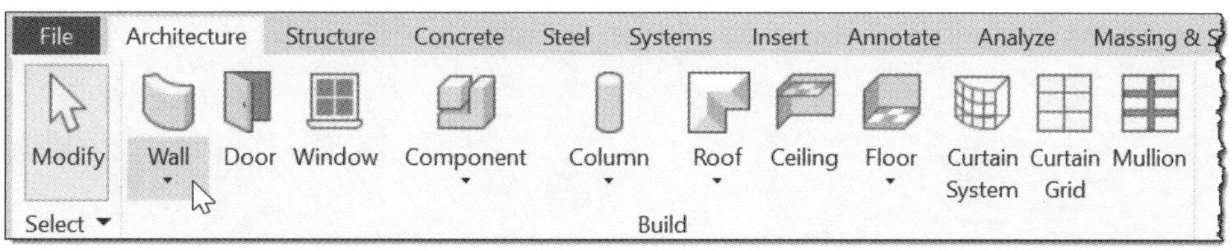

The *Architecture* tab on the *Ribbon* contains most of the tools the architect needs to model a building, essentially the things you can put your hands on when the building is done.

Each tab starts with the *Modify* tool, i.e., the first button on the left. This tool puts you into "selection mode," allowing you to select elements to modify. Clicking this tool cancels any active command and unselects elements. With the *Modify* tool selected, you may select elements to view their properties or edit them. Note that the *Modify* tool, which is a button, is different than the *Modify* tab on the *Ribbon.*

The *Ribbon* has three types of buttons: *button*, *drop-down button,* and *split*, as covered on the previous page. In the previous image, you can see that the *Wall* tool is a **split button**. Most of the time, you would simply click the top part of the button to draw a wall. Clicking the down-arrow part of the button, for the *Wall* tool example, gives you the option to draw a *Wall, a Structural Wall, a Wall by Face, a Wall Sweep, or* a *Reveal.*

TIP: The Model Text tool is only for placing 3D text in your model, not for adding notes!

Ribbon – Annotate Tab

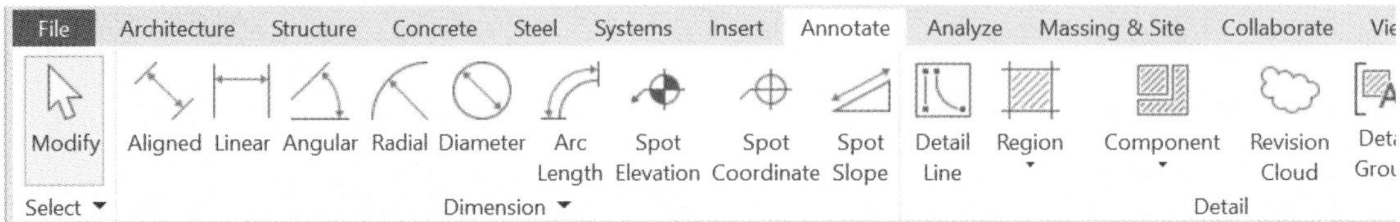

To view this tab, simply click the label "Annotate" near the top of the *Ribbon.* This tab presents a series of tools that allow you to add notes, dimensions, and 2D "embellishments" to your model in a specific view, such as a floor plan, elevation, or section. All of these tools are **view-specific**, meaning a note added in the first floor plan will not show up anywhere else, not even another first floor plan: for instance, a first floor electrical plan.

Notice in the image above that the Dimension panel label has a down arrow next to it. Clicking the down arrow reveals an **extended panel** with additional related tools.

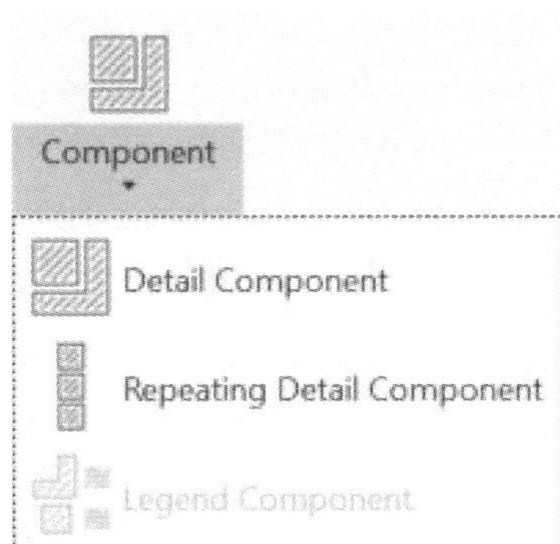

Finally, notice the *Component* tool in the image above; it is a **split button** rather than a *drop-down button.* Clicking the top part of this button will initiate the *Detail Component* tool. Clicking the bottom part of the button opens the fly-out menu, revealing related tools. Once you select an option from the fly-out, that tool becomes the default for the top part of the split button for the remainder of the current Revit session (see the image to the right).

Ribbon – Modify Tab

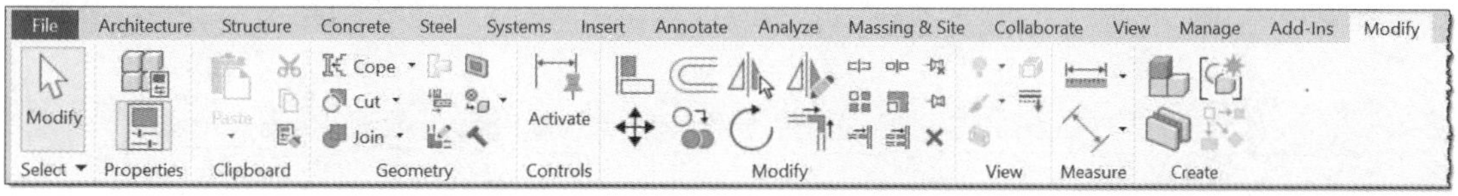

Several tools for manipulating and deriving information from the current model are available on the *Modify* tab. Additional *Modify* tools are automatically appended to this tab when elements are selected in the model (see *Modify Contextual Tab* on the next page).

> *TIP: Do not confuse the Modify tab with the Modify tool when following instructions in this book.*

Ribbon – View Tab

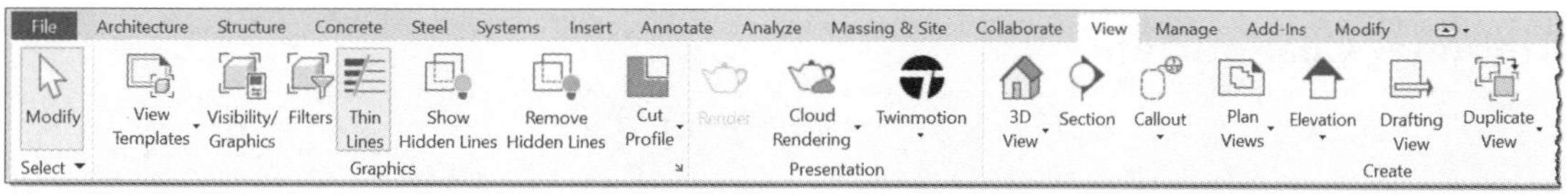

The tools on the *View* tab allow you to create new views of your 3D model, including 2D views (e.g., floor plans, elevations, and sections) and 3D views (e.g., isometric and perspective views).

The *View* tab also gives you tools to control how views look, including which elements are shown (e.g., Plumbing Fixture, Furniture, or Section Marks) and line weights.

> *NOTE: Line weights are controlled at a project-wide level but may be overridden.*

Finally, notice the little arrow in the lower-right corner of the *Graphics* panel. When you see an arrow like this, you can click on it to open a dialog box with settings that relate to the panel's tool set (*Graphics* in this example). Hovering over the arrow reveals a tooltip that tells you which dialog box will be opened.

Ribbon – Modify Contextual Tab

The *Modify* tab is displayed when certain tools are active or elements are selected in the model; this is called a *contextual tab*. The first image below shows the *Place Wall* tab, which presents various options while adding walls. The next example shows the *Modify Walls* contextual tab, which is accessible when one or more walls are selected.

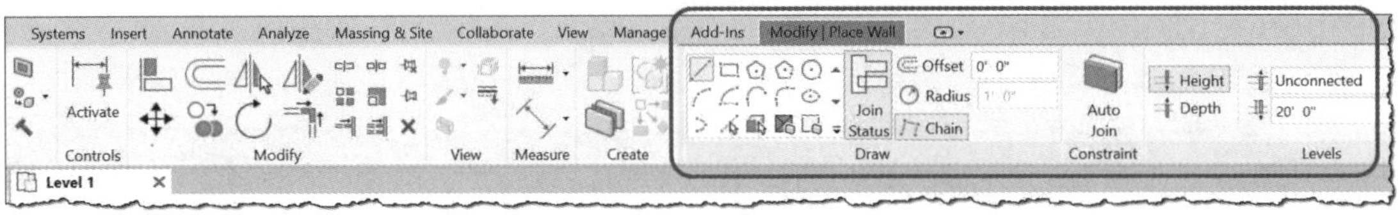

Place Wall contextual tab – visible when the Wall tool is active.

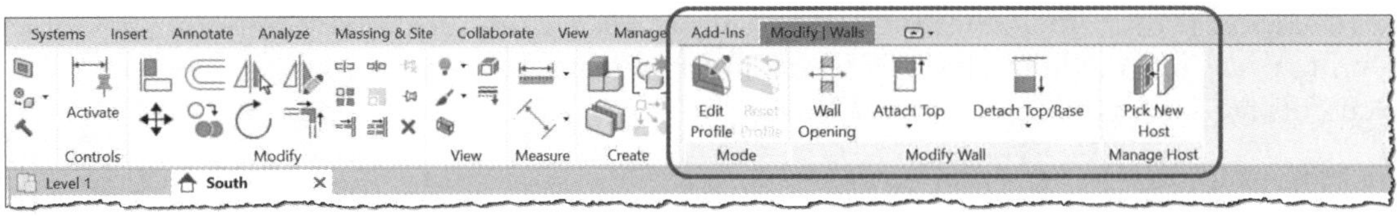

Modify Walls contextual tab – visible when a wall is selected.

Ribbon – Customization

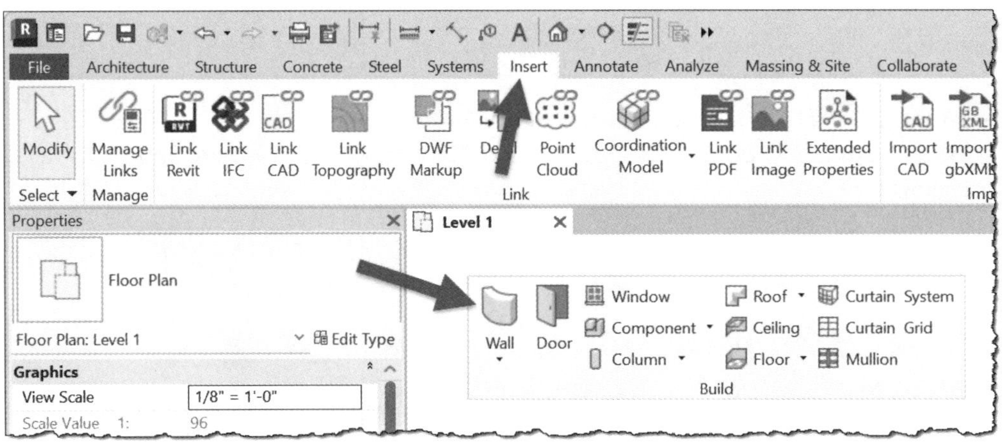

There isn't much customization that can be done to the *Ribbon*. One of the only things you can do is pull a panel off the *Ribbon* by clicking and holding down the left mouse button on the titles listed, e.g., "Link" or "Build," across the bottom. This panel can be placed within the *drawing window* or on another screen if you have a dual monitor setup.

The image above shows the *Build* panel, from the *Architecture* tab, detached from the *Ribbon* and floating within the drawing window. Notice that the *Insert* tab is active. Thus, you have constant access to the *Build* tools while accessing other tools. Note that the *Build* panel is not available on the *Architecture* tab as it is literally moved, not just copied.

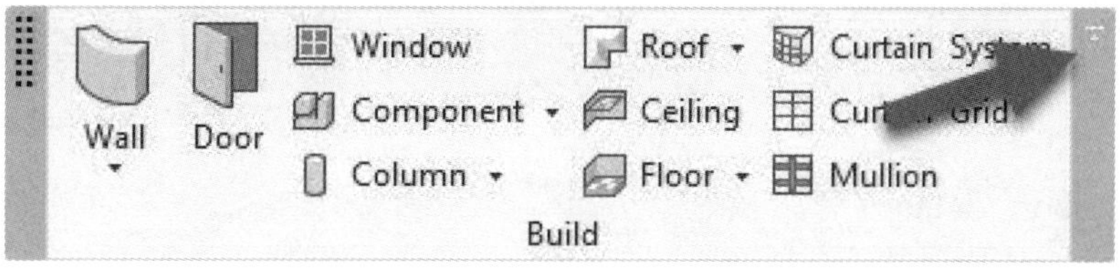

When you need to move a detached panel back to the *Ribbon,* do the following: hover over the detached panel until the sidebars appear, then click the "Return panels to ribbon" icon in the upper right (as shown in the image above). Panels cannot be moved to other tabs.

> ***FYI:*** *Whenever the resolution of your monitor is too low or you don't have the Revit application maximized on the screen, the buttons may be modified to take up less room on the Ribbon; typically, the words are removed. Compare the image to the right with the Build panel above.*

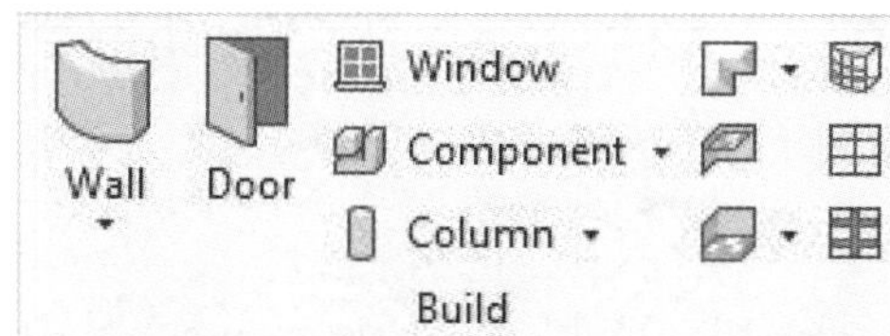

If you install a Revit add-in on your computer, you will likely see a new tab appear on the Ribbon. Some add-ins are free, while others require a subscription. If an add-in only has one tool, it will likely be added to the catch-all tab called Add-Ins (shown in the image below). Some firms have custom tools they developed, and may have their own tab, like LF Tools.

Tab Visibility

This is not really customizing the User Interface, but in the Options dialog, there are several adjustments one can make, such as turning off tabs and tools not used.

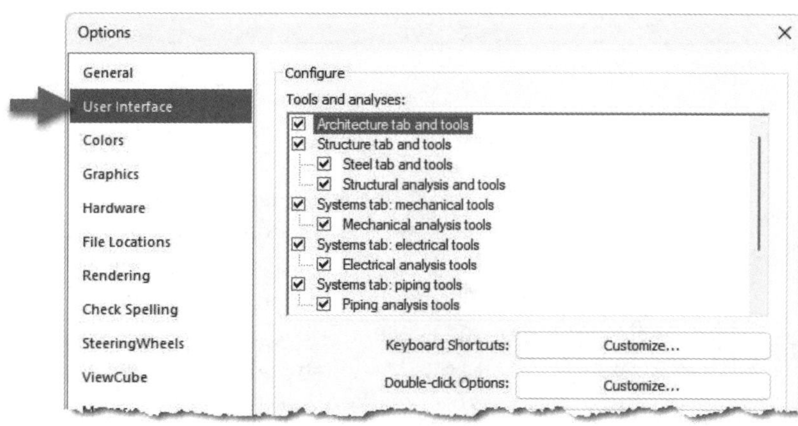

> **TIP:** When Revit is first opened, you are prompted to indicate your role, or what type of work you do. This will turn off tabs here.

Ribbon – States

The *Ribbon* can be displayed in one of four states:

- Full Ribbon (default)
- Minimize to Tabs
- Minimize to Panel Tiles
- Minimize to Panel Buttons

The intent of this feature is to increase the size of the available drawing window. It is recommended, however, that you leave the *Ribbon* fully expanded while learning to use the program. The images in this book show the fully expanded state. The images below show the other three options. When using one of the minimized options, you simply hover (or click) your cursor over the Tab or Panel to temporarily reveal the tools.

FYI: Double-clicking on a Ribbon tab will also toggle the states.

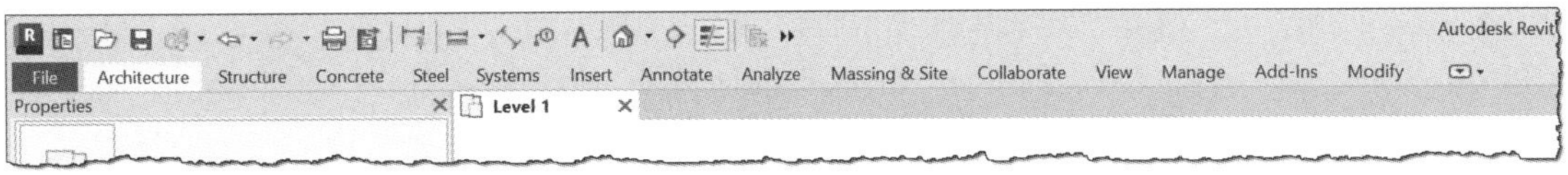

Minimize to Tabs

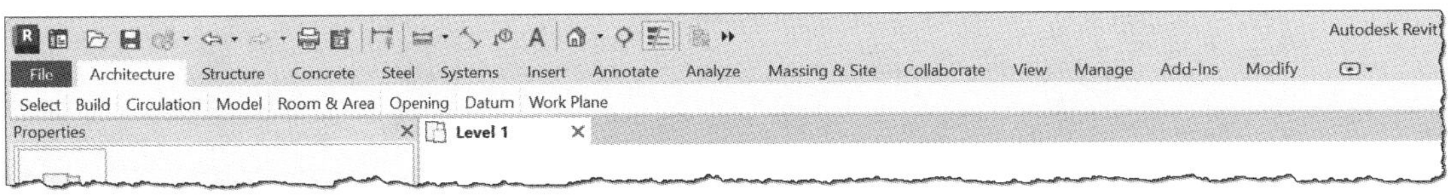

Minimize to Panel Tiles

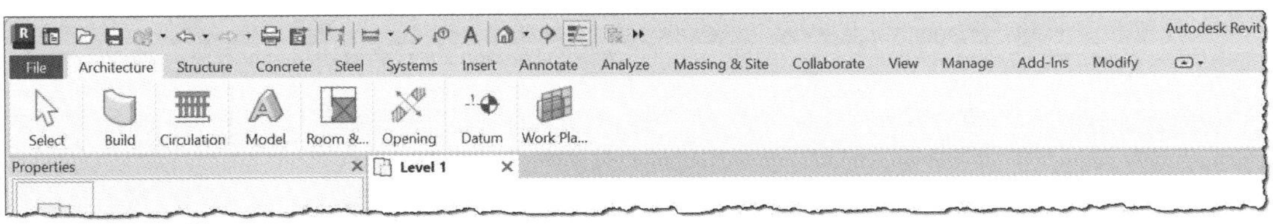

Minimize to Panel Buttons

Elevation Marker

This item is not actually part of the Revit UI but is visible in the drawing window by default through the various templates you can start with, so it's worth mentioning at this point. The four elevation markers point to each side of your project and ultimately indicate the drawing sheet where you'll find an elevation drawing of each side of the building. All you need to know right now is that you should generally place your building in the center of the four elevation markers shown in each plan view; DO NOT delete them, as doing so will remove the related view from the Project Browser.

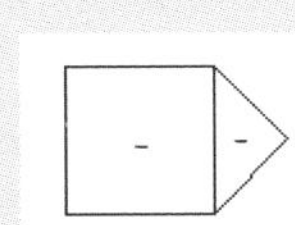

Ribbon – References in this Book

When the exercises refer to tools in the Ribbon, a consistent approach is used to eliminate unnecessary wording and save space. Take a moment to understand this so that things go smoothly for you later.

Throughout the textbook, you will see an instruction similar to the following:

23. Select **Architecture → Build → Wall**

This means click the ***Architecture*** tab, and within the ***Build*** panel, select the ***Wall*** tool. Note that the *Wall* tool is actually a split button, but a subsequent tool was not listed, so you are to click on the primary part of the button. Compare the above example to the one below:

23. Select **Architecture → Build → Wall → Structural Wall**

The above example shows that you should click the down arrow on the Wall tool to select the *Structural Wall* option.

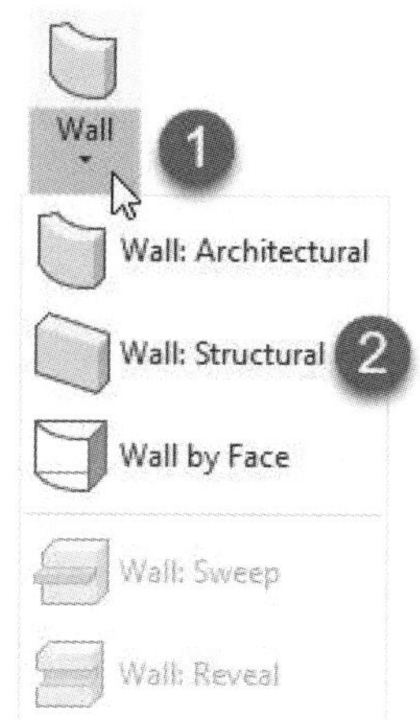

Thus, the general pattern is this:

Tab → Panel → Tool → drop-down list item

#1 *Tab:* This will get you to the correct area within the *Ribbon.*

#2 *Panel:* This will narrow down your search for the desired tool.

#3 *Tool:* Specific tool to select and use.

Drop-down list item: This is specified only for drop-down buttons and sometimes for split buttons.

The image below shows the order in which the instructions for selecting a tool are given; note that you do not actually click the panel title.

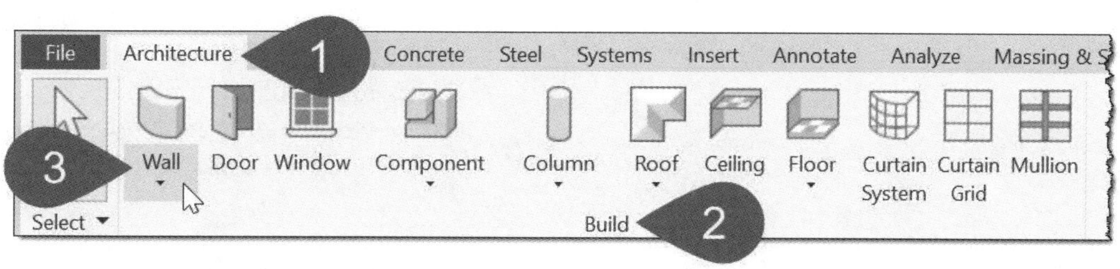

Options Bar

Note that the previous version of Revit had a contextual area just below the Ribbon, and above the View Tabs, called the Options Bar. This has been removed from Revit, and all related features have been moved to the Ribbon and/or Properties Palette.

Properties Palette – Element Type Selector

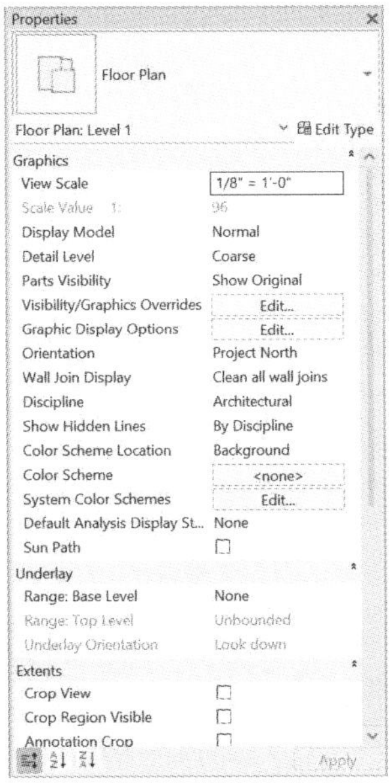

Properties Palette; nothing selected

The *Properties Palette* provides instant access to settings related to the element selected or about to be created. When nothing is selected, it shows information about the current view. When multiple elements are selected, the common parameters are displayed.

The *Element Type Selector* is an important part of the *Properties Palette.* Whenever you are adding elements or have them selected, you can select from this list to determine how a wall to be drawn will look, or how a wall previously drawn should look (see lower left image). If a wall type needs to change, you never delete it and redraw it; you simply select it and pick a new type from the *Type Selector.*

The **Selection Filter** drop-down list below the *Type Selector* shows the type and quantity of the currently selected elements. When multiple elements are selected, you can narrow the properties to a single element type (aka Category), such as *wall.* Notice that the image below shows seven doors are in the current selection set. Selecting **Doors (7)** will cause the *Palette* to only show *Door* properties, even though many other elements are selected (and remain selected).

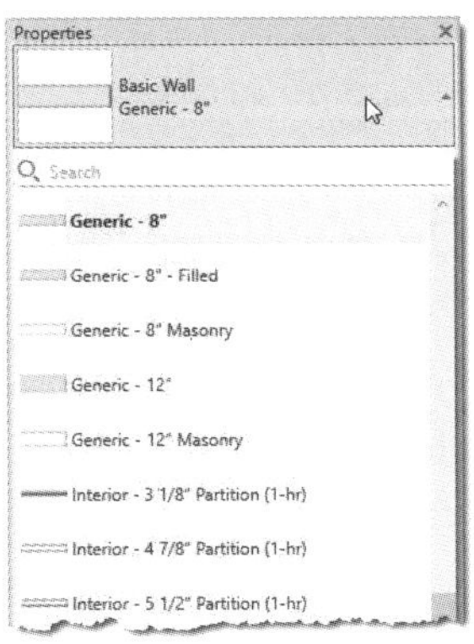

Type Selector; Wall tool active or a Wall is selected

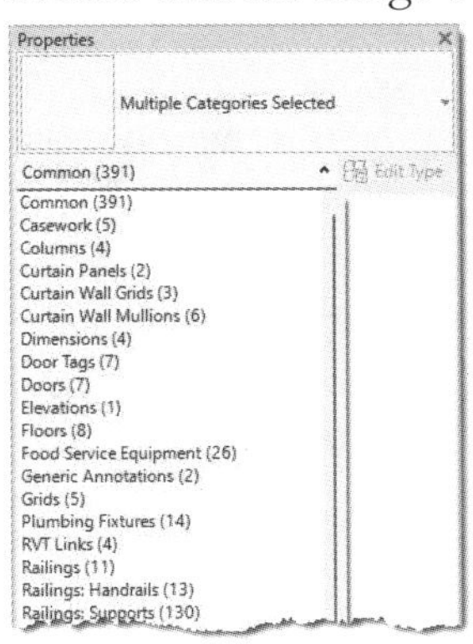

Selection Filter; multiple elements selected

The width of the *Properties Palette* and the center column position can be adjusted by dragging the cursor over that area. You may need to do this at times to see all the information. However, making the *Palette* too wide will reduce the usable drawing area.

The *Properties Palette* should be left open; if you accidentally close it, you can reopen it by **View → Window → User Interface → Properties** or by typing **PP** on the keyboard.

Project Browser

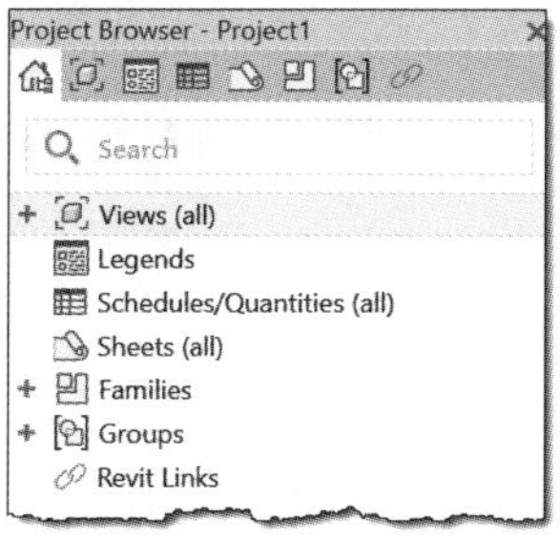

Primary nodes in project browser

The *Project Browser* is the "Grand Central Station" of the Revit project database. All the views, schedules, sheets, and content are accessible through this hierarchical list. The first image on the left shows the seven major categories; any item with a "plus" next to it contains subcategories or items (each with a filter icon across the top – Home is the default).

Double-clicking a View, Legend, Schedule, or Sheet opens it for editing; the current item open for editing is bold (**Level 1** in the example to the left). An empty box indicates the view is not placed on a sheet. Right-clicking displays a pop-up menu with options such as *Delete* and *Copy*.

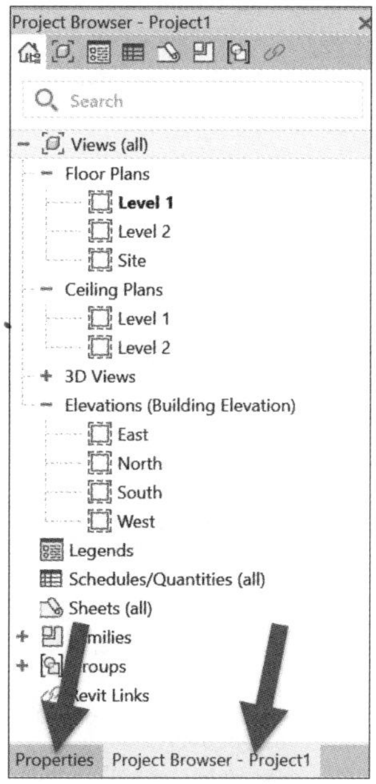

Alternative configuration

Right-click on *Views (all)*, at the top of the *Project Browser*, and you will find a **Search** option in the pop-up menu. This can be used to search for a *View*, *Family*, etc., a useful tool when working on a large project with 100s of items to sift through.

Like the *Properties Palette*, the width of the *Project Browser* can be adjusted. When the two are stacked above each other, they both move together. You can also stack the two directly on top of each other; in this case, you will see a tab for each at the bottom, as shown in the second image to the left.

The *Project Browser* should be left open; if you accidentally close it by clicking the "X" in the upper right, you can reopen it by
View → Window → User Interface → Project Browser.

The *Project Browser* and *Properties Palette* can be repositioned on a second monitor, if you have one, when you want more room to work in the drawing window.

Status Bar

This area will display, on the far left, information about the current command or list information about a selected element. The right-hand side of the *Status Bar* shows the number of elements selected. The small funnel icon to the left of the selection number can be clicked to open the *Filter* dialog box, which lets you narrow your current selection to a specific category; for example, you could select the entire floor plan and then filter it down to just the doors. This is different than the *Selection Filter* in the *Properties Palette,* which keeps everything selected.

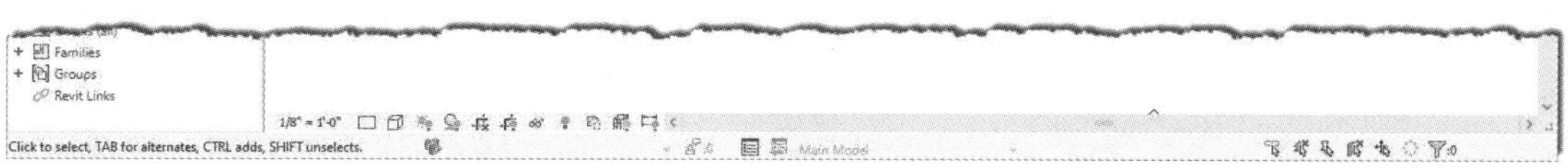

On the *Status Bar*, the first five icons on the right, shown in the image below, control how elements are **selected**. From left to right, these are:

- Select Links
- Select Underlay Elements
- Select Pinned Elements
- Select Elements by Face
- Drag Elements on Selection

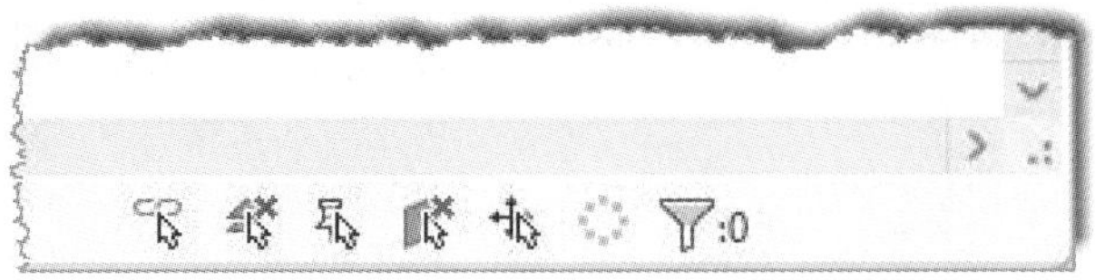

Hover your cursor over an icon for the name and for a brief description of what it does. These are toggles that are on or off; **the red 'X' in the upper right of each icon means you cannot select that type of element within the model**. These controls help prevent accidentally moving or deleting things. Keep these toggles in mind if you are having trouble selecting something; you may have accidentally toggled one of these on.

Finally, the two drop-down lists toward the center of the Status Bar control, Design Options and Worksets (see the image on the previous page). Design Options facilitate multiple design solutions in the same area, and *Worksets* enable more than one designer to be in the model at a time.

View Control Bar

This feature gives you convenient access to tools that control each view's display settings (e.g., scale, shadows, detail level, graphics style). The options vary slightly between view types: 2D view, 3D view, Sheet, and Schedule. The important thing to know is that these settings only affect the current view, the one listed on the *Application Title Bar*. Most of these settings are available in the *Properties Palette*, but this toolbar cannot be turned off (i.e., hidden) as the *Properties Palette* can.

Context Menu

The *context menu* appears near the cursor whenever you right-click (see image at right). The options on that menu will vary depending on what tool is active or what element is selected.

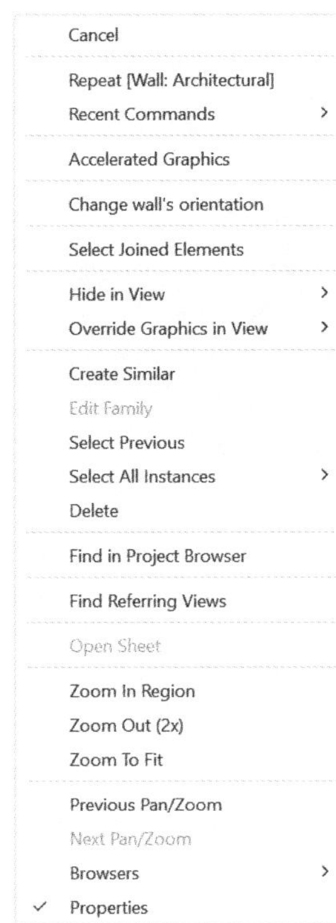

Context menu example with a wall selected

Canvas (aka Drawing Window)

This is where you manipulate the Building Information Model (BIM). Here you will see the current view (plan, elevation, or section), schedule, or sheet. Any changes made are instantly propagated to the entire database.

Autodesk Assistant (with Autodesk AI)

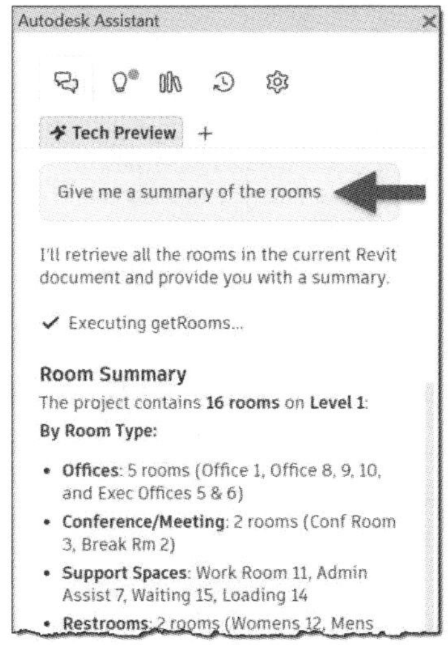

This feature has primarily been an advanced help feature across Autodesk products. But that changes significantly with the integration of **Autodesk AI**. While the early version of this AI tool offers model interrogation and some creation and editing options, the feature will surely enable significant advancements in creativity, efficiency, and accuracy within Revit specifically and the AEC industry in general. Remember, AI can make mistakes!

Example prompts:

- What can you do for me?
- Check sheets naming consistency
- Create a door schedule sorted by level

A summary of rooms was requested in the example shown here.

Revit Options

There are several User Interface settings that are not tied to the current model. That is, these settings apply to the installation of Revit on your computer, rather than to just one model or project file. A few of these settings will be briefly discussed here. It is recommended that you don't make any changes here right now.

Click on **Options** in the *File* tab. The options under File Locations specify where Revit finds templates and content. In the Hardware section, verify that your graphics card and display driver meet Autodesk's minimum requirements. If Revit is crashing or exhibits strange behavior, it often relates to your graphics driver. You can bypass this problem by turning off *Use Hardware Acceleration*, but this will make Revit run slower when panning and zooming.

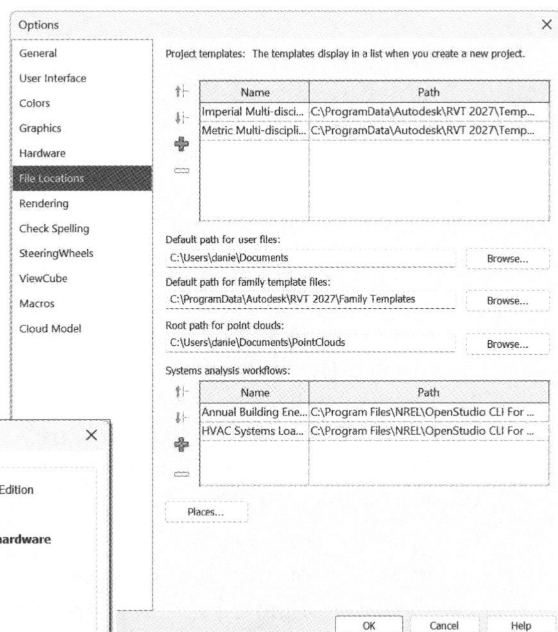

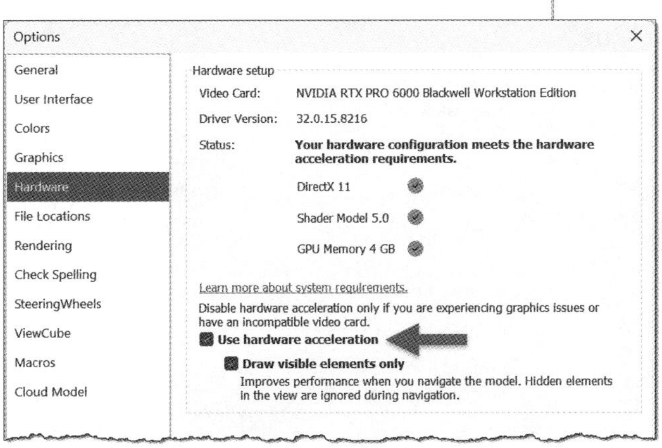

Efficient Practices

The *Ribbon* and menus are really helpful when learning a program like Revit; however, most experienced users rarely use them! The process of moving the mouse to the edge of the screen to select a command, then back to where you were, is very inefficient, especially for those who do this all day, five days a week. Here are a few ways experienced BIM operators work:

- Use the wheel on the mouse to Zoom (spin the wheel), Pan (press and hold the wheel button while moving the mouse), and Zoom Extents (double-clicking the wheel button). All this can be done while in another command; so, if you are in the middle of drawing walls and need to zoom in to see which point you are about to Snap to, you can do it without canceling the Line command and without losing focus on the area you are designing by having to click an icon near the edge of the screen.

- Revit conforms to many of the Microsoft Windows operating system standards. Most programs, including Revit, have several standard commands that can be accessed via keyboard shortcuts. Here are a few examples (press both keys at the same time):
    - Ctrl + S   Save   *(saves the current model)*
    - Ctrl + A   Select All   *(selects everything in the text editor)*
    - Ctrl + Z   Undo   *(undoes the previous action)*
    - Ctrl + X   Cut   *(Cut to Windows clipboard)*
    - Ctrl + C   Copy   *(does not replace Revit's Copy tool)*
    - Ctrl + V   Paste   *(used to copy between models/views/levels)*
    - Ctrl + Tab   Change View   *(toggles between open views)*
    - Ctrl + P   Print   *(opens print dialog)*
    - Ctrl + N   New   *(create new project file)*
    - F7   Spelling   *(launch spell check feature)*
    - ENTER   Previous Command   *(repeat previous command)*

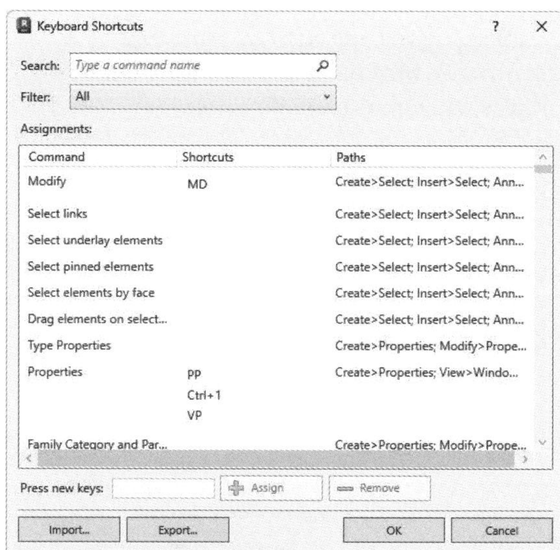

Keyboard shortcuts dialog

- If you recall, the *Open Documents* area, on the *File Tab,* lists all the views that are currently open on your computer. By clicking one of the names in the list, you "switch" to that view. A shortcut is to press **Ctrl + Tab** to quickly cycle through the open drawings.

- Many Revit commands also have keyboard shortcuts. So, with your right hand on the mouse (and not moving from the "design" area), your left hand can type **WA** when you want to draw a Wall, for example. You can see all the preloaded shortcuts and add new ones by clicking *View (tab)* → *User Interface (drop-down)* → *Keyboard Shortcuts.*

It should be noted that any customized keyboard shortcuts are specific to the computer you are working on, not the project. You can use the *Export* button (see image to the right) to save the entire keyboard shortcuts list to a file, and then *Import* it into another computer's copy of Revit.

View Tabs

Revit displays a tab for each open view. Clicking a tab is a quick way to switch between open views. Click the "X" in each view tab to close that view. Drag a tab to change its position. Tabs can also be pulled outside of the main Revit application window – even to a second monitor. In the second image below, the schedule could be filling a second computer screen while reviewing the same information in the floor plan.

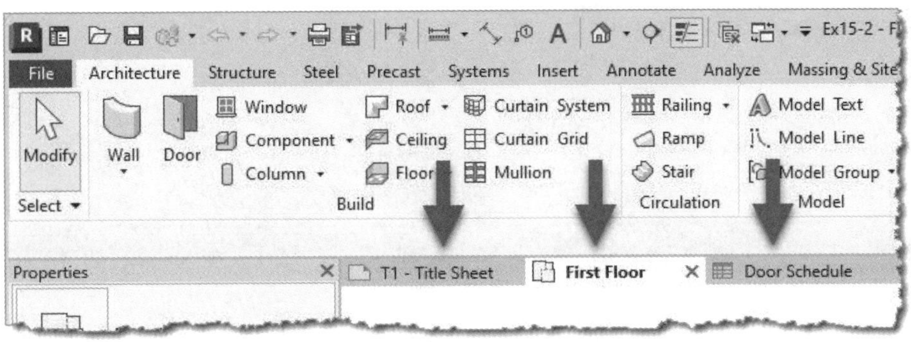

View Tabs; one for each open view

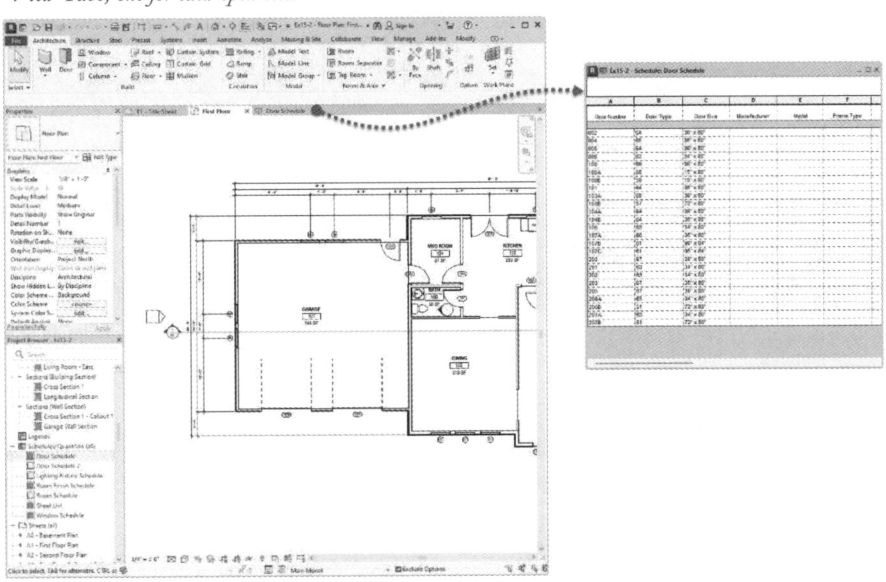

View Tabs can be pulled outside of the main Revit application window, even to a second screen

This concludes your brief overview of the Revit user interface. Many of these tools and operations will be covered in more detail throughout the book.

Exercise 1-3:
Open, Save, and Close a Revit Project

To *Open* **Revit 2027** in Windows 11, select Start and then click Revit 2027 or search for it.

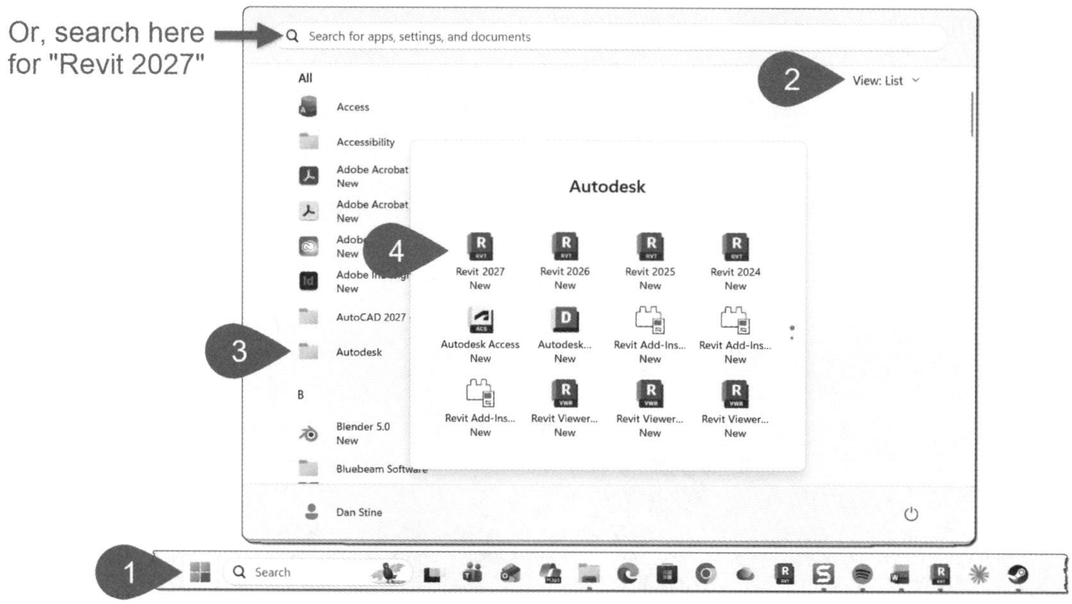

Or double-click the Revit icon on your desktop.

How to Open a Revit Project

By default, Revit opens to the Home screen, which displays thumbnails of recent projects you have worked on. Clicking the thumbnail opens the project.

1. Click the **Open** button under *Models* as shown to the right.

FYI: If the preview is for a *Central* file (aka Worksharing) it will automatically open a *Local* file. Worksharing allows multiple people to work in the same file.

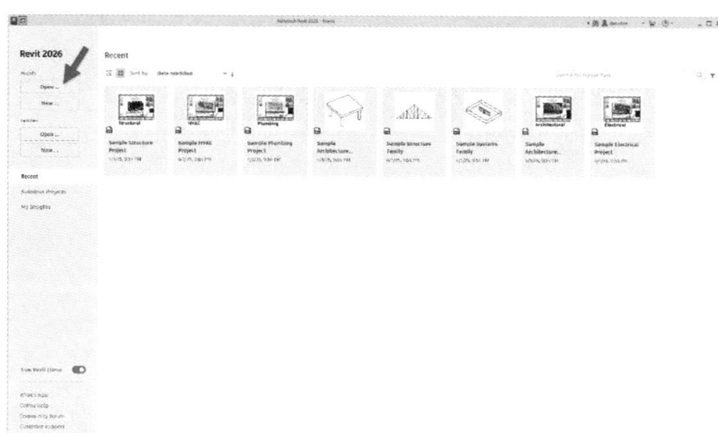

FIGURE 1-3.1 Revit Home screen

Next, you will open an existing Revit project file. You will select a sample file provided online at SDCpublications.com; see the inside front cover for more information.

2. Click the drop-down box at the top of the *Open* dialog (Figure 1-3.2). Browse to your downloaded files (provided files must be downloaded from www.SDCpublications.com; see the backside of the front cover of this book for more info).

   TIP: *If you cannot access the online sample files, you can substitute any Revit file you can find. Some sample files may be found here on your computer's hard drive: C:\Program Files\Autodesk\Revit 2027\Samples, or via* ***File*** *(tab)* **→** ***Open*** *(fly-out)* **→** ***Sample Files.***

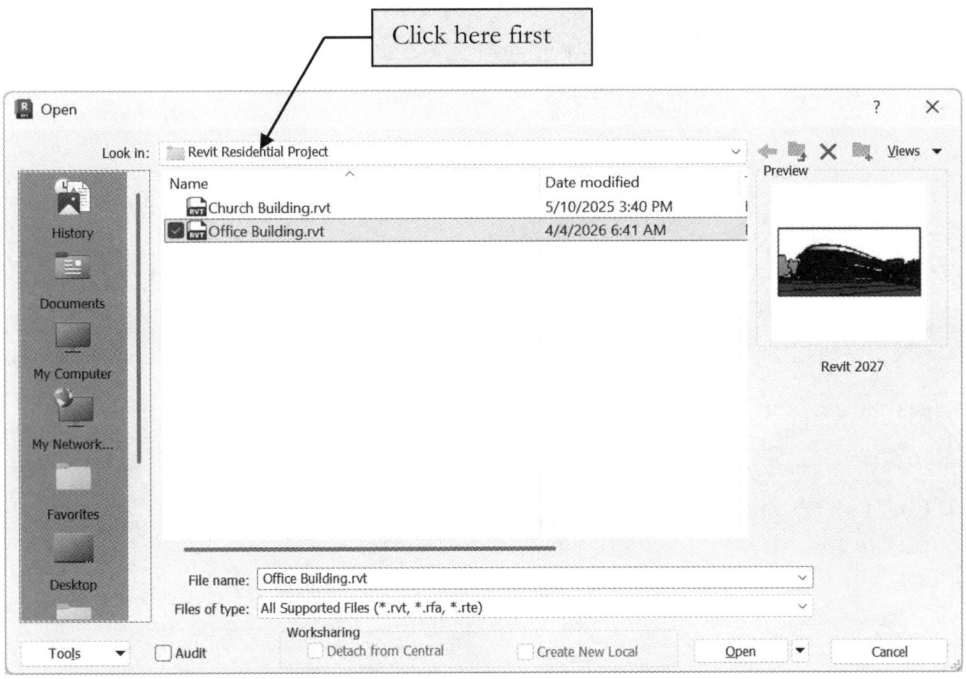

FIGURE 1-3.2 Open dialog; downloaded content from SDCpublications.com

3. Select the file named **Office Building.rvt** and click **Open**.

FYI: *Notice the preview of the selected file. This will help you select the correct file before taking the time to open it.*

The *Office Building.rvt* file is now open, and the last saved view is displayed in the drawing window (Figure 1-3.3).

FIGURE 1-3.3 Sample file "Office Building.rvt"

FYI: The Autodesk Assistant can be closed if additional screen space is needed. To open it later: **View → User Interface → Autodesk Assistant.**

The *File Tab* lists the projects and views currently open on your computer (Figure 1-3.4).

4. Click **File Tab → Open Documents (icon)** (Figure 1-3.4).

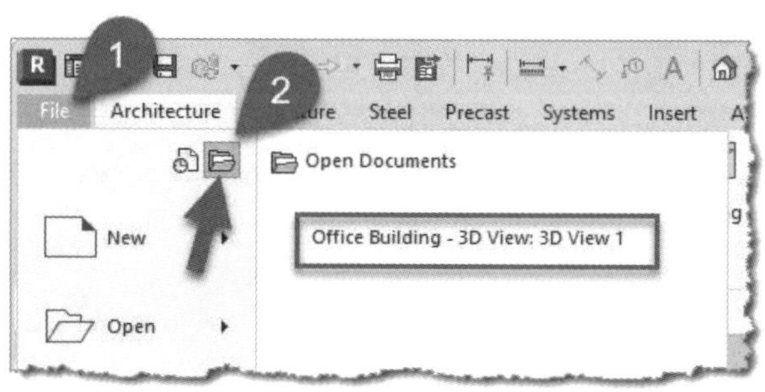

FIGURE 1-3.4 File Tab: Open Documents view

Notice that the *Office Building.rvt* project file is listed. Next to the project name is the name of a view open on your computer (e.g., floor plan, elevation).

Additional views will be added to the list as you open them. Each view has the project name as a prefix. The current view, the view you are working in, is always at the top of the list. You can toggle between open views from this menu by clicking on them, but this is normally done via the View tabs above the drawing window.

Opening Another Revit Project

Revit allows you to have more than one project open at a time.

5. Click **Open** from the *Quick Access Toolbar.*

6. Per the instructions previously covered, browse the downloaded online files.

7. Select the file named **Church Building.rvt** and click **Open** (Figure 1-3.5).

   TIP: If you cannot locate the online files, substitute one of the Autodesk sample files.

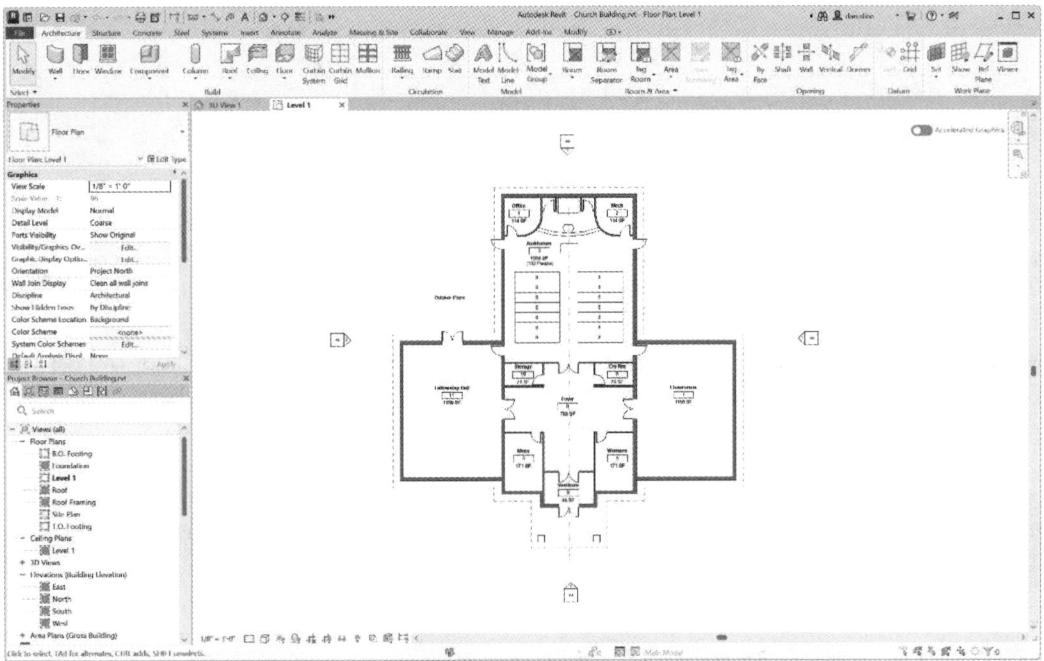

FIGURE 1-3.5 Sample file "Church Building.rvt"

8. Click **Open Documents** from the *File Tab* (Figure 1-3.6).

Notice that the *Church Building.rvt* project is now listed along with a view: Floor Plan: Level 1.

Try toggling between projects by clicking on *Office Building.rvt – 3D View: 3D View 1.*

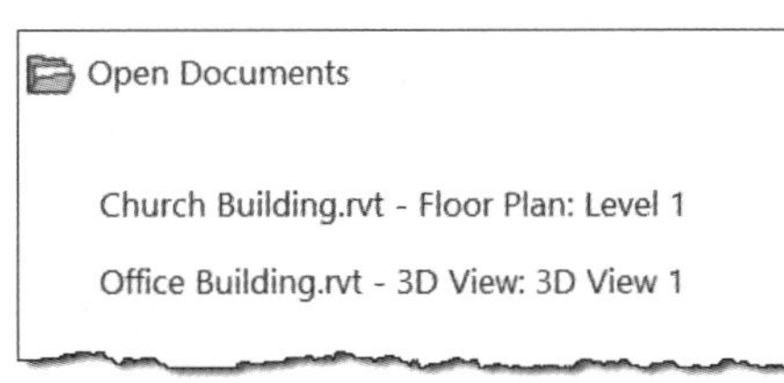

FIGURE 1-3.6 Open Documents

Close a Revit Project

9. Select **File Tab → Close**; click **No** if prompted to save.

This will close the current project/view. If more than one view is open for a project, only the current view will close. The project and the other open views will not close until you get to the last open view.

10. Repeat the previous step to close the other project file.

If you made changes and have not saved your project yet, you will be prompted to save your project before Revit closes the view. **Do not save at this time**. When all open project files are closed, you find yourself back in the *Revit Home* screen – which is where you started.

Saving a Revit Project

At this time, you will not actually save a project.

To save a project file, simply select *Save* from the *Quick Access Toolbar*. You can also select *Save* from the *File Tab* or press *Ctrl* + *S* on the keyboard.

You should get in the habit of saving often to avoid losing work due to a power outage or program crash. Revit offers a reminder to save; the notification is based on how long it has been since your last save. The **Save Time Interval** is set in *Options*.

You can also save a copy of the current project by selecting **Save As** from the File Tab. Once you use the Save As command, you are in the new project file, and the file you started in is closed.

Closing the Revit Program

Finally, from the *File Tab,* select **Exit Revit**. This will close any open projects/views and shut down Revit. Again, you will be prompted to save, if needed, before Revit closes the view. **Do not save at this time**.

You can also click the "X" in the upper-right corner of the *Application* window to close Revit.

Exercise 1-4:
Creating a New Project

Open **Autodesk Revit**.

Creating a New Project File

The steps required to set up a new Revit model project file are very simple.

To manually create a new project (maybe you just finished working on a previous assignment and want to start the next one):

1. Select **New** under "Models" on the Home Screen (not New "Families").

FYI: *If the Home screen is not visible, you can also select File tab → New → Project.*

After clicking *New,* you will get the ***New Project*** dialog box (Figure 1-4.1).

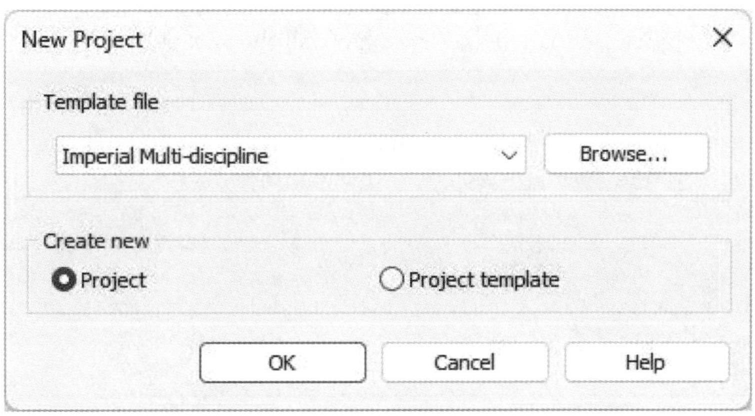

FIGURE 1-4.1 New Project dialog box

The *New Project* dialog box lets you specify the template file you want to use, or not use a template at all via the <None> option (which is not recommended). You can also specify whether you want to create a new project or a new template file.

2. Select the **Imperial Multi-discipline** option in the drop-down list. Leave *Create new* set to **Project** (Figure 1-4.1).

3. Click **OK**. You now have a new unnamed/unsaved project file.

To name an unnamed project file you simply *Save*. The first time an unnamed project file is saved you will be prompted to specify the name and location for the project file.

4. Select **File → Save** from the *Ribbon.*

5. Specify a **name** and **location** for your new project file.
   Your instructor may specify a location or folder for your files if in a classroom setting.

What is a Template File?

A template file allows you to start your project with specific content and certain settings preset the way you like or need them.

For example, you can have the units set to *Imperial* or *Metric*. You can have the door, window and wall families you use most loaded and eliminate other less often used content. Also, you can have your company's title block preloaded and even have all the sheets for a project set up.

A custom template is a must for design firms and contractors using Revit and will prove useful to the student as they become more proficient with the program.

> ***Be Aware:***
> It will be assumed from this point forward that the reader understands how to create, open and save project files. Please refer back to this section as needed. If you still need further assistance, ask your instructor for help.

Exercise 1-5:
Using Zoom and Pan to View Your Drawings

Learning to *Pan* and *Zoom* in and out of a drawing is essential for accurate and efficient design, drafting, and visualization. We will review these commands now so you are ready to use them with the first design exercise.

Open **Revit**.

You will select a sample file from the SDC Publications-provided online files.

1. Select **Open** from the *Quick Access Toolbar.*
2. Browse to the **downloaded online files**.
3. Select the file named **Church Building.rvt** and click **Open** (Figure 1-5.1).

    TIP: If you cannot locate the online files, substitute any of the training files that come with Revit, found at C:\Program Files\Autodesk\Revit 2027\Samples.

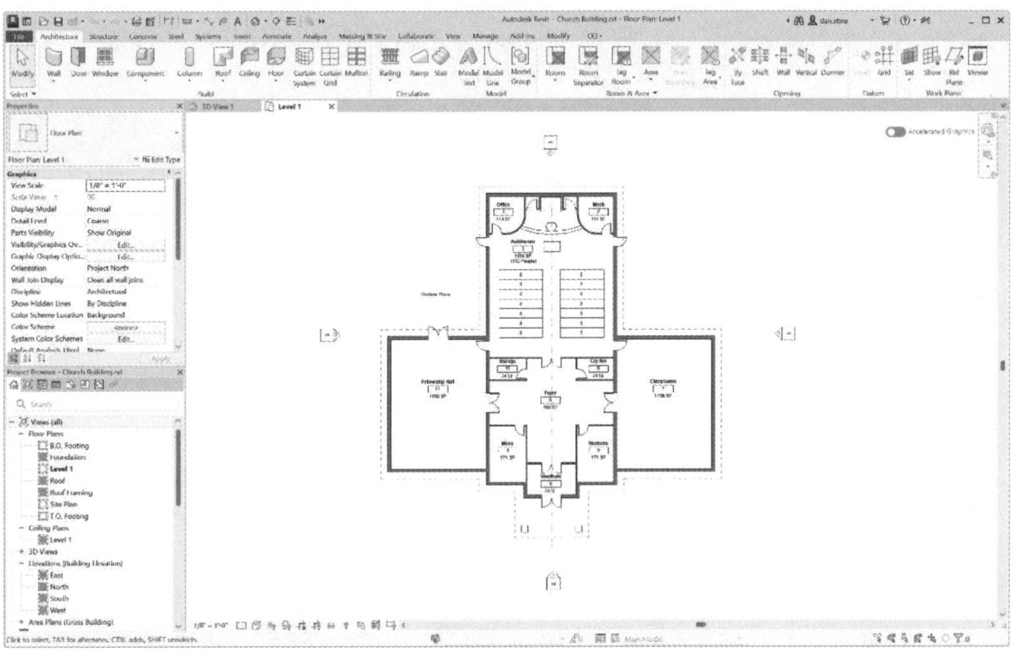

FIGURE 1-5.1 Church Building.rvt project

If the default view that is loaded is not **Floor Plan: Level 1**, double-click on **Level 1** under **Views\Floor Plans** in the *Project Browser*. Level 1 will be bold when it is the active or current view in the drawing window.

Using Zoom and Pan Tools

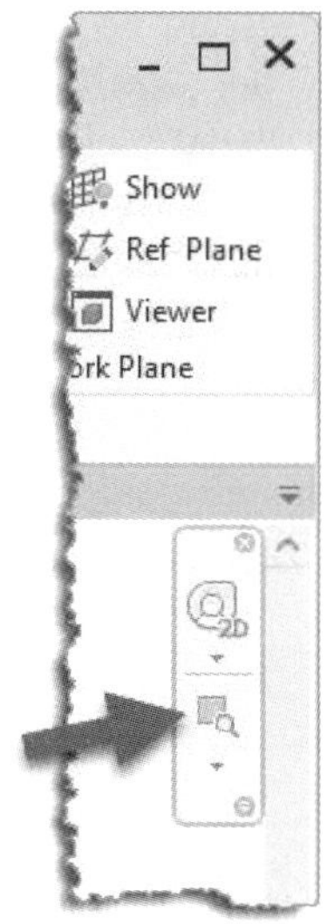

You can access the *Zoom* tools from the ***Navigation Bar*** or use the *scroll wheel* on your mouse.

The *Zoom* icon contains several zoom-related tools:

- The default (i.e., visible) icon is *Zoom in Region*, which allows you to window an area to zoom into.
- The *Zoom* icon is a **split button**.
- Clicking the down-arrow part of the button reveals a list of related *Zoom* tools.
- You will see the drop-down list on the next page.

Zoom In

4. Select the top portion of the *Zoom* icon (see image to right).

5. Drag a window over your plan view (Figure 1-5.2).

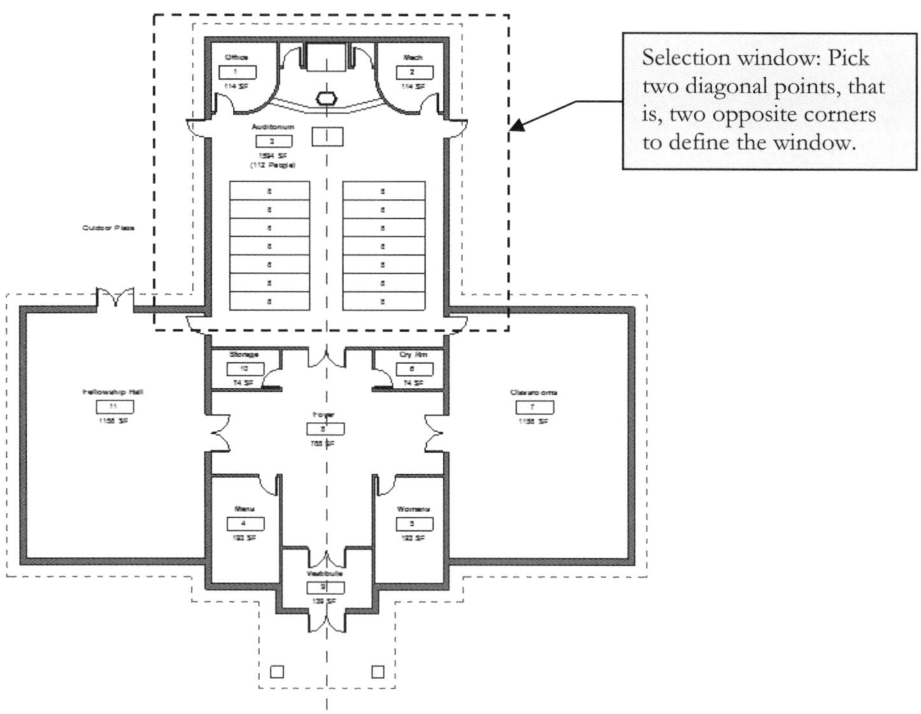

FIGURE 1-5.2 Zoom In window

You should now be zoomed in to the specified area (Figure 1-5.3).

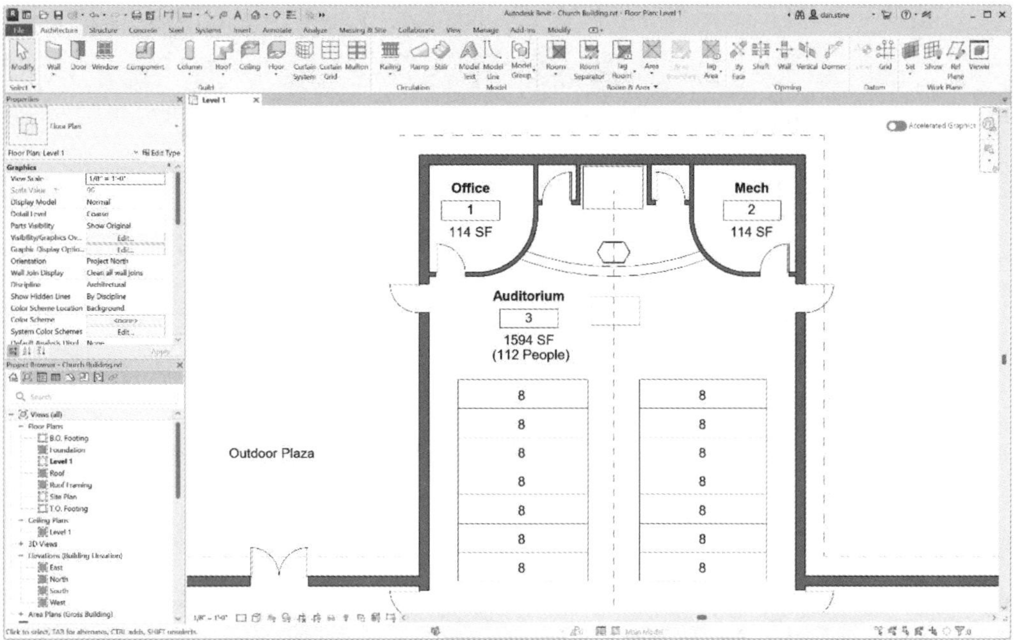

FIGURE 1-5.3 Zoom In results

Zoom Out

6. Click the down-arrow next to the zoom icon (Figure 1-5.4). Select **Previous Pan/Zoom**.

You should now be back where you started. Each time you select this icon, you are resorting to a previous view state. Sometimes you have to select this option multiple times if you did some panning and multiple zooms.

7. **Zoom** into a smaller area, and then **Pan**, i.e., adjust the portion of the view seen, by holding down the scroll wheel button.

The Pan tool just changes the portion of the model you see on the screen; it does not actually move it.

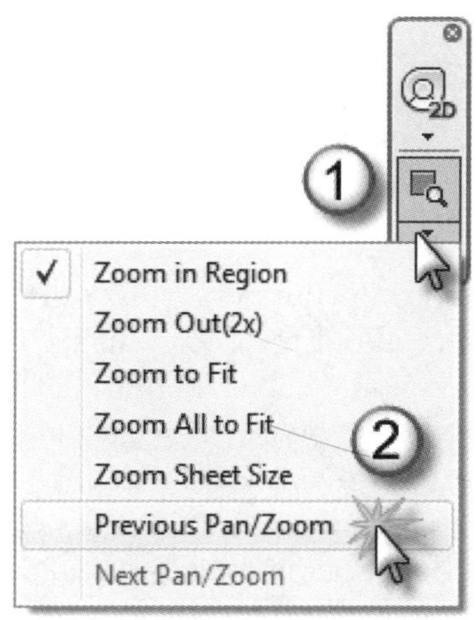

FIGURE 1-5.4 Zoom Icon drop-down

Take a minute and try the other *Zoom* tools to see how they work. When finished, click **Zoom to Fit** before moving on.

TIP: *You can double-click the wheel button on your mouse to* Zoom Extents *in the current view.*

Default 3D View

Clicking on the *Default 3D View* icon on the *QAT* loads a 3D View. This allows you to quickly switch to a 3D view.

8. Click on the **Default 3D View** icon.

9. Go to the **Open Documents** listing in the *File Tab* and notice that the *3D View* and the *Floor Plan* view are both listed at the bottom.

   REMEMBER: *You can toggle between views here.*

10. Click the **Esc** key to close the *File Tab.*

ViewCube

The *ViewCube* provides convenient control over the 3D view. This technology has been implemented across many of Autodesk's programs to make the process seamless for its customers.

11. You should notice the ***ViewCube*** in the upper right corner of the drawing window (Figure 1-5.5). If not, you can turn it on by clicking *View → Windows → User Interface → ViewCube.*

    TIP: *The ViewCube is only visible in 3D views.*

Hovering your cursor over the *ViewCube* engages it. As you move about the *Cube,* you see various areas highlight. If you click, you will be taken to that highlighted area in the drawing window. You can also click and drag your cursor on the *Cube* to "roll" the model in an unconstrained fashion. Click and drag the mouse on the disk below the Cube to spin the model without rolling. Finally, you have a few options in a right-click menu, and the **Home** icon, just above the *Cube*, gets you back to where you started if things get disoriented!

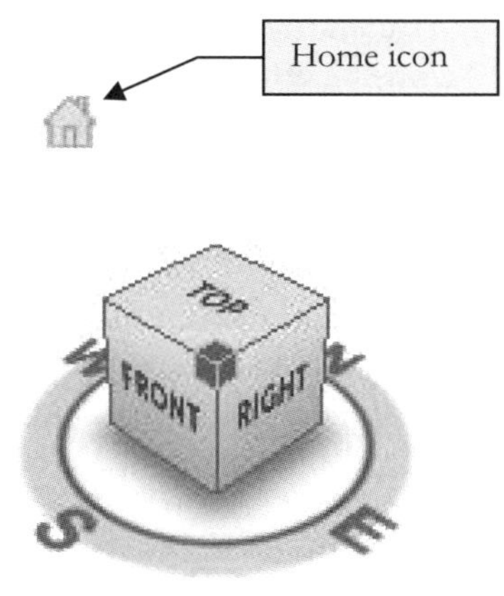

FIGURE 1-5.5 ViewCube

12. Give the *ViewCube* a try, then click the **Home** icon when you are done.

    REMEMBER: *The* Home *icon only shows up when your cursor is over the ViewCube.*

Navigation Wheel

Similar to the *ViewCube*, the *Navigation Wheel* helps you navigate your model. With the *Navigation Wheel,* you can walk through your model, going down hallways and turning into rooms. Revit has not advanced to the point where the doors will open for you; thus, you walk through closed doors or walls as if you were a ghost!

The *Navigation Wheel* is activated by clicking the upper icon on the *Navigation Bar.*

Unfortunately, it is way too early in your Revit endeavors to learn to use the *Navigation Wheel.* You can try this in the chapter on creating photorealistic renderings and camera views. You would typically use this tool in a camera view.

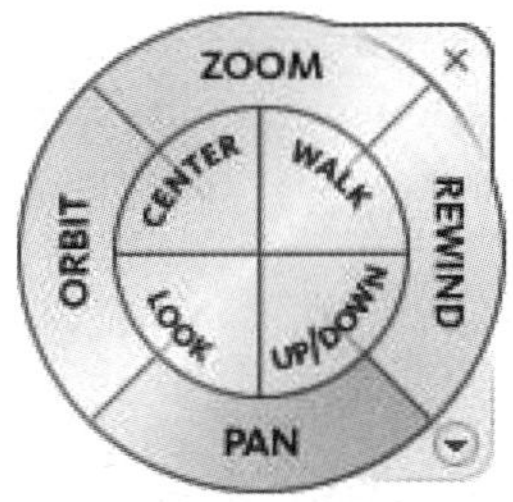

FIGURE 1-5.6 Navigation Wheel

13. **Close** the *Church Building* project **without** saving.

Using the Scroll Wheel on the Mouse

The scroll wheel on the mouse is a must for those using BIM software. In Revit, you can *Pan* and *Zoom* without even clicking a zoom icon. You simply **scroll the wheel to zoom** and **hold the wheel button down to pan**. This can be done while in another command (e.g., while drawing walls). Another nice feature is that the drawing zooms into the area near your cursor, rather than zooming only at the center of the drawing window. Give this a try before moving on. Once you get the hang of it, you will not want to use the icons. Also, double-clicking the wheel button zooms *to Fit* so everything is visible on the screen.

Exercise 1-6:
Using Revit's Help System

This section of your introductory chapter will provide a quick overview of Revit's *Help System*. This will allow you to study topics in more detail if you want to know how something works beyond the introductory scope of this textbook.

1. Click the **round question mark** icon in the upper-right corner of the screen.

You are now in Revit's Help site (Figure 1-6.1). This is a website which opened in your web browser. The window can be positioned side by side with Revit, which is especially nice if you have a dual-screen computer system. This interface requires an internet connection. As a website, Autodesk can add and revise information at any time, unlike files stored on your hard drive. This also means the site can change quite a bit, potentially making the following overview outdated. If the site has changed, just follow along as best you can for the next three pages.

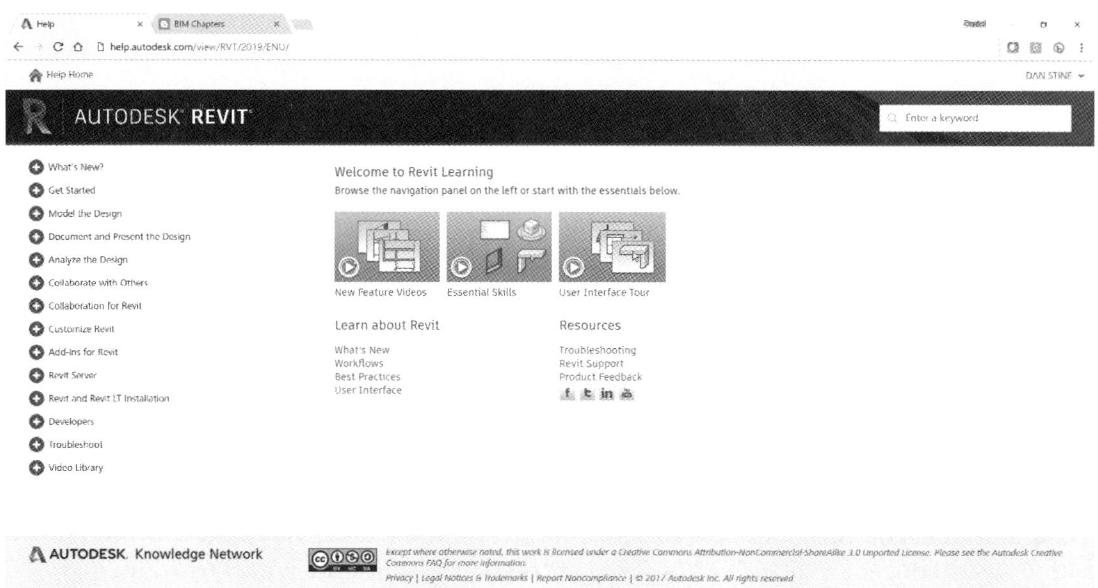

FIGURE 1-6.1 Autodesk Help site

Tip: Remember that the **Autodesk Assistant** can also be used to learn more about specific commands, and, with its AI-powered capabilities, it can even execute some of them for you.

In the upper right, you can click the search field and search the *Help System* for a word or phrase. You may also click any one of the links to learn more about the topic listed. The next few steps will show you how to access the *Help System's* content on the Revit user interface, a topic you have just studied.

2. On the left, click the **plus symbol** next to **Get Started**.

3. Now, click the **plus symbol** next to **User Interface** (Figure 1-6.2).

Notice the tree structure on the left. You can use this to quickly navigate the help site.

4. Finally, click directly on **Ribbon**.

You now see information about the *Ribbon* as shown in the image below. Notice additional links are provided below on the current topic. You can use the browser's *Back* and *Forward* buttons to move around in the *Help System*.

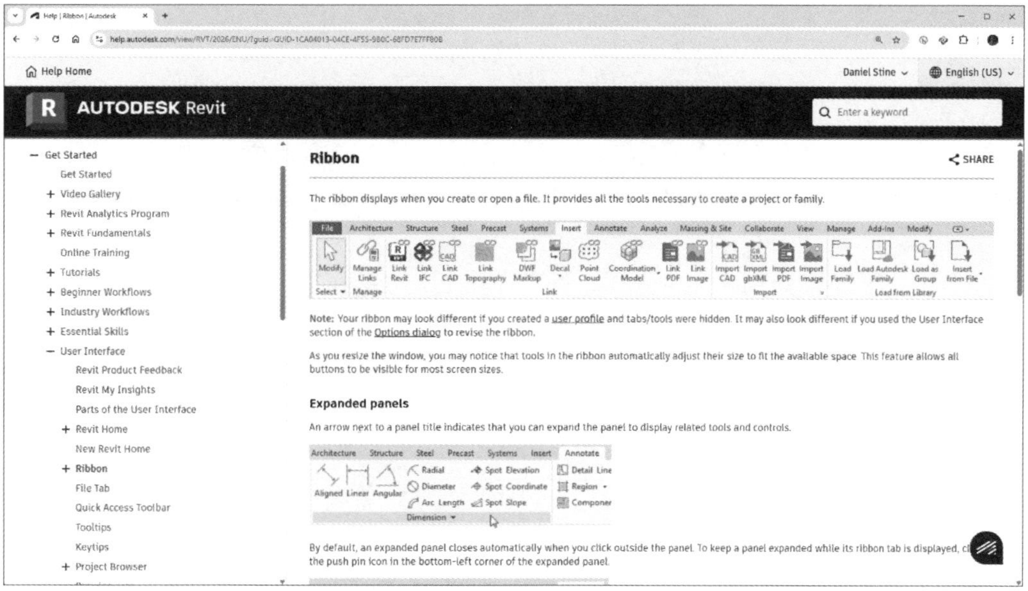

FIGURE 1-6.2 Help window; Ribbon overview

Next, you will try searching the Revit *Help System* for a specific Revit feature. This is a quick way to find information if you have an idea of what it is you are looking for.

5. In the upper right corner of the current *Help System* web page, click in the search text box and then type **gutter**.

6. Press **Enter** on the keyboard.

The search results are shown in Figure 1-6.3. Each item in the list is a link that will take you to information on that topic.

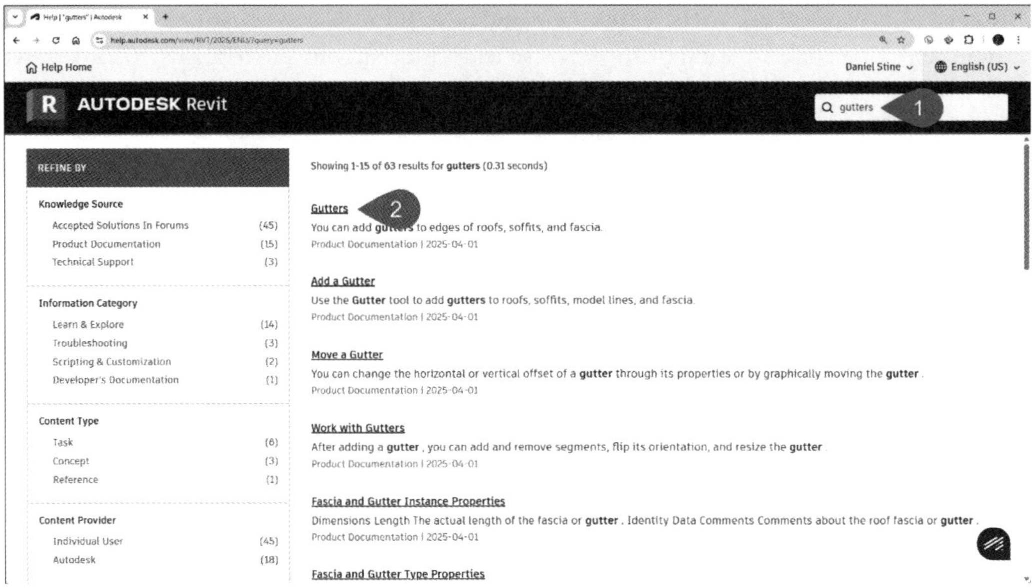

FIGURE 1-6.3 Help search results

The *Help System* can be used to complement this textbook. It is a reference resource, not a tutorial. As you work through the tutorials in this book, you may want to use the Help System to fill in the blanks if you have trouble or want more information on a topic.

Exercise 1-7:
Introduction to Autodesk Drive

We will finish this chapter with a look at Autodesk Drive, which is an integral foundation for much of Autodesk's **Cloud Services**. You do not necessarily need to use Autodesk's cloud services to complete this book successfully.

AUTODESK® **DRIVE**

Here is how Autodesk describes *Autodesk Drive* on their website:

Autodesk Drive is a cloud storage solution that allows individuals and small teams to organize, preview, and share any type of design or model data.

You can use Autodesk Drive to:

- Upload data to a personal cloud drive.
- Organize and manage your data into folders.
- View 2D and 3D designs and models within the browser on any device.
- Share files & folders with others for viewing, editing, uploading, and managing data.
- You can also access, view, and edit data that others have shared with you.
- With Desktop Connector installed, you can also view and organize files stored in Drive from your desktop and desktop applications.

The Cloud, Defined

Before we discuss *Autodesk Drive* with more specificity, let's define what the *Cloud* is. **The Cloud is a service, or collection of services, which exists partially or completely online.** This is different from the *Internet*, which mostly involves downloading static information, in that you are creating and manipulating data. Most of this happens outside of your laptop or desktop computer.

The cloud gives the average user access to massive amounts of storage space, computing power, and software they could not otherwise afford if they had to actually own, install, and maintain these resources in their office, school, or home. In one sense, this is similar to a *Tool Rental Center*, in that the average person could not afford, nor would it be cost-effective to own, a jackhammer. However, for a fraction of the cost of ownership and maintenance, we can rent it for a few hours. In this case, everyone wins!

Creating an Autodesk Account

The first thing an individual needs to do in order to gain access to *Autodesk Drive* is create a free Autodesk account at drive.autodesk.com. If you are already using an Autodesk product, you likely already have an Autodesk account.

This account is for an individual person, not a computer, not an installation of Revit or AutoCAD, nor does it come from your employer or school. Each person who wishes to access *Autodesk Drive* services must create an account, which will give them a unique username and password.

Generally speaking, there are two ways you can access *Autodesk Drive* cloud services:

- Autodesk Drive website
- Within Revit or AutoCAD; local computer

Autodesk Drive Website

When you have documents stored in the *Cloud,* you can access them via your web browser. Here you can manage your files, view them without the full application (some file formats are not supported), and share them. These features use advanced browser technology, so make sure your browser is up to date; Chrome works well.

Using the website, you can upload files from your computer to store in the *Cloud.* To do this, create or open a Folder, then click the **Upload** option (Fig. 1-7.1).

FIGURE 1-7.1 Viewing files stored in the cloud

Tip: If using a modern browser, you can drag and drop documents onto the window. This is a great way to create a secure backup of your documents.

You can share files stored in the *Cloud* with others. Simply hover over a file within *Autodesk DRIVE* and click the **Get Link** icon to see the Share dialog (Figure 1-7.2). Anyone with this link can view and download the shared files (if Allow Downloads is toggled on).

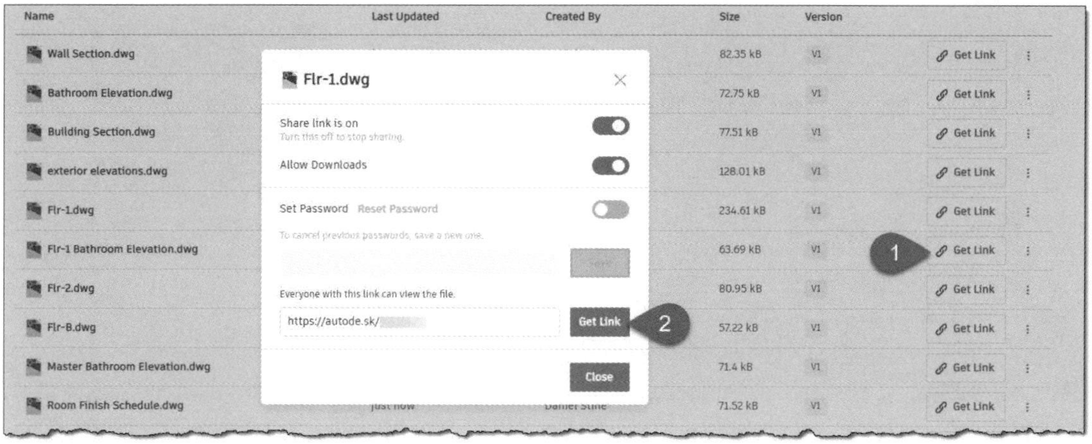

FIGURE 1-7.2 Sharing files stored in the cloud

Installing Autodesk Desktop Connector

To sync the Autodesk Drive files with your local computer and work directly on these files, you must first download Autodesk Desktop Connector. This tool creates an environment similar to OneDrive or Dropbox, but with enhanced features supporting Autodesk-specific CAD and BIM workflows.

To install Desktop Connector, first close any open Autodesk products, such as AutoCAD. Then click the **Get Desktop Connector** button (Fig. 1-7.1) to access the download page. Download the latest version and install it.

Files are now synced locally and appear in This PC in Windows Explorer (Fig. 1-7.3).

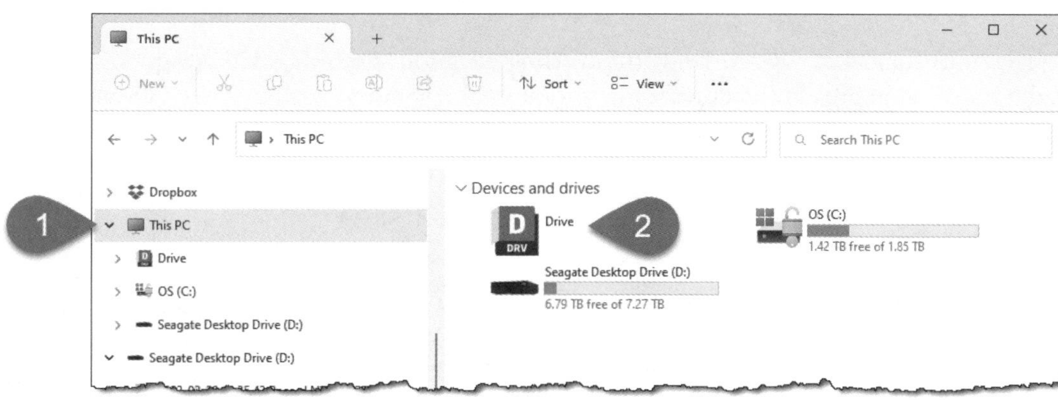

FIGURE 1-7.3 Accessing Drive files via Desktop Connector

The same cloud-based files appear locally, as shown below (Fig. 1-7.4).

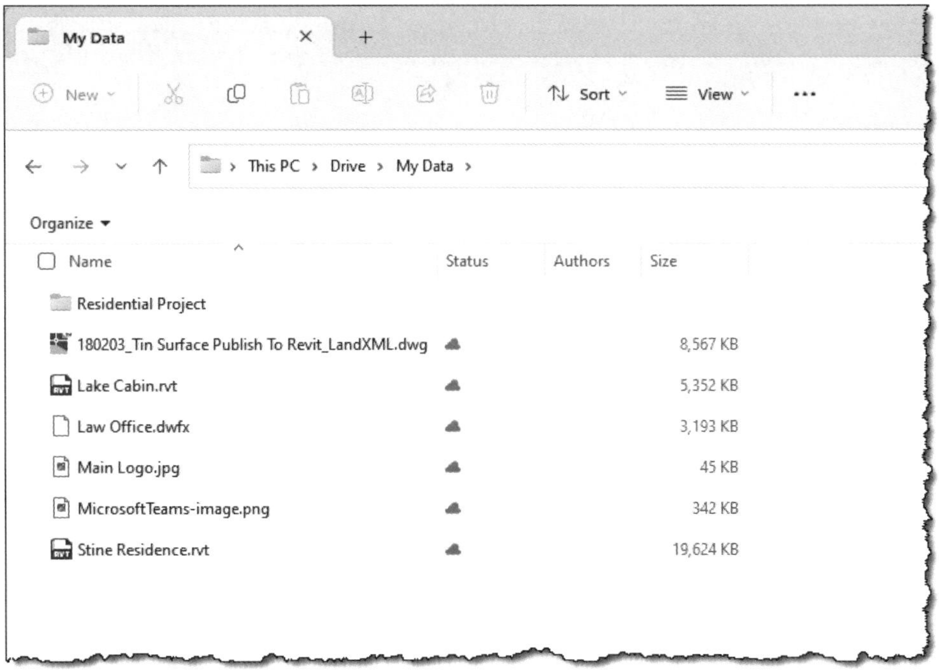

FIGURE 1-7.4 Accessing Drive files via Desktop Connector

Accessing Autodesk DRIVE within your CAD/BIM application

Another way to access your cloud-stored data is from within your Autodesk application, such as Revit or AutoCAD. This is typically the most convenient, as you can open, view, and modify your drawings. Once logged in, you will also have access to any *Cloud Services* available to you from within the application, such as rendering services or *Green Building Studio.*

To sign into your *Autodesk Account* within your application, simply click the **Sign In** option in the notification area in the upper right corner of the window. You will need to enter your student email address and password, or your work/personal email if you are not a student. When properly logged in, you will see your username or email address listed, as shown in Figure 1-7.5 below. Note: you are most likely already signed in, as this is required to use most Autodesk products.

FIGURE 1-7.5 Example of user logged into their Autodesk account

The files within Autodesk Drive may be accessed via the **Open** dialog, as shown in Figure 1-7.6 below. Working on the files in this location ensures they are automatically backed up every time you save your work.

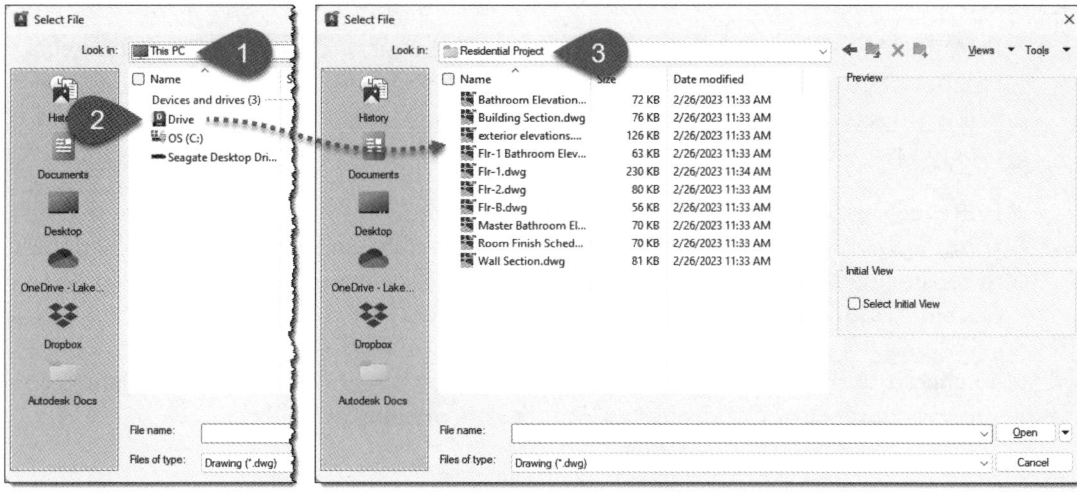

FIGURE 1-7.6 Accessing Autodesk Drive within AutoCAD or Revit

Notice that once a file has been modified, you can tell by the **Version** being incremented in Autodesk Drive when viewed in your browser, as shown below (Fig. 1-7.7).

FIGURE 1-7.7 Accessing Autodesk Drive within AutoCAD or Revit

When using AutoCAD and when sharing files with others via Drive, only one person may modify a DWG file at a time. Similarly, when working with Revit models, an additional paid service called **Forma Design Collaboration** (previously BIM 360 Collaborate Pro) is required for multiple users to work within the same BIM.

As you work through this book, it is recommended that you save all your work in the Cloud via Autodesk Drive, so you have a safe, secure location for your files. These files can then be accessed from several locations via the two methods discussed here. It is still important to maintain a separate copy of your files on a flash drive, a portable hard drive, or in another cloud-based service such as *Dropbox*. This will be important if your main files ever become corrupt. You should manually back up your files to your backup location so a corrupt file does not automatically corrupt your backups.

TIP: If you have a file that will not open, try one of the following:

- In AutoCAD: Open AutoCAD and then, from the *Application Menu*, select Drawing Utilities → Recover → **Recover**. Then browse to your file and open it. AutoCAD will try to recover the drawing file. This may require some things to be deleted, but it is better than losing the entire file.

- In Revit: Open Revit and then, from the *Application Menu*, select Open, browse to your file, and select it. Click the **Audit** checkbox, then click Open. Revit will attempt to repair any problems with the project database. Some elements may need to be deleted, but this is better than losing the entire file.

Be sure to check out the Autodesk website to learn more about Forma Design Collaboration and the growing number of cloud services Autodesk is offering.

Self-Exam:

The following questions can be used as a way to check your knowledge of this lesson. The answers can be found at the bottom of this page.

1. The *View* tab allows you to save your project file. (T/F)
2. You can zoom in and out using the wheel on a wheel mouse. (T/F)
3. Revit is a parametric architectural design program. (T/F)
4. A ______________ file allows you to start your project with specific content and certain settings preset the way you like or need them.
5. Autodesk Drive allows you to save your files safely in the ____________ .

Review Questions:

The following questions may be assigned by your instructor as a way to assess your knowledge of this section. Your instructor has the answers to the review questions.

1. The *Ribbon* dynamically changes to show options that complement the current operation. (T/F)
2. Revit is strictly a 2D drafting program. (T/F)
3. The Projects/Views listed in the *Open Documents* list allow you to see which Projects/Views are currently open. (T/F)
4. When you use the *Pan* tool you are actually moving the drawing, not just changing what part of the drawing you can see on the screen. (T/F)
5. Revit was not originally created for architecture. (T/F)
6. The icon with the floppy disk picture () allows you to _________________ a project file.
7. Clicking on the ____________ next to the *Zoom* icon will list additional zoom tools not currently shown in the *View* toolbar. 
8. You do not see the *ViewCube* unless you are in a ________________ view.
9. Creating an *Autodesk* user account is free. (T/F)
10. The *Views/Schedules cannot be positioned outside of the Revit application window.* (T/F)

SELF-EXAM ANSWERS:
1 – F, **2** – T, **3** – T, **4** – Template, **5** – Cloud

Notes:

Autodesk User Certification Exam
Be sure to check out Appendix A for an overview of the official Autodesk User Certification Exam and the available study book and software, sold separately, from SDC Publications and this author.

Successfully passing this exam is a great addition to your resume and could help set you apart and help you land a great job. People who pass the official exam receive a certificate signed by the CEO of Autodesk, the makers of Revit.

Lesson 2
Lake Cabin: FLOOR PLAN (The Basics):

In this lesson, you will get a down-and-dirty overview of the functionality of Autodesk® Revit® for architectural design. We will cover the basics of creating the primary components of a floor plan: walls, doors, windows, roof, annotations, and dimensions. This lesson will show you the amazing "out-of-the-box" features in Autodesk Revit: powerful yet easy to use. It should make you very excited about learning this industry-leading software program. Future lessons will cover these features in more detail and introduce other editing tools and related concepts along the way.

Exercise 2-1:
Walls

In this exercise, you will draw the walls, starting with the exterior. Read the directions carefully; everything you need to do is clearly listed.

Rough Sketch of Lake Cabin Plan:

This sketch is intended to give you an idea of what you'll be creating in this chapter.

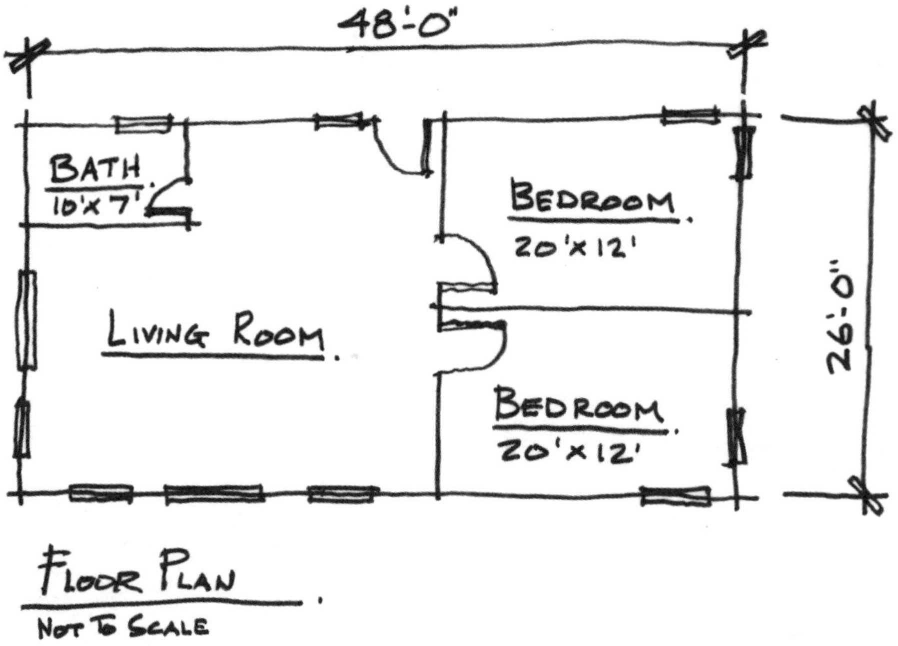

Exterior Walls:

1. Start a new project named **Lake Cabin.** <u>Steps:</u> *Click New (Models) → Browse → Default → Open, then OK. (Fig. 2-1.1)*

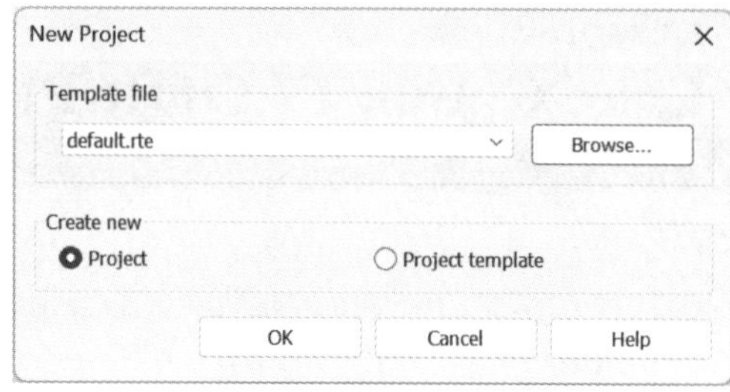

FIGURE 2-1.1 Generic template selected

2. Click **Architecture → Build→ Wall**

   (i.e., the upper part of the icon, not the down-arrow part). See Figure 2-1.2.

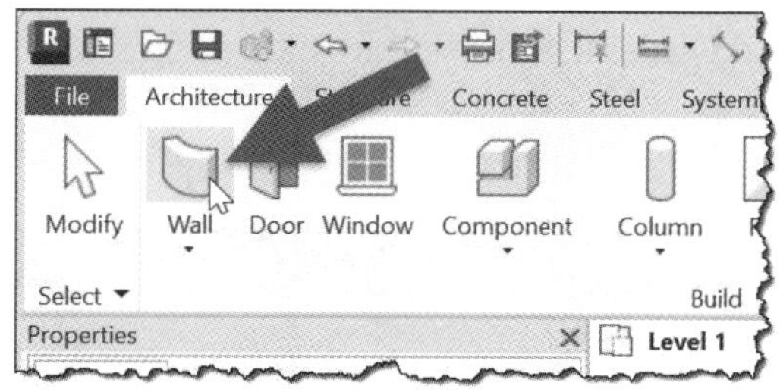

FIGURE 2-1.2 Wall tool

Notice that the *Ribbon* and *Properties Palette* have changed to show options related to drawing walls. Next, you will modify those settings.

3. Modify the *Ribbon* to the following (Figure 2-1.3):
   a. *Change Element Type:* click the down-arrow and select **Generic – 12″**. *(Type Selector)*
   b. *Location Line:* Set this to **Finish Face: Exterior**. *(Properties Palette)*
   c. *Height:* Change the height from 20′-0″ to **9′-0″**. *(Ribbon)*

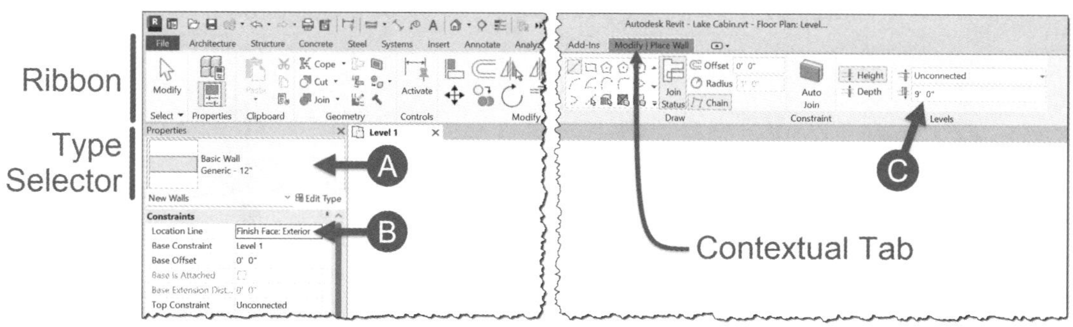

FIGURE 2-1.3 Ribbon and Type Selector

You are now ready to draw the exterior walls in the *Level 1* view.

4. In the drawing window, **click** in the upper left corner.

   TIP: Remember to draw within the four elevation symbols (see the image to the right).

5. Start moving the mouse to the right. **Click** when the wall is **48′-0″** long and horizontal.

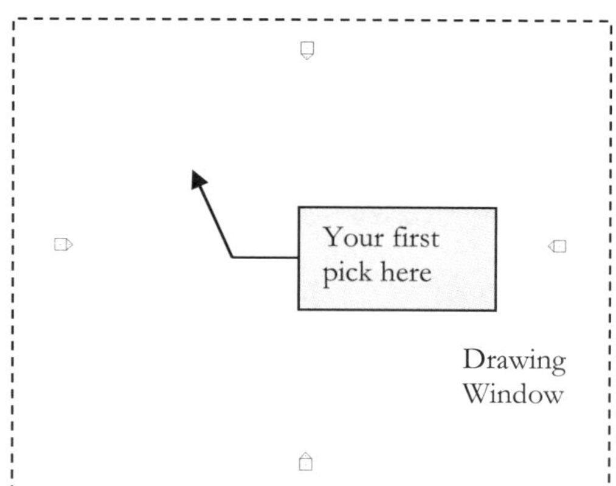

FIGURE 2-1.4 First pick point

Notice, as you move the mouse, Revit dynamically displays a length and an angle. To draw a horizontal line, move the mouse straight across the screen; a dashed line and a tooltip will appear when the line is snapped to the horizontal (Figure 2-1.5).

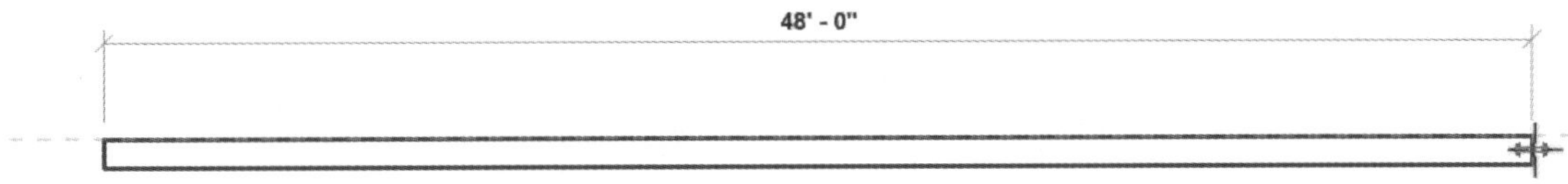

FIGURE 2-1.5 Horizontal tooltip displayed

> *TIP: If your mouse moved slightly when you clicked and the wall is not exactly 48-0, click the dimension, type 48, and press Enter. You do not need to type the foot symbol.*

You are now ready for your second wall.

6. Start moving your mouse straight down, or South, until the dashed line and tooltip appear (indicating a vertical line); type **26** and press **Enter**.

> *TIP: Once the wall is drawn, the temporary dimension will read 25'-6" because it is measured to the wall's centerline at the north corner.*

Typing the length allows you to accurately input a length without having to spend a lot of time setting the mouse in just the right position. However, you can still adjust the dimension after the wall is drawn.

7. Draw the other two exterior walls to create a closed rectangle.

Interior Walls:

The same tool is used to draw both interior and exterior walls.

8. Select the *Wall* tool and modify the ***Ribbon*** and ***Properties Palette*** as follows:
    a. *Type Selector:* Click the down-arrow and select **Generic – 5"**.
    b. *Location Line:* Set this to **Wall Centerline**.

9. Drawing a wall between bedrooms: *Snap* (you will see a triangle symbol appear before clicking) to the midpoint of the east wall (Figure 2-1.6). Do not click the second point yet; see the next step to finish the wall.

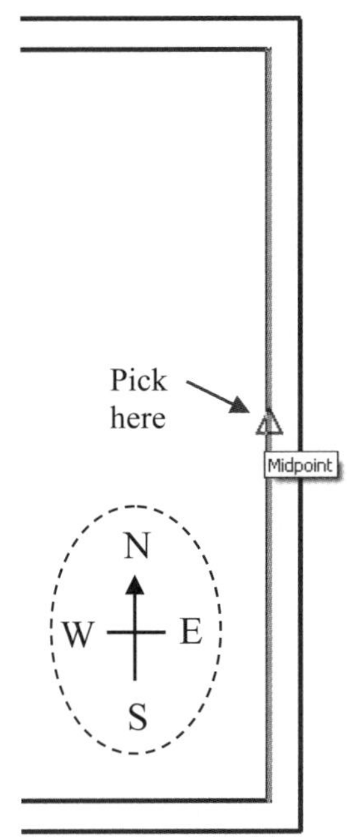

FIGURE 2-1.6 Interior wall start point

10. While moving the mouse to the West (left) and snapping to the horizontal plane; Type **20 2 ½** and press **Enter**.

TIP: Type the length as shown; you don't need a dash, the foot, or the inch symbols as they are assumed here. You do need two spaces – after the feet and before the fraction.

11. Press Esc once to start a new wall segment. Draw the perpendicular wall to close off the bedrooms. Revit allows you to do this with a single wall segment by selecting your points in a specific order. See Figure 2-1.7 for a graphical description of this process. Press Esc twice to unselect the new wall (first Esc) and cancel the Wall command (second Esc).

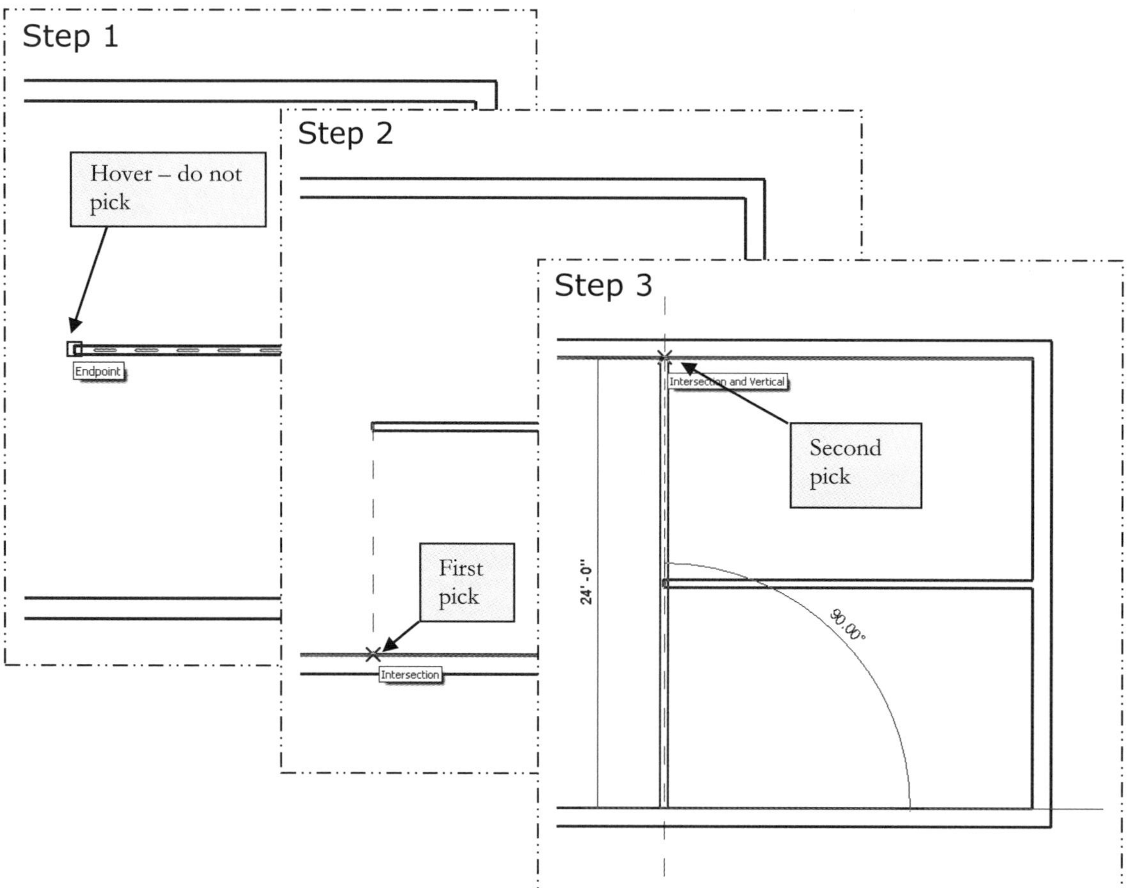

FIGURE 2-1.7 Draw wall with object tracking

12. **One More Step:** Draw the two interior walls for the bathroom to complete the interior walls; dimensions are to the center of the walls (Figure 2-1.1). ***Tip:*** add the two walls. Press Esc twice, then edit the temporary dimensions for the selected wall.

13. **Save** your project (*Lake Cabin.rvt*) via the *QAT*.

Exercise 2-2:
Doors

In this exercise you will add doors to your cabin floor plan.

1. Open **Lake Cabin.rvt** created in Exercise 2-1.

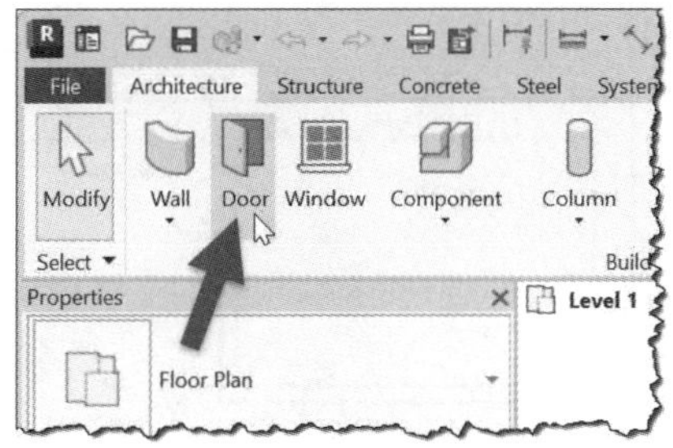

FIGURE 2-2.1 Door tool

Placing Doors:

2. Click **Architecture → Build → Door** (Figure 2-2.1).

Notice that the *Ribbon* and *Properties Palette* have updated to show options for doors. Next, you will modify those settings.

The *Type Selector* indicates the door style, width, and height. Clicking it displays all the doors loaded into the current project.

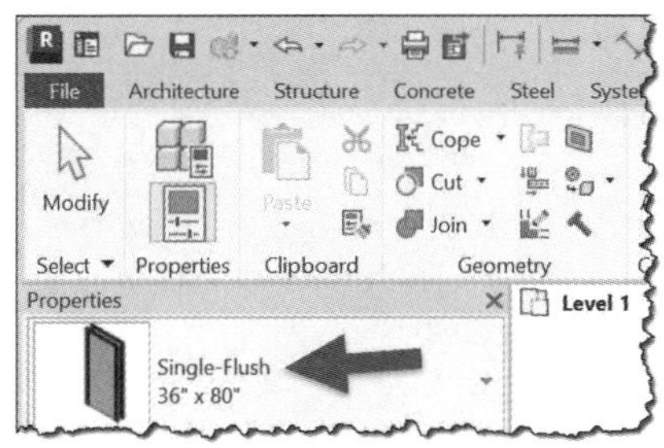

FIGURE 2-2.2 Door type selected

The default project template you started from includes several sizes for a single-flush door. Notice that there are two standard heights in the list. The 80″ (6′-8″) doors are the standard residential height, and the 84″ (7′-0″) doors are the standard commercial height.

3. On the *Ribbon*, click **Tag on Placement** so it is highlighted, meaning on (see image to the right), and then change the *Type Selector* to **36″ x 80″**; see Fig. 2-2.2.

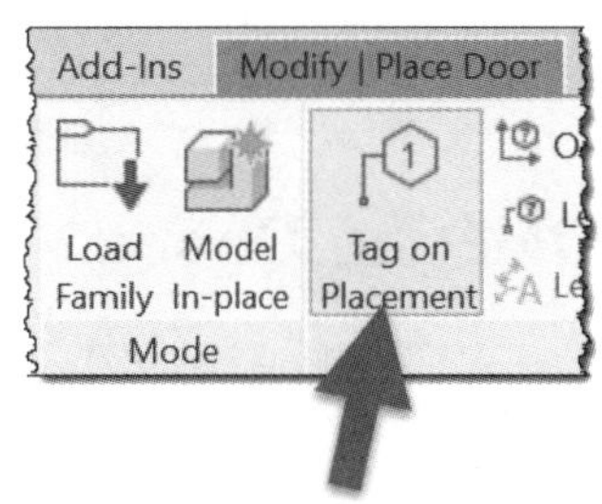

4. Move your cursor over a wall and position the door as shown in **Figure 2-2.4**. Notice that the swing of the door changes depending on what side of the wall your cursor is favoring (look ahead to Figure 2-2.4).

5. Click to place the door, and Revit will automatically trim the wall.

6. While the door is still selected, click on the *change swing (control arrows)* symbol to make the door swing against the wall (Figure 2-2.3).

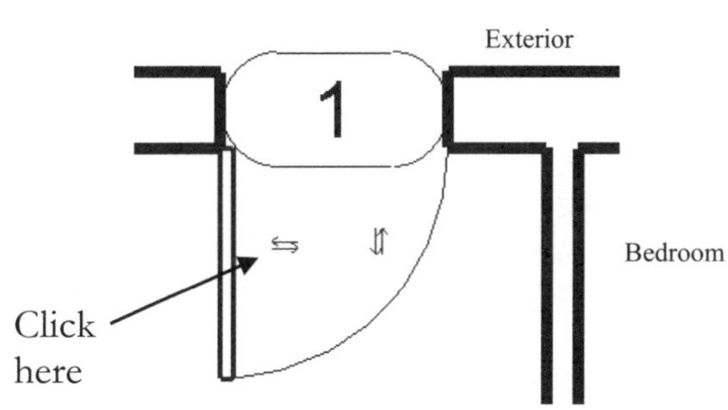

FIGURE 2-2.3 Changing door swing

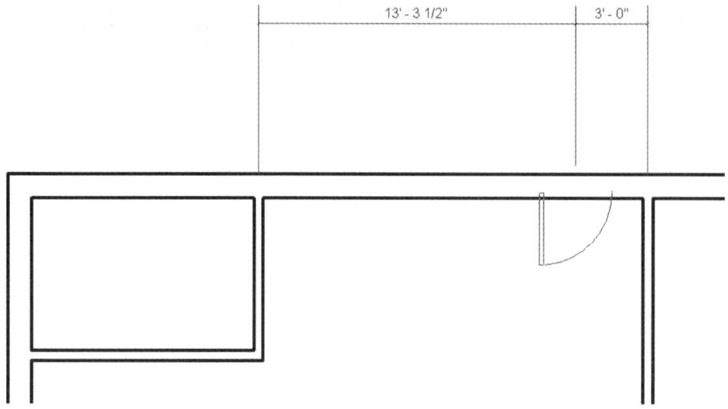

FIGURE 2-2.4 Dynamic graphical info during door insertion

Revit lets you keep inserting doors until you select a different tool from the *Ribbon* or press *Esc.*

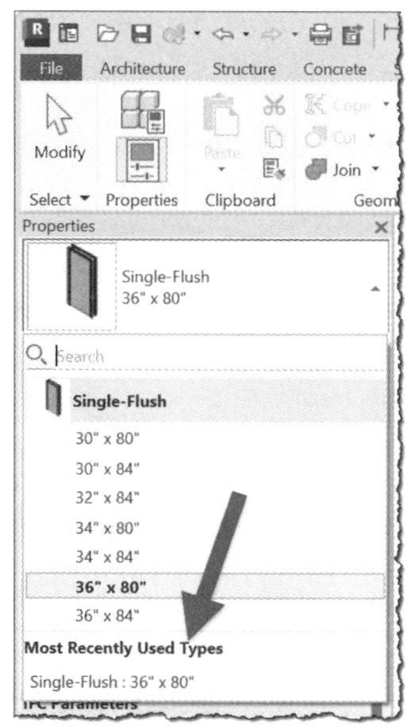

FIGURE 2-2.5
Door Element Types

7. Insert the doors into the bedrooms as shown in **Figure 2-1.1**. The exact position is not important in this exercise.

8. Change the *Type Selector* to **30″ x 80″**.

9. Insert a door into the bathroom.

Notice that the door types recently used are listed at the bottom of the list (Figure 2-2.5). Also, notice the Search box near the top—this allows the list to be shortened on large projects with several doors and door types to choose from.

Deleting Doors:

Next, you will learn how to delete a door. This process works for most objects (e.g., walls, windows, text) in Revit.

10. Insert a door between the two bedrooms, any size.

11. Press the **Esc** key twice.

Tip: You can also click the Modify button on the far left of each tab on the Ribbon.

12. Click on the door you just inserted, between bedrooms, and press the **Delete** key on your keyboard (selecting Delete from the right-click menu also works).

13. **Save** your project (*Lake Cabin.rvt*).

Exercise 2-3:
Windows

In this exercise, you will add windows to your cabin floor plan, keeping in mind that you are creating a 3D model, which you will explore soon.

1. Open **Lake Cabin.rvt** created in Exercise 2-2.

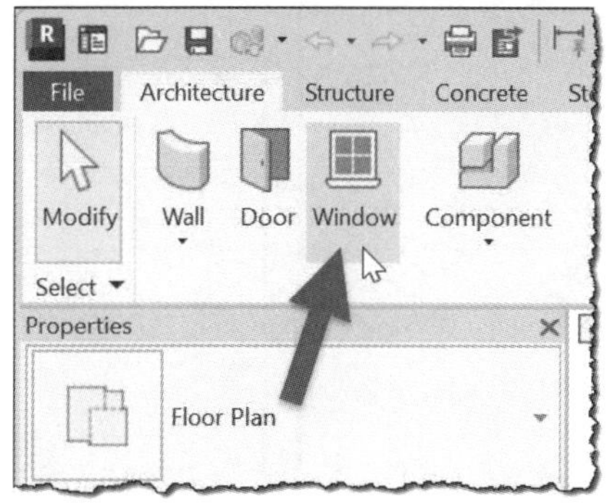

FIGURE 2-3.1 Window tool

Placing Windows:

2. Click **Architecture → Build → Window** (Figure 2-3.1).

Again, notice that the *Ribbon* and *Properties Palette* have changed to show options related to windows. Next, you will modify those settings.

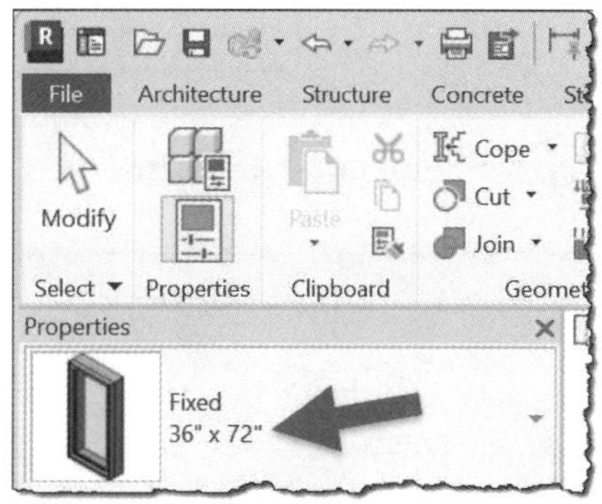

FIGURE 2-3.2 Window types

The *Type Selector* indicates the window style, width, and height. Clicking the *Type Selector* lists all the windows loaded in the current project.

3. On the *Ribbon*, click **Tag on Placement** so it is highlighted and then change the *Type Selector* to **36″ x 72″** (Figure 2-3.2).

4. Move your cursor over a wall and place two windows as shown in **Figure 2-3.3**. Notice, as you move your cursor near a wall, that the position of the window changes depending on which side of the wall your cursor is favoring.

5. With the Window tool still active, change the *Type Selector* to **24″ x 72″**.

6. Place the other four windows in the living room area as shown in **Figure 2-1.1**. Again, in this exercise, we are not concerned with the exact placement of the windows.

7. Change the *Type Selector* to **24″ x 48″**.

8. Place the remaining five windows: two in each bedroom and one in the bathroom, as shown in **Figure 2-1.1**.

9. **Save** your project (*Lake Cabin.rvt*).

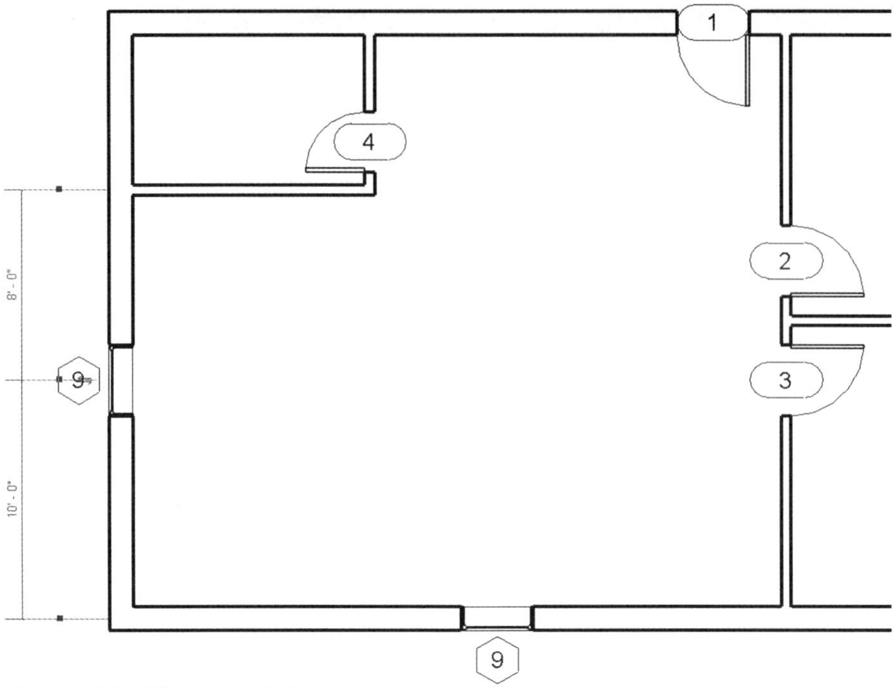

FIGURE 2-3.3 Two large windows

Object Snap Symbols:

By now, you should be well aware of the snaps that Revit suggests as you move your cursor about the drawing window.

If you hold your cursor still for a moment while a snap symbol is displayed, a tooltip will appear on the screen. However, when you become familiar with the snap symbols, you can pick sooner (Figure 2-3.4).

Tapping the **TAB** key cycles through the available snaps near your cursor.

The keyboard shortcut disables the other snaps for a single pick. For example, if you type **SE** (snap endpoint) on the keyboard while in the Wall command, Revit will only look for an endpoint for the next pick.

Finally, typing **SO** (snaps off) turns all snaps off for one pick.

See Exercise 3-2 for more information.

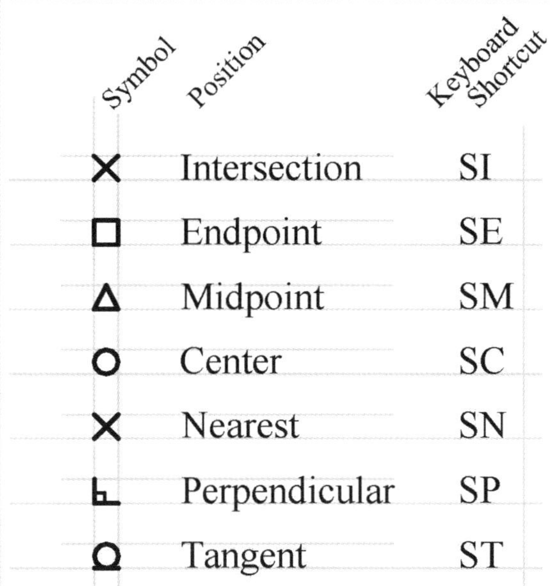

FIGURE 2-3.4 Snap Reference Chart

Exercise 2-4:
Roof

You will now add a simple roof to your lake cabin.

1. Open **Lake Cabin.rvt** created in Exercise 2-3 (if necessary).

Sketching a Roof:

2. Click **Architecture → Build → Roof** (click the bottom part of the button); a fly-out menu will appear (Figure 2-4.1).

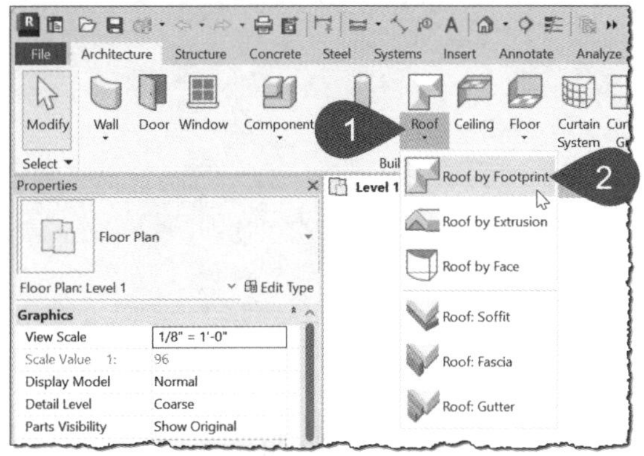

FIGURE 2-4.1 Roof tool

The fly-out prompts you for the method you want to use to create the roof.

3. Click **Roof by footprint**.

When Revit detects an issue that might not be appropriate, a warning is displayed. In this case, you see *Roof is on the Lowest Level* warning.

Revit notices that you are on Level 1 and asks you if you want to move the roof to another level. In our case we want to move it to Level 2 (Figure 2-4.2).

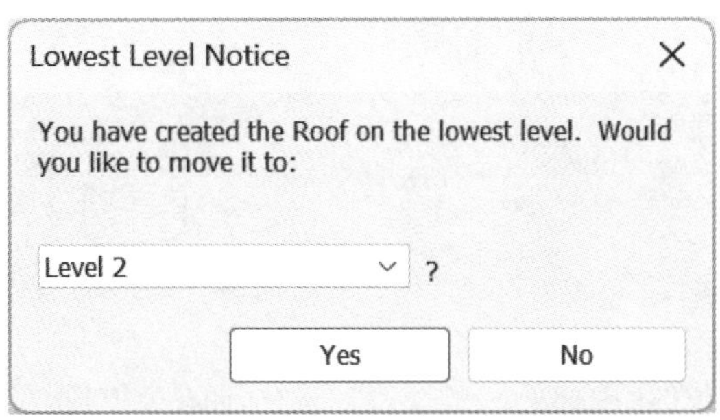

FIGURE 2-4.2 Roof is on the Lowest Level prompt

4. Make sure **Level 2** is selected and click **Yes** (Figure 2-4.2).

You are still on Level 1, but Revit will move the roof to Level 2 once you are finished drawing it. The entire model is grayed out at the moment because you are in "Sketch Mode"; when finished sketching, the roof and everything will return to normal. You will not see the roof as it will be above the current view (i.e., Level 1); you will learn more about this on the next page.

Also, notice that the contextual tab **Create Roof Footprint** has temporarily been added to the *Ribbon*, which provides creation options for the roof (Figure 2-4.3).

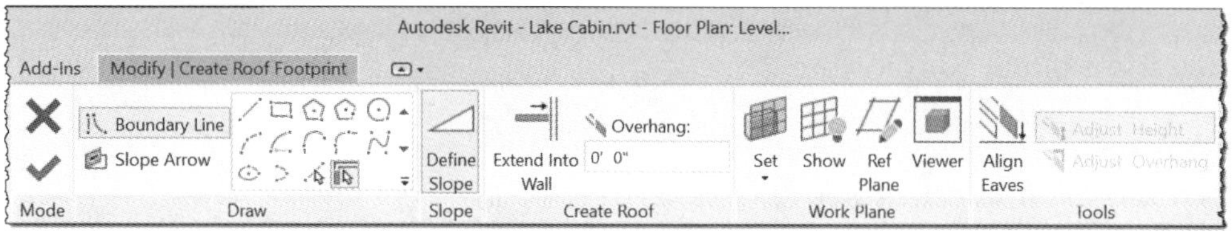

FIGURE 2-4.3 Roof sketch options on the *Ribbon*

5. Pick each of the exterior walls to specify the roof footprint.
   Be sure to pick the exterior side of the wall.

6. Click **Finish Edit Mode** via the green checkmark on the *Ribbon.*

You should be on Level 1. You can see this in the *Project Browser*, as Level 1 is bold.

7. To see the roof click the **Default 3D View** icon on the *QAT* (Figure 2-4.4).

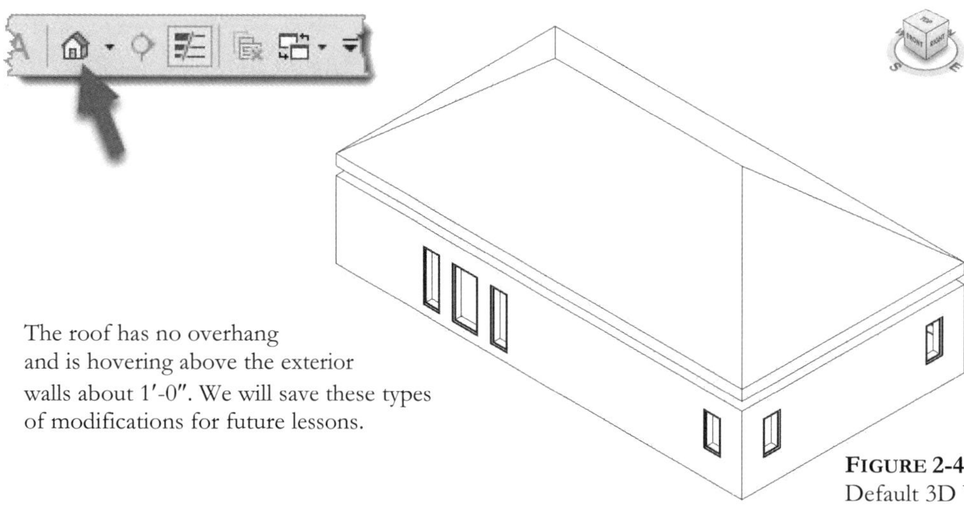

The roof has no overhang and is hovering above the exterior walls about 1′-0″. We will save these types of modifications for future lessons.

FIGURE 2-4.4
Default 3D View

8. Click the **X** on the {3D} drawing tab to close that view. This will close the 3D view but not the project or the Level 1 view. ***NOTE:*** *Clicking the X on the Titlebar closes Revit.*

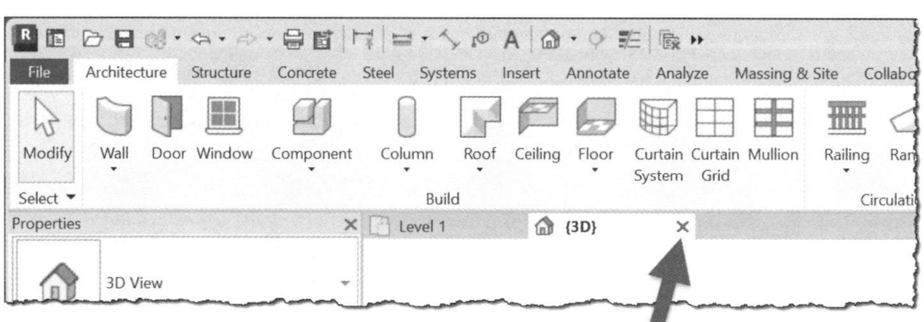

Exercise 2-5:
Annotation and Dimensions

Adding text and dimensions is very simple in Revit. In this exercise, you will add room tags to each room in the lake cabin floor plan. You will also place two dimensions.

Placing Text:

1. Open **Lake Cabin.rvt** created in Exercise 2-4, if not already open.

2. Make sure your current view is **Level 1**. The word "Level 1" will be bold under the heading *Floor Plans* in your *Project Browser*. If Level 1 is not current, simply double-click on the "Level 1" text in the *Project Browser* (Figure 2-5.1).

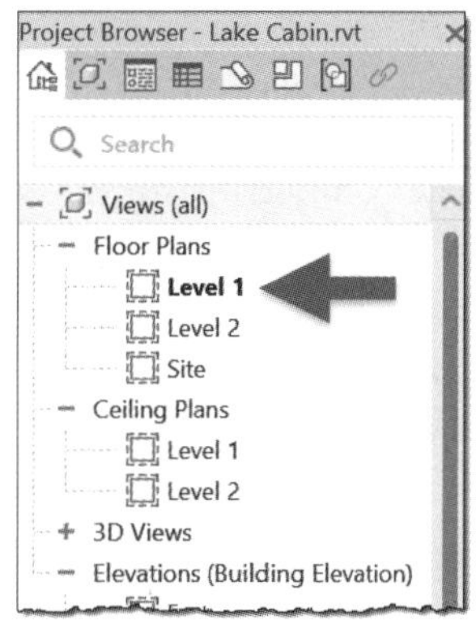

FIGURE 2-5.1 Project Browser

3. Select **Annotate → Text → Text**; do not select *Model Text* from the *Architecture* tab of the *Ribbon*.
   TIP: You can also select the Text *tool from the Quick Access Toolbar (QAT).*

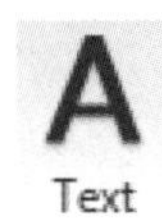

Once again, notice the *Ribbon* has changed to display some text options; all of this falls under a *contextual tab* named *Modify | Place Text* (Figure 2-5.2).

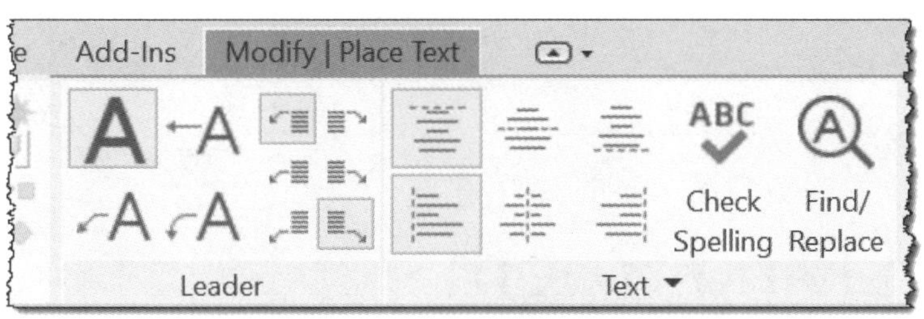

FIGURE 2-5.2 Ribbon: contextual tab for Text tool

The *Type Selector* indicates the text size. From this *Contextual Ribbon,* you can also place text with arrow lines, or leaders, and set the text alignment: Left justified, Centered, or Right justified. You will not adjust these settings at this time.

4. You will now place the words "Living Room." **Click** within the living room area to place the text (Figure 2-5.3).

5. Type **Living Room**, then click somewhere in the plan view to finish the text.

You may notice that the text seems too large. This is a good time to explain what the text height is referring to in the *Type Selector (i.e., ¼" Arial).* The text height, in the *Properties Palette,* refers to the size of the text on a printed piece of paper. For example, if you print your plan you should be able to place a ruler on the text and measure ¼" in height when the text is set to ¼" in the *Type Selector.*

This can be a complicated process in other CAD programs; Revit makes it very simple. All you need to do is change the *View Scale* for **Level 1**, and Revit automatically adjusts the text and annotation to match that scale. Currently, the *View Scale* is set to ⅛" = 1'-0"; you want the *View Scale* to be ¼" = 1'-0". With the *View Scale* set to ⅛" = 1'-0" our text is twice as big as it should be. Next, you will change the *View Scale* for Level 1.

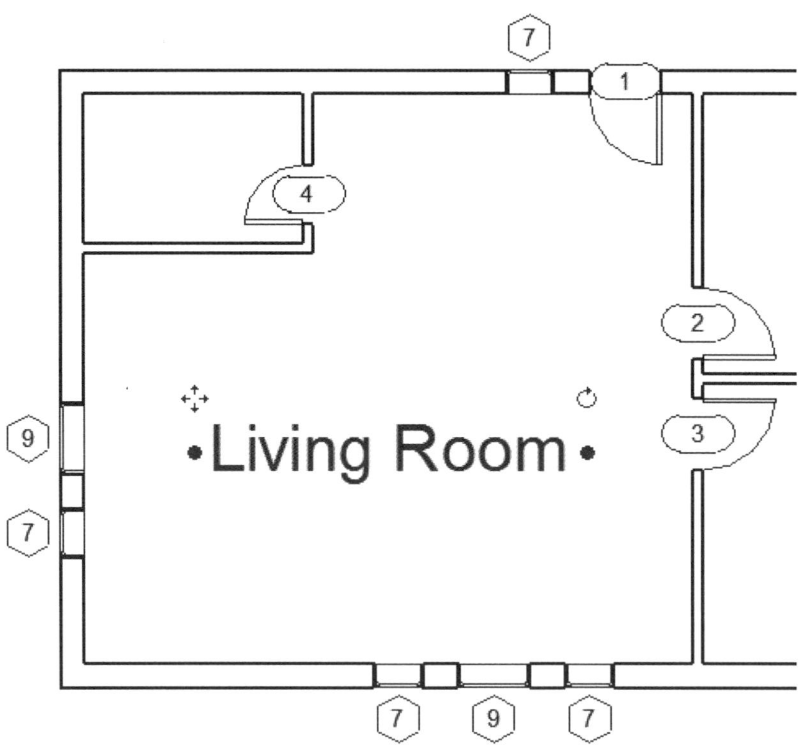

FIGURE 2-5.3 Placing text

6. In the lower-left corner of the drawing window, on the *View Control Bar*, click on the text of the listed scale, which is currently set at ⅛″ = 1′-0″.

7. In the pop-up menu, which lists several standard scales, select **¼″ = 1′-0″** (Figure 2-5.4).

You should now notice that your text and even your door and window tags are half the size they used to be (Figure 2-5.5).

Keep in mind that this scale adjustment only affected the current view (i.e., Level 1). If you switched to Level 2, you would notice that it is still set to ⅛″ = 1′-0″. This is nice because you may, on occasion, want a larger-scale plan to show more detail.

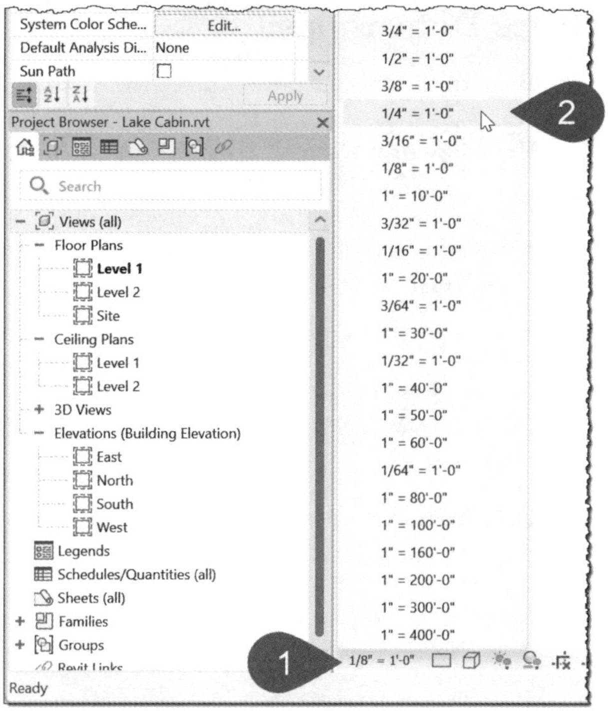

FIGURE 2-5.4 Changing View Scale

8. Finally, using the ***Text*** tool, place a room name label in each room as shown in **Figure 2-1.1** and **Figure 2-5.5** below.

9. **Save** your project.

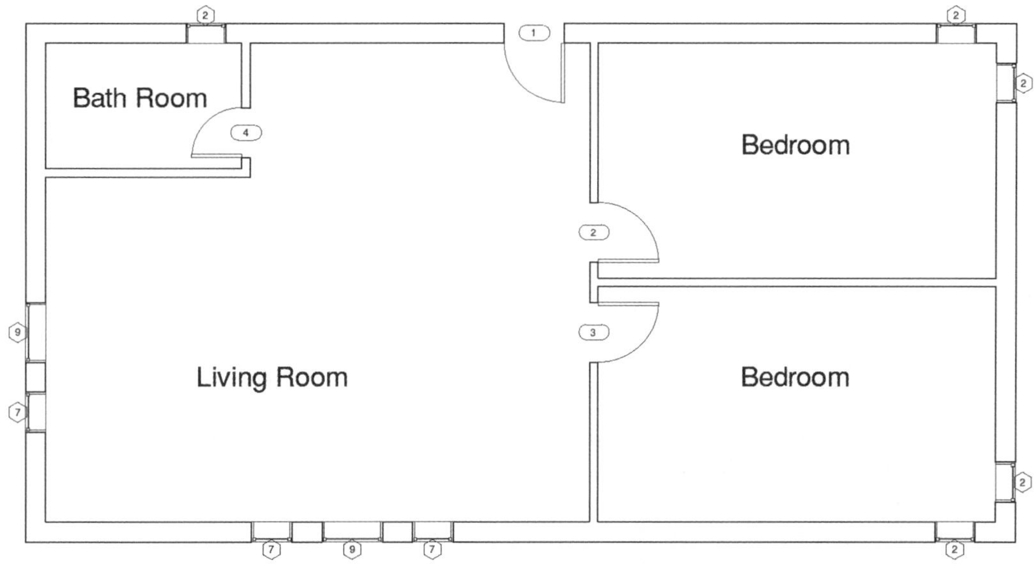

FIGURE 2-5.5 Floor Plan with text at ¼″ = 1′-0″

Place Dimensions:

To finish this exercise, you will place two overall plan dimensions.

10. Select **Annotate → Dimension → Aligned** (see icon to right).

11. On the *Ribbon*, change the drop-down list that says *Wall centerlines* to **Wall faces**. This option will allow you to dimension to the outside face of your building, as you would normally do when dimensioning the overall footprint of your building.

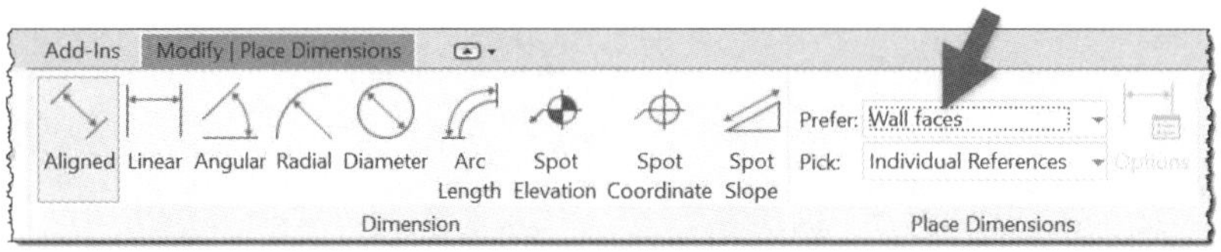

12. Place a dimension by selecting two walls and then clicking a third point to specify where the dimension line should be located relative to the walls (Figure 2-5.6).

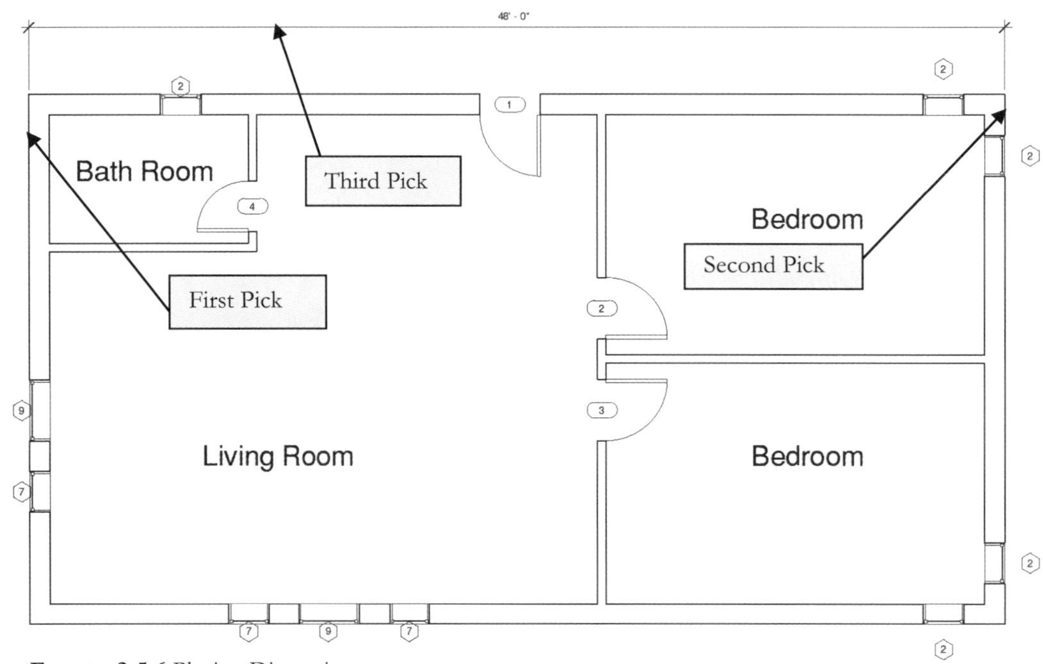

FIGURE 2-5.6 Placing Dimensions

13. Place one more dimension indicating the depth of the building.

The *Dimension* tool, as just used, places permanent dimensions; however, they can be deleted. Revit also provides a tool to list a distance but not actually place a permanent dimension; this is called the **Measure** tool. The *Measure* tool is convenient when you simply want to know what a dimension is, but do not need to document it for the construction drawings.

14. **Save** your project.

Exercise 2-6:
Printing

The last thing you need to know to round off your basic knowledge of Revit is how to print the current view. Printing will be covered in more detail later in the book; this section will only scratch the surface of the process.

Printing the Current View:

1. Select **File Tab → Print** (hover) **→ Print.**

2. Adjust your settings to match those shown in **Figure 2-6.1**.

    - Select a printer from the list that you have access to.
    - Set *Print Range* to **Visible portion of current window**.

FIGURE 2-6.1 Print dialog

3. Click on the **Setup** button to adjust additional print settings.

4. Adjust your settings to match those shown in **Figure 2-6.2**.

    - Set Zoom to **Fit to page**.

5. Click **OK** to close the *Print Setup* dialog and return to *Print.*

6. Click **No** if you get the following prompt (Figure 2-6.3).

7. Click the **Preview** button in the lower left corner. This will save paper and time by verifying the drawing will be correctly positioned on the page (Fig 2-6.5, next page).

8. Click the **Print** button at the top of the preview window.

9. Click **OK** to print to the selected printer.

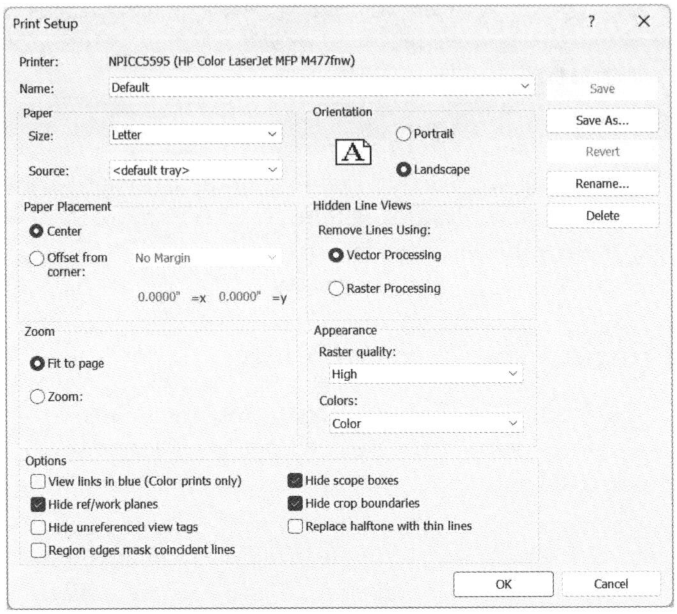

FIGURE 2-6.2 Print Settings dialog

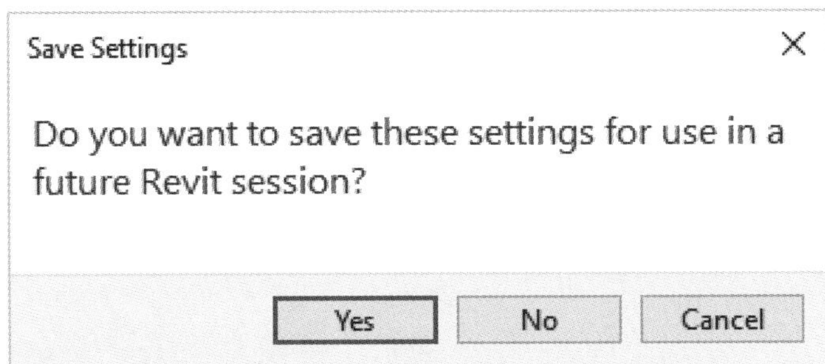

FIGURE 2-6.3 Save Print Settings prompt

In addition to physically printing on paper, it is also possible to export a PDF file using Revit's built-in tool. This is accessed from **File → Export → PDF** or via the *Quick Access Toolbar* (Figure 2-6.4). The PDF file can be emailed to clients, contractors, consultants, and more. The PDF file is also a good way to save progress versions of your drawings.

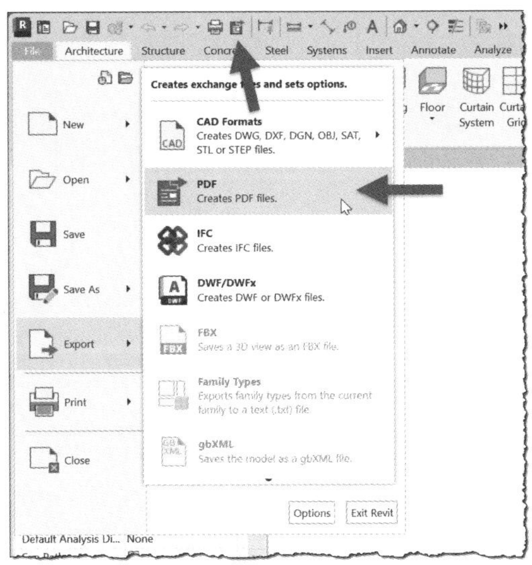

FIGURE 2-6.4 Export PDF file

FYI:
Notice you do not have the option to set the scale (i.e., ⅛″ = 1′-0″). As noted in the previous exercise, the scale is set in the properties for each view.

If you want a quick half-scale print, set the zoom factor to 50%. You could also select **Fit to Page** to get the largest image possible, but not to scale, which is selected above, since the plan will not fit on 8½″ x 11″ (letter) sized paper at ¼″ = 1′-0″.

Printer versus Plotter?

Revit can print to any printer or plotter installed on your computer.

A **Printer** is an output device that uses smaller paper (e.g., 8½″x11″ or 11″x17″). A **Plotter** is an output device that uses larger paper; plotters typically have one or more rolls of paper ranging in size from 18″ wide to 42″ wide. A roll-fed plotter has a built-in cutter that can, for example, cut paper from a 36″ wide roll to make a 24″x36″ sheet.

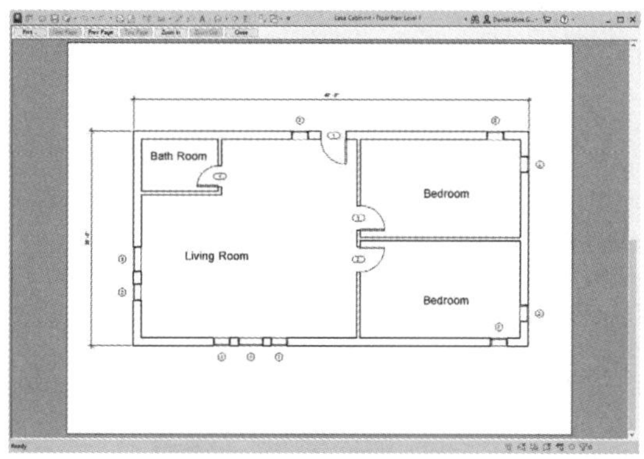

FIGURE 2-6.5 Print Preview

Plotter with three paper rolls

Color **printer**/copier

Self-Exam:

The following questions can be used as a way to check your knowledge of this lesson. The answers can be found at the bottom of the page.

1. The Wall tool uses the same command interface for creating both interior and exterior walls. (T/F)
2. When drawing walls, Revit displays temporary dimensions that can be edited after placement. (T/F)
3. Setting the Location Line to Finish Face: Exterior affects where the wall is drawn relative to its thickness. (T/F)
4. Pressing the Esc key once exits Revit entirely from the current project. (T/F)
5. Door elements automatically cut openings in walls when they are placed. (T/F)

Review Questions:

The following questions may be assigned by your instructor as a way to assess your knowledge of this section. Your instructor has the answers to the review questions.

1. The swing direction of a door can be reversed after placement using on-screen controls. (T/F)
2. Recently used door sizes appear at the top of the Type Selector list. (T/F)
3. Window placement in Revit depends on which side of the wall the cursor is positioned. (T/F)
4. The TAB key allows you to cycle through available object snaps before selecting a point. (T/F)
5. Typing keyboard shortcuts such as SE or SO temporarily overrides Revit's default snapping behavior. (T/F)
6. Creating a roof by footprint requires sketching the roof boundary before it is generated. (T/F)
7. The Default 3D View button on the Quick Access Toolbar opens a new project window. (T/F)
8. Text size in a plan view changes automatically when the View Scale is adjusted. (T/F)
9. Overall building dimensions are typically placed using wall centerlines rather than wall faces. (T/F)
10. The print scale is controlled in the Print dialog box rather than in the view properties. (T/F)

SELF-EXAM ANSWERS:
1 – T, **2** – T, **3** – T, **4** – F, **5** – T

Lesson 3
Overview of Linework and Modify Tools:

It may seem odd to you that, in an industry-leading 3D design program, you will begin by learning to draw and edit 2D lines and shapes. However, any 3D object requires, at a minimum, detailed information in at least two of the three dimensions. Once two dimensions are defined, Autodesk® Revit® can begin to automate much of the third dimension for you. Many building components and features will require you to draw the perimeter using 2D lines.

Many of the edit tools that are covered in this lesson are the same tools that are used to edit the 3D building components.

Exercise 3-1:
Lines and Shapes

Drawing Lines:

You will draw many 2D lines in Autodesk Revit, typically in what is called *Sketch* mode. Two-dimensional lines in Autodesk Revit are extremely precise drawing elements. This means you can create very accurate drawings. Lines, or any drawn object, can be as precise as 8 decimal places (i.e., 24.999999999) or 1/256.

Autodesk Revit is a vector-based program. That means each drawn object is stored in a numerical database. When geometry needs to be displayed on the screen, Autodesk Revit reads the project database to determine what to show. This ensures that the line will be very accurate at any scale or zoom magnification.

A raster-based program, in contrast to vector based, is comprised of dots that infill a grid. The grid can vary in density and is typically referred to as resolution (e.g., 600x800, 1600x1200, etc.). This file type is used by graphics programs that typically deal with photographs, such as Adobe Photoshop. There are two reasons this type of file is not appropriate for Computer-Aided Design (CAD) programs:

- A raster-based line, for example, is composed of many dots on a grid, representing the line's width. When you zoom in, magnifying the line, it starts to become pixilated, meaning you actually start to see each dot on the grid. In a vector file you can "infinitely" zoom in on a line, and it will never become pixilated because the program recalculates the line each time you zoom in.

- A CAD program, such as Revit, only needs to store the start and end coordinates for each wall. For example, the dots needed to draw the wall are calculated on-the-fly for the current screen resolution, whereas a raster file must store each dot that represents the full length and width of the line, or lines in the wall, for example. This can vary from a few hundred dots to several thousand dots, depending on the resolution, for the same line.

The following graphic illustrates this point:

Vector vs. Raster Lines:

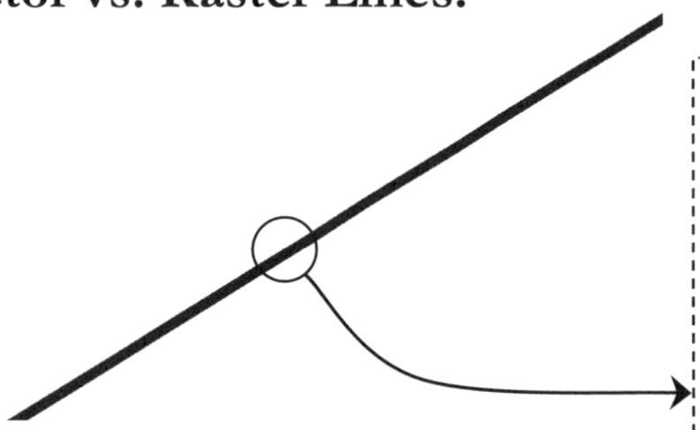

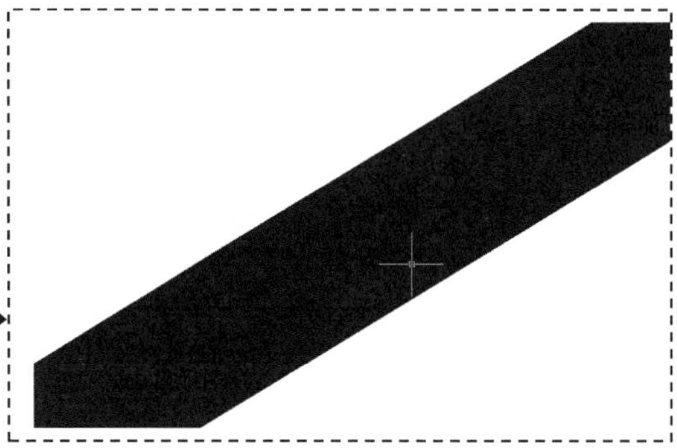

FIGURE 3-1.1 Vector Line Example
File Size: approx. 33kb

FIGURE 3-1.1A Vector Line Enlarged 1600%

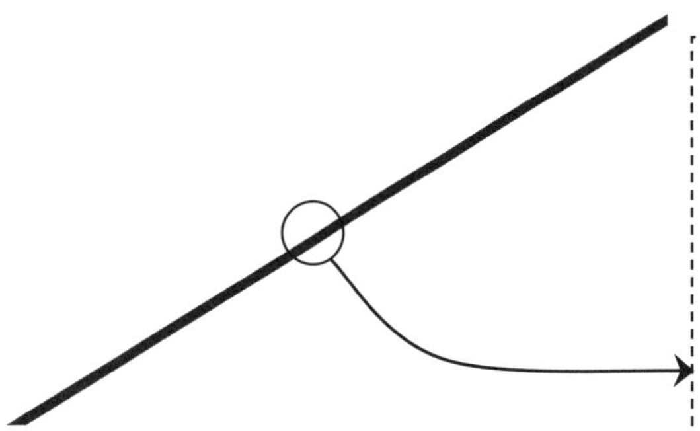

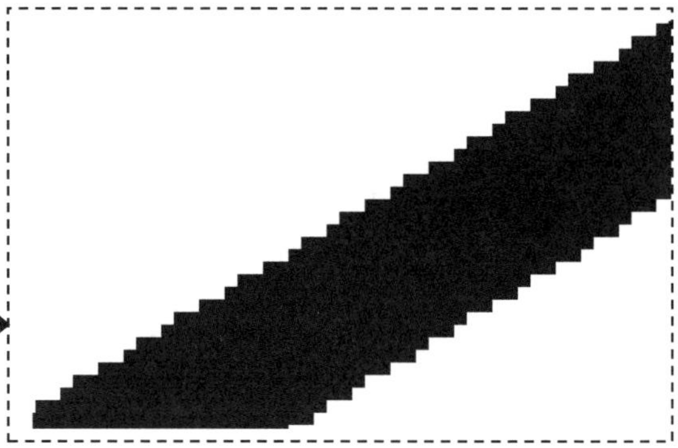

FIGURE 3-1.2 Raster Line Example
File Size: approx. 4.4MB

FIGURE 3-1.2A Raster Line Enlarged 1600%

The Detail Lines Tool:

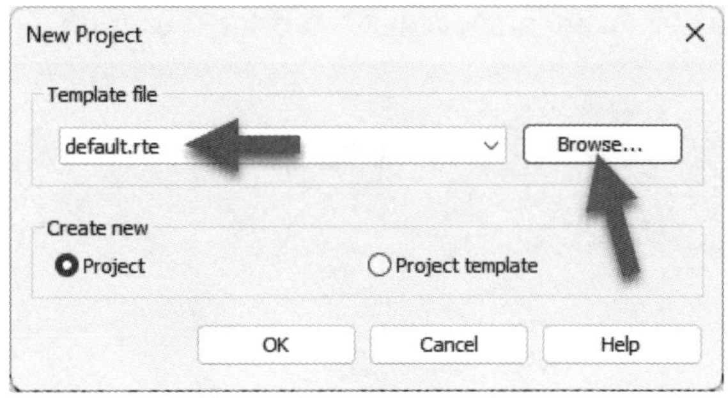

You will now study the *Detail Lines* tool.

1. **Open** Revit.

Each time you start Revit, you are in the *Recent Files* view. This view is closed automatically when a new or existing project is opened.

2. Start a new project: select **File Tab → New → Project**, click **Browse**, select **default.rte**, and then click **Open** and then **OK**.
   a. Or, click **New…** (Models) from the *Home* screen.

The drawing window is set to the *Level 1 Floor Plan* view. The 2D drafting will be done in a drafting view. Next you will learn how to create one of these views.

3. Select **View → Create → Drafting View**.
   (Remember: this means *Tab → Panel → Icon* on the *Ribbon.*)

4. In the *New Drafting View* dialog box, type **Ex 3-1** for the *Name* and set the *Scale* to **3/4″ = 1′-0″** by clicking the down-arrow at the right (Figure 3-1.3).

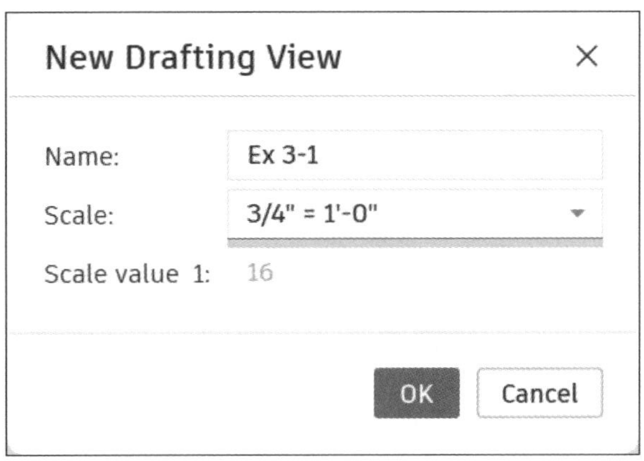

FIGURE 3-1.3 New Drafting View dialog

You are now in the new view and the *Project Browser* will contain a node labeled *Drafting Views (Detail)*. Here, each *Drafting View* created will be listed.

5. In the *Project Browser*, click the plus symbol next to the label **Drafting Views (Detail)**; this will display the *Drafting Views* that exist in the current project (Figure 3-1.4).

You are now ready to start looking at the *Detail Lines* tool:

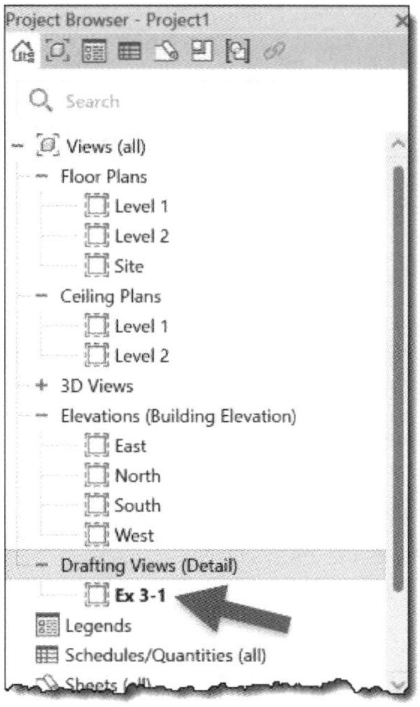

FIGURE 3-1.4 Project Browser: Drafting Views

6. Select the ***Annotate*** tab on the *Ribbon.*

7. On the *Detail* panel, select **Detail Line** (Figure 3-1.5).
   TIP: Do not use the "Model Line" tool on the Architecture tab.

8. **Draw a line** from the lower left corner of the screen to the upper right corner of the screen, by simply clicking two points on the screen within the drawing window (Figure 3-1.6).

   NOTE: Do not drag or hold your mouse button down; just click.

After clicking your second point, you should notice the length and the angle of the line are graphically displayed; this information is temporary and will disappear when you move your cursor.

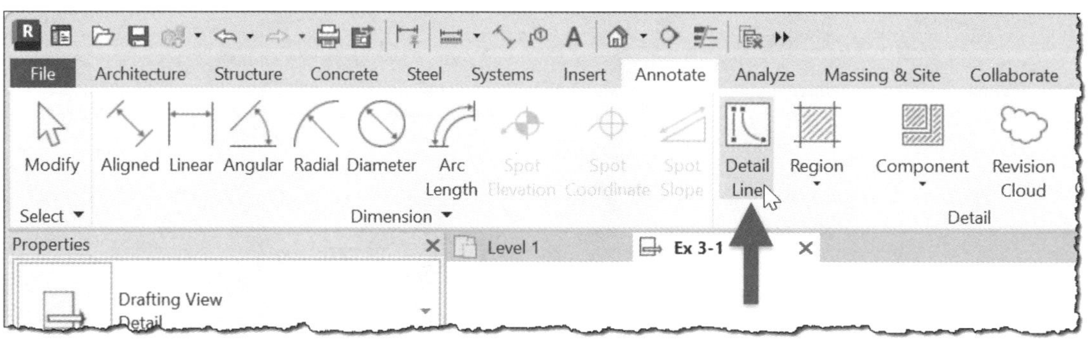

FIGURE 3-1.5 Annotate tab

You should also notice that the *Detail Line* tool is still active, which means you could continue to draw additional lines on the screen.

9. After clicking your second point, select the ***Modify*** tool from the left side of the *Ribbon*.

Selecting *Modify* cancels the current tool and allows you to select portions of your drawing for information or editing. Revit conveniently places the *Modify* tool in the same location on each tab so it is always available no matter which tab on the *Ribbon* is active.

TIP: Pressing the Esc key twice reverts Revit back to Modify mode.

Did You Make a Mistake?

Whenever you make a mistake in Revit you can use the **UNDO** command, via the *QAT*, to revert to a previous drawing state. You can perform multiple UNDOs all the way to your previous *Save*.

Similarly, if you press Undo a few too many times, you can use **REDO**. 

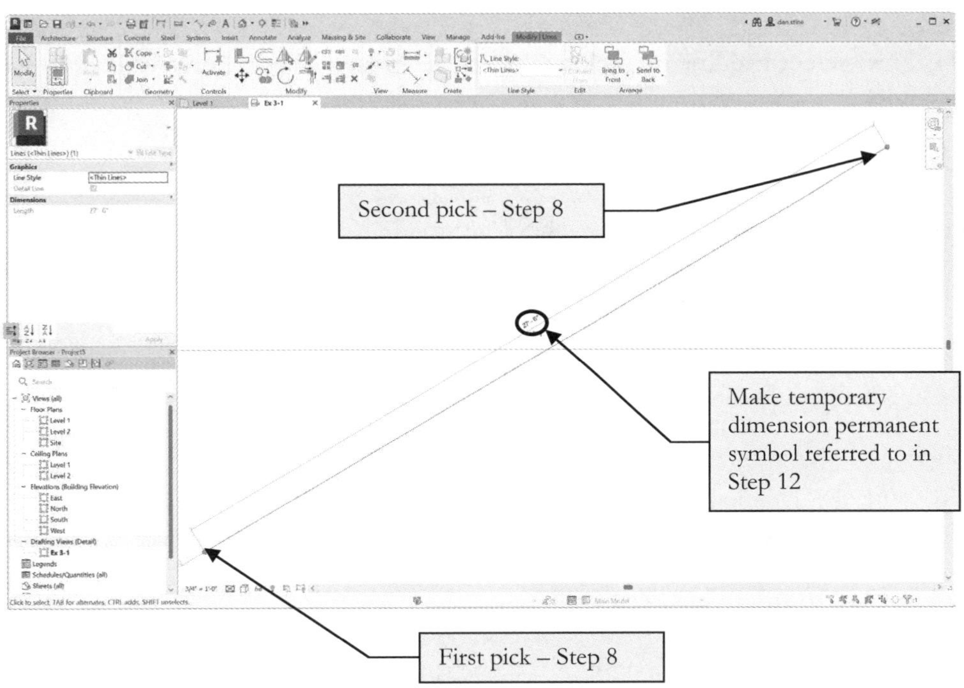

FIGURE 3-1.6 Your first detail line; exact dimensions are not important at this point.

Notice in the image above that while the *Detail Line* tool is active, the *Modify | Place Detail Line* contextual tab is shown. As soon as you click the *Modify* button or press Esc, the tab reverts to the basic *Modify* tab.

This constitutes your first line! However, as you are probably aware, it is not very accurate in terms of length and angle. Your line will likely be a different length due to where you picked your points and the size and resolution of your monitor.

Typically, you need to provide information such as length and angle when drawing a line; you rarely pick arbitrary points on the screen as you did in the previous steps. Revit allows you to get close with the on-screen dimension and angle information. Most of the time, you also need to accurately pick your starting point. For example, how far one line is from another, or picking the exact middle point on another line.

Having said that, however, the line you just drew still has precise numbers associated with its length and angle; this information is displayed after the line is drawn. The dimension and angle information is displayed until you begin drawing another line or select another tool. You can also select the line. While the dimensions are still visible, you can use them to modify the line's length and angle; you will try that later.

10. If not already selected, click the **Modify** tool from the *Ribbon.*

Notice that the temporary dimensions have disappeared.

While you are in *Modify* mode, you can select lines and objects in the current view.

11. Now **select the line** by clicking the mouse button with the cursor directly over the line.

FYI: *Always use the left button unless the right button is specifically mentioned.*

Notice that the temporary dimensions have returned.

The following step shows how to make a temporary dimension permanent:

If, at any point, you want to make a temporary dimension permanent, you simply click the "make this temporary dimension permanent" symbol near the dimension. You will try this now.

12. With the diagonal line still selected, click the "make this temporary dimension permanent" symbol near the dimension (Figure 3-1.6).

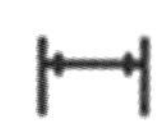

13. Select **Modify** to unselect the line.

The dimension indicating the length of the line is now permanent (Figure 3-1.7). The value of your dimension will not be the same as the one in this book as the size of your monitor and the exact points picked can vary greatly.

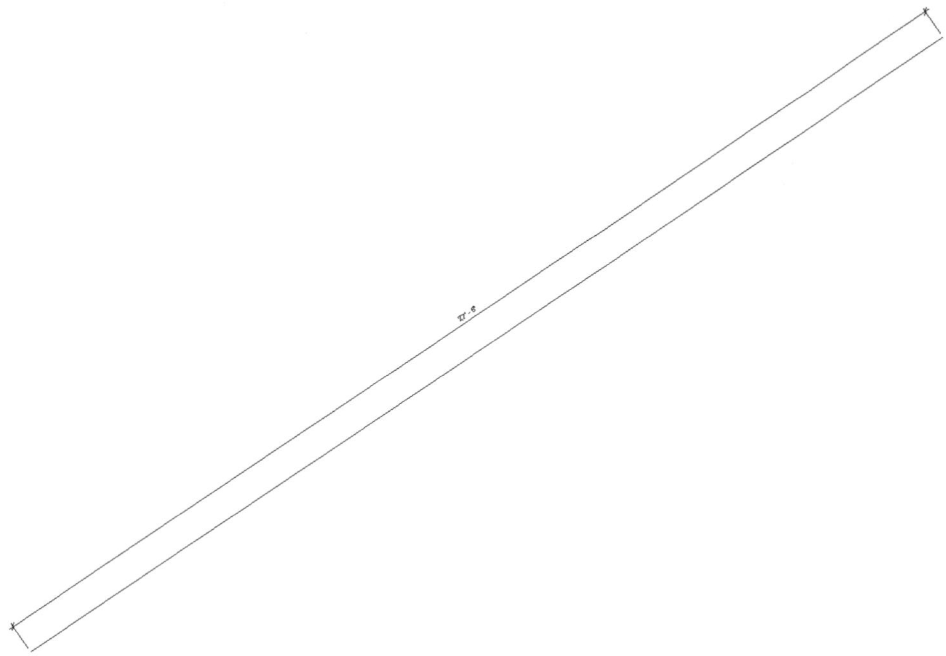

FIGURE 3-1.7 Temp dimension converted to permanent dimension

The following shows how to change the length of the line:

Currently, the line is approximately 20 - 30′ long (27′-6″ in Figure 3-1.7). If you want to change the length of the line to 22′-6″, you select the line and then change the dimension text, which in turn changes the line length. This can also be done with the temporary dimensions; the key is that the line has to be selected. You will try this next.

FYI: *Your detail line length will vary slightly depending on the size and resolution of your computer monitor, as you will be seeing more or less of the drawing area. This also assumes you have not performed any zooming, including spinning the wheel button on your mouse. If your line is way off, you should Undo or start over so the next several steps work out as intended.*

14. In *Modify* mode, select the diagonal line.

15. With the line currently selected, click on the dimension-text.

A dimension-text edit box appears directly over the dimension, within the drawing window. Whatever you type as a dimension changes the line to match.

16. Type **22 6** (i.e., 22 *space* 6) and press **Enter** (Figure 3-1.8).

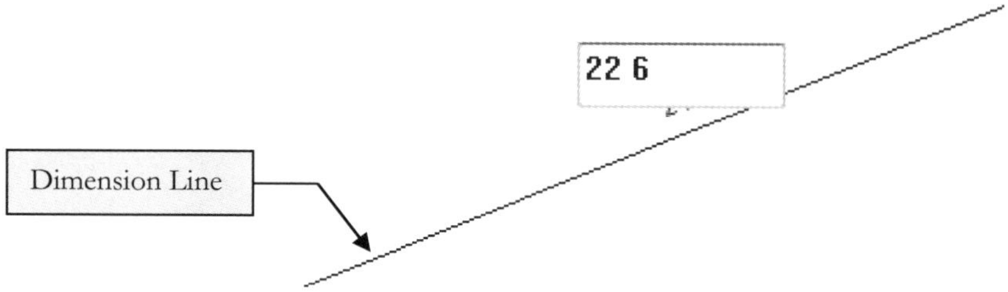

FIGURE 3-1.8 Editing dimension to change line length

You should have noticed the line's length changed. Revit assumes you want the line to change length equally at both ends, so the midpoint does not move. Try changing the dimension to 100′ and then Undo.

Locking Dimensions:

Revit allows you to *Lock* a dimension, which prevents the dimension and line length from changing. You will investigate this now to help avoid problems later.

17. Make sure the line is *not* selected; to do this, press Esc or click *Modify*.

18. Select the dimension, not the line, and note the following about the selected dimension (Figure 3-1.9).

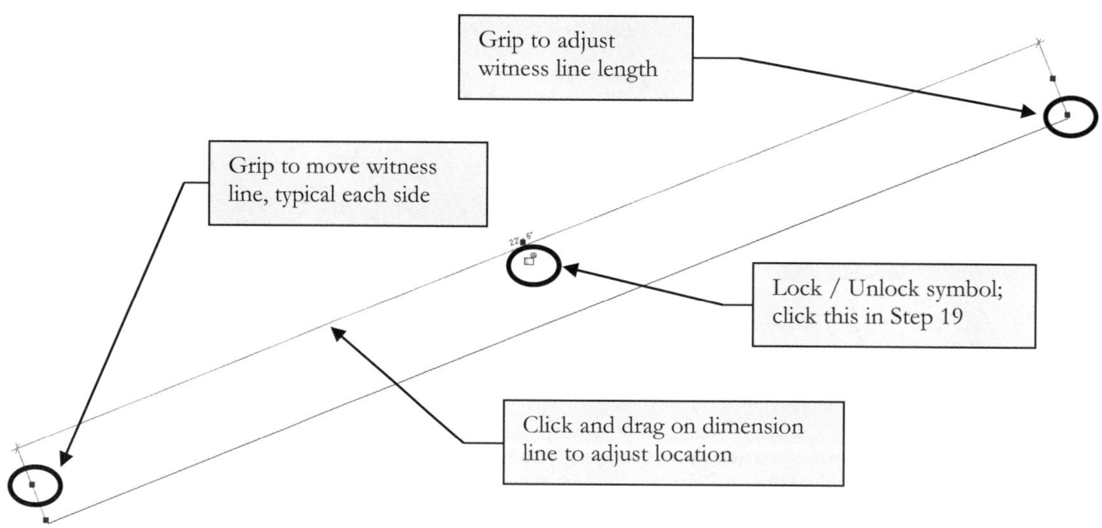

FIGURE 3-1.9 Selected dimension

19. Click on the **Lock/Unlock** padlock symbol to lock the dimension (Figure 3-1.9).

The dimension is now locked. Again, this means that you cannot change the dimension OR the line, though you can move it. The dimension is attached to the line so that changing one affects the other. Next, you will see what happens when you try to modify the dimension while it is locked.

Any time the line or dimension is selected, you will see the lock or unlock symbol in the locked position.

FYI: *Clicking the dimension's padlock icon anytime it is visible will toggle the setting between locked and unlocked.*

20. Select **Modify** to unselect the *Dimension.*

21. Select the line (not the dimension).

22. Click on the dimension text and attempt to modify the line length to **21′**.

As you can see, Revit will not let you edit the text.

Even though your current view is showing a relatively small area, i.e., your *Drafting View,* it is actually an infinite drawing board.

In architectural CAD drafting, everything is drawn to true life size, or full scale, ALWAYS! If you are drawing a building, you might draw an exterior wall that is 600′-0″ long. If you are drawing a window detail, you might draw a line that is 8″ long. In either case, you are entering that line's actual length.

You could, of course, have an 8″ line and a 600′-0″ line in the same *Drafting View*. Either line would be difficult to see at the current drawing magnification (i.e., approximately 22′ x 16′ area; also recall that your diagonal line is 27′-6″ long). So, you would have to zoom in to see the 8″ line and zoom out to see the 600′-0″ line. Next, you will get to try this.

When the diagonal line is selected, notice the *Properties Palette* lists the type of entity selected (i.e., Lines), the *Style* (i.e., Thin Lines), and the *Length* (i.e., 22′-6″). See Chapter 1 for more information on the *Properties Palette* and how to open it if you accidentally closed it.

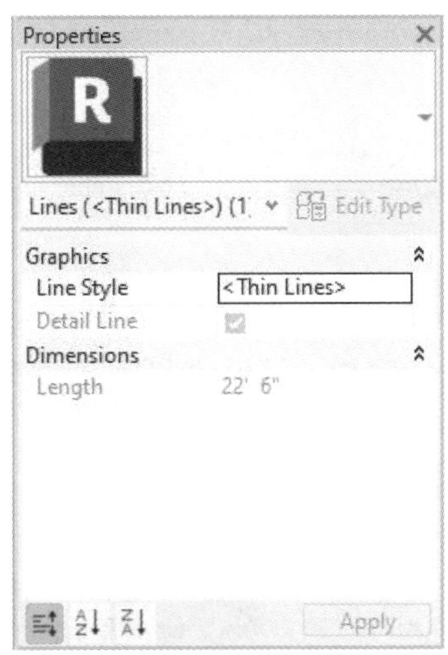

FIGURE 3-1.10 Properties Palette with diagonal line selected

Draw an 8″ Line:

The next steps will walk you through drawing an 8″ horizontal line. Revit provides multiple ways to do this. You will try one of them now.

23. Select **Annotate → Detail → Detail Line**.

24. Pick a point somewhere in the upper left corner of the drawing window.

25. Start moving the mouse towards the right and generally horizontal until you see a dashed reference line extending in each direction of your line appear on the screen, as in Figure 3-1.11.

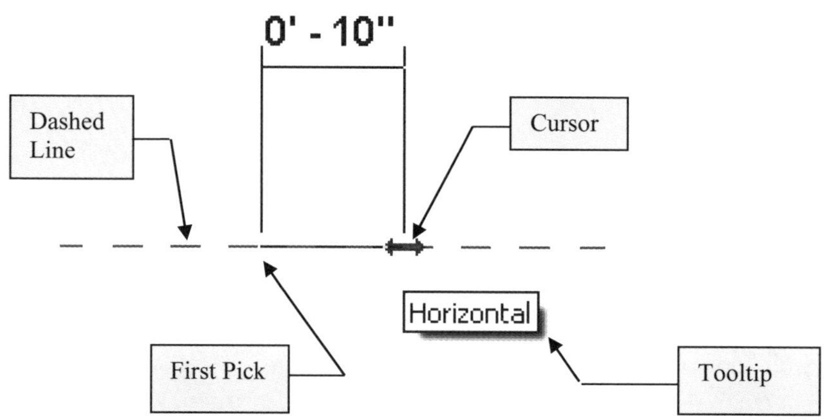

FIGURE 3-1.11 Drawing a line with the help of Revit

TIP: You will see a dashed horizontal line and a tooltip when the line is horizontal.

As you move the mouse left and right, you will notice that Revit displays various dimensions that let you quickly draw your line at these often-used increments. See the next exercise to learn more about how to control the increments shown.

26. With the dashed line and *tooltip* visible on the screen, take your hand off the mouse, so you do not accidentally move it, and type **8″** and then press **Enter**.

    TIP: Remember, you have to type the inch symbol; Revit always assumes you mean feet unless you specify otherwise. A future lesson will review the input options in more detail.

You have just drawn a line with a precise length and angle!

27. Use the ***Measure*** tool to verify it was drawn correctly. Click *Modify* → *Measure* → *Measure (down arrow)* → *Measure Between Two References*

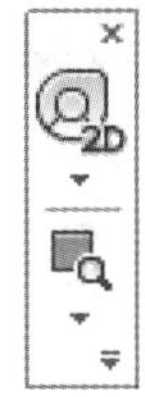

28. Use the ***Zoom In Region*** tool to enlarge the view of the 8″ line via the *Navigation Bar* (image to the right).

29. Now use the ***Zoom to Fit*** or ***Previous Pan/Zoom*** tools so that both lines are visible again.

Draw a 600′ Line:

30. Select the ***Detail Line*** tool and pick a point in the lower right corner of the drawing window.

31. Move the cursor straight up from your first point so that the line snaps to the vertical and the dashed line appears (Figure 3-1.12).

32. With the dashed line and *tooltip* visible on the screen, take your hand off the mouse so you do not accidentally move it; type **600** and then press **Enter**.

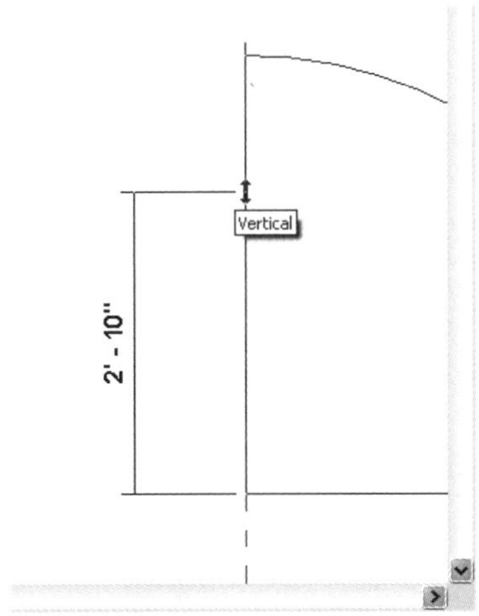

FIGURE 3-1.12 Drawing another Detail Line; 600′-0″ vertical line – lower right

TIP #1: Notice this time you did not have to type the foot symbol (′).

TIP #2: You do not need to get the temporary dimension close to reading 600′; the temporary dimension is ignored when you type in a value.

33. Press the **Esc** key twice to exit the *Detail Line* tool and return to the *Modify* mode.

Because the visible portion of the drawing area is only about 16′ tall, you obviously would not expect to see a 600′ line. You need to change the drawing's magnification by zooming out to see it.

34. Use ***Zoom to Fit*** to see the entire drawing (Fig. 3-1.13).

TIP: Double-click your wheel button to Zoom Extents.

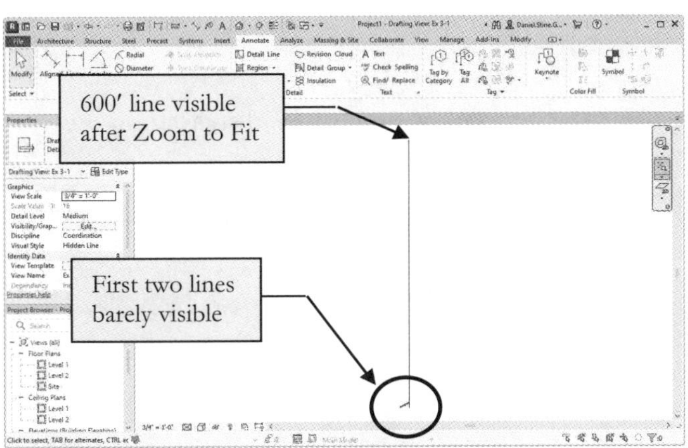

FIGURE 3-1.13 Detail view with three lines

Drawing Shapes:

Revit provides several tools for drawing common shapes such as squares, rectangles, circles, and ellipses. These tools can be found on the *Ribbon* while the *Detail Line* tool is active. You will take a look at *Rectangle* and *Circle* now.

Creating a Rectangle:

35. Use ***Previous Pan/Zoom***, or *Zoom Region*, to get back to the original view where the diagonal line spans the screen.

36. Select the ***Detail Line*** tool.

Notice the *Ribbon* and *Properties Palette* have changed to show various options related to *Detail Lines* (Figure 3-1.14).

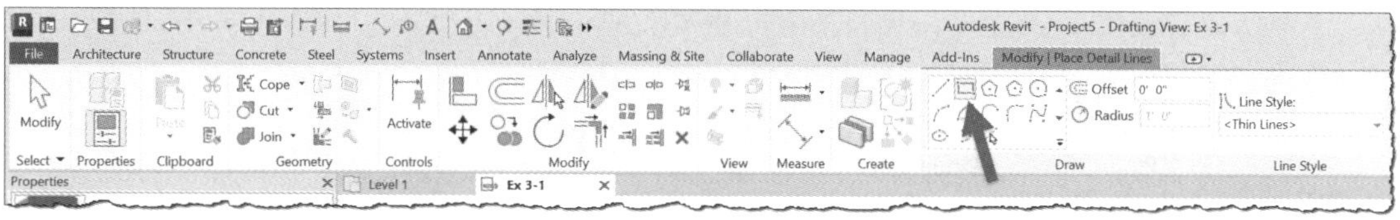

FIGURE 3-1.14 Place Detail Lines contextual Tab on Ribbon

37. Select the **Rectangle** tool from the *Ribbon.*

TIP: Hover your cursor over the icon to see the tooltip until you learn what tools the icons represent.

38. Pick the "**first corner point**" somewhere near the lower center of the drawing window (Figure 3-1.15).

Notice that the temporary dimensions display a dimension for both width and height. At this point, you can pick a point on the screen, trying to get the dimensions correct before clicking the mouse button. If you do not get the rectangle drawn correctly, you can click each dimension-text and change the dimension while the temporary dimensions are displayed; see the next two steps for the rectangle dimensions.

39. Draw a 2′-8″ x 4′-4″ rectangle using the temporary dimensions displayed on the screen; if you do not draw it correctly, do the following:

    a. Click the dimension-text for the horizontal line, then type **2′-8″** and then press **Enter**.

    b. Type **4′-4″** and then press **Enter** for the vertical dimension.

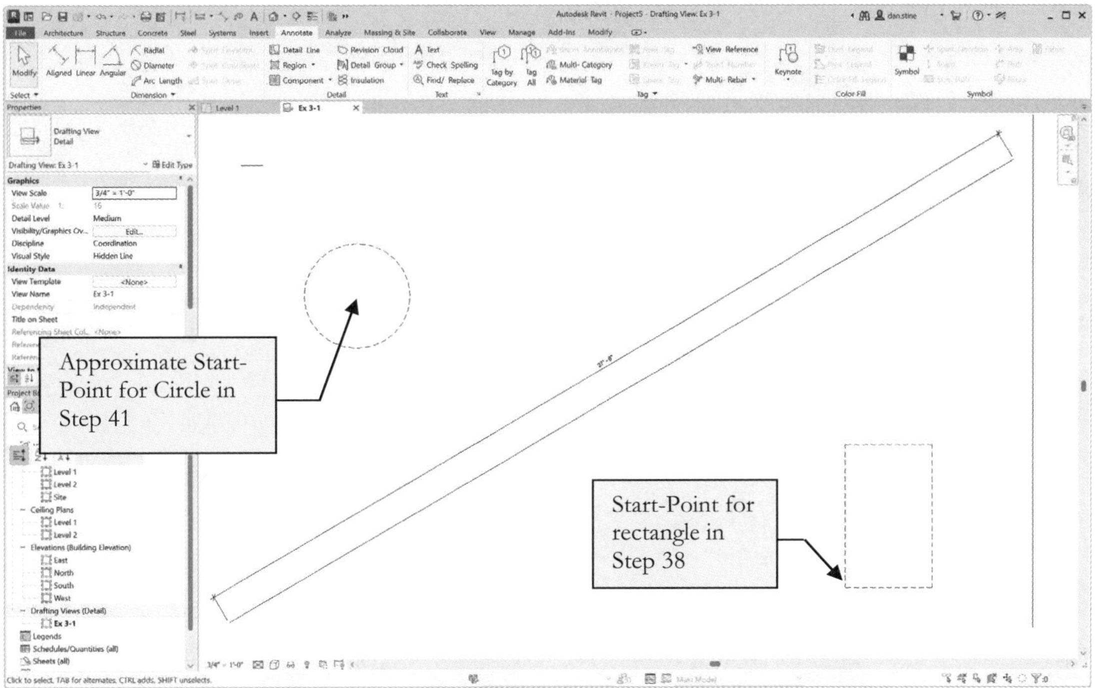

FIGURE 3-1.15 Drawing with Rectangle and Circle to be added (shown dashed for clarity)

Creating a Circle:

40. With the *Detail Line* tool active, select **Circle** from the *Ribbon* (Figure 3-1.16).

41. You are now prompted to pick the center point for the circle; pick a point approximately as shown in Figure 3-1.15.

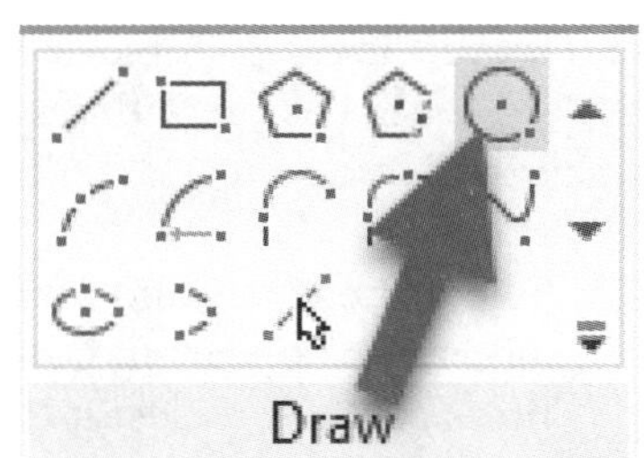

FIGURE 3-1.16 Detail Line shapes

You should now see a dynamic circle and a temporary dimension attached to your cursor, which allows you to visually specify the circle's size. Move your mouse around to see that you could arbitrarily pick a point on the screen to create a quick circle if needed, then proceed to Step 42 where you will draw a circle with a radius of 1′-6⅝″.

42. Type **1 6 5/8** and then press **Enter** (Figure 3-1.17).

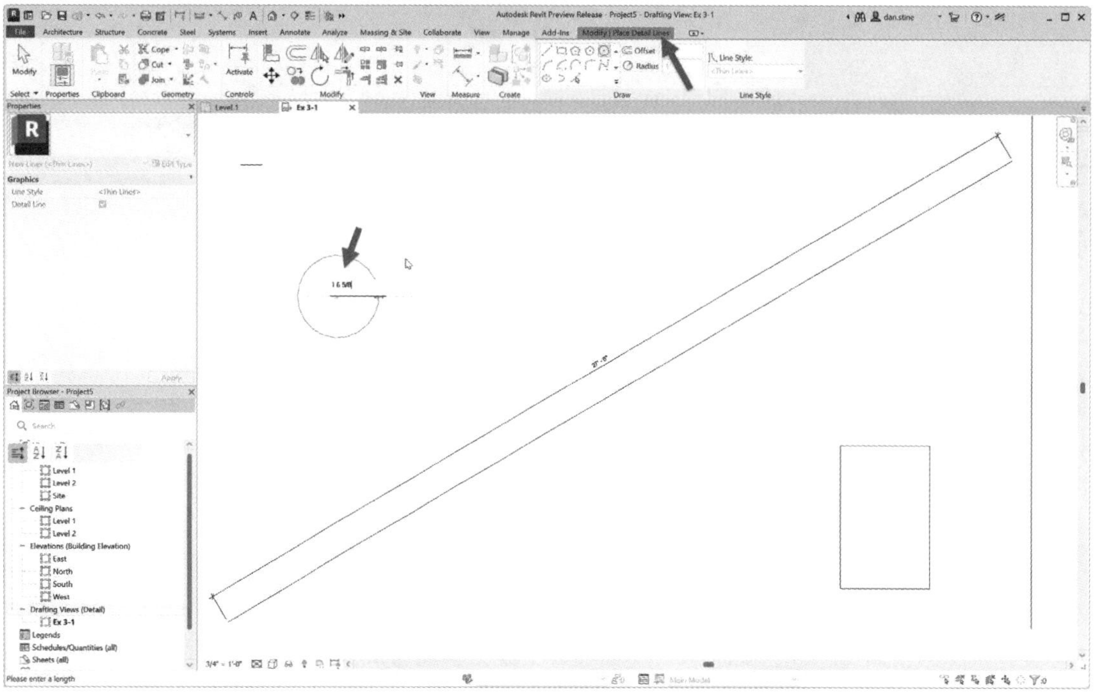

FIGURE 3-1.17 Drawing with Rectangle and Circle added

Notice in the image above, the *Detail Line* is still active because the *contextual tab*, **Modify | Place Detail Lines**, is visible and the *Status Bar* is prompting to "Click to enter circle center." You need to press **Esc** or click *Modify* to cancel the command; clicking another command will also cancel the current command.

43. **Select the circle** and notice a temporary dimension appears indicating the circle's radius. Press **Esc** to unselect it (Figure 3-1.18).

    TIP: This temporary dimension can be used to change the radius of the circle while the circle is selected.

44. **Save** your project as "**ex3-1.rvt**".

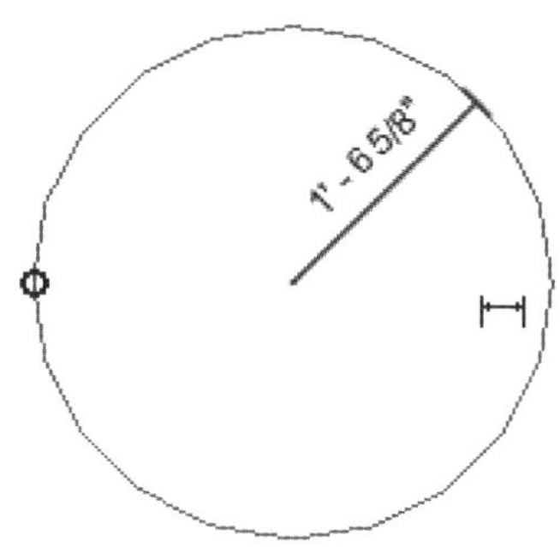

FIGURE 3-1.18
Circle selected

Exercise 3-2:
Snaps

Snaps are tools that allow you to accurately pick a point on an element. For example, when drawing a line you can use *Object Snap* to select, as the start-point, the endpoint or midpoint of another line or wall.

This feature is absolutely critical to drawing accurate technical drawings. Using this feature allows you to be confident you are creating perfect intersections, corners, etc. (Figure 3-2.1).

Object Snaps Options:

You can use *Object Snaps* in one of two ways.

- "Normal" mode
- "Temporary Override" mode

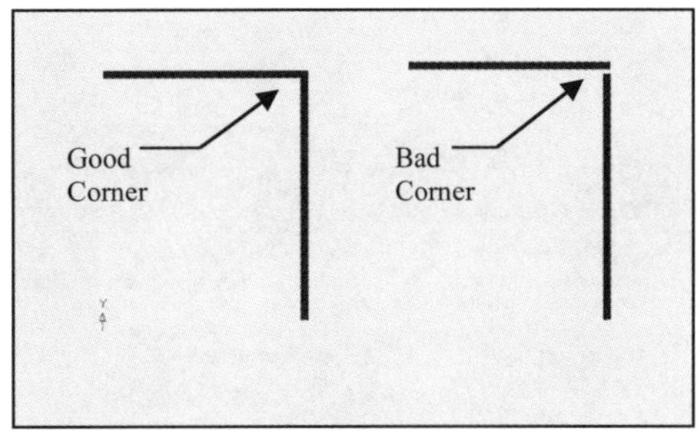

FIGURE 3-2.1 Typical problem when *Snaps* are not used

"Normal" *SNAP* mode is a feature that constantly scans the area near your cursor when Revit is looking for user input. You can configure which types of points to look for.

***NOTE:** The term "normal" is not a Revit term, rather it is simply a description used in this book to differentiate this portion of the Snaps feature from the Temporary Override portion discussed next.*

Using a "Temporary Override" *Object Snap* for individual pick-points allows you to quickly select a particular point on an element. This option will temporarily disable the other *Object Snap* settings, which means you tell Revit to just look for the endpoint on an object, for the next pick-point only, rather than the three or four types being scanned for by the "normal" *Object Snaps* feature.

Overview of the Snaps Dialog Box:

Revit provides a *Snaps* dialog box where you specify which *Object Snaps* you want enabled. Next you will take a look at it.

1. Open project **Ex3-1** and select **Manage → Settings → Snaps**.

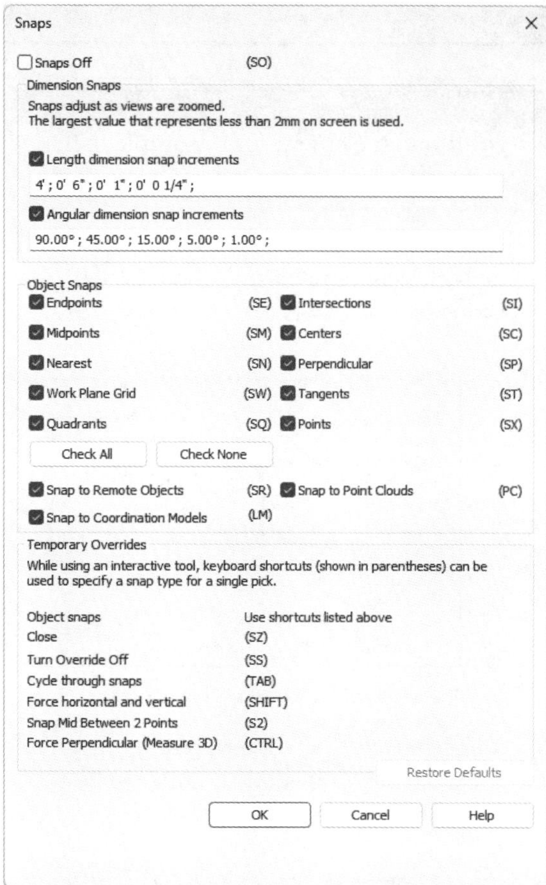

FIGURE 3-2.2 Snaps dialog box; default settings

You should now see the *Snaps* dialog box (Figure 3-2.2). Take a minute to study the various settings that you can control with this dialog box. Notice the check box at the top that allows you to turn this feature off completely.

<u>*Dimension Snaps*</u>
This controls the automatic dimensions that Revit suggests when you are drawing. Following the given format you could add or remove increments. If you are zoomed in close, only the smaller increments are used.

<u>*Object Snaps*</u>
This controls the "normal" *Object Snaps* that Revit scans for while you are drawing. Unchecking an item tells Revit not to scan for it anymore. Currently, all *Object Snaps* are enabled (Figure 3-2.2).

<u>*Temporary Overrides*</u>
This area is really just information on how to use Temporary Overrides.

While drawing you will occasionally want to tell Revit you only want to *Snap* to an Endpoint for the next pick. Instead of opening the *Snaps* dialog and un-checking every *Object Snap* except for Endpoint, you can specify a *Temporary Override* for the next pick. You do this by typing the two letters, in parentheses, in the *Object Snaps* area of the *Snaps* dialog (Figure 3-2.2).

2. Make sure the *Snaps Off* option is unchecked in the upper-left corner of the dialog box; this turns Snaps completely off.

3. Click on the **Check All** button to make sure all *Snaps* are checked.

4. Click **OK** to close the *Snaps* dialog box.

Understanding Snap Symbols:

Again, you should be well aware of the *Object Snap* symbols that Revit displays as you move your cursor about the drawing window while you are in a tool like *Wall* and Revit is awaiting your input or pick-point.

If you hold your cursor still for a moment, while a snap symbol is displayed, a tooltip will appear on the screen. However, when you become familiar with the snap symbols you can pick sooner, rather than waiting for the tooltip to display (Figure 3-2.3).

The TAB key cycles through the available snaps near your cursor.

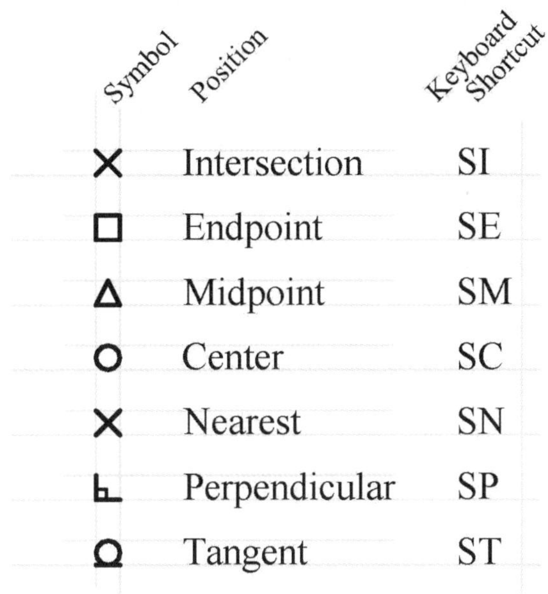

FIGURE 3-2.3 Snap symbols

Finally, typing **SO** turns all snaps off for one pick.

FYI: *The Snaps shown in Figure 3-2.2 are for Revit in general, not just the current project. This is convenient; you don't have to adjust to your favorite settings for each Project or View, existing or new.*

Setting Object Snaps:

You can set Revit to have just one or all Snaps running at the same time. Let us say you have Endpoint and Midpoint set to be running. While using the *Wall* tool, you move your cursor near an existing wall. When the cursor is near the end of the wall you will see the Endpoint symbol show up; when you move the cursor towards the middle of the line you will see the Midpoint symbol show up.

The next step shows you how to tell Revit which Object Snaps you want it to look for. First you will save a new copy of your project.

5. Select **File Tab → Save-As → Project**.

6. Name the project **ex3-2.rvt**.

7. As discussed previously, open the ***Snaps*** dialog box.

8. Make sure only the following *Snaps* are checked:
   a. Endpoints
   b. Midpoints
   c. Centers
   d. Intersections
   e. Perpendicular

9. Click **OK** to close the dialog box.

> **For More Information:**
> For more on using Snaps, search Revit's *Help System* for **Snaps**. Then double-click **Snap Points** or any other items found by the search.

Now that you have the *Snaps* adjusted, you will give this feature a try.

10. Using the ***Detail Line*** tool, move your cursor to the lower-left portion of the diagonal line (Figure 3-2.4).

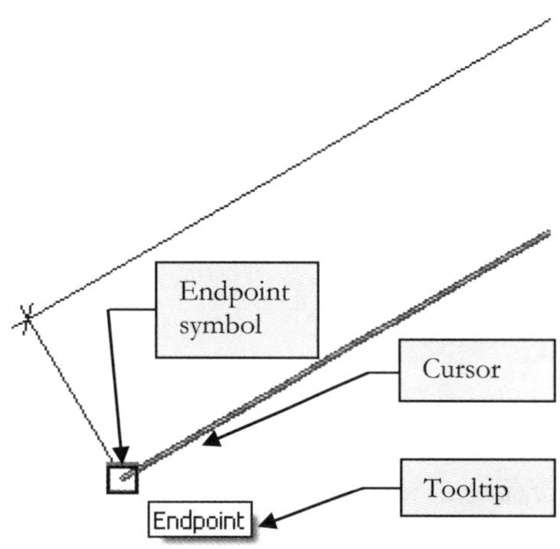

FIGURE 3-2.4 Endpoint SNAP symbol visible

11. Hover the cursor over the line's endpoint (without picking); when you see the *Endpoint* symbol you can click to select that point.

> **Just So You Know**
> It is important that you see the *SNAP* symbol before clicking. Also, once you see the symbol you should be careful not to move the mouse too much.
>
> These steps will help to ensure accurate selections.

While still in the Detail Line tool, you will use Snaps to draw lines and sketch accurately.

12. Draw the additional lines shown in **Figure 3-2.5** using the appropriate *Object Snap,* changing the selected Snaps as required to select the required points.

TIP #1: At any point while the Line tool is active, you can open the SNAP dialog box and adjust its settings. This will not cancel the Line command.

TIP #2: Also, remember you can press Tab to cycle through the various snap options below or near your cursor.

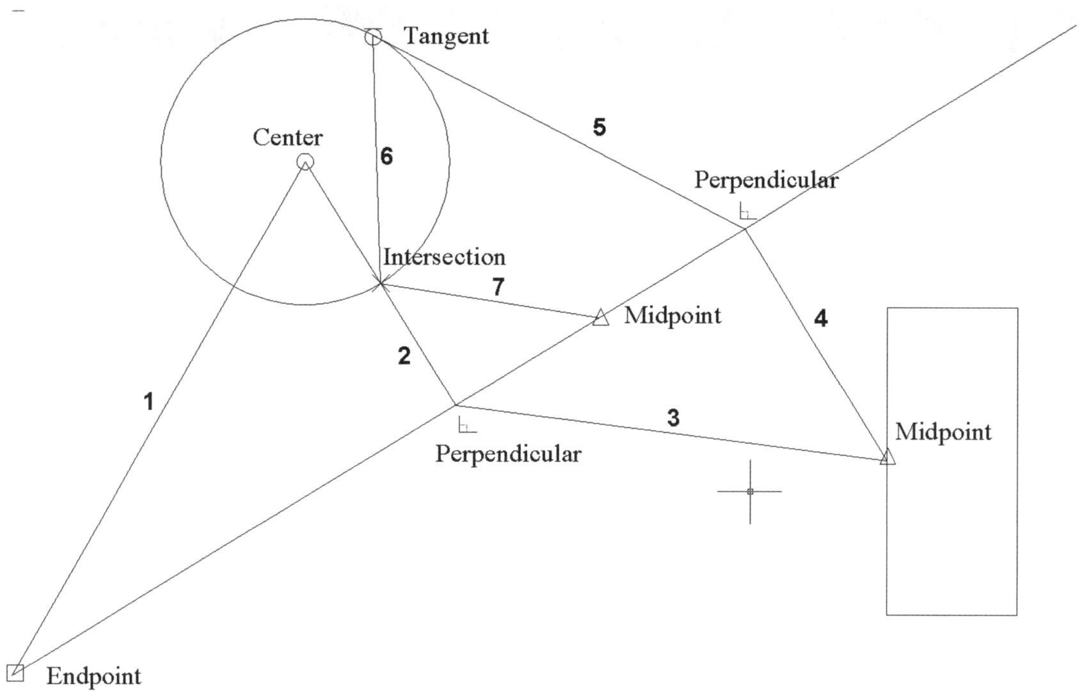

FIGURE 3-2.5 Lines to draw and Snap to use

13. **Save** your project.

Your drawing might look slightly different depending on where you drew the rectangle and circle in the previous steps.

> **This is a Residential Example?**
>
> OK, this is not really an architectural example yet. However, the point here is to focus on the fundamental concepts and not architecture just yet.

Save Reminders:

Revit is configured to remind you to save every 30 minutes to prevent you from losing any work (Figure 3-2.6).

It is recommended that you do not simply click *Cancel*; instead, click the **Save the project** option.

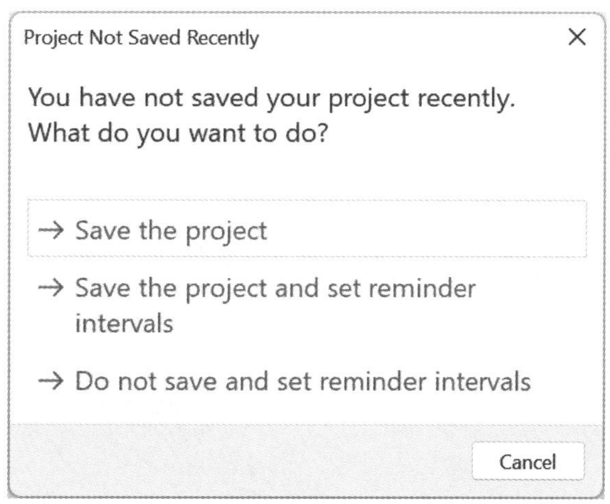

FIGURE 3-2.6 Save reminder

Exercise 3-3:
Edit Tools

The *edit tools* are often used in Revit. A lot of time is spent tweaking designs and making code and client-related revisions.

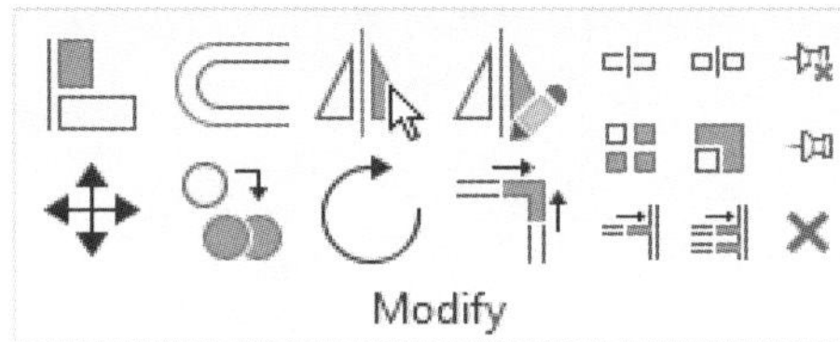

FIGURE 3-3.1 Modify panel

Example: you use the *design tools* (e.g., Walls, Doors, Windows) to initially draw the project. Then you use the *edit tools* to *Move* a wall so a room becomes larger, *Mirror* a cabinet so it faces in a different direction, or *Rotate* the furniture per the owner's instructions.

You will usually access the various edit tools from the Modify tab on the *Ribbon*. You can probably visualize what most of the commands do by the graphics on the icons; see Figure 3-3.1. When you hover over an icon, the tool name will appear. The two letters shown to the right are its keyboard shortcut; pressing those two keys, one at a time, activates that tool.

In this exercise, you will get a brief overview of a few of the edit tools by manipulating the tangled web of lines you have previously drawn.

1. **Open** project **ex3-2.rvt** from the previous lesson.

2. **Save-As** "**ex3-3.rvt**".

FYI: You will notice that instructions or tools that have already been covered in this book will have fewer "step-by-step" instructions.

Delete Tool:

It is no surprise that the *Delete* tool is a necessity; things change and mistakes are made. You can *Delete* one element at a time or several. Deleting elements is very easy: you select the elements, and then pick the *Delete* icon. You will try this on two lines in your drawing.

3. While holding the **Ctrl** key, select the lines identified in **Figure 3-3.2**.

   TIP: See the section below Figure 3-3.2 on Selecting Entities.

4. Select **Delete** from the *Ribbon* (or press the **Delete** key on the keyboard).

The lines are now deleted from the project.

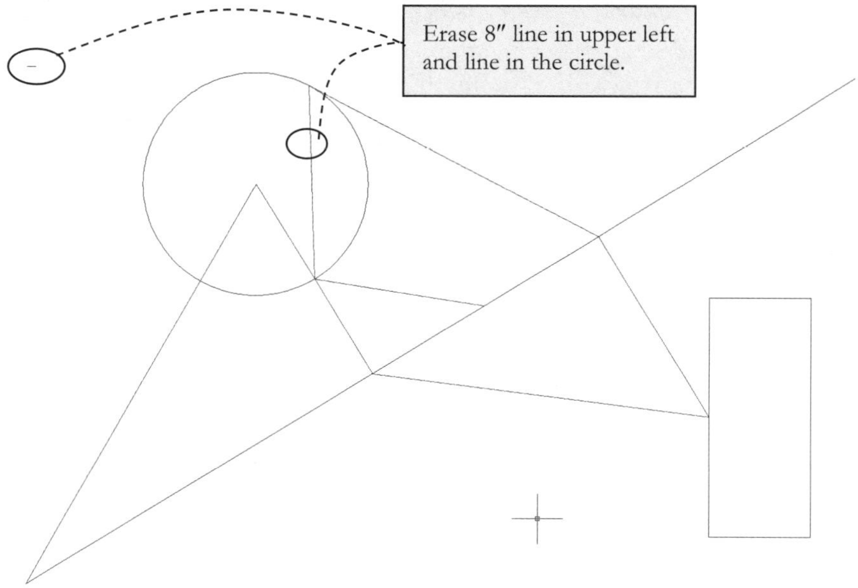

FIGURE 3-3.2 Lines to be erased

Selecting Objects:

At this time, we will digress and take a quick look at the various techniques for selecting entities in Revit. Most tools work the same way when selecting elements.

When selecting entities, you have two primary ways to select them:

- Individually select entities one at a time
- Select several entities at a time with a window

You can use one or a combination of both methods to select elements when using the *Copy* tool.

Individual Selections:
When prompted to select entities to copy or delete, for example, you simply move the cursor over the element and click; holding the **Ctrl** key you can select multiple objects. Then you typically click the tool you wish to use on the selected items. Press **Shift** and click on an item to subtract it from the current selection set.

Continued on next page

<u>Window Selections</u>:
Similarly, you can pick a *window* around several elements to select them all at once. To select a *window*, rather than selecting an object as previously described, you select one corner of the *window* you wish to define. That is, you pick a point in "space" and hold the mouse button down. Now, as you move the mouse, you will see a rectangle on the screen that represents the windowed area you are selecting; when the *window* encompasses the elements you wish to select, release the mouse.

You actually have two types of windows you can select. One is called a **window** and the other is called a **crossing window**.

Window:
This option allows you to select only the objects that are completely within the *window*. Any lines that extend out of the *window* are not selected.

Crossing Window:
This option allows you to select all the entities that are completely within the *window* and any that extend outside the *window*.

Using Window versus Crossing Window:
To select a *window* you simply pick and drag from left to right to form a rectangle (Figure 3-3.3a).

Conversely, to select a *crossing window*, you pick and drag from right to left to define the two diagonal points of the window (Figure 3-3.3b).

Selecting a chain of lines (hover, tab, click):
Revit provides a quick and easy way to select a chain of lines, that is, a series of lines (or walls) whose endpoints are perfectly connected. You simply hover your cursor over one line so it highlights, then press the Tab key once, and then click the mouse button. This trick can be used to quickly select all the exterior walls on a building, for example.

Turning off **Drag Element on Selection** on the *Status Bar* helps to avoid accidentally clicking directly on an element and moving it rather than starting the intended first corner of a selection window.

Remember, all these draw, modify and select tools have direct application to working with Revit's 3D building components, not just the 2D geometry being covered in this chapter.

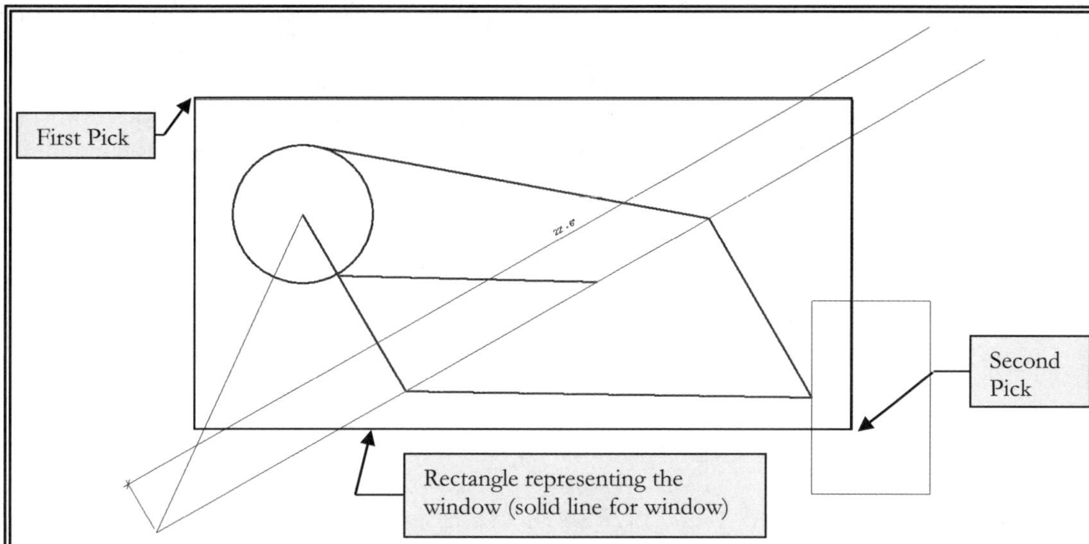

FIGURE 3-3.3A Six items selected using *window;* only the lines completely within the window are selected.

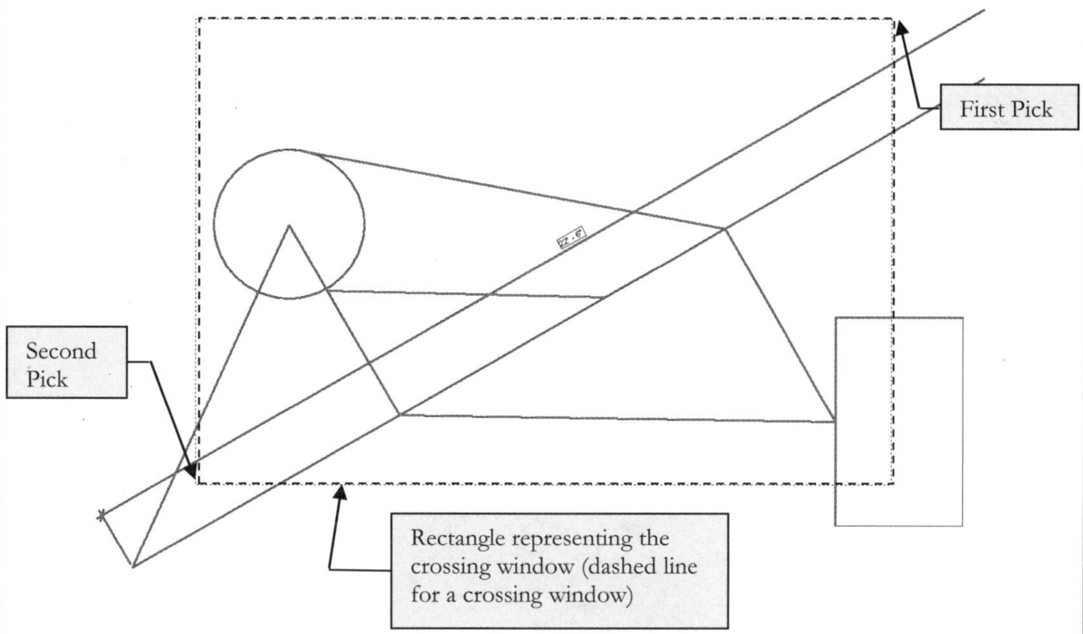

FIGURE 3-3.3B Everything selected using a *crossing window;* all lines within crossing are selected.

Copy Tool:

The *Copy* tool allows you to accurately duplicate an element(s). You select the items you want to copy and then pick two points that represent an imaginary vector, which provides both length and angle, defining the path used to copy the object. You can also type in the length if there are no convenient points to pick in the drawing. You will try both methods next.

5. **Select the circle.**

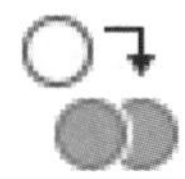

6. Select **Copy** from the *Ribbon.*

Notice the prompt on the Status Bar: Click to enter move start point.

7. Pick the **center** of the **circle** (Figure 3-3.4).

   FYI: *You actually have three different Snaps you can use here: Center, Endpoint, and Intersection. All occur at the exact same point.*

Notice the prompt on the Status Bar: Click to enter move end point.

8. Pick the **endpoint** of the angled line in the lower left corner (Figure 3-3.4).

   FYI: *If you want to make several copies of the circle, select* Multiple *on the Ribbon.*

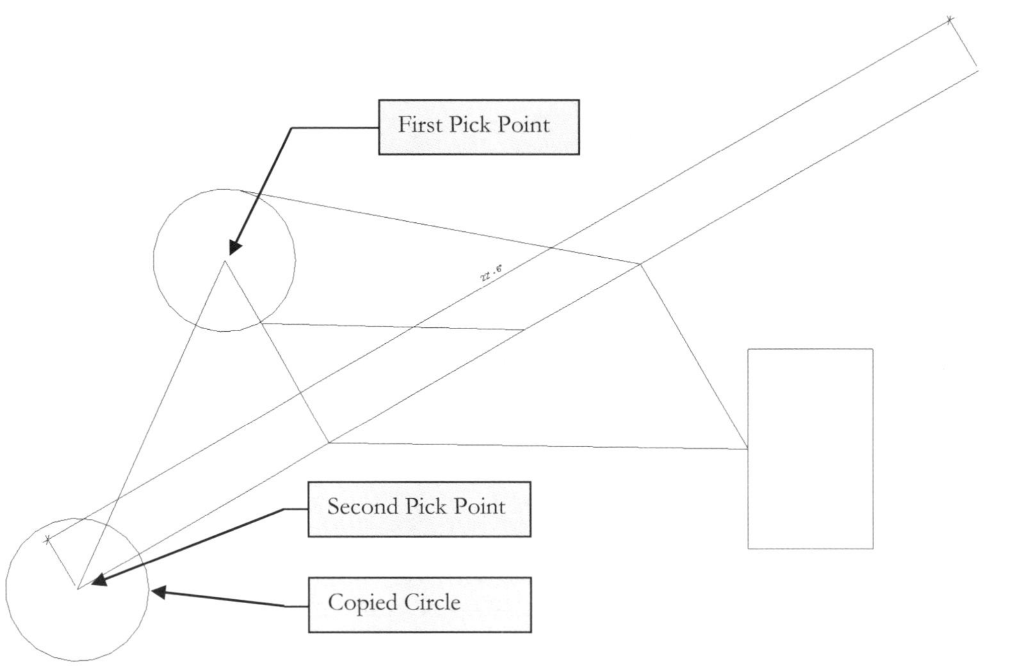

FIGURE 3-3.4 Copied circle; also indicates points selected

9. **Select the rectangle** *(all four lines).*

   TIP: *Try the "hover, tab, click" method discussed on page 3-22.*

10. Select **Copy**.

11. Pick an arbitrary point on the screen. In this scenario, it makes no difference where you pick; you will see why in a moment.

At this point, move the mouse in the direction you want to copy the rectangle until the correct angle is displayed, then type the distance instead of picking a second point on the screen.

12. Move the mouse towards the upper right until 45 degrees displays, then type **6'** and then press **Enter** (Figure 3-3.5).

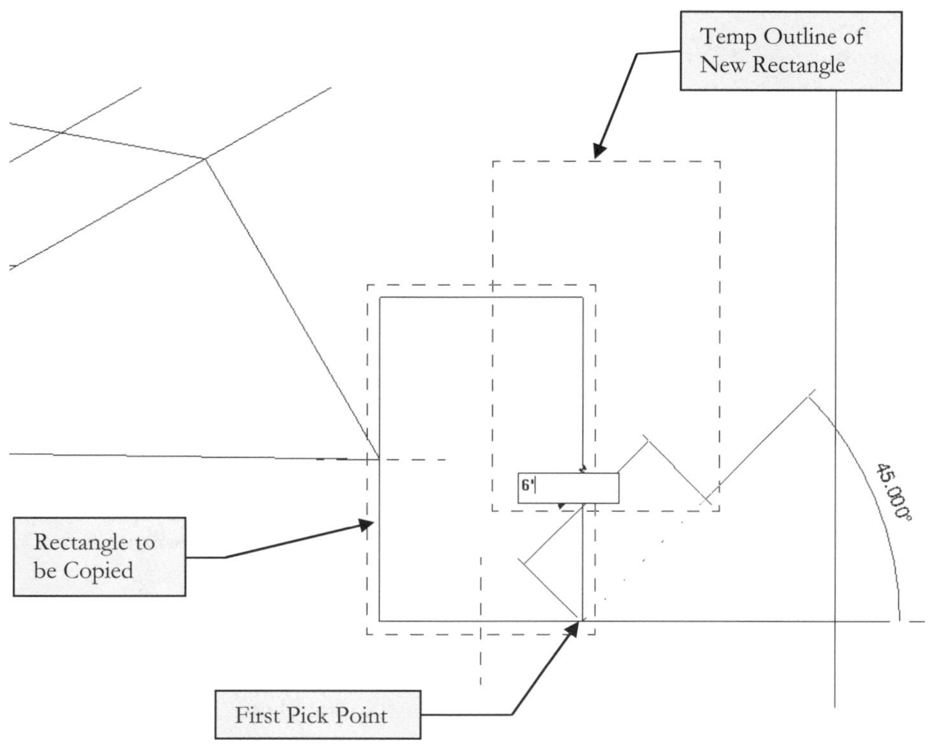

FIGURE 3-3.5 Copying rectangle; angle set visually and distance typed in

NOTE: *Your drawing may look a little different from this one because it is not completely to scale.*

Move Tool:

The *Move* tool works exactly like the *Copy* tool except, of course, you move the element(s) rather than copy it. Given the similarity to the previously covered tool, the *Move* tool will not be covered now. You are encouraged to try it yourself; just Undo your experiments before proceeding.

Rotate Tool:

With the *Rotate* tool, you can arbitrarily or accurately rotate one or more objects in your drawing. When you need to rotate accurately, you can pick points that define the angle, assuming points exist in the drawing to pick, or you can type a specific angle.

Rotate involves the following steps:

- Select element(s) to be rotated
- Select *Rotate*
- Determine if the Center of Rotation symbol is where you want it.
    - If you want to move it:
        - Simply drag it, or
        - Click *Place* on the *Ribbon*
- Select a point to define a reference line and begin rotation.
- Pick a second point using one of the following methods:
    - By selecting other objects or using the graphic angle display *or*
    - You can type an angle and press **Enter**.

13. **Select the new rectangle** you just copied *(all four lines)*.

14. Select **Rotate** on the *Ribbon*.

Notice that the "Center of Rotation" grip, by default, is located in the center of the selected elements. This is the point about which the rotation will occur. See Figure 3-3.6.

You will not change the "Center of Rotation" at this time.

15. Pick a point directly to the right of the "Center of Rotation" grip; this tells Revit you want to rotate the rectangle relative to the horizontal plane (Figure 3-3.6).

Now, as you move your mouse up or down, you will see the temporary angle dimension displayed. You can move the mouse until the desired angle is displayed, then click to complete the rotation, or type the desired angle and press **Enter**. If you recall, the *Snaps* dialog box controls the angle increments Revit displays; they are all whole numbers. So if you need to rotate something 22.45 degrees, you must type it as Revit will never display that number as an option.

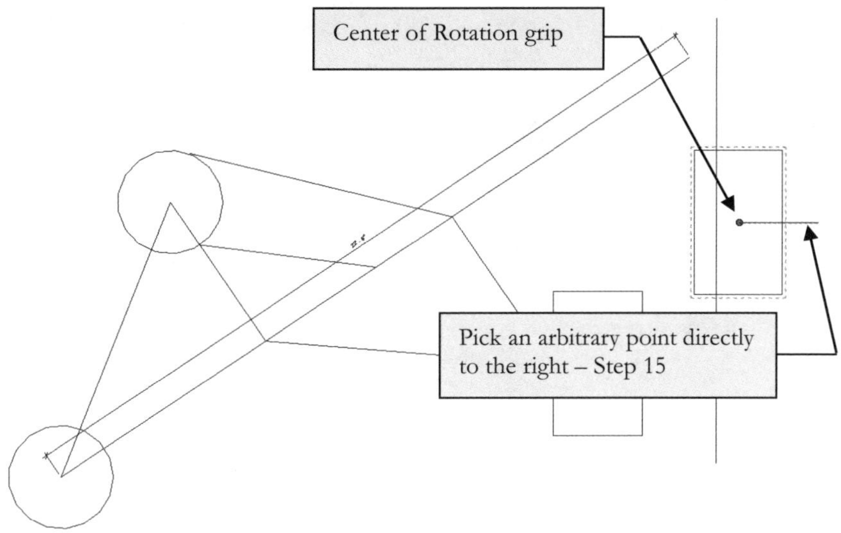

FIGURE 3-3.6 Rotate tool; first step – select lines and then click Rotate

16. Move the mouse up and to the left until 90 degrees is displayed and then click to complete the rotation (Figure 3-3.7).

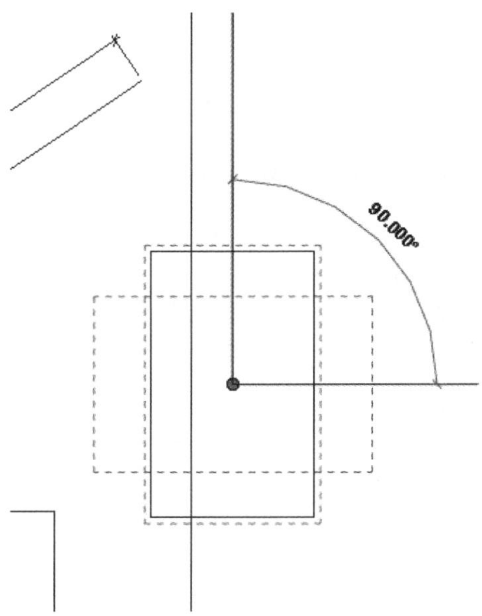

FIGURE 3-3.7 Rotate tool; last step – select angle visually or type angle

The previous steps just rotated the rectangle 90 degrees counter-clockwise about its center point (Figure 3-3.8).

17. Select the **Undo** icon. 

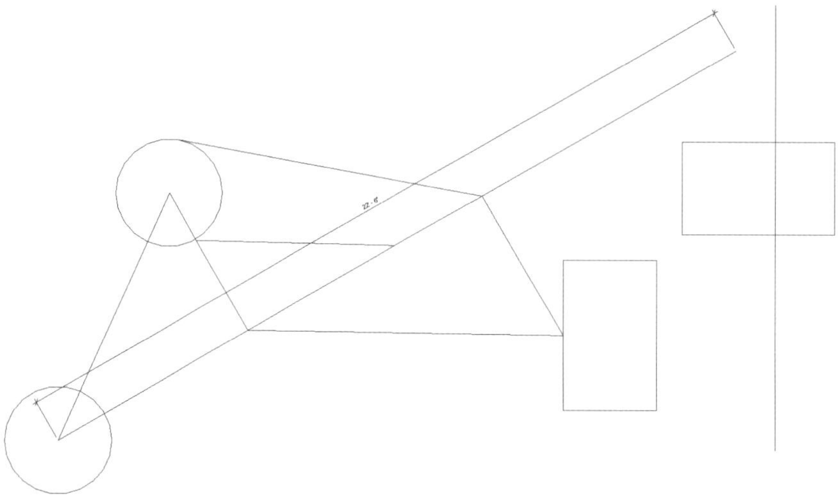

FIGURE 3-3.8 Rotate tool; rectangle rotated about its center point

Now you will do the same thing, but with a different angle and a different "Center of Rotation."

18. **Select the rectangle** and then pick **Rotate.**

19. Click and drag the "Center of Rotation" grip to the left and *Snap* to the midpoint of the vertical line (Figure 3-3.9).

    ***TIP:** You can also click the* **Place** *button on the Ribbon (see the image to the right).*

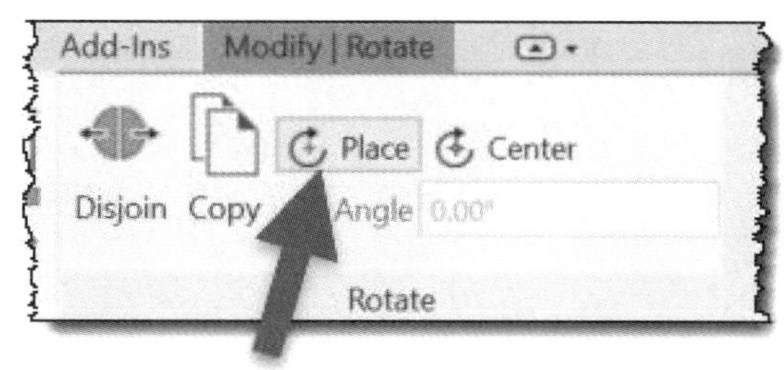

20. Pick a point to the right, creating a horizontal reference line.

21. Start moving your mouse downward, then type **22.5** and then press **Enter** (Figure 3-3.10).

The rectangle is now rotated 22.5 degrees clockwise (Figure 3-3.11).

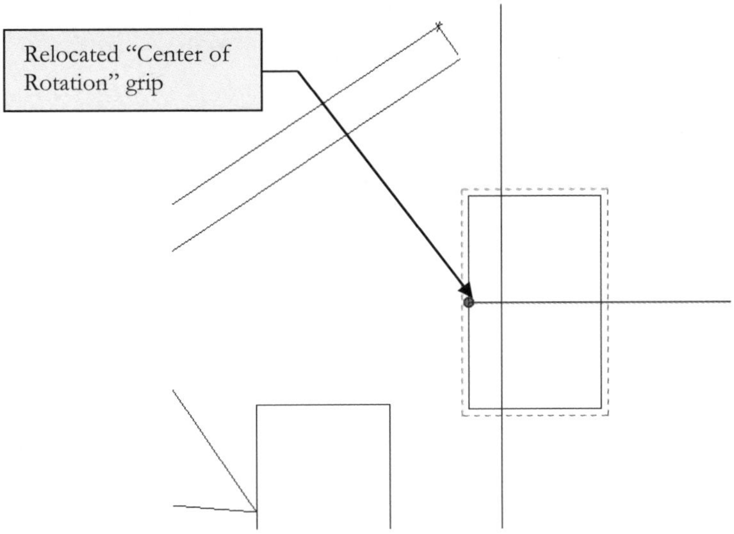

FIGURE 3-3.9 Rotate tool; relocated Center of Rotation grip

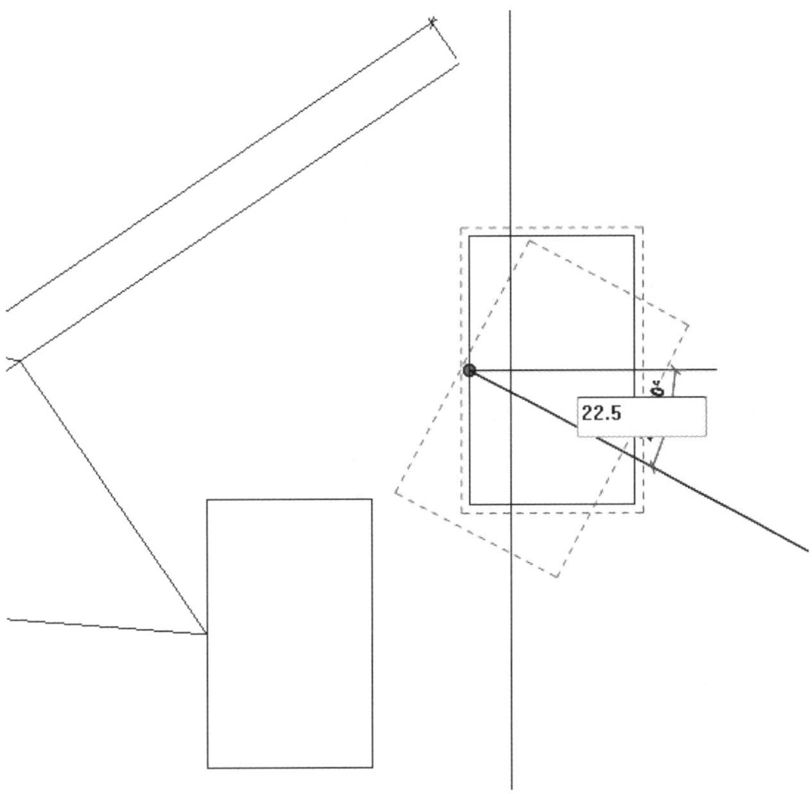

FIGURE 3-3.10 Rotate tool; typing in exact angle

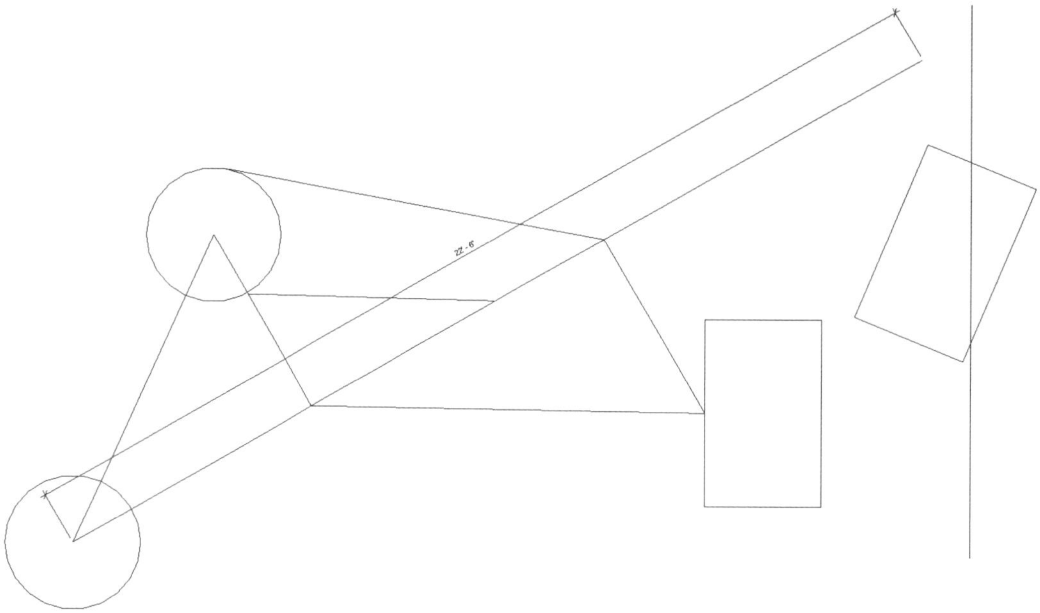

FIGURE 3-3.11 Rotate tool; rectangle rotated 22.5 degrees

Scale Tool:

The *Scale* tool has steps similar to the *Rotate* tool. First, you select what you want to scale or resize, specify a scale factor, and then you pick the base point. The scale factor can be specified by selecting points on the screen or by entering a numerical scale factor (e.g., 2 or .5, where 2 is twice the original size and .5 is half the original size).

Next, you will use the *Scale* tool to adjust the size of the circle near the bottom.

Before you resize the circle, use the Modify tool/mode to measure its diameter. Select the circle and view its temporary dimensions. After resizing the circle, you will refer back to the temporary dimensions to note the change. This step is meant to teach you how to verify the accuracy and dimensions of entities in Revit.

22. Select the bottom circle.

23. Select the **Scale** icon from the *Ribbon*.

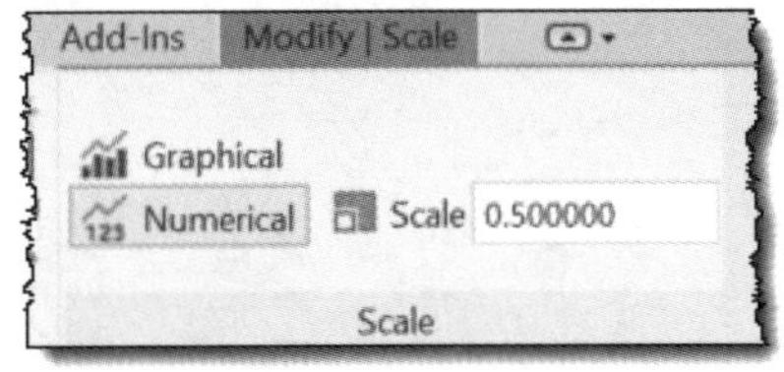

On the *Ribbon,* you will specify a numeric scale factor of .5 to resize the circle to half its original size.

24. Click **Numerical** and then type **.5** in the textbox *(see the Ribbon to the right).*

You are now prompted **Click to enter origin** on the *Status Bar.* This is the base point about which the circle will be scaled; see examples in Figure 3-3.13 on the next page.

25. Click the center of the circle.

You just used the *Scale* tool to change the circle's radius from 1-6 5/8 to 9 5/16. A scale factor of .5 reduces the entities to half their original scale (Figure 3-3.12).

> **Selecting the Correct Center of Rotation *(Base Point)*:**
> You need to select the appropriate *Center of Rotation*, or Base Point, for both the *Scale* and *Rotate* commands to get the results desired. A few examples are shown in Figure 3-3.13. The dashed line indicates the original position of the entity being modified. The black dot indicates the base point selected.

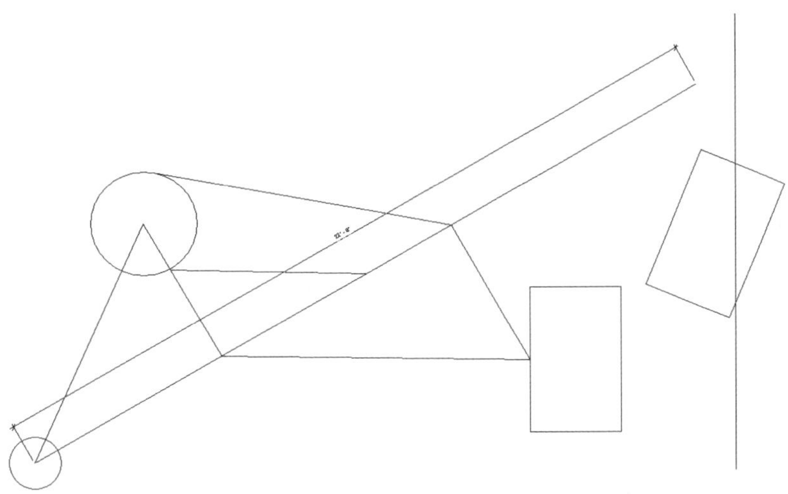

FIGURE 3-3.12 Resize circle; notice it is half the size of the other circle

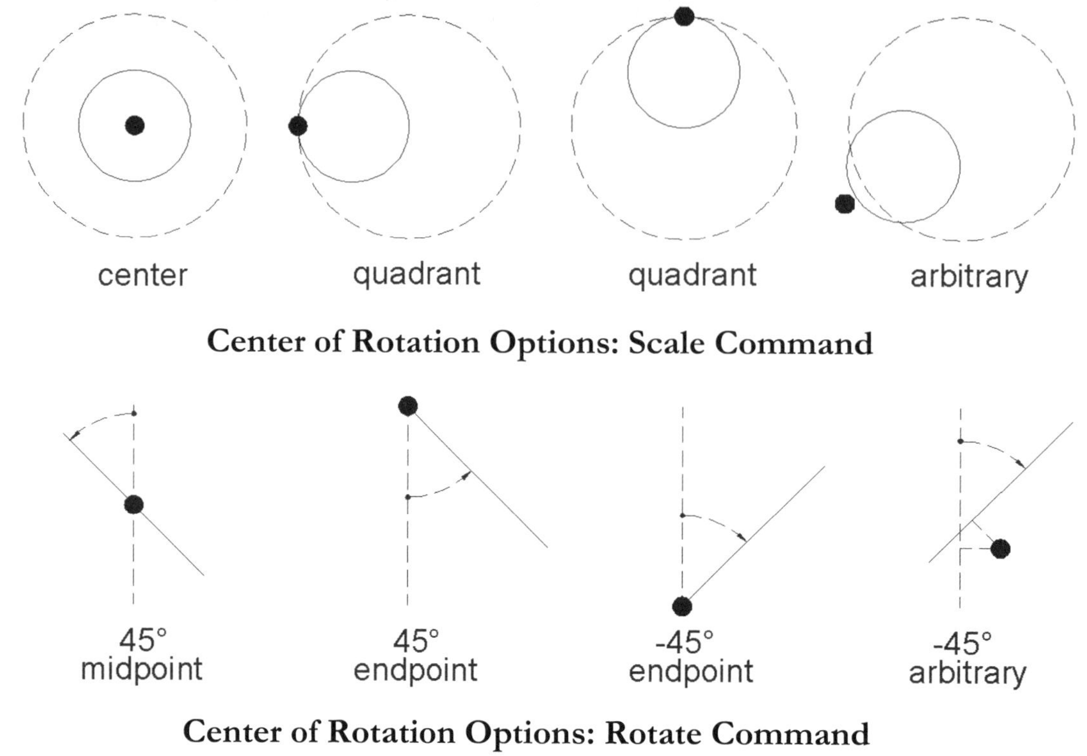

FIGURE 3-3.13 Center of Rotation Options and the various results

This will conclude the brief tour of the *Edit* tools. Do not forget, even though you are editing 2D lines, the edit tools work the same way on 3D elements such as walls, floors, roofs, etc. Exception: you cannot *Scale* walls, doors, etc.; these objects have to be modified by other methods. You would not typically change the door thickness when changing its width and height, as would happen if you could use the *Scale* tool on it.

As you surely noticed, the *Modify* panel on the *Ribbon* has a few other tools that have not been investigated yet. Many of these will be covered later in this book.

26. **Save** the project. Your project should already be named "ex3-3.rvt" per Step 2 above.

Exercise 3-4:
Annotations

Annotations, or text and notes, allow the designer and technician to accurately describe the drawing. Here you will take a quick look at this feature set. There is a chapter, later in the book, dedicated to annotation which covers these tools in greater detail.

Annotations:

Adding annotations to a drawing can be as essential as the drawing itself. Often the notes describe a part of the drawing that would be difficult to discern from the drawing alone.

For example, a wall framing drawing showing a bolt may not indicate, graphically, how many bolts are needed or at what spacing. The note might say "*5/8" anchor bolt at 24" O.C.*"

Next you will add text to your drawing.

1. **Open** project **ex3-3.rvt** from the previous lesson.

2. **Save-As** "**ex3-4.rvt**".

3. Use **Zoom** if required to see the entire drawing, except for the 600' line which can run off the screen.

4. Select **Annotate → Text → Text**.

   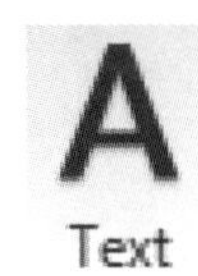

   Note that the *Model Text* tool on the *Architecture* tab is only for drawing 3D text; *Drafting Views* are only 2D so that command is not even an option currently.

From the *Text* icon tooltip (see image to the right) you can see that the keyboard shortcut for the *Text* tool is **TX**. Thus, at any time you can type T and then X to activate the *Text* tool; if you have another command active, Revit will cancel it.

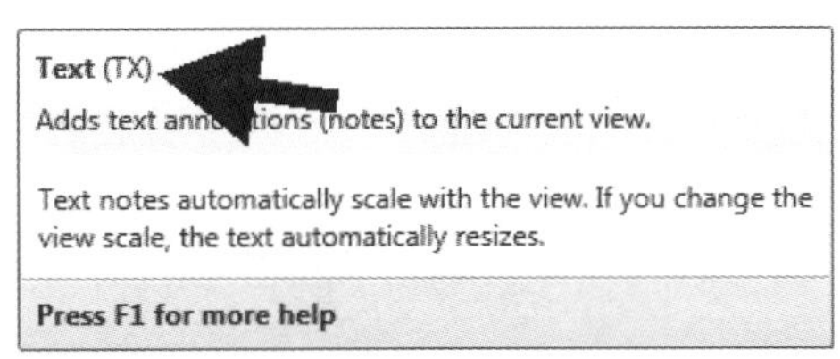

Text icon's tooltip (hover cursor over icon)

Experienced and efficient designers use a combination of keyboard shortcuts and mouse clicks to save time. For example, while your left hand is typing TX, your right hand can be moving toward the location where you want to insert the text. This process is generally more efficient than switching between tabs on the *Ribbon* and clicking icons, or fly-out icons which require yet another click of the mouse.

Notice the current *prompt* on the *Status Bar* at the bottom of the screen; you are asked to "Click to start text or click and drag rectangle to create wrapping text." By clicking on the screen you create one line of text, starting at the point picked, and press **Enter** to create additional lines. By clicking and dragging a rectangle you specify a window, primarily for the width, which causes Revit to automatically move text to the next line. When the text no longer fits within the window it is pushed below, or what is called "text wrapping" (Figure 3-4.1).

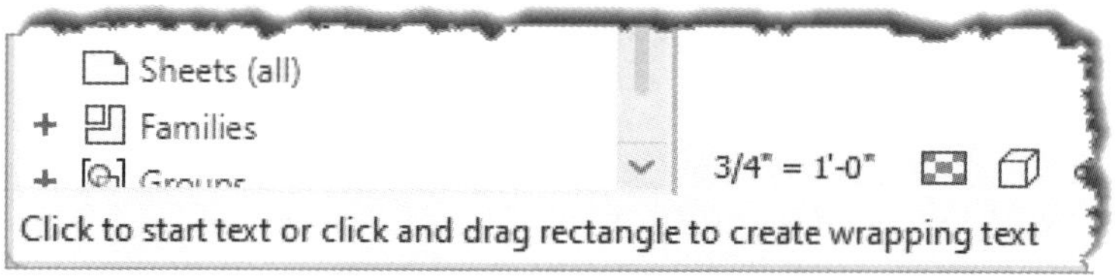

FIGURE 3-4.1 Status Bar while Text tool is active

You should also notice the various text options available on the *Ribbon* while the *Text* tool is active (Figure 3-4.2). You have two text heights loaded from the template file you started with, text justification icons (Left, Center, Right) and the option to attach leaders, or pointing arrows, to your drawings. The *Text* tool will be covered in more detail later in this book.

***FYI:** The text heights shown (i.e., ¼", 3/32" via Type Selector) are heights the text will be when printed on paper, regardless of the view scale.*

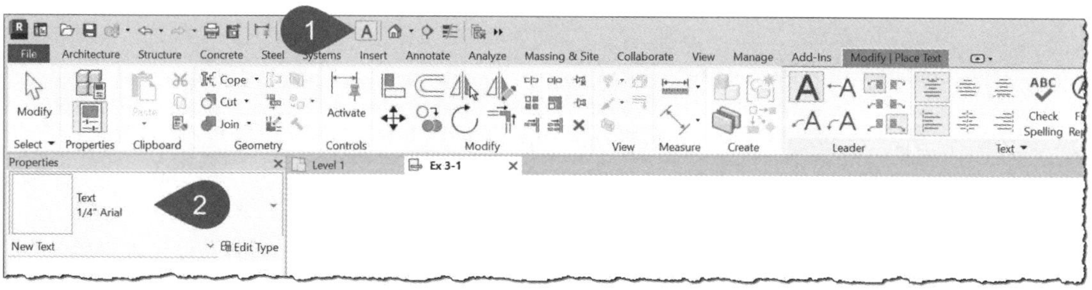

FIGURE 3-4.2 Ribbon and Properties Palette with the Text tool active

5. Pick a point in the upper left portion of the view as shown in Figure 3-4.3.

6. Type "**Learning Revit is fun!**"

7. Click anywhere in the view, except on the active text, to finish the *Text* command; pressing **Enter** will only add new lines.

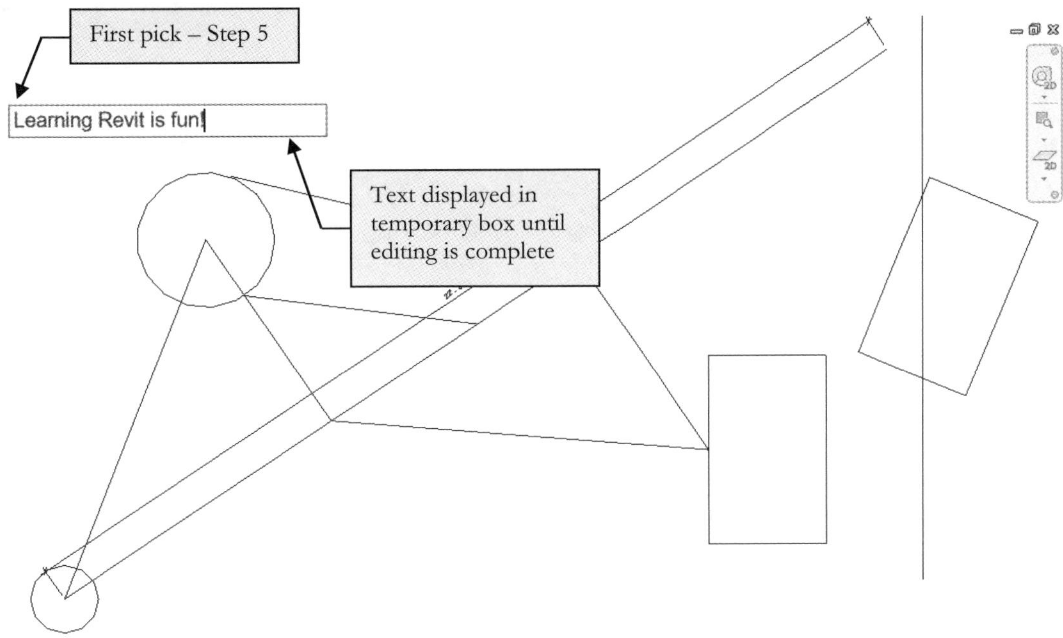

FIGURE 3-4.3 Text tool; picking first point and typing text.

As soon as you complete the text edit, the text will still be selected, and the *Move* and *Rotate* symbols will be displayed near the text; this allows you to more quickly *Move* or *Rotate* the text after it is typed (Figure 3-4.4).

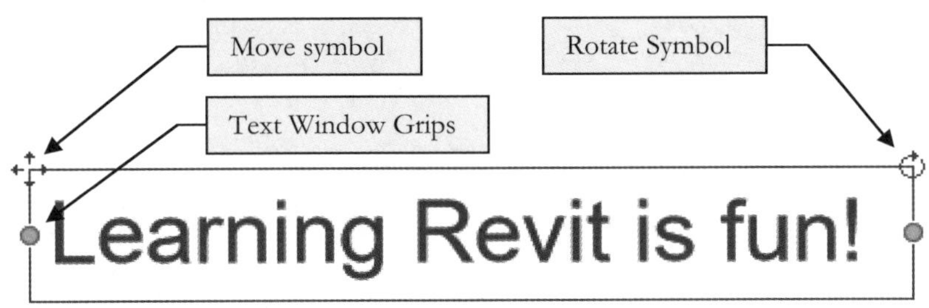

FIGURE 3-4.4 Text tool; text typed with Move and Rotate symbols showing.

8. Finish the *Text* tool completely by pressing *Modify* or clicking in the drawing.

TIP: Notice that the text is no longer selected, the symbols are gone, and the contextual tab disappears from the Ribbon.

Your text should generally look similar to Figure 3-4.5.

9. Print your drawing; refer back to page 2-15 for basic printing information. Your print should fit the page and look similar to Figure 3-4.5.

10. **Save** your project.

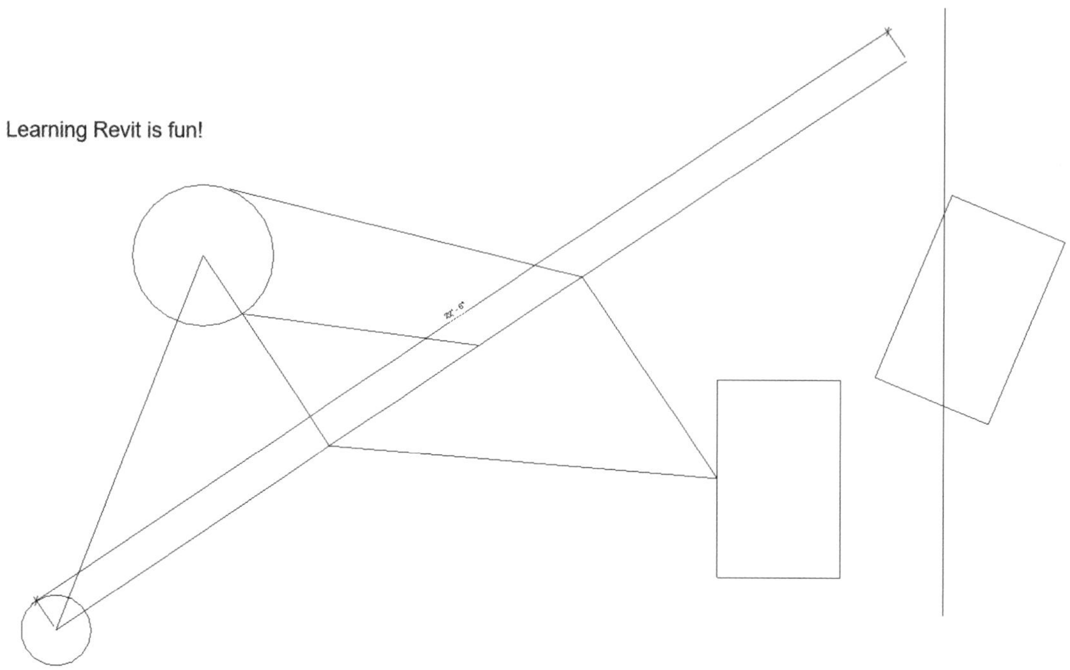

FIGURE 3-4.5 Text tool; text added to current view

Self-Exam:

The following questions can be used as a way to check your knowledge of this lesson. The answers can be found at the bottom of the page.

1. Revit is only accurate to three decimal places. (T/F)
2. The triangular-shaped Snap symbol represents the Midpoint snap. (T/F)
3. You can move or rotate text via its modify symbols when text is selected. (T/F)
4. Use the ____________ tool to duplicate objects.
5. When selecting objects, use the ____________________ to select all the objects in the selection window and all objects that extend through it.

Review Questions:

The following questions may be assigned by your instructor as a way to assess your knowledge of this section. Your instructor has the answers to the review questions.

1. Revit is a raster-based program. (T/F)
2. The "Center of Rotation" you select for the *Rotate* and *Scale* commands is not important. (T/F)
3. Entering 16 for a distance actually means 16′-0″ to Revit. (T/F)
4. Use the *Detail Line* tool, with ______________ selected on the *Ribbon*, to create squares.
5. You can change the height of the text from the *Type Selector*. (T/F)
6. Pressing the _____________ key cycles you through the snap options.
7. Where do the two predefined text heights come from? _______________
8. Specifying degrees with the *Rotate* tool, you must type the number when Revit does not display the number you want; the increments shown on-screen are set in the

   ______________________ dialog box.
9. List all the Snap points available on a circle (ex. Line: endpoint, midpoint,

   nearest): ____.
10. The Snaps Off option must not be checked in the Snaps dialog box to automatically and accurately select snap points while drawing. (T/F)

SELF-EXAM ANSWERS:
1 – F, **2** – T, **3** – T, **4** – Copy, **5** – Crossing Window

Notes:

Lesson 4
Drawing 2D Architectural Objects:

This lesson is intended to give you practice drawing in Autodesk® Revit®; while doing so, you will become familiar with the various shapes and sizes of the more common symbols used in a residential design.

Do not forget that learning to draw 2D is important in Autodesk Revit. You often define 3D items, like walls, in 2D floor plans, while Autodesk Revit takes care of the third dimension automatically. Additionally, you will often want to embellish a view with 2D lines; for example, the exterior elevation, which is a 2D projection of a 3D model.

If you have used other design programs, such as AutoCAD or AutoCAD Architecture, these lessons will help you understand how to draw in Autodesk Revit, which uses a more visual, graphic-based input system.

Each drawing will be created in its own *Drafting View.*

For some of the symbols to be drawn, you will have step-by-step instructions and a study on a particular tool that would be useful in the creation of that object. Other symbols to be drawn are for practice by repetition and do not provide step-by-step instructions.

Do NOT draw the dimensions provided; they are for reference only.

Exercise 4-1:
Sketching Rectilinear Objects

Overview:

All the objects you will draw in this exercise consist entirely of straight lines, either orthogonal or angular.

As previously mentioned, all the objects MUST BE drawn in SEPARATE *Drafting Views.* Each object will have a specific name provided, which is to be used to name the *Drafting View.* All views will be created in one Revit project file, which should be saved in your personal folder created for this course.

view name: Bookcase

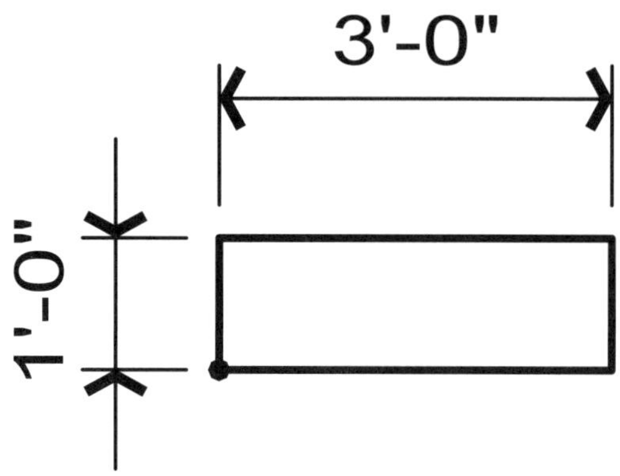

This is a simple rectangle that represents the size of a bookcase.

1. **Open** a new project; **Save** the project as **Ex4-1.rvt**.
   Tip: use the *default.rte* template again.

2. Create a new *Drafting View* named **Bookcase** (Figure 4-1.1) *(from the View tab)*.

3. Select **Detail Line** from the *Annotate* tab.

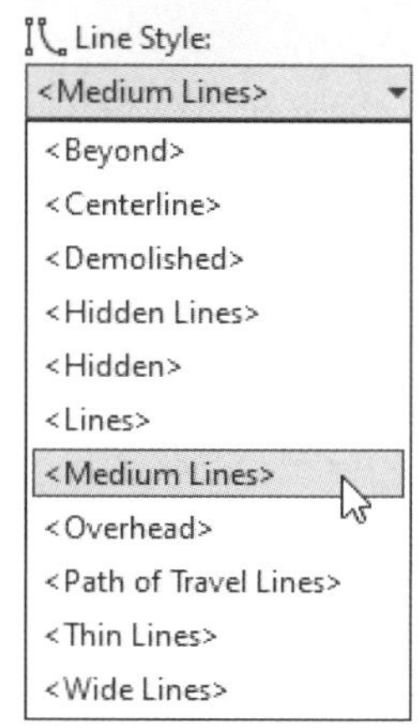

By default, the current line thickness is set to *Thin Lines*. You can see this on the *Ribbon* when the *Detail Line* tool is active. You will change this to *Medium* next.

4. Set the line thickness to **Medium Lines** (Figure 4-1.2; also see image to the right).

   NOTE: Use this setting for all the drawings in this chapter.

5. Click the **Rectangle** button on the *Ribbon* (Figure 4-1.2).

6. **Draw a rectangle**, per the dimensions shown above, generally in the center of the drawing window.

   TIP: You should be able to accurately draw the rectangle using the temporary dimensions; if not, click on the dimension text to change it.

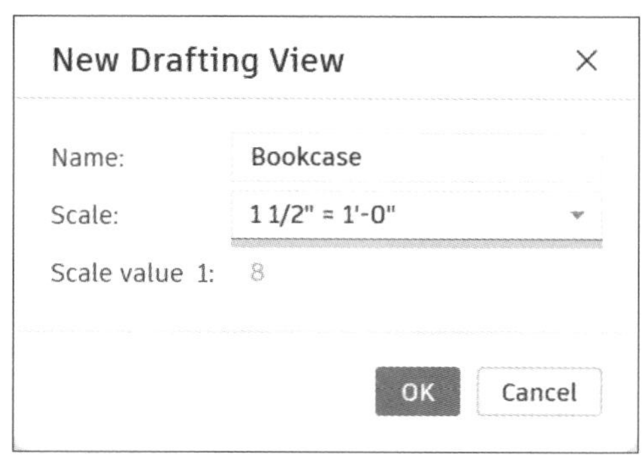

FIGURE 4-1.1 New Drafting View dialog

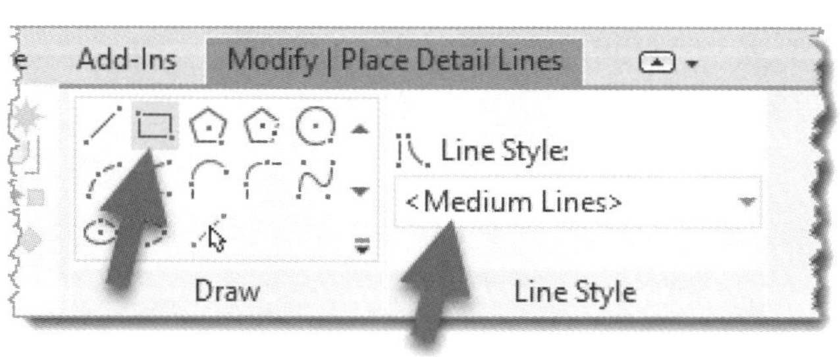

FIGURE 4-1.2 Ribbon; Medium Lines and Rectangle selected

view name: Coffee Table

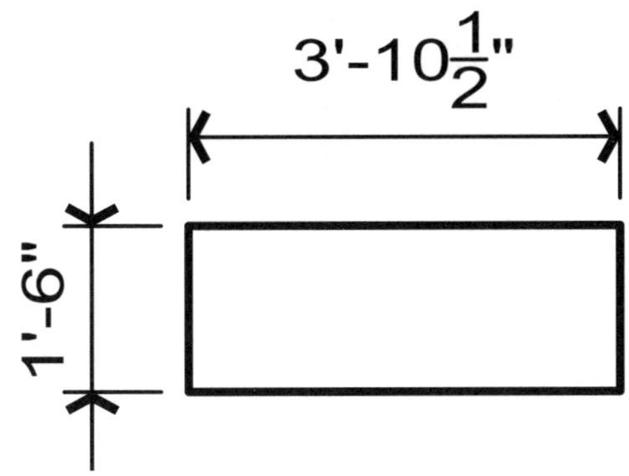

7. Create a new *Drafting View.*

   NOTE: *This step will be assumed for the rest of the drawings in this exercise.*

8. Similar to the steps listed above, plus the suggestions mentioned below, create the coffee table shown to the left.

Draw the rectangle as closely as possible using the visual aids; you should be able to get the 1′-6″ dimension correct. Then click on the text for the temporary horizontal dimension and type in 3′-10 1/2″.

Entering fractions: the 3′-10½″ can be entered in one of four ways.

o	3 10.5	*Notice there is a space between the feet and inches.*
o	3 10 1/2	*Two spaces separate the feet, inches and fractions.*
o	0 46.5	*This is all in inches; that is 3′-10½″ = 46.5″.*
o	46.5″	*Omit the feet and use the inches symbol.*

view name: Desk-1

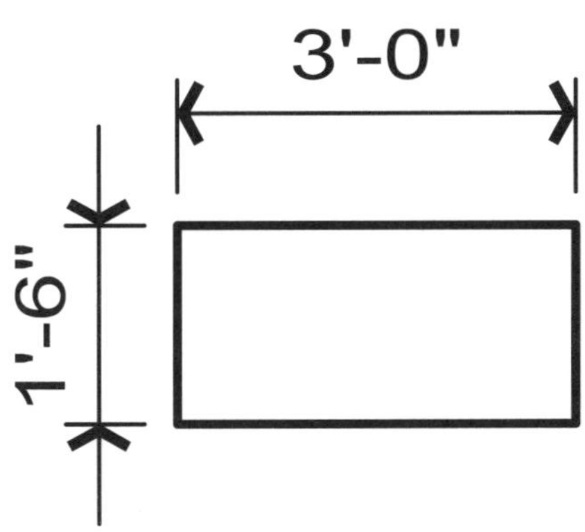

9. Draw the *Desk* in its own view, similar to the steps outlined above.

TIP: *You should double-check your drawing's dimensions using the* Measure *tool. Pick the icon from the* Modify *tab and then pick two points. A temporary dimension will display.*

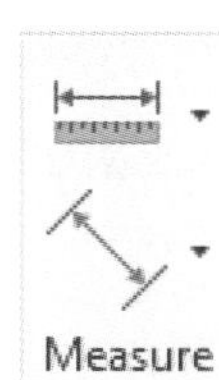

view name: **Night Table**

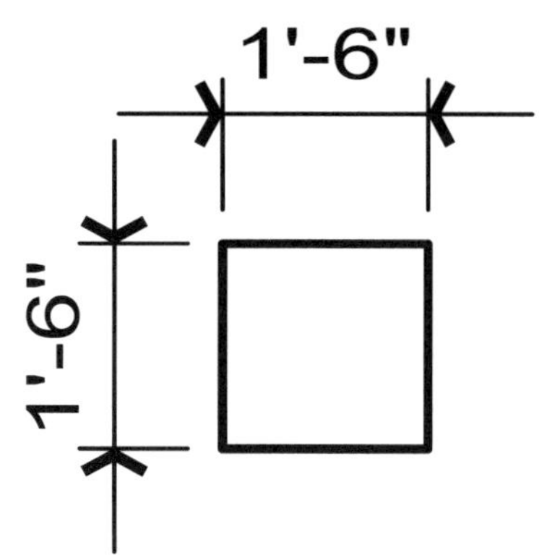

Obviously, you could draw this quickly per the previous examples. However, you will look at copying a Drafting View and modifying an existing drawing.

You will use the *Move* tool to stretch the 3′-0″ wide desk down to a 1′-6″ wide night table.

First, you will look at *Drafting Views* and how they are organized in the *Project Browser*, and then you will copy the *Desk-1 Drafting View* to start the *Night Table* drawing/view.

10. Locate the ***Drafting Views*** section in the *Project Browser* and expand it by clicking on the "plus" symbol.

Notice that the three views you previously created are listed (Figure 4-1.3). The *Desk-1* view is shown with bold text because it is the current view. All *Drafting Views* are listed here and can be renamed, copied, or deleted at any time by right-clicking on the item in the list. You will copy the *Desk-1* view next.

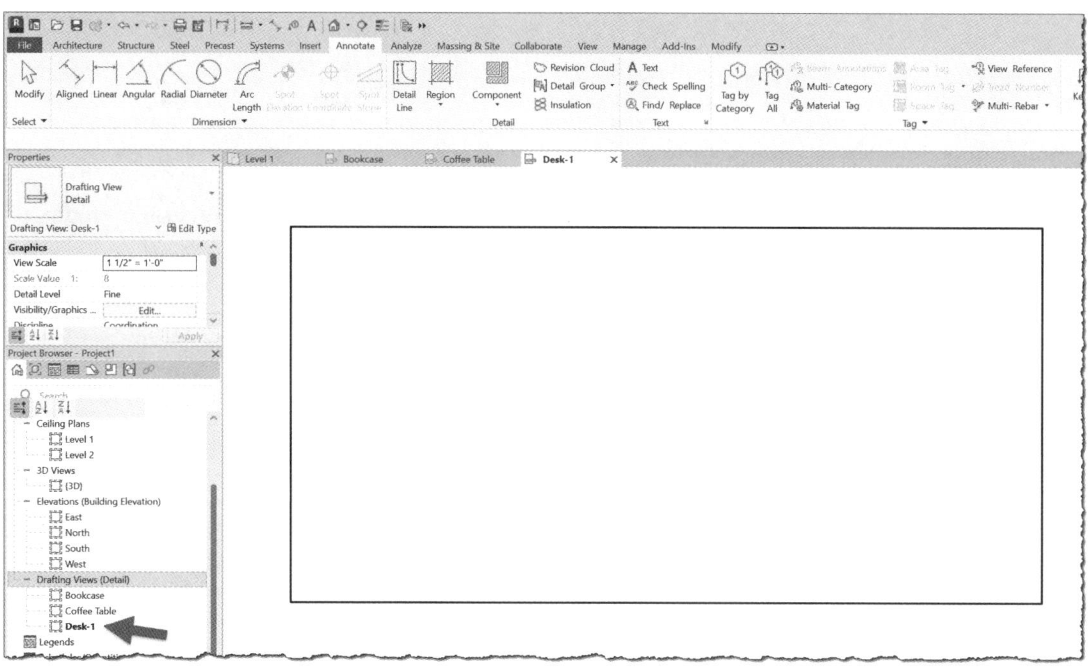

FIGURE 4-1.3 Project Browser: Drafting Views section expanded

11. Right-click on the *Desk-1* view (Figure 4-1.4).

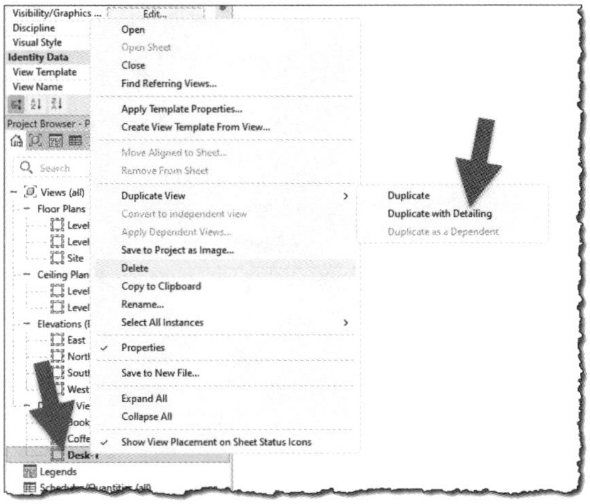

FIGURE 4-1.4 Drafting Views list – Right click on Desk-1 view for menu

Next, you will select *Duplicate with Detailing*, which will copy the *View* and the *View's* contents, whereas the *Duplicate* option will only copy the *View* and its settings, but without any line work.

12. Select **Duplicate View → Duplicate with Detailing** from the pop-up menu (Figure 4-1.4).

You now have a new View named *Copy of Desk-1* in the *Drafting Views* list. This *View* is open and current.

13. **Right-click** on the new view name, ***Copy of Desk-1***, and select **Rename** from the pop-up menu.

14. Type **Night Table** and then press **Enter** (Figure 4-1.5).

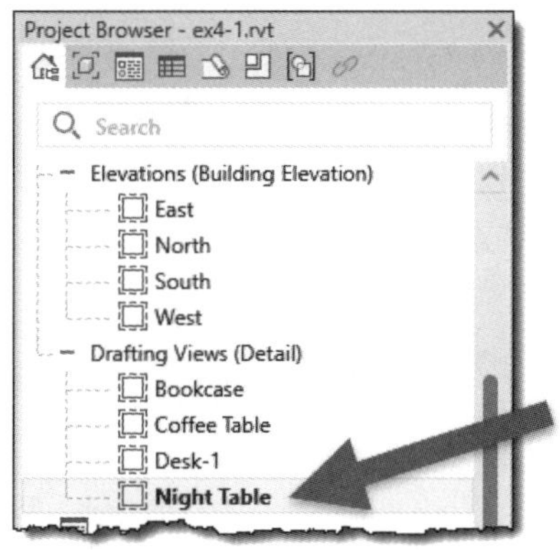

FIGURE 4-1.5
Rename View dialog – Night Table entered

You are now ready to modify the copy of the *Desk-1* linework. You will use the *Move* tool to change the location of one of the vertical lines, which will cause the two horizontal lines to stretch with it. Autodesk Revit *Detail Lines* automatically have a parametric relationship to adjacent lines when their endpoints touch them.

15. Select the vertical line on the right and then click the **Move** icon on the *Ribbon*.

16. Pick the midpoint of the vertical line, then move the mouse 1′-6″ to the left and click again (Figure 4-1.6).

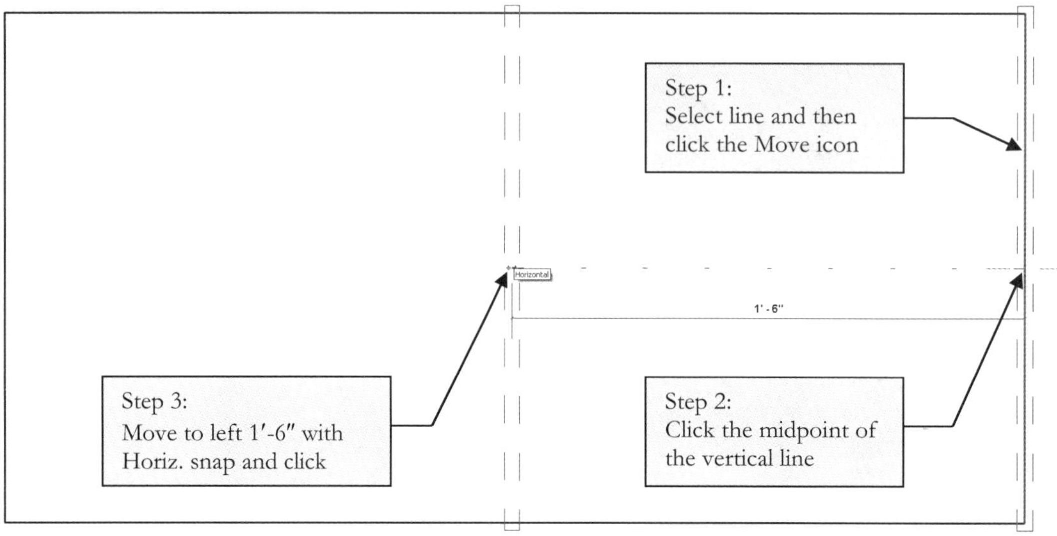

FIGURE 4-1.6 Move tool used to stretch a rectangle

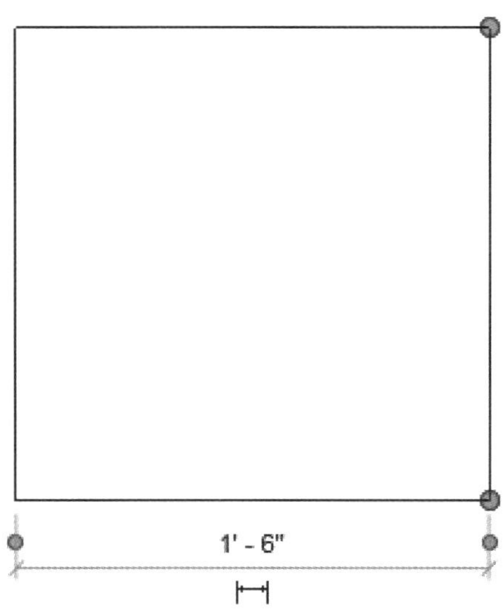

FIGURE 4-1.7 Stretched rectangle (using Move tool)

The rectangle is now resized to half its original width.

You will notice that the horizontal lines automatically adjust.

Revit assumes a special relationship between a line being edited and any line whose endpoint is directly touching it.

TIP: *You can select "Disjoin" on the Ribbon while in the Move command if you don't want other lines to move or stretch with it. You will not do that here, though.*

17. **Save** your project.

view name: **Dresser-1**

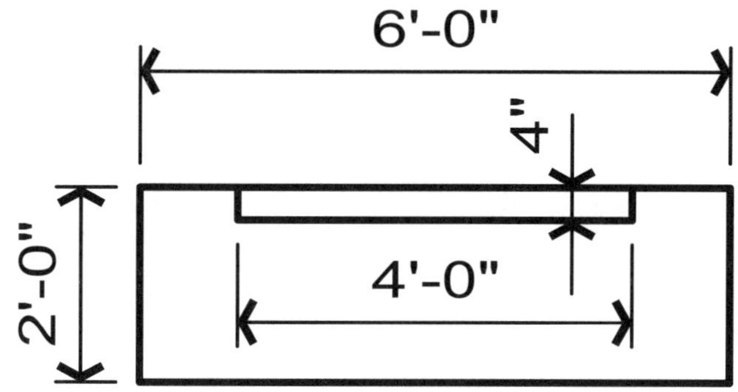

18. Draw the dresser using the following tip:

    TIP: Simply draw two rectangles. Move the smaller rectangle into place using the Move tool and Snaps.

view name: **Dresser-2**

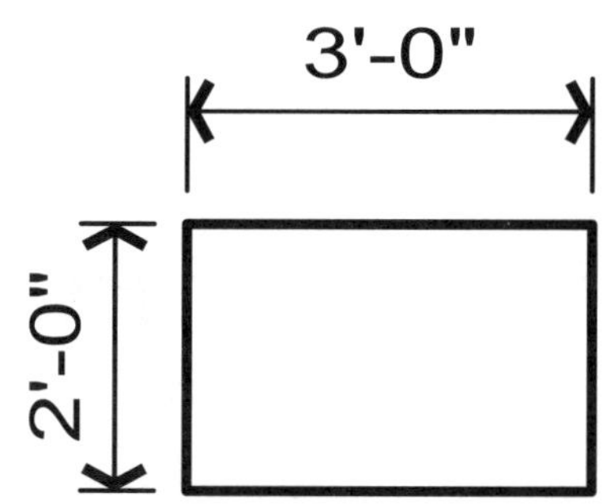

19. Draw this smaller dresser.

view name: **Desk-2**

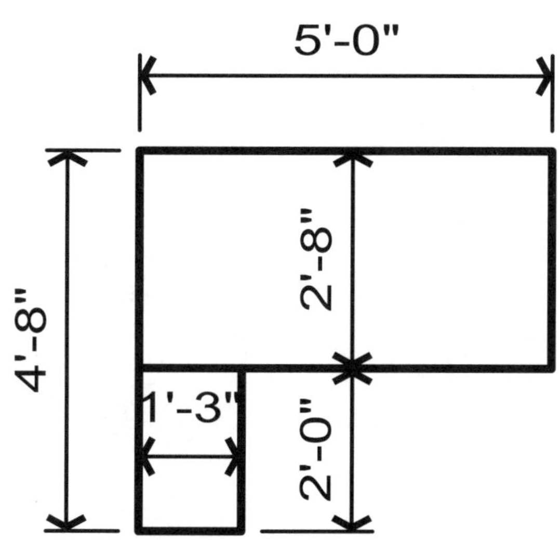

20. Draw this desk in the same way you drew *Dresser-1*.

view name: **File Cabinet**

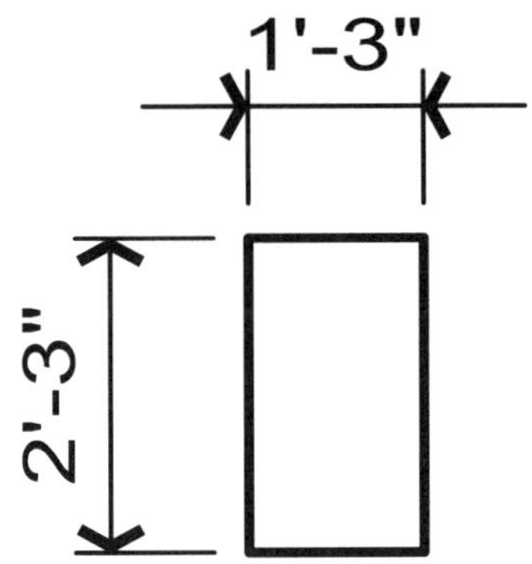

21. Draw this file cabinet.

view name: **Chair-1**

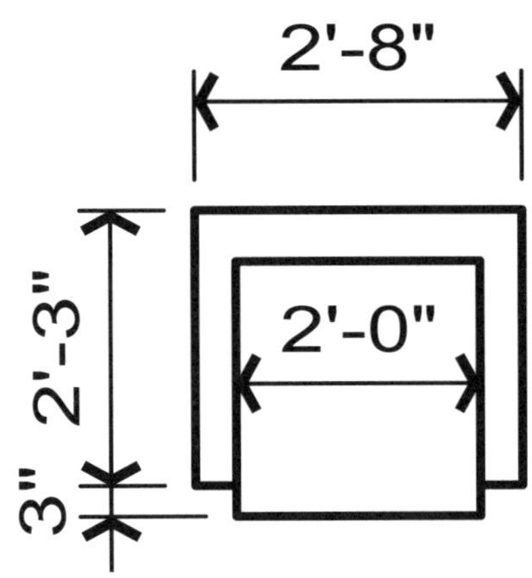

22. Draw this chair per the following tips:

Draw the 2′x2′ square first, and then draw three separate rectangles as shown to the right. Move them into place with *Move* and *Snaps*. Next, delete the extra lines so your drawing looks like the one shown on the left. Pay close attention to the dimensions!

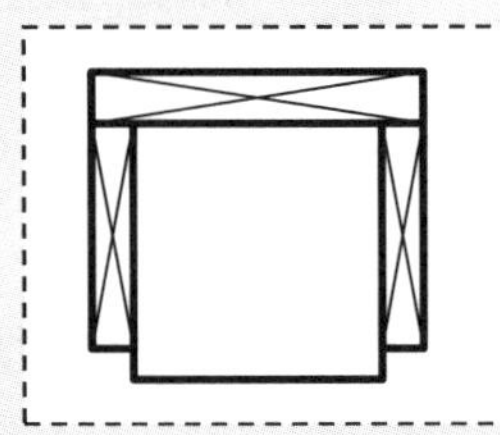

view name: **Sofa**

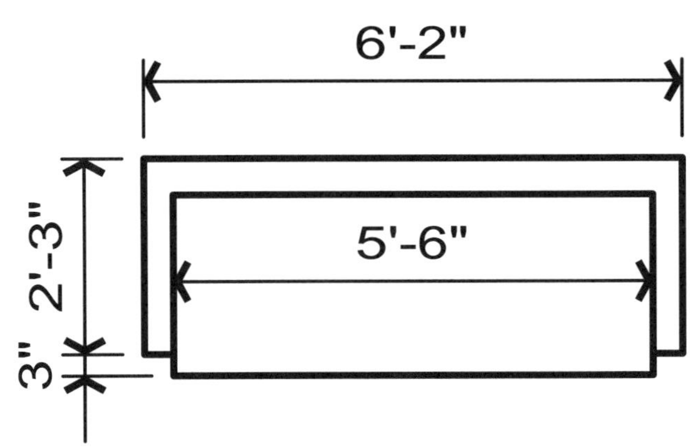

23. *Duplicate* and *Rename* the *Chair-1* view to start this drawing.

Tip: *See the next page for more information on creating this drawing.*

You can create the *Sofa* in a similar way that you created the *Night Table*; that is, you will use the *Move* tool. Rather than selecting a single vertical line, you will select all the lines on one side of the chair.

You can select all the lines on one side in a single step, rather than clicking each one individually while holding the Ctrl key. You will select using a *window* selection, not a *crossing window* selection.

24. **Select** all the lines on the right side (Figure 4-1.8).

    TIP: Pick from left to right for a window *selection.*

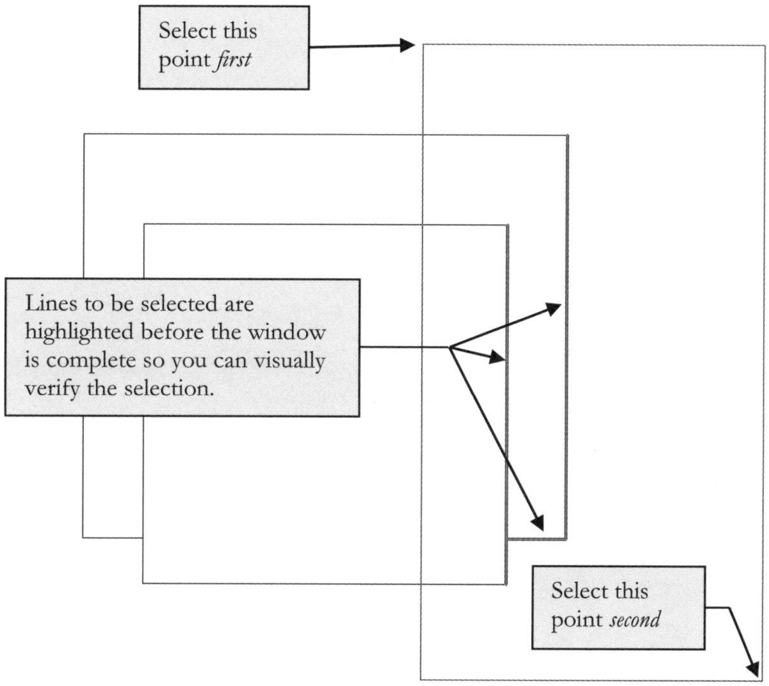

FIGURE 4-1.8 Stretch chair using Move tool

25. Use the ***Move*** tool to extend the chair into a sofa.

    TIP: The difference between the chair width and the sofa width is the distance the lines are to be moved.

You have just successfully transformed the chair into a sofa! Do not forget to *Save* often to avoid losing work. Also, use the *Measure* tool to verify the accuracy of your drawing.

view name: **Bed-Double**

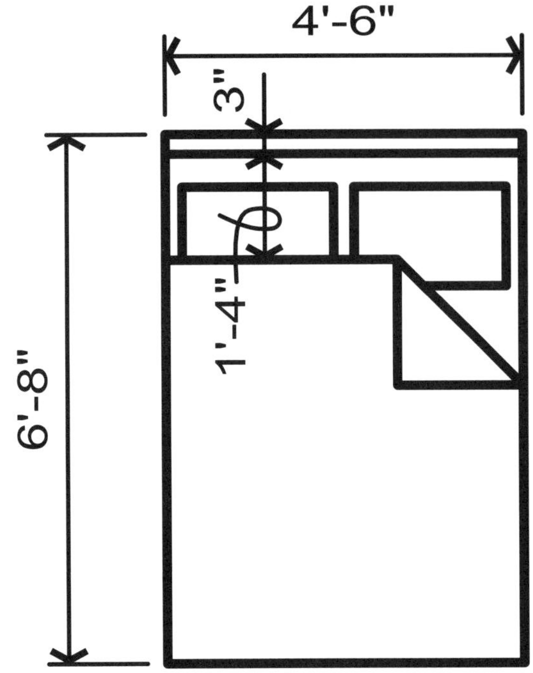

26. Draw this bed using lines and rectangles; the exact sizes of items not dimensioned are not important.

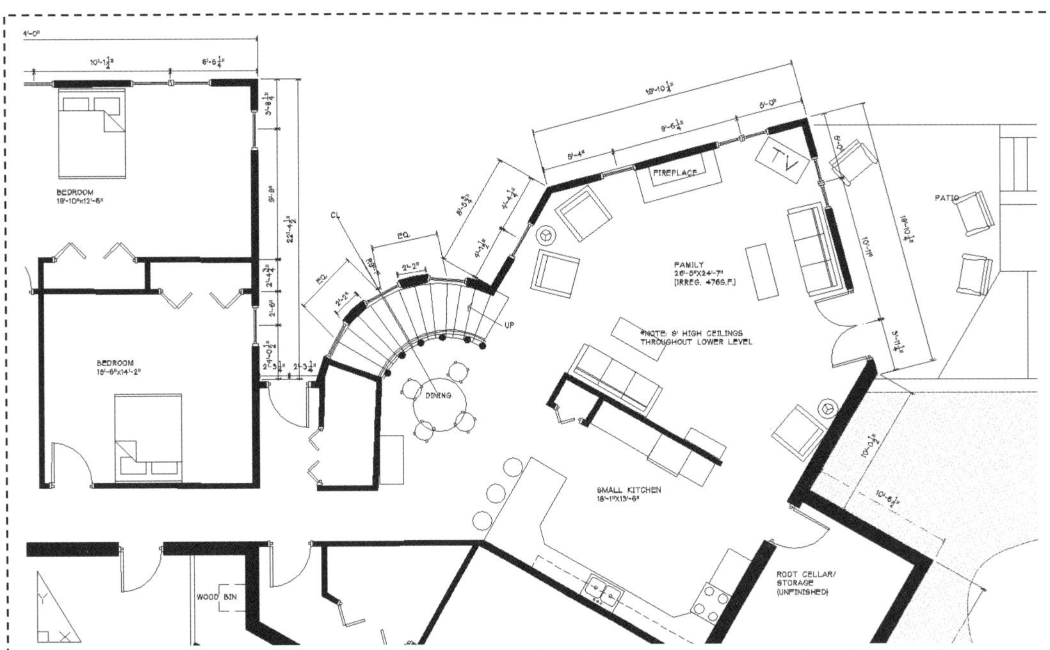

FIGURE 4-1.9 Floor Plan example using similar furniture to that drawn in this exercise.

Image courtesy of Stanius Johnson Architects
www.staniusjohnson.com

Exercise 4-2:
Sketching Objects with Curves

Similar to the previous exercise, you will draw several shapes; this time, they will have curves.

You will look at the various commands for creating curves, such as *Arc*, *Circle,* and *Fillet.*

Again, you will not draw the dimensions as they are for reference only; each drawing should be drawn in its own *Drafting View*. Name the view with the label provided.

Finally, you can ignore the black dot on each drawing below. This dot simply represents the location from which the symbol would typically be inserted or placed.

view name: Laundry-Sink

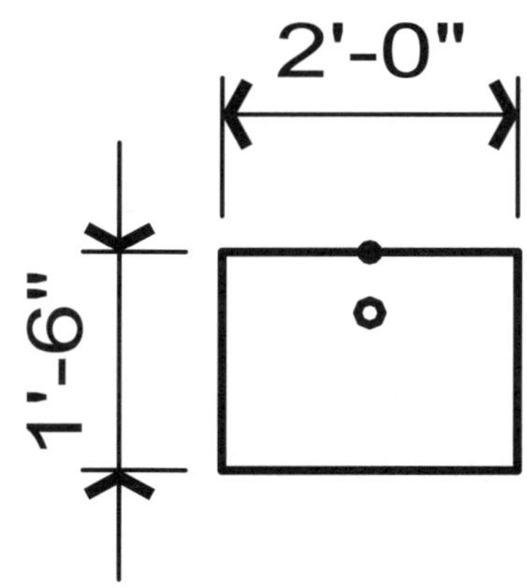

This is a simple rectangle representing the size of a laundry sink, with a circle representing the drain.

1. **Open** a new Revit project and name it **Ex4-2.rvt**.

2. Draw the rectangle shown; refer to Exercise 4-1 for more information.

3. Use the ***Measure*** tool to verify the size of your rectangle.

Next, you will draw a circle for the drain. The drain needs to be centered left and right and 5" from the back edge. The following steps show you one way to do this.

4. Select the ***Detail Line*** tool from the *Annotate* tab.

5. Select the ***Circle*** icon from the *Ribbon* (Figure 4-2.1).

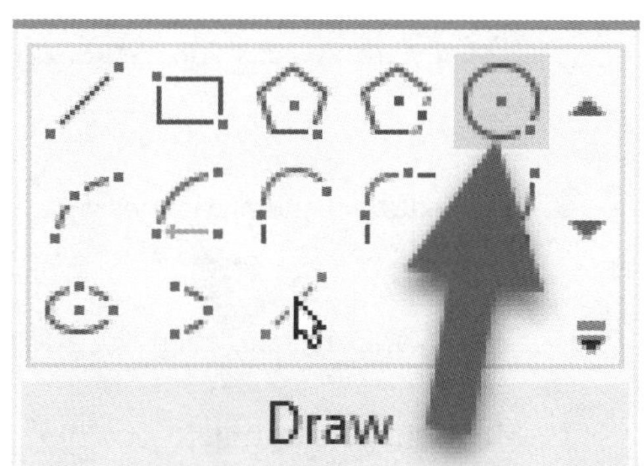

FIGURE 4-2.1 Sketch Options for detail lines

6. Pick the midpoint of the top line (Figure 4-2.2).

   FYI: This is the center of the circle.

7. Type **0 1** for the radius and press **Enter** (0 1 = 0′ – 1″).

   FYI: This creates a 2″ diameter circle.

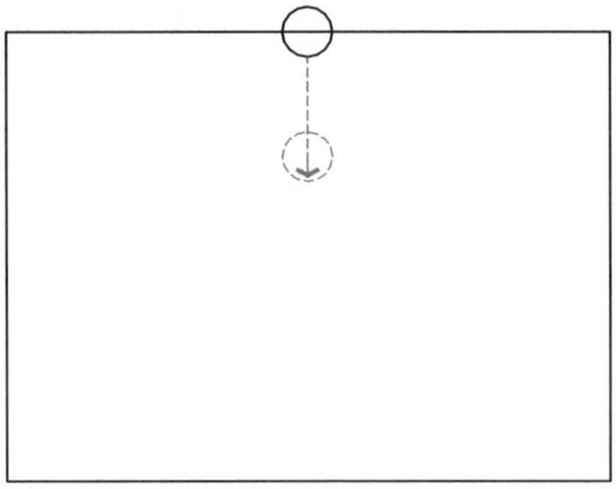

FIGURE 4-2.2 Creating a circle and moving it into place.

At this point, you may get an error indicating the "Line is too short" or "Element is too small on screen" (Figure 4-2.3). This is supposed to prevent a user, like yourself, from accidentally drawing a very small line when you click the mouse twice right next to each other, or trying to change the dimension of a previously drawn line to something less than 1/32″. If you get this error, you simply zoom in on your drawing more so that the circle is more prominently visible on the screen.

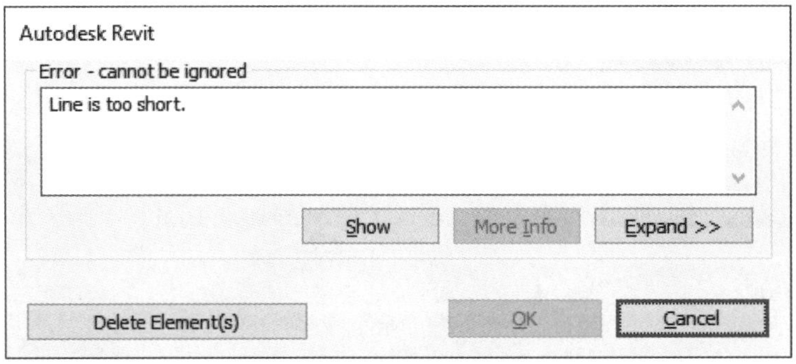

FIGURE 4-2.3 Possible Revit error message when creating the circle

8. If you did get the error message just described, click *Cancel*, *Zoom In* and then draw the circle again.

9. Select the circle and then the ***Move*** tool.

10. **Move** the circle straight down 5″ (Figure 4-2.2).

That's it! Do not forget to save your *Ex4-2* project often.

view name: **Dryer**

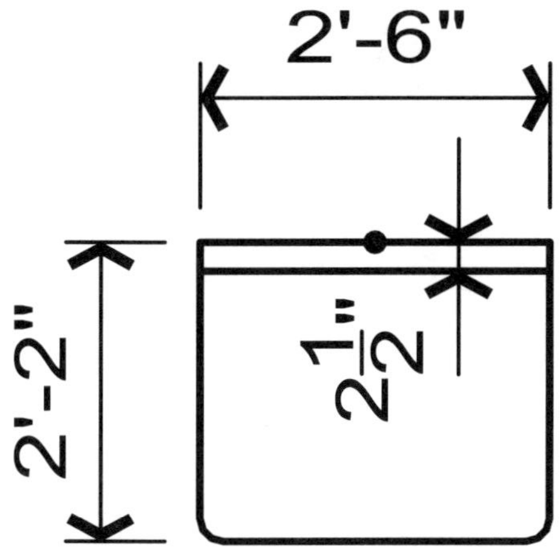

Here you will draw a dryer with rounded front corners. This, like all the other symbols in this lesson, is a plan view symbol, as in "viewed from the top."

11. Draw a 30″x26″ Rectangle.

12. Use the ***Measure*** tool to verify your dimensions.

Next, you will draw the line that is 2½″ from the back of the dryer. You will draw the line in approximately the correct position, then use the temporary dimensions to fine-tune the location.

13. Select the **Detail Line** tool and then pick a point approximately 3″ down from the upper-left corner; a temporary dimension will be displayed before you click your mouse button (Figure 4-2.4).

14. Complete the horizontal line by picking a point perpendicular to the vertical line on the right (Figure 4-2.4).

15. With the temporary dimensions still displayed, click the text for the 0′-3″ dimension, type **0 2.5**, and then press **Enter** (Figure 4-2.5).

16. Click ***Modify*** to clear the selection and make the *Temporary Dimensions* go away.

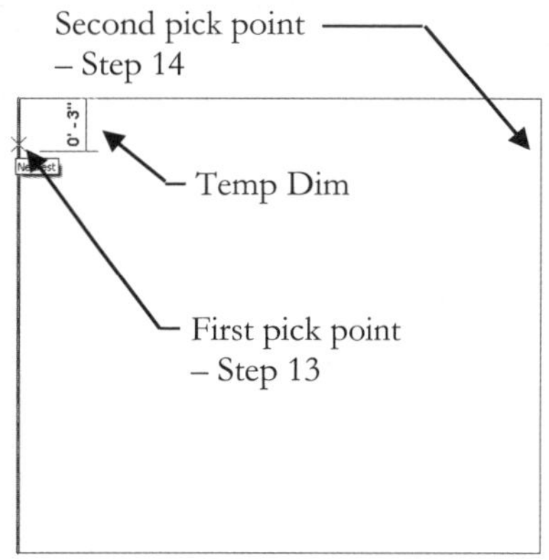

FIGURE 4-2.4 Drawing a line

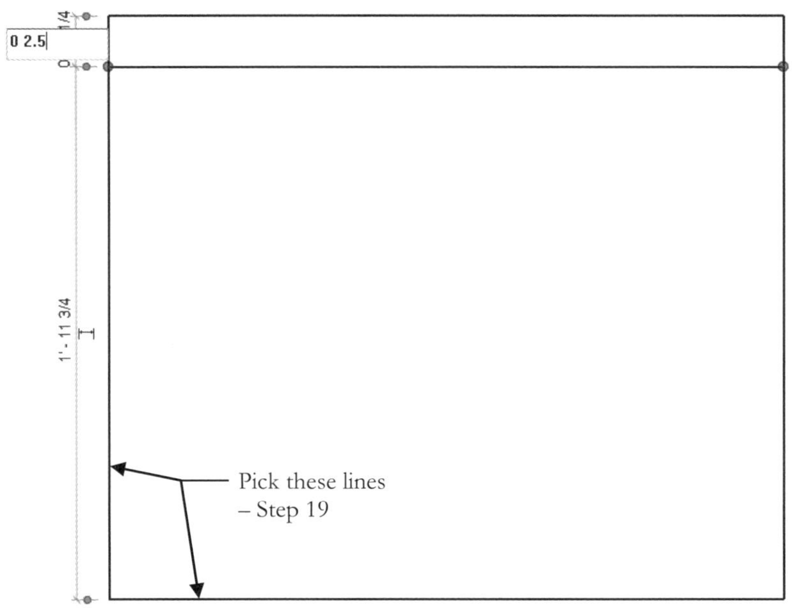

FIGURE 4-2.5 Adjusting new lines position via temporary dimensions

Next, you will round the corners. You still use the *Detail Line* tool, but use a *Draw* option called *Fillet Arc*, pronounced "Fill it." You will try this next.

17. With the ***Detail Lines*** tool active, select the **Fillet Arc** *Draw* option on the *Ribbon* (Figure 4-2.6).

18. Check **Radius** and enter **0′ 2″** in the text box on the *Ribbon* (Figure 4-2.6).

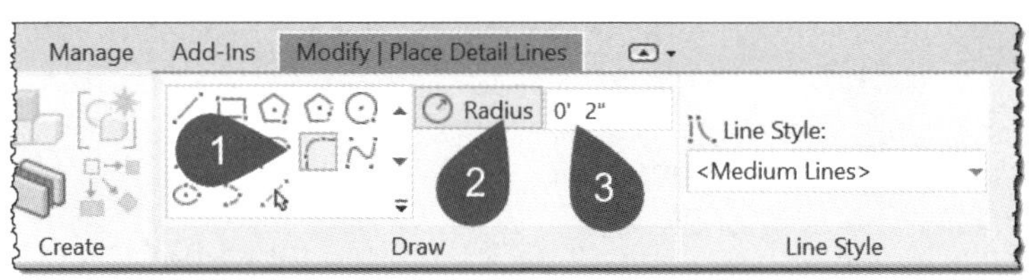

FIGURE 4-2.6 Ribbon and *Ribbon*; options for Detail Lines in Fillet mode

19. Pick the two lines identified in Figure 4-2.5.

The intersection of the two lines is where the arc is placed; notice the two lines you picked have been trimmed back to the new *Fillet Arc*.

20. Repeat the previous step to **Fillet** the other corner.

view name: **Washer**

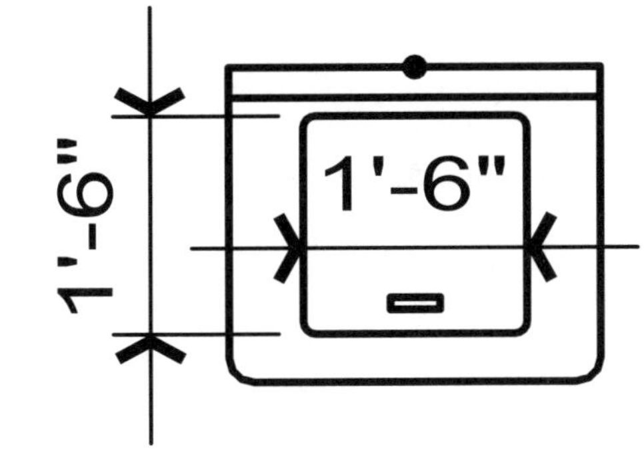

This drawing is identical to the *Dryer* except for the door added to the top. You can duplicate the *Dryer Drafting View* to get a jump start on this drawing.

To draw the door you will use the **Offset** option, which is part of the *Detail Line* tool.

The ***Offset*** tool is easy to use; to use it, you:

- Select the *Detail Line* tool
- Select the *Pick Lines* icon on the *Ribbon*
- Enter the *Offset* distance on the *Ribbon*
- Select near a line, and on the side to offset

21. Select the ***Detail Line*** tool.

22. Select the **Pick Lines** icon on the *Ribbon* (Figure 4-2.7).

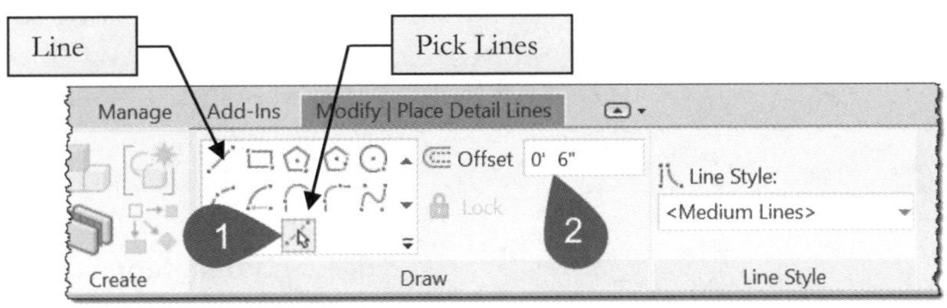

FIGURE 4-2.7 Ribbon and *Ribbon*: options for Detail Lines in Pick Lines mode

Note that the *Pick Lines* icon toggles you from *Draw* mode to *Pick Lines* mode. The *Pick Lines* mode allows you to use existing linework to quickly create new linework. You should notice that the available options on the Ribbon change after selecting *Pick Lines*; you can switch back by selecting the *Draw* icons on the *Ribbon* (Figure 4-2.7).

23. Enter **0′ 6″** for the *Offset* distance (Figure 4-2.7).

Next, you will need to select a line to offset. Which side of the line you click on will indicate the direction the line is offset. Revit provides a visual reference line indicating which side the line will be offset to and its location based on the offset distance entered.

Without clicking the mouse button, move your cursor around the drawing and notice the visual reference line. Move your mouse from side-to-side over a line to see the reference line move to correspond to the cursor location.

24. **Offset** the left vertical line towards the right.

TIP: Make sure you entered the correct offset distance in the previous step (Figure 4-2.8).

You will need to look at the washer drawing and the dryer drawing dimensions to figure out the door size.

25. **Offset** the other three sides; your sketch should look like Figure 4-2.9.

26. Use the ***Fillet Arc*** sketch mode, in the *Detail Line* tool, to create a 1″ radius on the four corners.

27. Click ***Modify*** to finish the current command.

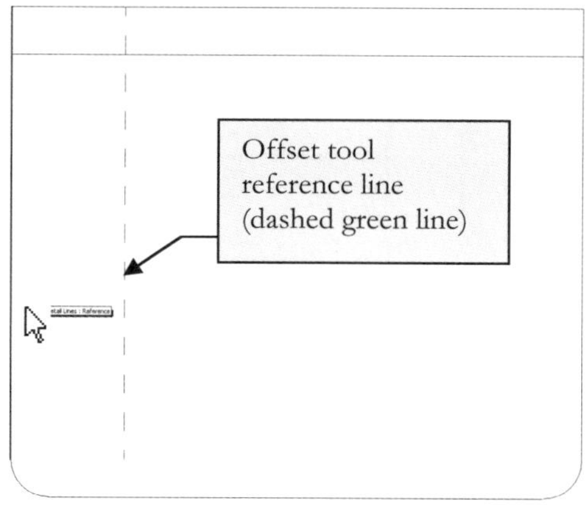

FIGURE 4-2.8 Offset left vertical line towards the right 6″

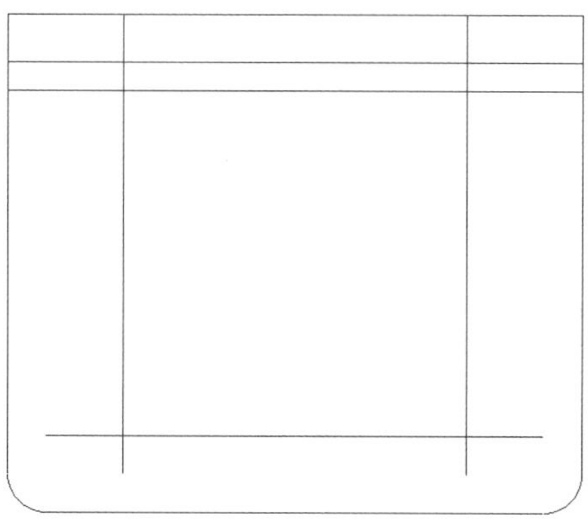

FIGURE 4-2.9 All four lines offset inward to create outline for washer door

All four corners should now be rounded off.

28. Draw a small 4″x1″ rectangle to represent the door handle. Draw it anywhere. Then using *Snaps*, move it to the midpoint of the bottom door edge, and then move the handle 2″ up.

29. **Save** your project. Make sure the view name is *Washer*.

TIP: Revit also provides an Offset *tool on the* Modify *tab of the* Ribbon. *The steps required are very similar to those just described.*

view name: **Range**

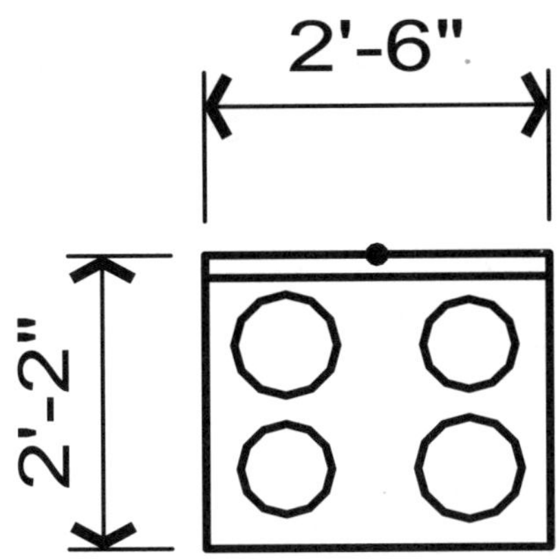

Now you will draw a kitchen *Range* with four circles that represent the burners.

In this exercise you will have to draw temporary lines, called *construction lines*, to create reference points needed to accurately locate the circles. Once the circles have been drawn, the construction lines can be erased.

30. Draw the range with a 2″ deep control panel at the back; refer to the steps described to draw the dryer if necessary.

31. Draw the four construction lines shown in Figure 4-2.10. Use the ***Ref Plane*** tool on the *Architecture* tab.

32. Draw two 9½″ Dia. circles and two 7½″ Dia. circles using the intersection of the construction lines to locate the centers of the circles (Figure 4-2.10).

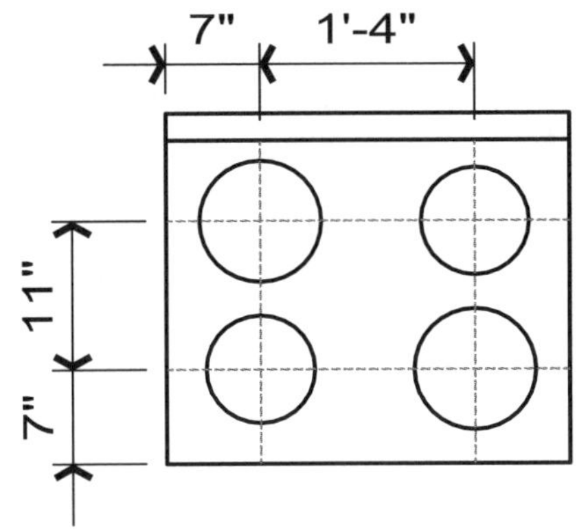

FIGURE 4-2.10 Range with four temporary construction lines (shown dashed for clarity)

TIP: Refer back to the Laundry-Sink for sketching circles.

33. **Erase** the four **Ref Plane** lines (construction lines).

34. **Save** your project.

TIP: When using the Measure *tool, you can select* Chain *on the* Ribbon *to have* Revit *calculate the total length of several picks. For example, you can quickly get the perimeter of a rectangle by picking each corner. Notice, as you pick points, the* Total Length *is listed on the* Ribbon.

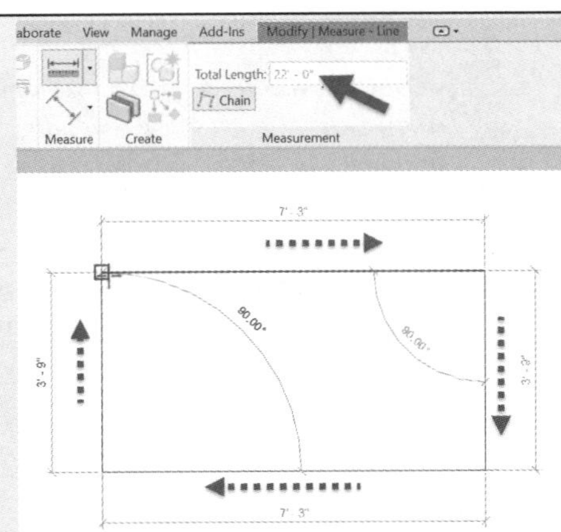

view name: **Chair-2**

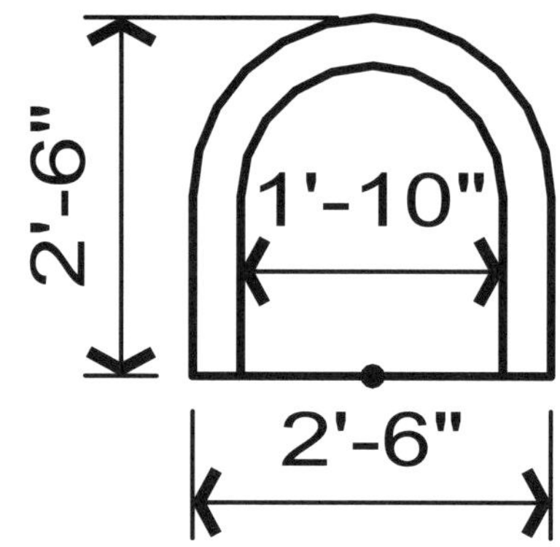

Now you will sketch another chair. You will use *Detail Line* with *Offset* and the *Arc* settings.

First, you will draw the arc at the perimeter.

35. Select *Detail Line* and then **Center – Ends Arc** from the *Ribbon* (Figure 4-2.1).

Notice on the *Status Bar,* you are prompted to "**Click to enter arc center**."

36. *First Pick*: Pick a point somewhere in the middle of a new *Drafting View* named *Chair-2* (Figure 4-2.11).

You are now prompted, on the *Status Bar*, "**Drag arc radius to desired location**."

37. *Second Pick*: Move the cursor towards the left, while snapped to the horizontal, until the temporary dimension reads **1′-3″** (Figure 4-2.11).

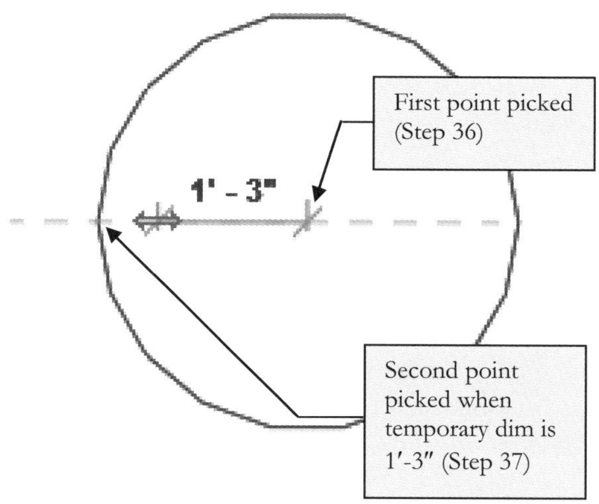

FIGURE 4-2.11 Sketching an arc; picking second point

NOTE: *As you can see, Revit temporarily displays a full circle until you pick the second point. This is because Revit does not know which direction the arc will go or what the arc length will be. The full circle allows you to visualize where your arc will be (Figure 4-2.11).*

38. *Third Pick*: Move the cursor to the right until the arc is 180 degrees and snapped to the horizontal again (Figure 4-2.12).

TIP: *Notice that your cursor location determines which direction or side the arc is created; move the cursor around before picking the third endpoint to see how the preview arc changes on screen.*

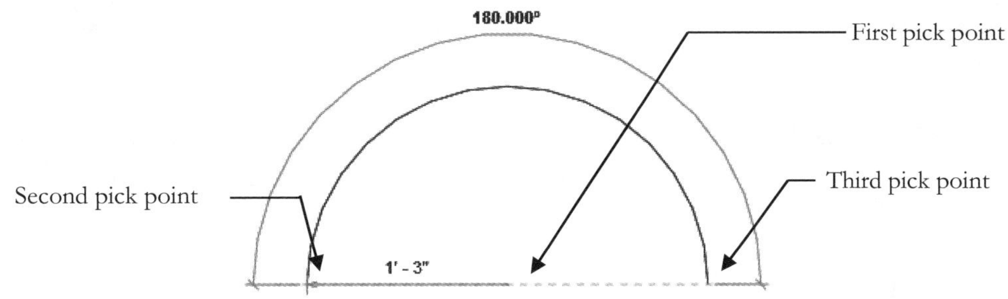

FIGURE 4-2.12 Pick points for arc command

Next, you will draw the three *Detail Lines* to complete the chair's perimeter.

39. Draw two vertical lines **1′-3″** long, attached to the arc endpoints.

    TIP: *Do not forget to use* Medium Lines *when sketching detail lines; if you forget, you can select the lines while in Modify mode and choose* Medium Lines *from the* Element Type Selector *on the* Ribbon.

40. Draw the **2′-6″** line across the bottom.

Notice the radius is 1′-3″. You did not have to enter that number because the three points you picked were enough information for Revit to determine it automatically.

If you had drawn the three lines in Steps 39 and 40 before the arc, you would not have had the required center point to pick while creating the arc. However, you could have drawn a temporary horizontal line across the top to set up a center pick that would allow you to draw the circle in its final location; or even better, use the **Start-End-Radius** *Detail Line* option.

You have now completed the chair's perimeter.

41. Use the ***Offset*** tool to offset the arc and two vertical lines the required distance to complete the sketch.

42. **Save** your project.

view name: **Love-Seat**

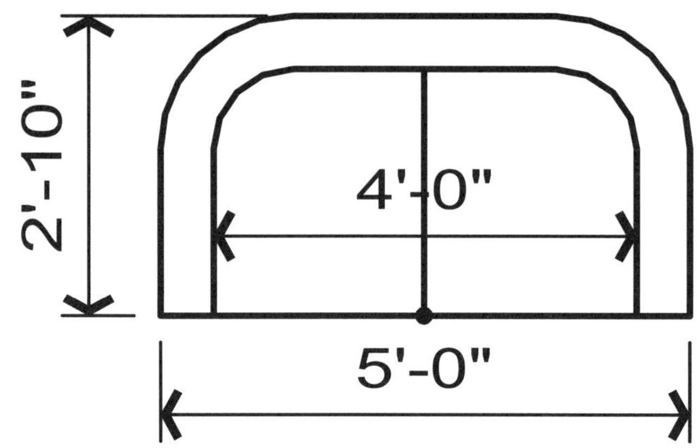

You should be able to draw this *Love-Seat* without any further instruction. Use the same radius as *Chair-2*.

You can create the drawing using a combination of the following tools:

- *Detail Line*
- *Fillet Arc*
- *Offset*
- *Move*

view name: **Tub**

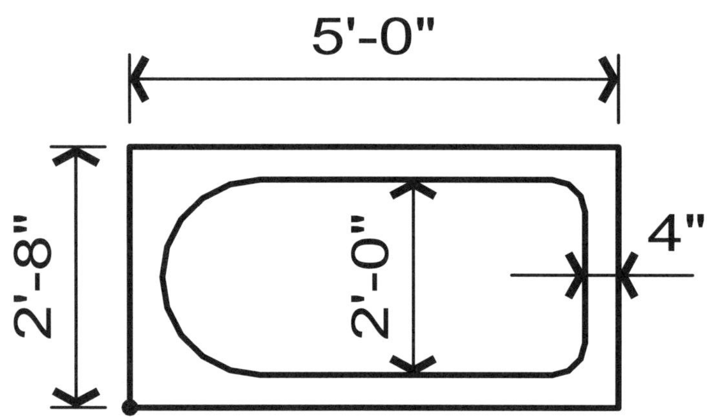

Now you will draw a bathtub. You will use several commands previously covered.

You will use the following tools:

- *Detail Line*
- *Fillet Arc*
- *Offset*
- *Move*

You may also wish to draw one or more construction lines to help locate things like the large radius, although it can be drawn without them.

view name: **Lav-1**

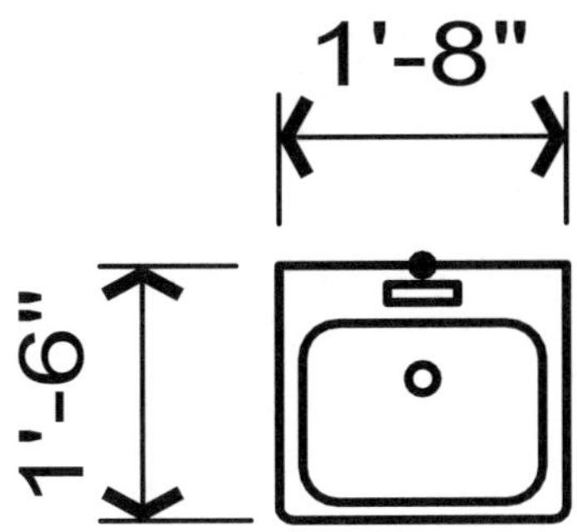

Draw this lavatory per the following specifications:

- Larger arcs shown shall have a 2½″ radius
- Smaller arcs shown shall have a 1″ radius, outside corners
- Sides and Front of sink to have 1½″ space, offset
- Back to have 4″ space, offset
- Small rectangle to be 4½″x1″ and 1½″ away from the back
- 2″ Dia. drain, 8″ from back

view name: **Lav-2**

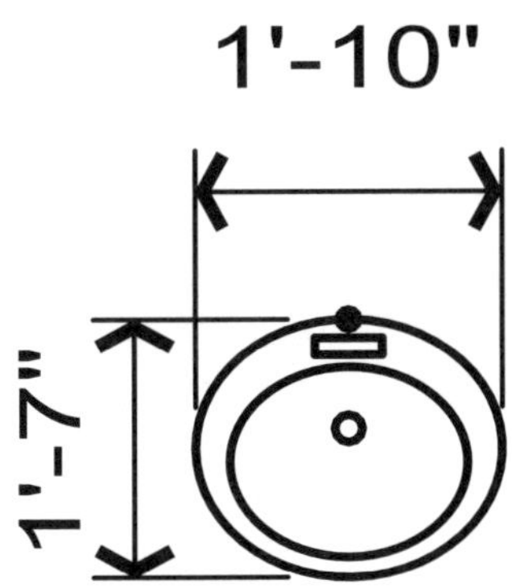

Next, you will draw another lavatory. This time, you will use the *Ellipse* tool.

43. Create a new *Drafting View.*

44. Select *Detail Lines* and then **Ellipse** from the *Ribbon* (Figure 4-2.1).

Notice the *Status Bar* prompt: "**Click to enter ellipse center**."

45. Pick near the middle of the screen.

46. With the cursor snapped to the vertical, point the cursor straight down and then type **0 9.5**; press **Enter**.

NOTE: 9½″ is half the HEIGHT, which is 1′-7″.

Now you need to specify the horizontal axis of the ellipse.

47. Again, snapping to the horizontal plane, position the cursor towards the right then type **0 11** and then press the **Enter** key.

NOTE: 11″ is half the width: 1′-10″.

That's all it takes to draw an ellipse!

48. ***Copy*** the ellipse vertically downward **3½"** (Figure 4-2.13).

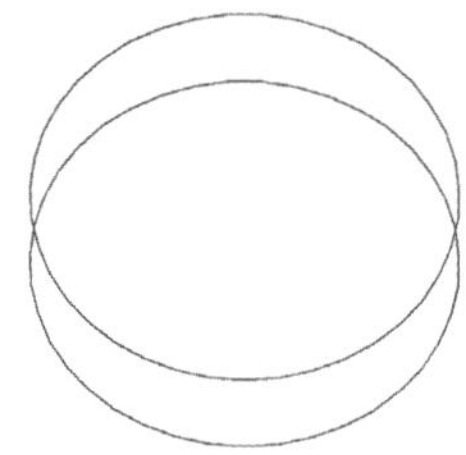

FIGURE 4-2.13 Ellipse copied downward 3½″

Next, you will use the *Scale* tool to reduce the size of the second ellipse. To summarize the steps involved:

- Select the ellipse to be resized
- Select the *Scale* icon
- Pick the origin
- Pick the opposite side of the ellipse
- Enter a new value for the ellipse.

49. Select the lower ellipse.

50. Select the **Scale** icon on the *Ribbon,* on the *Modify* tab.

Notice the *Status Bar* prompt: "**Pick to enter origin.**" The origin, or base point, is a point on, or relative to, the object that does not move.

51. *First Pick:* Pick the top edge, midpoint, of the selected ellipse (Figure 4-2.14).

52. *Second Pick:* Pick the bottom edge, midpoint, of the same ellipse (Figure 4-2.14).

53. Type **1 2** (i.e., 1′-2″) and press **Enter**; this will be the new distance between the two points picked.

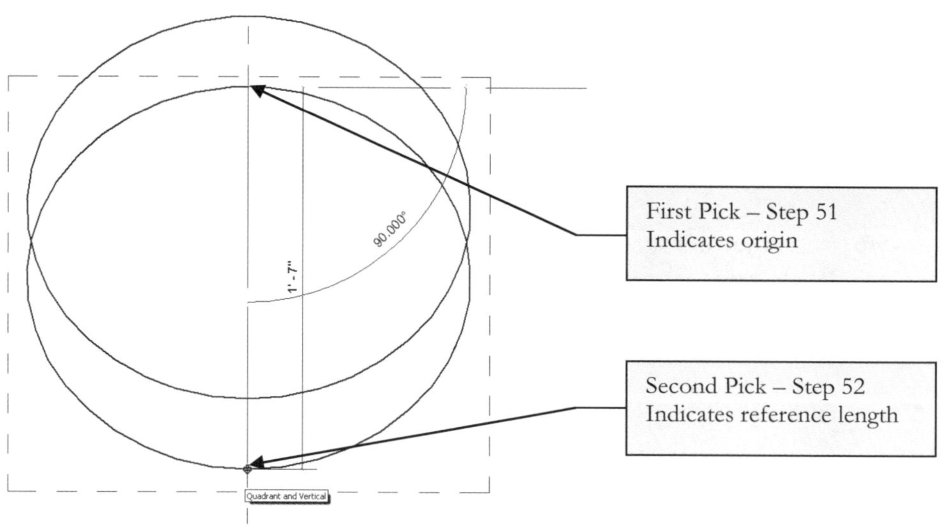

FIGURE 4-2.14 Scaling the ellipse

Next, you need to draw the faucet and drain. As it turns out, the faucet and drain for *Lav-1* are in the same position relative to the middle and back (black dot). So to save time, you will *Copy/Paste* these items from the *Lav-1* drafting view into the *Lav-2* view.

54. Open **Lav-1** *Drafting View.*

55. Select the entire *Lav-1* sketch.

56. Pick **Modify | Lines → Clipboard → Copy** while the *Lav-1* linework is selected.

57. Switch back to the *Lav-2* view and press **Ctrl + V** on the keyboard. Press both keys at the same time.

58. Pick a point to the side of the *Lav-2* sketch (Figure 4-2.15).

59. Select the faucet, the small rectangle, and the drain (i.e., the circle).

    TIP: Use a window *selection, picking from left to right.*

60. Select the ***Move*** tool; pick the middle/back of the *Lav-1* sketch and then pick the middle/back of the *Lav-2* sketch.

    NOTE: These two points represent the angle and distance to move the selected items.

61. **Erase** the extra *Lav-1* linework from the *Lav-2* view.

You should now have the faucet and drain correctly positioned in your *Lav-2* view.

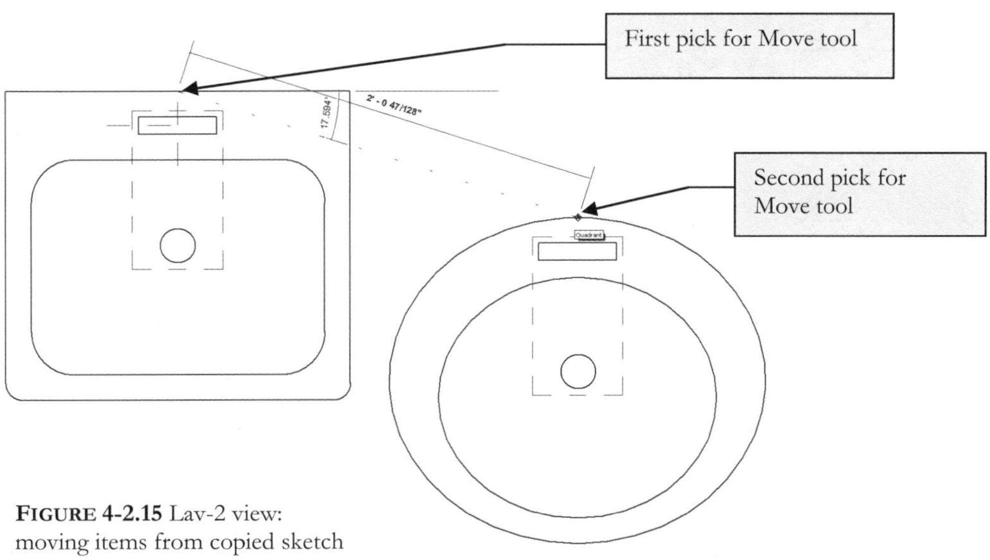

FIGURE 4-2.15 Lav-2 view: moving items from copied sketch

view name: **Sink-1**

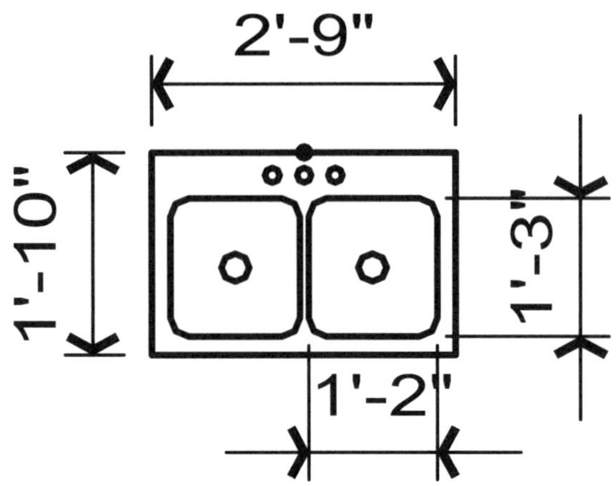

Draw this lavatory per the following specifications:

- 2″ space, offset at sides and front
- 3″ Dia. Circles centered in sinks
- 2″ rad. for Fillets
- 1½″ Dia. at faucet spaces; 3½″ apart

view name: **Water-Closet**

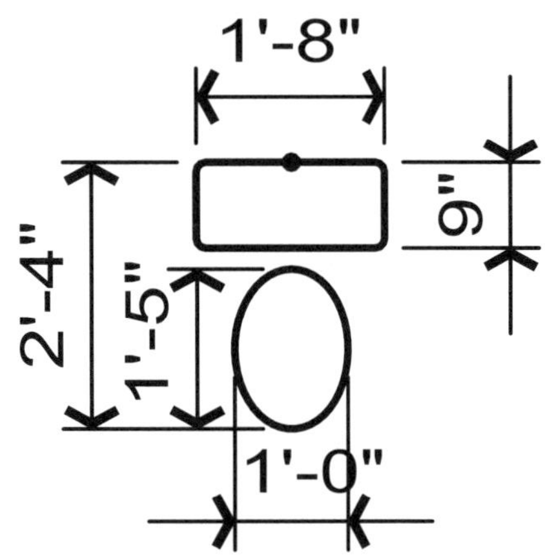

You should be able to draw this symbol without any help.

TIP: *Draw a construction line from the Origin (i.e., black dot) straight down 11″ (2′-4″ – 1′-5″ = 11″). This will give you a point to pick when drawing the ellipse.*

view name: **Tree**

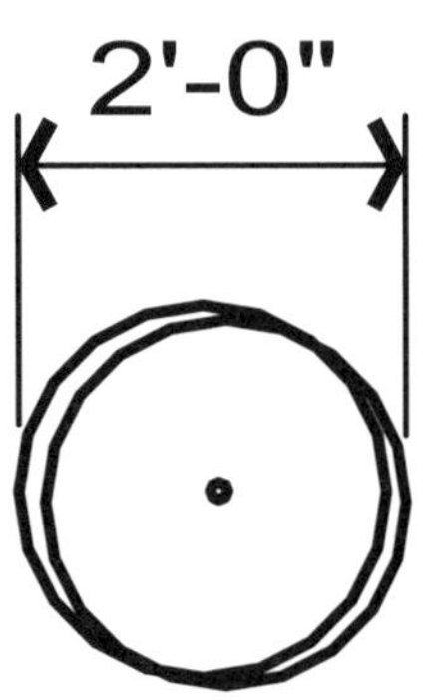

62. Draw one large circle and then copy it similar to this drawing.

63. Draw one small 1″ diameter circle at the approximate center.

64. **Save** your project.

view name: **Door-36**

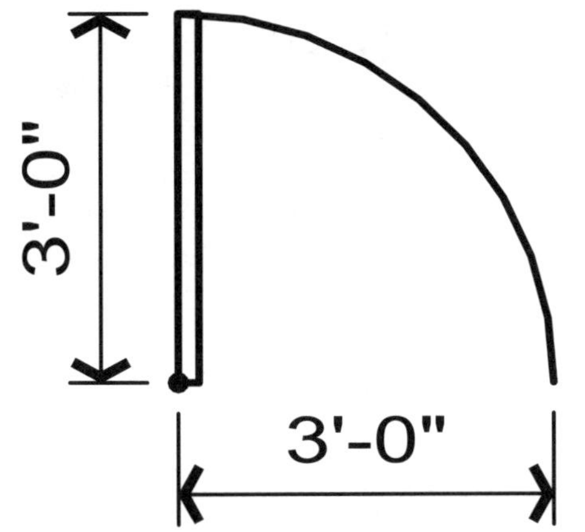

This symbol is used to show a door in a floor plan. The arc represents the path of the door as it opens and shuts.

A symbol like this, 90 degrees open, helps to avoid the door conflicting with something in the house like cabinets or a toilet. Existing doors are typically shown open 45 degrees so it is easier to visually discern new from existing.

Revit has an advanced door tool, so you would not actually draw this symbol very often. However, you may decide to draw one in plan that represents a gate in a reception counter or one in elevation to show a floor hatch. Refer back to Figure 4-1.9 for a floor plan example with door symbols.

65. Draw a **2″x3′-0″ rectangle**.

66. Draw an arc using **Center – Ends Arc**; select the three points in the order shown in Figure 4-2.16.

TIP: Be sure your third pick shows the cursor snapped to the horizontal plane.

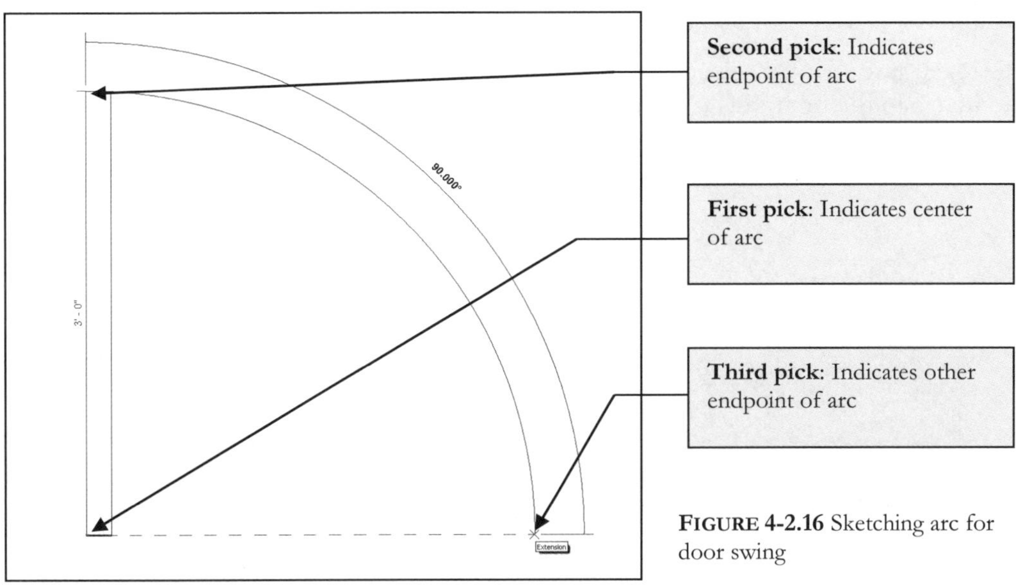

FIGURE 4-2.16 Sketching arc for door swing

view name: **Door2-36**

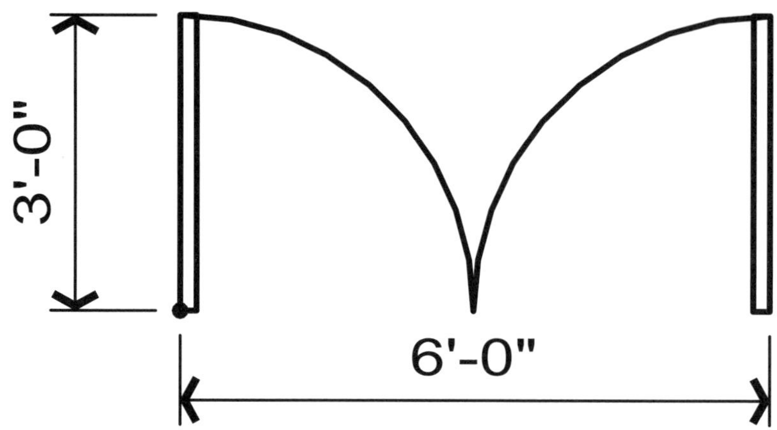

Here you will use a previous drawing and the *Mirror* tool to quickly create this drawing showing a pair of doors in a single opening.

67. Right-click on **Door-36** view label in the *Project Browser*, select "**Duplicate with detailing"** from the pop-up menu.

68. **Rename** the new *Detail View* **Door2-36**.

Next you will mirror both the rectangle and the arc. By default, Revit wants you to select a previously drawn line to be used as the "axis of reflection," but you do not have a line that would allow you to mirror the door properly to the left, so you have to pick the "*Draw Mirror Axis*" option on the *Ribbon.*

69. Select the rectangle and the arc, use a *crossing window* by picking from right to left, and then pick the **Modify | Lines → Modify → Mirror - Draw Axis** tool from the *Ribbon.*

70. Make sure ***Copy*** is selected on the *Ribbon.* See image to the right; this is the default.

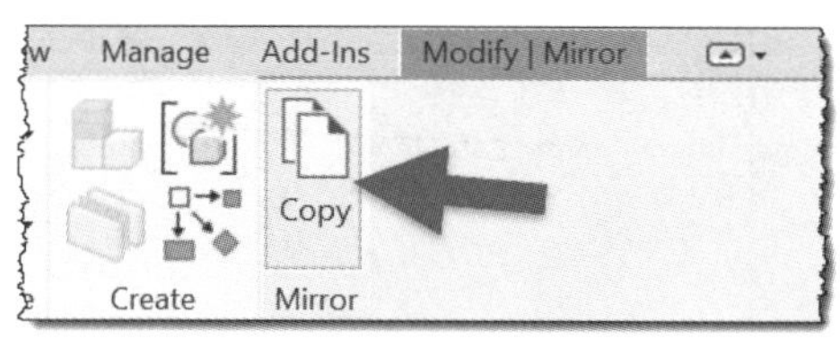

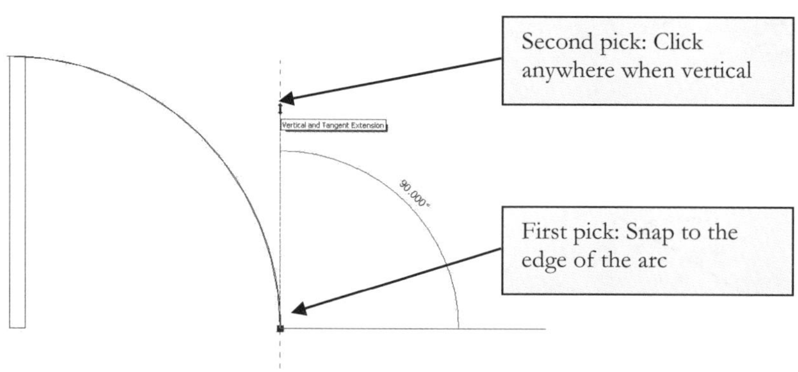

FIGURE 4-2.17 Creating axis of reflection

Notice the *Status Bar* is prompting you to "**Pick Start Point for Axis of Reflection**."

71. Pick the two points shown in **Figure 4-2.17**.

At this point the door symbol, the rectangle and arc, is mirrored and the *Mirror* tool is done.

72. Select ***Modify*** to end the command and unselect everything.

73. **Save** your project as "Ex4-2.rvt".

view name: Clg-Fan-1

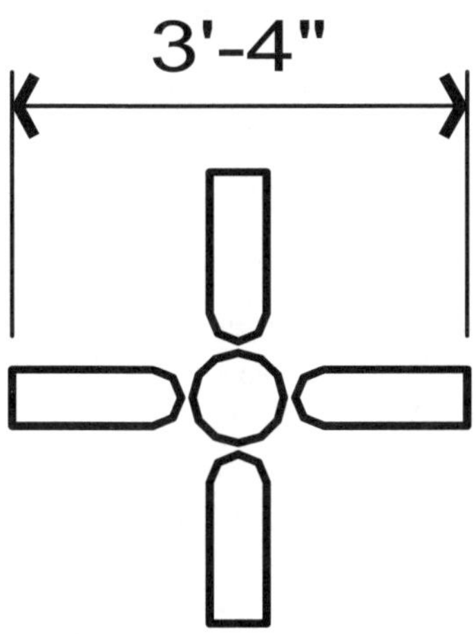

You will use the *Array* command while drawing this ceiling fan.

The *Array* command can be used to array entities in a rectangular pattern (e.g., columns on a grid) or in a polar pattern (i.e., in a circular pattern).

You will use the polar array to rotate and copy the fan blade all in one step!

74. Start a new drawing and create the portion of drawing shown in the figure to the right.

75. Select the fan blade and then select **Array** from the *Ribbon.*

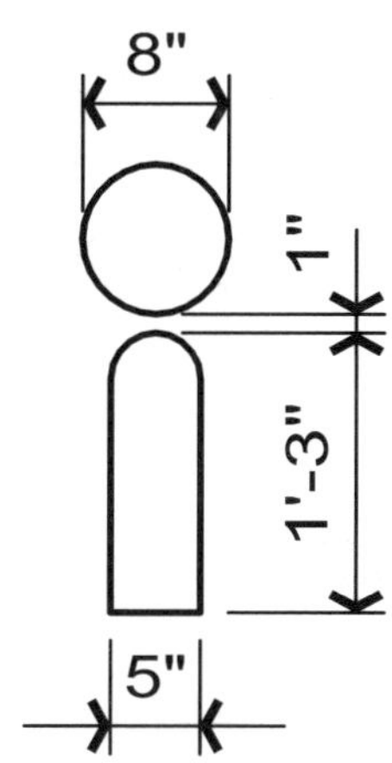

Similar to the *Rotate* tool, you will relocate the *Center of Rotation Symbol* to the center of the 8″ circle. This will cause the fan blade to array around the circle rather than the center of the first fan blade.

76. Click *Radial* on the *Ribbon* and then click and *drag* the **Rotation grip** to the center of the 8″ circle (or click the *Place* button on the *Ribbon*); make sure Revit snaps to the center point before clicking (see Figure 4-2.19).

77. Make the following changes to the *Ribbon* (Figure 4-2.18).

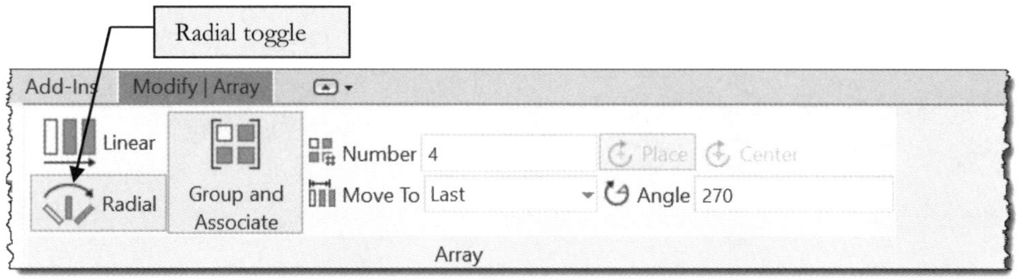

FIGURE 4-2.18 Array options on the Ribbon

78. After typing the angle in the *Ribbon*, press **Enter**.

You should now see the three additional fan blades and a temporary array number. This gives you the option to change the array number if desired.

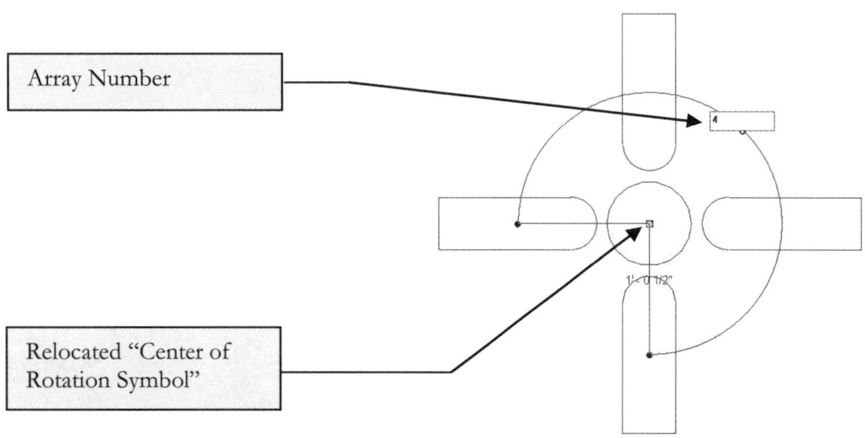

FIGURE 4-2.19 Arraying fan blades

79. Click **Modify** to complete the *Array* and finish the ceiling fan.

Because you left *Group and Associate* checked on the *Ribbon* when you created the array, you can select any part of a fan blade and the array number will appear, like a temporary dimension, and allow you to change the number. You can select *Ungroup* from the *Ribbon* to make each item individually editable as if you had drawn everything from scratch.

80. **Save** your project.

FYI: *You can export each Drafting View to a file and import it back into any project file. It can then be placed as a symbol into floor plans. This would make for smaller files on large projects, such as a large hospital complex. The major downside is that you would not see anything in your 3D views for furniture. Thus, you will not likely use these for your Revit plans, but you will be able to utilize every skill learned in this section!*

Self-Exam:

The following questions can be used as a way to check your knowledge of this lesson. The answers can be found at the bottom of the page.

1. Revit does not allow you to copy *Detail Views*. (T/F)

2. Entering 4 3.25 in Revit means 4′-3¼″. (T/F)

3. Reference Planes (aka, construction lines) are useful drawing aids. (T/F)

4. Use the ____________ tool to sketch an oval shape.

5. When you want to make a previously drawn rectangle wider you would use

   the ____________ tool.

Review Questions:

The following questions may be assigned by your instructor as a way to assess your knowledge of this section. Your instructor has the answers to the review questions.

1. Use the *Offset* option to quickly create a parallel line(s). (T/F)

2. If Revit displays an error message indicating a line is too small to be drawn, you simply zoom in more and try again. (T/F)

3. Use the ____________ command to create a reverse image.

4. With the *Move* tool, lines completely within the selection window are actually only moved, not stretched. (T/F)

5. You can relocate the "center of rotation" when using *Radial Array*. (T/F)

6. Occasionally you need to draw an object and then move it into place to accurately locate it. (T/F)

7. The ____________ is an option within the *Detail Line* tool which allows you to create a rounded corner where two lines intersect.

8. When using the *Mirror* tool, you occasionally need to draw a temporary line that represents the *Axis of Reflection*. (T/F)

9. Which line style was required to be selected in the *Type Selector*, in the *Properties Palette*, for all the linework in this Lesson? ____________

10. In the *Detail Line* tool, how many options allow you to draw arcs? ______

SELF-EXAM ANSWERS:
1 – F, **2** – T, **3** – T, **4** – Ellipse, **5** – Move

Notes:

Lesson 5
FLOOR PLAN (First Floor):

In this lesson, you will draw the first floor plan of a single-family residence. The project will be further developed in subsequent chapters. It is recommended that you spend adequate time on this lesson, as later lessons build upon this one.

Exercise 5-1:
Project Setup

The Project:

You will model a two-story residence located in a suburban setting. Just to the North of the building site is a medium-sized lake. For the sake of simplicity, the property is virtually flat.

The main entry is from the South side of the building. You enter the building into a large foyer. The second floor has a railing that overlooks the foyer.

This building is not meant to meet any particular building code. It is strictly a tool to learn how to use Autodesk Revit. That said, there are some general comments on how codes may affect a particular part of the design; each must be verified against your local rules and regulations.

Creating the Project File:

As previously mentioned, a Building Information Model (BIM) consists of a single file. This file can be quite large. For example, the prestigious architectural design firm SOM used Autodesk Revit to design One World Trade Center (also known as Freedom Tower) in New York City. As you can imagine, a skyscraper would be a large BIM file, whereas a single-family residence would be much smaller.

Large databases are only now entering the architectural design realm. However, banks, hospitals, etc., have been using them for years, even with multiple users accessing the same data simultaneously!

When Autodesk Revit is launched on your computer, the *Home* screen is loaded. The provided template files include several items set up and ready to use (e.g., some wall, door, and window types). Starting with the correct template can save you significant time.

Autodesk Revit provides a handful of templates for specific project types. They are *Commercial*, *Construction,* and *Residential.*

In this exercise, you will use the *Residential* template. It has several aspects of the project file pre-set up and ready for use. A few of these items will be discussed momentarily.

As your knowledge of Revit increases, you will be able to start refining a custom template that probably originated from a standard template. The custom template will include a firm's custom title block and a cover sheet with abbreviations, symbols, etc., all set up and ready to go.

Next, you will create a new project file. **The next 5 steps are very important!**

1. From the Home screen, click **New...** under MODELS, or, if not at the Home screen, select ***File Tab → New → Project***.

   You are now in the *New Project* dialog box. Rather than clicking *OK*, which would use a non-residential default architectural template, you will select *Browse* to choose a specialized template (Figure 5-1.1).

2. Click the **Browse...** button.

3. Select the template named **Residential-Default.rte** from the list of available templates (Figure 5-1.2).

4. Click **Open** to select the highlighted template file.

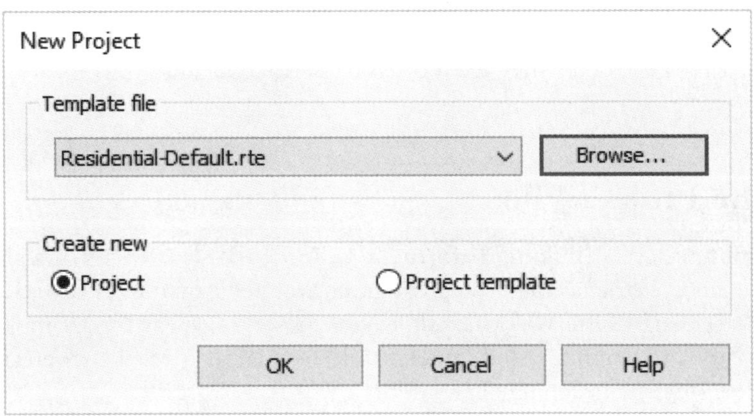

FIGURE 5-1.1 New Project dialog

5. Click **OK** to complete the *New Project* dialog.

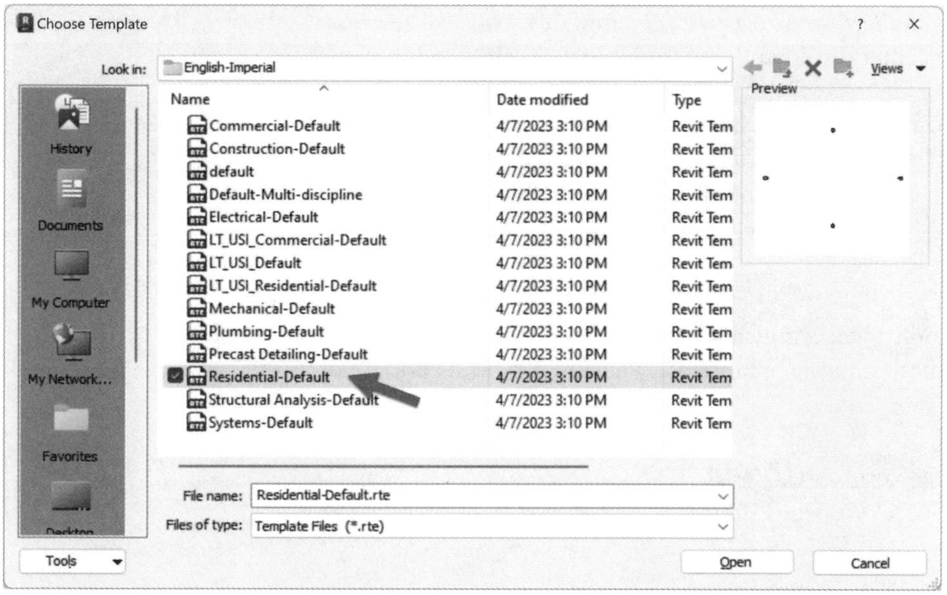

FIGURE 5-1.2 Choose Template dialog

You have just set up a project file that you will use for the **remainder of this book**, so be sure you selected the correct template file!

Next, you will take a look at the predefined wall types that have been loaded with the template file.

6. Select **Architecture → Build → Wall.**

7. Click the ***Type Selector*** down-arrow on the *Properties Palette* (Figure 5-1.3). When done looking at the wall types, press the **Esc** key three times to close the *Type Selector* and cancel the command.

Wall Types:

Notice the wall types preloaded in the *Residential* template. These wall types are among those one would expect to find on a typical residential construction project.

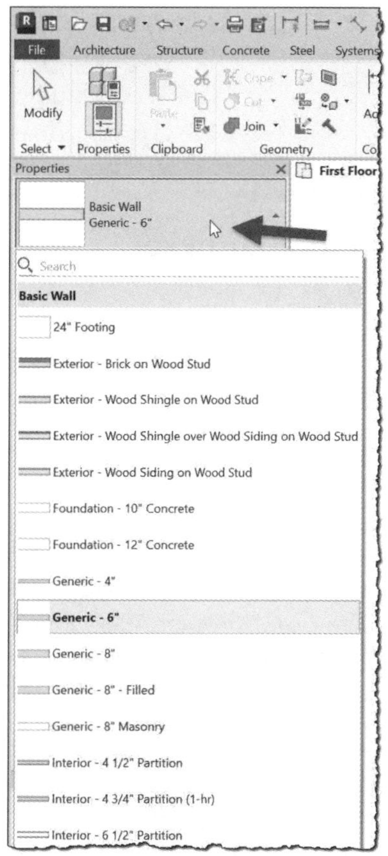

FIGURE 5-1.3 Preloaded wall types

The walls are mostly wood stud walls, both interior and exterior. If you look at the *Default* or *Commercial* templates, you will see that they mostly use metal stud and concrete block (CMU) wall types.

Additionally, material thicknesses can vary between commercial and residential applications; this is also accounted for in the templates. For example, gypsum board is typically ⅝″ thick on commercial projects, whereas it is usually only ½″ on residential work.

To reiterate the concept, consider the following comparisons between a typical commercial interior wall and a typical residential interior wall.

- <u>Typical Commercial Wall</u>
    - ⅝″ Gypsum Board
    - 3⅝″ Metal Stud
    - ⅝″ Gypsum Board
        - Total thickness: **4⅞″**

- <u>Typical Residential Wall</u>
    - ½″ Gypsum Board
    - 2x4 Wood Stud (3½″ actual)
    - ½″ Gypsum Board
        - Total Thickness: **4½″**

Project Browser:

Take a few minutes to review the Project Browser and note the views and sheets set up in the template file you started from (Figure 5-1.4).

Many of the views you need to start designing a residence are set up and ready to go.

Practically all the sheets typically found on a residential project have been created; see Figure 5-1.4 under the *Sheets (all)* heading of the *Project Browser*. Also, notice the sheets with a plus symbol next to them. These are sheets that already have views placed on them. You will study this more later, but a view, such as your *East Elevation* view, is placed on a sheet at a scale you select. This means your title block sheets will have printable information as soon as you start sketching walls in one of your plan views.

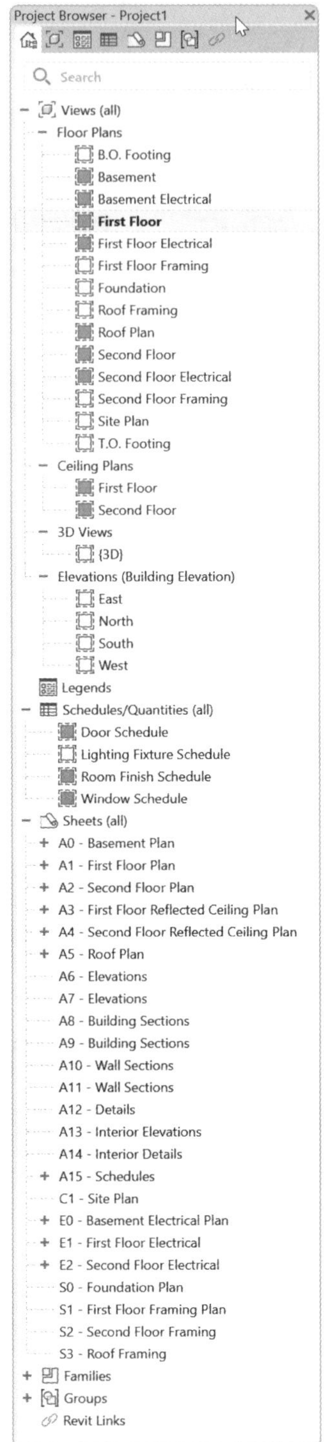

FIGURE 5-1.4 Project Browser: various items preloaded

Project Information:

Revit provides a dialog to enter basic project information, such as the client name and project address. Next, you will enter this information.

8. Select **Manage → Settings → Project Information**.

9. Enter the *Project Information* shown in Figure 5-1.5.

FYI: For now, you will enter three question marks for the date.

Project Issue Date:	**???**
Project Status:	**Preliminary**
Client Name:	**John Brown**
Project Name:	**New Residence**
Project Number:	**2016-048**

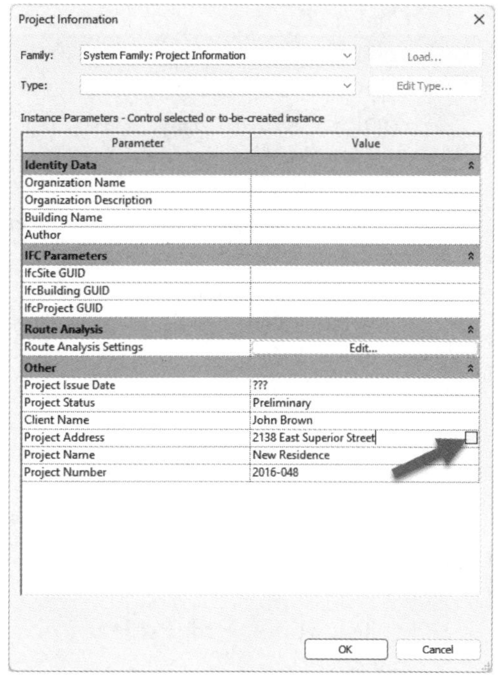

FIGURE 5-1.5 Project Information dialog

10. Click in the field next to the *Project Address* parameter and then click the small icon that appears to the right (Figure 5-1.5).

11. Enter the project address shown in Figure 5-1.6.

FYI: This is the address where the house is going to be built, not the client's current address.

Enter:
2138 East Superior Street
Duluth, MN 55812

NOTE: You can enter any address you want at this point; the suggested address is made up.

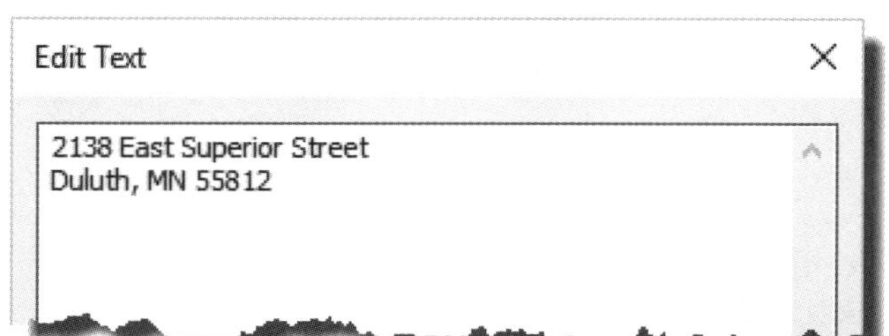

FIGURE 5-1.6 Adding Project Address (partial view)

12. Click **OK**.

13. Click the **Edit** button next to Route Analysis Settings (Figure 5-1.7). Review the settings.

    FYI: Route Analysis is a feature that finds a walking path through your building, between a start and end point you select.

14. Click **OK**.

15. Click **OK**, again, to close the *Project Information* dialog box.

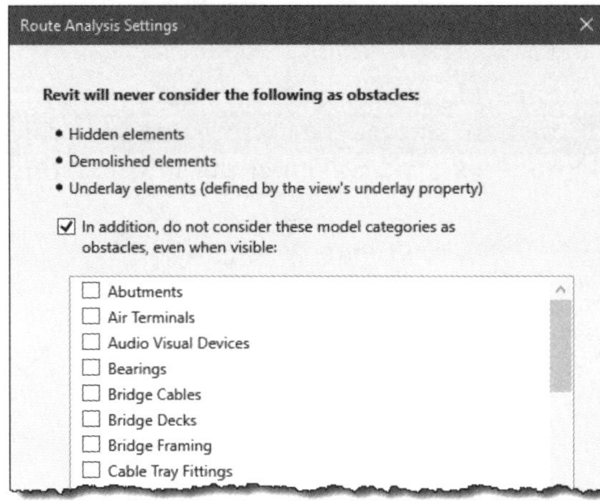

FIGURE 5-1.7 Route Analysis dialog (partial view)

Next, you will specify the project's location on Earth using Revit's *Location* command.

16. Click **Manage → Project Location → Location.**

17. In the *Project Address* field, enter **Duluth, MN** (or your city/state) (Figure 5-1.8).

18. Click **OK** to close the Location dialog.

Note that the *Weather Station* data are used to perform accurate daylighting and energy analyses. Using Revit in conjunction with Autodesk Insight can help create more energy-efficient buildings by allowing you to study the design's impact on energy consumption earlier in the project, when changes are still possible.

For daylighting, additional tools such as *Autodesk Lighting, Autodesk Solar,* or *ElumTools* by Lighting Analysts, Inc. can be used to analyze light levels for a specific day in time or annual.

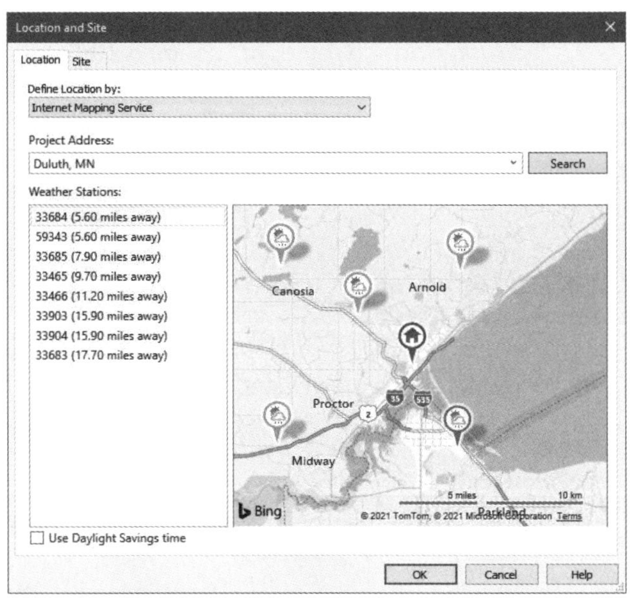

FIGURE 5-1.8 Specify Project Location

The project information is now saved in your Revit project database. Revit has already used some of this information to complete a portion of your title block on each sheet. You will verify this next.

19. Under the **Sheets** heading, in the *Project Browser*, double-click on the sheet **A1 – First Floor Plan**.

    TIP: If needed, click the plus symbol next to the Sheets node to expand it and reveal the project's sheets. You do not need to click the plus symbol next to the sheet name/number currently.

20. **Zoom** in to the lower right area of the title block (Figure 5-1.10).

    Reminder: To zoom, place your cursor in the area you wish to zoom into and scroll the wheel on your mouse. If your mouse/input device does not have a scroll wheel, use the Zoom tools in the upper-right corner of the drawing area.

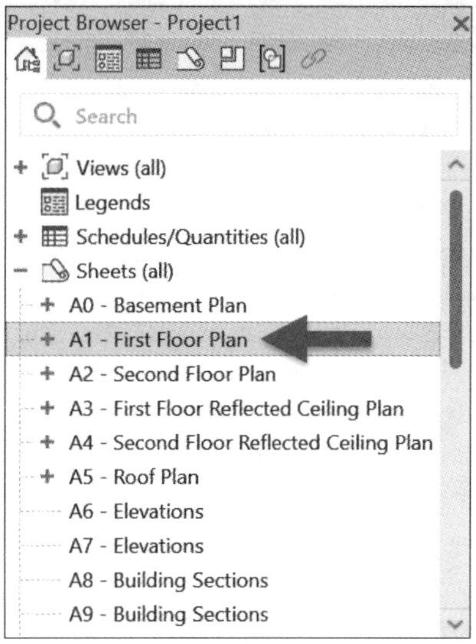

FIGURE 5-1.9 Sheet to open from project browser

Notice that much of the information is automatically filled in, and this is true for every sheet!

Your project database (that is, your BIM file) is now set up.

21. **Save** your project as **Ex5-1.rvt**.

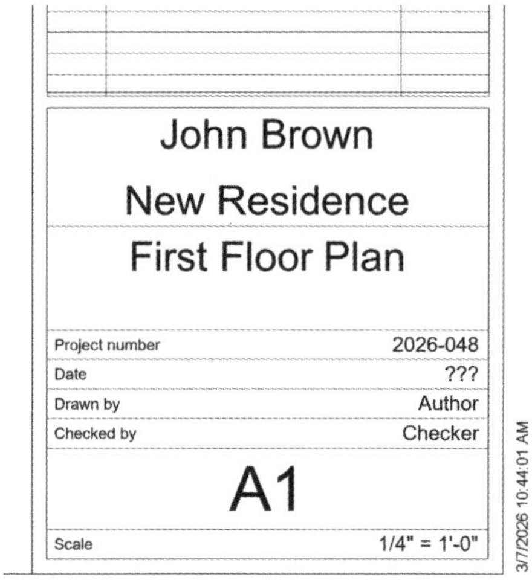

FIGURE 5-1.10 Sheet with Project Information added automatically

Exercise 5-2:
Exterior Walls

You will begin the first floor plan by drawing the exterior walls. Like many projects, you might not be certain what the exterior walls will be like early on. So you will start with the generic wall styles. Then you will change them to a custom wall style, which you will create once you have decided on the wall construction.

Often, a residence is designed with a specific site in mind. However, to align with most drafting and design classes, in which floor plans are studied before site plans, you will develop the plans now.

Completed Plans – For Reference:

The following two images show the floor plans as they will look when you finish this book. You should not need to use any information from these images; they are simply meant to introduce you to the project.

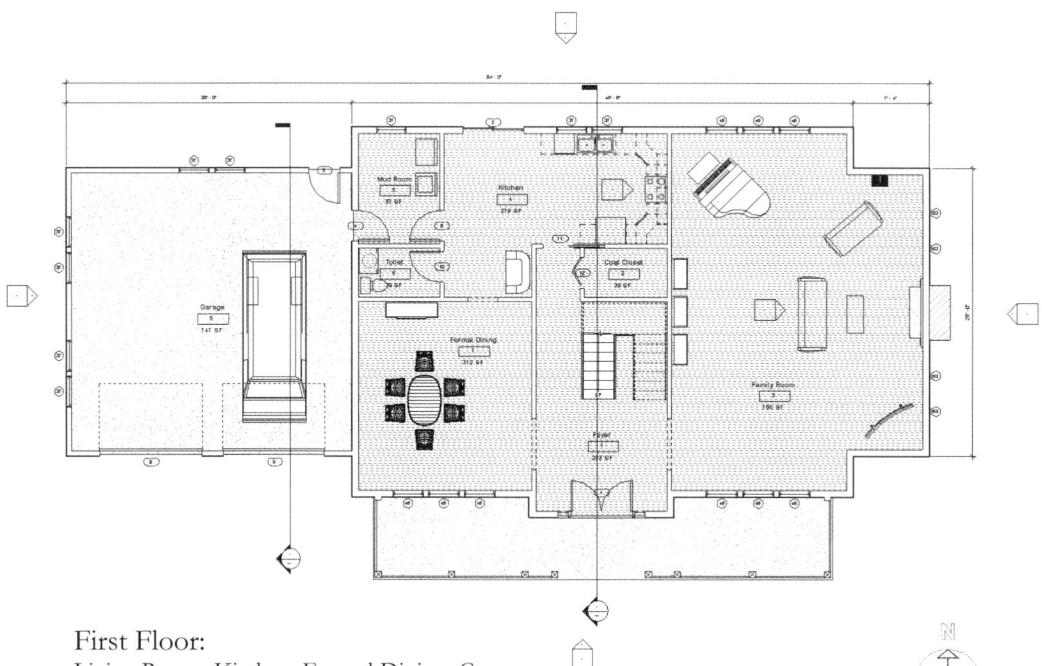

First Floor:
Living Room, Kitchen, Formal Dining, Coat Closet, ½ Bath, Mud Room, Garage

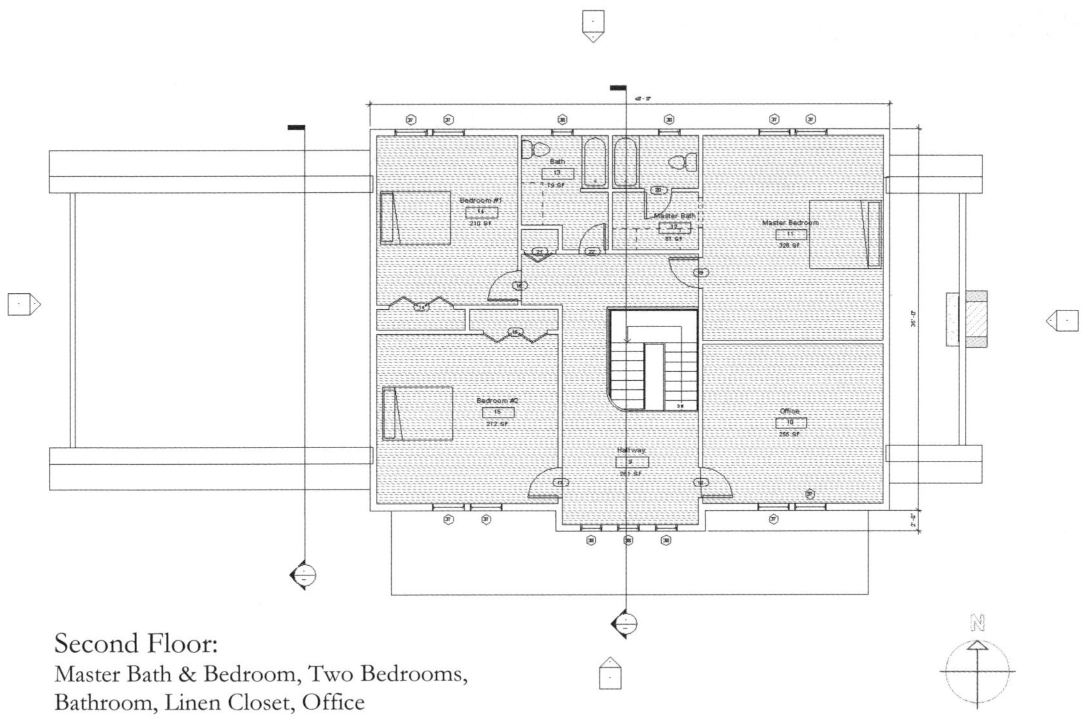

Second Floor:
Master Bath & Bedroom, Two Bedrooms,
Bathroom, Linen Closet, Office

Adjust Wall Settings:

1. In your project, Ex5-1.rvt, switch to ***First Floor*** 'floor plan' view; select **Wall** from the *Architecture* tab.

2. Make the following changes to the wall options within the *Ribbon* and *Properties Palette* (Figure 5-2.1):
   - *Wall style:* *Basic Wall:* **Generic – 8″** [203.2 mm]
   - *Height:* **Unconnected**
   - *Height:* **19′ 0″** [5791.2 mm]
   - *Location Line:* **Finish Face; Exterior**
   - *Chain:* **checked**

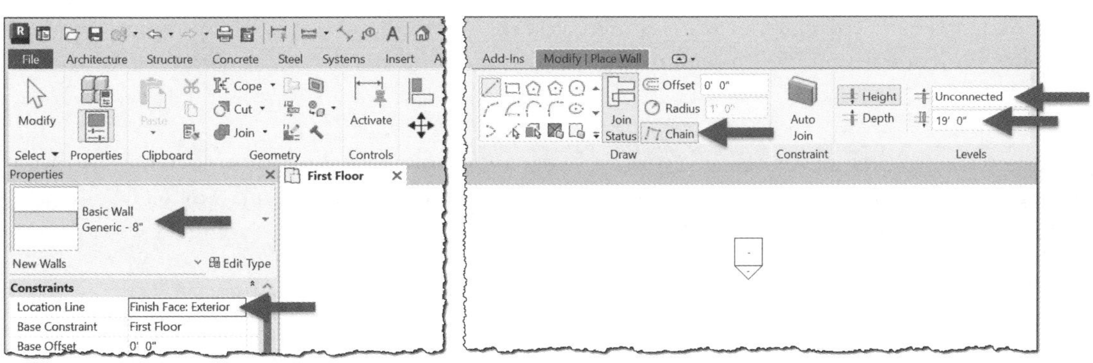

FIGURE 5-2.1 Ribbon and Properties Palette – Wall command active

Draw the Exterior Walls:

3. **Draw** the walls shown in Figure 5-2.2. Make sure your dimensions are correct. Use the *Measure* tool on the *QAT* to double-check your dimensions. Center the building between the elevation tags (see Figure 1-2.1). Move the elevation tags as needed by selecting the square part of the tag and using the *Move* tool (do not delete them).

   NOTE: If you draw clockwise, your walls will have the exterior side correctly positioned. You can also use the spacebar to toggle which side the exterior face is on during creation.

   TIP: On the Ribbon, while you are in the Wall tool, you can click Chain to continuously draw walls. When Chain is not selected, you have to pick the same point twice: once where the wall ends and again where the next wall begins.

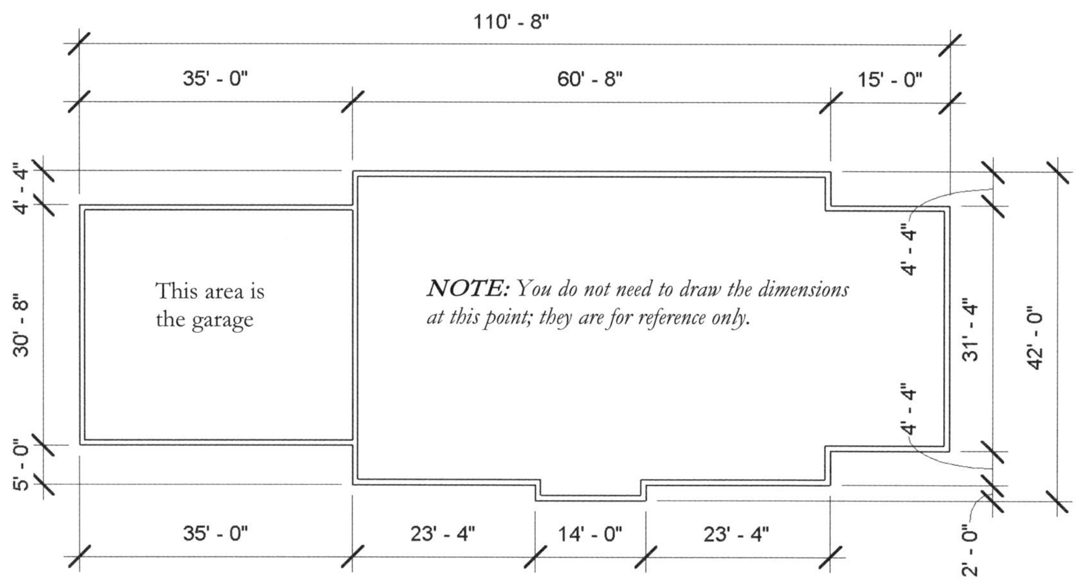

FIGURE 5-2.2 Exterior walls

Modifying Wall Dimensions:

Now that you have the exterior walls drawn, you might decide to adjust the building size for masonry coursing if you have a concrete block foundation, or subtract square footage to reduce cost.

Editing walls in Revit is very easy. You can select a wall and edit the temporary dimensions that appear, or you can use the *Move* tool to change the position of a wall. Any walls whose endpoints touch the modified wall are also adjusted automatically (i.e., they grow or shrink).

Next, you will adjust the dimensions of the walls just drawn. You will assume the house will have a concrete block (CMU) foundation due to the cold-climate location.

4. Click the **Modify** button (not the tab) and then select the far-left wall (Figure 5-2.3).

Clicking *Modify* cancels the current command and deselects everything. Sometimes you have to press it twice to clear everything completely.

5. Select the temporary dimensions text (35′-0″) and then type **34 8** (Figure 5-2.3).

FYI: Remember, you do not need to type the foot or inch symbol; the space distinguishes between them.

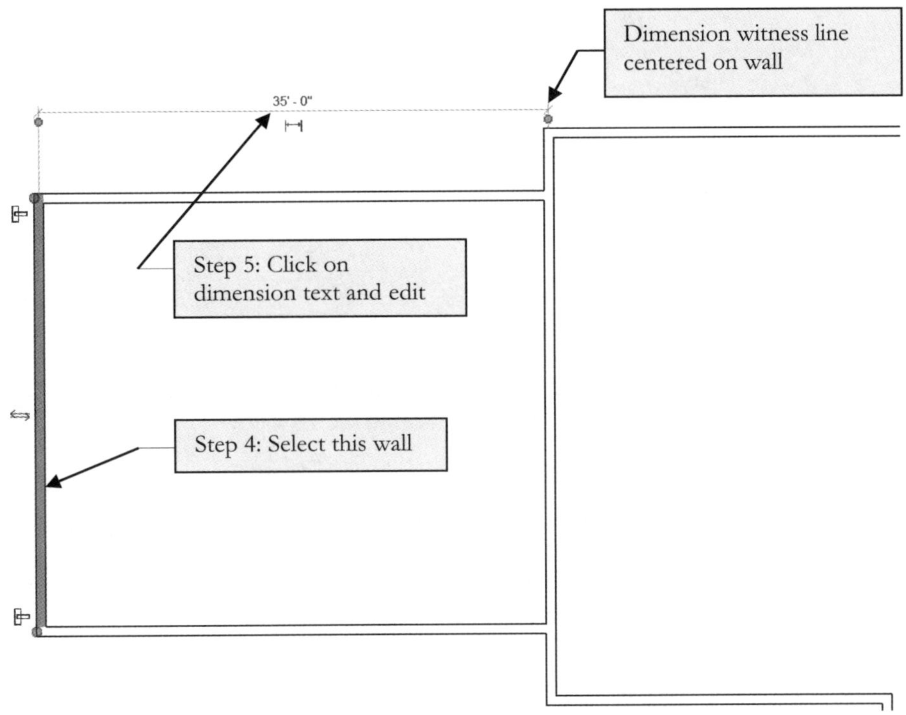

FIGURE 5-2.3 Editing wall dimensions

TIP: Whenever you want to adjust the model using temporary/permanent dimensions, select the object you want to move first, then select the text or number of the temporary or permanent dimension.

6. In the lower right corner of the floor plan, select the wall shown in Figure 5-2.4.

7. Edit the 4′-4″ dimension to **4′-0″**.

TIP: Just type 4 and press Enter; Revit will assume feet when a single number is entered.

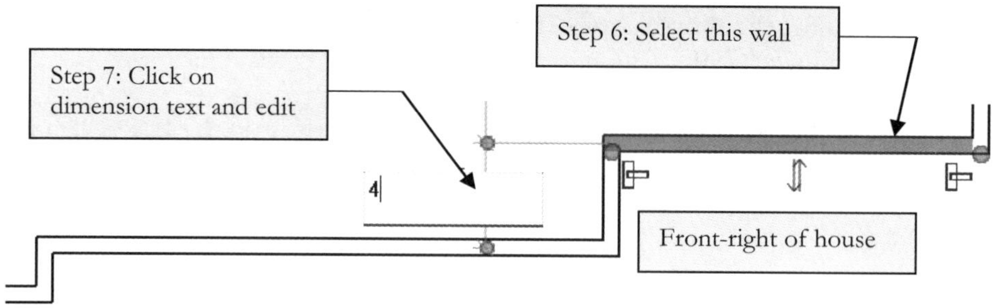

FIGURE 5-2.4 Editing exterior walls

FYI: You can edit the location of the witness lines if desired by going to Manage → Additional Settings → Annotations → Temporary Dimensions. Here, you can set the default to "Faces" rather than "Centerlines." Do not change any settings at this time.

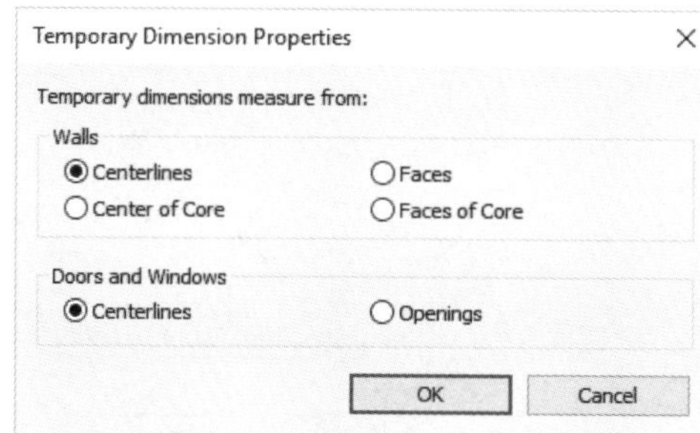

> **TIP:**
> Concrete blocks (or CMU) come in various widths, and most are 16″ long and 8″ high. When drawing plans, there is a simple rule to keep in mind to make sure you are designing walls to coursing. This applies to wall lengths and openings within CMU walls.
>
> Dimension rules for CMU coursing in floor plans:
> - ***e***′-0″ or ***e***′-8″ where ***e*** is any even number (e.g., 6′-0″ or 24′-8″)
> - ***o***′-4″ where ***o*** is any odd number (e.g., 5′-4″)

Using the Align Tool with Walls:

Revit has a tool called *Align* that lets you quickly align one element with another. You will make the South wall of the garage align with the wall you just modified. After they are aligned, you will lock the relationship so the two walls will always move together, which is great when you know you want two walls to remain aligned but might accidentally move one, maybe while zoomed in, and you cannot see the other wall.

8. Select the **Modify** (tab) → **Modify** (panel) → **Align** icon. 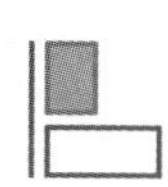

TIP: Or just type **AL** to start the Align tool

Notice the *Status Bar* is asking you to select a reference line or point. This is the wall, or linework, that is in the correct location; the other wall(s) will be adjusted to match the reference plane.

9. Select the exterior face of the horizontal wall you just modified: Set *Prefer* to **Wall Faces** on the *Ribbon* (Figure 5-2.5).You should notice a temporary dashed line appear on screen. This will help you to visualize the reference plane.

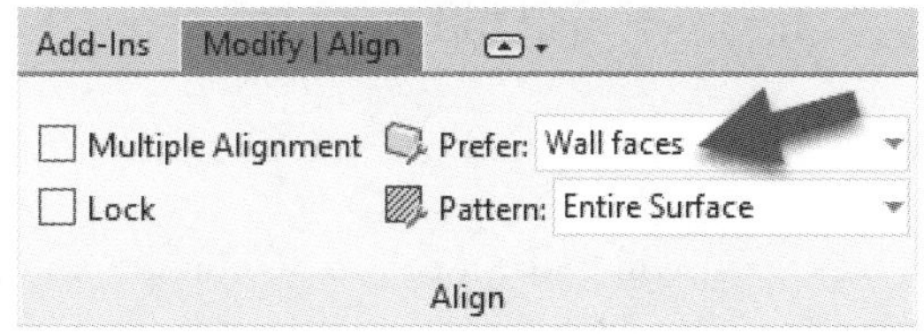

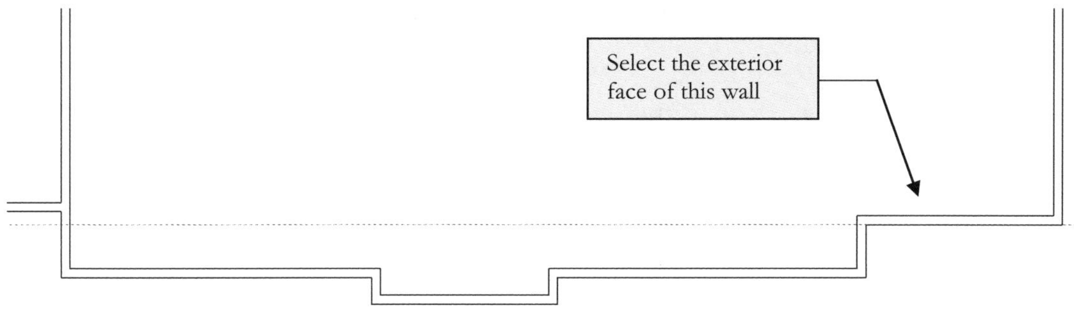

FIGURE 5-2.5 Align tool: wall selected

Notice the *Status Bar* is prompting you to select an entity to align with the temporary reference plane.

10. Now, select the exterior face of the South garage wall (Figure 5-2.6).

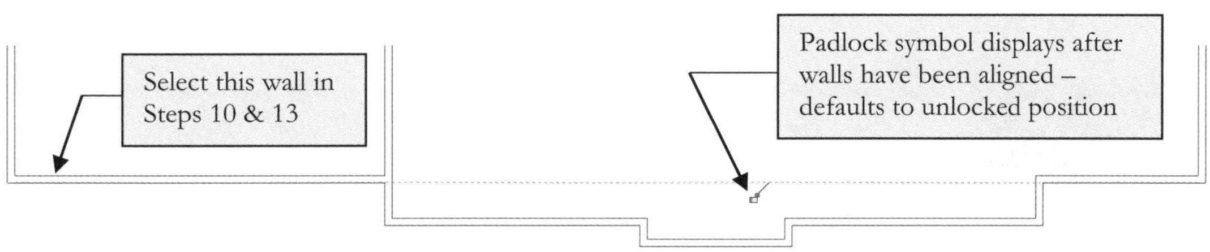

FIGURE 5-2.6 Align tool: select wall(s) to be aligned

Note that if you had selected the interior face of the wall, that side of the wall would have aligned with the reference plane rather than the exterior as it did. If you made a mistake, click *Undo* and try it again.

Also, notice that you have a padlock symbol showing. Clicking the padlock symbol will maintain the alignment relationship as a parametric relationship. Next, you will lock the alignment relationship and experiment with a few edits to see how modifying one wall affects the other.

11. Click on the **padlock** symbol (Figure 5-2.6). 

The padlock symbol is now in the locked position.

12. Click the **Modify** button to unselect the walls (or just press the **Esc** key).

13. Select the garage wall identified in Figure 5-2.6.

Next you will make a dramatic change so you can clearly see the results of that change on both locked walls.

14. Change the 4′-0″ dimension to **20′-0″** (Figure 5-2.7). After reviewing the information below, click **Undo**.

Notice that both walls moved together (Figure 5-2.7). Also notice that when either wall is selected, the padlock is displayed, which helps in identifying "locked" relationships while you are editing the project. Whenever the padlock symbol is visible, you can click on it to unlock it or remove the aligned relationship.

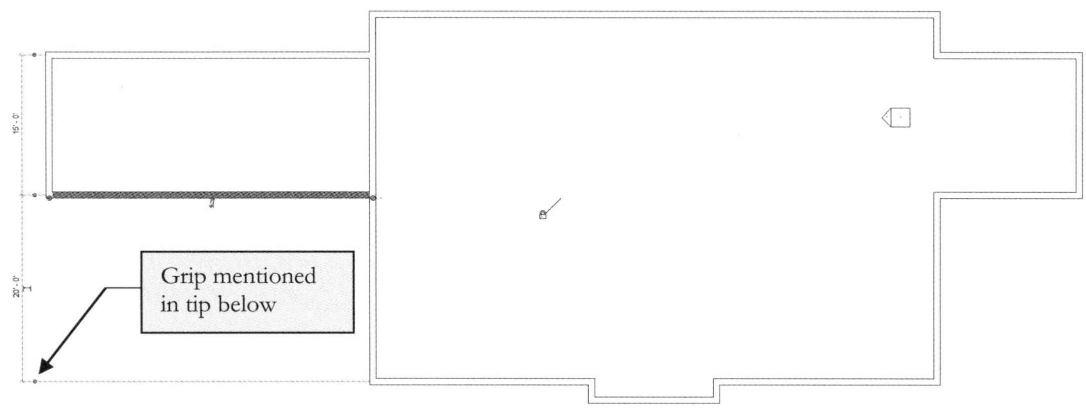

FIGURE 5-2.7 Wall edit: Both walls move together

Next, you will make a few more wall modifications on your own to bring the building perimeter to masonry coursing.

15. Modify wall locations by selecting a wall and modifying the temporary dimensions; the selected wall will move to match Figure 5-2.8; do not draw the dimensions at this time.

TIP: Use the Measure *tool to verify all dimensions before moving on!*

TIP: Clicking the grip on the witness line of a Temporary Dimension toggles the witness line between locations on the wall (i.e., exterior face, interior face, and center). You can also drag the grip to a different wall. *See page 5-27 for more information on this.*

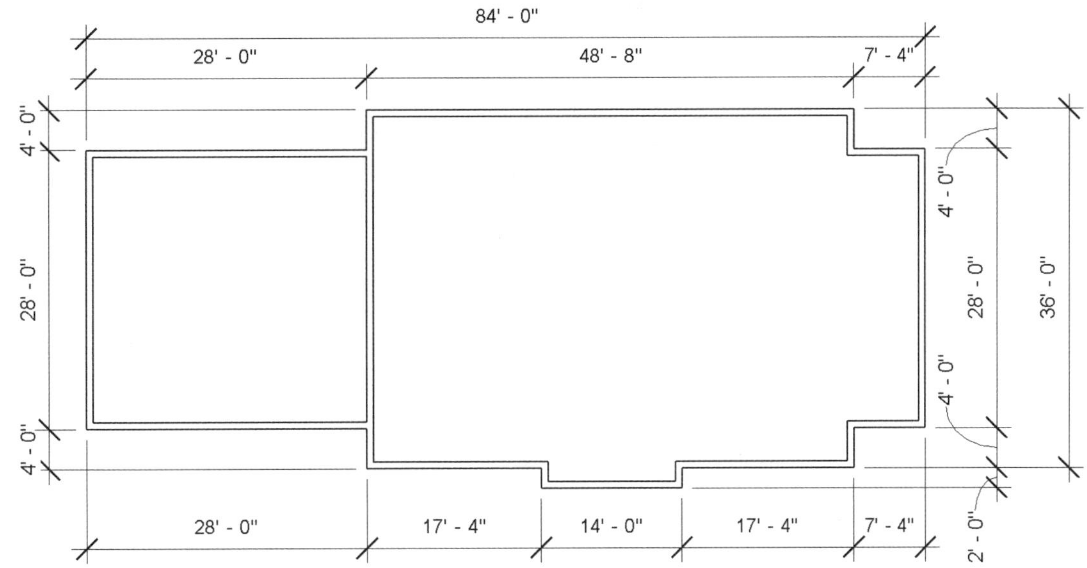

FIGURE 5-2.8 Exterior walls with final dimensions

Changing a Wall Type:

In the next several steps, you will learn how to change the generic walls into a more refined wall type. Basically, you select the wall(s) you want to change, then choose a different wall type from the *Type Selector* on the *Properties Palette*. Remember, the *Ribbon* and *Properties Palette* are context-sensitive, which means the wall types are only listed in the Type Selector when you are using the Wall tool or have a wall selected.

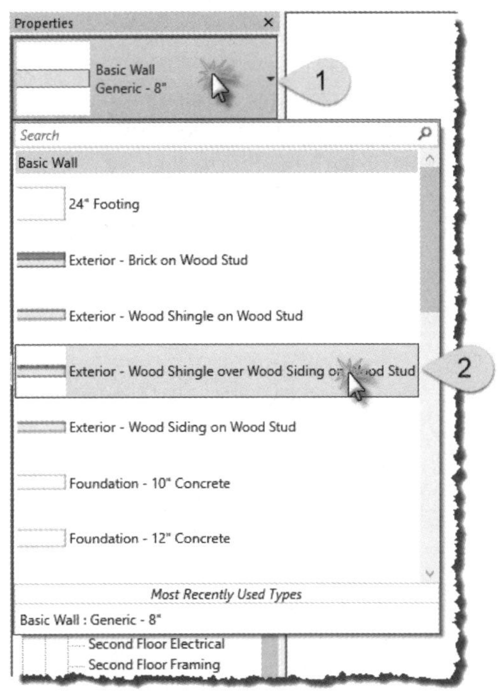

FIGURE 5-2.9 Type Selector

16. Select all the walls in your *First Floor* plan view.

    TIP: You can select all the walls at once: click and drag the cursor to select a window. *Later in the book, you will learn about "Filter Selection," which also aids in the selection process.*

17. From the *Type Selector* on the *Properties Palette*, select **Exterior – Wood Shingle over Wood Siding on Wood Stud** (Figure 5-2.9).

18. Click **Modify** to unselect the walls.

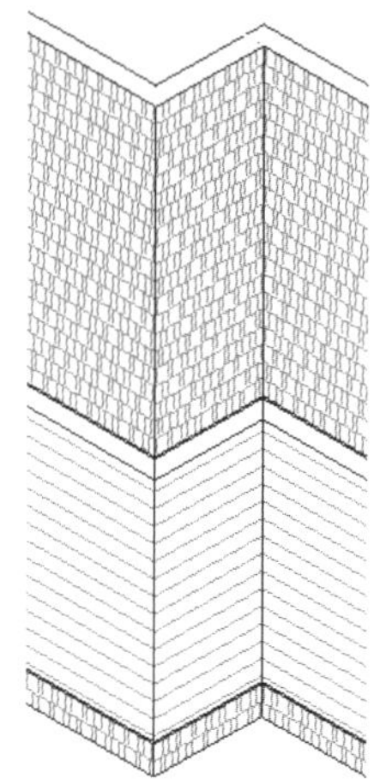

If you zoom in on the walls, you can see their graphic representation has changed a little. It would have changed a lot, of course, if you had selected a brick and CMU cavity wall. But you typically try to start with a wall closest to the one you think you will end up with, though you may never even have to change the wall type.

Even though the wall did not change much graphically in this plan view, it did change quite a bit. In a 3D view, which you will look at in a moment, the wall now has siding and trim! The image to the right is a snapshot of the 19′-0″ tall wall you now have in your model.

Next, you will create a custom wall type for the walls around the garage. You will need a wall type similar to the one you just selected, but with 2x4 studs rather than 2x6s. You will start by making a copy of the existing wall type and then modify the copy.

Create a Custom Wall Type:

As previously mentioned, Revit provides several predefined wall styles, from wood studs with gypsum board to concrete block and brick cavity walls. However, you will occasionally need a wall style that has not yet been predefined by Revit. You will study this process next.

First, you will take a close look at the predefined wall type you are using for the exterior walls.

19. Select the *Wall* tool, pick the wall type **Exterior – Wood Shingle over Wood Siding on Wood Stud** from the *Type Selector* drop-down list (Figure 5-2.9).

20. Click the **Edit Type** button on the *Properties Palette* (Figure 5-2.10).

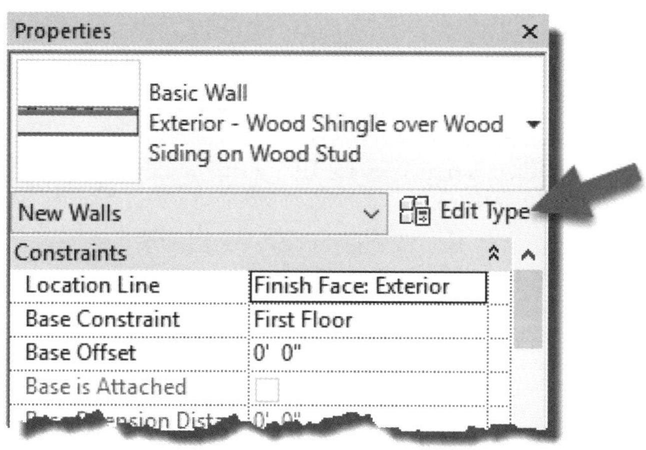

FIGURE 5-2.10 Edit Type button

21. You should be in the *Type Properties* dialog box (Figure 5-2.11).

22. Click the **Edit** button next to the *Structure* parameter.

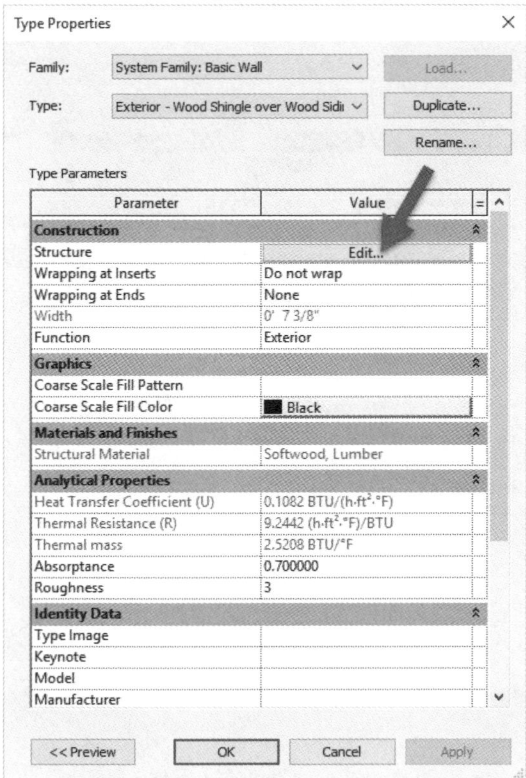

FIGURE 5-2.11 Type Properties

> **FYI:**
> Here is the difference between the two Element Properties dialogs:
>
> Properties Palette (Instance Properties): This information can vary by instance (e.g., individual walls, doors, windows, etc.). For example, the height to the bottom of a window or the fire rating of a wall or door; these values can vary from instance to instance.
>
> Type Properties: This is information that is the same for every instance of a specific type. For example, the width and height of window type "W1" should be the same for all, and the width of wall type "S6" should be the same for all. Any changes to these values affect all previously drawn and to-be-drawn objects in the model.

23. Finally, you are in the *Edit Assembly* dialog box. This is where you can modify existing wall types. Click **<<Preview** to display a preview of the selected wall type (Figure 5-2.12).

Here, the *Edit Assembly* dialog box allows you to change the composition of an existing wall or to create a new wall.

Things to notice (Figure 5-2.12):

- The exterior side is labeled at the top and interior side at the bottom.
- You will see horizontal lines (i.e., *Layers*) identifying the core material. The core material can be used to place walls and dimension walls. For example, the *Wall* tool will let you draw a wall with the interior or exterior core face as the reference line. On an interior wall you might dimension to the face of stud (i.e., the core face) rather than to the finished face of gypsum board; this would give the contractor the information needed for the part of the wall he will build first.
- Each row is called a *Layer*. By clicking on a *Layer* and picking the **Up** or **Down** buttons, you can reposition materials (i.e., layer) within the wall assembly.
- Wall layers automatically join between walls when the Material and Priority match.

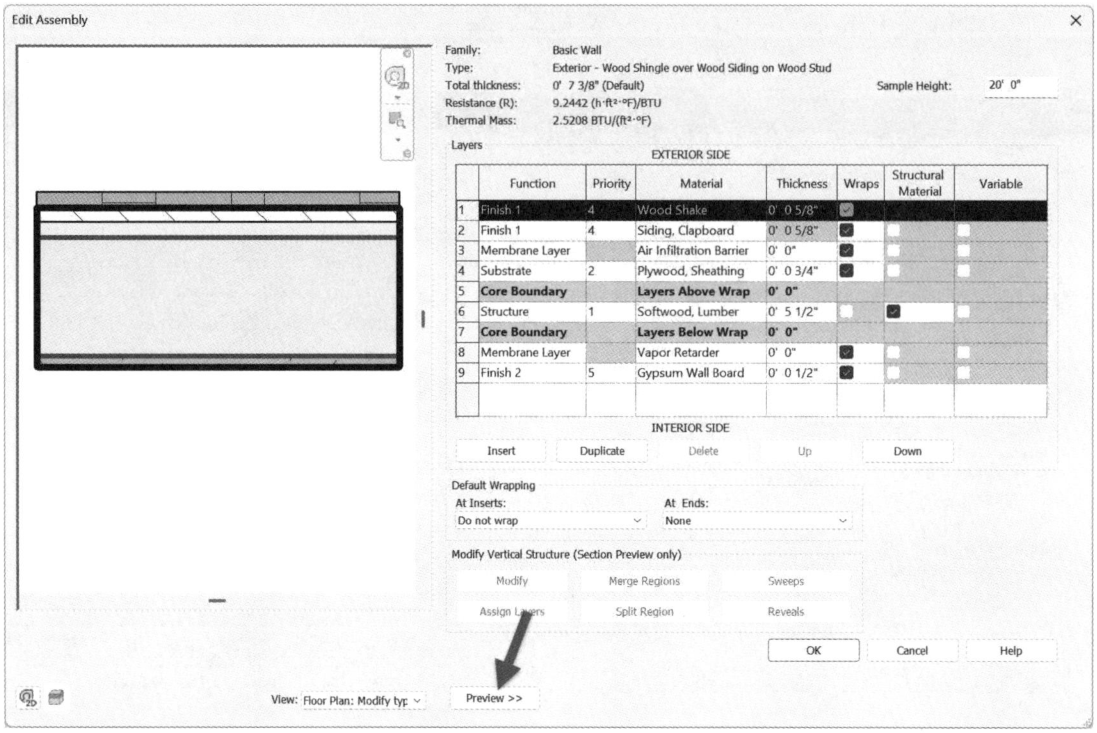

FIGURE 5-2.12 Edit Assembly

24. Click **Cancel** to close the *Edit Assembly* dialog box (leave the *Type Properties* dialog open).

Next, you will instruct Revit to create a new wall type based on a copy of the currently selected wall type.

25. Click the **Duplicate** button (Figure 5-2.11).

26. Enter **Exterior – Wood Shingle over Wood Siding on 2x4 Wood Stud** for the new wall type name, and then click **OK** (Figure 5-2.13).

FYI: Notice that you have simply added "2x4" as a descriptor, making the name distinguishable from the others. Be sure to remove the "2" at the end, which was automatically added by Revit in case you did not change the name.

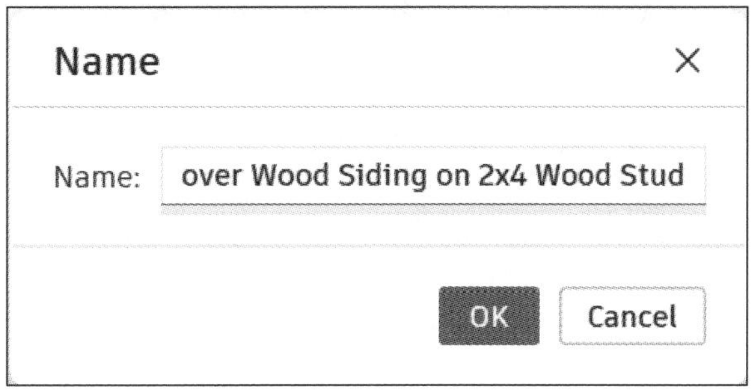

FIGURE 5-2.13 New wall type name

27. Click the **Edit** button next to the *Structure* parameter.

Next, simply change the size of the wood stud layer, then save your changes.

28. Change the *Thickness* of the **Softwood, Lumber** *Layer* (Row 6) to **0′ 3 ½″**.

29. Your dialog should look like **Figure 5-2.14**. Notice the total wall thickness is listed near the top. Also note that the Total Thickness and R-Value have been updated.

30. Click **OK** to close all dialog boxes.

You now have access to your newly defined wall. You can sketch new walls using the *Wall* tool, or you can change existing walls to your new wall type using the *Modify* tool.

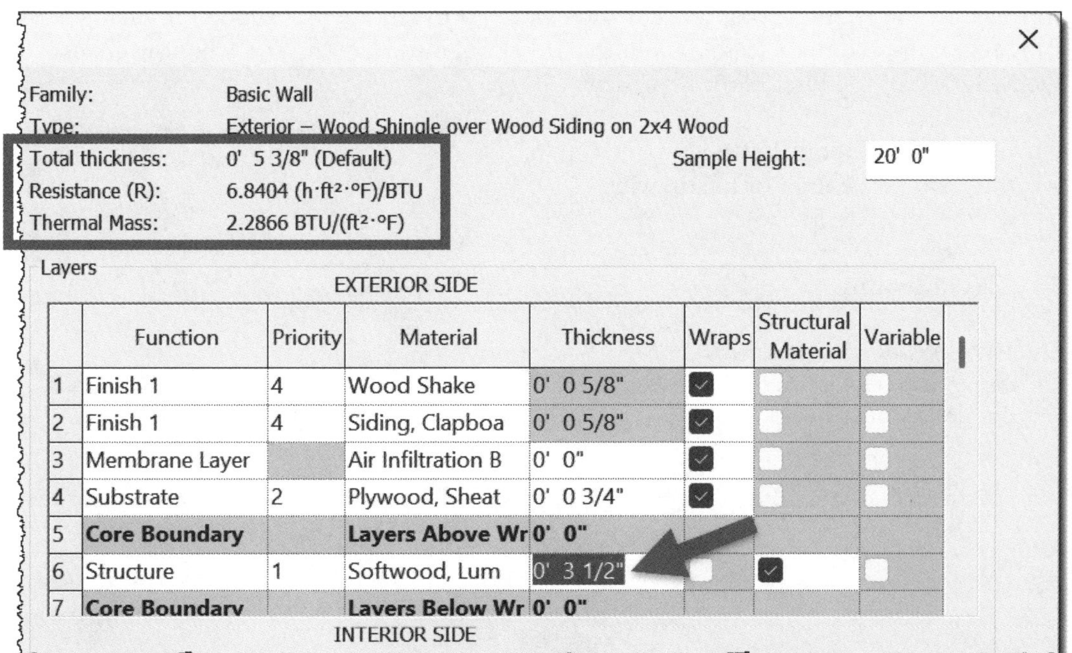

FIGURE 5-2.14 Edit Assembly; change stud size to 2x4

The next step is to change the wall type for the three walls around the garage.

31. Select the **Modify** button from the *Ribbon*; this cancels any active commands and allows you to select elements in your model.

32. **Zoom out** so you can see the entire plan. Dragging your mouse from the upper-right to the lower-left, make a *crossing window* to select the three garage walls, **or** hold down **Ctrl** and click each wall (these are the three walls on the far left).

33. With the walls selected, pick **Basic Wall: Exterior – Wood Shingle over Wood Siding on 2x4 Wood Stud** from the *Type Selector* drop-down; see tip below.

You should notice a change in wall thickness; the **location line** (face, center, etc.) does not move. You had *Finish Face: Exterior* selected when you drew the walls, so the exterior side of the wall does not move, which is good.

> ***TIP:*** *If, after selecting all the walls, the* Type Selector *is grayed out and the contextual tab says* Multi-Select, *you have some other type of element selected, such as text or dimensions (although you have not been instructed to draw anything but walls yet) or one of the four elevation tags. Try to find those objects and delete them, but DO NOT delete the elevation tags. You can also click the Filter button on the Ribbon when objects are selected and uncheck the types of elements to exclude from the current selection.*

For many walls, Revit can display more refined linework and hatching within the walls. This is controlled by the *Detail Level* option for each view. At the moment, making this change will only reveal the exterior sheathing, but this is helpful information. You will now change the Detail Level for the First Floor Plan view.

34. Click on the **Detail Level** icon in the lower-left corner of the drawing window (Figure 5-2.15).

35. Select **Medium**.

    FYI: *This view adjustment is only for the current view, as are all changes made via the* View Control Bar.

FIGURE 5-2.15 Detail Level; set to medium

You may need to zoom in, but you should now see a line added for the exterior sheathing. If you did not pay close enough attention when drawing the walls originally, some of your walls may show the sheathing to the inside of the building.

> *TIP: On the View tab, you can select* Thin Lines *to temporarily turn off the line weights; this has no effect on plotting.*

36. Select **Modify** (or press **Esc**); select a wall. You will see a symbol that allows you to flip the wall orientation by clicking it (Figure 5-2.16).

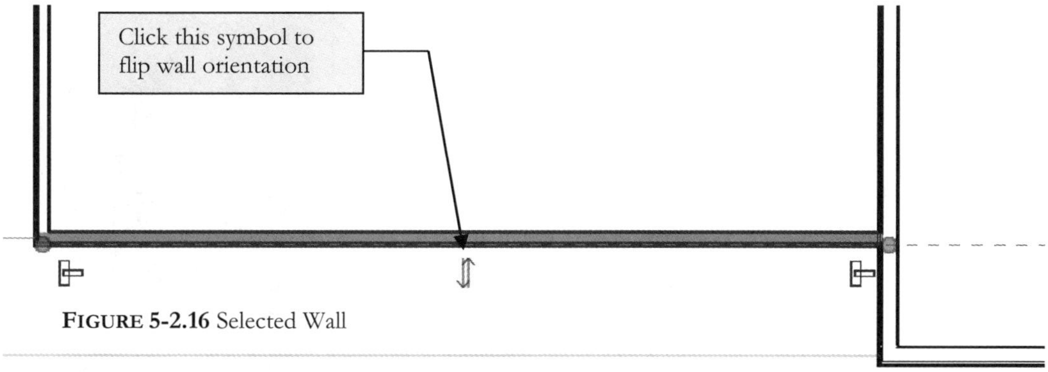

FIGURE 5-2.16 Selected Wall

37. Whether you need to adjust walls or not, click on the flip symbol to experiment with its operation.

> *TIP: The flip symbol is always on the exterior side, or what Revit thinks is the exterior side, of the wall.*

38. If some walls do need to be adjusted so the sheathing and flip symbol are to the exterior, do it now. You may need to select the wall(s) and use the Move tool to reposition them to match the required dimensions.

> *TIP: Walls are flipped about the Location Line, which can be changed via the Properties Palette. So changing the Location Line to Wall Centerline before flipping the wall will keep the wall in the same position. Be sure to change the Location Line back to Exterior Face.*

TIP: You can use the **Move** *tool on the Ribbon to accurately move walls. The steps are the same as in the previous chapters!*

Follow these steps to move an element:

- *Select the wall*
- *Click the Move icon*
- *Pick any point on the wall*
- *Start moving the mouse in the correct direction; do not click!*
- *Start typing the distance you want to move the wall and press Enter.*

39. You can see your progress nicely with a 3D view. Click the **Default 3D View** icon on the *QAT*. In the enlarged image, walls are shaded to make the image clearer (Figure 5-2.17).

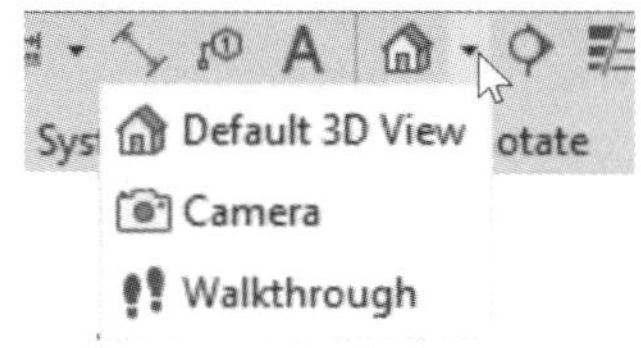

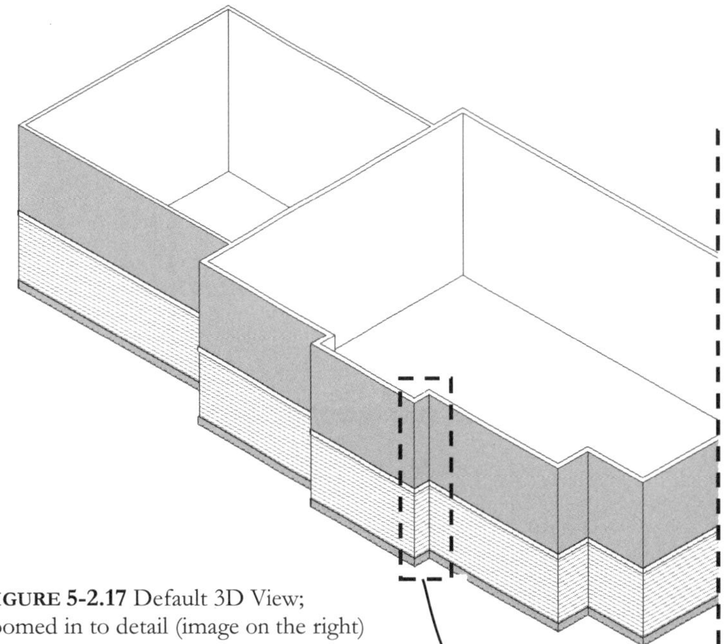

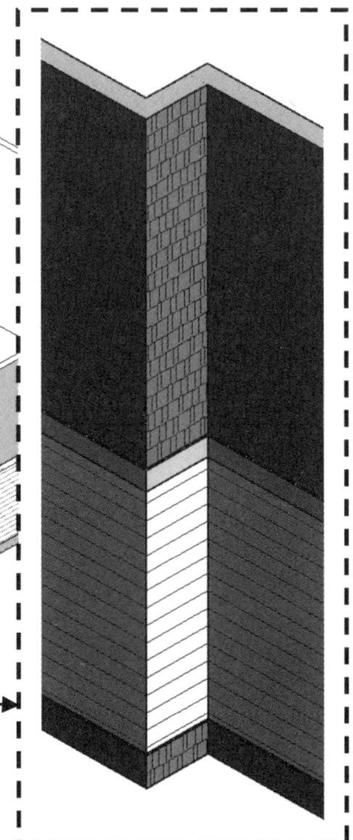

FIGURE 5-2.17 Default 3D View; zoomed in to detail (image on the right)

If you zoom in on the walls, you can see how much detail Revit can store in a wall type. By picking a few points, you defined the wall's width, height, and exterior finish materials.

The last thing you will do in this exercise is to adjust the height of the walls at the garage and a portion of the living room; refer to the image on the book's cover. Revit allows you to modify the building model in any view. You will make the wall height adjustments in the current 3D View, per the following steps.

40. In the *3D View*, click to select the three exterior garage walls.

> ***TIP:*** *Holding down the Ctrl key allows you to select multiple elements, while holding down the Shift key allows for subtraction from the current selection set. The total number of selected items is listed in the lower right, on the Status Bar; make sure it says "3."*

You will notice, similar to other views, when an element is selected in a 3D view the entire object temporarily turns blue and becomes transparent. This helps to see which objects are in the current selection set when several items are selected.

You should also see that the *Properties Palette* and *Ribbon* have been populated with options for the selected walls, just like the plan views. You will adjust the height setting in the *Properties Palette* next.

41. In the *Properties Palette*, change the *Unconnected Height* parameter to **12′-0″** and then click **Apply** (or, simply move your cursor back into the drawing area).

42. Make the same height adjustment to the three exterior walls at the Eastern most (i.e., right) portion of the living room (Figure 5-2.18).

43. Close the *3D View* and switch back to the *First Floor Plan* view.

44. Using the **Save As** command, save your project as **ex5-2.rvt**.

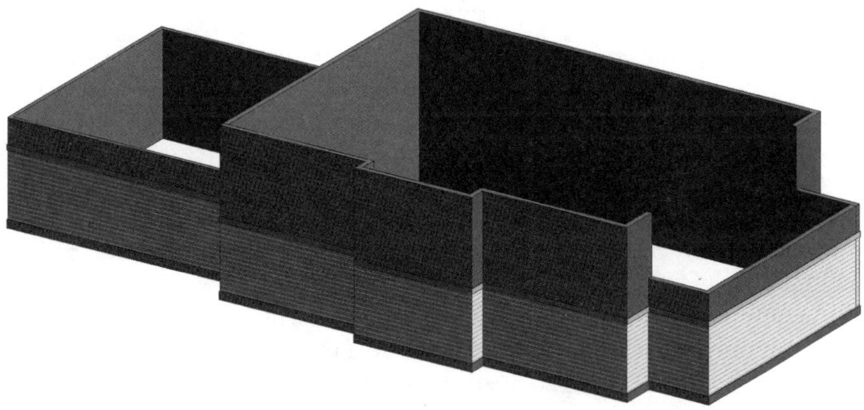

FIGURE 5-2.18 Completed exercise

TIP: *Holding down the Shift key while pressing the mouse wheel button lets you orbit the building. You will have to experiment with how the mouse movements relate to the building orbit. Selecting an item first causes that item to remain centered on the screen during orbit.*

Exercise 5-3:
Interior Walls

In this lesson you will draw the interior walls for the first floor. Using the line sketching and editing techniques you have studied in previous lessons, you should be able to draw the interior walls with minimal information.

Overview on How Plans are Typically Dimensioned:

The following is an overview of how walls are typically dimensioned in a floor plan; however, this can vary widely by region and design firm. This information is intended to help you understand the dimensions you will see in the exercises, as well as prepare you for the point when you dimension your plans, in a later lesson.

Wood or metal stud walls are typically dimensioned to the centers of the walls. Here are a few reasons why you should dimension to the center of the stud rather than to the face of the gypsum board:

- The contractor is laying out the walls in a large "empty" area. The most useful dimension is to the center of the stud; that is where they will make a mark on the floor. If the dimension was to the face of the gypsum board, the contractor would have to stop and calculate the center of the stud, which is not always the center of the wall thickness; for example, a stud wall with one layer of gypsum board on one side and two layers of gypsum board over resilient channels on the other side of the stud.

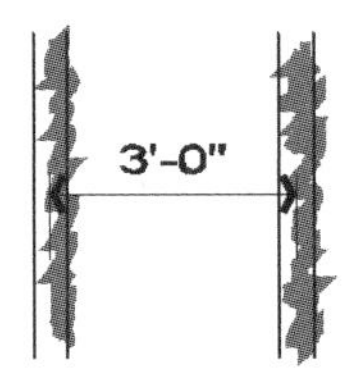

Dimension Example – Two Stud Walls

- When creating a continuous string of dimensions, the extra dimensions indicating the thickness of the walls would take up an excessive amount of room on the floor plans, space that would be better used by notes.

Occasionally, you should dimension to the face of a wall rather than the center; here's one example:

- When indicating design intent or building code requirements, you should reference the exact points/surfaces. For example, if you have uncommonly large trim around a door opening, you may want a dimension from the edge of the door to the face of the adjacent wall. Another example would be the width of a hallway; if you want a particular width you would dimension between the two faces of the wall and add the text "clear" below the dimension to make it known without question that the dimension is not to the center of the wall (maybe this is required by code for egress).

Dimensions for masonry and foundation walls:

- Foundation and masonry walls are dimensioned to the nominal face and not the center. These types of walls are modular (e.g., 8″x8″x16″) so it is helpful, for both designer and builder, to have dimensions that relate to the masonry wall's "coursing."

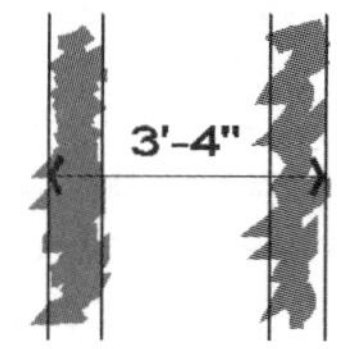

Dimension Example
– Two masonry Walls

Dimensions from a stud wall to a masonry wall:

- The rules above apply for each side of the dimension line. For example, a dimension for the exterior foundation wall to an interior stud wall would be from the exterior face of the foundation wall to the center of the stud on the interior wall.

Again, you will not be dimensioning your drawings right away, but Revit makes it easy to comply with the conventions above.

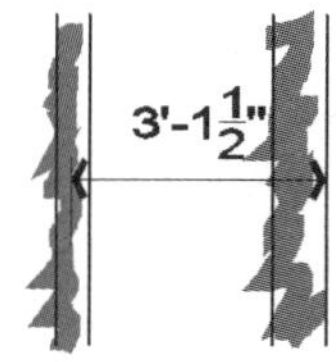

Dimension Example
– Stud to masonry

Adjust Wall Settings:

1. In the First Floor 'floor plan' view, select **Wall** from the *Architecture* tab on the *Ribbon.*

2. Make the following changes to the wall options in the *Properties Palette* and *Ribbon* (similar to Figure 5-2.1):
    - Wall style: **Interior – 4 ½″ partition**
    - Top Constraint: **Second Floor** (rather than unconnected)
    - Location Line: **Wall Centerline**

Contos Residence

Image courtesy of Anderson Architects
Alan H. Anderson, Architect, Duluth, MN

Drawing the Interior Walls:

Now that you have the perimeter drawn, you will draw a few interior walls. When drawing floor plans it is good practice to sketch out the various wall systems you think you will be using; this will help you determine what thickness to draw the walls. Drawing the walls at the correct thickness helps later when you are fine-tuning things.

Although Revit provides most of the wall types required, it is a good idea for the student to understand exactly what is being drawn.

Take a moment to think about the basic interior wall in a residential project. It typically consists of the following:

- 2x4 wood studs
  (actual stud size is 1½″ x 3½″)
- ½″ gypsum board

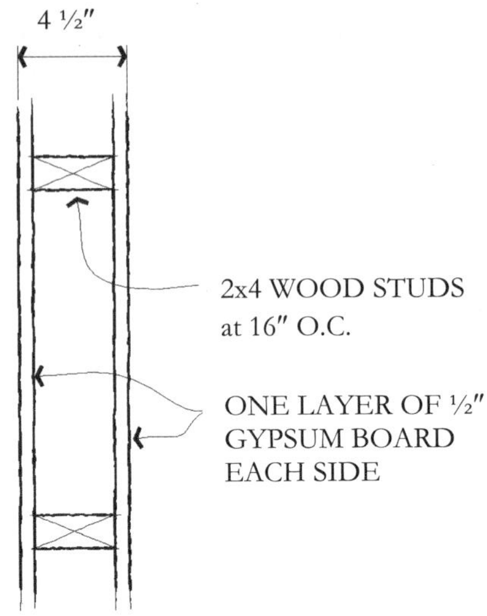

FIGURE 5-3.1
Sketch – Plan view of interior wall system

The wall system described above is shown in Figure 5-3.1.

Note: All your interior walls should be drawn **4½″** <u>for each floor</u>.

3. Draw a wall approximately as shown in Figure 5-3.2. You will adjust its exact position in the next step. ***TIP:*** *Click near the center of each exterior wall and make sure the wall is snapped to the vertical reference plane (vertical relative to the computer screen).*

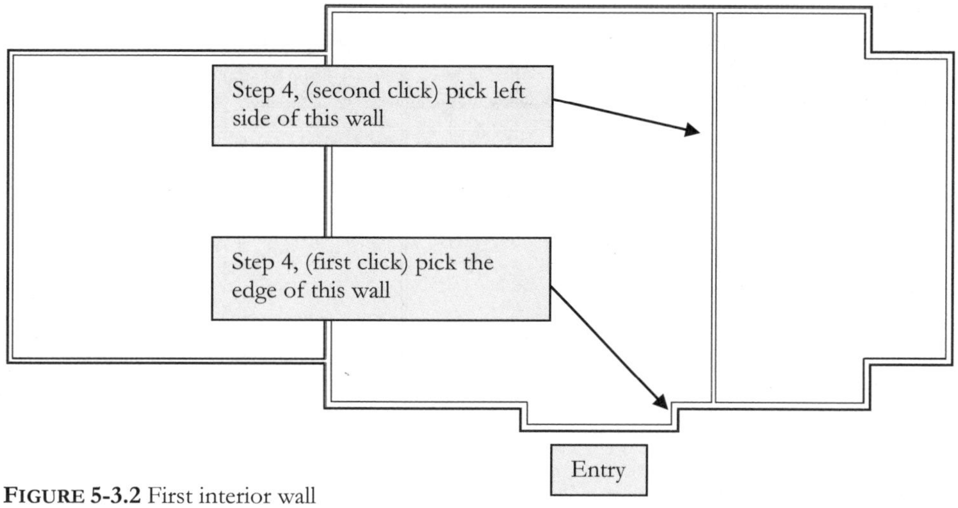

FIGURE 5-3.2 First interior wall

4. Use the ***Align*** tool to align the interior wall you just drew with the edge of the exterior wall (Figure 5-3.2). Set *Prefer* to *Wall Faces* on the *Ribbon*. When you are done, the wall should look like Figure 5-3.3.

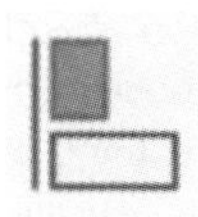

FYI: You do not need to lock this alignment.

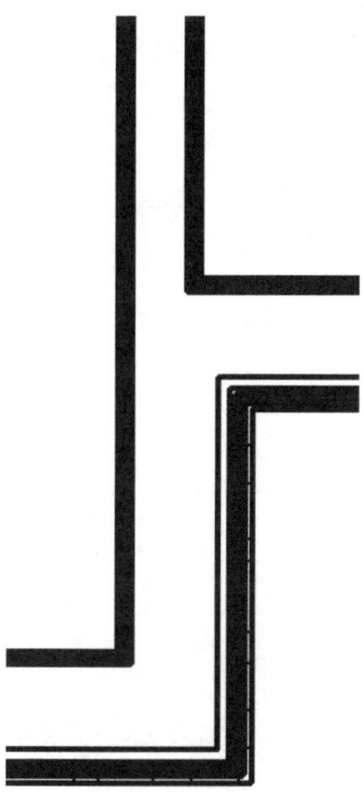

FIGURE 5-3.3 Aligned wall

5. Create the same wall for the West side of the entry, repeating the steps above.

Next, you will draw a handful of walls per the given dimensions. You will use the same partition type (4½″ partition).

6. Draw the interior walls shown in Figure 5-3.4; see the tips below to help you sketch the walls more accurately.
   a. All dimensions are from the exterior face of exterior walls and the centerline of interior walls.

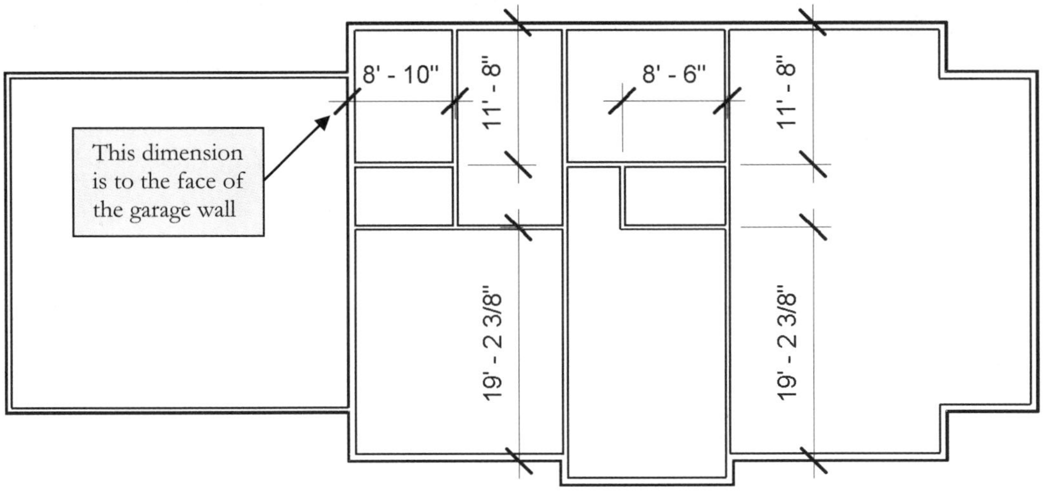

FIGURE 5-3.4 Layout dimensions for first floor interior walls

TIP - DIMENSION WITNESS LINE CONTROL:

When sketching walls, you can adjust the exact position of the wall after its initial placement. However, the temporary dimensions do not always reference the desired wall location (left face, right face, or center). You will see how easy it is to adjust a dimension's witness line location so you can place the wall exactly where you want it.

First, you will be introduced to some dimension terminology. The two "boxed" notes below are only for permanent dimensions, the others are for both permanent and temporary.

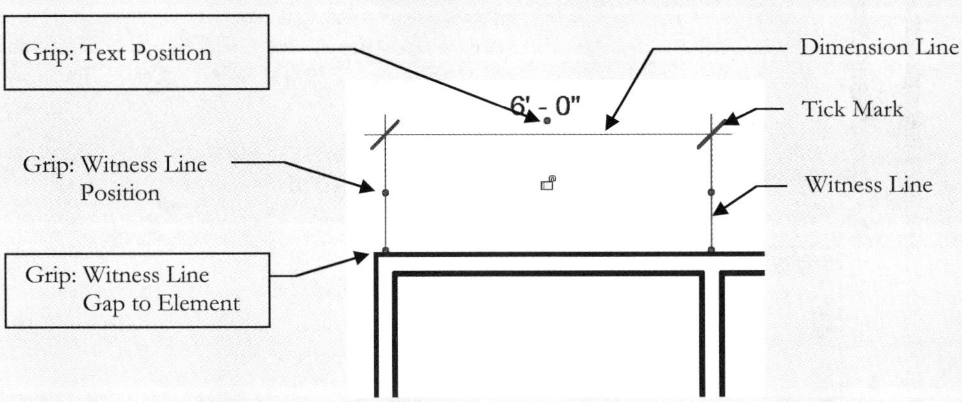

Next, you will adjust the witness lines to modify the inside clear dimension between the walls in the illustration above.

When you select a wall, you will see temporary dimensions, as shown in the image on the next page.

TIP - DIMENSION WITNESS LINE CONTROL: (CONTINUED FROM PREVIOUS PAGE)

NOTE: *Some elements do not display temporary dimensions; in that case, you can usually click the "Activate Controls and Dimensions" button on the Ribbon to see them.*

Clicking, not dragging, on the witness line grip toggles the witness line between the location options (left face, right face, center). In the example below, the grip for each witness line has been clicked (not dragged) until both witness lines refer to the "inside" of the room.

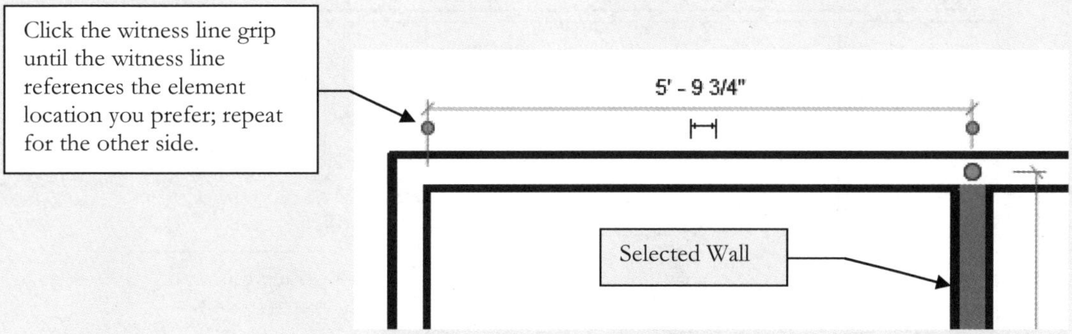

In the above example, the temporary dimension could now be modified, which would adjust the wall's location to a specific inside or clear dimension.

Not only can you adjust the witness line about a given element, but you can also move the witness line to another element. This is useful because Revit's temporary dimensions, for a selected element, do not always refer to the desired element. You can relocate a witness line (temporary or permanent) by clicking and dragging the grip; see example below.

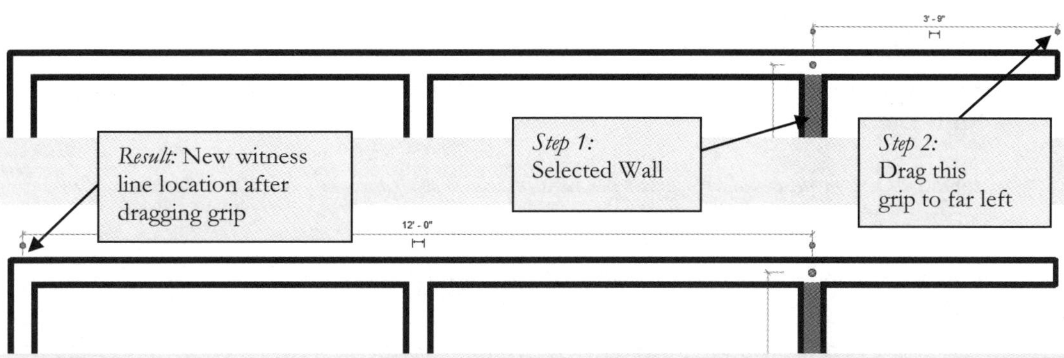

Next, you will use the *Trim* tool to remove a portion of the wall that is not needed.

7. Select **Trim** from the *Modify* tab.

8. Select the two walls identified in Figure 5-3.5.

FYI: The walls can be selected in either order.

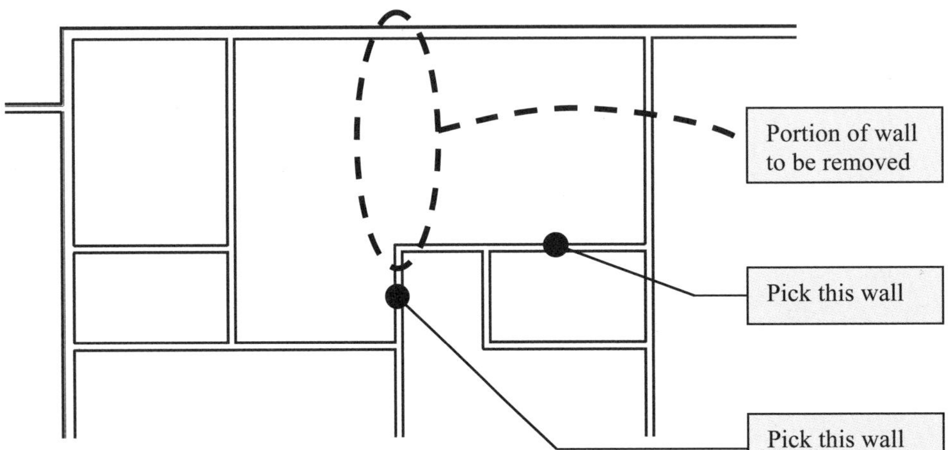

FIGURE 5-3.5 Trimmed wall

Modify an Existing Wall:

Next, you want to change the portion of wall between the house and the garage. Currently, the wall is your typical exterior wall which includes siding on the garage side. The entire wall is one element, so to only change the interior portion you will need to split the current wall, trim the corners and then draw a new interior wall.

9. **Zoom** in on the interior garage wall and select the **Modify → Modify → Split Element** tool.

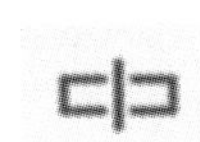

FYI: This will break a wall into two; when used in plan it splits the wall vertically and when used in a section a horizontal split results.

10. Pick somewhere in the middle of the wall (Figure 5-3.6a).

11. Use the **Trim** tool to trim the corners so the exterior wall only occurs at exterior conditions. Select **Unjoin Elements** (see "Warning Prompt" section on the next page).

TIP: Select the portion of wall you wish to retain (Figure 5-3.6b).

Warning prompt:
While trimming the exterior walls, you will get a warning message when you try to trim the wall that touches the two (horizontal) interior walls. Revit is pointing out that these walls are joined and, in order to proceed, need to be un-joined.

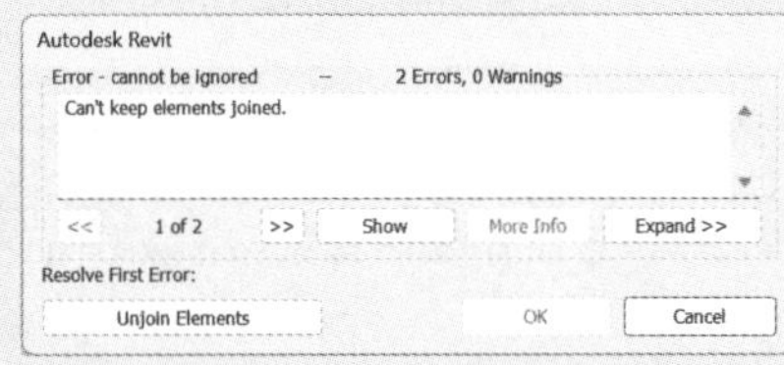

In this case you can click the *Unjoin Elements* button to allow Revit to proceed with the *Trim* operation. The walls will be re-joined to the new interior wall that you will sketch in a moment.

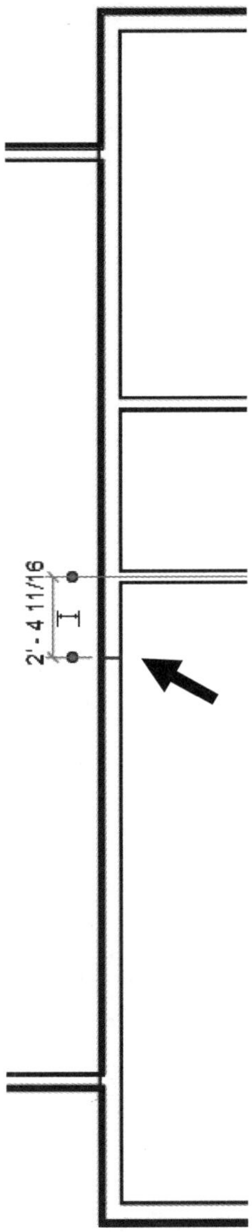

FIGURE 5-3.6A Split wall

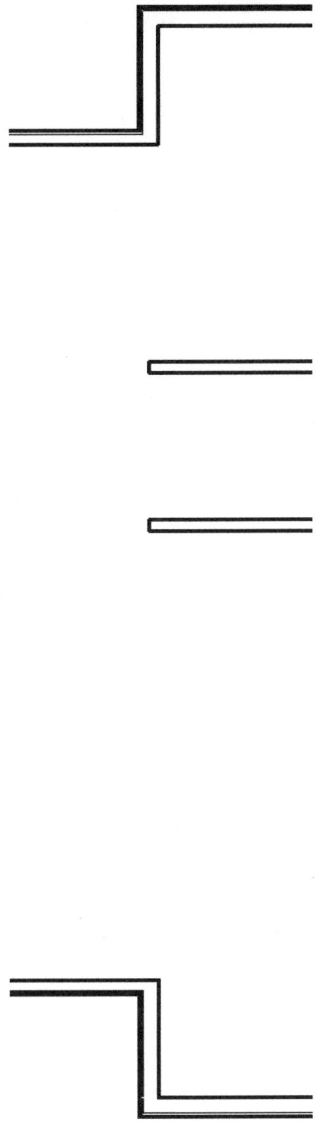

FIGURE 5-3.6B Trim wall

Additional Custom Wall Types:

Next, you will create a new interior partition type using a copy of the original exterior wall type as a starting point. It is easier to start with a wall that is similar to the one you wish to create.

Structurally, this wall could probably only require 2x4 studs. However, directly above this wall will be an exterior wall (the portion above the garage roof) that needs to have 2x6 studs to allow for adequate insulation. Additionally, you will want to insulate the interior garage wall; this helps with noise and heat loss when the large garage door is opened in -20 F degree weather!

Truthfully, in this case it may be easier to start with a new wall, given the complexity of the exterior wall you are about to modify. However, this will give you a little more insight on how the exterior wall is constructed and the interworking of Revit's wall assembly.

12. Using wall type **Exterior – Wood Shingle over Wood Siding on Wood Stud** as a starting point, create a new wall type named **Exterior – Garage Wall (Interior)**. *(Remember to click Edit Type and then Duplicate; see page 5-16.)*

13. Click the **Edit** button next to the *Structure* parameter.

Typically, you will want to give walls more generic names so they can be used elsewhere in the project. Because you know this wall will only be used once, it is easier to give it a more descriptive name so it is not confused with other wall types later.

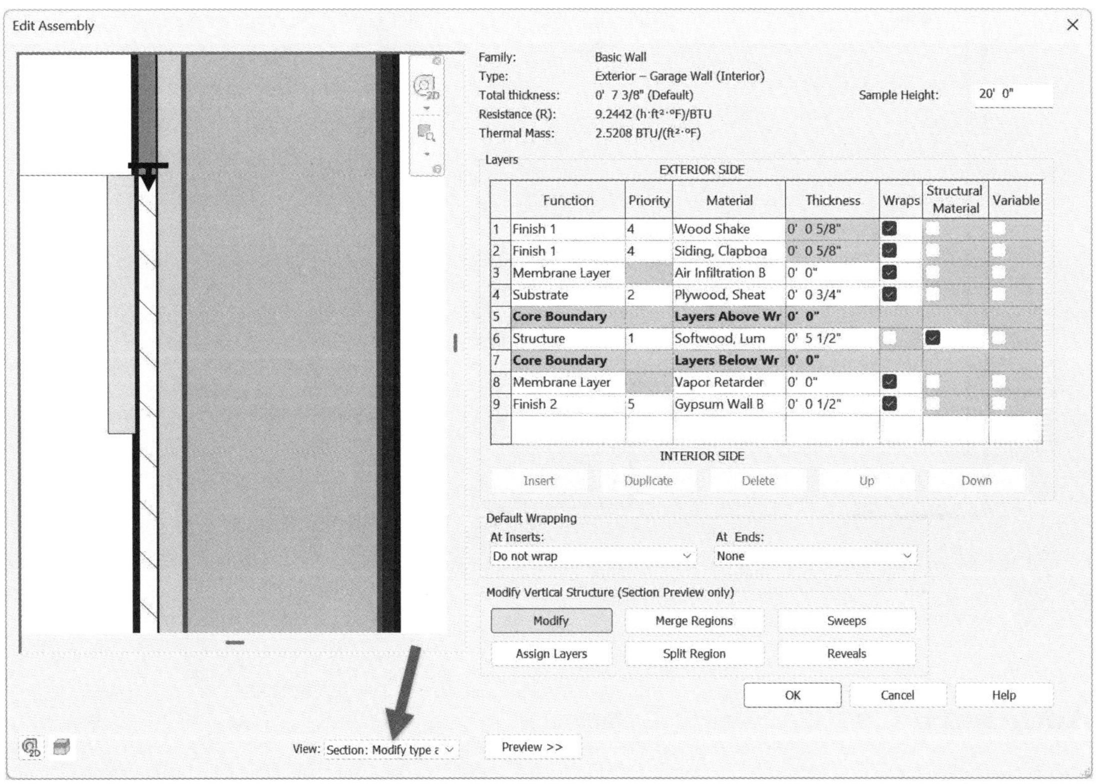

FIGURE 5-3.7 Edit Assembly dialog (see step 14)

The *Edit Assembly* dialog shown in Figure 5-3.7 will be modified as follows (starting in step 14). This is just an overview; the detailed instructions will follow:

- First, you will delete the horizontal sweeps.
  - A sweep is a closed 2D shape that is extruded along the length of a wall at a given height; a unique material can be specified.
  - This wall type currently has two sweeps (refer back to Figure 5-2.17): one at the base of the wall and another near the second floor line.

- Second, you will merge the two "vertically stacked" exterior finish layers so you can delete the exterior finish layers.
  - A layer can be split vertically into multiple regions; the exterior layer of this wall style is split into two regions. One has the material "Wood-Shake" assigned, and the other has "Siding, Clapboard" assigned.
  - Looking at Figure 5-3.7, you can visually see which layers are split vertically by looking at the Thickness column; the shaded "Thickness" cells are "vertically stacked" layers.
  - Vertically stacked layers must be *Merged* back into one region before they can be deleted from the layers list.

- Finally, you will change the plywood sheathing to gypsum board and move the air barrier between the gypsum board and the studs.

14. In the *Edit Assembly* dialog, make sure the *Preview* pane is visible (*click on the <<Preview button*) and then select **Section: modify type attributes** from the *View* list (Figure 5-3.7).

15. Click the **Sweeps** button to load the *Wall Sweeps* dialog.

16. Delete both *Wall Sweeps*: click on the row number to select the row, and then click the **Delete** button (Figure 5-3.8). Click **OK** to close the dialog box when done.

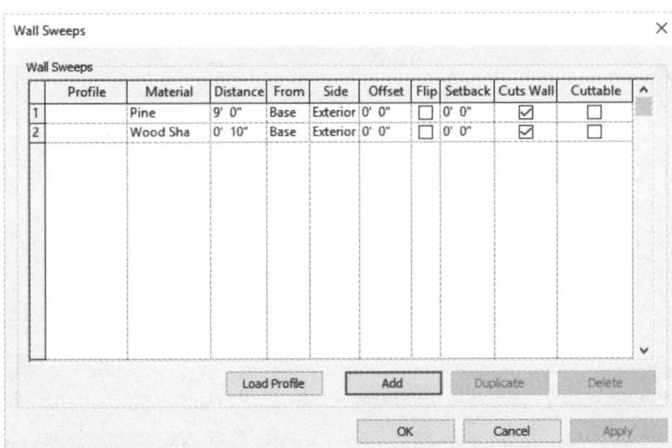

FIGURE 5-3.8 Wall Sweeps to be deleted

The two rectangular sweeps that represented the horizontal trim are now removed from the preview section.

Also, notice in Figure 5-3.8, this is where the material is assigned to the sweep.

Next, you will merge the two "vertically stacked" layers into one region. The tricky part here is that Revit will let you merge any two regions, so you need to keep an eye on the cursor and the pop-up tooltip.

17. Select the **Merge Regions** button.

18. Using the *scroll wheel* on the mouse, zoom in on the region split line at the top edge of the vertical dimension; you need to click in the *Preview* window to activate that area first (Figure 5-3.7).

19. Move your cursor over the short horizontal line and then tap the **Tab** key until the cursor changes to a horizontal line with an arrow pointing downward and the tooltip states that **Layer 1 and Layer 2 will be merged** (see Figure 5-3.7), and then click.

FYI: *You can also* Pan *in the Preview pane using your scroll wheel button.*

20. Individually select the *Layer* numbers 1 and 2 to select the row, and **Delete** them. This will delete the two exterior finish layers: shakes and siding.

FYI: *Watch the Preview pane while you do this.*

21. Click the *Air Infiltration Barrier* **Membrane Layer** (row 1) and then click the **Down** button to move the location of the air barrier within the wall.

22. Do not change the wood stud layer; leave it at 5½″.

23. Change the ¾″ sheathing layer by clicking in each cell in that row and then clicking the down-arrow that appears to the right; change the *Function* to **Finish 1** , *Priority* to **4**, *Material* to **Gypsum Wall Board**, *Thickness* to **½″** (Figure 5-3.9). **OK** to close the dialogs.

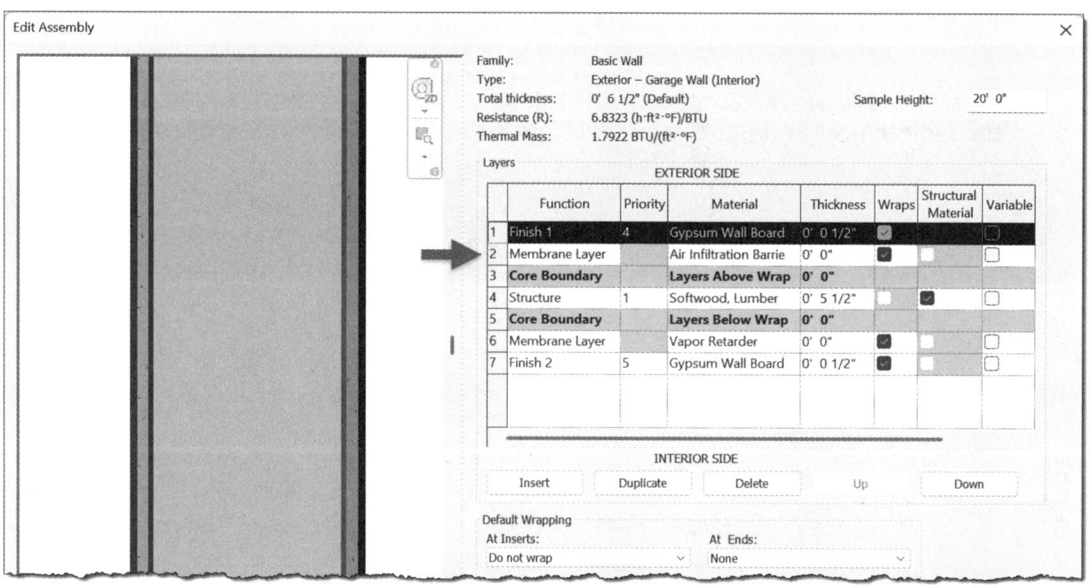

FIGURE 5-3.9 Modified edit assembly dialog

Now that you have created a new wall type, you can sketch the wall in the first floor plan view.

24. With your new wall type selected in the *Type Selector*, use the ***Wall*** tool to sketch a wall between the garage and the house.
    a. Set the wall's *Top Constraint* to **Second Floor**.
    b. Set the *Location Line* to **Finish Face**: **Interior**, and then select the interior corner of the exterior wall.

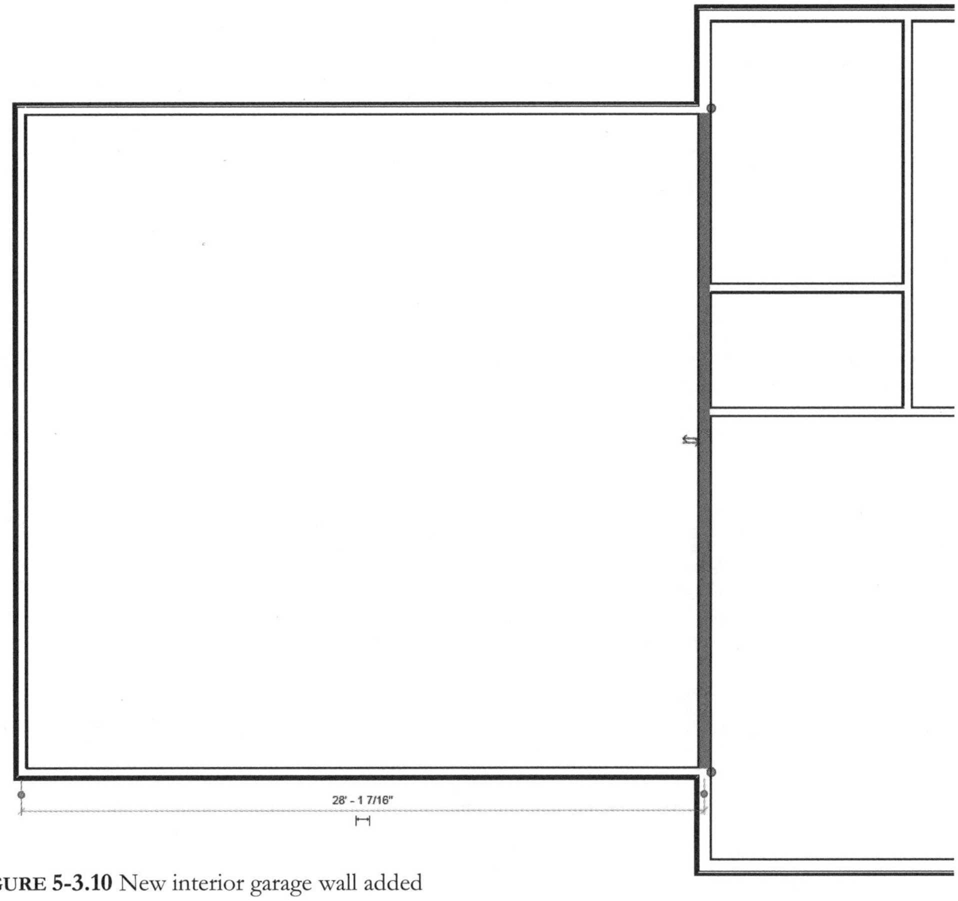

FIGURE 5-3.10 New interior garage wall added

It is important to remember that the "flip control" symbol is displayed on the exterior side of the wall when the wall is selected; this corresponds to the *Exterior Side* and *Interior Side* designations within the wall type editor. If your symbol is on the wrong side, click it to flip the wall and the symbol to the other side. You will then have to *Move* or *Align* the wall so it is flush with the adjacent exterior wall.

25. Save your project as **Ex5-3.rvt**.

Exercise 5-4:
Doors, Openings, and Windows

This lesson will take a closer look at inserting doors and windows.

Now that you have sketched the walls, you will add some doors. A door symbol, in a floor plan view, indicates which side the hinges are on and the direction the door opens.

New doors are typically shown open 90 degrees in floor plans to avoid conflicts, such as the door hitting an adjacent base cabinet. Additionally, to make it clear graphically, existing doors are often shown open only 45 degrees.

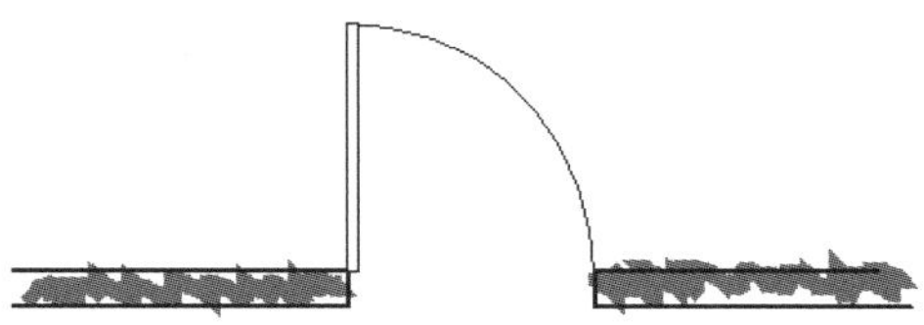

Door symbol Example – New Door drawn with 90 degree swing

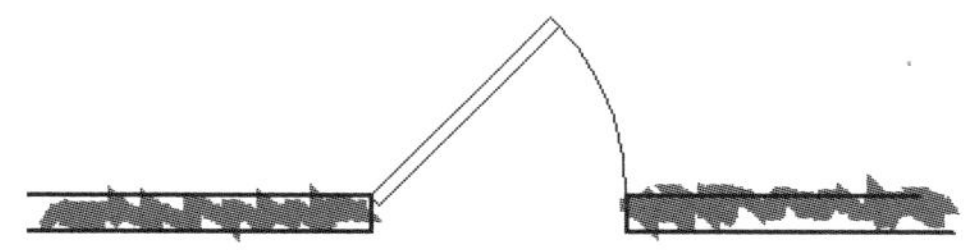

Door symbol Example – Existing Door shown with 45 degree swing

One of the most powerful features of any CAD program is its ability to reuse previously drawn content. With Revit, you can insert entire door systems (door, frame, trim, etc.). You drew a 2D door symbol in Lesson 4; however, you will now use Revit's powerful *Door* tool, which is fully 3D.

Doors in stud walls are dimensioned to the center of the door opening. On the other hand, doors in masonry walls are dimensioned to the face, similar to dimensioning masonry walls (see example below).

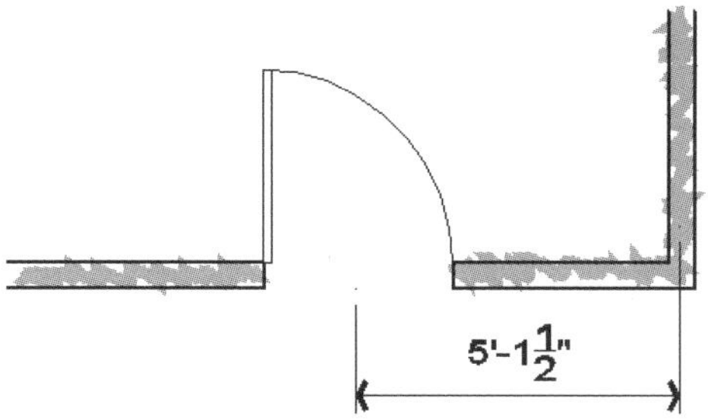

Door Dimension Example – Dimension to the center of the door opening

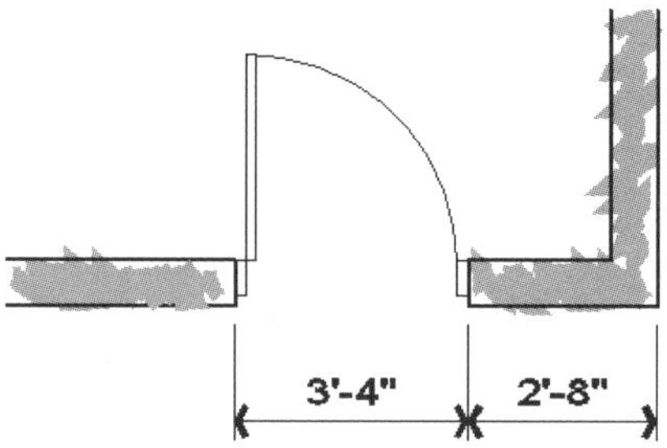

Door Dimension Example – Dimension the opening size and location

Loading Additional Door Families:

Revit has done an excellent job providing several different door families. This makes sense, seeing as doors are an important part of an architectural project. Some of the provided families include bi-fold, double, pocket, sectional (garage), and vertical rolling, among others.

Important: Be sure to download the content provided with this book as described on the inside front cover. You will also need some Autodesk Content from the Load Autodesk Content tool on the Insert tab, alternatively downloaded from https://autode.sk/30EJYkX.

The default template you started with *(Residential-Default.rte)* only provides four door *families*; each family contains multiple door sizes. If you want to insert other styles, you will need to load additional *families* from the library. This step is necessary because when you load a family, Revit actually copies the data into your project file. If every possible family were loaded into your project at the beginning, not only would it be hard to find what you want in a large list of doors, but also the project file would be several megabytes in size before you even drew the first wall.

You will begin this section by loading a few additional families into your project.

1. Open project ex5-3.rvt and **Save-As ex5-4.rvt.**

2. On the Insert tab, select **Load Autodesk Family** (Figure 5-4.1). **FYI:** This tool requires an internet connection, as the content is coming from the cloud.

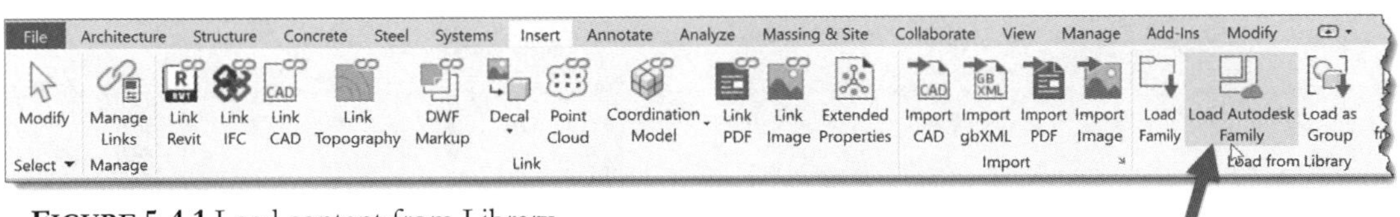

FIGURE 5-4.1 Load content from Library

3. Browse through the ***Doors \ Residential*** category for a moment.

   If you have manually downloaded the Autodesk content, the *Doors* folder is a sub-folder of the *English-Imperial* library. Using the Insert → Load Family tool, Revit should have taken you there by default; if not, you can browse to C:\ProgramData\Autodesk\RVT 2027\Libraries\English-Imperial\Doors.

Each file represents a *family*, each having one or more *Types* of varying sizes (Figure 5-4.2).

4. Leave the *Load Autodesk Family* dialog open for now.

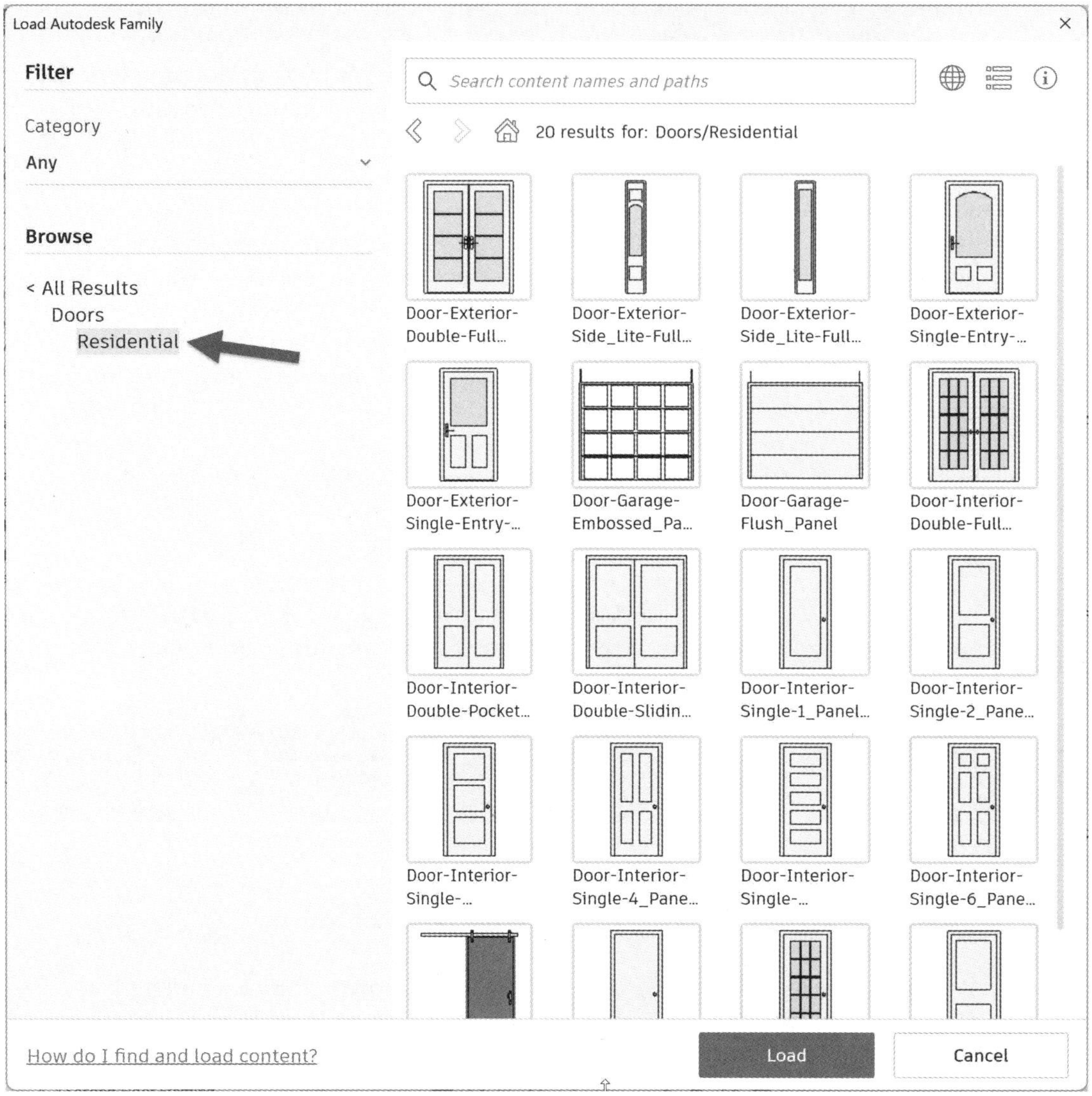

FIGURE 5-4.2 Load Autodesk Family tool

While loading some content a Type Catalog will appear listing available types; for doors, this will be a list of standard sizes. Since there are many options, it is often preferred to only load options required for the current project. More options can be loaded as needed, but limiting the options makes selection lists shorter and helps avoid selecting the wrong size. In the next step, you will see the Type Catalog and should select only the options indicated.

Load Content:

Next, you will load some content provided with Revit.

5. Load the following Door families, one at a time, selecting the specified sizes:
   a. Door-Exterior-Double-Full Glass-Wood_Clad
      - **72" x 80"**
   b. Door-Exterior-Side_Lite-Full Arch Glass-Wood_Clad
      - **15" x 80"**
   c. Door-Exterior-Single-Entry-Half Arch Glass-Wood_Clad
      - **36" x 80"**
   d. Door-Exterior-Single-Entry-Half Flat Glass-Wood_Clad
      - **36" x 80"**
   e. Door-Garage-Embossed_Panel
   f. Door-Interior-Single-2_Panel-Wood
      - **34" x 80"**
      - **36" x 80"**
   g. Door-Interior-Single-Pocket-2_Panel-Wood
      - **36" x 80"**

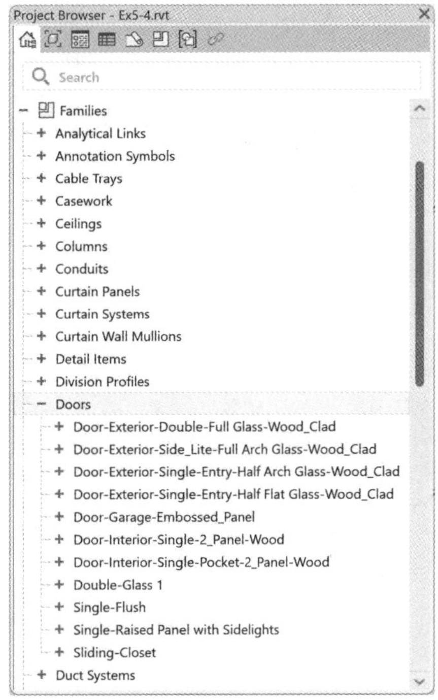

FIGURE 5-4.3 Loaded door families

6. In the *Project Browser*, expand the *Families* category and then *Doors* to see the loaded door families (Figure 5-4.3).

If you expand the *Doors* families in the *Project Browser,* you see the predefined door sizes (i.e., Family Types) associated with that family. Right-clicking a door size lets you rename, delete, or duplicate it. To add a door size, you duplicate the item and then modify its properties, as you did when creating a new wall.

You may want to create a folder to save all the families you download. This would make future access more convenient, especially if you did not have internet access at that time. This folder should probably not be in Revit's standard folder location, as it may be difficult to migrate the data after an upgrade (e.g., sorting custom files from default files).

Revit content can be found at various locations on the internet. You can try an internet search with text that reads something like "*Autodesk Revit families.*" As Revit's popularity grows, more and more product manufacturers are making families available for their products, making it easier for designers to incorporate those products into a project. For example, one can also download an extensive wall and ceiling library from United States Gypsum (USG) at www.usgdesignstudio.com. Additionally, you can visit www.augi.com (Autodesk Users Group International) or www.revitcity.com for Revit-related resources and content.

Next, you will start inserting the doors into the first floor plan.

7. With the *Door* tool selected, pick **Door-Exterior-Single-Entry-Half Flat Glass-Wood_Clad: 36" x 80"** from the *Type Selector* on the *Properties Palette.*

8. Select **Tag on Placement** on the *Ribbon* to toggle it on if needed (it is on when highlighted), and then place one door in the North exterior wall of the garage as shown in Figure 5-4.4.

Immediately after inserting the door, or when the door is selected, you can click the horizontal or vertical flip controls to position the door as desired.

Since "Tag on placement" was selected on the *Ribbon*, Revit automatically adds a *Door Tag* near the newly inserted door. The door itself stores information about the door, which can then be compiled into a door schedule. The doors are automatically numbered in the order they are placed. The number can be changed at any time to suit the designer's needs; you will do this later in the door schedule section. Most architects and designers use 1x or 1xx (e.g., 12 or 120) for first-floor door numbers and 2x or 2xx for second-floor door numbers.

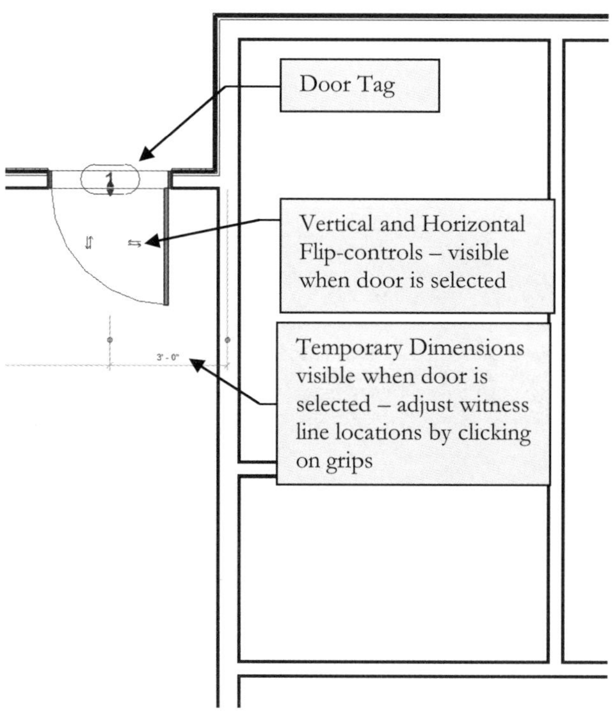

The *Door Tag* can be selected by clicking it, then dragging it to its new location. You may need to press the *Tab* key to pre-highlight the tag before you can select it.

Also, with the *Door Tag* selected, you can set the vertical/horizontal orientation and whether a leader is displayed when the tag is moved in the *Properties Palette.* The tag must be selected.

Tip: when the tag is selected, it can be repositioned using the arrow keys on the keyboard.

FIGURE 5-4.4 First door placed at rear of garage

9. Click *Modify* and then select the newly placed door; take a moment to review the information displayed in the *Properties Palette.*

> ***TIP:** If the Properties Palette is not visible, simply type "pp" on the keyboard; do not press Enter.*

Notice, in Figure 5-4.5, you see the *Instance Parameters,* which are options that can vary with each door, for example, *Sill Height* and *Door Number (Mark).* These parameters control the selection of elements during initial placement.

The *Type Parameters* are not visible in this dialog. To be sure you want to make changes that affect all doors of that type, Revit forces you to click the *Edit Type* button and make changes in the *Type Properties* dialog. Also, in the *Type Properties* dialog, you can add additional pre-defined door sizes to the *"Door-Exterior-Single-Entry-Half Flat Glass-Wood_Clad"* door family by clicking the *Duplicate* button, providing a new name and changing the "size" parameters for that new *Type.*

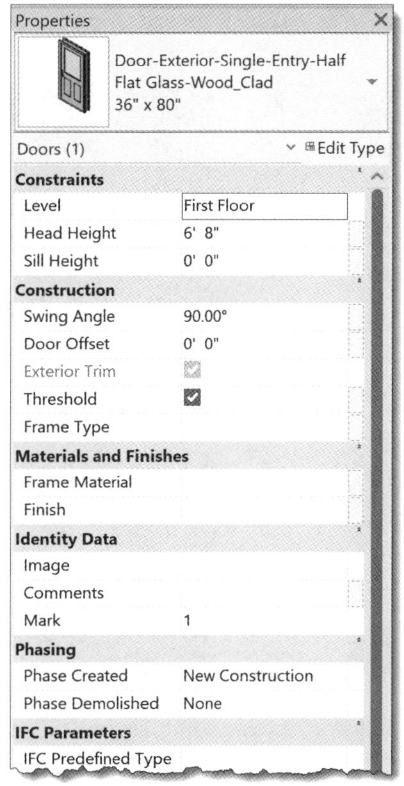

FIGURE 5-4.5
Properties for door

10. Finish inserting doors for the first floor as shown in Figure 5-4.6 per the following guidelines:

    h. Use the door types shown in Figure 5-4.6; the prefix "Door" and Interior/Exterior" have been omitted from the image due to limited space.

    i. Place **Door-Exterior-Side_Lite-Full Arch Glass-Wood_Clad: 15" x 80"** on each side of the front door.

    j. Doors across from each other in the *Mud Room* should align with each other.

    k. Place doors approximately as shown; exact location is not important.

    l. See the next page for information on sliding pocket doors.

    m. While inserting doors, you can control the door swing by moving the cursor to one side of the wall or the other and by using the spacebar on the keyboard.

    n. The order in which the doors are placed does not matter; this means your doors may have different numbers than the ones shown below.

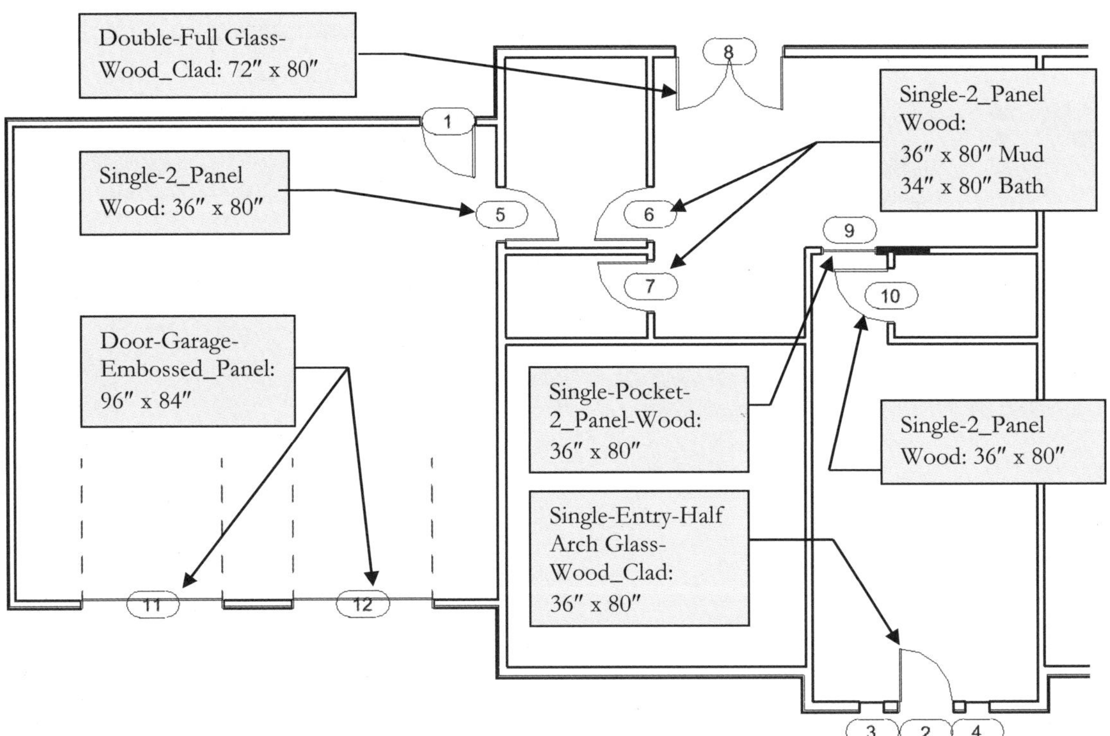

FIGURE 5-4.6 Doors to be inserted

Sliding Pocket Doors:

Sliding pocket doors are doors that slide into the wall rather than swinging open into a room. This type of door is convenient when the door will be open most of the time and you do not want, or have room for, an open door. On the other hand, if the door will be used often, like the door from the hallway into the bathroom, you should use a swinging door for ease of use and long-term durability.

One important thing to keep in mind when designing a room with a sliding door: the entire width of the door is in the wall when the door is fully open. That means you need space in the wall next to the door that equals the width of the door plus a few inches depending on the manufacturer. This includes plumbing and electrical that might be in the wall.

POCKET DOOR EXAMPLES – Double door and Single door photos (top); Installation illustration (bottom)

Images used by permission, KrisTrack www.kristrack.com

Insert Openings:

With the first floor doors in place, you will add three openings. An opening is similar to a door in that, when placed, it removes a portion of the wall, automatically creating a circulation route.

One common mistake is to split/break a wall, so the floor plan appears to have an opening. However, when a section is cut through the opening, there is no wall above the opening. This is also problematic when it comes to placing *Rooms* and the *Ceiling*.

One key to working successfully in Revit is to model the building project as you would build it, because that is how Revit is designed to work.

Next, you will place two larger openings in the walls between the *Foyer* and the *Living Room* and the *Dining Room*. A smaller opening will be placed in the wall between the *Dining Room* and the *Kitchen*. All three openings will be created using the built-in *Wall Opening* command.

11. Select **Architecture → Opening → Wall**; (Figure 5-4.7).

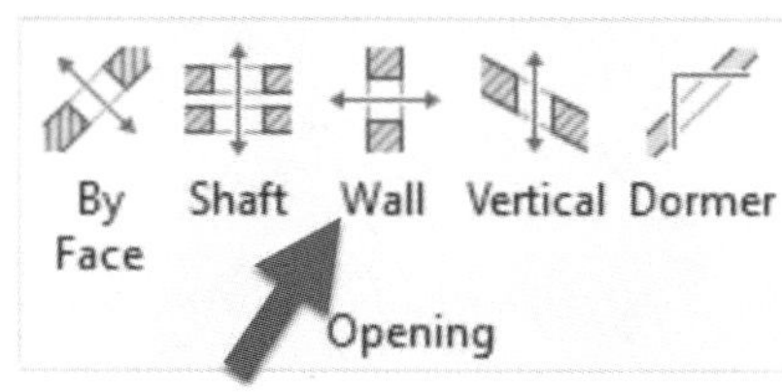

FIGURE 5-4.7 Opening panel

12. Place the three **openings** as shown in Figure 5-4.9.

    a. Select the wall to add an opening in.

    b. Pick two points along the wall to define the opening width (the exact value can be edited in the next step).

    c. Click *Modify*, select the opening, and edit the width using the temporary dimension; **5'-0"** <u>width</u>.

    d. While the opening is still selected, specify the height in the *Properties Palette* (Figure 5-4.8); <u>**Unconnected Height**</u> of **6'-8"**.

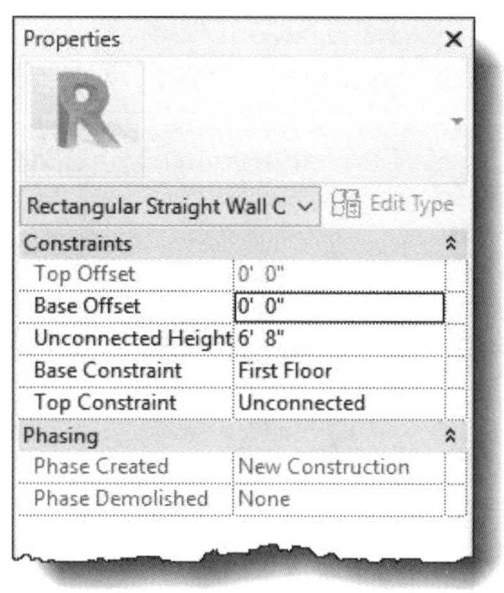

FIGURE 5-4.8 Wall opening properties

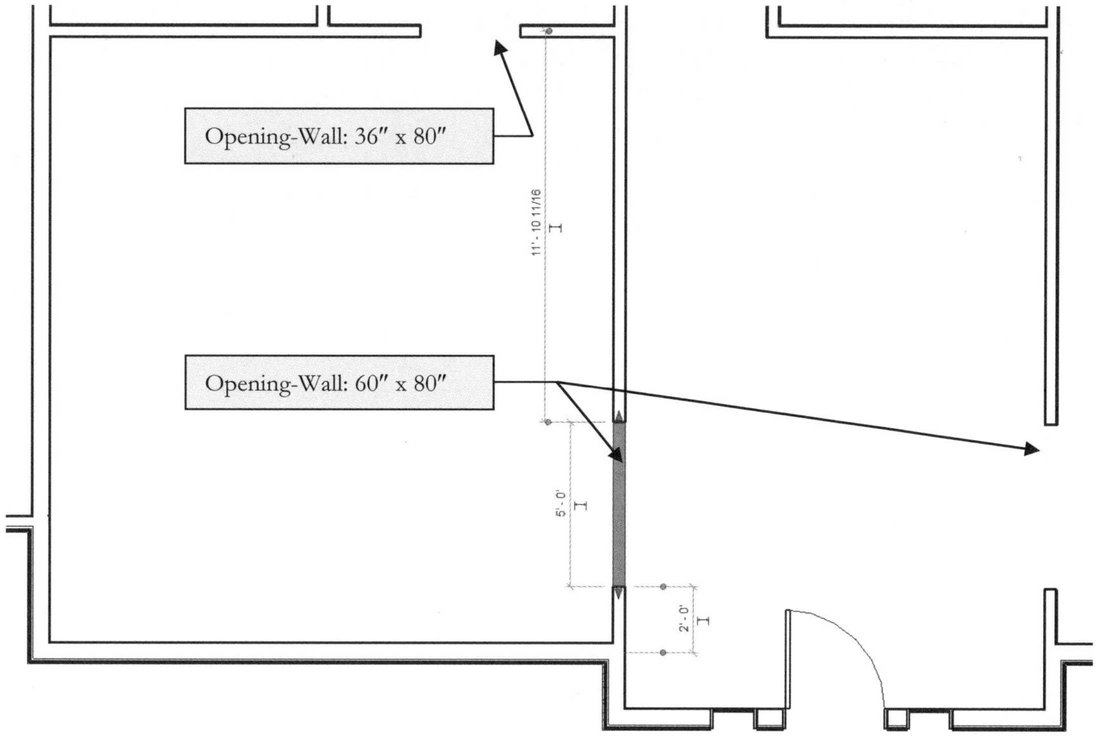

FIGURE 5-4.9 Openings placed in first floor plan

Insert Windows:

Adding windows to your project is very similar to adding doors. The template file you started from has three families preloaded into your project: Window-Casement-Double, Window-Double-Hung, and Fixed with Trim. Looking at the *Type Selector* drop-down, you will see the various sizes (Types) available for insertion. Additional families can be loaded in the same way you loaded the doors.

13. Similar to the steps just completed for the doors, load the window family **Window-Double-Hung** into your project, selecting **38" x 46"** and **38" x 62"** from the *Type Catalog* (Hold down the CTRL key to select multiple; select **Overwrite the existing version** when prompted).

14. Click the ***Window*** command on the *Architecture* tab, select **Window-Double-Hung: 38" x 62"** in the *Type Selector,* and make sure **Tag on Placement** is on, via the *Ribbon.*

15. Insert 9 windows as shown in **Figure 5-4.10**; be sure to adjust the window locations to match the dimensions shown, but do not add the dimensions. Be sure to click towards the exterior side of the wall, so the window has the proper orientation.

TIP: To edit location: Modify → select window → adjust temporary dimension witness lines → edit temporary dimension text.

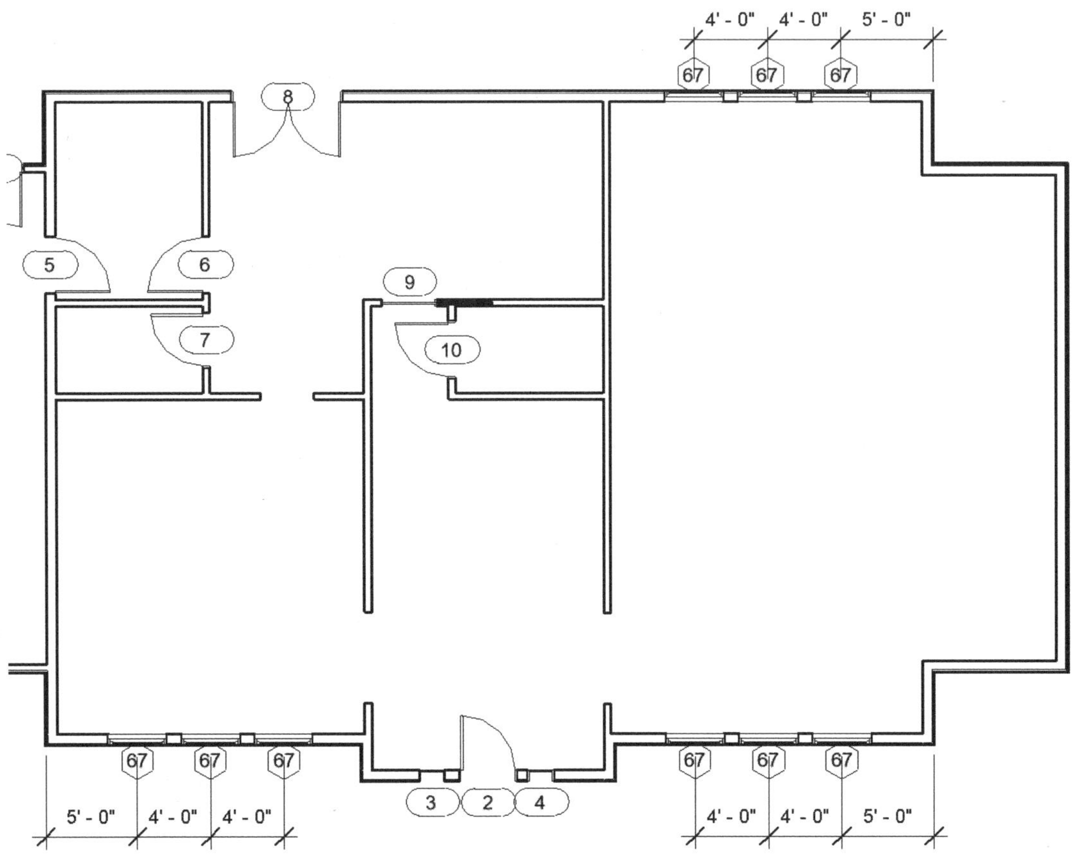

FIGURE 5-4.10 Nine windows added: Window-Double-Hung: 38" x 62"

With a window *Type*, within a family, not only is the window size pre-defined, but the vertical distance off the floor is as well. Next, you will see where this setting is stored.

16. Select one of the windows that you just placed in the walls, and then notice the information presented in the *Properties Palette.*

As previously discussed, this palette shows the various settings for the selected item: a window in this case (Figure 5-4.11). The sill height will be adjusted in the next step.

As you might guess, the same window type can have more than one sill height (i.e., the distance from the floor to the bottom of the window). So, Revit lets you adjust this setting on a window-by-window (instance) basis; this is called an *Instance Parameter.*

Another setting you might have noticed by now is *Phase Created.* This is part of what makes Revit a 4D program; the fourth dimension is time. Again, you might have several existing windows and several new ones in a building addition, all the same size. Revit lets you do that!

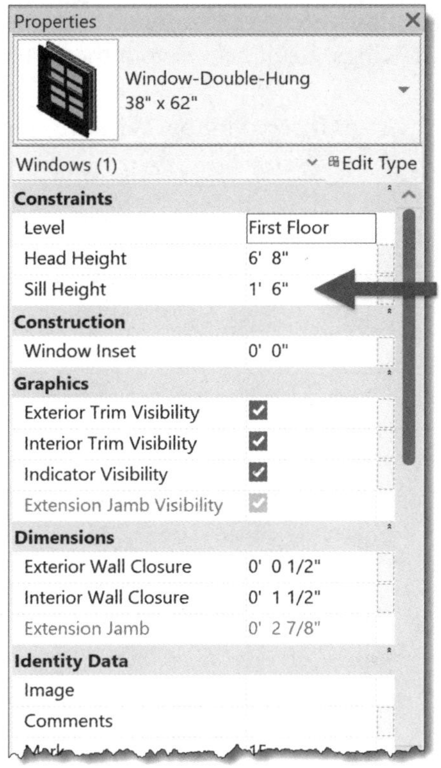

FIGURE 5-4.11 Element Properties

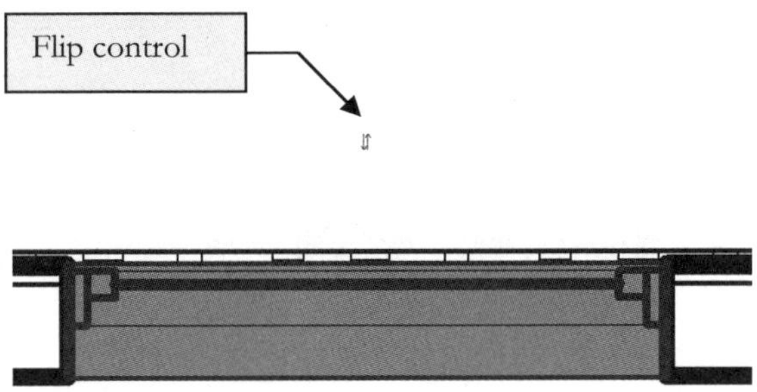

FIGURE 5-4.12 Window selected

Notice that a *Flip Control* icon is shown when the window is selected, similar to doors (Figure 5-4.12). This icon should be on the exterior side of the wall. If not, simply click on the icon to flip the window's orientation within the wall.

17. For all windows, change the *Sill Height* to **1′-6″** and make sure the **Flip Control** icon is on the exterior side of the wall; do this for all nine windows.

Next, you will insert several double-hung windows that are not as tall in the less prominent rooms, including the Kitchen, so the cabinets will fit below the windows. However, if you did place the tall windows in the *Kitchen*, you would realize it as soon as you tried to place the base cabinets and generate interior elevations or sections. This is because the entire Revit project is one 3D database.

Compare the above-mentioned conflict with traditional CAD, where 2D elevations have nothing to do with floor plans, sections, or interior elevations. With traditional CAD, you could draw the exterior elevations with the tall windows and place cabinets under it in plan view, and then draw an interior elevation showing the cabinets and a shorter window. The windows are usually ordered and rough openings framed based on the exterior elevation drawings. Revit helps avoid these costly mistakes.

18. Insert window **Window-Double-Hung: 38″ x 46″** as shown in **Figure 5-4.13**; use *Instance Properties* to set the *Sill Height* to **2′-10″**; place 9 windows total.

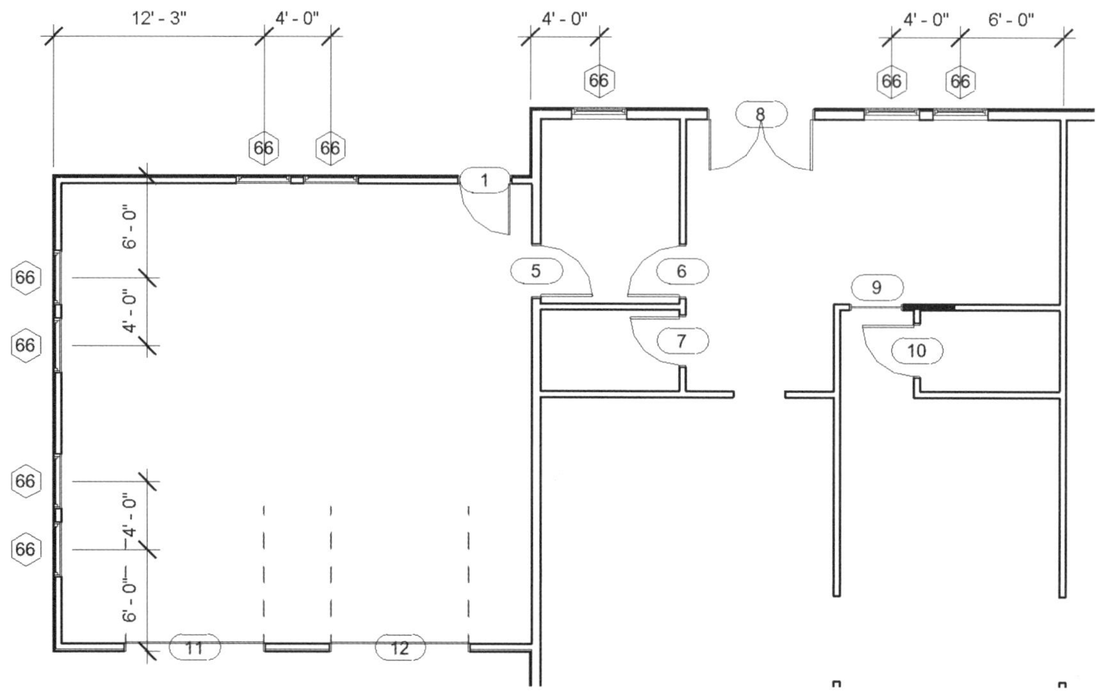

FIGURE 5-4.13 Nine more windows added to the first floor plan

Creating a New Window Type:

You will add four more windows to the East wall. These will be high windows, two on either side of a fireplace. Rather than using one of the predefined window sizes, you will create a new size within a family already loaded in the project.

These windows will be fixed, non-operable, so you will be adding a new type to the <u>*Fixed with Trim*</u> family.

19. Select the ***Window*** tool and then select the **Edit Type** button on the *Properties Palette.*

20. Set the *Family* drop-down to **Fixed with Trim** and then set the *Type* drop-down to **36″ x 24″** (Figure 5-4.14). **Do not select the Double Hung window!**

FYI: You could have selected this in the Type Selector *before clicking the* Edit Type *button.*

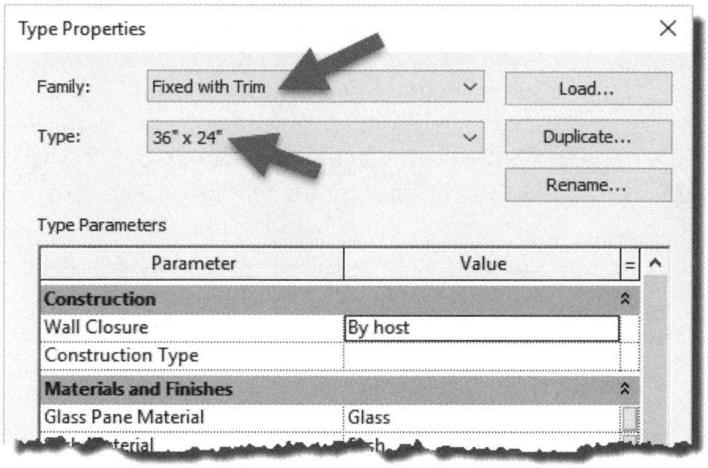

FIGURE 5-4.14 Type Properties – *Family*: Fixed with Trim; *Type*: 36″ x 24″

21. Click the **Duplicate** button.

22. Enter **36″ x 20″** for the name and then click **OK**.

You are now viewing the *Type Properties* for the new 36″ x 20″ type you just created. However, the name has nothing to do with actually changing the window size. You will do this next.

23. Change the *Height* parameter to **1′-8″** (Figure 5-4.15).

24. Change the *Default Sill Height* to **5′-4″**. *(This makes the top of all your windows align at 7′-0″.)*

25. Click **OK** to close the *Type Properties* dialog.

26. Add the windows as dimensioned in Figure 5-4.16.

    a. Before placing the first window, make sure the *Sill Height* is set to **5'-4"** in the *Properties Palette.*

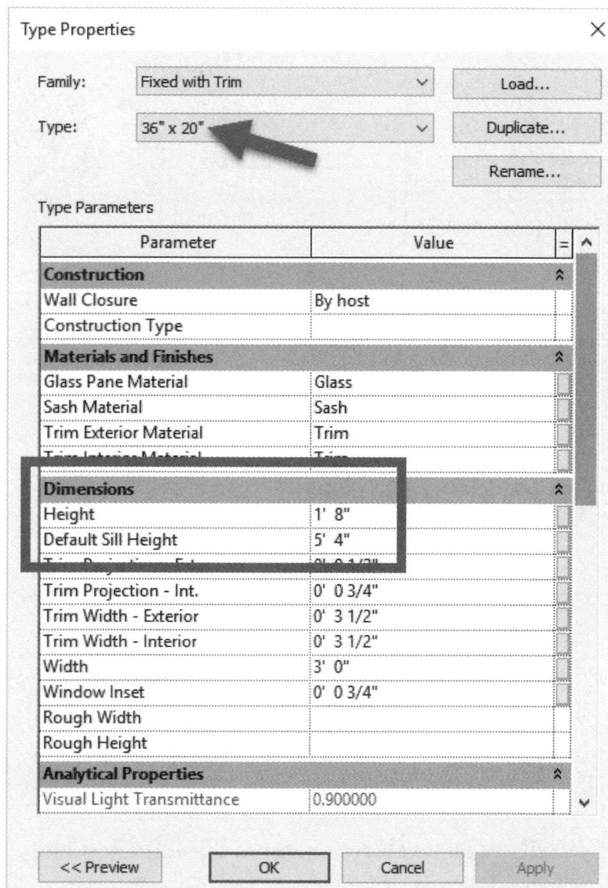

FIGURE 5-4.15 Type Properties: New predefined window size

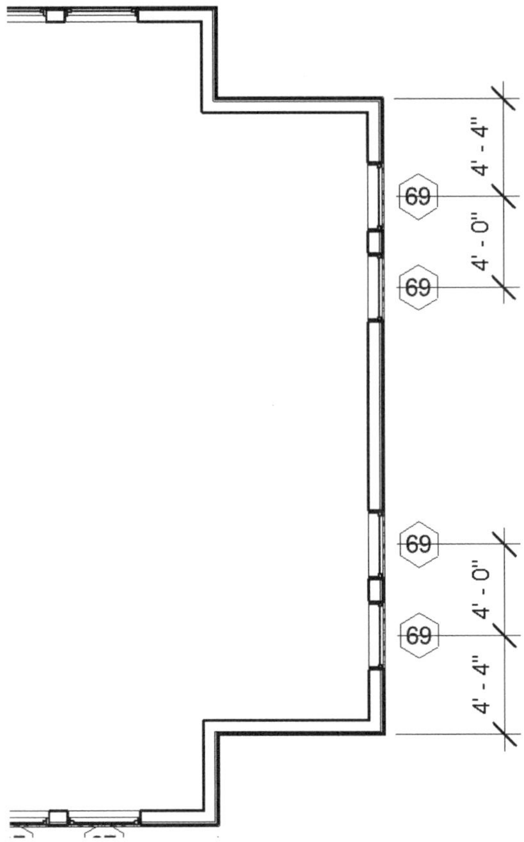

You are probably wondering where the windows are? They are tagged and you can select them. However, they are not visible.

With your project being a 3D model, Revit has to cut through the model at a certain elevation when generating the plan view. The default *Cut Plane* is 4'-0" above the floor line.

As you should recall, the sill of the new window type you just created is 5'-4" (Figure 5-4.15). If it is not, you should select the 36"x20" windows and adjust the sill height in the *Properties Palette*, so the window occurs above the cut line.

The windows will show up just fine in elevation and section views. Next you will see where the *Cut Plane* is set for each plan view.

POWER TIP: *If you want the windows to be visible, or a high stair landing to show, you can create a* Plan Region, *which allows you to override the cut plane within the selected area. See Help for more on this.*

FIGURE 5-4.16
First floor plan: last four windows added

27. Click the ***Modify*** tool on the *Ribbon* to unselect elements and cancel any active commands. This will cause the *Properties Palette* to show information about the current view.

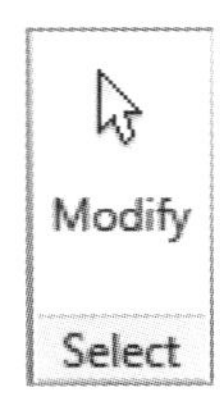

28. Scroll down, in the *Properties Palette*, and select **Edit** next to *View Range.*

Notice the *Cut Plane* is set to 4'-0" (Figure 5-4.17). Try changing it to 5'-6" and closing the dialog to see the various effects it has on your *Floor Plan* view; also look at the high windows.

Be sure to set the *Cut Plane* back to 4'-0" before proceeding.

29. Click **OK** to close the *View Range* dialog box.

FIGURE 5-4.17 View Range properties

Cleaning House:

As previously mentioned, you can view the various *Families* and *Types* loaded into your project via the *Project Browser*. The more families and types you have loaded the larger your file is, whether or not you are using them in your project. Therefore, it is a good idea to get rid of any door, window, etc., that you know you will not need in the current project. You do not have to delete any at this time, but this is how you do it:

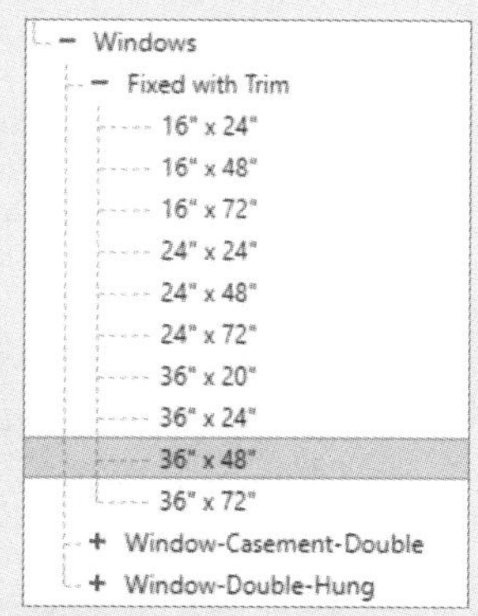

Figure: Project Browser

- In the *Project Browser*, navigate to Families → Windows → Fixed with Trim. Right-click on **36″ x 48″** and select **Delete.**

Another reason to delete types is to avoid mistakes. As you have seen, loading a door family has the potential of creating multiple door types. On a residential project you would rarely use 7′-0″ tall doors, so it would be a good idea to delete them from the project, so you don't accidentally pick them.

That concludes the exercise on adding doors, openings and windows to the first floor plan.

30. Save your project as **Ex5-4.rvt**

Exercise 5-5:
Adding a Fireplace

The last thing you will do in this lesson is to add a fireplace to the living room. Creating a fireplace family is beyond the scope of this introductory book, so you will use one provided with this book.

1. Using techniques previously described to download doors from SDC Publications, download the following items (Figure 5-5.1):
    a. **Mantel 1**
    b. **Masonry Chimney-Wall**

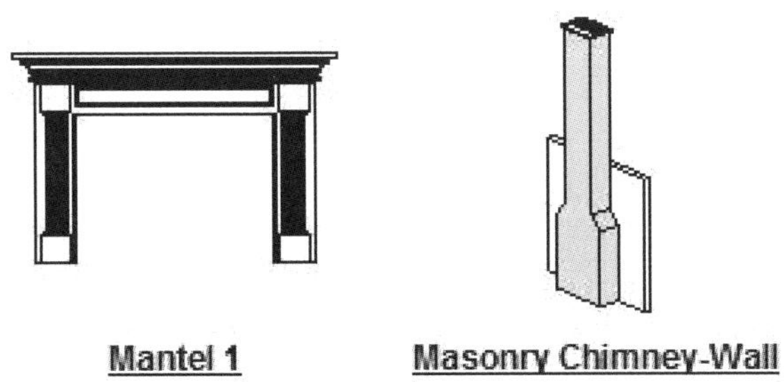

FIGURE 5-5.1 Mantel and Chimney to be used

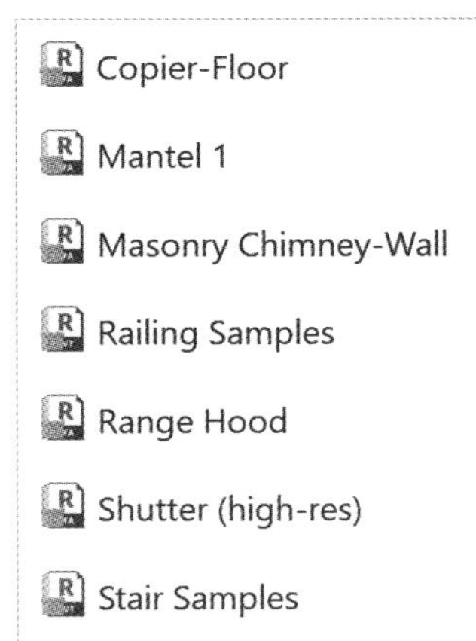

2. **Load** the downloaded families, provided with this book, into your project (see inside front cover).

You are now ready to place the fireplace in the first floor plan.

3. With the *First Floor Plan* view current, select **Architecture → Build → Component** from the *Ribbon.*

4. From the *Type Selector*, pick **Masonry Chimney-Wall : Chimney**.

The chimney will be scanning for a wall to be inserted into; it is a *wall hosted family*. When your cursor is near a wall, you will see a "ghost" graphic of the chimney to help you visually place it; when the cursor is not near a wall, Revit does not display the "ghost" graphic because it is not a valid location to place it.

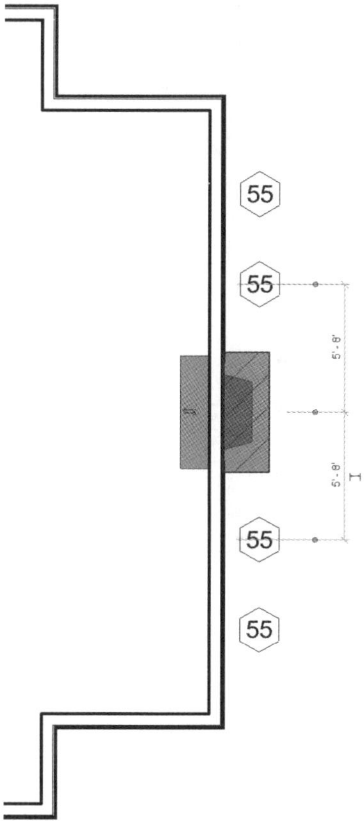

FIGURE 5-5.2 Chimney added

Try moving the cursor around the plan for a minute. Notice, again, that when the cursor is near a wall, you see the "ghost" graphic and the element orients itself with the wall (e.g., vertical, horizontal, angled). When the family encounters another element placed within a wall, you will see a small circle with a diagonal line through it, indicating the two elements cannot overlap. Furthermore, the element flips to the side of the wall where the cursor is. Try moving the cursor from one side of the wall to the other and observe the image flip back and forth.

5. Move your cursor to the middle portion of the easternmost (far right) wall, between the high windows; with your cursor on the exterior side of the wall, click to place the fireplace.

6. Adjust the temporary dimensions so the chimney is centered on the wall (Figure 5-5.2).

Next, you will place the mantel in the plan view. This is less automatic as it does not attach to the wall, so you will insert the mantel in the middle of the living room, rotate it, and then move it into place.

7. Use the **Component** tool to insert **Mantel 1: 80″ x 58¾″** into the middle of the *Living Room.*

8. Select the *Mantel* and use the ***Rotate*** tool to rotate the mantel 90 degrees in the clockwise direction.

TIP: You could have also pressed the spacebar during placement in step 7, then skipped step 8.

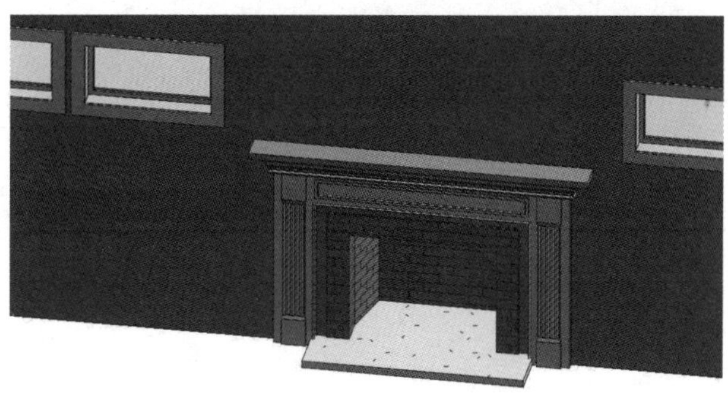

FIGURE 5-5.3 3D view of mantel

9. With the *Mantel* still selected, use the **arrow keys** on your keyboard to "nudge" the element into place, or try using the *Align* tool (Figure 5-5.4).

10. Take a minute to look at the *3D View* of all that you have completed so far (Figure 5-5.5).

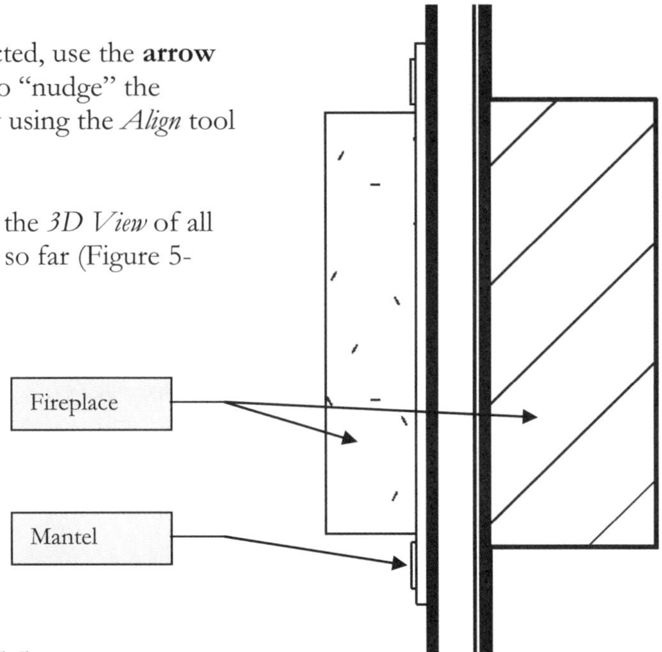

11. **Save** your project as **Ex5-5.rvt**.

FIGURE 5-5.4 Mantel added in plan view

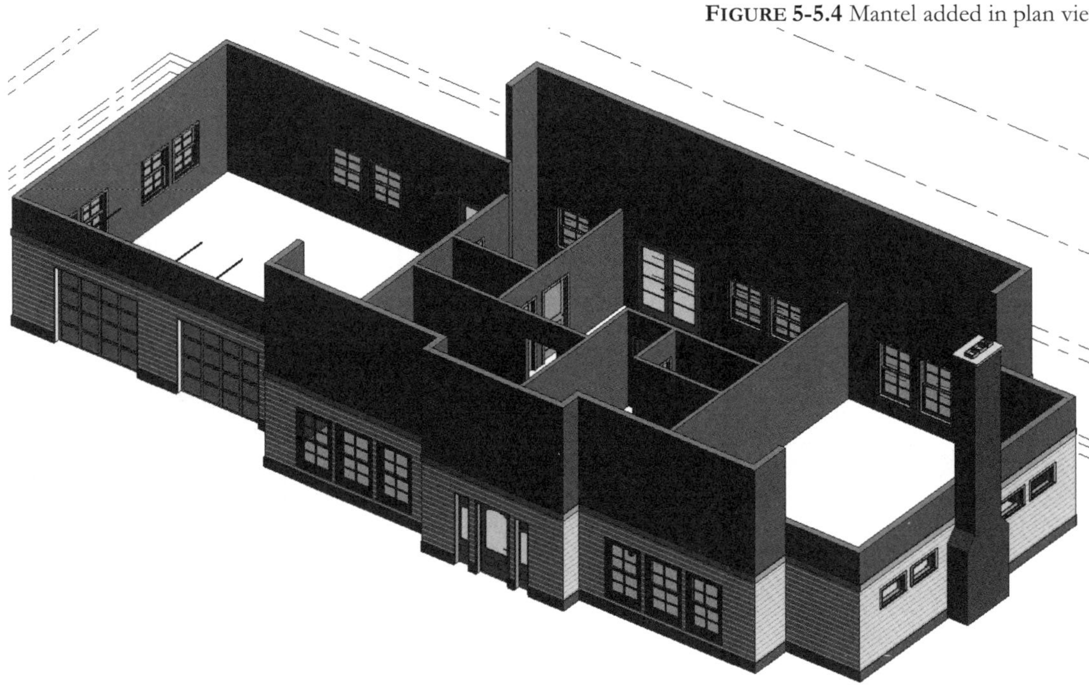

FIGURE 5-5.5 3D View of completed chapter

Self-Exam:

The following questions can be used as a way to check your knowledge of this lesson. The answers can be found at the bottom of the page.

1. The *Ribbon* allows you to select the height at which your wall will be drawn. (T/F)

2. It is not possible to draw a wall with the interior or exterior face of the core as the reference point. (T/F)

3. Objects cannot be moved accurately with the *Move* tool. (T/F)

4. The __________ tool, on the *Ribbon*, has to be selected in order to select an object in your project.

5. A wall has to be ____________ to see its flip icon.

Review Questions:

The following questions may be assigned by your instructor as a way to assess your knowledge of this section. Your instructor has the answers to the review questions.

1. Revit comes with many predefined doors and windows. (T/F)

2. The *Project Information* dialog allows you to enter data about the project, some of which is automatically added to sheet titleblocks. (T/F)

3. You can delete *families* and *types* in the *Project Browser*. (T/F)

4. It is not possible to add a new window *type* to a window *family*. (T/F)

5. It is not possible to select which side of the wall a window should be on while you are inserting the window. (T/F)

6. What tool will break a wall into two smaller pieces? ____________________

7. The ___________ tool allows you to match the surface of two adjacent walls.

8. Use the __________ key, on the keyboard, to flip the door swing while placing doors using the *Door* tool.

9. You adjust the location of a dimension's witness line by clicking on, or dragging, its ______________.

10. The ______________ file has a few doors, windows and walls preloaded in it.

SELF-EXAM ANSWERS:
1 – T, **2** – F, **3** – F, **4** – Modify, **5** – Selected

Notes:

Lesson 6
FLOOR PLANS (Second Floor and Basement Plans):

In this lesson, you will develop the second floor and the basement floor plans in Autodesk® Revit®. This will involve copying objects from the first floor with some modifications along the way. You will also add stairs and dimensions to your plans.

Exercise 6-1:
View Setup and Enclosing the Shell

Discussion: Second Floor View Current Conditions

1. Open **Ex5-5.rvt** and switch to the ***Second Floor*** view under *Floor Plans* in the *Project Browser*; double-click on the view name.

You should see a plan view similar to Figure 6-1.1. The geometry you are seeing is a result of two things:

- **First**, the height of the walls drawn on the first floor:
    i. Some of the exterior walls that you sketched on the first floor plan are 19′-0″ tall.
    ii. From the elevation views, you can see that the second floor is 9′-0″ above the first.
    iii. As you may recall from the last chapter, the default *View Range* – Cut Line is 4′-0″ above the floor.
    iv. So, relative to the first floor, the second floor Cut Plane is 13′-0″ above it (9′-0″ + 4′-0″).
    v. Therefore, the 19′-0″ tall walls extend past the second floor Cut Plane; that is why they are bold (elements in section automatically have a heavier line weight).
    vi. The exterior walls of the garage and east living room walls are only 12′-0″, which is below the Cut Plane. It is still within the *View Range*, so it shows up in "elevation" or projection. Elements in *projection* (i.e., beyond the Cut Plane) have lighter lines than those in section (i.e., at the Cut Plane).

- **Second**, the *Underlay* feature:
    i. In the *Properties Palette* (View Properties) for the *Second Floor Plan* view, you will see a section labeled *Underlay* (Figure 6-1.2).
    ii. The *Range: Base Level* is currently set to *First Floor.*

iii. The *Underlay* feature causes the selected level's walls to be displayed as light gray lines for reference, even though they are not within the current view's *View Range.*

iv. The walls shown as part of an underlay cannot be selected using a *window* selection but can be selected, and even deleted, by picking directly on a wall or anything else.

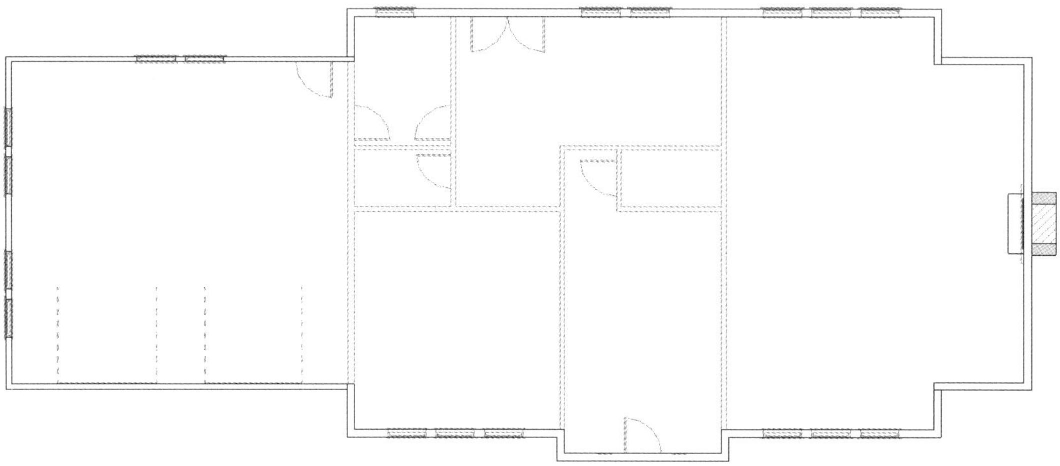

FIGURE 6-1.1 Second Floor: initial view

You do not need to see the first floor walls at the moment, so you will turn them off.

2. In the *Properties Palette* dialog, set (Underlay) **Range: Base Level** to **none**. *(Click Modify first if the View Properties are not currently shown.)*

Now you should only see the exterior walls (Figure 6-1.3).

Next, you will sketch two more exterior walls to enclose the second floor. These walls only occur above the second floor line, so they will only have wood shakes for siding.

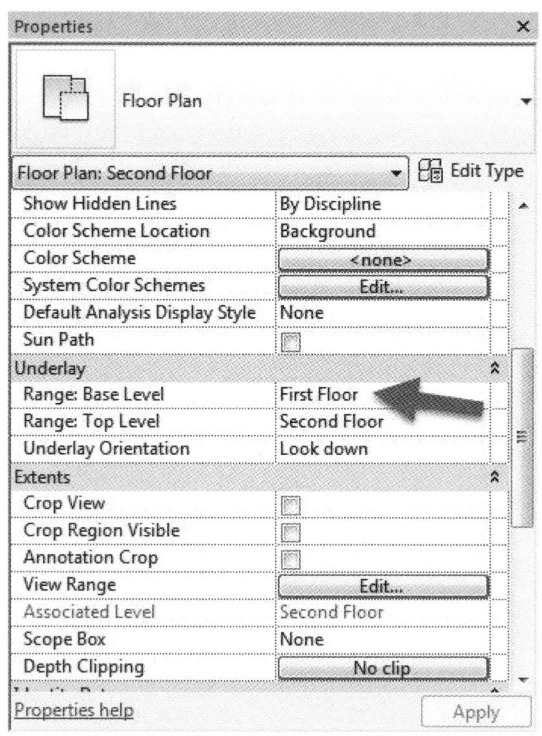

FIGURE 6-1.2 View Properties: Second Floor view

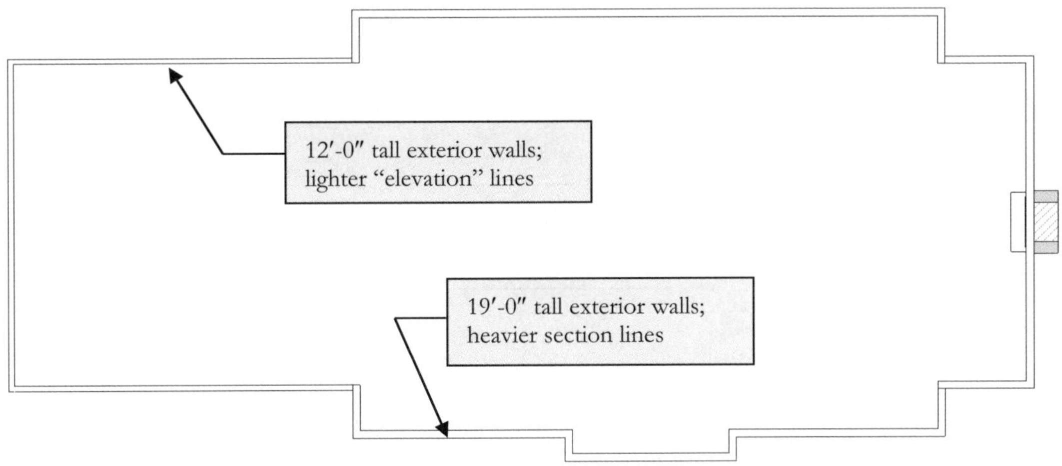

FIGURE 6-1.3 Second Floor: underlay turned off

3. Select the *Wall* command, select **Exterior – Wood Shingle on Wood Stud** from the *Type Selector*.

If you look at the properties for this wall, you will see that it is very similar to your primary exterior wall assembly. The main difference is that the vertical elements are stripped away: horizontal siding and two sweeps. You will also see another wall type with only horizontal siding. These two walls are loaded in the template for the reason you are about to use one: as infill between the main, more complex, wall type. The image to the right shows, from left to right, horizontal siding only, shakes only, and then the main wall you have previously used.

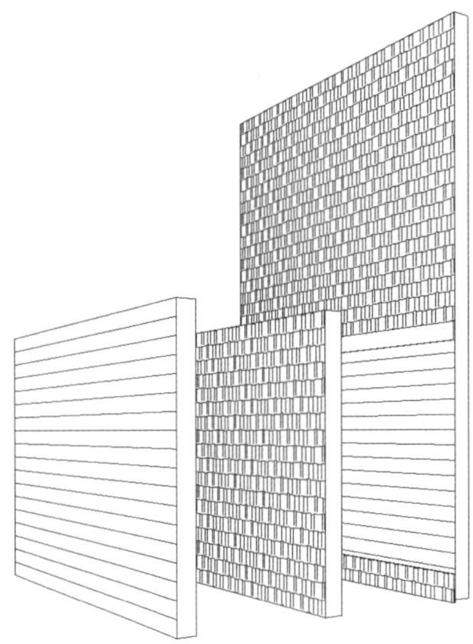

If you tried to use the wall type "Basic Wall: Exterior – Wood Shingle over Wood Siding on Wood Stud," the horizontal wood siding would start at the second floor line for any wall placed on the second floor. This is why you need a wall that just has wood shingles and no sweeps (i.e., horizontal trim boards).

4. Draw the two walls as shown in Figure 6-1.4, using the following information:
   - Set the *Height* to **Roof** (*Ribbon*).
   - Set the *Location Line* to **Finished Face: <u>Interior</u>** (*Properties Palette*).
   - Pick the interior side of the existing wall; press the *spacebar* if you need to flip the wall before picking the wall endpoint.

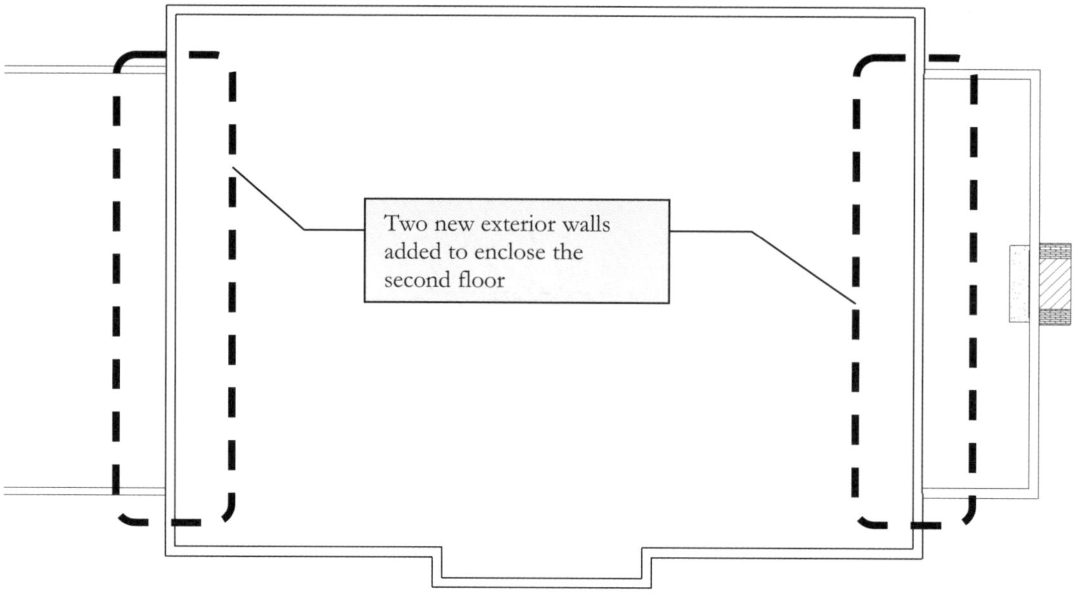

FIGURE 6-1.4 Second Floor: two exterior walls added

The height of the walls will change later when the roof is drawn. In fact, the height will vary as it extends to the underside of the gable-end roof; see the image on the book cover.

The two walls just drawn will be supported by the second floor, which has not yet been drawn. The bottom of the walls is aligned with *Level 2* because of the view you are in.

You may have noticed that the exterior wall face does not align perfectly with the adjacent walls. You will explore this problem and correct it in the next steps.

5. Select one of the walls just placed.

6. Click the **Edit Type** button on the *Properties Palette.*

7. In the *Type Properties* dialog, click **Edit** next to the ***Structure*** parameter.

8. Take note of the overall wall thickness and the thickness of the various layers (Figure 6-1.5A).

9. Close the dialog boxes, *Edit Assembly* and *Type Properties*, by clicking **OK**.

10. Follow the previous steps to look at the structure properties for the **Exterior – Wood Shingle over Wood Siding on Wood Stud**.

    NOTE: *The sheathing thickness is not the same (Figures 6-1.5a and b). You will change one so they both match.*

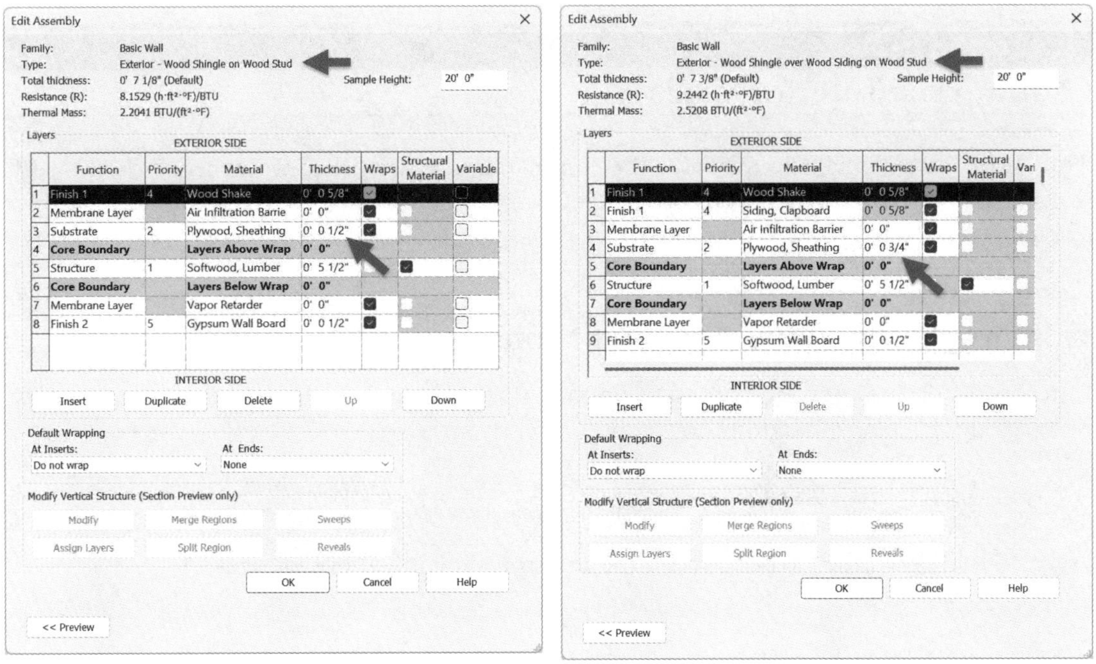

FIGURE 6-1.5A & B Comparing two walls' properties; sheathing thickness varies

11. Modify the *Sheathing* from ½" to ¾" for *Exterior – Wood Shingle on Wood Stud.*

The newly placed walls are now the same thickness as the adjacent walls.

12. **Save** your project as **Ex6-1.rvt**.

FYI:
Just as a reminder: the four elevation tags should not be deleted. You will study these more thoroughly later. This is what they represent:

> The default template has four elevation tags shown in plan view. These symbols represent what the four preset views listed in the *Project Browser* will see. Therefore, you should always start drawing your plan in the approximate center of the four symbols. The symbols can be moved by dragging them with your mouse.

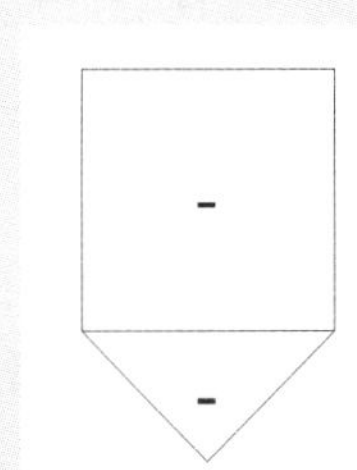

Again, do not delete these elevation tags as that will delete the actual views from the *Project Browser.*

Any view (e.g., plan, elevation or section) can be recreated, but all the notes and dimensions, which are view specific, would have to be manually recreated.

Exercise 6-2:
Adding the Interior Walls

This short exercise will help reinforce the commands you have already learned. You will add walls, doors, and windows to your project.

Copying Walls From the First Floor:

Often, walls occur in the same location on each floor. The easiest thing to do is copy/paste between floors. You will try this now.

1. Switch to the ***First Floor Plan*** view.

2. Hold down the **Ctrl** key; select the four walls identified in Figure 6-2.1.

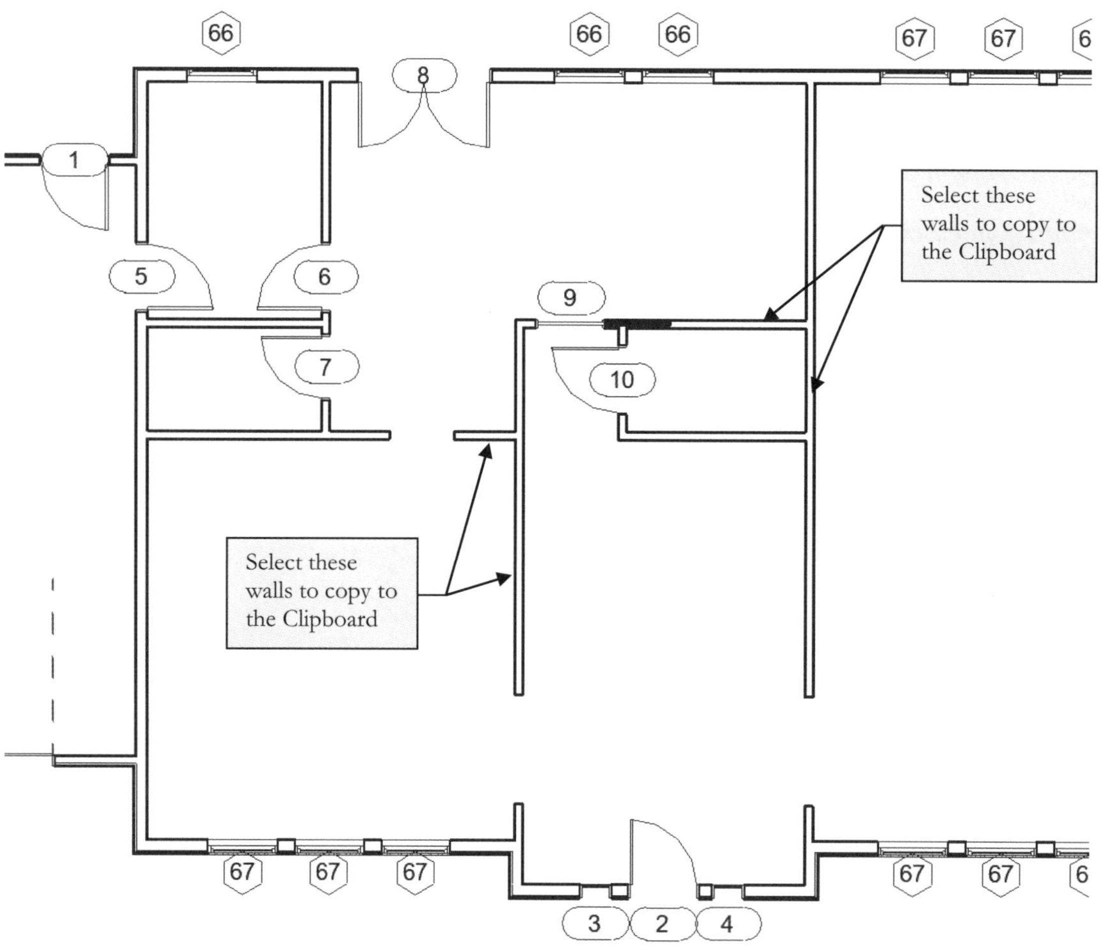

FIGURE 6-2.1 First Floor: Selected walls, (4) total, to be copied/pasted to the Second Floor

3. With the four walls selected, select **Modify | Walls → Clipboard → Copy to Clipboard**; this command is different than *Copy* in the *Modify* panel, which only works in the current view.

4. Click **Modify** to unselect the first floor walls and then switch back to the ***Second Floor Plan*** view.

TIP: Just click the Second Floor tab above the drawing window.

5. Select **Modify → Clipboard → Paste → Aligned to Current View** (Figure 6-2.2).

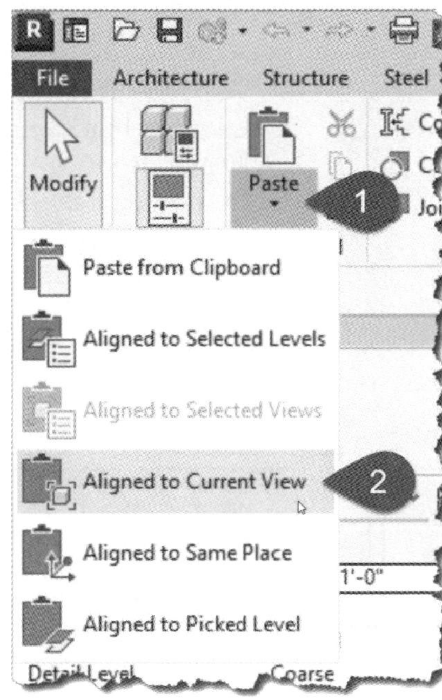

FIGURE 6-2.2
Modify tab: Paste Aligned fly-out

You should now see the four walls on the second floor *Plan* view (Figure 6-2.3).

Why did we not just draw these four first floor walls 19′-0″ high like the exterior walls?

Simulating real-world construction is ideal for several reasons. Most of the time, you can be sure exterior walls align from floor to floor. Although the four interior walls align, they do not have to, as they are separated by floor construction; this allows one floor to be easily modified in Revit. However, if an exterior wall is moved in any plan view, you want to make sure it moves everywhere, so these walls are drawn full height.

6. Select **Modify** to deselect the walls via the *Ribbon.*

Whenever a wall is copied or pasted, any hosted elements attached to the wall(s) are copied along with it. Next, you will delete the openings copied from the walls on the first floor.

7. Individually select each of the four doors/openings and delete them using the Delete key on the keyboard.

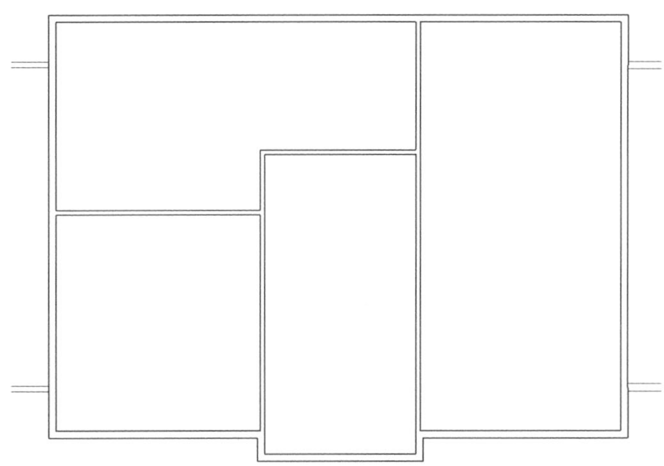

FIGURE 6-2.3 Second Floor: walls copied, doors deleted

Your first floor walls have their *top constraint* set to the second floor, so when you copied the walls from the first floor to the second floor, Revit automatically set the *top constraint* to the next level above the first floor: the *Roof* level. This is fine for now.

Next, you will add a few more interior walls.

8. Using the ***Wall*** tool, draw the walls shown in Figure 6-2.4 using the following information:
    a. Wall type: **Interior – 4½" Partition**
    b. Location Line: *use whatever is appropriate*
    c. Height: **Roof**
    d. Do not draw the dimensions at this time.
    e. Notice that one of the interior walls from Figure 6-2.3 gets extended and another gets trimmed; the walls previously created are shaded just for this image (Figure 6-2.4).

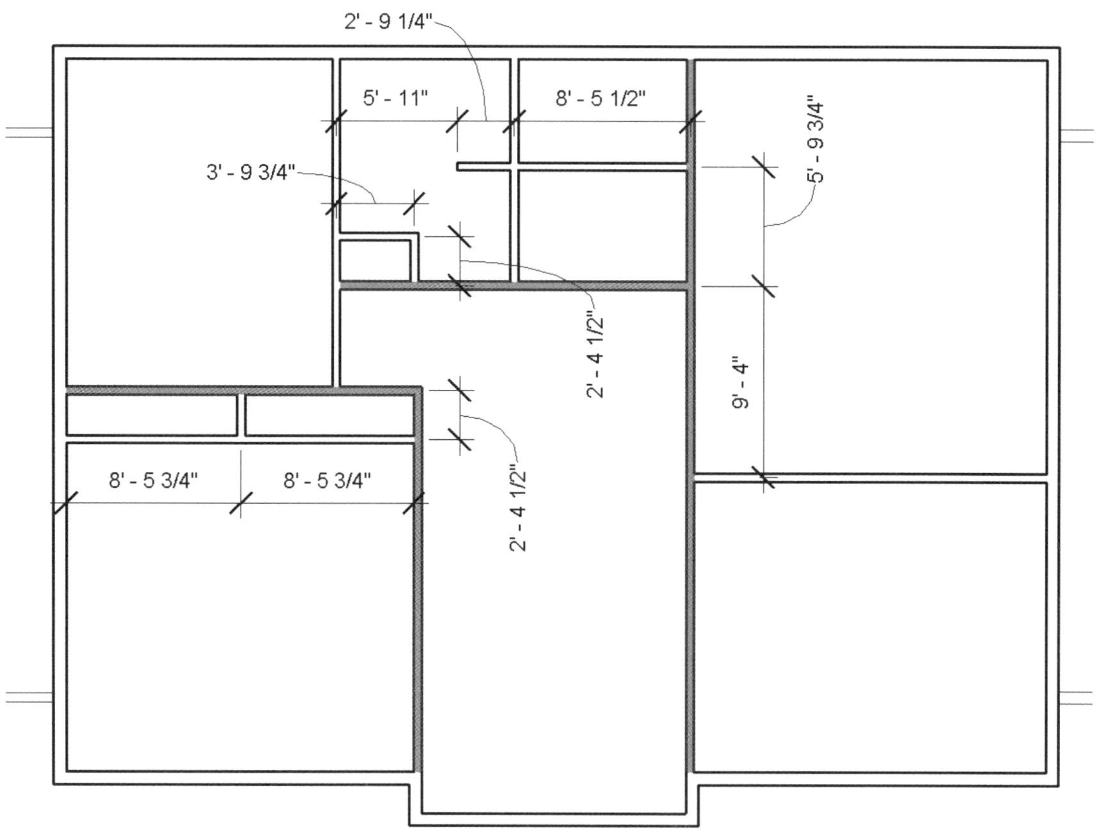

FIGURE 6-2.4 Second Floor: additional walls added

Joining Geometry:

Occasionally the intersection of two walls will not clean up, so you can use the *Join Geometry* icon on the *Ribbon*. The steps are as follows:

- Click *Modify* → *Geometry* → *Join.*
- Select the two walls.
- That's it; the walls are joined.

Intersecting walls

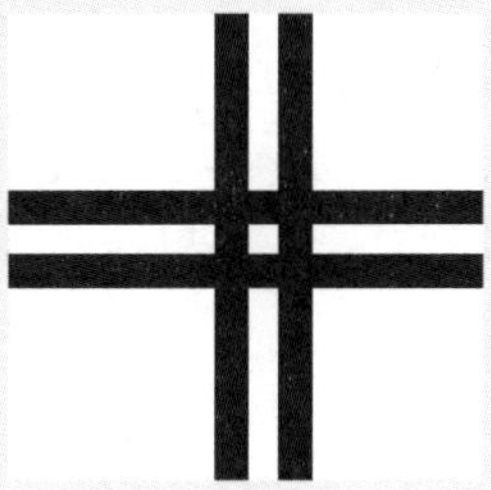

Walls joined

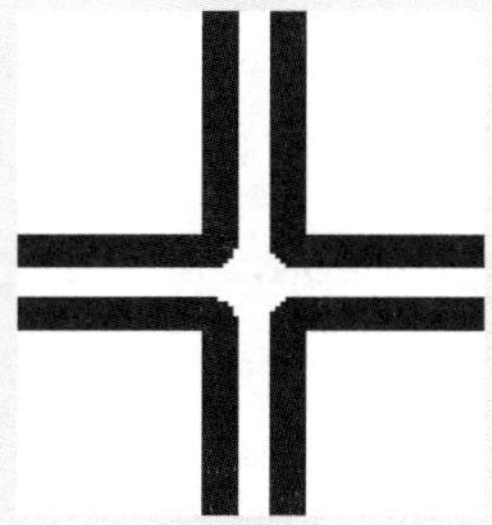

Controlling the View Scale

The size of the dimensions and door and window tags is controlled by the *View Scale*. Each *View* has its own scale setting. To facilitate the creation of this book, the *View Scale* has been set to 3/32″ = 1′-0″ typical. At that scale, Revit makes the text and symbols larger so it is legible at the smaller scale. However, the images in this book are not to scale.

The default *View Scale* is ¼″ = 1′-0″ for the plan views, floor, ceiling and framing plans. This is good and should not be changed for this tutorial. In addition to controlling the text and symbols, it also controls the size, or scale, of that drawing on the sheet (i.e., one of the sheets in a set of drawings). This only makes sense seeing as *View Scale* has everything to do with what scale that view is intended to be printed at.

The *View Scale* can be controlled via the *View Properties* dialog or more conveniently on the *View Control Bar* at the bottom of the drawing window (Figure 6-2.5).

9. Save your project as **ex6-2.rvt**.

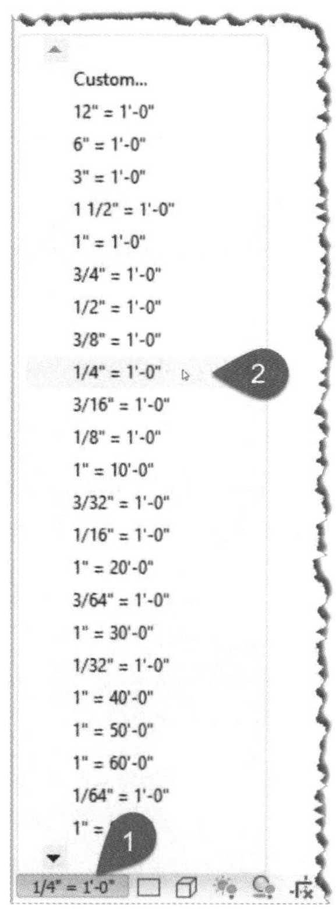

FIGURE 6-2.5
View Scale

Exercise 6-3:
Adding Doors, Openings, and Windows

Do not forget to keep a backup of your files on a separate disk (i.e., flash drive or external drive) or in the Cloud via Google Drive or Dropbox. Your project file should be about 14 MB when starting this exercise. Remember, your Revit project is a single large file, not many small ones. You do not want anything to happen to it. Make sure you have a copy of this file in two places at all times – do this daily!

Adding More Doors

Now you will add the second floor doors and openings, but first you must load one more door family and another door type to a family already loaded.

1. Open project ex6-2.rvt and **Save-As ex6-3.rvt**.

2. Load the following door families and types:

    a. **Door-Interior-Double-Sliding-2_Panel-Wood**, type **72" x 80"**

    b. Add another door type, **30" x 80"**, from **Door-Interior-Single-2_Panel-Wood.rfa** into your project. This new type will be added to the list of already-loaded types.

    c. Add another window type, **28" x 46"**, from **Window-Double-Hung.rfa**.

    Reminder: *Insert → Load Autodesk Family, then go to the Doors\Residential section.*

3. Add the doors as shown in Figure 6-3.1:

    a. Ensure Tag on Placement is toggled on so door tags are automatically added.

    b. Center the closet doors in the closet.

    TIP: *With the inserted door selected, you can "nudge" the door using the arrow keys.*

    FYI: *The more zoomed in you are, the more accurate the "nudge" increments are.*

Residential Door Sizes!

Doors come in many shapes and sizes.

Thickness: 1⅜″, 1¾″ and 2¼″

The 1⅜″ door is most often used in residential construction, and the 2¼″ door is typically used only on exterior doors for high-end projects (i.e., big budget).

Size: ranges from 1′-0″ x 6′-8″ to 4′-0″ x 9′-0″

The height of a residential door is usually 6′-8″. This writer once worked on a project where 7′-0″ high doors were specified. The contractor was so used to the standard 6′-8″ dimension that he framed all the exterior openings at 6′-8″. To top it off, the exterior walls were concrete (ICF system), so the openings could not be modified. Thus, 6′-8″ doors were used.

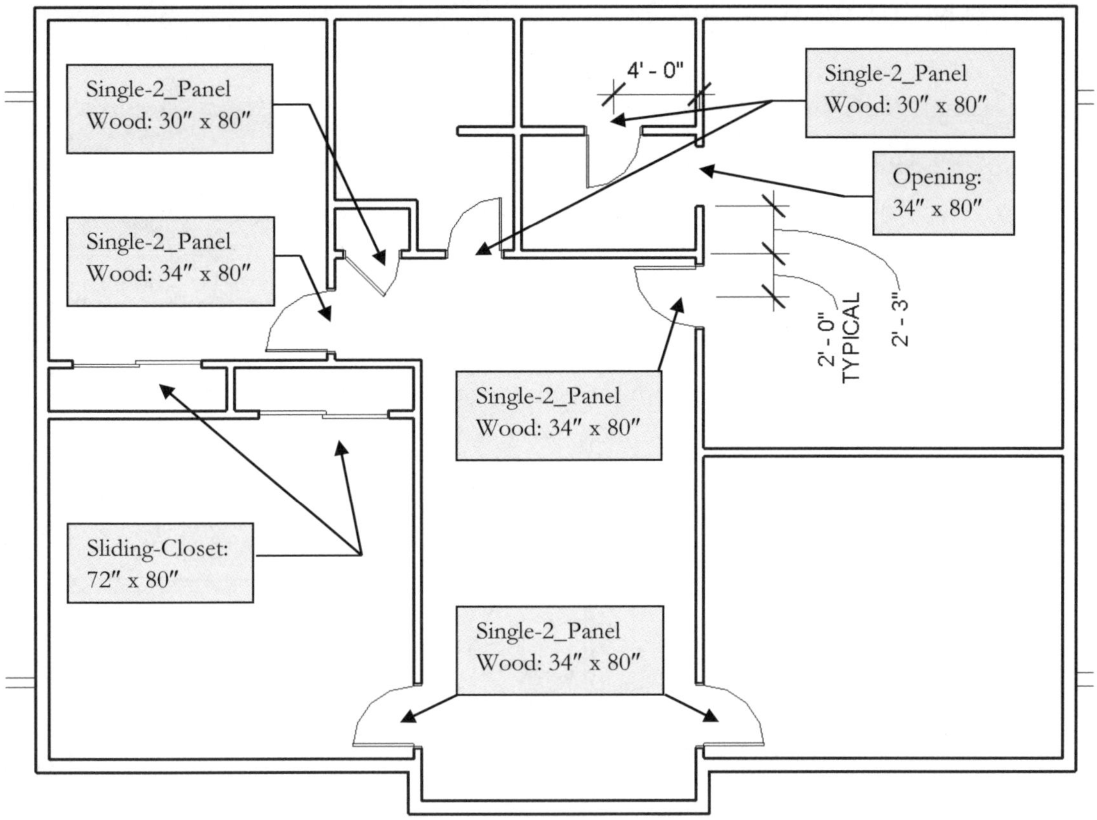

FIGURE 6-3.1 Second Floor; doors added

The door numbers were temporarily hidden from view for clarity. On your plans, you notice that the new doors have different numbers while the windows have the same number. Why is this? It relates to industry standards for architectural documentation. Each window that is the same size and configuration has the same *Type* number throughout the project. Each door has a unique number because it has so many variables (e.g., locks, hinges, closers, panic hardware, material, and fire rating). To make doors easier to find, many architectural firms align the door number to the room number it opens into. You can change the door number by selecting the tag and then clicking on the text. The door schedule will be updated automatically.

It is possible to use the AI feature in the **Autodesk Assistant** to adjust the door numbers by floor or to align with the room numbers. Any adjustments made to the model using AI need to be carefully reviewed.

Adding More Windows:

4. Add the windows as shown in Figure 6-3.2.
   a. Verify via the *Properties Palette* that each window's *Head Height* is set to 6′-10″.

      TIP: *Type* PP *if you accidentally closed the* Properties Palette.

   b. All windows are **Window-Double-Hung: 38" x 46"** unless otherwise noted in Figure 6-3.2.

   c. Like the previous image, the door and window tags have been temporarily hidden from view; you will learn how to do this next.

   d. All dimensions are from the center of the window to the exterior face of wall.

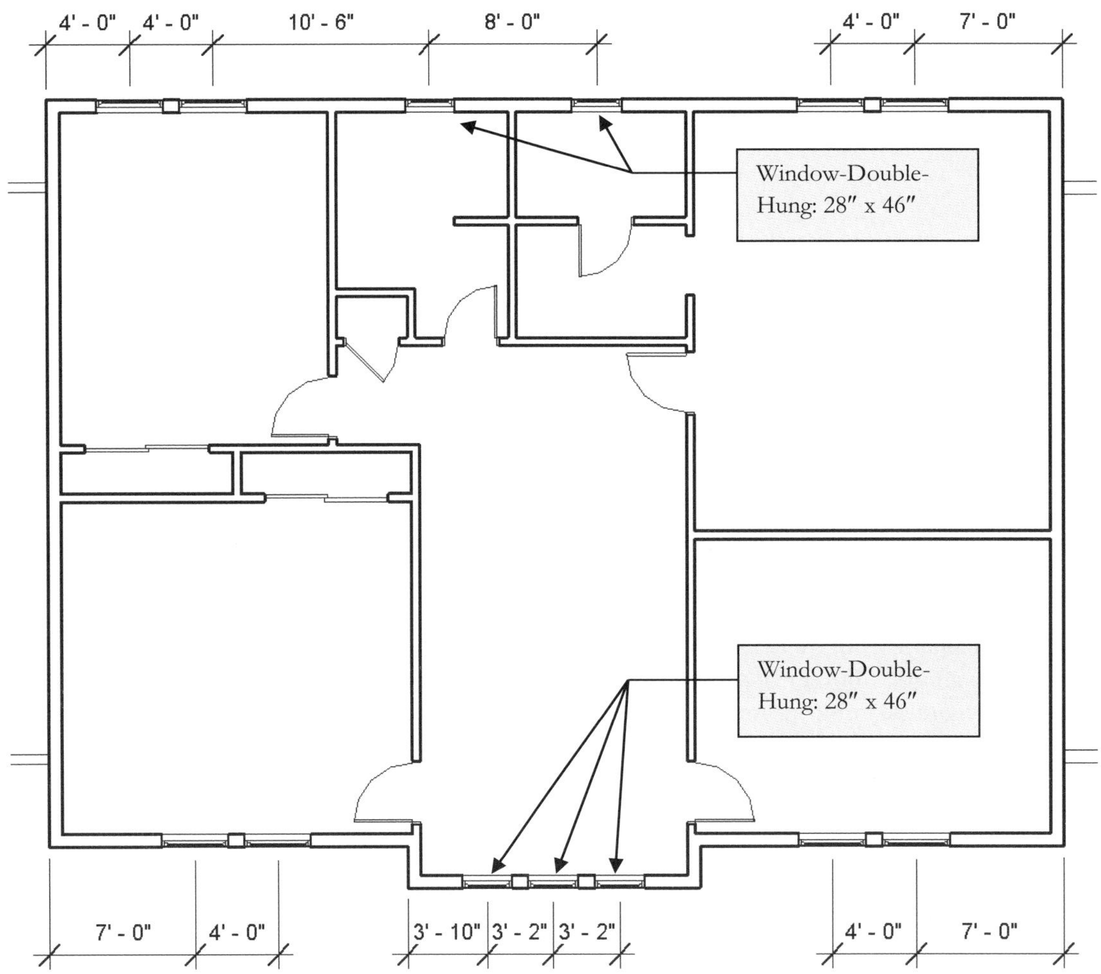

FIGURE 6-3.2 Second floor plan: windows added

Using Hide/Isolate to Control Visibility:

Now you will shift gears for a moment and look at the *Hide/Isolate* feature. This allows you to temporarily hide or isolate the selected elements, or all elements in the same category as the selected ones.

This feature is accessed via the *View Control Bar*, like the *View Scale* feature previously discussed.

5. Holding the **Ctrl** key, select one door tag and one window tag.

6. On the *View Control* bar click the **Temporary Hide/Isolate** icon (looks like sunglasses).

7. From the pop-up menu, select **Hide Category** (Figure 6-3.3).

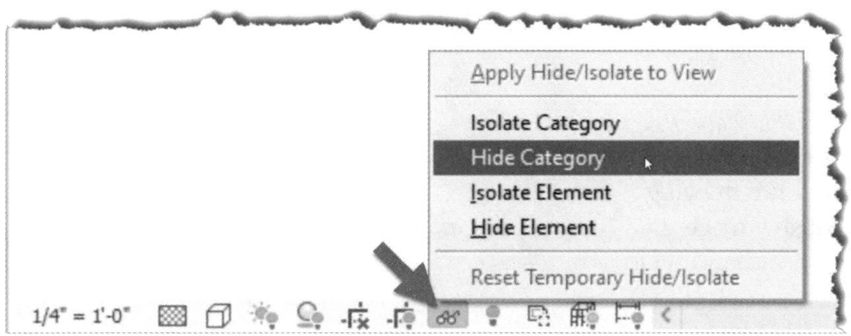

FIGURE 6-3.3 View Control bar: Hide/Isolate selected

You should notice two things. First, all the door and window tags are gone from the current view. Second, the *Hide/Isolate* icon has a cyan background, and the drawing window has a heavy cyan border around it, with text in the upper left stating "Temporary Hide/Isolate," which reminds you that something(s) is temporarily removed from the current view.

As implied by the feature name, the tags are temporarily hidden from view; they have not been deleted.

If you had selected *Hide Element*, only the selected elements would have been hidden from view rather than the entire category.

To restore this temporary setting, do the following:

8. Click the **Temporary Hide/Isolate** icon again (nothing has to be selected).

9. Select **Reset Temporary Hide/Isolate** from the pop-up menu.

   FYI: *Hiding items does affect printing. If you close the project and reopen it, the temporary override will be gone.*

The view is now back to normal. Try a few other variations on this feature and observe the results. Select *Reset Temporary Hide/Isolate* before proceeding.

Apply Hide/Isolate to View:

If you temporarily hide a few elements or categories and you want those items to be permanently hidden, you can select **Apply Hide/Isolate to View** from the *Hide/Isolate* icon menu – this option can be seen in Figure 6-3.3.

This feature allows you to hide (or isolate) individual items; for example, you could select a single window tag and hide it. The only way to see it again in that view is to select the **Reveal Hidden Elements** icon on the *View Control Bar* (Figure 6-3.4).

When *Reveal Hidden Elements* is toggled on, you should notice two things. First, all the hidden window tags are magenta, and everything else is light gray. Second, the *Reveal Hidden Elements* icon has a magenta background, and the drawing window has a heavy magenta border around it with a label in the upper left, which reminds you that the current view settings are being modified.

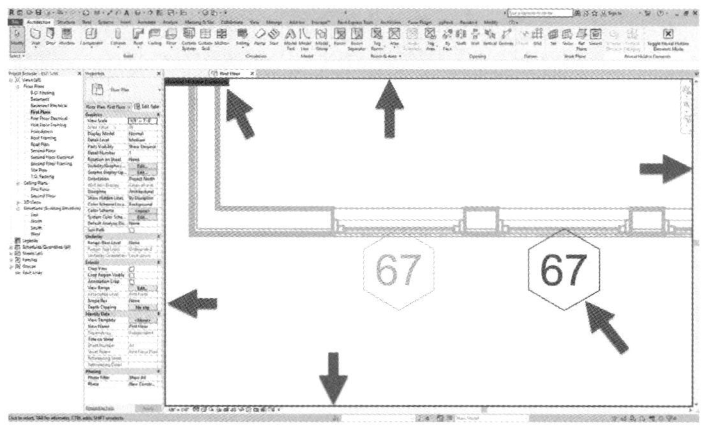

FIGURE 6-3.4 Reveal Hidden Elements mode active

Restoring Hidden Elements:

To restore a hidden item, you first click the *Reveal Hidden Elements* (Figure 6-3.4a) icon and then select the element(s) to be restored to view. Once the item(s) is selected, you click **Unhide Element** or **Unhide Category** from the *Ribbon (Figure 6-3.5).* Finally, you select the *Reveal Hidden Elements* icon again to return to the normal "current view" settings.

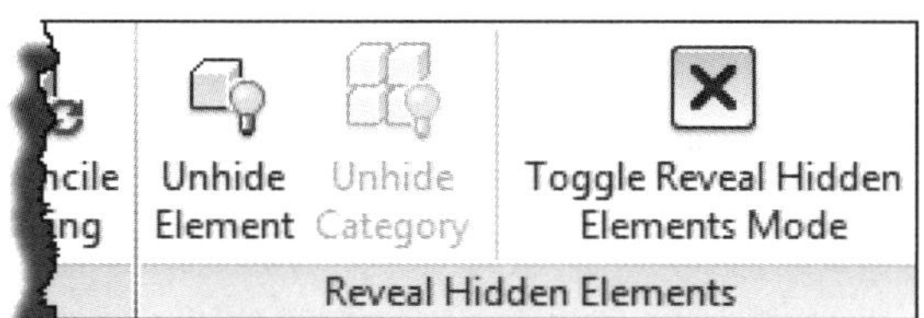

FIGURE 6-3.5
Ribbon: Reveal Hidden Elements panel

Exercise 6-4:
Basement Floor Plan

Basement Floor Plan:

Now you will sketch the basement floor plan. Not all residences have basements; they are most common in cold climates, where foundation walls are deep to avoid frost heave. Once you have dug out for the deep foundation walls along the entire perimeter of the building, it does not take much more effort or resources to create a basement. Designing a basement is the same as designing the other floors: you draw the exterior walls, the concrete foundation walls (in this case), the interior walls, etc. Once again, since the residential template you started with is set up for a typical residential project, it should not surprise you that the typical foundation wall type is predefined and ready to be sketched; both 10- and 12-wall types are available.

1. Open your project file ex6-3.rvt and **Save As ex6-4.rvt.**

2. Switch to the ***Foundation*** floor plan view, not the *Basement* plan.

You should see a grayed-out representation of the first floor.

3. In *View Properties*, do the following two steps:

   a. Note the *Underlay*, **Range:Base Level** parameter is set to **First Floor**; if not set properly, you should change it now so *First Floor* is the current *Underlay.*

   b. Change the **Discipline** parameter to **Architectural**.

This underlay setting gives you an outline of your building that can be used to sketch the foundation walls.

4. Using the ***Wall*** tool, draw the foundation walls using the following information (see *Type Selector* and *Ribbon* image below, Figure 6-4.1):

   a. *Wall type*: **Foundation – 12" Concrete**

   b. *Location Line:* **Finish Face: Exterior**

   c. *Depth:* **T.O. Footing** (i.e., Top of Footing).

   FYI: *Notice this setting on the Ribbon changes from "Height" to "Depth" when a "foundation" wall is selected!*

   d. Check **Chain** on the *Ribbon*.

   e. Start anywhere by snapping to one of the exterior corners of the *Underlay*; work in a clockwise direction.

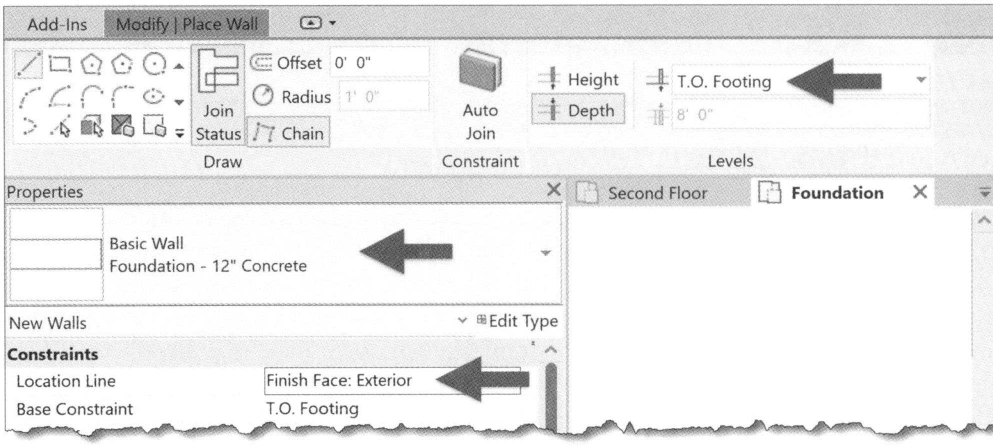

FIGURE 6-4.1 Properties Palette and Ribbon settings for foundation wall placement

When finished, your plan should look like Figure 6-4.2. The garage area will be slab-on-grade (i.e., no basement under it), so **make sure** you sketch a foundation wall between the garage and basement as shown.

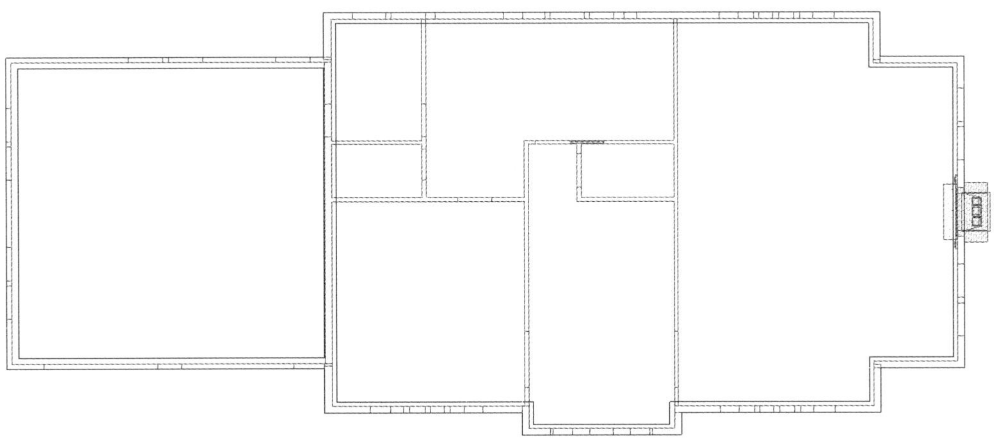

FIGURE 6-4.2 Foundation Floor Plan; with First Floor Underlay turned on

5. Set the 'Base Level' *Underlay* parameter for "Foundation" floor plan to **None** in the *Properties Palette.*

What Exactly Did You Just Draw?

You just drew a foundation with the top at the current level (named Foundation in this example), and the "Depth" parameter on the *Ribbon* controls the **bottom** of the wall (T.O. Footing in this example). The image on the next page should make this concept perfectly clear (Figure 6-4.3).

***FYI:** Each level datum has a corresponding floor plan view when the target is blue (as seen in the image on the next page). You may not need all of these views in a set of construction documents, but they are useful for creating the Building Information Model (BIM).*

Creating a New Foundation Wall Type:

Because the garage area is slab-on-grade, both sides of the foundation wall will be in contact with earth. The main basement walls act as retaining walls because they have earth on only one side. Therefore, you will change the three exterior foundation walls in the garage area to 8″ concrete. You will have to create a new wall type to accommodate this need.

6. Select the ***Wall*** tool and then select **Foundation – 12″ Concrete** from the *Type Selector.*

7. Create a new wall type based on the current selection; name it **Foundation – 8″ Concrete**.

   REMEMBER: *Properties Palette → Edit Type → Duplicate.*

8. Adjust the *Type Parameters* of the new wall so the Width is **8″**.

   FYI: *This is through* Properties Palette → Edit Type → Edit Structure.

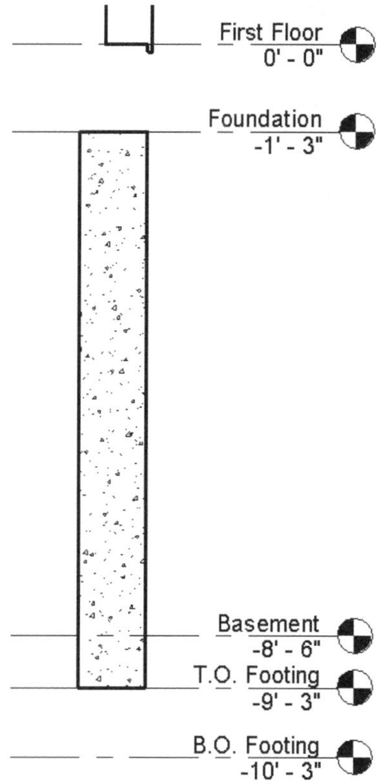

FIGURE 6-4.3
Foundation wall in section

9. Select the three exterior garage foundation walls while holding down the Ctrl key, and then select your new wall in the *Type Selector.*

   REMEMBER: *Click* Modify *first to cancel the* Wall *tool.*

   TIP: *Hover your cursor over one wall, press Tab to highlight all three walls (a chain of walls), and then click to select all three walls at once!*

10. Switch to the **Basement** floor plan view.

Your **basement** plan (not Foundation plan) should look like Figure 6-4.4.

Because the *Location Line* was set to Finish Face: Exterior, the exterior side of the foundation wall is stationary when walls of a different width are selected; this is the desired result in this situation.

FYI: *You will add footings below the foundation walls in Exercise 10-2.*

FIGURE 6-4.4 Basement Floor Plan; with 8″ foundation walls at the garage

Adding Interior Walls in the Basement:

To make things simple, for this tutorial and structurally, you will copy all the walls from the first floor to the basement. In the process of accomplishing this task, you will also study the selection **Filter** function.

First, switch to the first floor, select a large area using a crossing window (i.e., picking from right to left), then use the *Filter* function to strip the selection down to just the walls.

11. Switch to the ***First Floor*** view and select all the interior walls using a *crossing window* (Figure 6-4.5).

Everything within or passing through the *crossing window* is now selected. Next, you will filter out everything except for the walls.

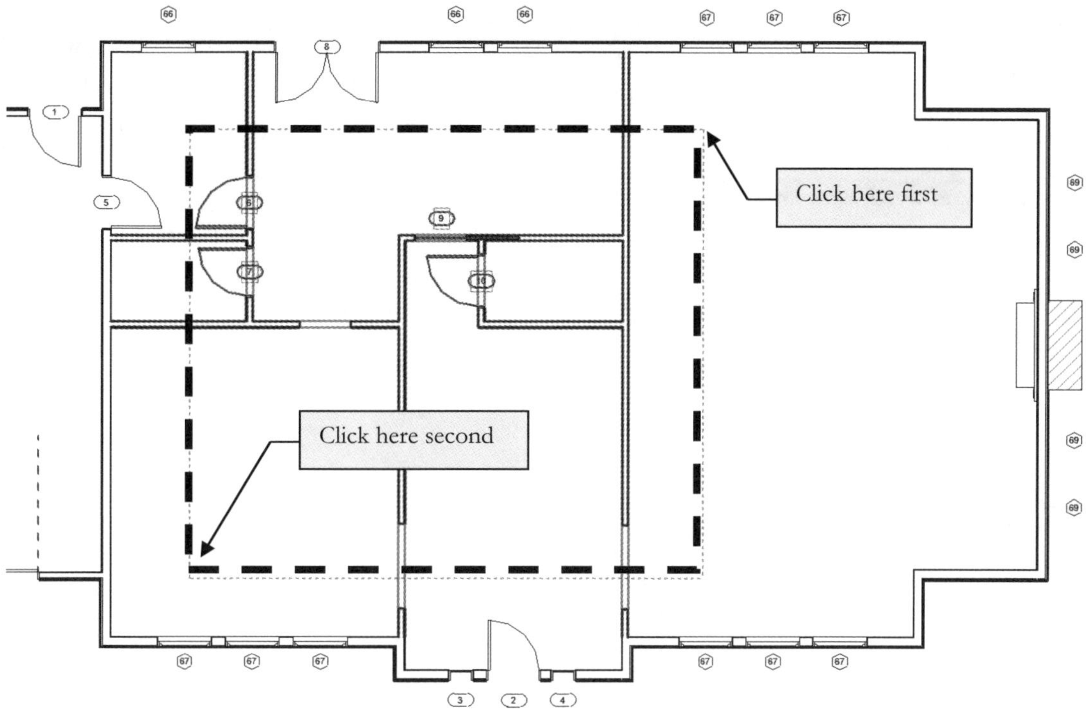

FIGURE 6-4.5 First Floor Plan; selecting all walls with a crossing window

12. With everything from the previous step still selected, click the **Filter** icon on the *Status Bar* (Figure 6-4.6).

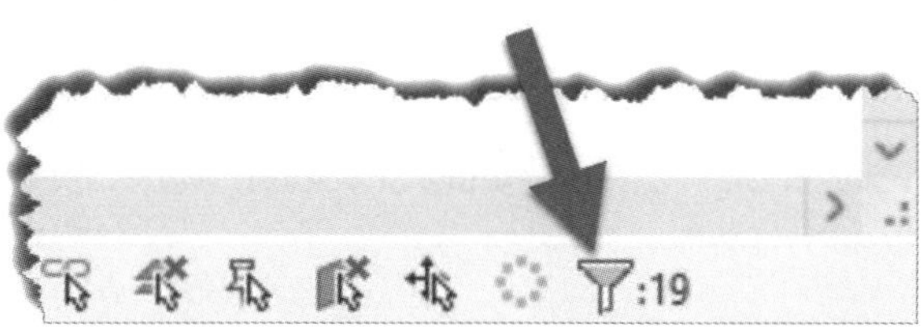

FIGURE 6-4.6 Filter Selection icon

You are now in the *Filter* dialog (Figure 6-4.7). This lists all element types or categories in the current selection set. When you click OK, only the checked items will be included in the current selection set.

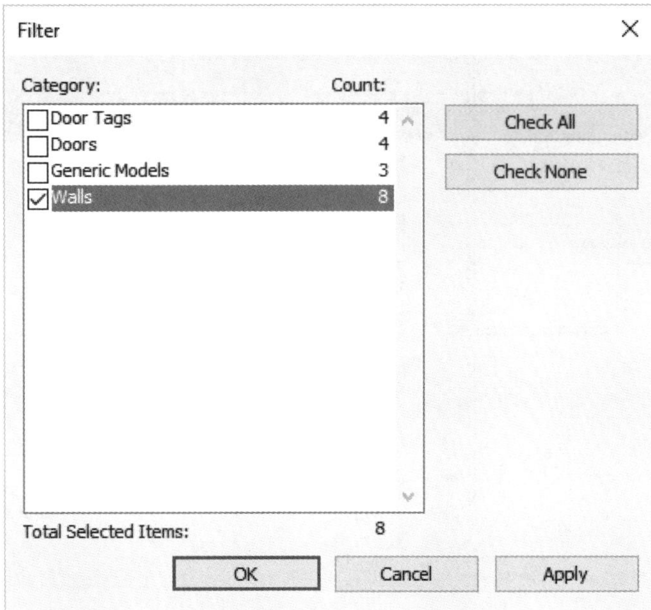

FIGURE 6-4.7 Filter dialog

> **TIP:**
> If you only wanted the walls selected, but had 20+ items in the list, you could click the "Check None" button and then check only "Walls" in the list. This would be faster than individually clicking each item in the list to unselect it.

13. Uncheck everything except the **Walls** item in the *Filter* dialog (Figure 6-4.7).

14. Click **OK** to update the current select set.

TIP: Notice the number of selected items is listed in the lower right corner of the program window (image to the right). If you know you want to delete 3 doors and the count shows 4 items, you would not want to click Delete before you unselect the fourth item!

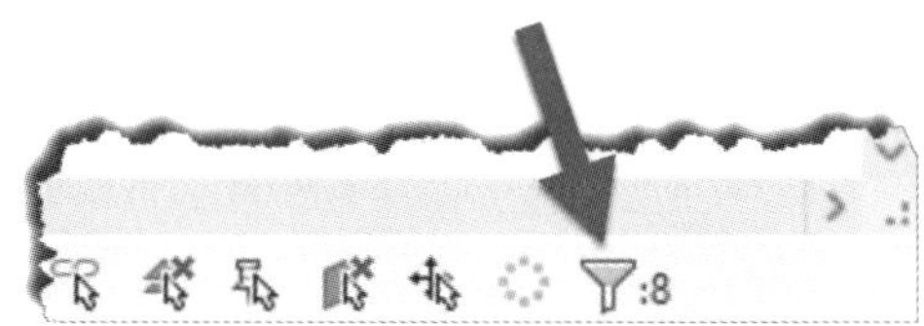

Now only the walls are selected. Next, you will copy them to the *Clipboard* and then *Paste* them into the basement floor plan.

This selection technique can be used in many ways. For example, you could select all the walls and change their *Top Constraint* via the *Properties* dialog.

15. From the *Ribbon,* select **Modify | Walls → Clipboard → Copy to Clipboard**.

16. Switch to the **Basement** view, not the Foundation view.

17. Select **Modify** on the *Ribbon*, and then **Modify → Clipboard → Paste → Aligned to Current View**.

You should get the following warning (Figure 6-4.8):

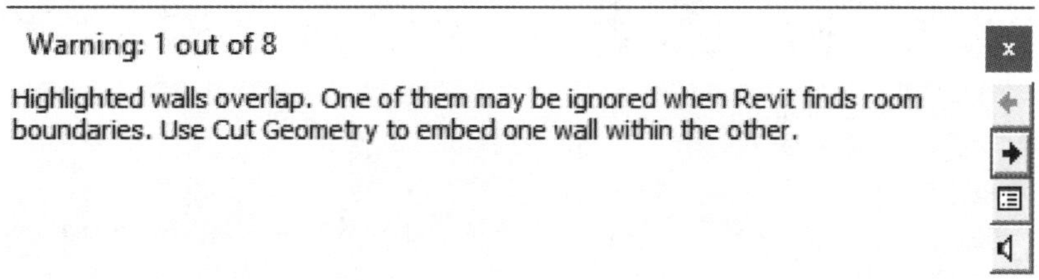

FIGURE 6-4.8 Wall placement warning

This error indicates that the wall(s) you just placed overlap another wall (vertically or horizontally). In this case, the Top Offset may be set to 6 rather than 0, causing the wall to extend 6 above the Top Constraint (the first floor line). So, if the first floor walls start at the first floor line, the basement walls extend up into the first floor walls by 6″, and the two walls would be overlapping vertically.

18. To resolve this warning, select all the interior walls in the basement and change the *Top Offset* to **0″** via the *Properties Palette.*

When finished, your plan should look like Figure 6-4.9.

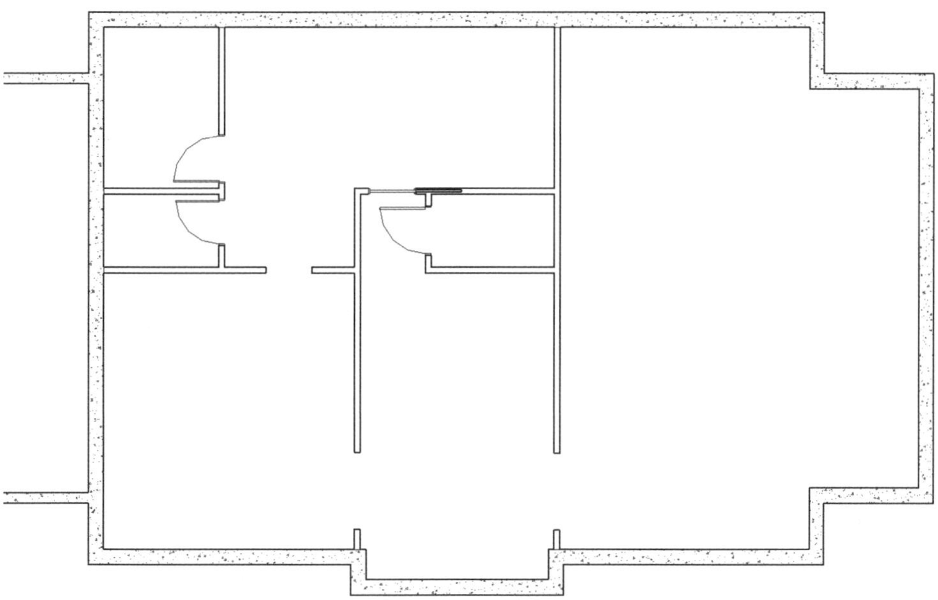

FIGURE 6-4.9 Walls added to the basement floor, copied from the first floor

Even though the doors were not selected, they were still copied with the walls just as before. This is fine; to save time, you will leave the doors as they are.

19. **Save** your project as **ex6-4.rvt.**

Exercise 6-5:
Stairs

Next, you will add stairs to your floor plans. Revit provides a powerful stair tool that lets you design stairs quickly, with constraints specified in the family loaded with the template you started from (e.g., 7 maximum risers).

Stair Type Parameters:

Before you draw the stairs, it's helpful to review the options available in the stair family.

1. Open ex6-4.rvt and *Save As* **ex6-5.rvt**. Open the **First Floor** plan.

2. From the *Project Browser*, expand the *Families* → *Stairs* → Assembled *Stair* (i.e., click the plus sign next to these labels).

3. Right-click on the stair type **Residential – Closed 2 Sides**, and select the **Type Properties…** option from the pop-up menu.

You should now see the options shown in Figure 6-5.1.

Take a couple of minutes to review the available options. We will quickly review a few below.

- Tread Depth: Treads are typically 12″ deep (usually code min.) and 1″ of that depth overlaps the next tread; so only 11″ is visible in plan view. This overlap is called the *nosing.*
- Riser: This provides Revit with the maximum dimension allowed (by code, or if you want it, less). The actual dimension will depend on the floor-to-floor height.
- Stringer dimensions: These dimensions usually vary per stair depending on the stair width, run and materials, to name a few.
- Cost: Estimating placeholder.

FYI: *Closed 2 Sides (part of the name of the stair family) means there will be a wall on each side of the stair; thus, a stringer will be visible above the stair.*

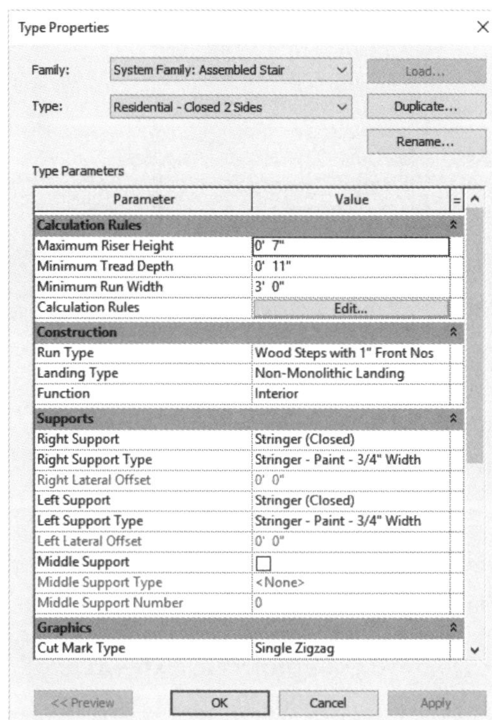

FIGURE 6-5.1 Stair type properties

Calculate Tread and Riser Size:

Although Revit automatically calculates the rise and tread dimensions for you, it is still a good idea to understand what is happening.

The *riser* is typically calculated to be as large as building codes will allow. Occasionally, a grand stair will have a smaller riser to create a more elegant stair.

Similarly, the *tread* is usually designed to be as small as allowable by building codes.

The largest riser and shortest tread create the steepest stair allowed. This takes up less floor space (Figure 6-5.2). A stairway that is too steep is uncomfortable and unsafe.

Building codes vary by location; for this exercise you will use 7″ (max.) for the risers and 11" (min.) for the treads.

Codes usually require that each tread be the same size, likewise with risers.

Calculate the number and size of the risers:

Given:
Risers: **7″** max. Floor to floor height: **9′-0″**.

Calculate the number of risers:
9′-0″ divided by 7″ (or 108″ divided by 7″) = 15.429

Seeing as each riser must be the same size we will have to round off to a whole number. You cannot round down because that will make the riser larger than the allowed maximum (9′-0″ / 15 = 7.2″). Therefore, you have to round up to 16. Thus: 9′-0″ divided by 16 = 6.75.

So you need **16** risers that are **6¾″** each.

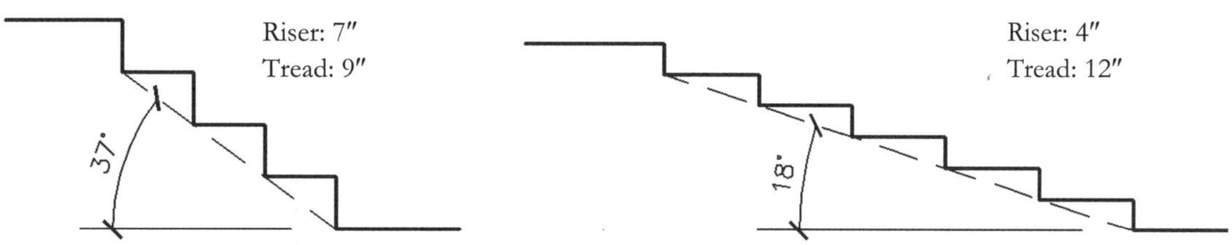

FIGURE 6-5.2 Stair rise/run comparison

Drawing the Stairs in Plan:

You will be drawing a U-shaped stair from the first floor to the second and an L-shaped stair from the basement to the first floor. At first, when using Revit to draw stairs, it may be helpful to manually figure out the number of risers and landings. That information will be helpful when drawing the stairs. As you become more familiar with the *Stair* tool, you will not need to do those calculations to draw a stair.

To get an idea about what you are going to draw next, take a moment to look at Figure 6-5.3. The image below is at the first floor, and the "UP" label indicates where you would access the stairs on the first floor. (Everything else rises from there, of course, to the second floor.)

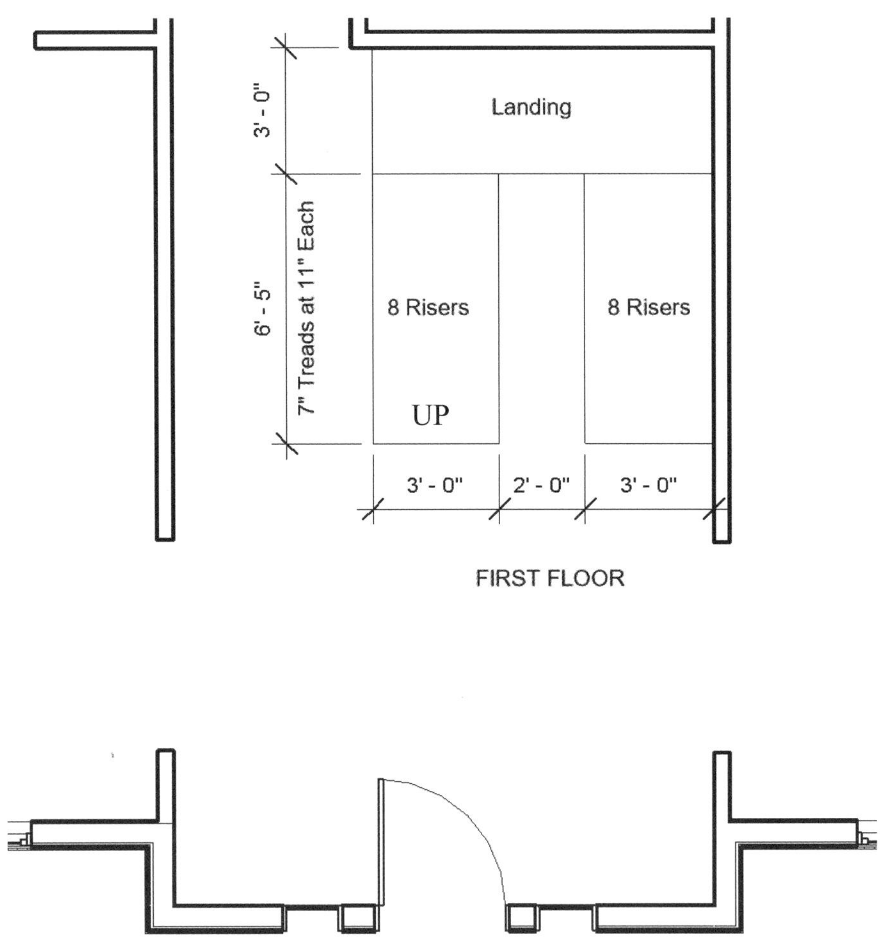

FIGURE 6-5.3 Stair information overview

The first thing you will do, to prepare to draw the stair from the first floor to the second floor, is to draw a temporary reference line. This line will be used to accurately pick a starting point while using the *Stair* command (you will be picking a starting point near the middle of the room – next to the "UP" label in Figure 6-5.3). After the stair is drawn, you will erase the line.

You have had plenty of practice drawing lines in previous chapters, so you will be given minimal instruction on how to draw the line.

4. Close the stair *Type Properties* dialog and make sure you are in the ***First Floor Plan*** view.

5. **Zoom in** to the front *Entry Foyer.*

6. Using the ***Detail Line*** tool from the *Annotate* tab, draw the temporary line in the ***First Floor Plan*** view, as shown in Figure 6-5.4.

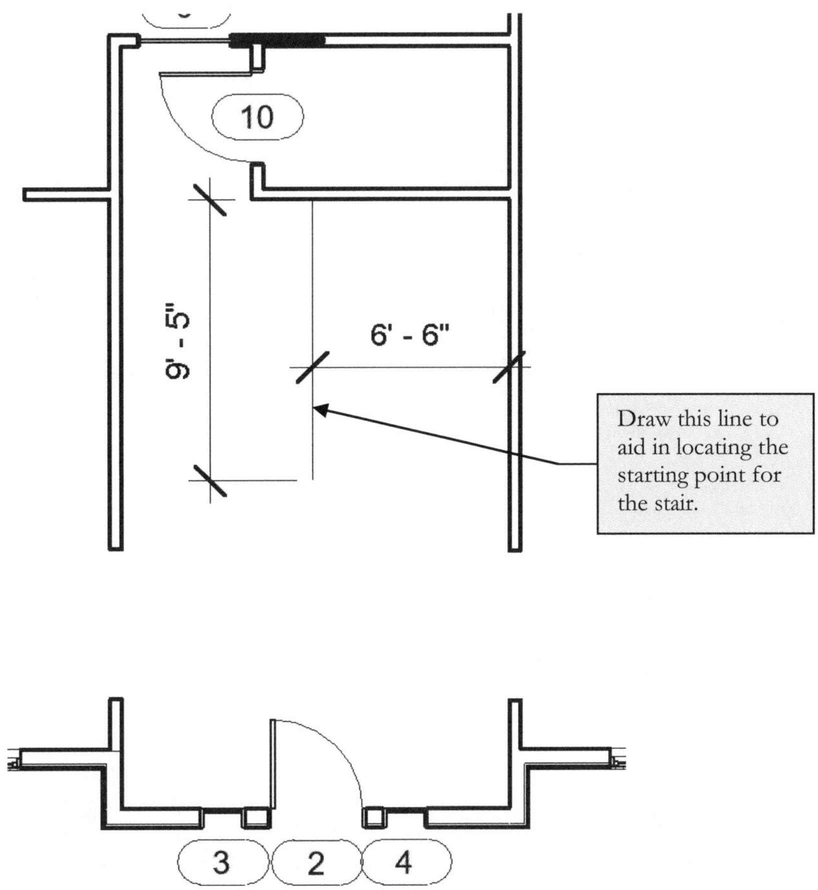

FIGURE 6-5.4 Draw a temporary detail line

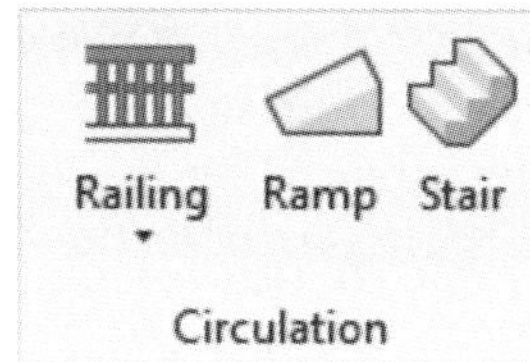

7. Click **Architecture → Circulation → Stair**.

8. On the *Ribbon*, make sure *Location Line* is set to **Run: Center** and *Actual Run Width* is set to **3'-0"** (Fig. 6-5.5).

9. Click the ***Edit Type*** button in the *Properties Palette*. Notice the *Minimum Run Width* is 3'-0". Click **OK**.

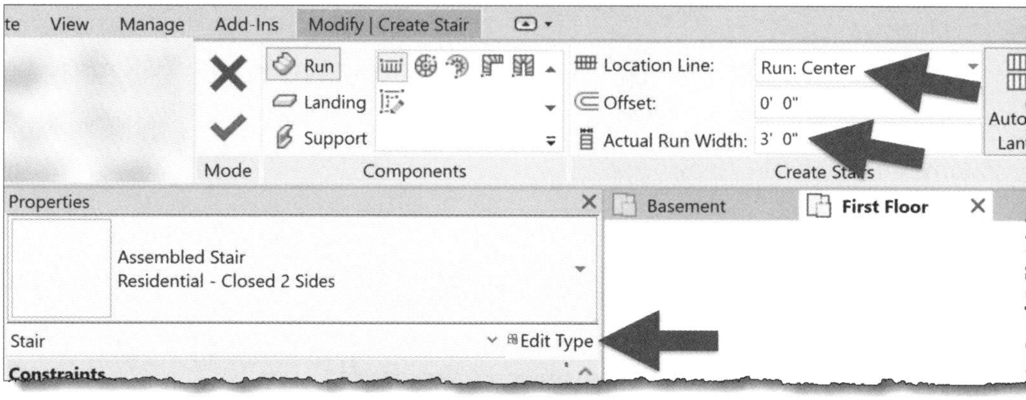

FIGURE 6-5.5 Stair tool active; Select Edit Type from the Properties Palette

10. Notice the *Top Level* is set to **Second Floor** (Figure 6-5.6).

11. Click the endpoint of your temporary detail line as shown in **Figure 6-5.7**; you are selecting the start point for the first step. Make sure you are snapping to the line for accuracy; a tooltip labeled "endpoint" will appear before you click.

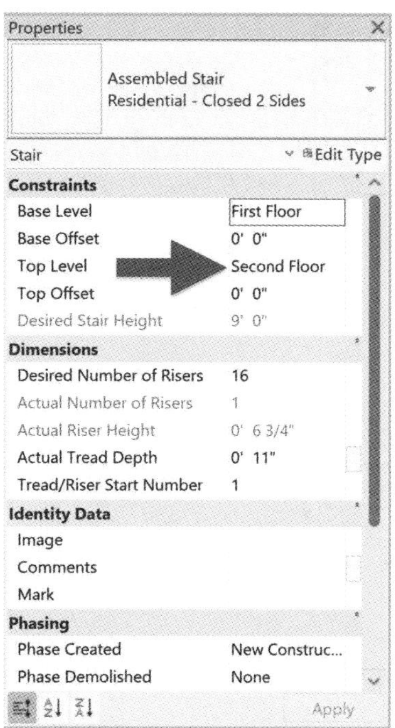

FIGURE 6-5.6 Stair instance properties

12. Pick the remaining points as shown in Figures 6-5.7, 6-5.8, and 6-5.9.

FYI: For the second run, set the Location Line to **Left** *on the Ribbon.*

> ***TIP:***
> *Notice the palette to the left is the* Instance Properties *which controls selected or to-be-created instances. In this case, of course, we are talking about a to-be-created instance.*
>
> *Clicking the* Edit Type *button here would make changes to this stair and any others previously created. Your project does not have any previously created stairs at this time.*

Notice that as you draw the stairs, Revit will display the number of risers drawn and the number of risers remaining to be drawn to reach the next level, or whatever level is selected as *Top Level* in *Properties.*

If you click *Finish Stairs*, the green check mark on the *Ribbon*, before drawing all the required risers, Revit will display a warning message. You can leave the problem to be resolved later.

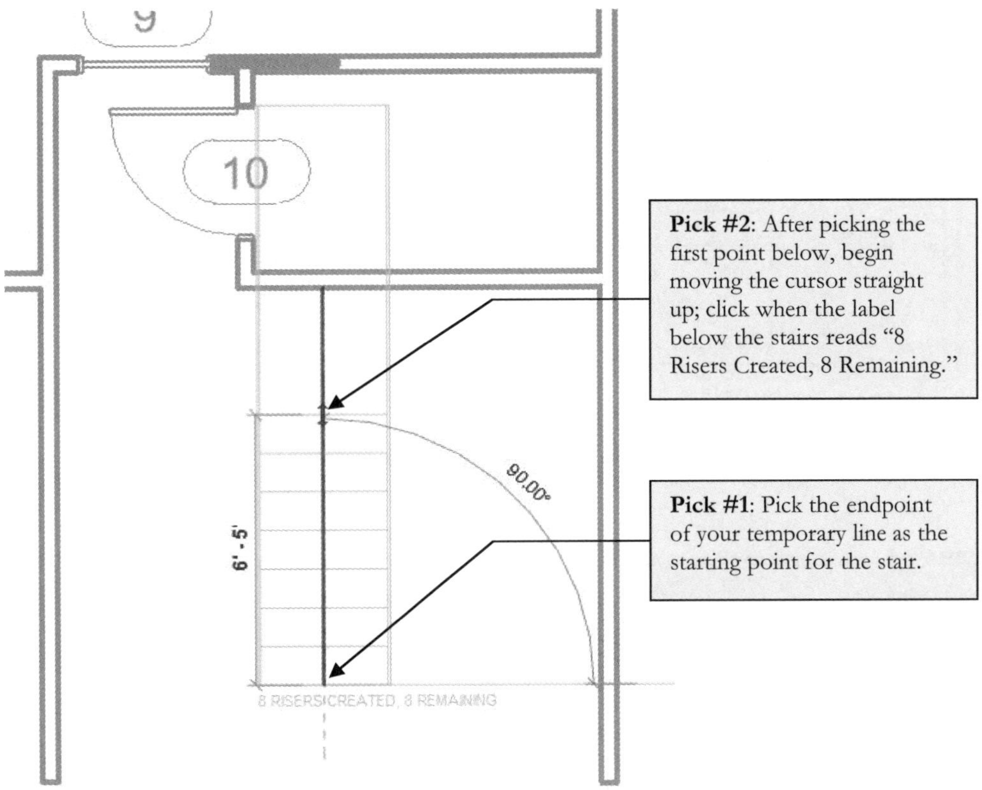

FIGURE 6-5.7 Beginning to sketch the stair

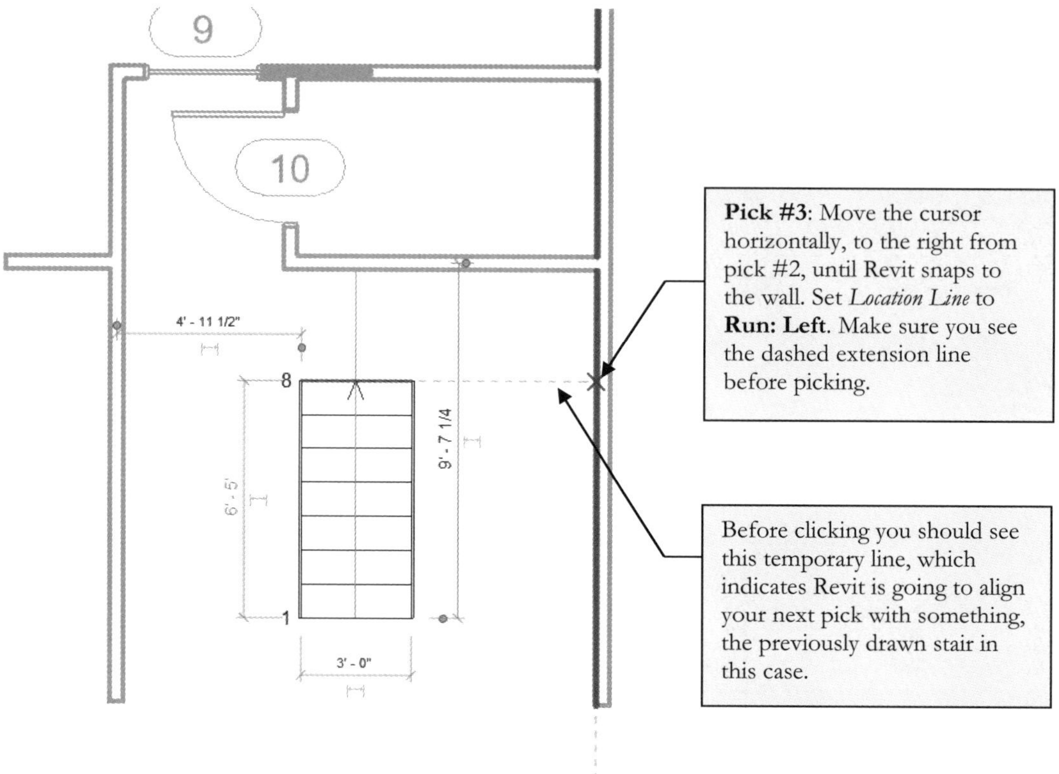

FIGURE 6-5.8 Continuing to sketch the stair

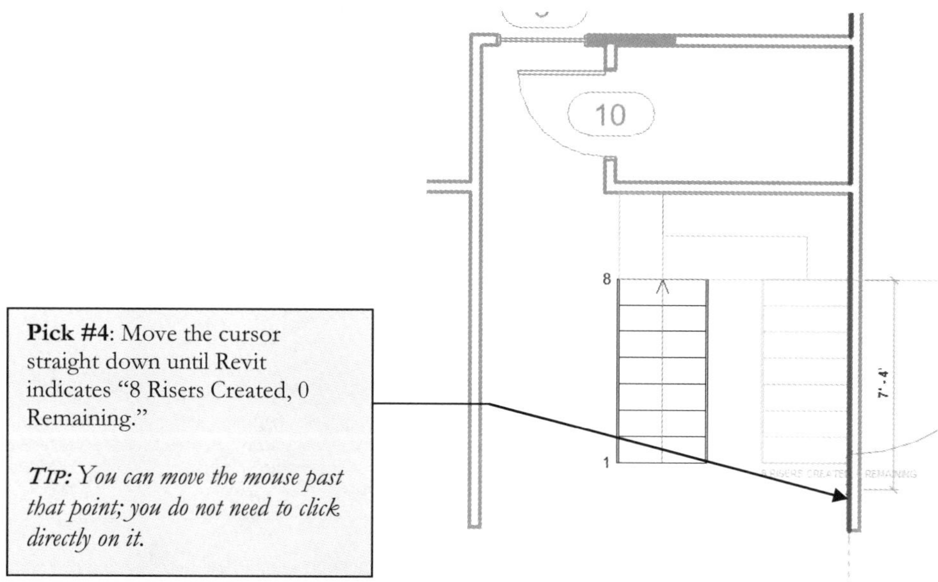

FIGURE 6-5.9 Last step in sketching the stair

13. Click the **green check mark** to *Finish* the stair on the *Ribbon* (Figure 6-5.5).

14. **Erase** the temporary detail line; you may need to tap the Tab key (i.e., tap, not hold down) to select it rather than the stair.

Your stairs should now look like Figure 6-5.10! Notice that Revit adds a break-line at the *Cut Plane,* and everything above that is dashed in.

As soon as you click *Finish Stair*, Revit will automatically add the landing, creating it between the two stair runs sketched. The landing width will match the stair width, which is 3′-0″. This is true for any stair configuration using the above method. You will see this momentarily when you sketch an L-shaped stair in the basement.

The second floor plan also shows this stair, but with a down arrow and no break lines because it does not pass through that view's *Cut Plane*!

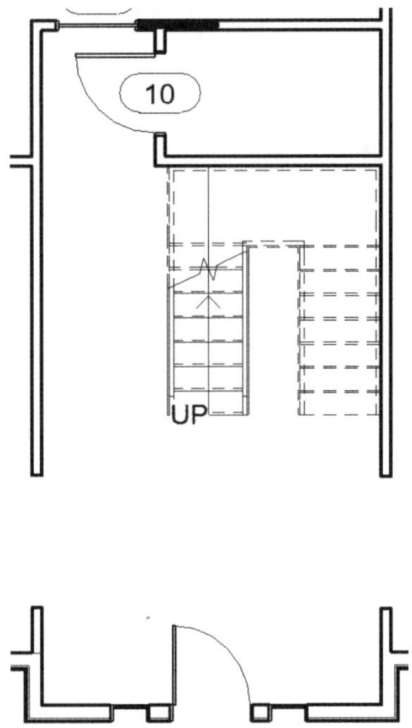

FIGURE 6-5.10 Finished stair

Modeling the Basement Stairs:

Now you will draw the L-shaped stairs from the basement to the first floor.

To get an idea about what you are going to draw next, take a moment to look at Figure 6-5.11. The image below is at the basement level, and the "UP" label indicates where you would access the stair on the basement level. Everything else rises from there, of course, to the first floor.

15. Save your project as **ex6-5.rvt**; remember to save often.

16. Switch to the **Basement** floor plan view.

17. Select the **Stair** tool.

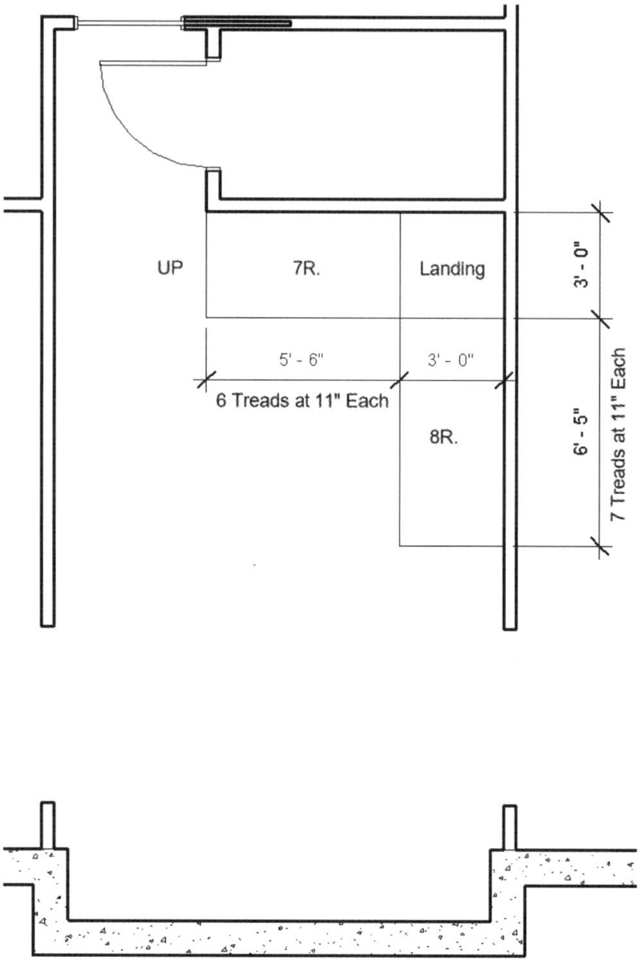

FIGURE 6-5.11 Stair information overview

18. In the *Properties Palette,* make the following changes:
    a. Change the *Type Selector* to **Residential – Open 2 Sides**.
    b. Make sure the *Top Level* is set to **First Floor**; the *Stair* tool defaults to the next *Level* up – which is "foundation" level and not "first floor" in your case.

19. Select the **Railing** button on the *Ribbon.*

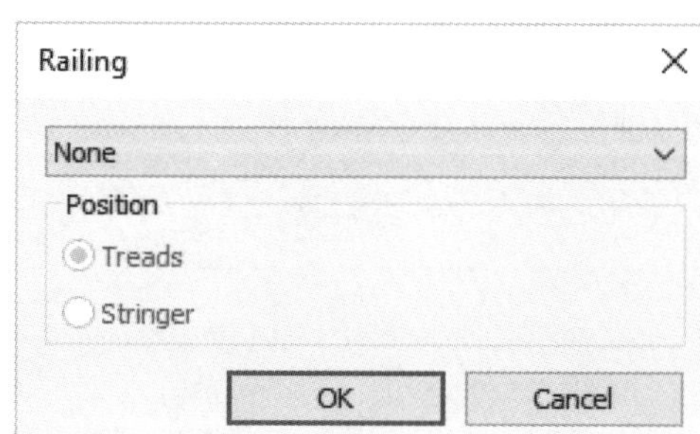

20. Select **None** and **OK** (see image to right).

21. Using the same techniques you employed to sketch the first floor stair, draw the basement stair per the information given in Figure 6-5.11.

***TIP:** While sketching the stairs, you can select a stair run (segment) and move it. Also, do not forget to draw a temporary line(s) if you think it will help.*

22. Click the **Green Check Mark** to finish the stair.

Your stair should look like Figure 6-5.12. If not, select one of the riser/tread lines and press the *Delete* key on the keyboard to erase the stair and try again. It can get a little frustrating when you are not familiar with the ins-and-outs of what Revit is doing or what information it needs to proceed. Take your time; take a break if necessary.

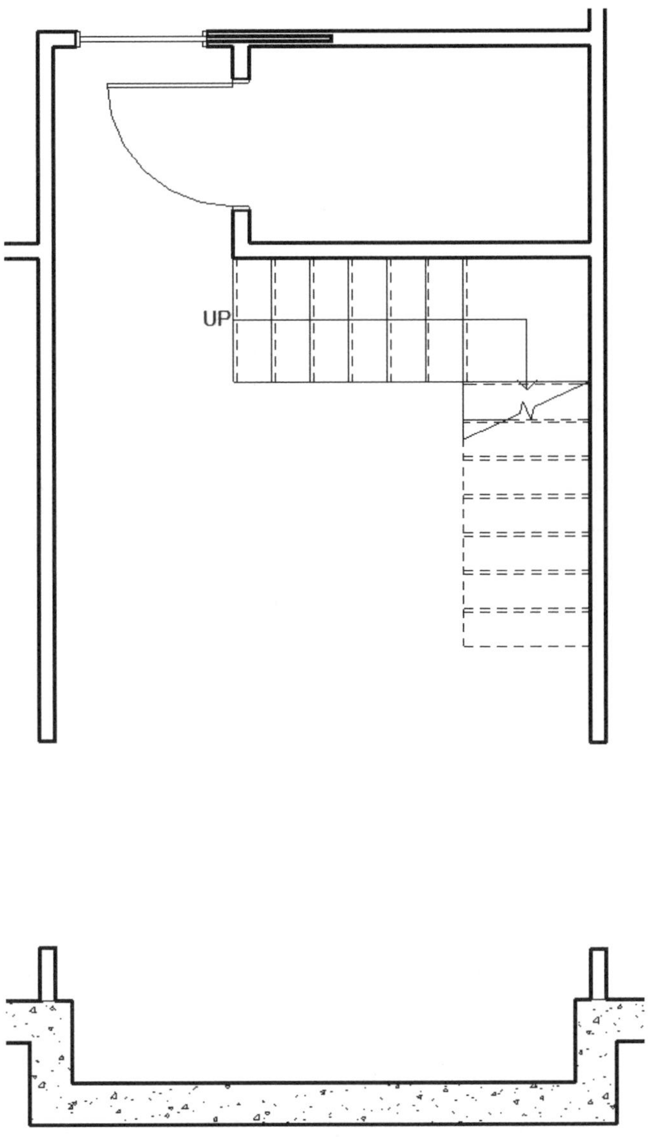

Next, you will draw three walls next to the stair. This will close off the two open sides and the bottom of the stair.

***TIP:** If a stair needs to be modified at any time in the future, you do not actually have to delete the stair and start over; the recommendation above is for practice only. If you select a stair, you can click the Edit Stairs icon on the Ribbon to re-enter Sketch mode for that stair.*

FIGURE 6-5.12 Finished basement stair

23. Using the ***Wall*** tool, draw the three interior walls as shown in **Figure 6-5.13**.

- Use the standard interior wall you used for the other floors.

  TIP #1: *You can select one and see its type in the Type Selector.*

  TIP #2: *You can also select a wall, right-click, and choose "Create Similar" from the pop-up menu to add another wall of the same type.*

- Click the *Chain* option if not already checked.
- Set *Location Line* to one of the finished wall faces.
- *Top Constraint* set to **First Floor**. (not the *Foundation* level, which will be the default)
- Click the inside points of the stair. Press the *spacebar* if needed to flip the wall so it is created outside of the stair footprint.
- Draw the third wall under the stair, at the fifth riser line.

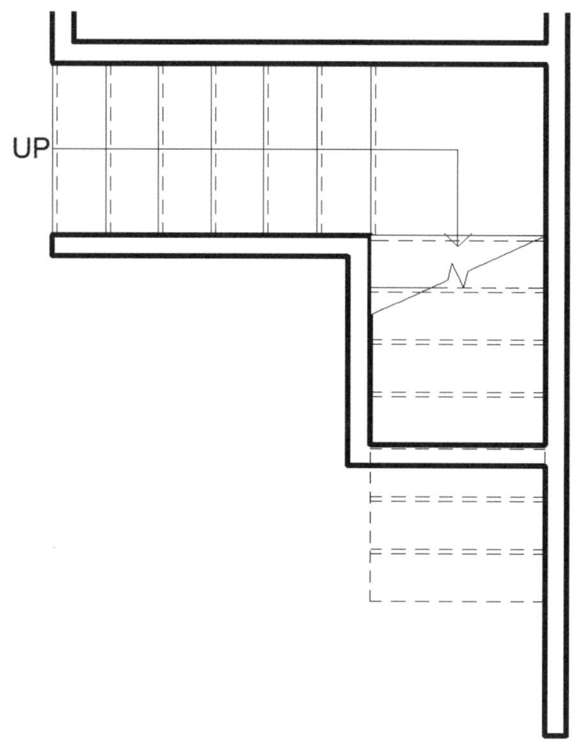

FIGURE 6-5.13 Three walls added at stairs

A cutaway 3D view of your model looks something like this; you will learn to do cutaway views later in the book.

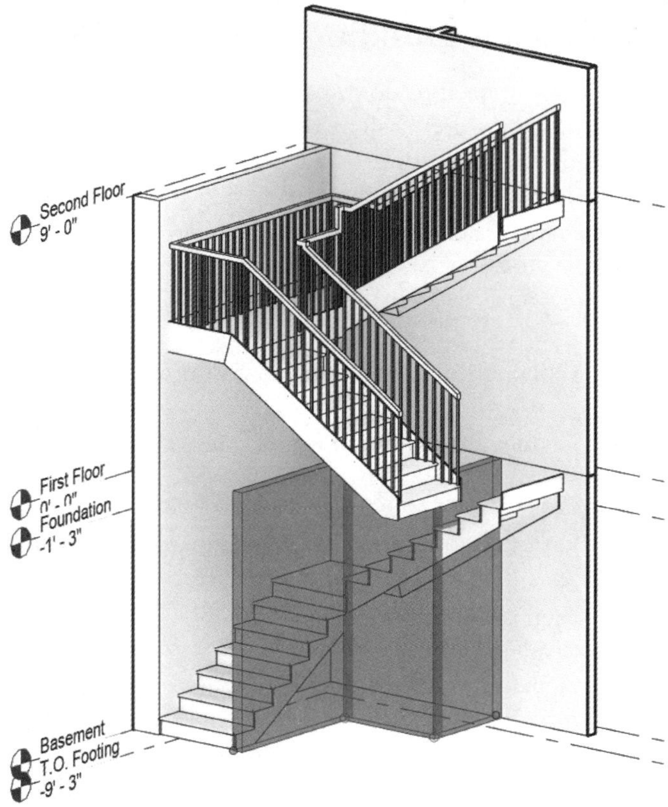

You should notice two things about this 3D view:

First: The basement wall you just added extends through the basement stair. You will fix that in the building sections lesson.

Second: No floors have been drawn yet. You will draw floor systems in a future chapter.

24. **Save** your project.

FYI: *Normally, you would not rename your project file. You do it here in the book for grading and restore options, should things get corrupted or messed up.*

Modify the Building's Floor-to-Floor Height:

You will not need to do this for this tutorial, but you can modify the building's floor-to-floor height (or Level). The reasons for doing this vary. Some examples might be to make the building shorter or taller, to accommodate ductwork in the ceilings or the depth of the floor structure; the longer the span, the deeper the structure. The default floor-to-floor height in the template file you started from is 9′-0″, which is fine for this project. However, should you want to change this for another project, here is how to do it:

- Open any exterior elevation from the *Project Browser.*
- Change the floor-to-floor height to be 12′-0″ for each level; in this example, to the right.
- Select the floor elevation symbol, and then select the text displaying the elevation. You should now be able to type in a new number. Press Enter to see the changes. Notice the windows move because the sill height has not been changed (Figure A).

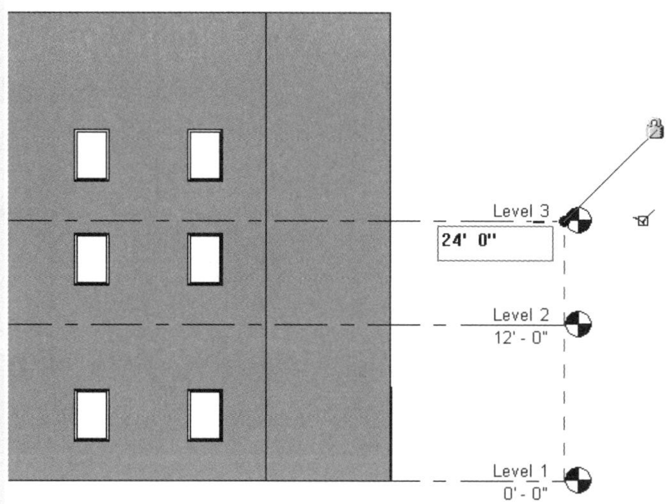

FIGURE A Exterior elevation: modifying Level 3 elevation

- The floor-to-floor height is a good thing to figure out, when possible, before drawing the stairs, as it affects the number of risers and treads required, not to mention floor area.

Self-Exam:

The following questions can be used as a way to check your knowledge of this lesson. The answers can be found at the bottom of the page.

1. The default settings for the floor plan view shows the walls for the floor below. (T/F)
2. Click the green check mark to finish the stair command. (T/F)
3. You should start drawing your floor plan generally centered on the default elevation marks in a new project. (T/F)
4. You can use the *Align* tool to align one wall with another. (T/F)
5. Where do you change the maximum riser height? ________________

Review Questions:

The following questions may be assigned by your instructor as a way to assess your knowledge of this section. Your instructor has the answers to the review questions.

1. It is not possible to copy/paste elements from one floor to another and have them line up (with the original objects). (T/F)
2. Changing an instance parameter affects the selected or to-be-created elements. (T/F)
3. Each Revit view is saved as a separate file on your hard drive. (T/F)
4. You select the part of the wall to be deleted when using the *Trim* tool. (T/F)
5. You cannot "finish stair" if you have not drawn all the treads or risers that are required between the two specified levels. (T/F)
6. What parameter should be set to none, in the *View Properties* dialog, if you

   do not want to see the walls from the floor below? ________________
7. Use the Temporary Hide/Isolate tool to get a better look at your model. (T/F)
8. You can use the ________________ tool to quickly select a certain type of element from a large group of selected objects.
9. The number of __________ remaining is displayed while sketching a stair.

SELF-EXAM ANSWERS:
1 – T, **2** – T, **3** – T, **4** – T, **5** – Type Properties

Notes:

Lesson 7
Annotation:

This chapter covers annotations in Revit: text, dimensions, tags, shared parameters, and keynotes. In print, the drawings are often insufficient to convey the design intent. These tools enable effective communication for those using the final printed drawings to both bid and build the building. Several of the chapters following this one will utilize many of these concepts.

All the tools covered in this chapter are found on the Annotate tab. Three of the tools on this tab are also on the Quick Access Toolbar because they are used often: **Dimension**, **Tag by Category**, and **Text**.

TIP: All the tools on the Annotate tab are 2D and view-specific.

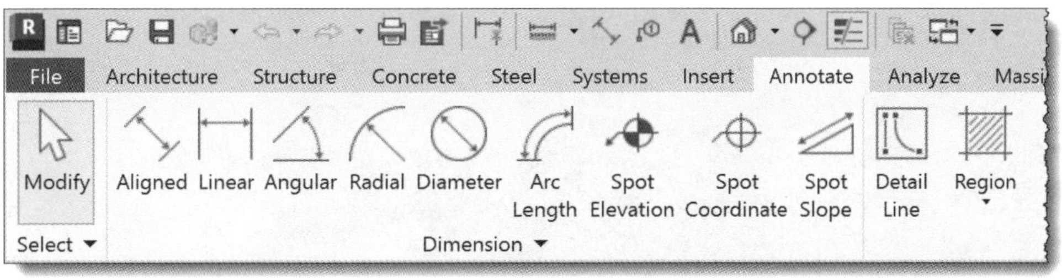

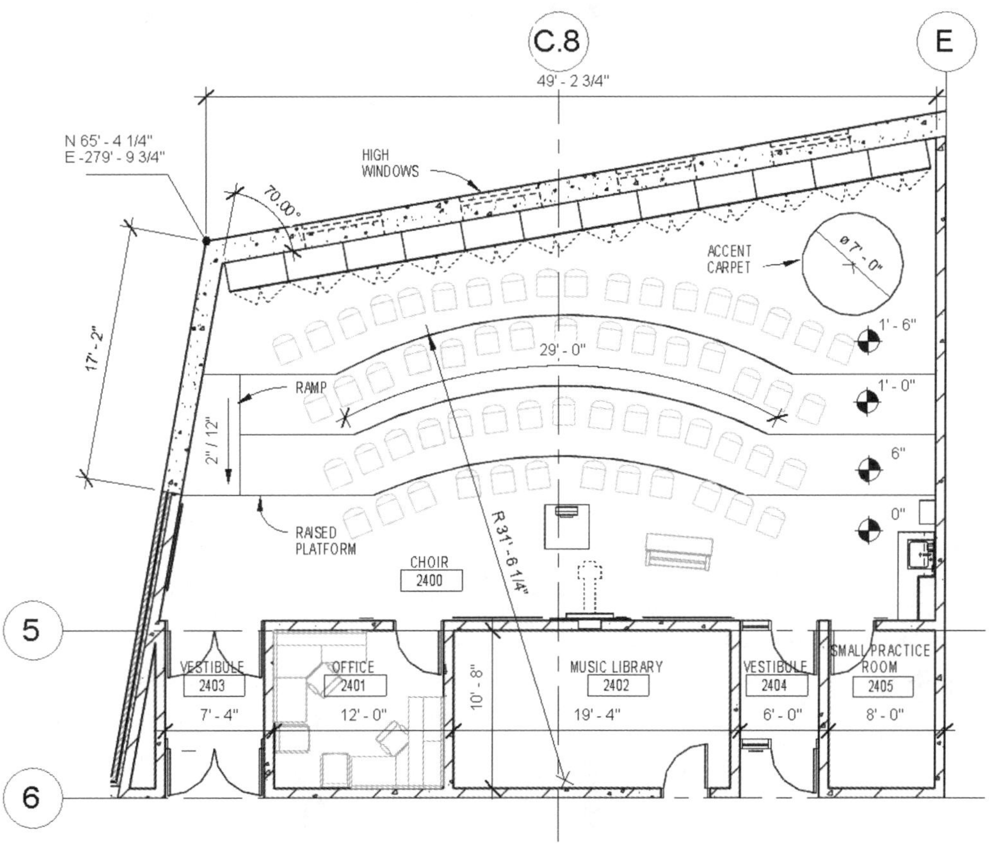

Exercise 7-1:
Text

This section covers placing notes using the **Text** command in Revit. We will also look at Revit's **Spell Check** and **Find/Replace** tools, including their limitations.

The first thing to know about the text tool is that it should be used as little as possible! Rather, dynamic tags, keynotes, and dimensions are preferred over static text to ensure the information is correct. Text will not update or move when something in the model changes—especially if the text is not visible or in the view where the model is being changed.

That said, the text command is still necessary and is often used in Revit.

Steps to add new Text to a view:

- Start the **Text** command
- Verify the **Text Style**
- Define the starting point; **click** *or* **click and drag**
- **Type** the desired text, typically without pressing *Enter*
- **Click away** from the text to finish the command

Steps to edit existing text:

- Select the text
- Click again to enter edit mode

Text

The Text tool can be started from the **Quick Access Toolbar**, the **Annotate** tab, or by typing **TX** on the keyboard.

The first step is to consider the current text type in the Type Selector (Figure 7-1.1). When creating new text types, the name of a text type should, at a minimum, contain the size and font name. The size is the **actual size on the printed page,** regardless of the drawing scale.

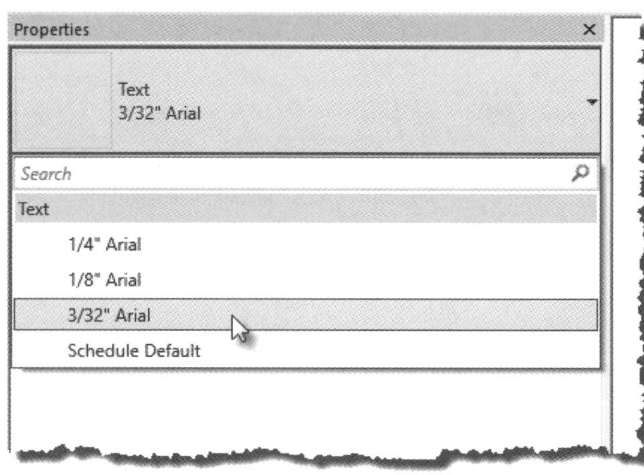

FIGURE 7-1.1 Type selector with text command active

There are additional steps that are optional, but at this point, you could click or click and drag within the drawing window and start typing your desired note.

Here is the difference between the **click** and **click and drag** options when starting text:

- **Click**: Defines the starting point for new text. No automatic return to next line while typing. An Enter must be pressed to start a new line; this is called a "hard return" in the word processing world.
- **Click and Drag**: This defines a windowed area where text will be entered. The height is not really important. The width determines when a line automatically returns to the next line while typing. Using this method allows paragraphs to be easily adjusted by dragging an edge of the selected textbox.

As long as "hard returns" are not used, the textbox width and number of rows adjust dynamically. To adjust the textbox, select the text, then use the round grip on the right (See Figure 7-1.2) to reposition it via click-and-drag with the left mouse button.

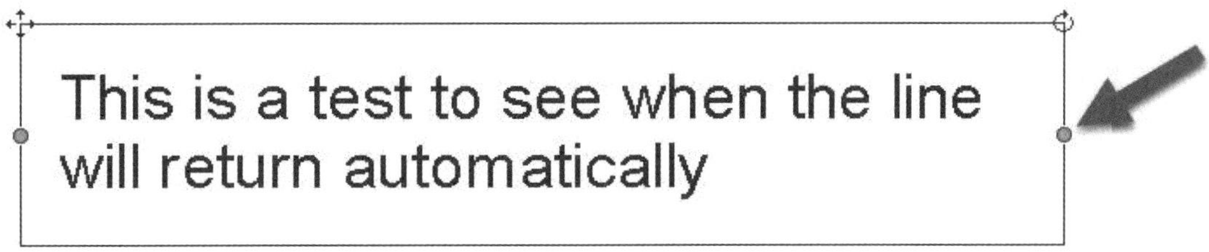

FIGURE 7-1.2 Selecting text and adjusting width of the textbox

The image to the right, Figure 7-1.3, shows the result of adjusting the width of the textbox—the text element went from two lines to four.

If an Enter is pressed at the end of each line of text when originally typed, the text will not automatically adjust as just described. An example of this can be seen in the following two images, Figure 7-1.4 & 5. Note that in some cases, this is desirable to ensure the text's formatting is not changed.

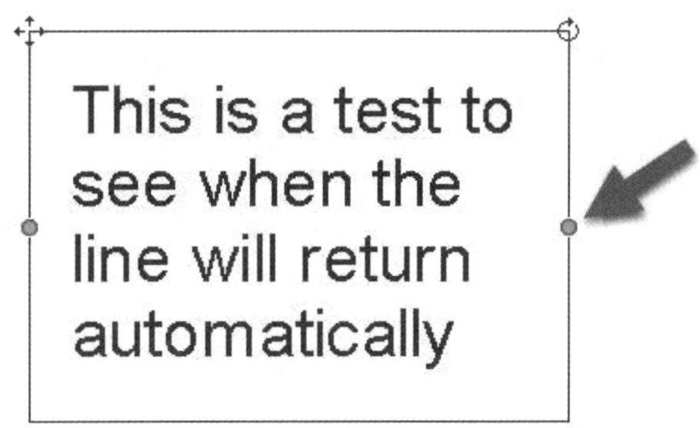

FIGURE 7-1.3 Text width adjusted

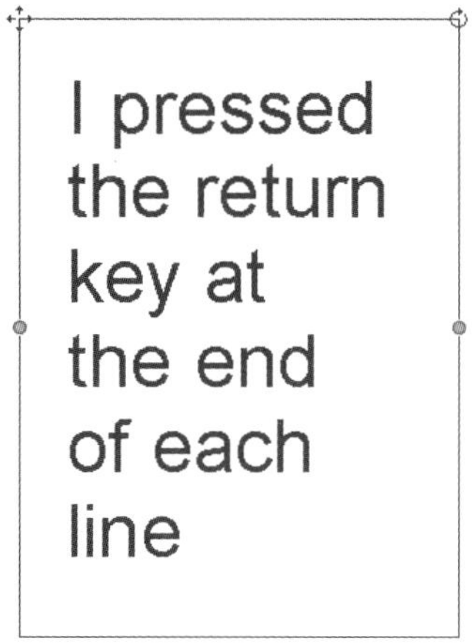

FIGURE 7-1.4
Text with hard returns

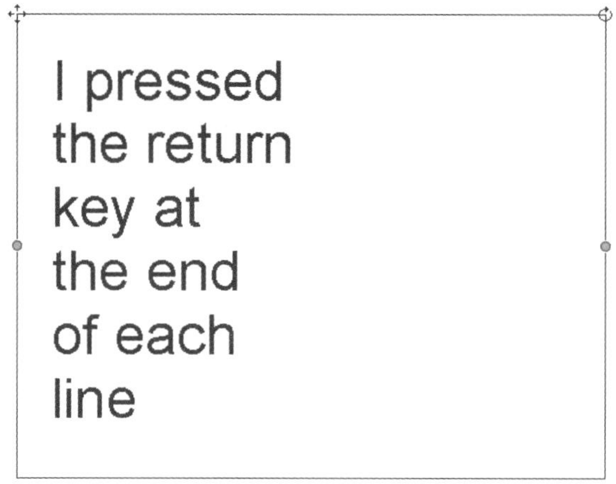

FIGURE 7-1.5
Text does not adjust when textbox width is modified

Keep in mind that this text tool is strictly 2D and view-specific. If the same text is required in multiple views, it either needs to be retyped or copied and pasted. However, for general notes that might appear on all floor plan sheets, a Legend View can be used.

Revit has a separate tool, on the Architecture tab, called **Model Text** for instances when 3D text is needed within the model. Model text is usually associated with something built by the contractor or manufacturer, such as a sign or the building's address.

Text Placement & Formatting Options

In addition to the basic topics covered, there are several options for text placement. These adjustments can be applied when creating the text initially or at any time later.

The formatting options are mainly found on the Ribbon immediately after activating the Text command.

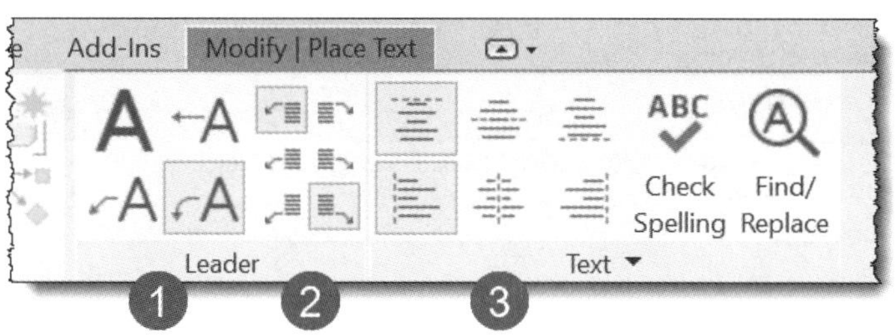

FIGURE 7-1.6 Formatting options on the Ribbon while creating text

The formatting options identified in the image are:

1. Leader options
2. Leader position options
3. Text Justification/Alignment

Leader Options

A leader is a line that extends from the text, with an arrow at its end, used to point to something in the drawing.

The default option, when using the text command, is no leader. This is the highlighted option in the upper left.

The remaining three options determine the graphical appearance of the leader: one segment, two segments, or curved, as seen in Figure 7-1.7. Often, a design firm will standardize one of these three options for a consistent look.

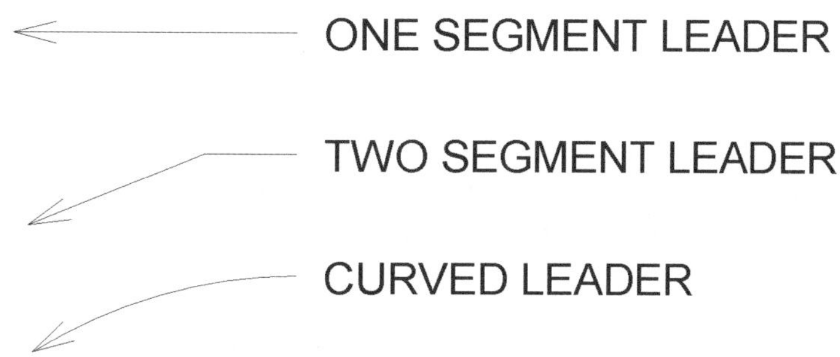

FIGURE 7-1.7 Leader formatting options

Here are the steps to include a leader with text:

- Start the **Text** command
- Select text type via **Type Selector**
- Select **Leader** option
- Specify **leader location** (2-3 picks)
- **Type** text
- Click **Close**, or click away from text, to finish

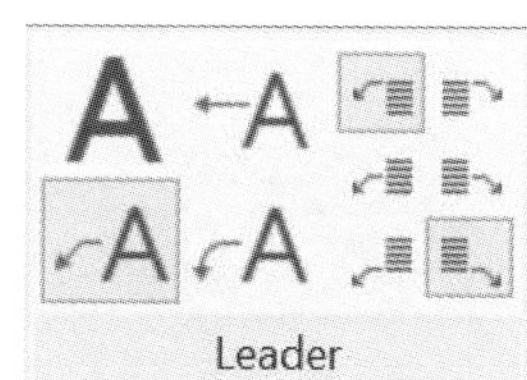

Leader Options

Once text with a leader is created, it can be selected and modified later if needed. In the next image, Figure 7-1.8, notice the two **circle grips** associated with the leader: at the arrow (magenta-colored grip) and the change in direction of the line (yellow-colored grip); the other two circle grips are for the textbox as previously described in this section. These two grips can be repositioned by clicking and dragging the left mouse button.

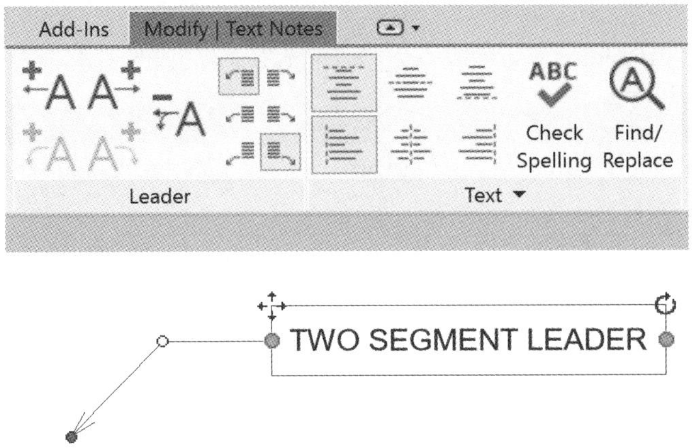

FIGURE 7-1.8 Text with leader selected; notice leader grips and Ribbon options

When text is selected, the Ribbon displays slightly different options for leaders as seen in the image above. It is possible to have multiple leaders (i.e., arrows) coming off the text—denoted by the green "plus" symbol. In the next image, Figure 7-1.9, a second leader was added on the left, and another on the right. It is not possible to have both curved and straight leader lines for the same text element. In this example, the curved leader options are grayed out as seen in Figure 7-1.8.

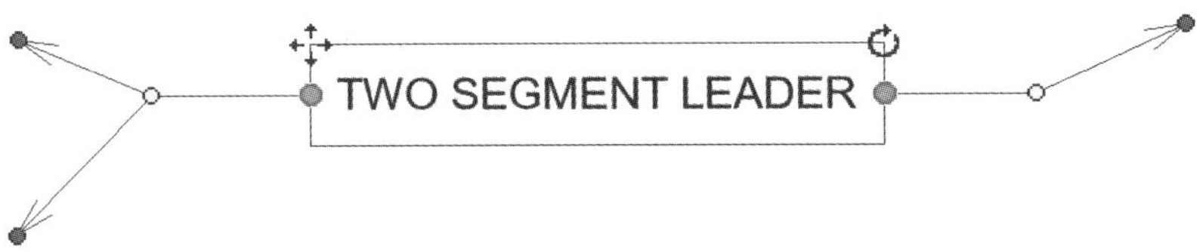

FIGURE 7-1.9 Multiple leaders added

Back in Figure 7-1.8, notice that leaders can be removed, even to the point where the text has no leaders. The one catch with the **remove leader** option is that they can only be removed in the reverse order in which they were added.

The **Leader Arrowhead** can be changed graphically (i.e., solid dot, loop leader, etc.). This will be covered in the section on Managing Text Types, as this setting is in the Type Properties for the text itself.

> ***Good to know…***
> Text can be placed in **any view** and on **sheets**. The only exception is that the Text command does not work in schedule views.
>
> Text can also be in a **Group**. When the group only has elements from the Annotate tab, it is a Detail Group. When the group also contains model elements, the text is in an Attached Detail Group. When a Model Group is placed, selecting it gives the option to add the Attached Detail Group.

Leader Position Options

These six toggles control the position of the leader relative to the text as seen in the two images below (Figures 7-1.10 and 11). These options also appear in the Properties Palette when text is selected, called **Left Attachment** and **Right Attachment**.

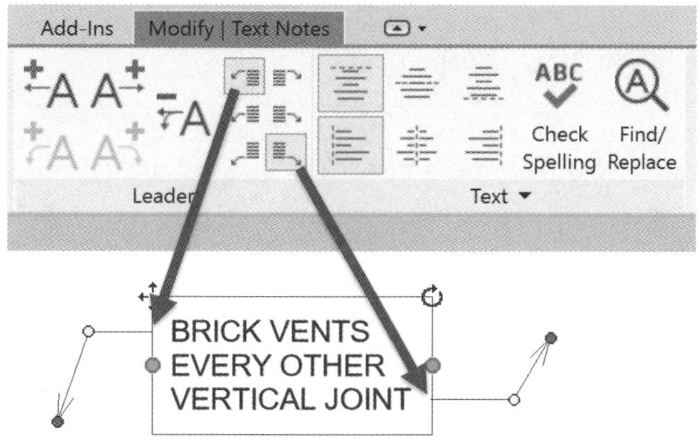

FIGURE 7-1.10 Leader position toggles – example A

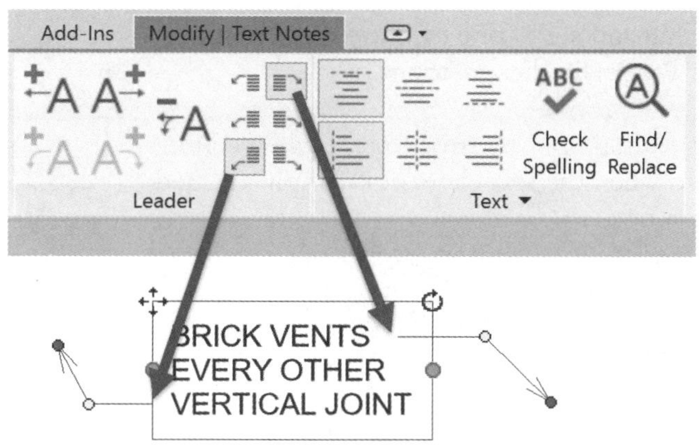

FIGURE 7-1.11 Leader position toggles – example B

Similar to a leader type, design firms will often select a standard that everyone is expected to follow so construction documents look consistent.

Text Justification

When text is selected, there are three options for horizontal justification on the Ribbon: Left, Center, and Right. The results are shown in the three images in Figure 7-1.12.

This option also appears in the Properties Palette when text is selected, called **Horizontal Align**. Keep in mind that all options in the Property Palette are instance parameters—meaning they only apply to the instance(s) selected. Thus, each text entity in Revit can have different settings.

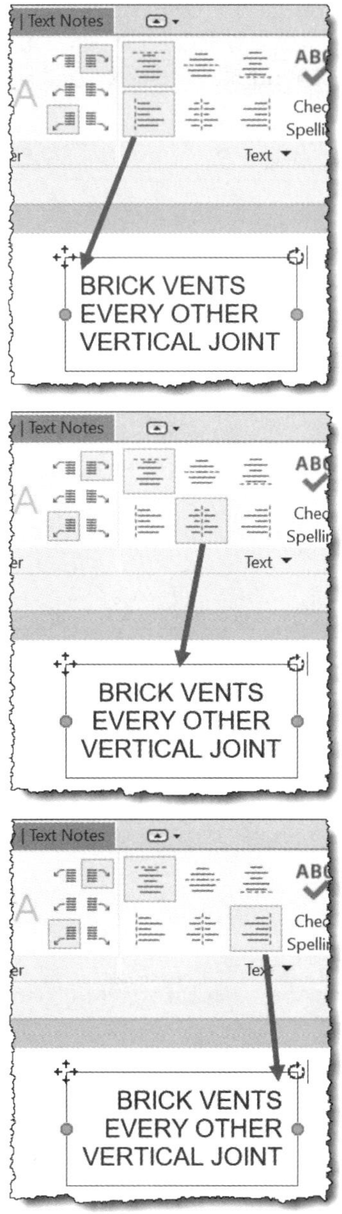

FIGURE 7-1.12 Text justification options

Text Formatting

The next section to cover is the options to make text Bold, Italic, or Underlined.

These options do not appear in the Properties Palette because they can be applied to individual words (or even individual characters). In the example below, the word "Brick" is bold, "other" is italicized, and "vertical" is underlined.

If all the text is selected and set to one of these three options, any future edits will also retain these settings.

FYI: Notice the formatting options are different when editing the text, compared to when the text element is simply selected.

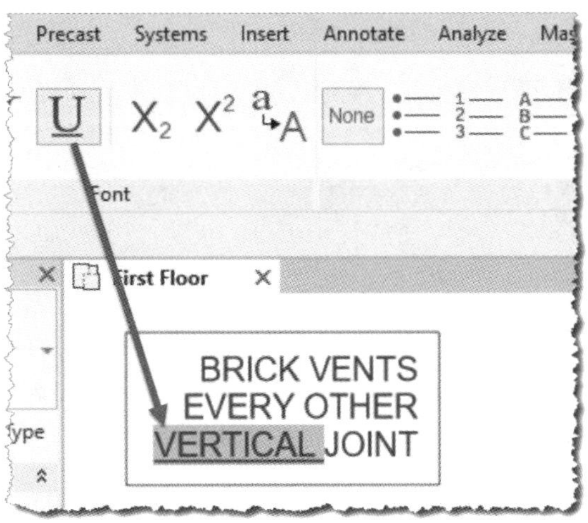

FIGURE 7-1.13 Text formatting

Text Formatting

The next section to cover is the **List** options on the Paragraph panel. This feature is only available while editing the textbox contents; to do so, select the text and click it to enter edit mode.

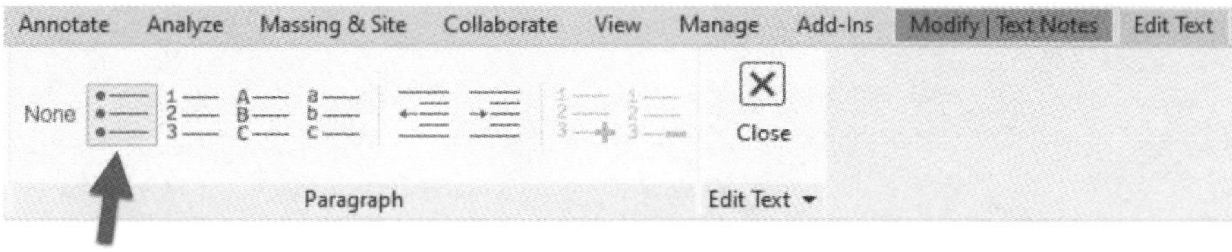

- 4" FACE BRICK
- 1" AIR SPACE
- 3" RIGID INSULATION
- 8" CONCRETE MASONRY UNIT (CMU)
- 3 5/8" MTL STUDS AT 16" O.C.
- 5/8" GYP BD

1. 4" FACE BRICK
2. 1" AIR SPACE
3. 3" RIGID INSULATION
4. 8" CONCRETE MASONRY UNIT (CMU)
5. 3 5/8" MTL STUDS AT 16" O.C.
6. 5/8" GYP BD

a. 4" FACE BRICK
b. 1" AIR SPACE
c. 3" RIGID INSULATION
d. 8" CONCRETE MASONRY UNIT (CMU)
e. 3 5/8" MTL STUDS AT 16" O.C.
f. 5/8" GYP BD

A. 4" FACE BRICK
B. 1" AIR SPACE
C. 3" RIGID INSULATION
D. 8" CONCRETE MASONRY UNIT (CMU)
E. 3 5/8" MTL STUDS AT 16" O.C.
F. 5/8" GYP BD

FIGURE 7-1.14 Four options to define a line within text

This is one case where you must press Enter to force the following text to a new line and automatically generate a list (i.e., bullet, letter, or number).

Clicking the **Increase Indent** tool will indent the list as shown below (Figure 7-1.15). To undo this later, click in that row and select **Decrease Indent**. There does not appear to be a way to change the indented list spacing. Using the backspace key, then indenting again, creates an indent without a number/letter.

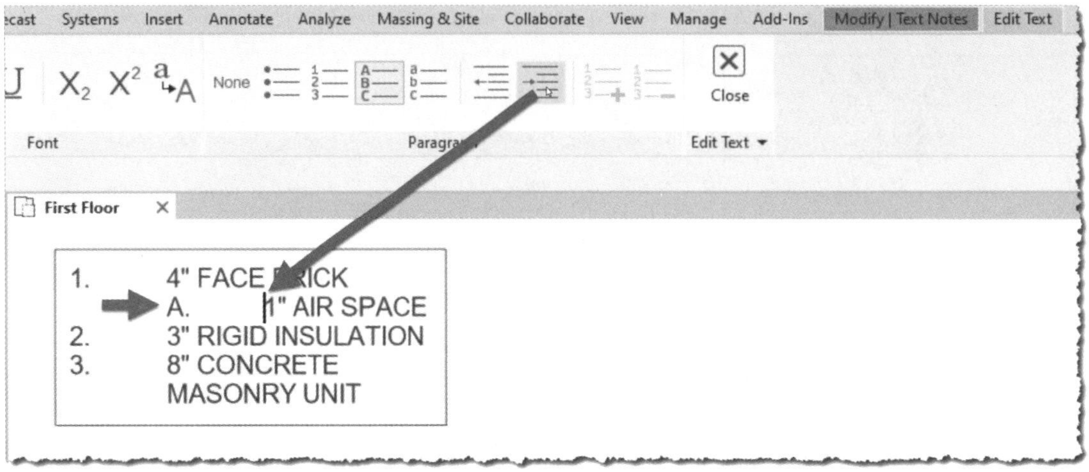

FIGURE 7-1.15 Indenting within a list

Clicking within the first row and selecting the plus or minus icons lets you change the starting number/letter of the list.

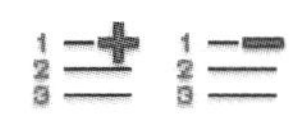

The text formatting options also allow for **subscript** and **superscript** as shown in the example below (Figure 7-1.16).

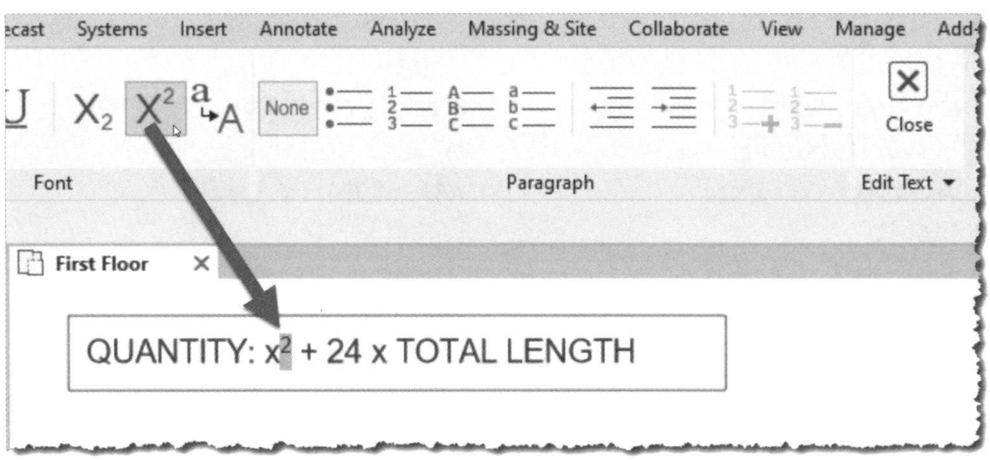

FIGURE 7-1.16 Superscript example

Also, notice the **All Caps** icon; clicking it will change the selected text to all uppercase. When this feature is used, Revit remembers the original formatting; toggling off the All Caps feature later restores the original formatting.

Managing Text Types

When using the text tool, the options in the Type Selector are determined by **Text Types** defined in the current project. Most design firms will have all the Text Types they need defined within their template.

There are two ways to access the text type properties. One is to start the Text command and then click **Edit Type** in the Properties Palette. The other is to click the arrow in the Text panel on the Annotate tab, as shown in the image below.

The **Type Properties**, as shown in the example to the right (Figure 7-1.17), are self-explanatory. Below is a brief description of each.

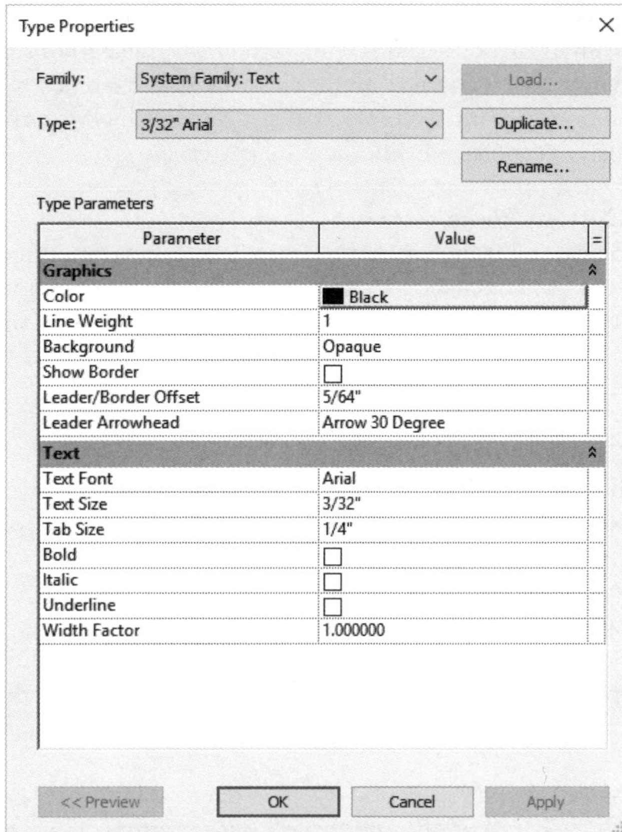

FIGURE 7-1.17 Text type properties

Command	*What it does…*
Color	This can affect printing, so it is often set to black.
Line Weight	This is only for the leader.
Background	*Toggle:* Opaque or Transparent
Show Border	*Check box:* Show or Hide
Leader/Border Offset	Space between text and border and leader – helpful when Background is set to Opaque.
Leader Arrowhead	Select from a list of predefined arrow types
Text Font	Select from a list of installed fonts on your computer
Text Size	Size of text on the printed page
Tab Size	Size of space when Tab is pressed (size on printed paper)
Bold	Default setting – can be changed while in edit mode
Italic	Default setting – can be changed while in edit mode
Underline	Default setting – can be changed while in edit mode
Width Factor	Adjusts the overall width of a line of text

Colors

The color applies to the text and the leader. The color is often set to black. If any other color is used, this can affect printing. For example, any color becomes a shade of gray when printed to a black-and-white printer—similar to printing a document from Microsoft Word, where green text is a darker shade of gray than yellow text. In the Print dialog, there is an option to print all colors as Black Lines, which can make colored text black. However, this also overrides gray lines and fill patterns.

Custom Fonts

Be careful using custom fonts installed on your computer, as others who do not have those fonts will likely not see the formatting the same as intended. Custom fonts can come from installing other software, such as Adobe InDesign. In fact, Autodesk also installs several custom fonts that are supposed to match some of the special SHX fonts that come with AutoCAD.

Custom Fonts

It is not possible to create custom arrowheads. However, the list of arrowheads is based on styles defined here: **Manage → Additional Settings → Arrowheads**. This provides many options for how these items look.

Width Factor

Some firms use a Width Factor like 0.75, 0.85, or similar to squish the text and fit more information on a sheet. Getting any narrower than this makes the text hard to read. This option actually changes the proportions of each letter, not just the space between them.

Misc.

Note that Text does not have a phase setting. Thus, the phase filters and overrides do not apply to text. It is sometimes desired to have text noting existing elements, such as ductwork, in a shade of gray rather than solid, and to reserve black for new elements.

Check Spelling

Revit has a tool that checks spelling. Keep in mind this only works on text created with the Text command and only for the current view. Revit cannot check the spelling of text in keynotes, tags, or families. Neither can it check the entire project.

The Spell Check tool can be found on the Annotate tab or on the Ribbon when text is selected. When Spell Check is selected, the dialog to the right appears if there are any misspellings found (Figure 7-1.18).

When Revit encounters a word not in the dictionary, it provides a list of possible correct words. Often, the first suggestion is the right one. If not, select from the list.

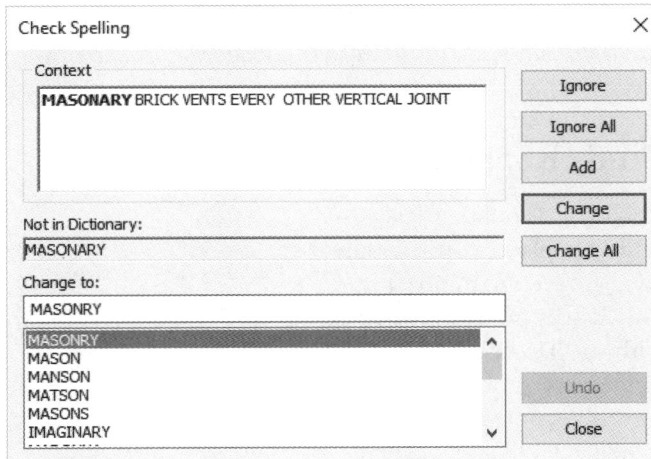

FIGURE 7-1.18 Check Spelling dialog

Clicking the **Change** button will correct the highlighted word. Clicking **Change All** will change all of the words with this same misspelling in the current view.

Sometimes Revit flags a word that isn't misspelled. This might be a company name, your name, a product name, or an industry abbreviation. In this case, one might select the **Add** option to add the word to the custom dictionary, so you don't have to deal with this every time you run spell check.

The image on the right shows the settings for the Spell Check engine. The options are self-explanatory. In an office, consider placing the custom dictionary on the server and pointing all users to it.

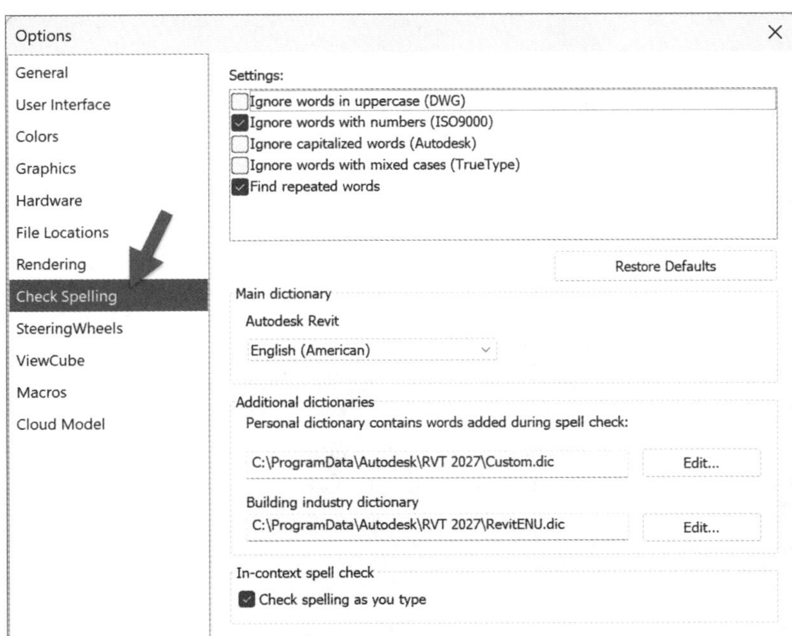

FIGURE 7-1.19 Check Spelling in Options dialog

Don't totally rely on Spell Check. A word may be spelled correctly but still be the wrong word. For example:

- Fill the **whole** with concrete and trowel level and smooth.
- Fill the **hole** with concrete and trowel level and smooth.

In this example, the word "whole" is wrong but spelled correctly. Also, keep in mind that Revit does not have a grammar-check system like popular word processing programs.

Find/Replace

Revit has a tool that lets you find or replace words within a view. Keep in mind, this only works on text created with the Text command. Revit cannot find or replace text in keynotes, tags, or families. Unlike the spelling tool, this tool can search the entire project.

When this tool is selected, the dialog to the right appears (Figure 7-1.20).

In this example, the current view is being searched for the brand name Sheetrock, so it can be replaced with the generic industry-standard term, **Gypsum Board**.

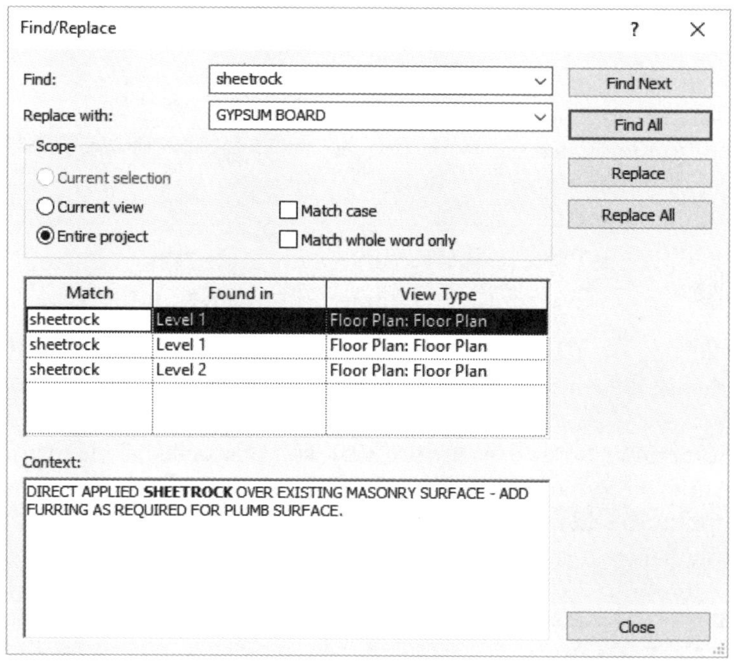

FIGURE 7-1.20 Find/Replace dialog

Selecting **Entire project** and then clicking **Find All** tells Revit to list all matches in the middle section of the dialog. For each row, you can click to select and see the context in which the found word(s) is used.

When items are found, the **Replace** or **Replace All** buttons can be used to swap out the text in one location or all. When clicking Replace, only the selected row is replaced.

This tool can be used to just find something and not replace it. For example, on a large project with hundreds of views in the Project Browser, using Find/Replace to search for details containing the word "roof drain" can significantly speed up locating the desired drawing.

Replacing a Text Type

In addition to replacing content within a text element, you can also replace the text type. For example, some imported details use a different font, and you want everything to match and be consistent. This is not really associated with the Find/Replace tool, but it is important to know how to accomplish this task.

> Replacing a Text Type within a view or project:
> - **Select** one text element within the project
> - **Right-click** (Fig. 7-1.21)
> - Pick **Select All Instances →**
>   - Visible in View
>   - In Entire Project
> - Select a different type from the **Type Selector**

This procedure will replace all the text in either the current view or the entire project. Even text that has been hidden with the "Hide in View" right-click option will be changed.

When a specific text type is selected, the selection count in the lower-right corner of the Revit window indicates the total number of elements selected (Figure 7-1.22). This can be used as a quick double check before replacing the text type. For example, if the intent was to replace only a few rogue text instances but the count was several hundred, this would be a clue that another view uses this text type and perhaps should not be changed, as it was created by someone else on the project. This can be especially true if multiple disciplines are working in the same project.

FIGURE 7-1.21 Select all instances via right-click

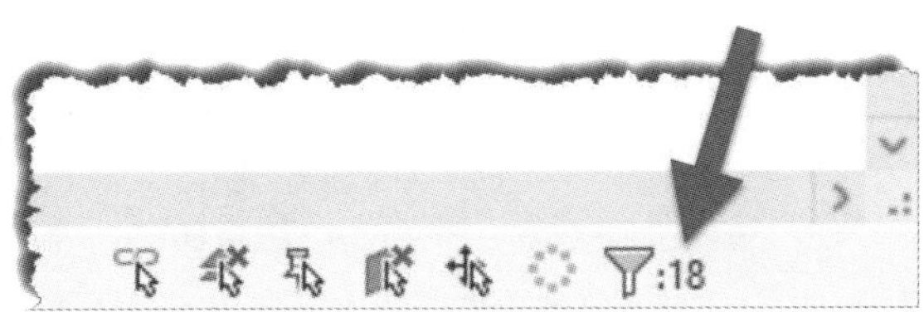

Exercise 7-2:
Dimensions

This exercise will cover the ins and outs of dimensioning in Revit.

The first thing to understand about dimensions is that they are 2D and view-specific—like all commands on the Annotate tab.

Dimension elements have an association with the thing(s) being dimensioned. If that thing(s) is deleted, the dimension will also be deleted, even if the dimension is not visible in the current view. For example, if a wall is deleted from a 3D view, then any dimensions associated with that wall, in a floor plan view, which may not even be open, will be deleted.

Because dimensions are associated with specific elements in the model, it is important to ensure the correct elements are selected when placing a dimension. In a floor plan, for example, the place to click to add a dimension may have several elements stacked on top of each other: grid line, wall edge, floor edge, window edge, and wall sweep. It may be necessary to tap the Tab key to cycle through the options and select the correct item (while tabbing, the highlighted element will appear in the status bar at the bottom of the screen).

Each dimension command will be covered in the order they appear on the Annotate tab, as seen in the image below.

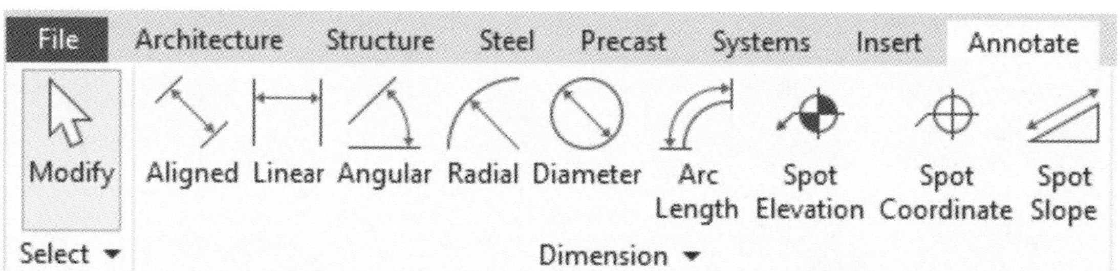

Command	*What it does (see image on next page)…*
1. Aligned	Most used dimension tool; dimension between parallel references (e.g., walls or ducts) or multiple points
2. Linear	Dimensions between points and always horizontal or vertical
3. Angular	Measures the angle between two references
4. Radial	Indicates the radius of a curved line or element
5. Diameter	Indicates the diameter of an arc or circle
6. Arc Length	Measures the length of a line/element along a curve
7. Spot Elevation	Lists the elevation at a selected point, on an element (e.g., floor, ceiling, toposolid)
8. Spot Coordinate	Indicates the N/S and E/W position of a selected point
9. Spot Slope	Used to indicate the slope of a ramp in plan or the pitch of a roof in elevation

The following floor plan example shows each dimension type used. This is a middle school choir room with various conditions in terms of dimensions, such as angled walls, curved lines, and multiple floor elevations.

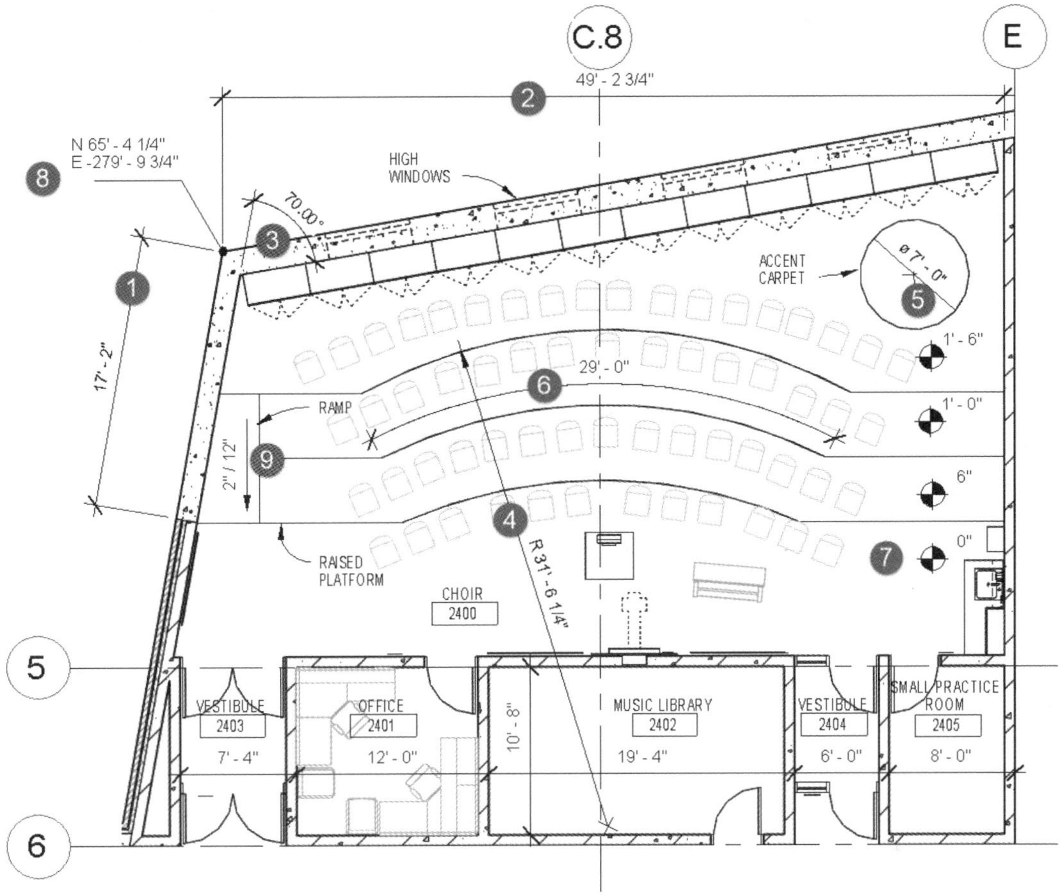

FIGURE 7-2.1 Example floor plan used for dimensioning study

Aligned - Dimension

This dimension tool is the most used of the dimension tools, and for this reason, it is also located on the Quick Access Toolbar (QAT).

Steps to add Aligned dimensions:

- Review **Type Selector** and **Ribbon options**
- **Select first reference**
  - Click on the element ***or***
  - Press tab to select a specific reference or intersection
- **Select second reference**
- Optional: Select additional references (creates a dimension string)
- **Click away** from anything dimensionable to finish the command

The **Align** dimension tool can create angled, horizontal, and vertical dimensions. When the tool is first started, the default "Prefer" option is to select **Wall Centerlines**, as indicated on the Ribbon. Clicking a wall starts a dimension line perpendicular to it. The second point could then be another wall at the same angle, or the endpoint or intersection of lines.

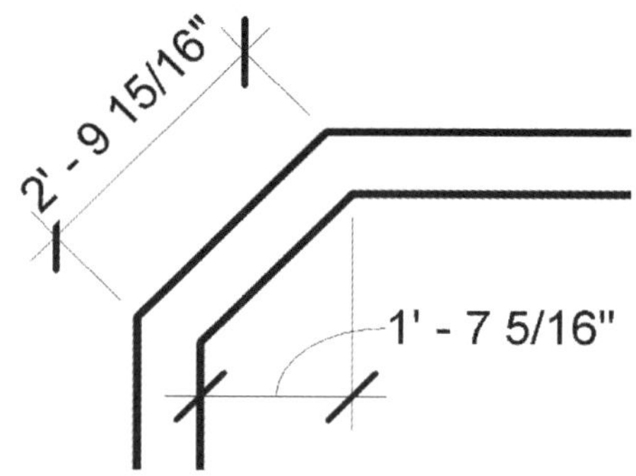

In the example to the right, if the vertical wall is rotated, the dimension will rotate with it. If the dimension must remain horizontal, use the Linear dimension option.

The image below shows the User Interface while the Aligned dimension tool is active.

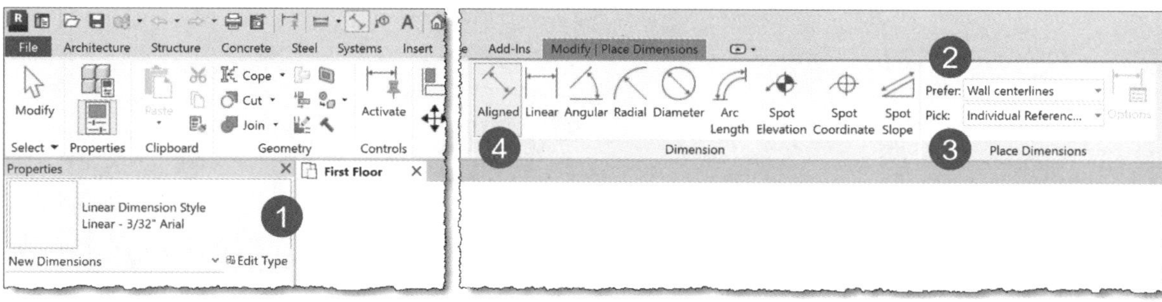

FIGURE 7-2.2 Using the Aligned dimension tool

Here is a description of the numbered items in the image above:

1. Type Selector
2. Selection Preference
3. Individual or Automatic Dimension
4. Switch to another dimension tool

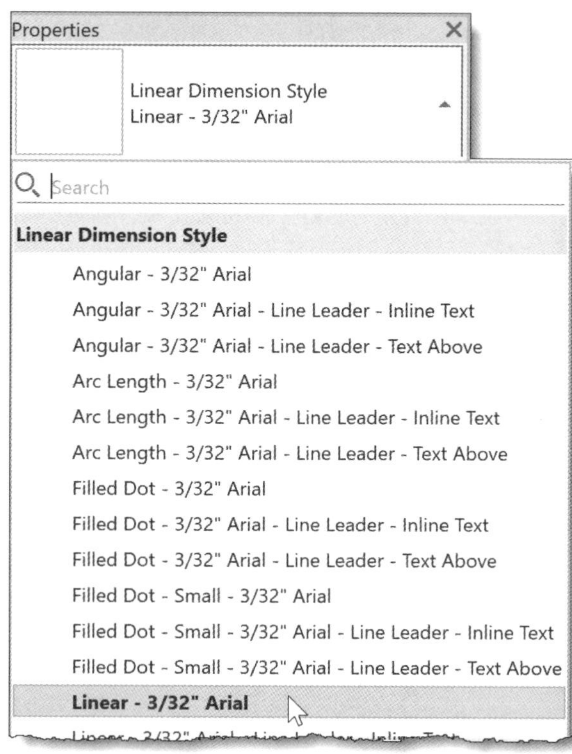

FIGURE 7-2.3 Selecting a dimension type

Type Selector:

Once the dimension tool is active, select the desired **Type** from the *Type Selector* (Figure 7-2.3). This list will vary depending on the template the project was started with and any modifications made.

Selection Preference:
The default is **Wall Centerlines**, which means that, even when zoomed way out, just clicking a wall will reference its centerline. The other options listed (Figure 7-2.4) are self-explanatory. Another option, rather than changing this drop-down list, is to hover the cursor over the desired face, e.g., **Wall faces**, and then tap the Tab key until that face is highlighted, and then click. This can save time by avoiding the need to keep moving the cursor all the way up to the Ribbon and changing the formal setting.

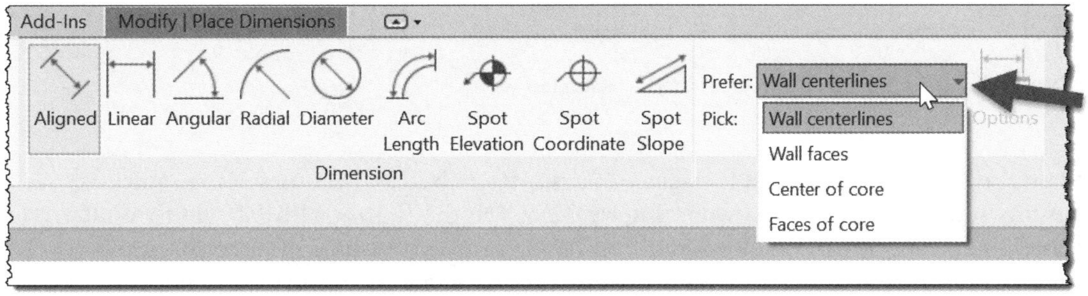

FIGURE 7-2.4 Specify the selection preference for dimensions

Individual versus Automatic Dimensions:
Revit defaults to the **Individual References** option so the designer can deliberately select each reference to dimension to (Figure 7-2.5).

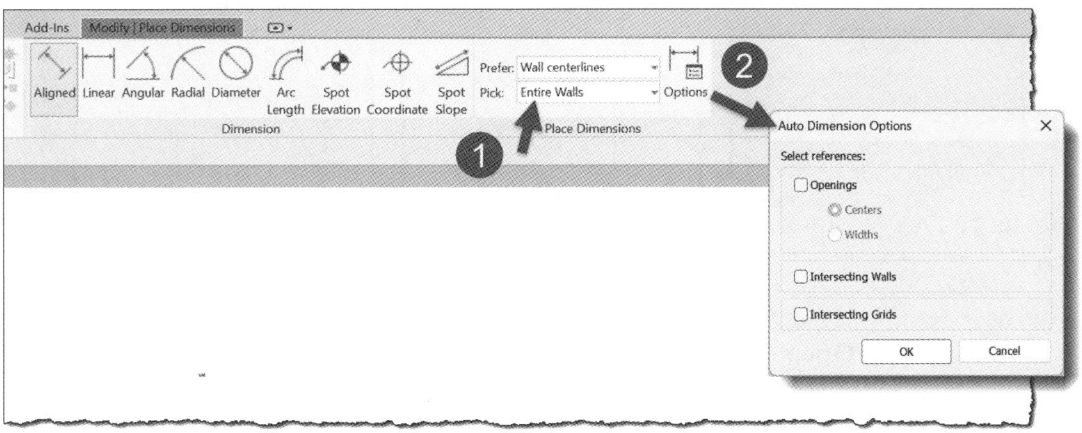

FIGURE 7-2.5 Specify individual or automatic dimensioning

Switching this option to **Entire Wall**, by default, will just add a dimension for the entire length of a selected wall. If **Wall Faces** is selected as well, the overall dimension is created as shown in the next image (Figure 7-2.6). Again, this dimension was created by simply clicking on the wall (with the door and windows); one click to specify the reference and another to position the line.

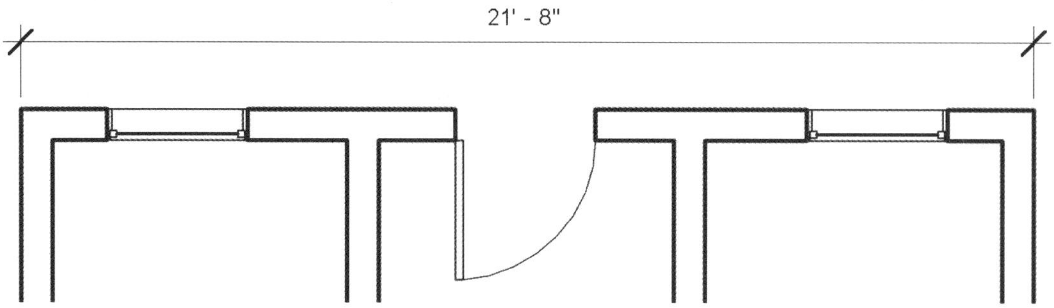

FIGURE 7-2.6 Automatic dimension created – example 1

When the **Entire Wall** option is selected, the **Options** button becomes active. Clicking this presents several options as shown in Figure 7-2.5. On the *Ribbon*, with *Pick* set to **Wall Centerlines** and the *Auto Dimension Options* dialog set to **Openings\Centerlines** and **Intersecting Walls**, the string of dimensions shown below is automatically created (Fig 7-2.7).

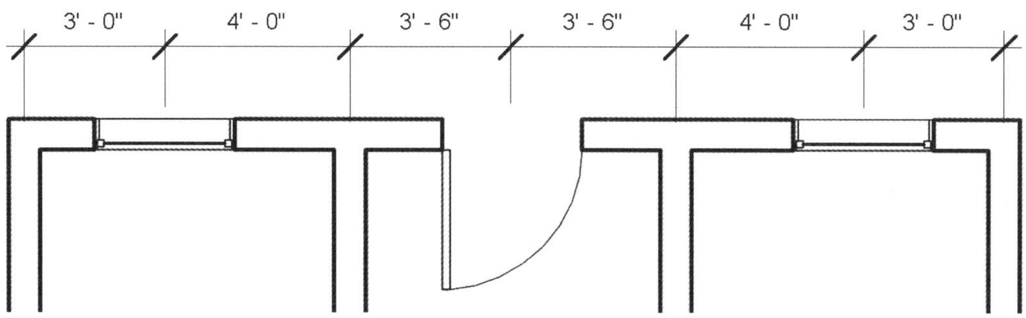

FIGURE 7-2.7 Automatic dimension created – example 2

In the next example (Figure 7-2.8), with the *Prefer* set to **Wall Faces** and the *Auto Dimension Options* dialog set to **Openings\Width** and **Intersecting Walls**, the string of dimensions shown below is automatically created.

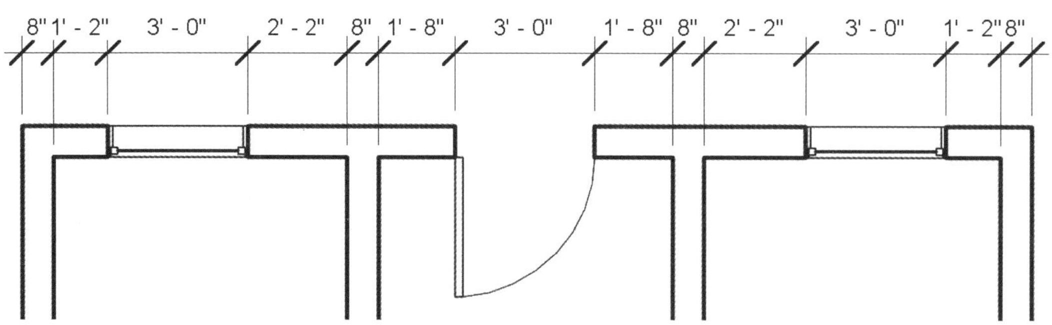

FIGURE 7-2.8 Automatic dimension created – example 3

Linear - Dimension

Use this tool to force Revit to maintain horizontal and vertical dimension segments or strings.

Steps to add Linear dimensions:

- Review **Type Selector** selection
- **Select first reference**
    - Intersection of walls and/or grids ***or***
    - Press tab to select a specific reference or intersection
- **Select second reference**
- Optional: Select additional reference
- **Click away** from anything dimensionable to finish command

This tool will automatically pick points rather than the element's face. In the example shown to the right, after selecting the two points to be dimensioned, the direction the mouse is moved (up or left) determines whether the dimension is horizontal or vertical—pressing the Space Bar also toggles between the two orientations.

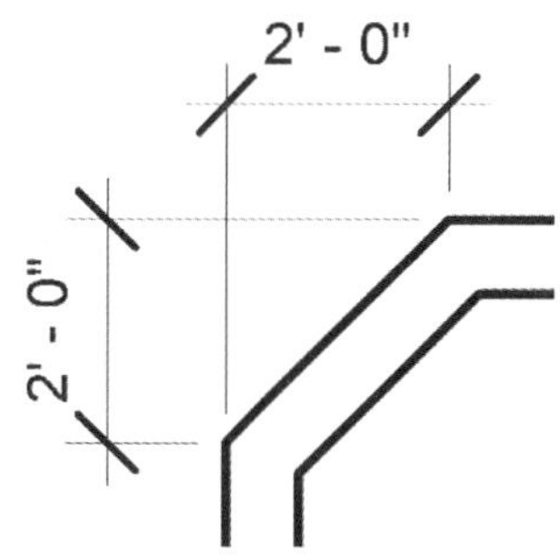

If the model is adjusted, these dimensions will automatically update regardless of which view they are in. Similarly, if one of these elements is deleted, these dimensions will also be deleted.

Angular - Dimension

Use this tool to indicate the angle between two references.

Steps to add Angular dimensions:

- Review **Type Selector** and **Ribbon** selections
- **Select first reference**
- **Select second reference**
- **Click** to place the location of the dimension line and text

Using the angular tool provides a way to measure the angle between two elements. In the example to the right, the dimension could be in three different positions: one where it is, one in the lower right and the larger obtuse angle on the left.

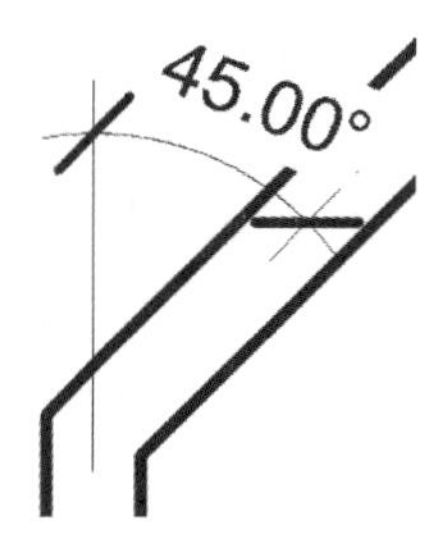

If the two references are modified the angular dimension will update no matter which view it is in.

Radius - Dimension

Use this tool to indicate the radius of an arc or circular reference. This can be the edge of a floor, wall, duct, or detail lines.

Steps to add a Radius dimension:

- Review **Type Selector** and **Ribbon** selections
- **Select the reference**
- **Click** to place the location of the dimension line and text

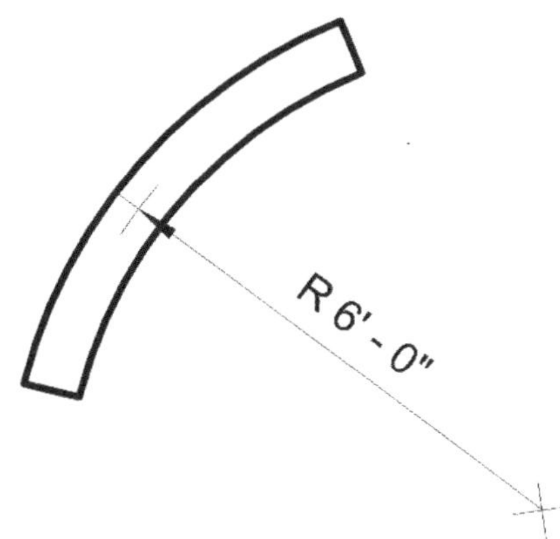

By default, the Radius dimension extends to the center point of the arc or circle. If a plan view is cropped, and Annotation Crop is active for the view, the center point must be visible within the cropped area.

Once the Radius is placed, the radius dimension can be selected, and the grip at the center point can be repositioned closer to the arc. Additionally, you can turn off the Center Mark symbol in the Type properties. However, in some cases, the center mark itself should be dimensioned so the contractor can accurately position the element within the building.

Diameter - Dimension

Use this tool to indicate the diameter of an arc or circular reference. This can be the edge of a floor, wall, duct, or detail lines.

Steps to add a Diameter dimension:

- Review **Type Selector** and **Ribbon** selections
- **Select the reference**
- **Click** to place the location of the dimension line and text

Arc Length - Dimension

Use this tool to measure the length of a line along a curved reference. This can be the edge of a floor, wall, duct, or detail lines.

Steps to add an Arc Length dimension:

- Review **Type Selector** and **Ribbon** selections
- **Select the reference**
- **Click** to place the location of the dimension line and text

Spot Elevation - Dimension

Use this tool to indicate the elevation of a surface.

> Steps to add a Spot Elevation dimension:
> - Review **Type Selector** and **Ribbon** selections
> - **Select the reference**
> - **Click** to place the location of the text and leader

The elevation listed is based on one of three options as listed below. This is a Type Property called Elevation Base. Thus, it is possible to use all three options, even right next to each other.

Elevation Base options for a Spot Elevation type:

- Project Base Point
- Survey Point
- Relative

Project Base Point:

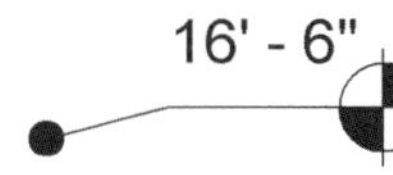

This option is related to the **level datum** numbers in the project. For example, the default templates that come with Revit set Level 1 to an elevation of 0'-0". In this example, all Spot Elevations set to Project Base Point will be relative to 0'-0" within a project.

Survey Point:

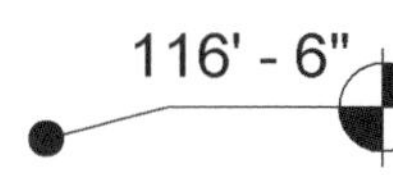

The Survey Base point is an **alternate coordinate system** used to align with the actual position on earth and elevation above sea level. Thus, any Spot Elevation set to Survey Point will display a value relative to the Survey Point settings. For example, where the Level 1 floor's Project Base Point is set to 0'-0" (or 100'-0"), the Survey value for Level 1 might be 650'-0" to match the elevation numbers shown for the contours on the Civil Engineer's grading plan. Revit can track both coordinate systems within the context of the Spot Elevation tool.

Relative:

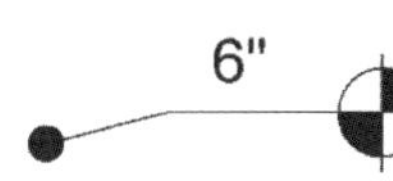

When a Spot Elevation has the Elevation Base set to Relative, the values listed are related to the plan view in which they are placed.

Spot Coordinate

Use this tool to indicate the North/South, East/West position of a point within the model.

> Steps to add a Spot Coordinate dimension:
> - Review **Type Selector** and **Ribbon** selections
> - **Select the reference point**
> - **Click** to place the location of the text and leader

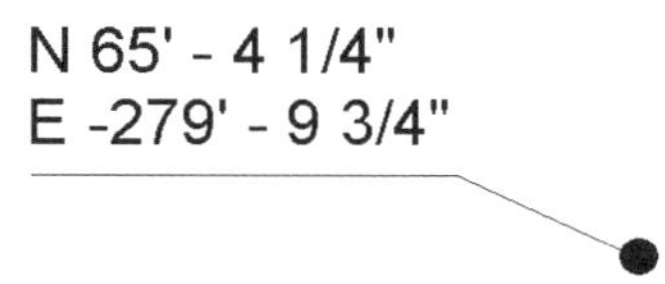

This feature can be used to indicate the positions of one or more building corners on the site. This is usually relative to a predefined Survey Point, which is relative to a benchmark or municipal coordinate system. On a typical commercial project, this information is provided only on the civil drawings and is therefore not required in the Revit model or documents.

Similar to the Spot Elevation tool, the Spot Coordinate can also be set to Relative or Project Base Point. This could be used to position items within the project, but it is not commonly used because the contractor or installer would need a direct line of sight between the two points.

Spot Slope

Use this tool to indicate the **Slope** in a floor plan view or the roof **Pitch** in an elevation view.

Steps to add a Spot Elevation dimension:

- Review **Type Selector** and **Ribbon** selections
- **Click** to both select a reference and place the location of the dimension element

Plan views:
In a plan view, the Spot Slope can indicate the slope of a sloped floor or a ramp.

Elevation View:
In an elevation view, the Spot Slope can be used to indicate the pitch of a roof, as shown in the example to the right.

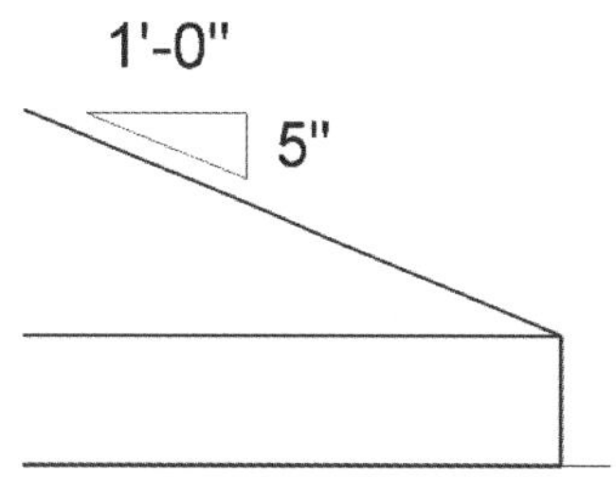

TIP: When placing the Spot Elevation on a hip roof, in elevation, use the Tab key to select the correct surface. By default, the hip line is selected, which has a different slope from the roof face itself.

The Spot Slope element has an Instance Parameter in the Properties Palette that toggles between Arrow and Triangle, the two options shown above.

Modifying a Dimension

When dimensions need to be modified, there are a few things to keep in mind.

Ways to Modify a Dimension:

- Edit Witness Lines
- Modify text
- Reposition text
- Lock a Dimension
- Drive the location of geometry
- Change type

Edit Witness Lines:
After a dimension is placed, a wall or opening may be added, and rather than deleting a dimension string and adding a new one, Revit provides the **Edit Witness Lines** tool. Simply select a dimension and click the Edit Witness Line button from the Ribbon. Once active, click new references to **add witness lines** and click existing references to **remove witness lines**.

Modify text:
When a dimension is selected, clicking the dimension value opens the Dimension Text dialog (Figure 7-2.9).

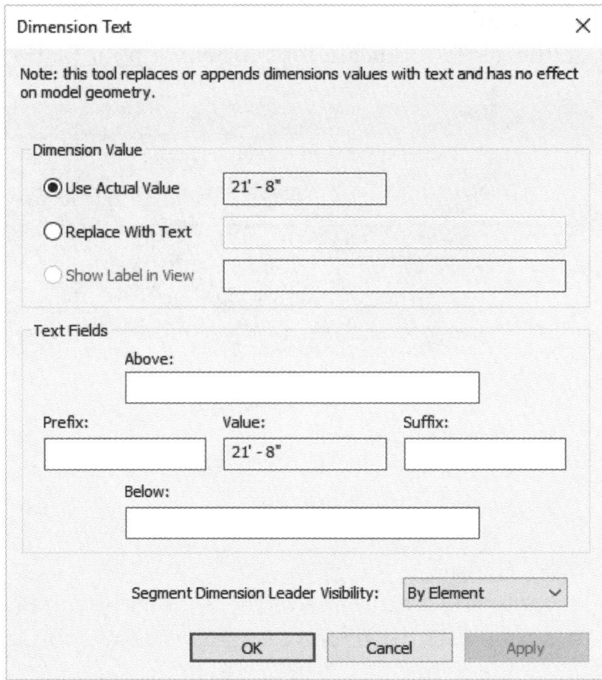

FIGURE 7-2.9 Dimension Text dialog

Figure 7-2.10 shows the relative position of each of the "text fields."

When **Replace With Text** is selected, the dimension value can be replaced with text. For example, "PAINT WALL" or "EXISTING CORRIDOR WIDTH – VERIFY IN FIELD."

Revit will not allow a dimension value in the text replacement box. The main reason for this restriction is to prevent faking dimensions rather than adjusting the model.

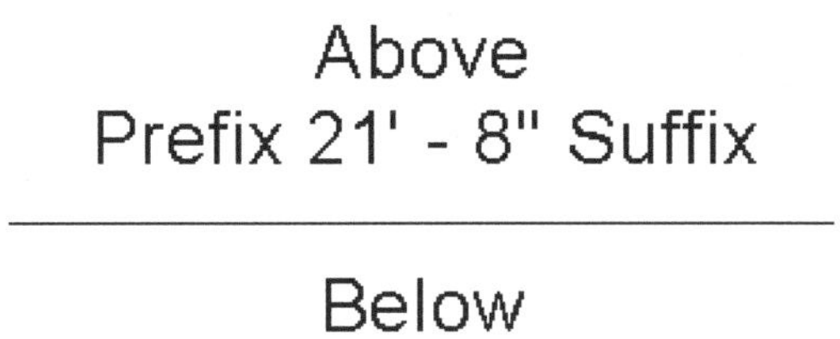

FIGURE 7-2.10 Dimension text field positions

<u>Reposition text:</u>
When a dimension is selected, clicking and dragging on the text grip allows the text to be repositioned.

When the text is moved past one of the witness lines, Revit will add a leader by default as shown to the right (Figure 7-2.11). Right-clicking on a dimension reveals related commands on the pop-up menu (Figure 7-2.12); selecting **Reset Dimension Text Position** will move the text back to the original location.

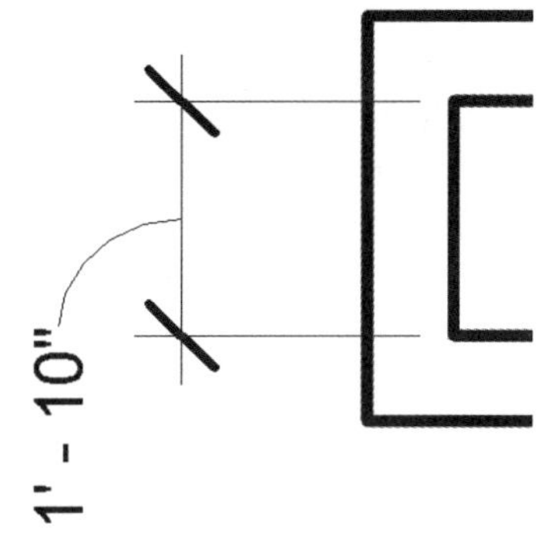

FIGURE 7-2.11 Dimension Text leader

<u>Lock a Dimension:</u>
When a dimension is selected, clicking the lock icon (Figure 7-2.13) will prevent that dimension value from changing. This will not prevent model elements from moving, but to maintain the dimension value, both reference elements will move. For example, if a dimension is locked between two walls which define a corridor, moving one wall will move the other wall to ensure the corridor width does not change.

When elements are selected which are in some way constrained, Revit will show the lock symbol. This is true even if the locked dimension is not visible in the current view (Figure 7-2.14). Clicking this icon will unlock the constraint.

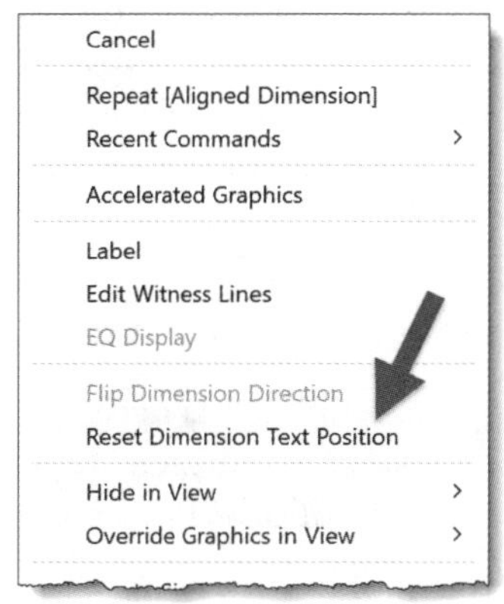

FIGURE 7-2.12 Right-click options

When a locked dimension is deleted, Revit asks if the constraint should also be removed. Thus, it is possible to delete the dimension but leave the constraint in place.

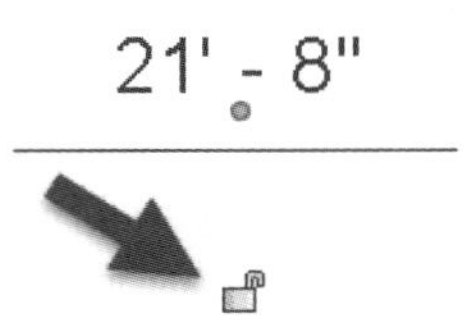

FIGURE 7-2.13 Dimension selected

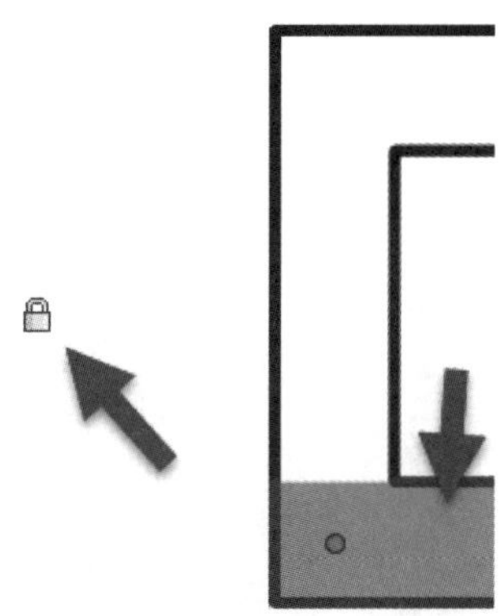

FIGURE 7-2.14 Locked element

Drive the location of geometry:
Like temporary dimensions, permanent dimensions can also be used to reposition geometry, such as walls, ducts, and more. The key is to select the element to be repositioned first, then click the dimension text. A common mistake is selecting the dimension directly and then clicking the text. This only opens the Dimension Text dialog. Also, consider that Revit would not know which referenced element to move if just selecting the dimension and not the element: move the left one, move the right element, or both equally?

TIP: A temporary dimension can be turned into a permanent dimension by clicking the "dimension icon" below the temporary dimension text, pointed out in Figure 7-2.15.

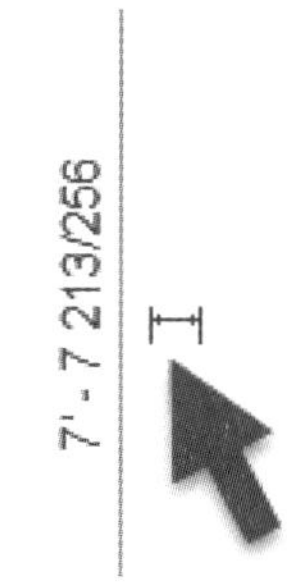

FIGURE 7-2.15 Temporary dimension selected

Change Dimension Type:
When a dimension is selected, click the Type Selector and select from the available options. Changing the type can affect the graphic appearance, the rounding, and when alternate units appear (e.g., metric).

Create and Modify Dimension Types

Sometimes it is necessary to modify a dimension type to match a design firm's graphical standard or a client requirement. Revit allows dimension types to be created and modified. Use caution when changing a dimension type, as all dimensions of that type will be updated in the current project. These changes will not affect any other projects or templates.

To modify existing types, either start the dimension command and click Edit Type or select one of the "Types" options in the extended panel area of the dimension panel on the Annotate tab (Figure 7-2.16).

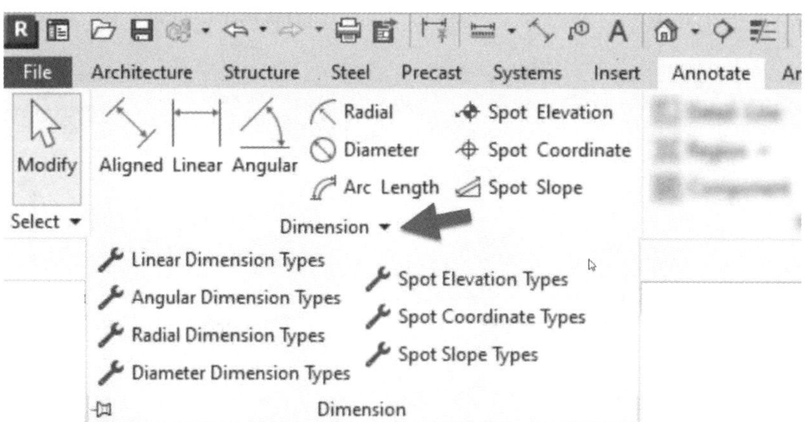

FIGURE 7-2.16 Editing Dimension types

To create a new Type, click the **Duplicate** option in the Type Properties dialog.

Figure 7-2.17 shows the various options that can be changed.

One option is **Units Format**. Selecting this option opens the Format dialog shown in Figure 7-2.18. Notice that a dimension style can be tied to the Project Units as set on the Manage tab. Un-checking this option allows this dimension style to round in a specific way and do a few other things, like "Suppress 0 feet:" and control the symbol (e.g., monetary symbol).

Setting up all the dimension styles typically needed in a template file will save a lot of time and help enforce a firm's standards.

TIP: To see how many instances use a specific dimension style in a project, select one and then right-click and pick Select All Instances → In Entire Project. The total number of selected items will be displayed in the lower-right corner of the screen, next to the filter icon on the status bar.

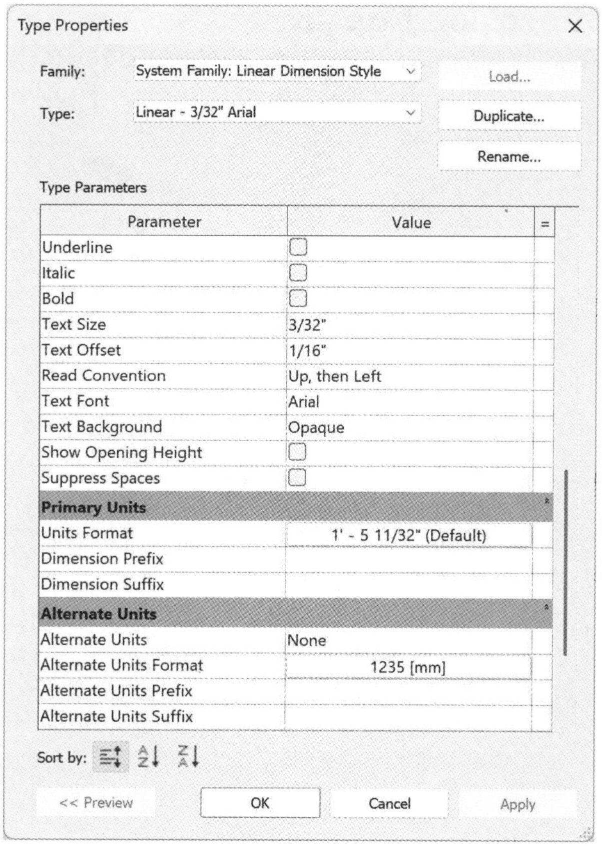

FIGURE 7-2.17 Dimension type properties

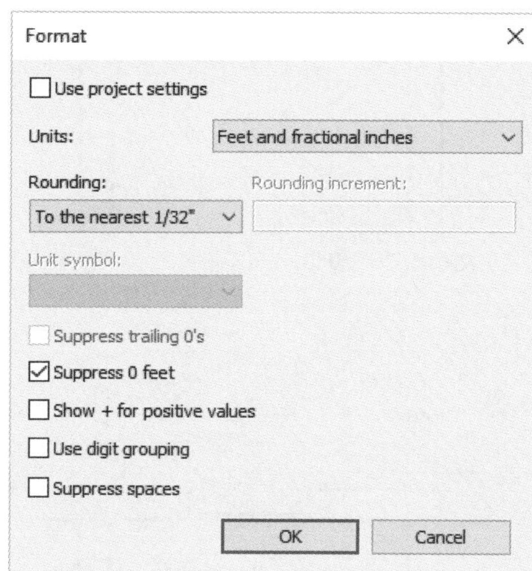

FIGURE 7-2.18 Dimension unit format

Dimension Equality

When a dimension string is selected, an **EQ** symbol appears with a red slash through it as seen in Figure 7-2.19. Clicking this toggle will make all dimension segments in that string equally spaced between the two ends.

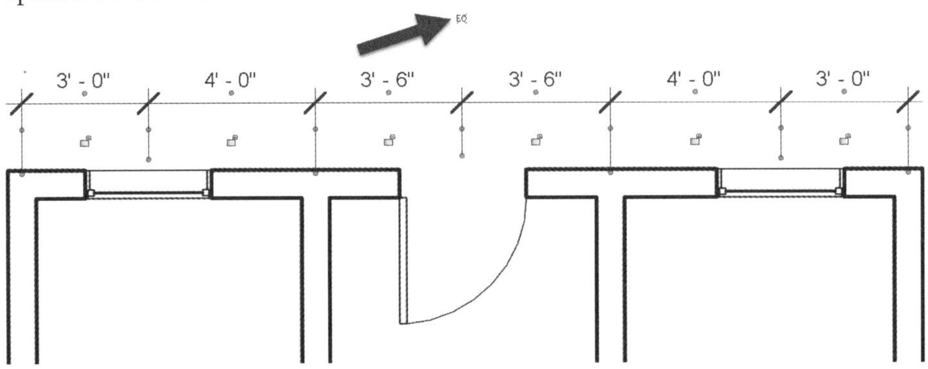

FIGURE 7-2.19 Dimension string selected and EQ symbol pointed

The image below (Figure 7-2.20) shows the result of clicking the EQ icon; the walls, windows, and door all moved with the now equally spaced witness lines. Notice the EQ icon no longer has a slash through it. If one of the end walls is moved, all elements are moved to maintain equal spacing. Setting the Dimension's **Equality Display** property to Value shows the dimension value rather than the "EQ" abbreviation.

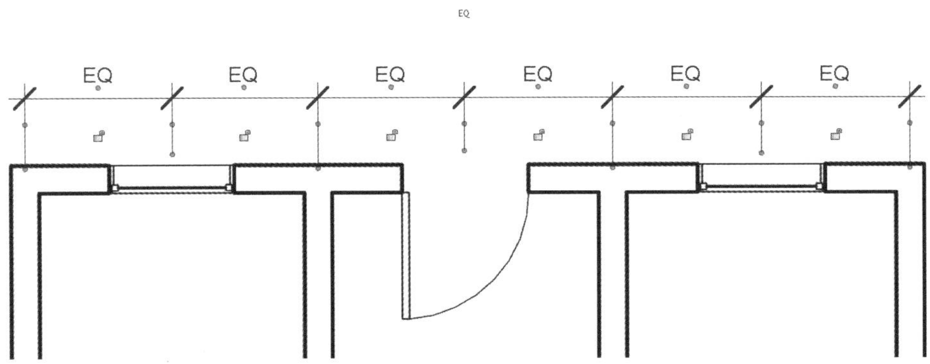

FIGURE 7-2.20 Dimension string with equality activated

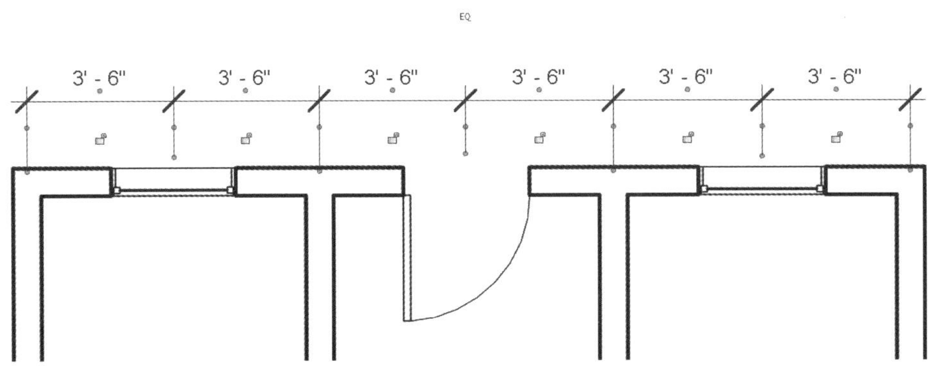

FIGURE 7-2.21 Dimension string with equality activated and dimension value shown

Exercise 7-3:
Tagging

This section will study how **tags** work in Revit. This is an important feature in Revit, one that designers use extensively. This feature is often used on furniture, doors, windows, casework, and ductwork, as well as many other elements within the Revit model.

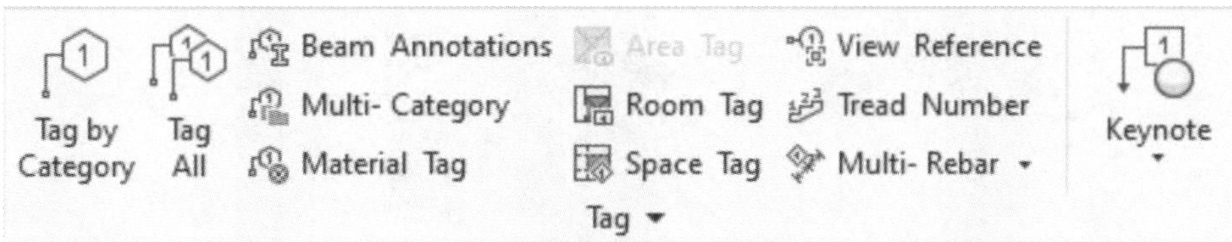

The basic premise of a *tag* is to be able to textually represent, in a drawing view, information found within an element, that is, an *Instance* or *Type Parameter*. One example found in nearly every set of construction documents is the door tag. This Revit tag has been set up to list the contents of a specific door's ***Mark*** parameter, which is an *Instance Parameter*.

> The process to tag an element is simple:
> - Select the ***Tag by Category*** tool from the *Quick Access Toolbar*.
> - Adjust the settings on the *Ribbon* if needed.
> - Click the element(s) to be tagged.
>
>   *FYI: Different tags are placed based on the category of the element selected.*
> - Click the *Modify* button or press the Esc key when done.

A *tag* is view-specific, meaning that if you add it to the Level 1 Finish Plan, it will not automatically appear in the **Level 1 Furniture Plan**. If you want the tag to appear in two Level 1 plan views, you need to add it twice. *(TIP: Use Copy/Paste.)* The advantage is that you can adjust the tag location independently in each view. One view may show furniture, and the other floor finishes. Each view might require the tag to be in a different location to keep it readable.

Tags are dependent on the element selected during placement. You cannot simply move a tag near another similar element and expect Revit to recognize this change. Similarly, if an element is deleted, the tag will also be removed from the model, even if the tag is in another view in the project.

The image below has several tags added to a floor plan view. All the listed information is coming from the properties of the elements that have been tagged. For example, the "M1" tag within the diamond shape is listing the wall type (i.e., *Type Mark*). Because the wall tag(s) is/are listing a *Type Parameter*, all wall instances of that type will report the same value, i.e., "M1." The door number "1" reports the element's Mark value, which is an *Instance Parameter*. Therefore, each door instance may have a different number. Notice some tags have the *Leader* option turned on. This is especially helpful if the tag is outside the room. Any 3D element visible in a view may be tagged, even the floor. In this case, the *Floor Tag* reports the *Type Name* listed in the *Type Selector*. The leader can be modified to have an arrow or a dot.

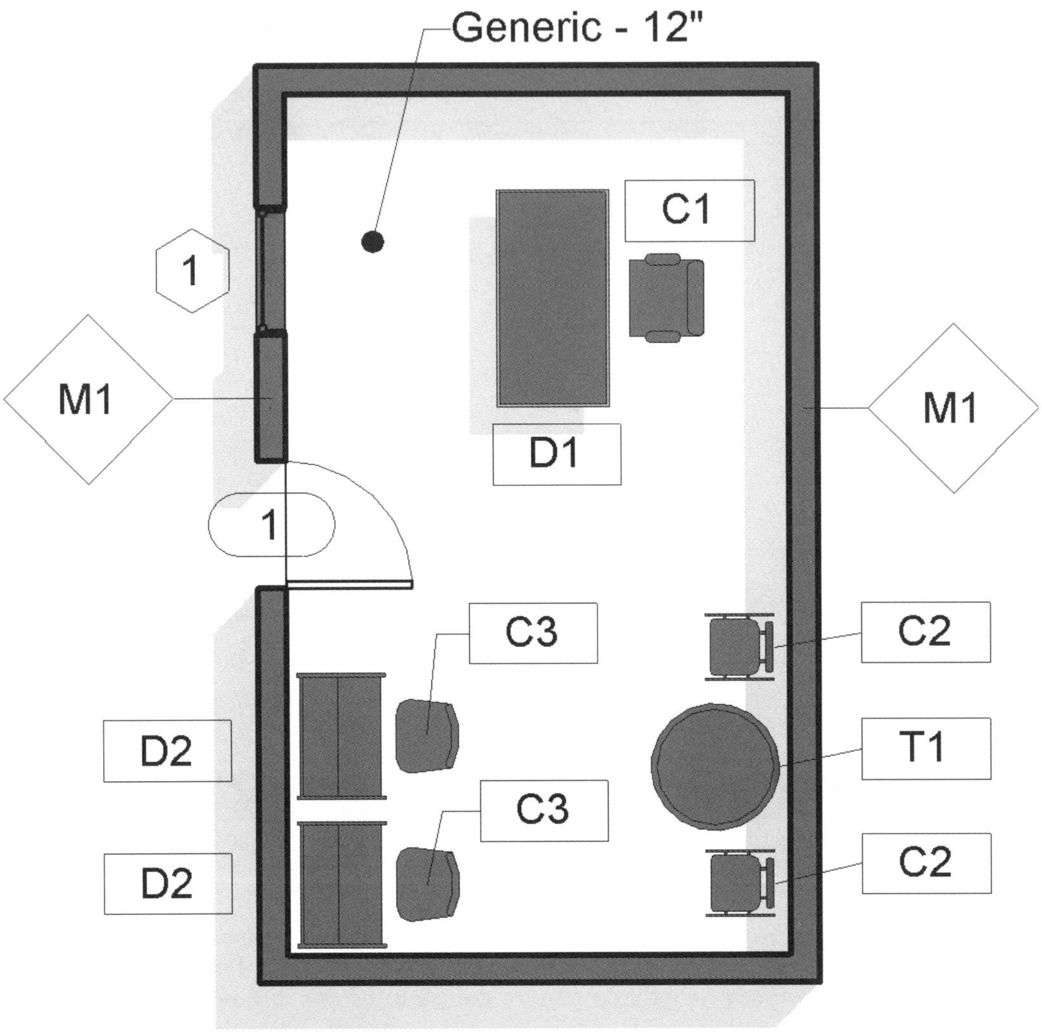

FIGURE 7-3.1 Floor plan with tags added

All of these tags were placed using the same tool: *Tag by Category*. Later, you will learn how to specify which tag gets used for each category (e.g., walls, furniture, floors, windows, etc.).

The section/interior elevation below (Figure 7-3.2) shows many of the same elements tagged as in the floor plan view above. If the wall's *Type Mark* is changed, the wall *Tag* will be instantly updated in all views: plans, elevations, sections, and schedules.

The tags had to be manually added to this view. They are not added here automatically just because you added one in the floor plan view, unlike when you add a section mark (where the section appears in other views automatically). If the view is deleted from the project, all these tags will automatically be deleted.

Some tags can actually report multiple parameter values found within an element. For example, the ***Ceiling Tag*** used in this example lists the *Type Name* and the ceiling height, and includes fixed text that reads "A.F.F.". Many tags can be selected and directly edited, which actually changes the values within the element. Changing the 8′-0″ ceiling height will change the ceiling position vertically.

It is possible to tag an element multiple times. You could add the same tag multiple times. In the example below, you could place a ***Wall Tag*** on each side of the door. You can also add different tags that report different information from the same element. The ***Wall Tag*** "M1" and the ***Material Tag*** "PT-1" are two separate tags that extract different information from the same wall.

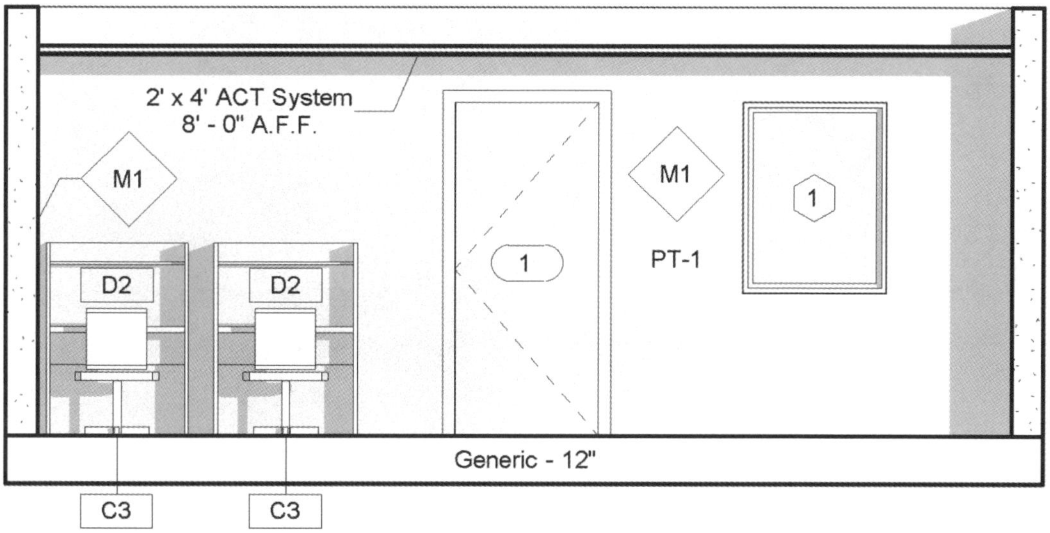

FIGURE 7-3.2 Section / interior elevation with tags added

Most design firms spend a little time adjusting the provided tags to make the text a little smaller and modify or delete the line work. This can easily be done by selecting a tag and then clicking ***Edit Family*** on the *Ribbon*. Revised tags can then be loaded back into the project and/or saved to a company template for future use.

It is also possible to add tags in 3D views (Figure 7-3.3b). Before tagging a 3D view, you must ***Lock*** it (Figure 7-3.3a) to prevent changing the view and interfering with the position of the tags relative to the elements being tagged.

FIGURE 7-3.3A Locking a 3D view

When the *Leader* option is off, the tag is placed at the center of the selected element. This initial position is not always desirable (e.g., note the D1 and C1 tags below), and you must move each tag so it is readable.

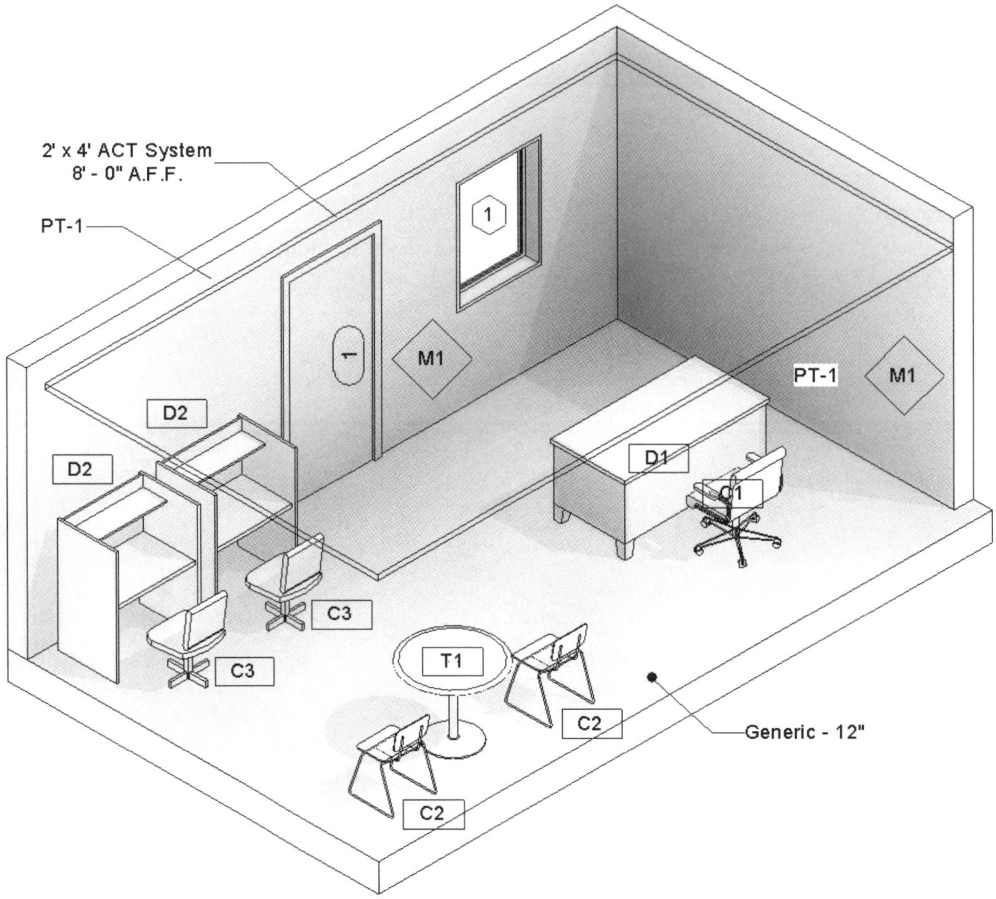

FIGURE 7-3.3B Locked 3D view with tags added

It is not possible to add *Room Tags* to 3D views.

It is helpful to understand where the information displayed in tags is stored. It is often necessary to change these values. In Figure 7-3.4, you can see that “PT-1” is the *Description* for the *Material* assigned to the wall type.

> ***TIP:** To find the* Material *assigned to a specific wall type: Select the wall → Edit Type → Edit Structure → observe the Material column.*

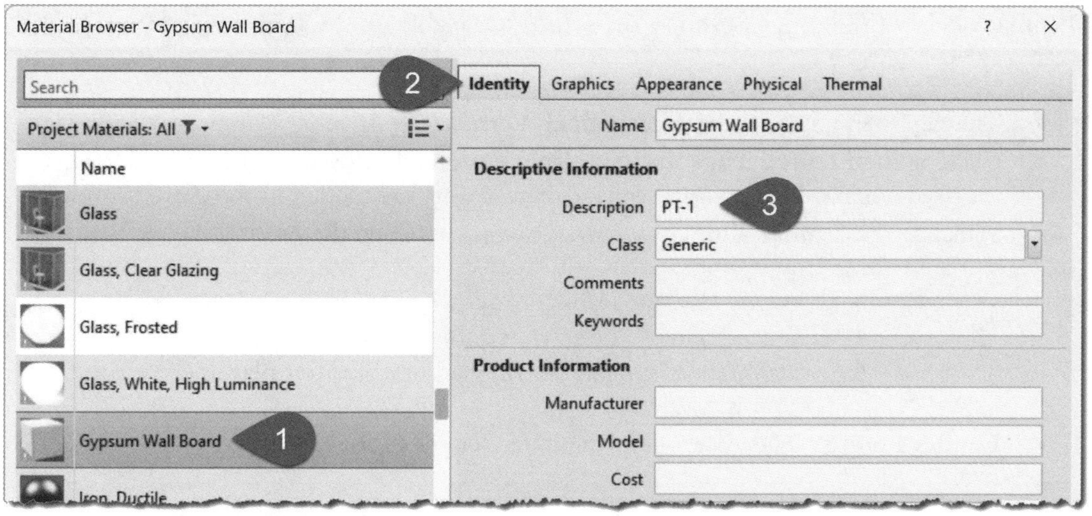

FIGURE 7-3.4 Material description value used in Material Tag

FYI: In the image above, the preview icons on the left with a gold triangle in the lower left corner are legacy materials, which are superseded by newer, physically accurate materials. However, many design firms still exclusively use the legacy materials.

A wall's *Type Mark* is found in the *Type Properties* dialog; select a wall → *Edit Type* from the *Properties Palette*. Notice in Figure 7-3.5 that the *Type Mark* is set to "M1." If you were to edit this value, all the tags for this wall will be updated instantly.

Seeing as all the information displayed in a tag is only stored in the element being tagged, you will never lose any information by deleting a tag.

FYI: A tag will move with the element even if the element is moved in another view where the tag is not visible.

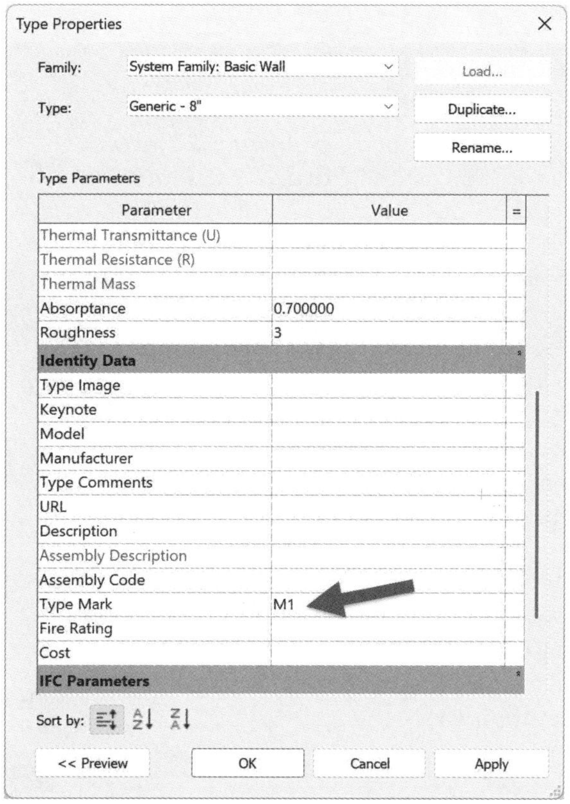

FIGURE 7-3.5 Selected wall's *Type Mark* value used in wall tag

The image below (Figure 7-3.6) shows the settings available on the *Ribbon* when the *Tag* tool is active.

- The tag orientation can be ***Horizontal*, *Vertical*, or *Model*** *(the latter may be rotated).*
- Clicking the **Loaded Tags and Symbols** button allows you to specify which tags are used when multiple tags for the same category are loaded in the current project.
- Selecting the ***Leader Line*** option draws a line between the tag and the element.
    - Leader End options:
        - *Attached End:* the leader always touches the tagged element.
        - *Free End:* allows you to move the end of the leader.
        - *Leader Start* is similar, but only adjustable after placement via the properties palette.
- **Leader Length**: This determines the initial length of the leader.

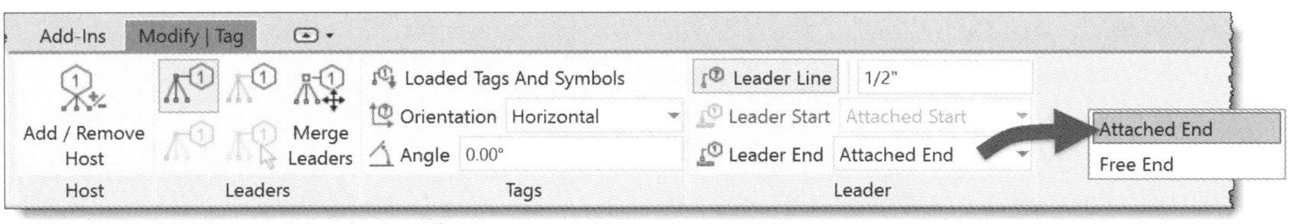

FIGURE 7-3.6 Tag options during placement

When clicking the *Loaded Tags and Symbols* button, you get the ***Loaded Tags and Symbols*** dialog as shown in Figure 7-3.7.

Notice that some categories do not have a tag family loaded. If you tried to tag a *Casework* element, Revit would prompt you to load a tag.

Clicking a tag name in the Loaded Tags column lets you select from multiple tag types/families loaded in the current project.

If you use one tag type in plan views and another in elevation views, you could open this dialog just before tagging in plan views, then adjust it again before tagging in elevation views.

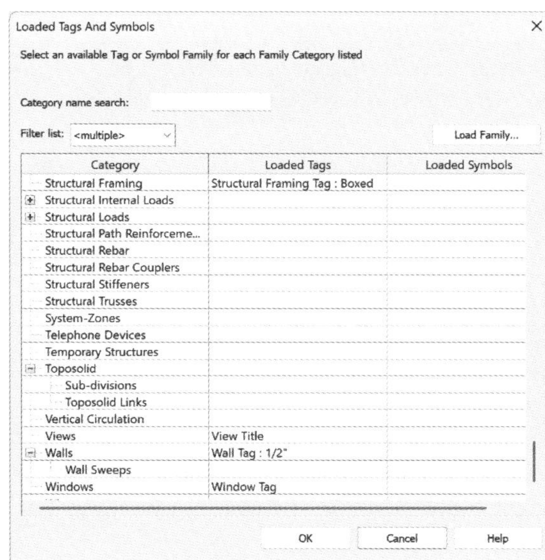

FIGURE 7-3.7 Loaded tags dialog

FYI: It is possible to let Revit place the default tag, then select the placed tag and swap it out via the Type Selector.

TIP: If you want to swap several tags with another type: Select one of the tags → right-click → **Select All Instances** *and then pick either* **Visible in View** *or* **In Entire Project**. *You now have all the tags selected and can pick something else via the* Type Selector.

The reader should be aware that some tags may be automatically added when content is added to the model. For example, when placing a window, the *Ribbon* has a toggle called ***Tag on Placement*** (Figure 7-3.8). When this option is selected (which it is NOT by default), a door tag is placed next to every door. Note that the tag is added only to the current view, which could be an elevation, a plan, etc.

You typically want this option off in the early design stages, since the tags will just get in the way as things move around. Also, existing elements are not usually tagged; thus, you would toggle this option off, so you do not have to come back and delete the tag later.

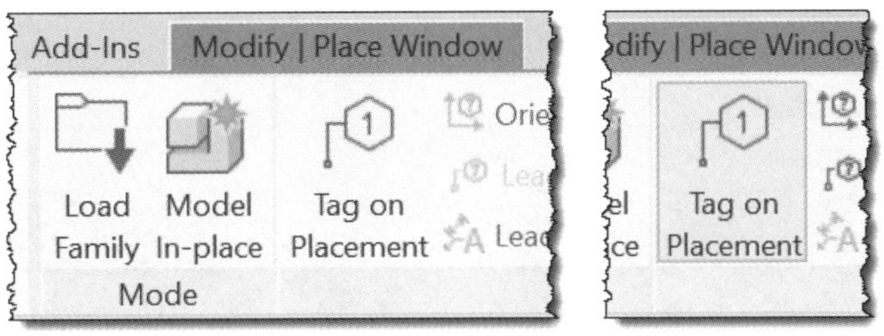

FIGURE 7-3.8 Tag on Placement option; **off** (shown on left) and **on** (on right)

If you did not add tags or some were deleted along the way, you will need to add them later. The easiest way to do this is to use the Tag All tool; it used to be called *Tag All Not Tagged*. When you use this tool, you can add a door tag to every door in the current view that does not already have a door tag. This is great for large projects with hundreds of doors, and you want to make sure you do not miss any. You may still have to go around and rotate and reposition a few tags, but overall, this is much faster!

Before concluding this introduction to tags, we will briefly look at how tags are created. If you select a tag and click Edit Family on the Ribbon, you will open the tag for editing in the *Family Editor*. Keep in mind that your project is still open in addition to the tag family.

If you select a furniture tag and edit it, you will see text (sample value shown) and four lines (Figure 7-3.9). Here, the lines can be selected and deleted if desired. Also, you can select the text, then click Edit Type to change its properties (e.g., height, font, width factor, etc.).

If you select the text and then click the ***Edit Label*** option on the *Ribbon*, you can change the parameter being reported, or report multiple parameters (Figure 7-3.9).

TIP: *Open a tag family, edit it, and then do a* Save-As *to make a new tag type.*

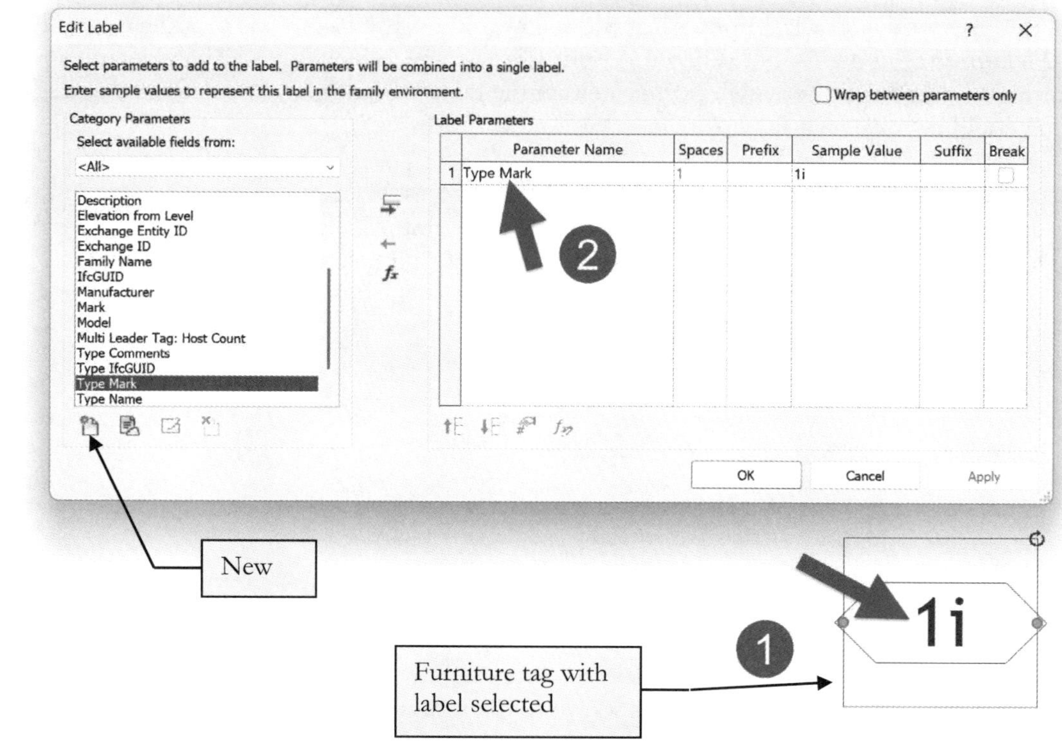

FIGURE 7-3.9 Editing a tag label in the family editor

In the *Edit Label* dialog above, you can click the **New** icon in the lower-left corner to load a Shared Parameter, which lets you create a tag that reports custom information. See the next section for more on this topic. Also, several icons to the right of the "New" icon is the *Edit Parameter's Units Format* tool that allows you to override the formatting for numeric parameters (Figure 7-3.10).

This concludes the introduction on using tags in Revit. The next section continues this discussion with a more advanced concept called *Shared Parameters.*

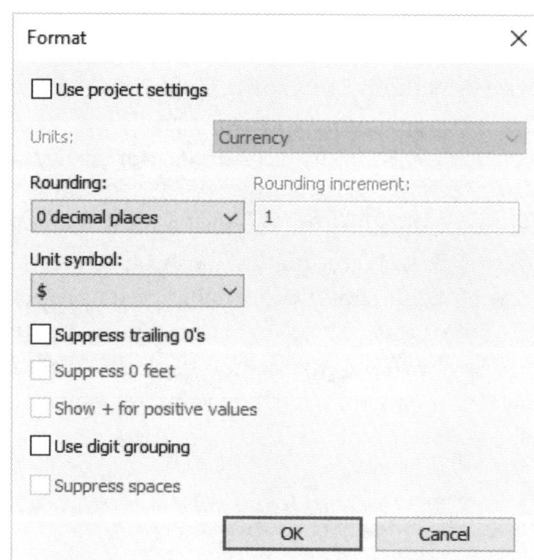

FIGURE 7-3.10 Editing a label's format

Exercise 7-4:
Shared Parameters

FYI: You will not be using Shared Parameters in the tutorial, but this information is essential for a designer to be proficient and properly leverage Revit's power.

Introduction

Revit has many features that are unique when compared to other building design programs; one of these is *Shared Parameters*. The main idea behind Shared Parameters is to manage parameters across multiple projects, schedules, families, and template files. This feature allows Revit to recognize that you are referring to the same piece of information across multiple unconnected files. Here, we will cover the basics of setting up Shared Parameters, common problems encountered, and a few related tips and tricks.

The main reason for using ***Shared Parameters*** is to display custom information in tags; however, there are a few other uses that will be mentioned later. In contrast, a ***Project Parameter*** is slightly easier to make in a project, but cannot appear in a tag; Revit has no way of knowing that the parameter created in the family, the info to be tagged, and the parameter created in the tag are the same bit of information. Both *Project* and *Shared Parameters* may appear in schedules.

The image below illustrates the concept of a common storage container (i.e., the Shared Parameter file) from which uniquely coded parameters can be loaded into content, annotations, and projects. This creates a connected common thread between several otherwise disconnected files.

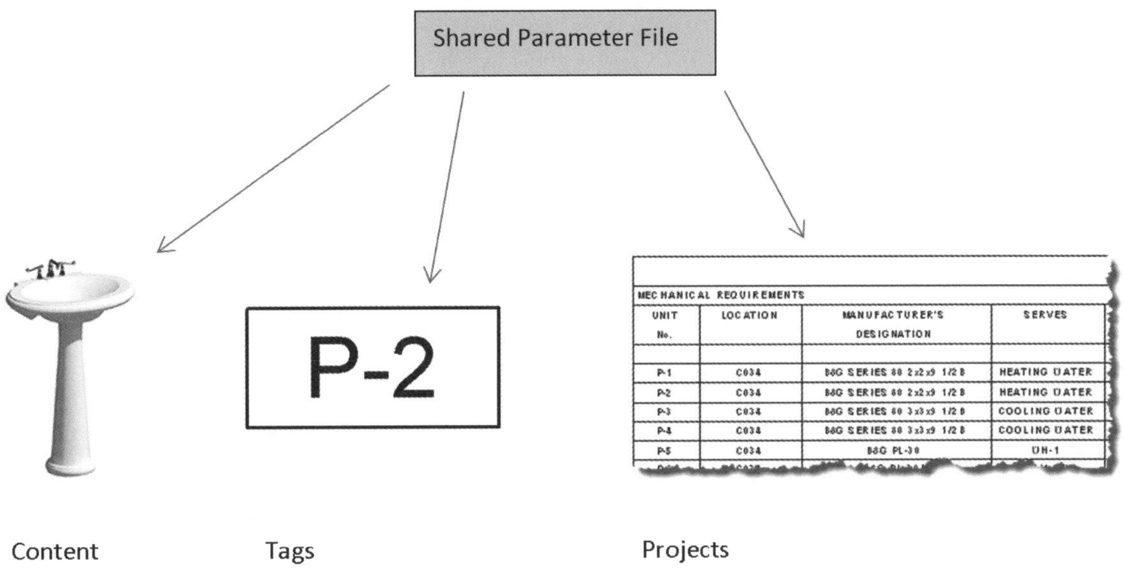

Shared Parameter File

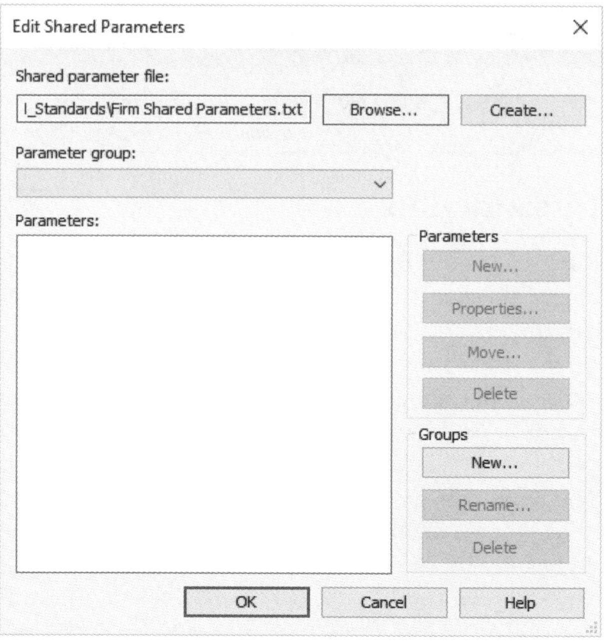

FIGURE 7-4.1 Edit Shared Parameters dialog

Creating a *Shared Parameter* is fairly straightforward, but afterwards, managing them can be troublesome. Select **Manage → Shared Parameters** from the *Ribbon* to open the *Shared Parameters* dialog box (Figure 7-4.1). This dialog basically modifies a simple **text file**, which should not be edited manually. If a text file has not yet been created, you will need to select the ***Create*** button and provide a file name and location for your *Shared Parameter* file.

It is important to keep in mind that this file will be the main record of all your *Shared Parameters*. From this file, you create *Shared Parameters* within Projects, Templates, and Families. Therefore, it is ideal to only maintain one file for the entire firm, even if you have multiple locations. Of course, there is always an exception to the rule. This single file should be stored on the server, and the software deployment should be set up to automatically point user computers to the *Shared Parameters* file. This can also be done manually by clicking the *Browse* button in the *Shared Parameters* dialog.

Once a *Shared Parameter* is loaded into a project, template, or family, the text file is no longer referenced. So you technically do not need to send this file with your project file when transmitting to a consultant or contractor.

The file name should be simple and easy to find. Create a new text file for each version of Revit you are using; include the version number in the file name. Some newer parameter types will cause older versions of the software to reject the text file.

Creating a Shared Parameter

Open the *Shared Parameters* dialog box. Here you can easily create *Groups* and *Parameters*. *Groups* are simply containers, somewhat like folders, used to organize the multitude of parameters you will likely create over time. When starting from scratch, you must first create at least one *Group* before creating your first *Shared Parameter*.

To create a new *Group*, click the ***New*** button under the *Groups* heading. In a multi-disciplinary firm, you should have at least one group for each discipline. Parameters can be moved around later, so do not worry about that too much at first.

Click the ***New*** button under the *Parameters* heading to create a new parameter in the current *Group*. You only need to provide three pieces of information:

- Name
- Discipline
- Type of Parameter
- Tooltip (optional)

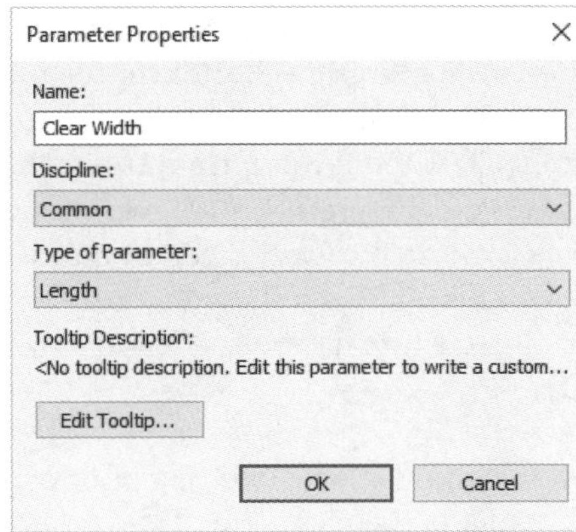

FIGURE 7-4.2 Setting Parameter Properties

In this example, see the image to the right (Figure 7-4.2). We will create a parameter called "Clear Width," which will be used in our door families (but can be used with other categories, as this is not specified at this level). The other standard options, such as *Instance* versus *Type*, are assigned when the parameter is set up in the project or family.

The **Discipline** option changes the options available in the *Type of Parameter* drop-down. The **Type of Parameter** drop-down lets Revit know what type of information will be stored in the parameter you are creating. Many programming languages require parameters to be declared before they are used and cannot be altered later. Revit is, in this sense, a graphical programming language.

The **Edit Tooltip** button allows an optional description of the parameter to be entered. Anyone working in the project will see the description when they hover their cursor over the parameter in the Properties Palette or Edit Type dialog.

When a new *Shared Parameter* is created, a unique code is assigned to it. The image below (Figure 7-4.3) shows the code created for the "Clear Width" parameter just created. For this reason, it is not possible to simply create another *Shared Parameters* file a few months from now and have it work the same.

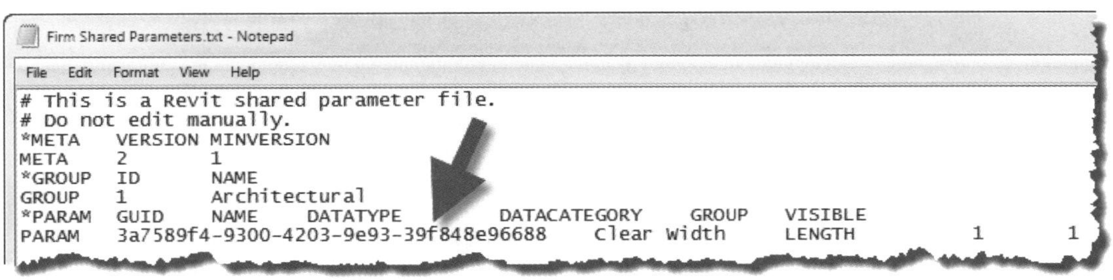

FIGURE 7-4.3 Shared Parameters text file

Creating a Shared Parameter in a Family

Now that you have created the framework for your *Shared Parameters*, i.e., the text file, you can begin to create parameters within content; the next section covers creating *Shared Parameters* in project files.

Open a family file – in this example, we will open the **Door - Single – Panel.rfa** file (download via Load Revit Family). Select the ***Family Types*** icon. Click the ***New Parameter*** icon on the lower-left (Figure 7-4.5). Now select the *Shared parameter*, then click the ***Select*** button (Figure 7-4.4). This will open the previously created shared parameter text file. Select "Clear Width" and then **OK**.

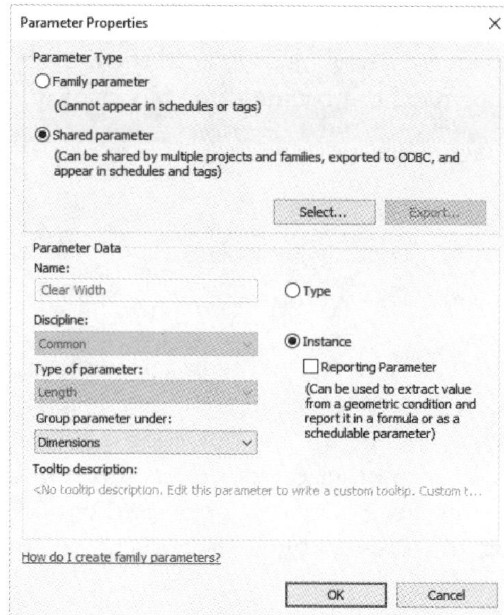

FIGURE 7-4.4 Parameter properties

Now you only have two bits of information left to provide. Is the parameter *Type* or *Instance*, and what is the "Group parameter under" option? This controls which section the parameter shows up under in the *Properties Palette.*

Notice how the bits of information specified in the *Shared Parameters* file are grayed out here. They cannot be changed, as doing so would create discrepancies between families and project files. Thus, this information is hard-wired.

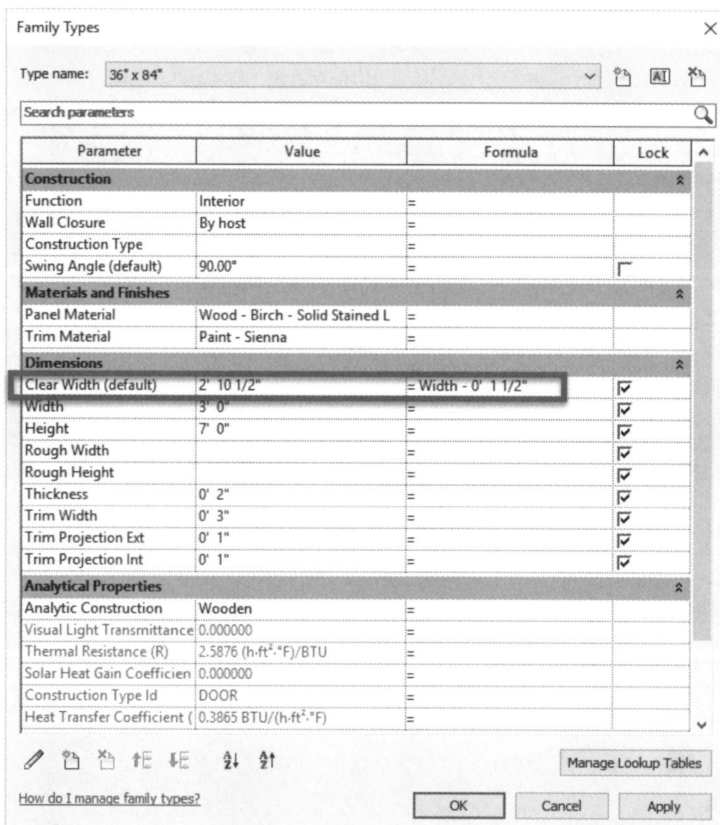

FIGURE 7-4.5 Family Types in family editor environment

Once the parameter has been created in the family, it can be used just like a *Family Parameter*. In this example, we created a formula to subtract the frame stops and the hinge/door imposition on the opening (Figure 7-4.5). Keep in mind that this value can now appear in a custom tag, if desired, listing the clear width for each door in a floor plan. Maybe the code official has required this. Using *Shared Parameters* is the only way to achieve this short of using "dumb text", that is, text manually typed which does not change automatically.

Next, we will look at creating a door tag that lists the clear width. This is similar to the steps just covered for the door family, since a tag is also a family. The only difference is that this parameter will be associated with a *Label*.

Note that the following steps are not required for the tutorial in this book: Open the default **Door Tag** family from within a Revit project (right-click it in the Project Browser and select Edit). Do a *Save As* and rename the file to **Door Tag – Clear Width.rfa**. Delete the linework, if desired. Select the text and click the *Edit Label* button on the *Ribbon*. In the *Edit Label* dialog, create a new parameter by clicking the icon in the lower-left corner; see the image below. Your only option here is to select a *Shared Parameter*, as previously mentioned, only *Shared Parameters* can be tagged. Once the new parameter is loaded, click to move it to the right side of the dialog, in the *Label Parameters* column. Next, select the original *Mark* parameter and remove it. Finally, edit the *Sample Value* to something like 2′-10″; this is what appears in the family to give you an idea of what the tag will look like in the project.

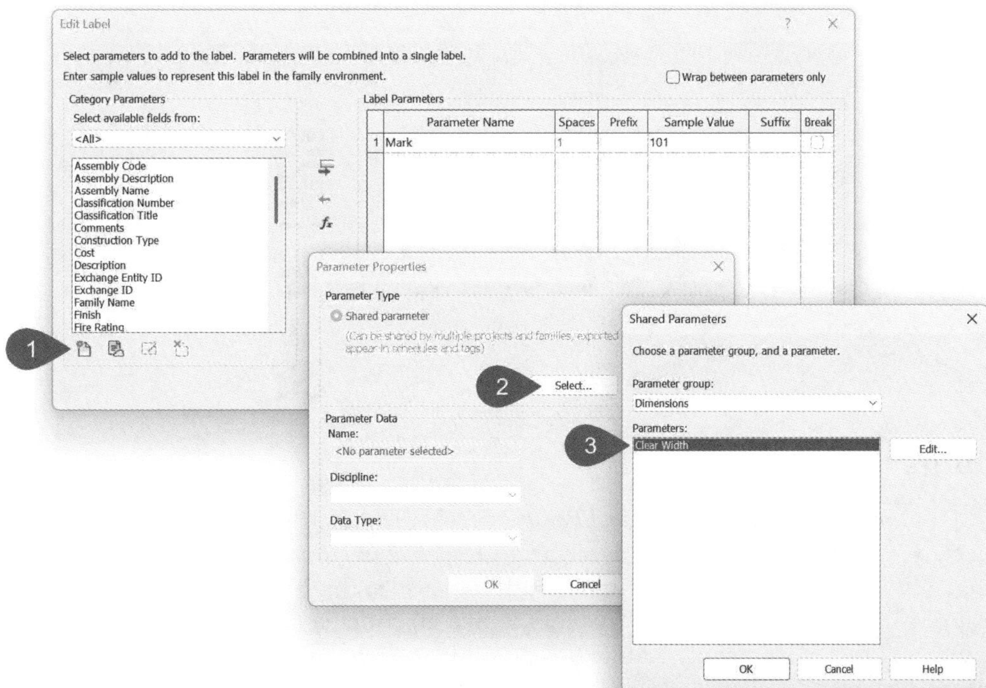

> ***FYI:*** *The* Mark *parameter could be left in the tag if you wanted both the* Mark *and* Clear Width *to appear together. The other option is to use two separate tags that can be moved independently. Keep in mind that it is possible to tag the same element multiple times. In this case, you would have two door tags on the same door, each tag being a different type.*

Load your new door and door tag families into a new project file. In the next section, you will see how these work in the project environment.

Using Shared Parameters in a Project

Now that you have your content and tags set up, you can use them in the project. First, draw a wall, then place an instance of the Single–Flush door (turn off *Tag on Placement*). Select the door and notice that the Clear Width parameter appears in the *Properties Palette*; it is an *Instance Parameter*. Add another door to the right of this one and change the width to 30″ via the *Type Selector*. Notice the *Clear Width* value has changed.

Next, you will tag the two doors. Select the ***Tag by Category*** icon from the *Quick Access Toolbar*. Uncheck the *Leader* option and select each door. Next, select each door tag, swap it with your new *Clear Width* option in the Type Selector, then set it to *Vertical* via the *Ribbon*.

> ***TIP:*** *If the text does not fit on one line, you have to go back into the family, increase the text box width, and reload the family into the project.*

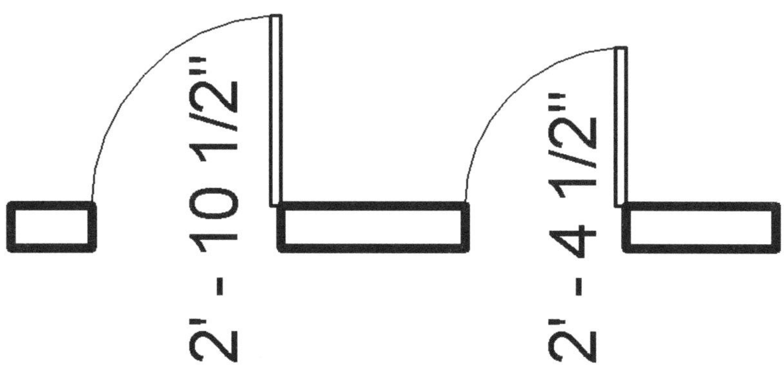

Things to Know

Only content that contains the *Shared Parameters* will display the parameter placeholder in a project. Try loading another door family (e.g., *Double–Flush*) into your test project without changing it in any way. Place an instance and then notice that the *Clear Width* option does not appear in the *Properties Palette*. This means that all content must have the Shared Parameter added in the family editor. It is possible to create a *Project Parameter* in the project/template file (that is based on a shared parameter) but you have to specify *Instance* or *Type*. If this varies, you cannot use a *Project Parameter*. The *Project Parameter* takes precedence and will change the loaded content.

Selectively associating parameters with content is a great trick when dealing with categories that have a variety of inputs, such as *Furniture* or *Mechanical Equipment*. Only loading *Shared*

Parameters into file cabinets or Air Handling Units (AHUs) will prevent those parameters from appearing in your lounge chairs or VAV boxes.

> ***FYI:** This also works with* Family Parameters, *but this information cannot be tagged or scheduled.*

Dealing with Problems

A number of problems can be created when *Shared Parameters* are not managed properly. The most common is when two separate *Shared Parameters* are created with the same name. This often happens when new users delete or otherwise lose a *Shared Parameter* file. They then try to recreate it manually, unaware that the previously mentioned unique code is different, and Revit will treat it as a different *Shared Parameter.* The first place this problem typically shows up is when a schedule in the project has blank spaces, even though the content (placed in the model) contains information. In this case, the schedule uses a specific version of the Shared Parameter, and only content that uses that same version appears in that schedule.

The fix for this problem is to open the bad content and re-associate the parameters with the correct *Shared Parameter.* It is not necessary to delete the bad parameter, which is good, as this could cause problems with existing formulas.

If you get content from another firm you are working with and they have used *Shared Parameters,* it is possible to export those parameters from the *Family Editor* into your *Shared Parameter* file. They will initially be located in the *Exported Parameters* group but can then be moved to a more appropriate location. This allows the unique code to be recreated in your project or content.

If you have a *Shared Parameter* with the same name as another firm's *Shared Parameter,* and you are working on the same model, that is a problem. You will have to decide whose version to use. There are third-party tools that can be used to add and modify Shared Parameters in batches of families.

Conclusion

Using *Shared Parameters* is essential to take full advantage of Revit's powerful features. Like any sophisticated tool, it takes a little effort to fully understand the feature and its nuances. Once you have harnessed the power of the feature and implemented it within your firm's content and templates, you can be much more productive and have less potential for errors and omissions on your projects.

Exercise 7-5:
Keynoting

This exercise will present an overview of the keynoting system in Revit. There are no steps to be applied to the project in this section.

Hybrid Method

A simple way to manage keyed notes is to use a custom Symbol family with a symbol and descriptive text, where the text visibility can be controlled per family instance. The keyed notes are placed in views with the text hidden, and the same keyed notes are also placed in a legend (or drafting view) with the text visible.

Notice in the plan view below that the keyed note is selected and that the custom instance parameter **Description Visible** is toggled off (Figure 7-5.1).

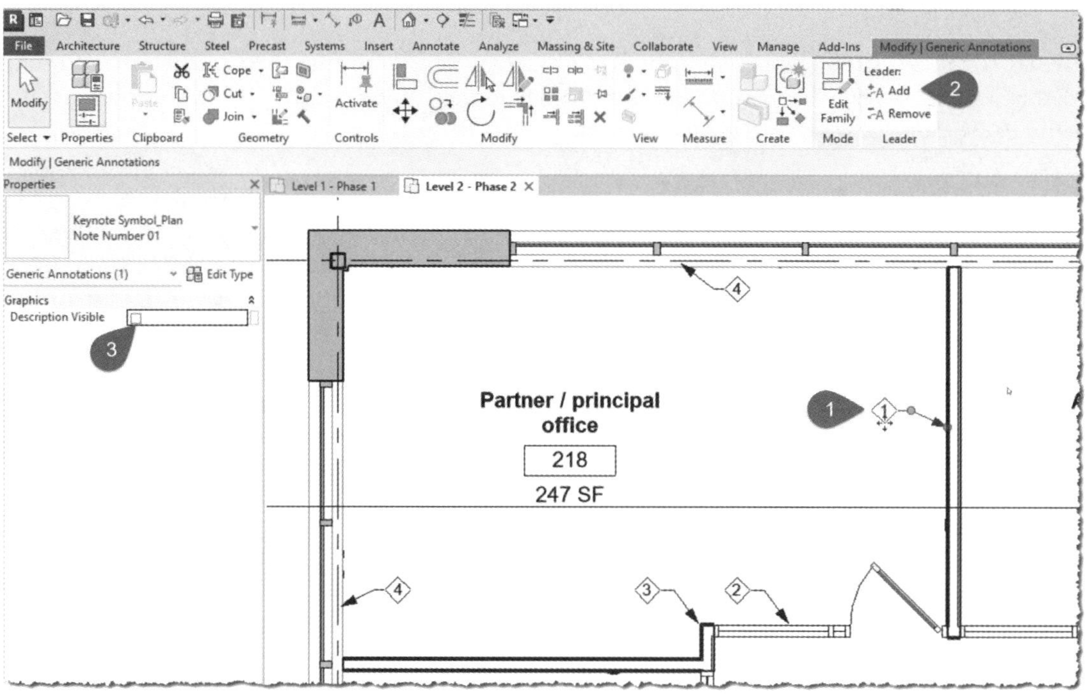

FIGURE 7-5.1 Keyed note in a floor plan view with 'Description Visible' toggled off

The next image shows the same family placed and then selected in a Legend view. In this view, the **Description Visible** is checked (Figure 7-5.2).

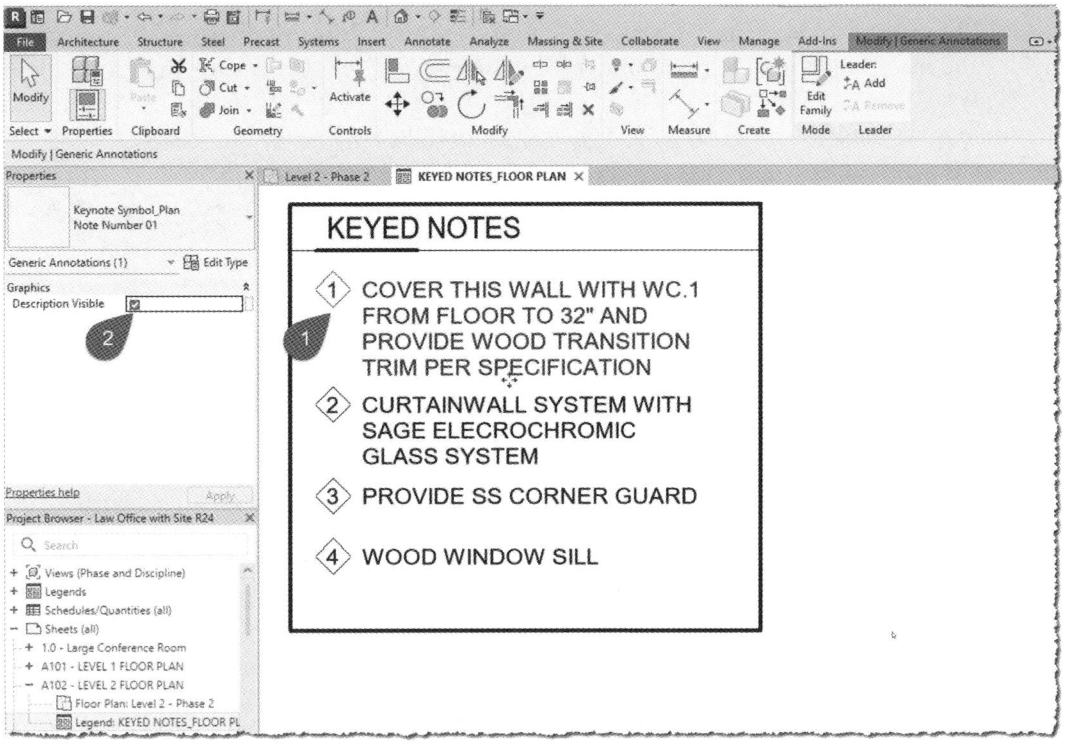

FIGURE 7-5.2 Keyed note in a legend view with 'Description Visible' toggled on

The image to the right shows the type properties for keyed note number 1. Notice the Keynote and Description are type parameters. This helps prevent someone from using the same number multiple times, each with a different description.

This method requires a different family for each plan type: e.g., Plan, Finish, Demo, Code, etc. Each family has one type for each note.

FYI: This example uses the **Multiline** parameter.

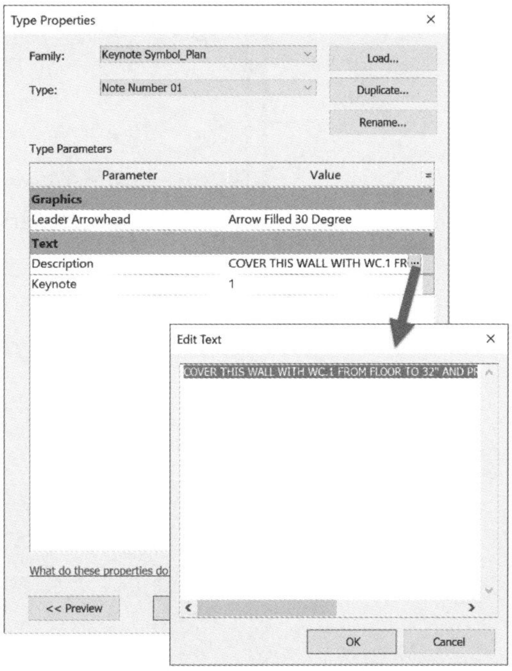

FIGURE 7-5.3 Type properties for selected keynote

Material Keynotes

We often want to identify a material in the model with "smart" text. In this case, we are talking about a Revit material defined within a **System Family** (e.g., Wall, Ceiling, Floor), a **Loadable Family** (e.g., Furniture, Casework, Doors, etc.), or **Painted** on a surface (which overrides the material defined in the Family).

There are two ways to identify materials within a Revit model (Figure 7-5.4):

- **Material Keynote**
- **Material Tag**

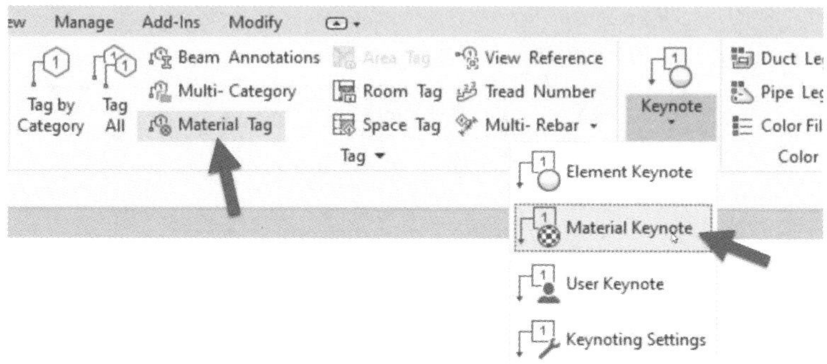

FIGURE 7-5.4 Material keynote and tag tools on the Annotate tab

> **FYI:** It should be pointed out that even though we can define multiple materials for some elements, e.g., several layers within a wall (Brick, Insulation, Studs, Gypsum Board, etc.), we can only keynote/tag a material visible in a view—i.e., we can click on it. Materials hidden within a wall or equipment family cannot be tagged.

The two examples, Material Keynote and Material Tag, are shown in the image below—referencing the wall and the wall/base cabinets (Figure 7-5.5). The boxed text is a Keynote, and the adjacent text is a Material Tag.

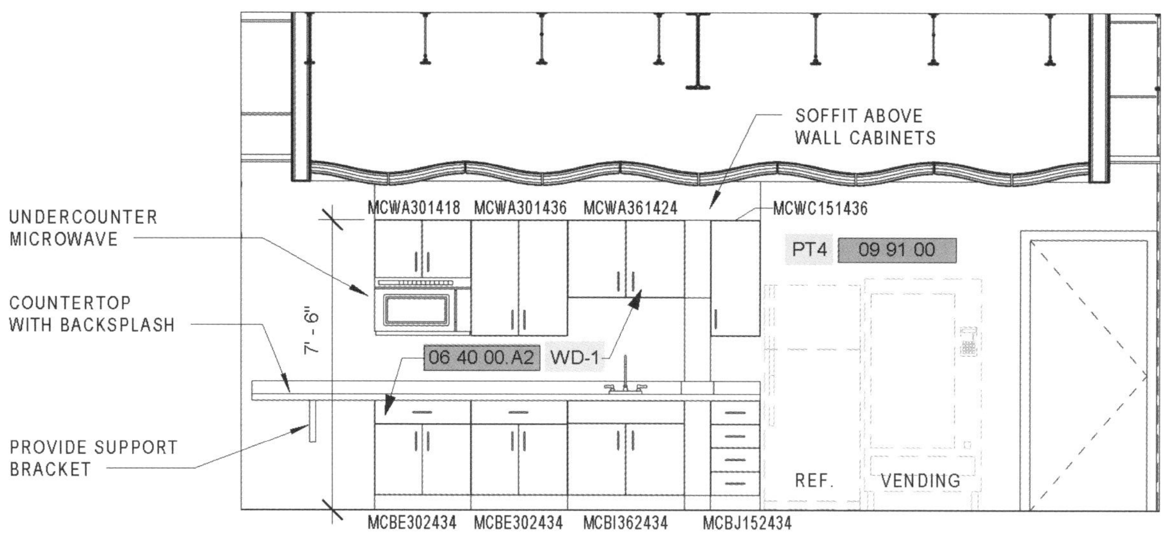

FIGURE 7-5.5 Material keynote applied to two elements (wall and cabinets)

Both values represented in the previous image are defined within the Material Browser as seen in the image below (Figure 7-5.6).

- Material Keynote → **Keynote**
  - *The value must be selected from the Keynote file (more on this later)*
- Material Tag → **Mark**
  - *The user can enter any value here*

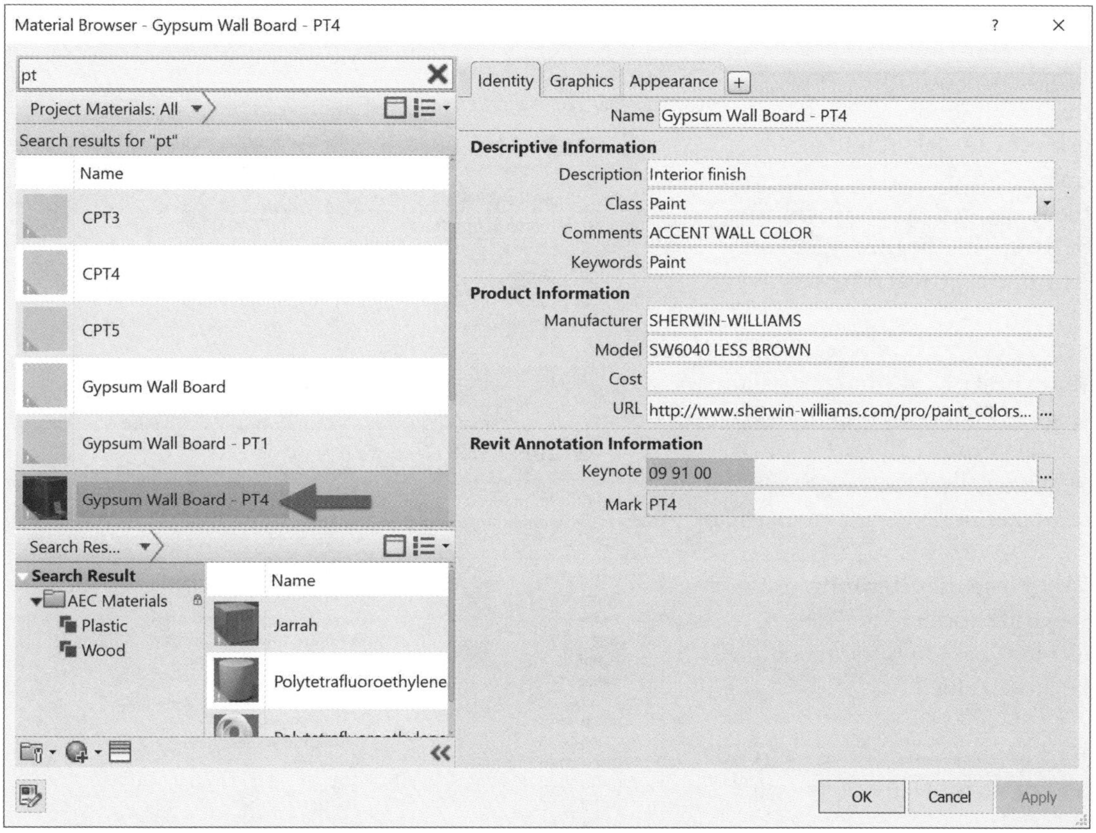

FIGURE 7-5.6 Annotation information within a Revit material

When either of these methods is used, the tags will update automatically if the family/type is changed (which also changes the material) or if a different material is painted on the elements being tagged.

When a Material is copied, the Keynote value is also copied (i.e. same keynote value is listed for the new material); however, the Mark value is not. The latter is preferred if you want to ensure the same value is not used for multiple materials.

Element Keynotes

Keynotes can be used to nearly eliminate "dumb" text in Revit. Here, we will quickly cover the basics of how keynotes work and then move on.

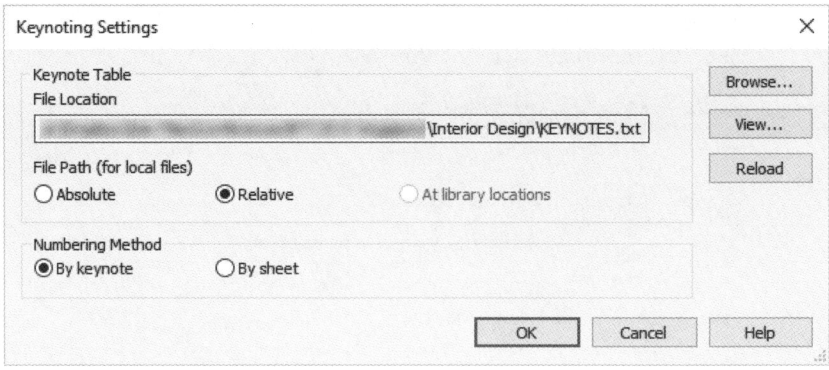

FIGURE 7-5.7 Keynoting settings dialog

First, the keynote information is stored in a simple text file (more on this in a minute). A Revit project can only reference one keynote file. The location of this file is defined in the **Keynoting Settings** file (Figure 7-5.7) via **Annotate → Keynotes**.

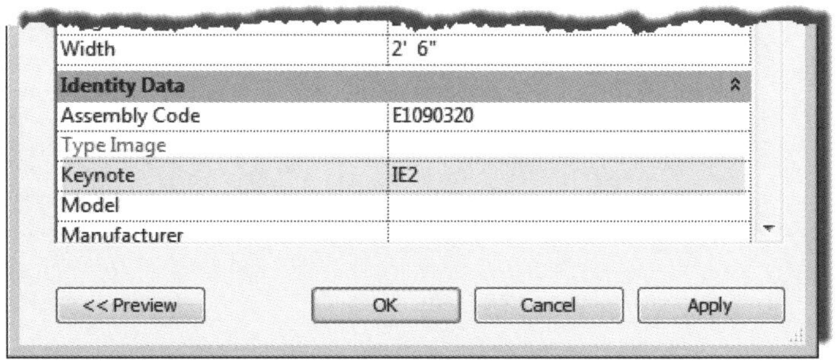

FIGURE 7-5.8 Keynote type parameter

Second, every model-based element in Revit has a **Keynote** type parameter (Figure 7-5.8). Editing this field opens the **Keynotes** dialog (Figure 7-5.9), which is a list based on the aforementioned external text file.

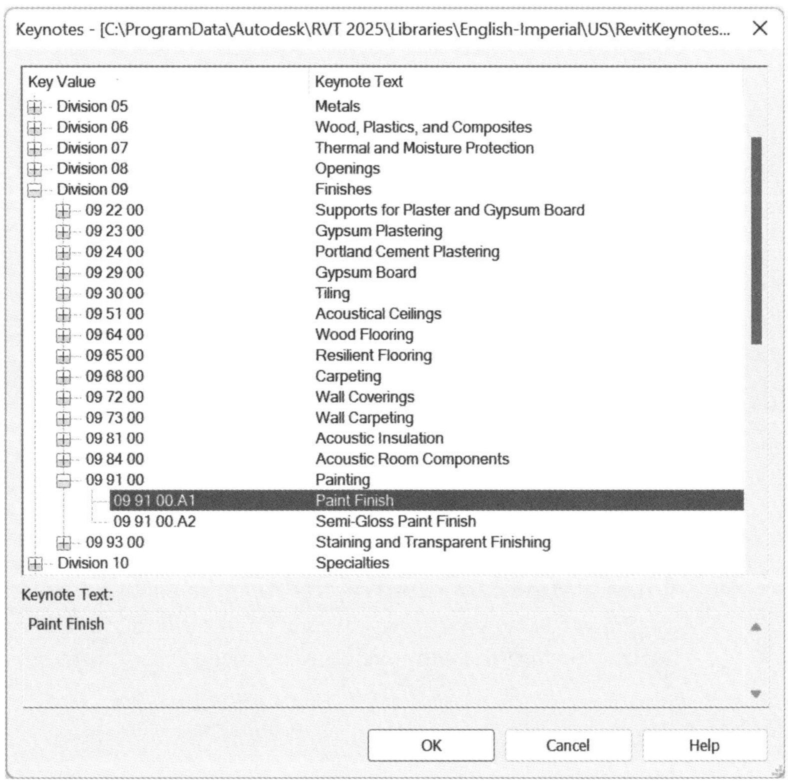

FIGURE 7-5.9 Keynotes dialog as viewed from within Revit

Third, use the **Element Keynote** tool to "tag" an element based on the predefined keynote value.

Fifth, create a **Keynote Legend** and place it on any sheets with keynoted views.

The result is shown in the sheet view below (Figure 7-5.10). The default keynote tag shows the keynote number, which corresponds to the same number and description in the legend. The result is "clean" looking drawings without excessive text.

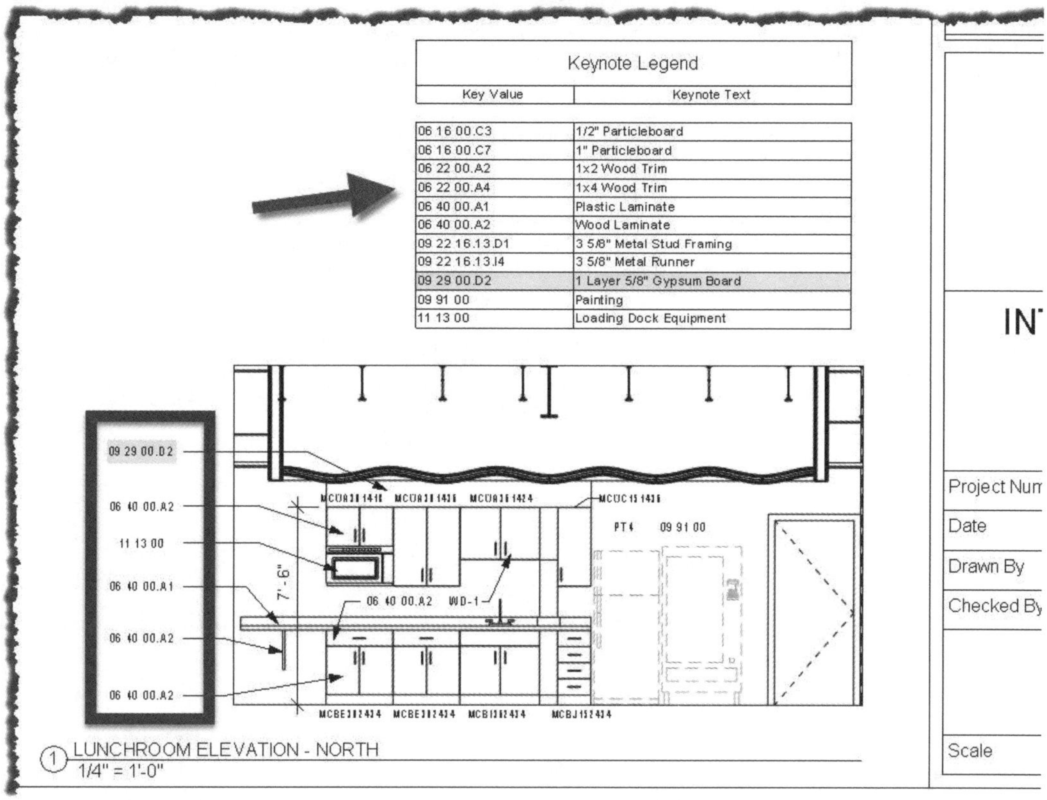

FIGURE 7-5.10 Example of a keynote legend and a view with keynotes

The keynote legend will only list keynotes that actually appear on a given sheet. Opening the keynote legend view directly will show all keynotes in the project. Keep in mind that the keynote legend lists only items that have been keynoted with the Keynote tool. It will not list a keynote just because an element's type property has a keynote value applied.

TIP: Use a Filter in Schedule Properties to limit the list if needed.

This concludes a basic overview of how keynotes work in Revit – with an emphasis on how they work out-of-the-box (OOTB). Next, we will look at a variation on this system that uses "normal" notes rather than product category numbers.

For this alternate method, we will start by creating a custom keynote file. Simply create an empty file using Microsoft Notepad and save it somewhere in your project folder (Figure 7-5.11).

To better understand the format of this file, note the following:

1. **Group definition**
    - unique number
    - descriptive text
2. **Keynote number**
3. **Keynote text**
4. **Group identifier**

The keynote text file must be stored on the server, accessible to all users (not necessarily with edit rights).

Results below explained on the next page…

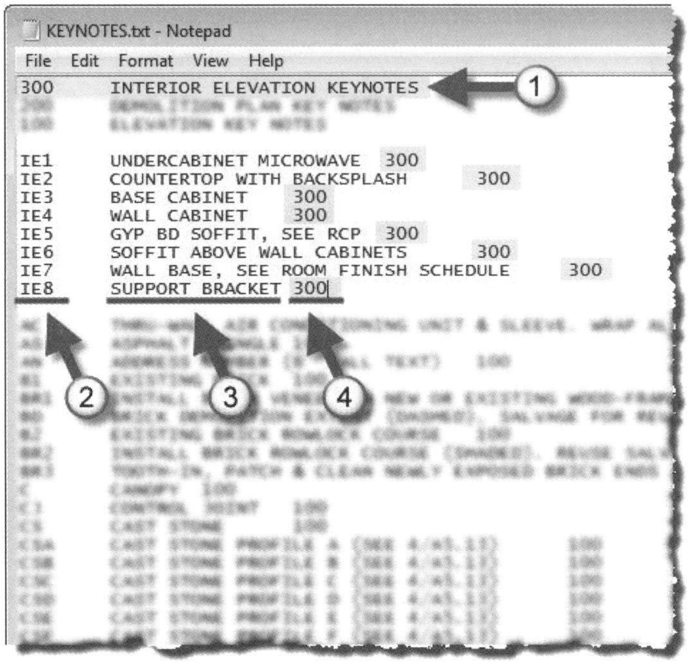

FIGURE 7-5.11 Anatomy of a keynote file

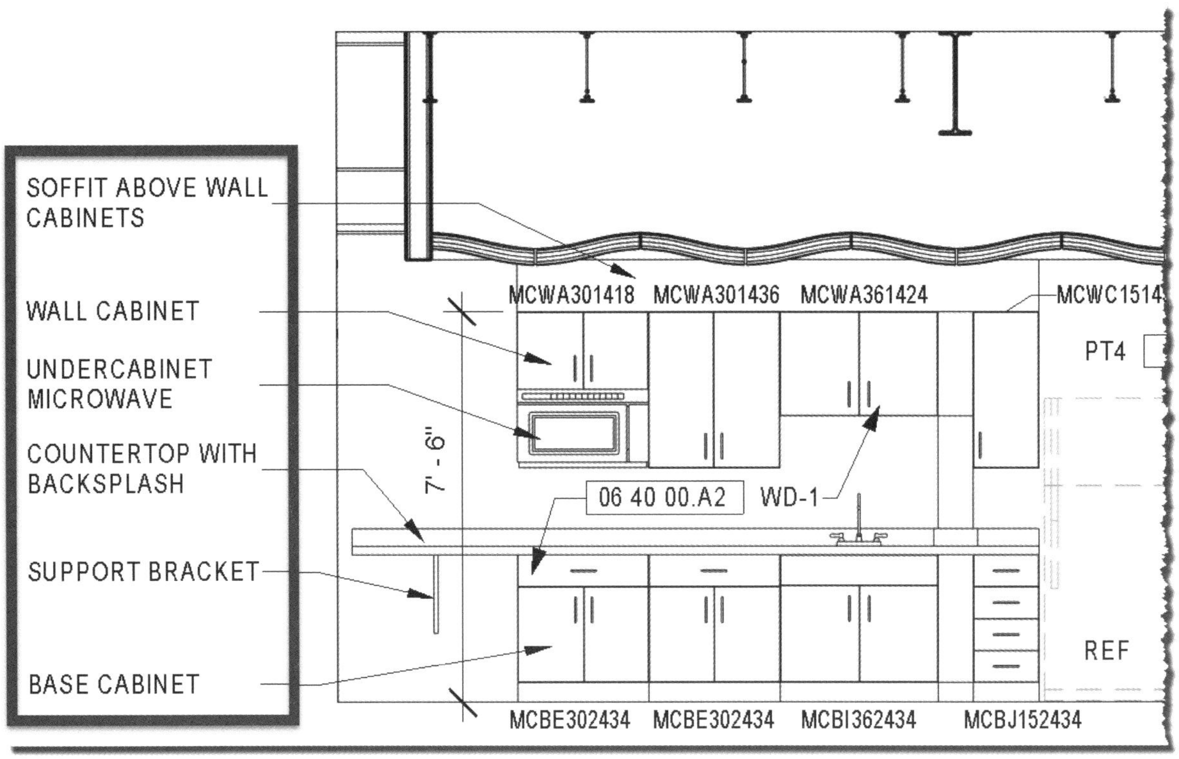

FIGURE 7-5.12 Keynotes added to elements in elevation - no “dumb” text

The elevation shown on the previous page includes Element Keynotes. The default Keynote tag has type properties to hide the keynote number & box and show the keynote number.

All the elements in the model have firm-approved standard notes applied to the Keynote type property. This information can be prepopulated in the content library (i.e., Revit families) to streamline production and ensure consistency across the firm.

Keynote Manager + Add-in for Revit

One challenge with maintaining the keynoting system in Revit is that the text file can only be edited by one person at a time. Also, after changes are made, they must be manually reloaded (note the Reload button in the Keynoting Settings dialog) to see them in the current Revit session (Figure 7-5.12).

Using **Keynote Manager +**, a third-party add-in for Revit, can help. This tool has the following features:

- Multiple users
- Auto reload
- Spellcheck
- Indicates keynotes used in the project (with house icon)
- Auto sequencing
- Add comments and URL links

FYI: To store the additional comments and external links, a same-named XML file is created right next to the keynote file.

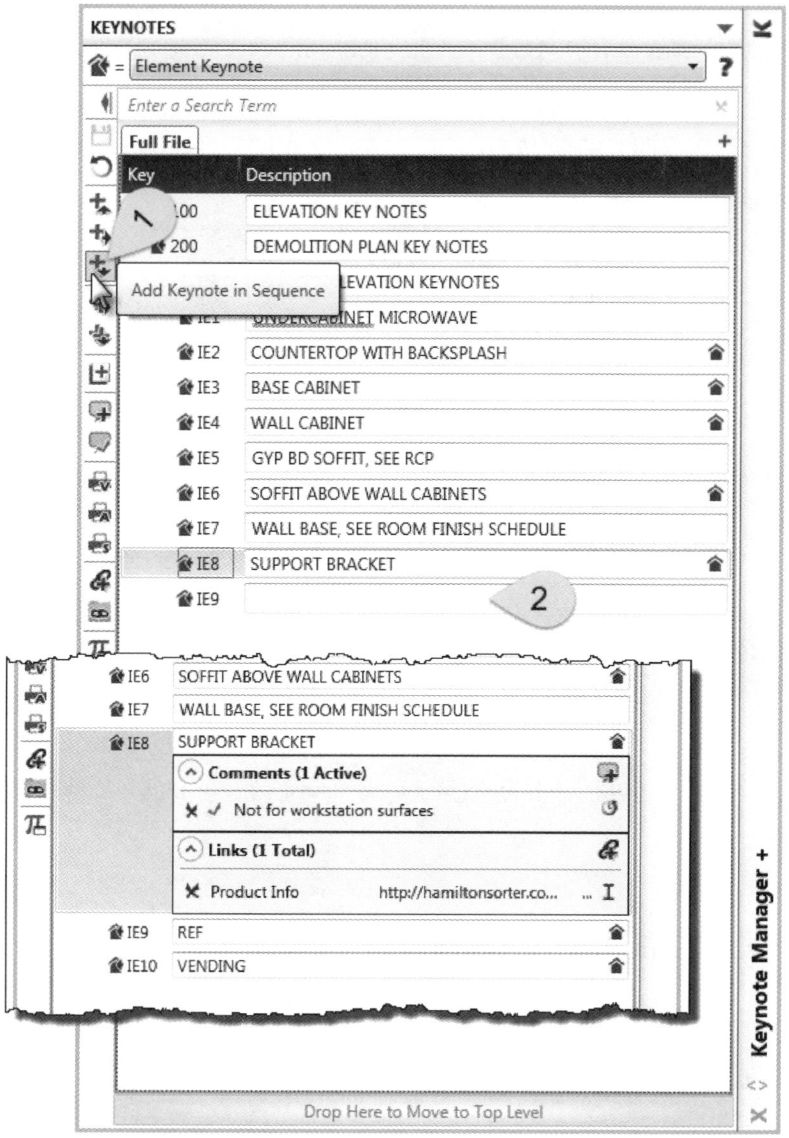

FIGURE 7-5.13 Keynote manager palette in Revit

Be sure to check out **Keynote Manager** by Revolution Design, Inc., for a powerful add-in that simplifies the use of Keynotes in Revit.
URL: http://revolutiondesign.biz/products/keynote-manager/features/

User Keynotes

User Keynotes work the same way as Element Keynotes, with one exception…

When the **User Keynote** tool is selected, the user is prompted to select an element to keynote. Next, a selection must be made from the keynote list (i.e., the text file).

Although this adds some flexibility to the process, it also provides an opportunity to select the wrong keynote. In the example below (Figure 7-5.14), the selected base cabinet is tagged with three keynotes (highlighted in yellow). One is an **Element Keynote**, and two are **User Keynotes**—both user keynotes indicate something completely different.

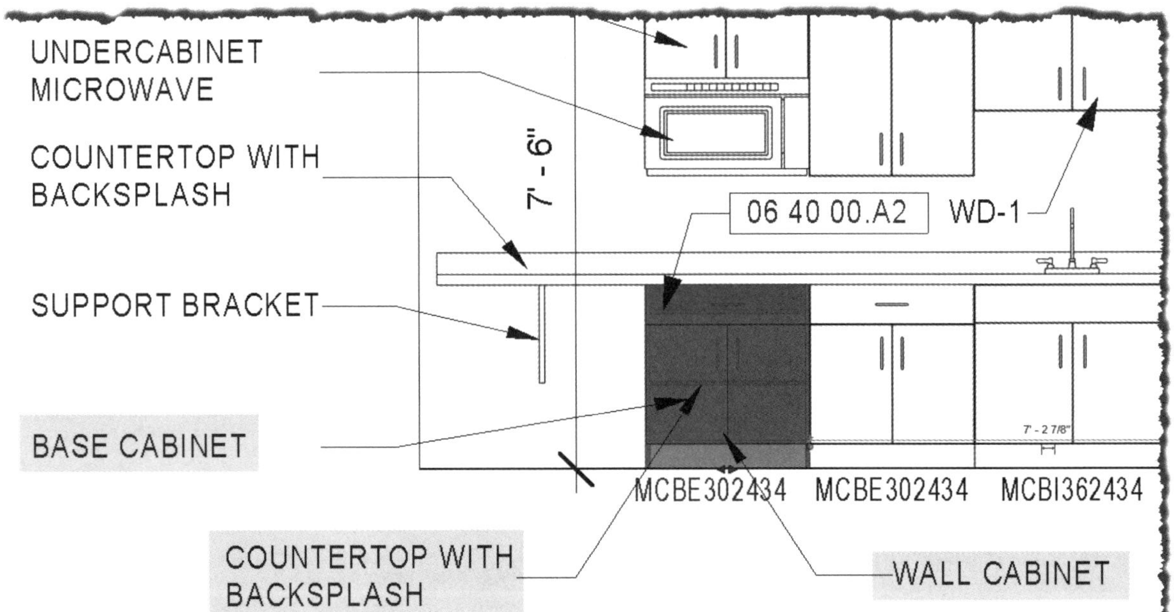

FIGURE 7-5.14 Multiple user keynotes applied to a single model element

Used correctly, the User Keynote tool can be helpful. However, those who use it must be trained and pick carefully each time they use it.

Exercise 7-6:
Adding Dimensions

Next, you will add dimensions to your floor plans. As covered earlier in this chapter, Revit provides a powerful dimensioning tool that lets you quickly dimension drawings. This process is much easier than other CAD programs. Revit has a dimension style all set up and ready to use, which works for most designers. Furthermore, the text and tick sizes are tied to the View Scale feature to ensure the dimensions always print at the correct size. For example, a dimension's text and ticks would get twice as big just by changing the *View Scale* from ¼″ = 1′-0″ to ⅛″ = 1′-0″. You will try this in a moment.

Industry standard dimensioning conventions were covered in the previous lesson. You may want to take a minute and review that information (see page 5-24).

Drawing dimensions in Revit involves the following steps:

- Select the *Aligned* dimension tool from the *Annotate* tab.
- *Ribbon* and *Type Selector*:
  - Select one of the predefined styles from the *Type Selector*.
  - Select the kind of dimension you want: Linear, Angular, Radial, Arch Length.
  - Tell Revit what part of the wall you want to dimension to: Wall centerlines, Wall Face, Center of Core, Face of Core; this can change for each side of a dimension's line.
- Select two or more walls to dimension between.
- Select a location for the dimension line.

Adding Dimensions to the First Floor Plan:

1. Open ex6-5.rvt and **Save-As ex7-6.rvt.**
2. Switch to the ***First Floor Plan*** view.
3. **Zoom in** on the North wall of the garage.
4. Select the **Annotate → Dimension → Aligned** tool.

Notice the *Ribbon* and *Type Selector* changes to give you control over the various options mentioned above (Figure 7-6.1).

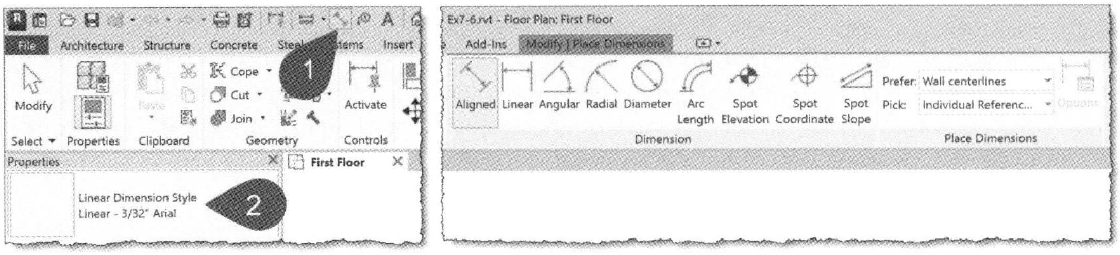

FIGURE 7-6.1 Ribbon and Type Selector: Dimension tool active

5. Set the *Type Selector* to **Linear – 3/32″ Arial**.

6. Click the **Edit Type** button on the *Properties Palette.*

Notice the various properties you can adjust for the selected dimension type (Figure 7-6.2).

Creating a new, custom dimension type is the same as for walls, doors, etc.; just click the *Duplicate* button, provide a name, and then adjust the properties.

All the dimensions you see here are multiplied by the *View Scale*. For example, the 3/32″ text is multiplied by 48 when the *View Scale* is set to ¼″ = 1′-0″; thus, the text is 4½″ tall in ¼″ drawings. When the ¼″ view is placed on a *Sheet*, Revit automatically scales it down by 1/48. At this point, the text is 3/32″ again. This makes the view actually a ¼″ = 1′-0″ on the *Sheet*, which is the actual sheet size – say 22″ x 34″. Finally, all this is automatically updated whenever the View Scale is changed: dimension and text sizes, as well as the *View* size on sheets! You will learn about *Sheets* later in the book.

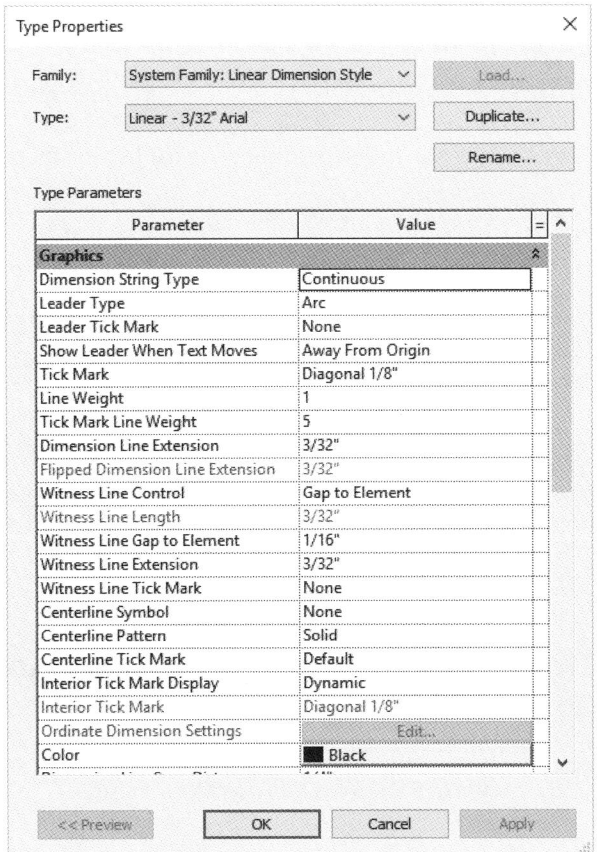

FIGURE 7-6.2 Properties for selected dimension type

7. Click **OK** to close the dialog box.

The Aligned dimension tool lets you place dimensions by selecting walls. You will try this now.

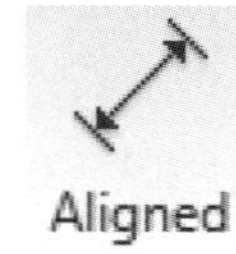

8. Next, select **Wall Faces** on the *Ribbon* (Figure 7-6.1).

9. Draw your first dimension by clicking the three points as identified in **Figure 7-6.3**.

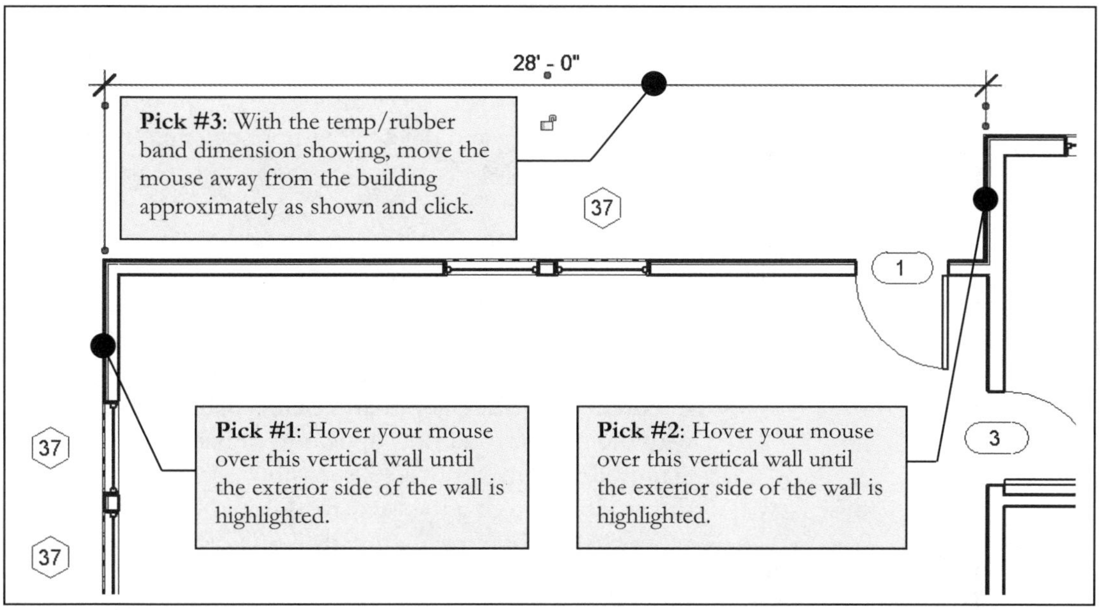

FIGURE 7-6.3 First Floor plan: first dimension added

***FYI:** In the figure above (7-6.3), you can select points 1 and 2 in the opposite order as well.*

10. Dimension the rest of the North exterior wall as shown in Figure 7-6.4. You may not be able to read the dimensions in the image provided, but you can still determine the number of dimensions required, and Revit provides the dimension text anyway. See the next page for dimension comments.

Once you have drawn one dimension, as in Step 9, the remaining dimensions in that "string" should align with the first. Revit helps you make the third pick (as in Figure 7-6.3) by automatically snapping to the previous dimension when you move your cursor to it.

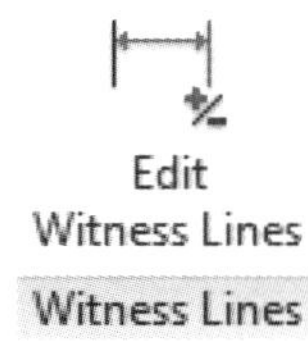

You can add a "string" of dimensions by simply clicking on parallel walls. When done, click somewhere away from any Revit elements to position and finish the dimension string. To edit a string of dimensions after it has been placed, simply select it and pick the **Edit Witness Lines** tool on the *Ribbon*. You can also *Tab/Select* a single dimension within a dimension string and delete it without deleting the entire string.

Yet another feature Revit offers that other programs do not is the ability to automatically snap to the center of a door or window opening. In other programs, you might have to draw a temporary line from one door jamb to the other; use the dimension command to snap to the midpoint of the line and then delete it. Then you are left with dimensions that only appear to dimension to the center. Remember, Revit's dimensions are able to modify the model, kind of a two-way road if you will, whereas other CAD programs are mostly a one-way road.

In addition to snapping to the center of doors and windows, Revit will also snap to the jambs, depending on where your mouse is relative to the element being dimensioned.

You will notice that Revit does not care if a dimension's witness line overlaps a door or window tag. The tags need to be selected and moved manually, individually or in groups.

Next, you will dimension the west side of the building.

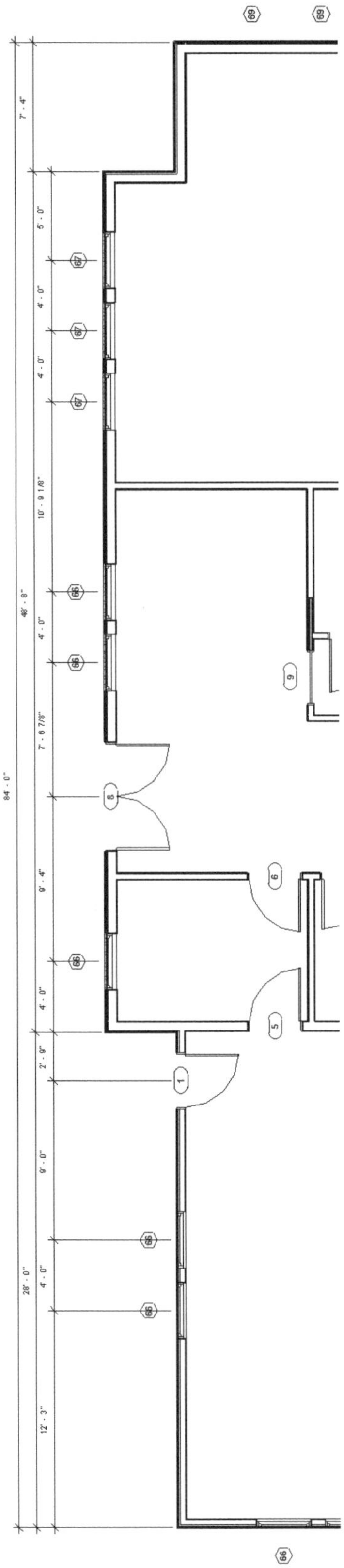

FIGURE 7-6.4
First Floor: rotated 90 degrees to increase image size in book

11. Dimension the West exterior walls and openings as shown in **Figure 7-6.5**.

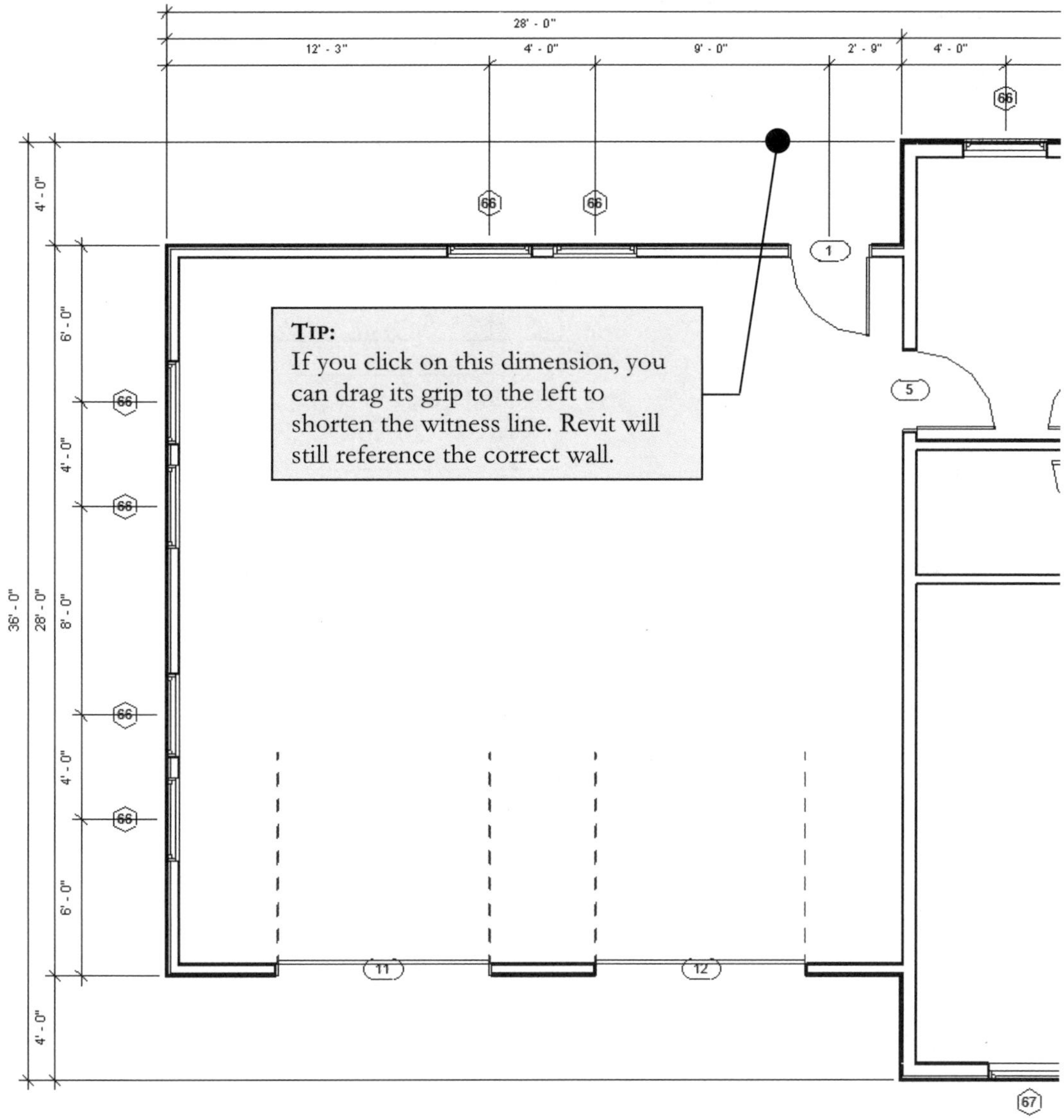

FIGURE 7-6.5 First Floor: dimensions added to the West wall

The last two images in the exercise give you an idea of what each dimension type loaded with the residential template looks like. Similar to other elements in Revit, you can select a dimension and verify what type it is by looking at the *Type Selector* on the *Properties Palette*. Also, you can change the type by selecting the desired type from the *Type Selector*.

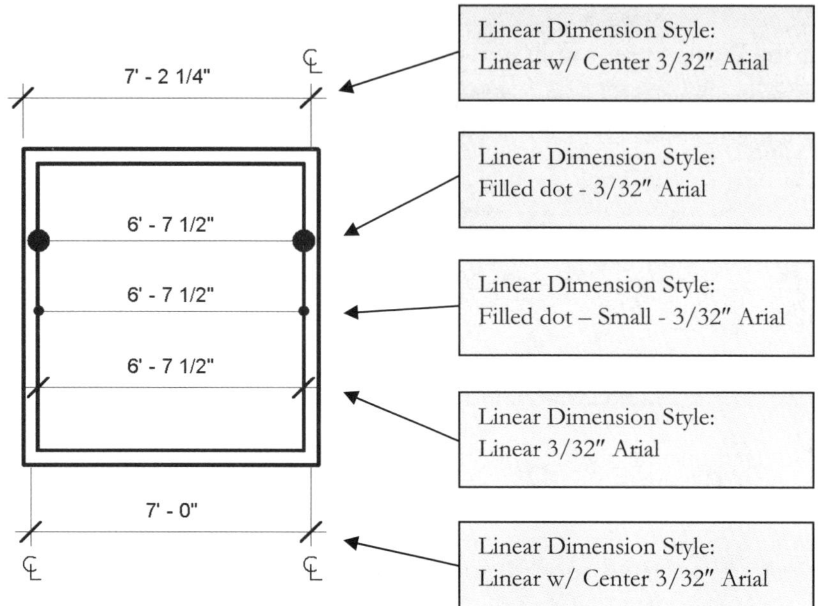

FIGURE 7-6.6 Dimension type comparison

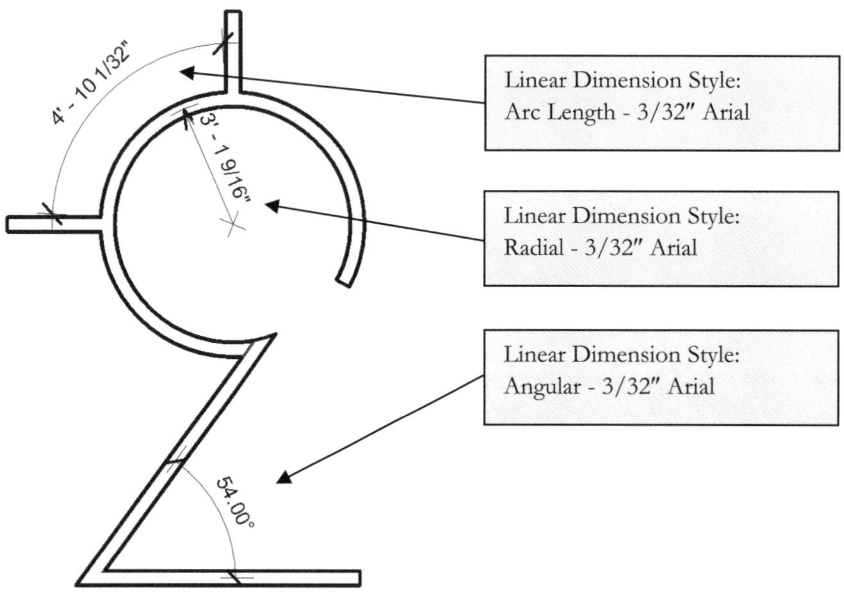

FIGURE 7-6.7 Dimension type comparison

This should be enough to help you understand how to dimension your plans. If you want more practice, you can dimension the rest of the *First Floor Plan* and then the other two floors; your instructor may require this. See Revit's *Help System* if you want to dig a little deeper into Revit's dimensioning options.

12. **Save** your Project as **ex7-6.rvt**.

Self-Exam:

The following questions can be used as a way to check your knowledge of this lesson. The answers can be found at the bottom of this page.

1. Deleting a dimension with equality toggled on will always also delete the constraint in the model. (T/F)
2. To move an element, simply click on the dimension and edit the text. (T/F)
3. Material Keynote and Material Tag are the two ways to annotate a material. (T/F)
4. Pressing Enter in a text element limits the ability to modify using the text box grips and have the number of rows adjust. (T/F)
5. To measure the length along a curved line, use this dimension tool:

   _______________________________ .

Review Questions:

The following questions may be assigned by your instructor as a way to assess your knowledge of this section. Your instructor has the answers to the review questions.

1. A dimension string set to Equality can only display 'EQ' and not the actual dimension value. (T/F)
2. A single text element can have both curved and straight leaders. (T/F)
3. Spell check only works on text elements, not tags or keynotes. (T/F)
4. The use of basic text should be minimized. (T/F)
5. The same element can be tagged more than once, even in the same view. (T/F)
6. Use a Linear dimension to ensure a dimension remains horizontal. (T/F)
7. Revit's keynoting system requires an external text file. (T/F)
8. Text leaders can only be removed in the reverse order they were added. (T/F)
9. Revit can dimension all the openings in a wall at once. (T/F)
10. A 'user keynote' presents an opportunity for user error by selecting the wrong item from a list each time this tool is used. (T/F)

SELF-EXAM ANSWERS:
1 – F, **2** – F, **3** – T, **4** – T, **5** – Arc Length

Notes:

Lesson 8
ROOF:

This lesson will look at various options and tools for designing a roof for your building. You will also add skylights.

Exercise 8-1:
Roof Design Options (Style, Pitch, and Overhang)

In this lesson, you will look at the various ways to use the *Roof* tool to draw the more common roof forms used in architecture today.

Start a New Revit Project:

You will start a new project for this lesson so you can quickly compare the results of using the *Roof* tool.

1. Start a new project using the **default.rte** template.

2. Switch to the **North** elevation view and rename the level named *Level 2* to **T.O. Masonry**. This will be the reference point for your roof. Click **Yes** to automatically rename the corresponding views.

   TIP: Just select the Level *datum and click on the level datum's text to rename.*

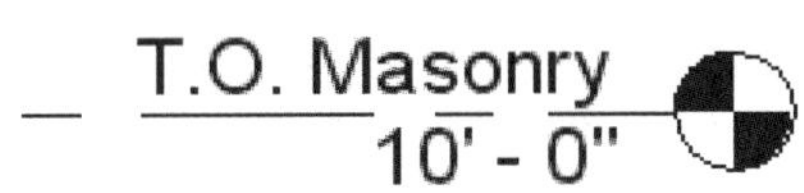

3. Switch to the ***Level 1 Floor Plan*** view.

Drawing the Buildings:

4. Set the Level 1 *"Detail Level"* to **Medium**, so the material hatching is visible within the walls.

   TIP: Use the View Control Bar at the bottom.

5. Using the ***Wall*** tool with the wall *Type* set to "**Exterior - Brick on Mtl. Stud**," and draw a **40'-0" x 20'-0"** building (Figure 8-1.1).

   FYI: The default Wall height is OK; it should be 20'-0".

Be sure to draw the building within the elevation tags.

TIP: You can draw the building in a single step by selecting the Rectangle *option on the Ribbon while using the* Wall *tool.*

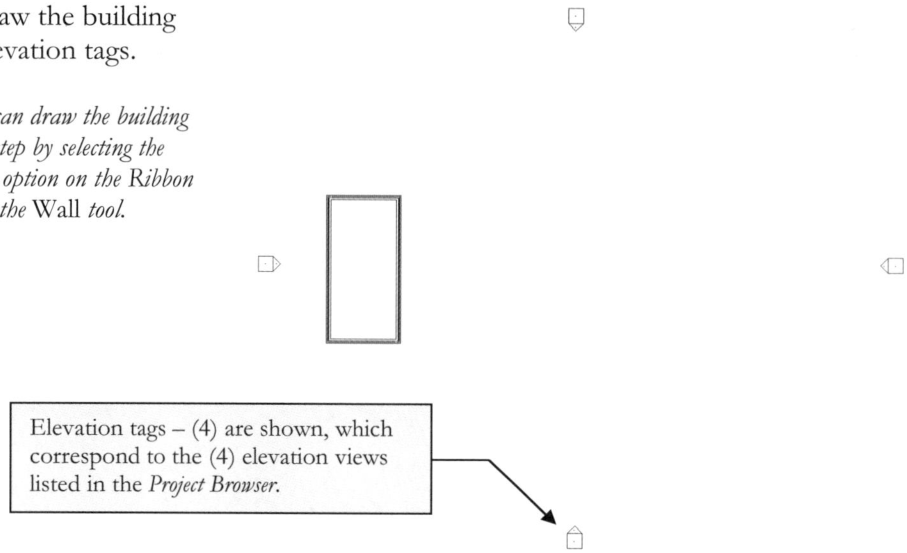

FIGURE 8-1.1 Bldg. and Elev. tags

You will copy the building to create a total of 4 buildings. You will draw a different type of roof on each one.

6. Drag a window around the walls to select them. Then use the **Array** command to set up four buildings **35′-0″ O.C.** (Figure 8-1.2). See the *Array Tip* below.

TIP: Zoom in and make sure the brick is on the exterior side of the wall. If not, you can select each wall and click its flip *icon.*

ARRAY TIP: Select the first building, select Array, and then, just like the Copy command, define a copy 35′ to the right, then enter the number of copies.

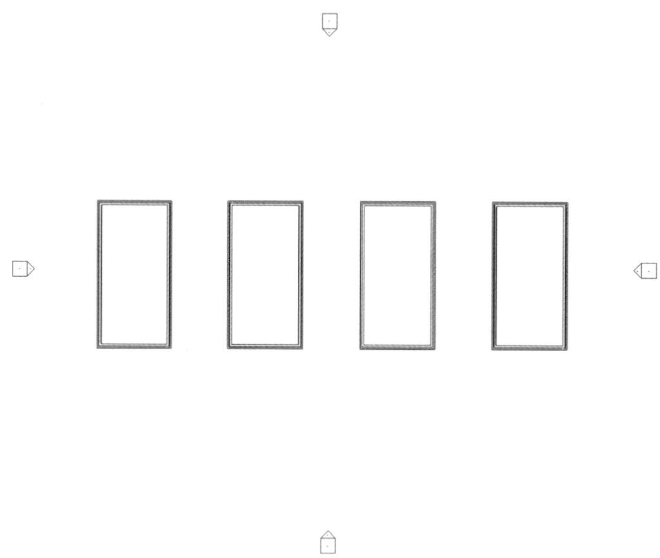

FIGURE 8-1.2 Four buildings

7. Select all of the buildings and click **Ungroup** from the *Ribbon*.

Hip Roof

The various roof forms are largely defined by the *"Defines slope"* setting. This is displayed in the *Ribbon* while the *Roof* tool is active. When a wall is selected, and the *"Defines slope"* option is selected, the roof above that portion of the wall slopes. You will see this more clearly in the examples below.

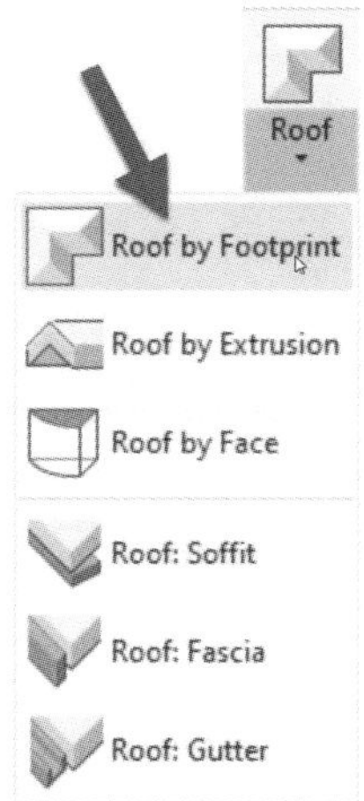

8. Switch to the **T.O. Masonry** *Floor Plan* view.

9. Select the **Architecture → Build → Roof** *(down-arrow)* → **Roof by Footprint** tool.

10. Set the overhang to **2′-0″** and make sure that the **Defines slope** option is activated (highlighted) on the *Ribbon.*

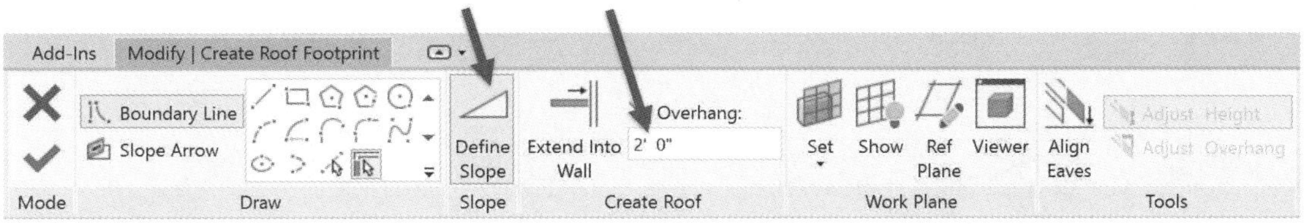

11. Select the four walls of the West (far left) building, clicking each wall one at a time.

    TIP: Make sure you select towards the exterior side of the wall; notice the review line before clicking.

12. Click **Finish Edit Mode** (i.e., the green check mark) on the *Ribbon* to finish the *Roof* tool.

13. Click the **Attach** button to attach the roof to the walls.

14. Switch to the **South** elevation (Figure 8-1.3).

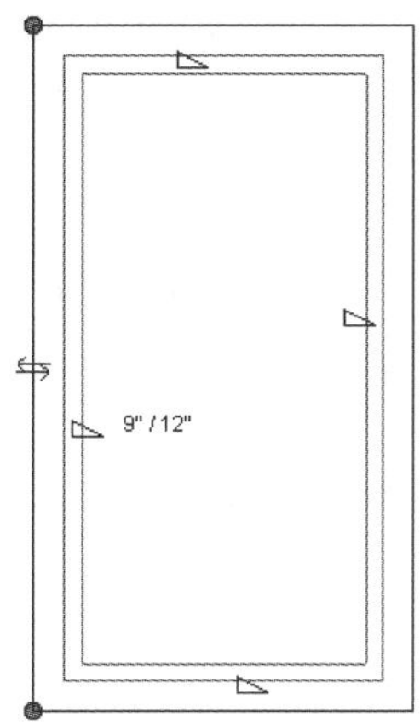

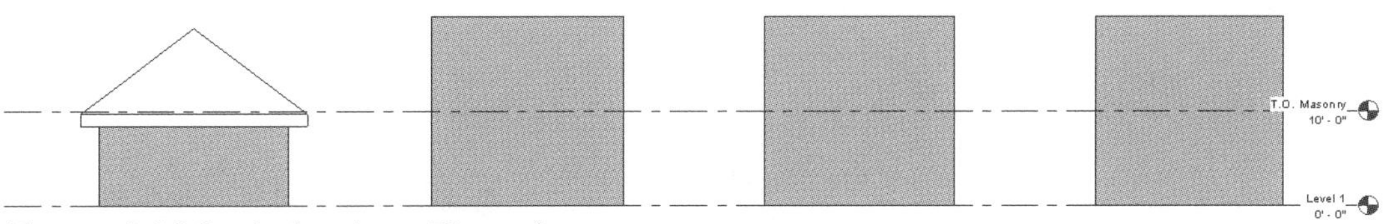

FIGURE 8-1.3 South elevation – Hip roof

You will notice that the default wall height is much higher than what we ultimately want. However, when the roof is drawn at the correct elevation, and you attach the walls to the roof, the walls automatically adjust to stop under the roof object. Additionally, if the roof is later raised or lowered, the walls will follow; you can try this in the South elevation view by simply using the *Move* tool. ***REMEMBER:*** *You can make revisions in any view.*

Switch to the **3D** view using the icon on the *QAT* (Figure 8-1.4).

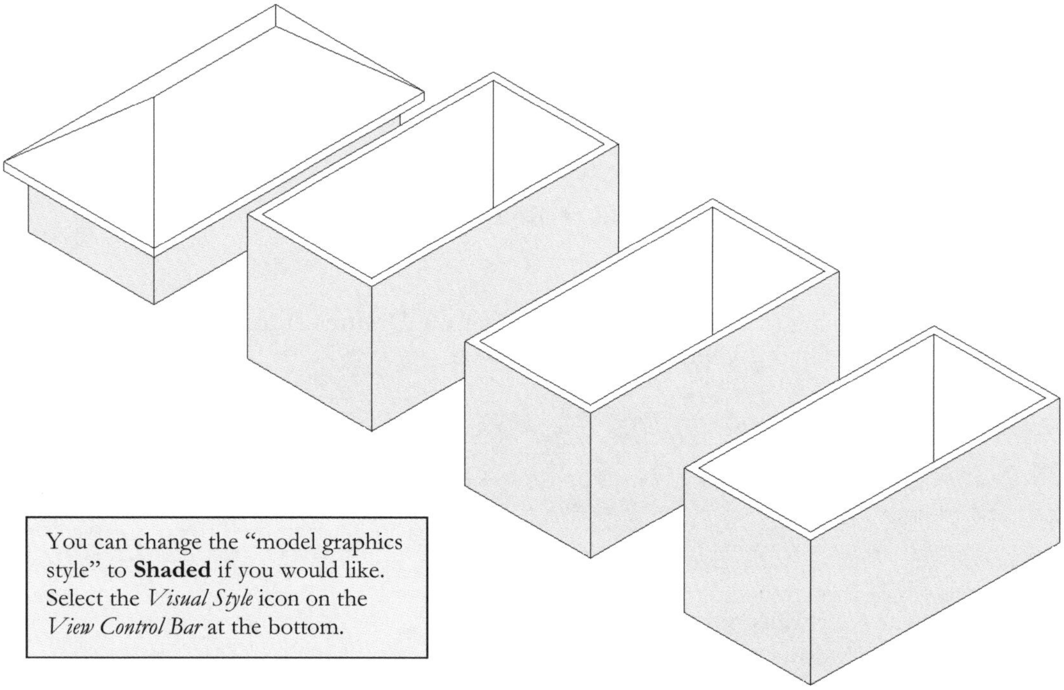

You can change the "model graphics style" to **Shaded** if you would like. Select the *Visual Style* icon on the *View Control Bar* at the bottom.

FIGURE 8-1.4 3D view – hip roof

Gable Roof

15. Switch back to the **T.O. Masonry** view (not the ceiling plan for this level).

16. Select the **Roof → Roof by Footprint** tool.

17. Set the overhang to **2′-0″** and make sure **Defines slope** is selected (highlighted) on the *Ribbon.*

18. Only select the two long (40′-0″) walls.

19. **Uncheck** the **Defines slope** option.

20. Select the remaining two walls (Figure 8-1.5).

21. Pick the **green check mark** on the *Ribbon* to finish the roof.

22. Select **Attach** to attach the walls to the roof.

23. Switch to the **South** elevation view (Figure 8-1.6).

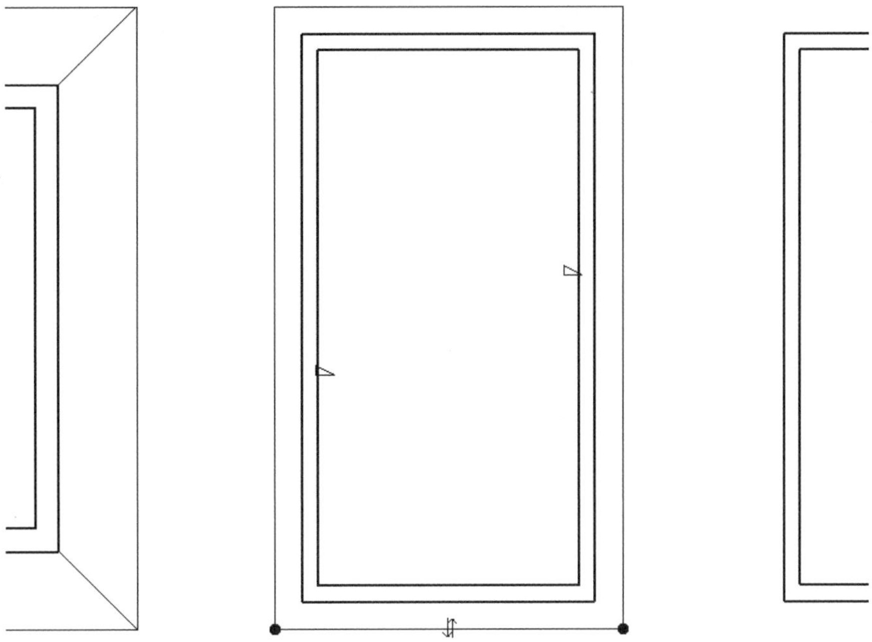

FIGURE 8-1.5 Gable – plan view

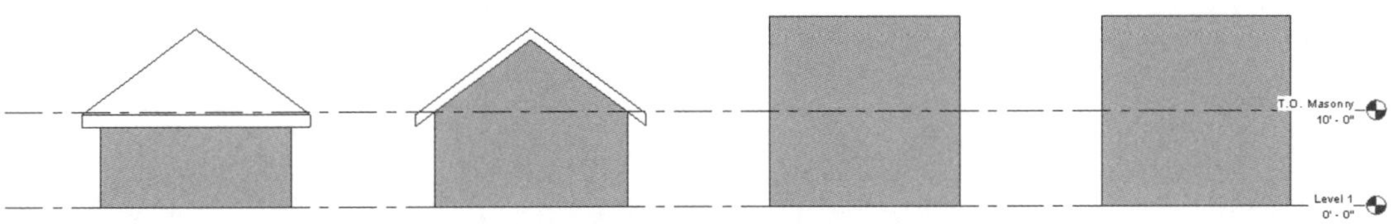

FIGURE 8-1.6 South elevation – gable roof

24. Switch to the **3D** view (Figure 8-1.7).

Notice the wall extends up to conform to the underside of the roof on the gable ends.

FYI: *You may be wondering why the roofs look odd in the floor plan view. If you remember, each view has its own* cut plane. *The* cut plane *happens to be lower than the highest part of the roof – thus, the roof is shown cut at the cut plane. If you go to Properties Palette → View Range (while nothing is selected) and then adjust the cut plane to be higher than the highest point of the roof, then you will see the roof's ridge line.*

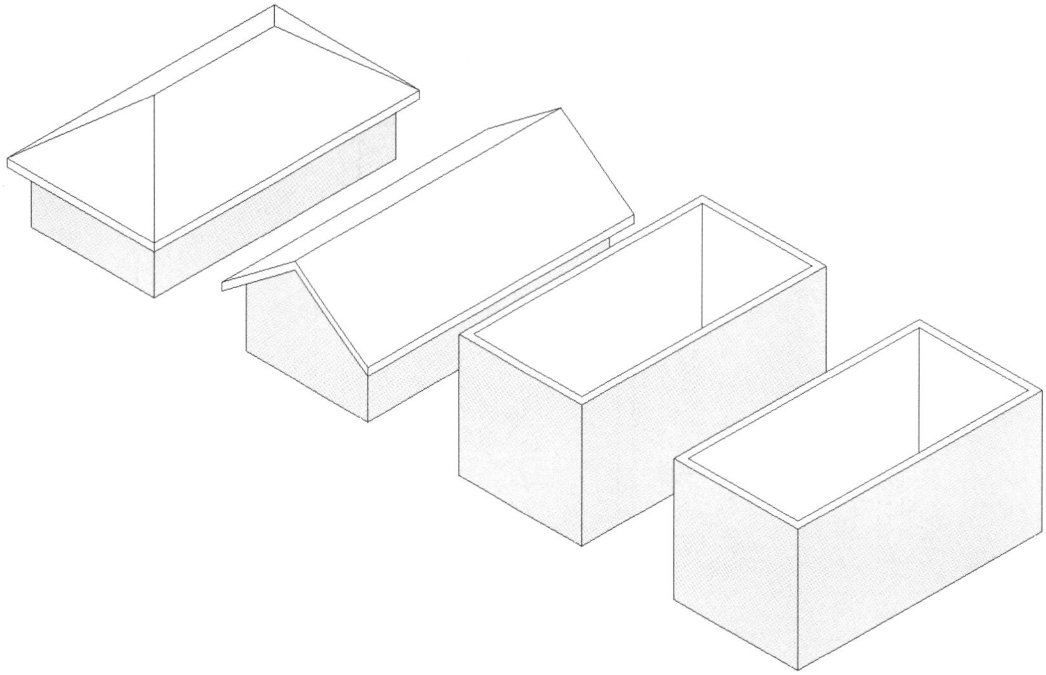

FIGURE 8-1.7 3D view – gable roof

Shed Roof

25. Switch back to the **T.O. Masonry** view.

26. Select the **Roof → Roof by Footprint** tool.

27. Check **Defines slope** on the *Ribbon.*

28. Set the overhang to **2′-0″** on the *Ribbon.*

29. Select the East wall (40′-0″ wall, right-hand side).

30. Toggle off **Defines slope** on the *Ribbon.*

31. Select the remaining three walls (Figure 8-1.8).

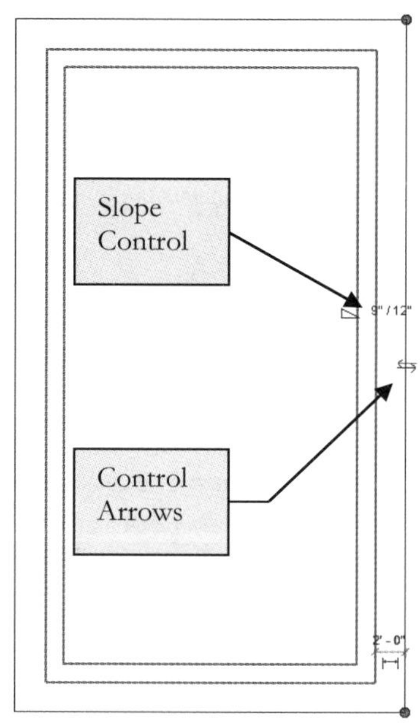

FIGURE 8-1.8 Selected walls

32. With nothing selected, set the **Slope**, aka roof pitch, to 3/12 (Figure 8-1.9) on the *Properties Palette.*

33. Click **Apply** on the *Properties Palette.*

34. Pick the **green check mark** on the *Ribbon* to finish the roof.

35. Select **Attach** to attach the walls to the roof.

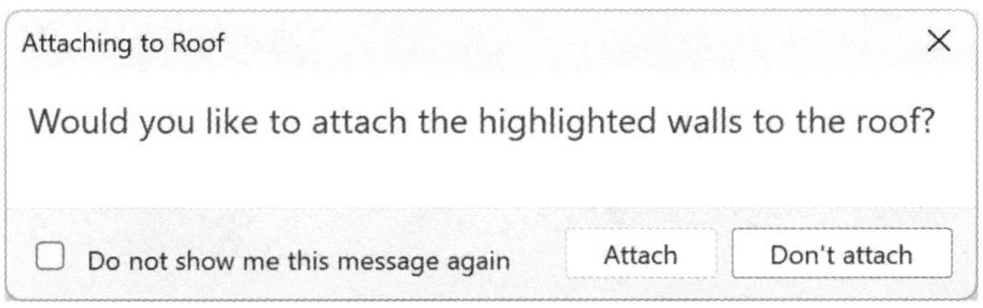

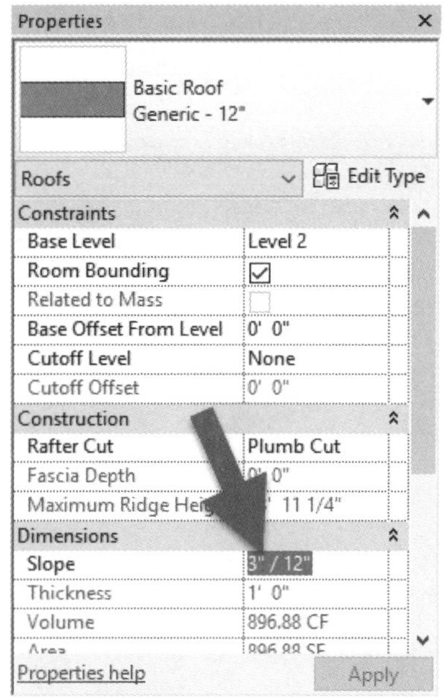

FIGURE 8-1.9
Properties for Roof tool

FYI: *You can also change the slope of the roof by changing the Slope Control text (see Figure 8-1.8); just select the text and type a new number.*

TIP: *You can use the Control Arrows, while the roof line is still selected, to flip the orientation of the roof overhang if you accidentally selected the wrong side of the wall and the overhang is on the inside of the building.*

36. Switch to the **South** elevation view (Figure 8-1.10).

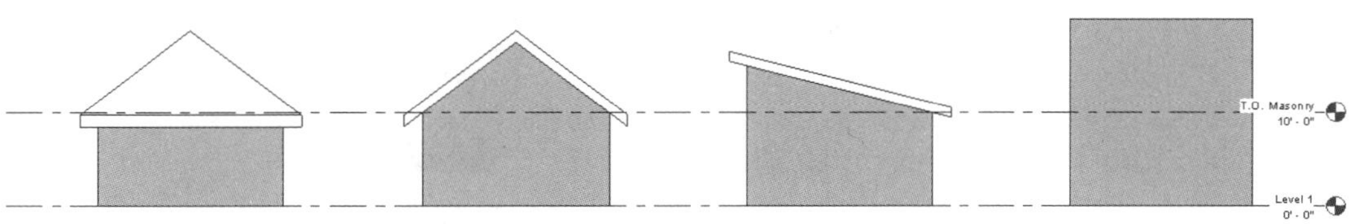

FIGURE 8-1.10 South elevation – shed roof

37. Switch to the ***Default 3D*** view (Figure 8-1.11).

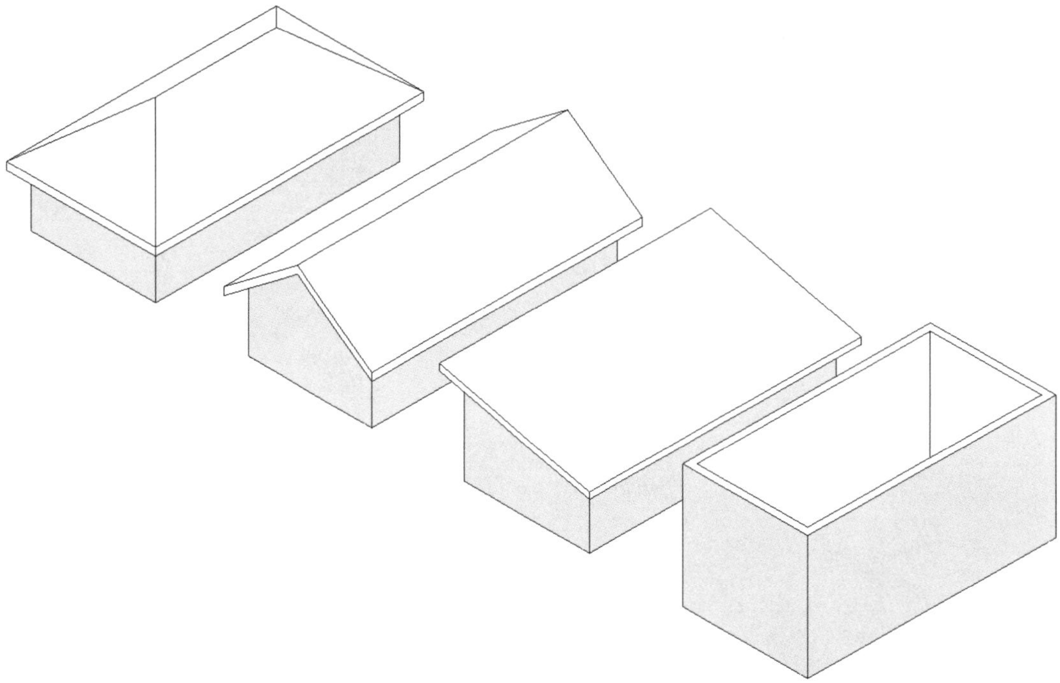

FIGURE 8-1.11 Default 3D view – shed roof

Once the roof is drawn, you can easily change the roof's overhang. You will try this on the shed roof. You will also make the roof slope in the opposite direction.

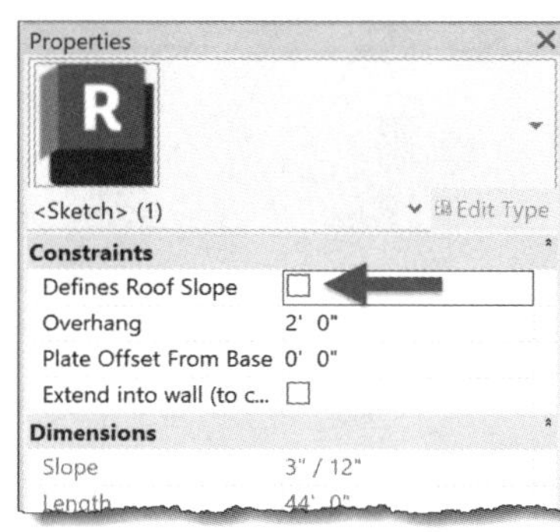

38. In **T.O. Masonry** view, select **Modify** from the *Ribbon*, and then select the shed roof.

39. Click **Edit Footprint** from the *Ribbon.*

40. Click on the East roof sketch-line to select it.

41. Uncheck **Defines slope** in properties.

42. Now select the West roofline and check **Defines slope**. Make sure the *Slope* is still set to **3"/12"**.

If you were to select the green check mark now, the shed roof would be sloping in the opposite direction. But, before you do that, you will adjust the roof overhang at the high side.

43. Click on the East roofline again to select it.

44. Change the overhang to **6′-0″** in properties.

Changing the overhang only affects the selected roofline.

45. Select the **green check mark.**

46. Switch to the South view to see the change (Figure 8-1.12).

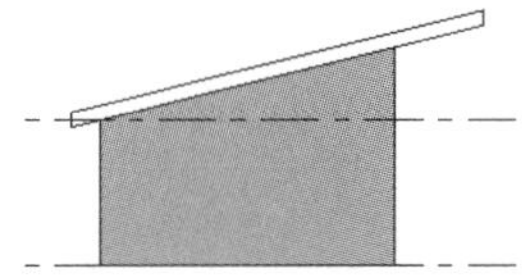

FIGURE 8-1.12 South elevation – shed roof (revised)

Thus, you can see it is easier to edit an object than to delete it and start over. Just remember you have to be in sketch mode (i.e., *Edit Sketch*) to make changes to the roof. Also, when a sketch line is selected, its properties are displayed in the *Properties Palette.* That concludes the shed roof example.

Flat Roof:

47. Switch back to the **T.O. Masonry** *Floor Plan* view.

48. Select the **Roof → Roof by Footprint** tool.

49. Set the overhang to **2′-0″** and make sure **Defines slope** is not active (i.e., un-highlighted) on the *Ribbon.*

50. Select all four walls, picking towards the exterior side of the wall.

51. Pick the **green check mark.**

52. Select **Attach** to attach the walls to the roof.

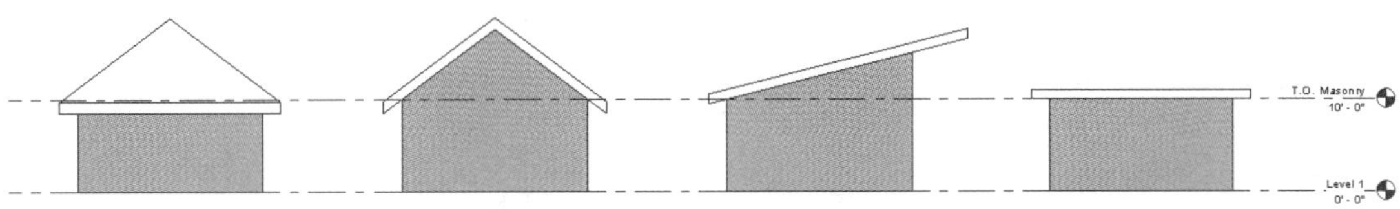

FIGURE 8-1.13 South elevation – flat roof

53. Switch to the South elevation view (Figure 8-1.13).

54. Also, take a look at the **Default 3D view** (Figure 8-1.14).

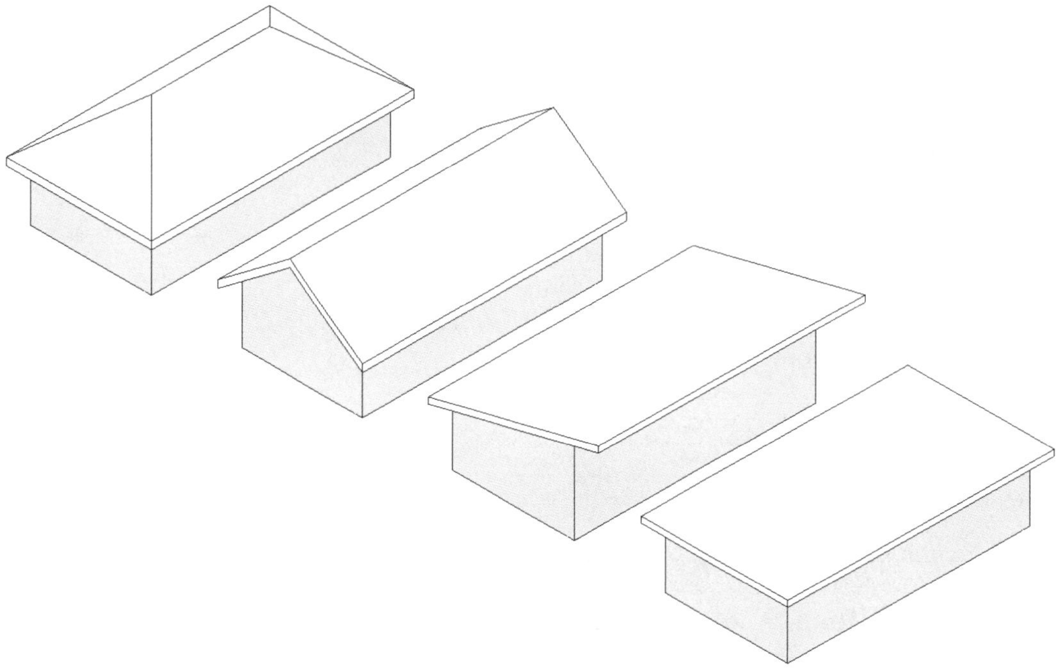

FIGURE 8-1.14 Default 3D view – flat roof

55. Save your project as **ex8-1.rvt**.

Want More?

Revit has additional tools and techniques available for creating more complex roof forms. However, that is beyond the scope of this book. If you want to learn more about roofs, or anything else, take a look at one of the following resources:

- Revit **Web Site:** www.autodesk.com
- Revit **Newsgroup** (potential answers to specific questions)
  www.augi.com; www.revitcity.com; www.autodesk.com; www.revitforum.org
- Revit **Blogs** information from individuals (some work for Autodesk and some don't)
  www.BIMchapters.blogspot.com, www.revitoped.com

Reference material: Roof position relative to wall

The remaining pages in this exercise are for reference only and do not need to be applied to your model. You are encouraged to study this information so you become more familiar with how the *Roof* tool works.

The following examples use a brick and concrete block wall. The image below shows the *Structure* properties for said wall type. Notice the only item within the *Core Boundary* section is the *Masonry – Concrete Block* (i.e., CMU), which is 7⅝″ thick (nominally 8″). Keep this in mind as you read through the remaining material.

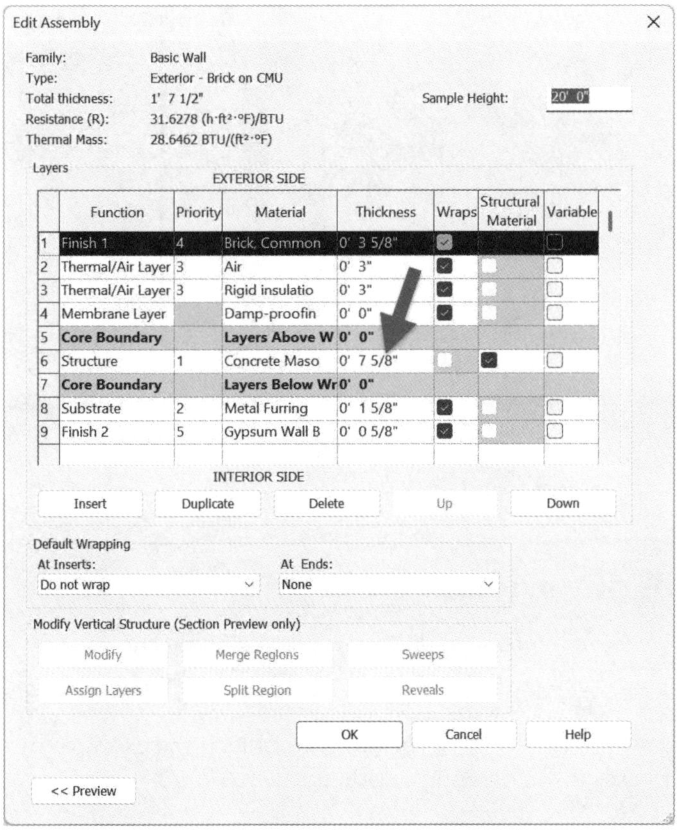

The following examples will show you how to control the position of the roof system relative to the wall below, both vertically and horizontally. The roof properties that dictate its position basically involve relationships between three things: the **Level Datum**, the exterior **Wall System**, and the bottom edge of the **Roof System**. There are several other properties (e.g., pitch, construction, fascia, etc.) related to the roof that will not be mentioned at the moment, so the reader may focus on a few basic principles.

The examples on this page show a sloped roof sketched with *Extend into wall (to core)* enabled and the *Overhang* set to 2′-0″. Because *Extend into wall (to core)* was selected, the bottom edge of the roof is positioned relative to the *Core Boundary* of the exterior wall rather than the finished face of the wall. See the discussion about the wall's *Core Boundary* on the previous page.

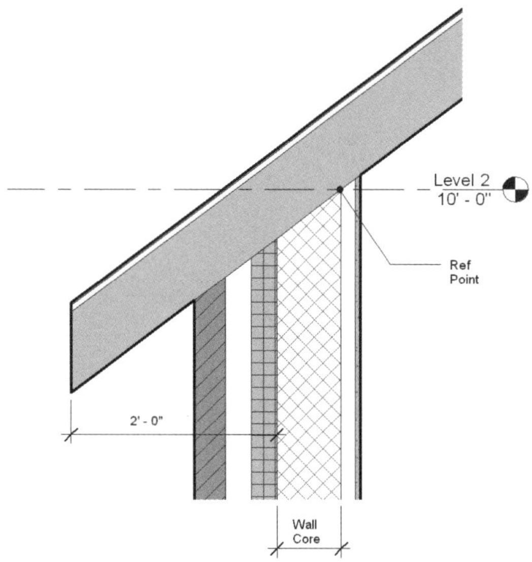

Extend to Core + Rafter

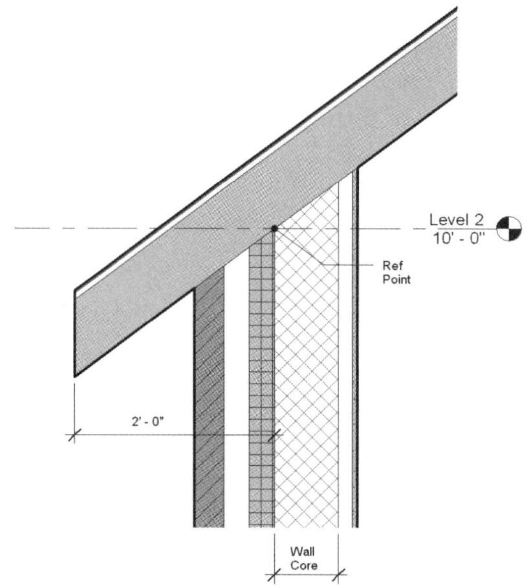

Extend to Core + Truss

Revit Roof Properties under Consideration:

Extend Into Wall: (To Core) This option was *highlighted* on the *Ribbon* while sketching the roof.

Rafter or Truss: This option is an *Instance Parameter* of the roof object; the example on the above left is set to *Rafter*, and the other is set to *Truss*.

***NOTE:** The* Extend into Wall (to core) *option affects the relative relationship between the wall and the roof, as you will see by comparing this example with the one on the next page.*

Base Level: Set to *Level 2*: By associating various objects to a level, it is possible to adjust the floor elevation (i.e., *Level Datum*) and have doors, windows, floors, furniture, roofs, etc., all move vertically with that level.

Base Offset: From Level Set to *0′-0″*: This can be a positive or negative number and will remain unchanged even if the level moves.

The examples on this page show a sloped roof sketched with *Extend into wall (to core)* NOT enabled, and the *Overhang* still set to 2′-0″. Notice that the roof overhang is derived from the exterior face of the wall (as opposed to the Core Boundary face in the previous example, where *Extend into wall* was enabled).

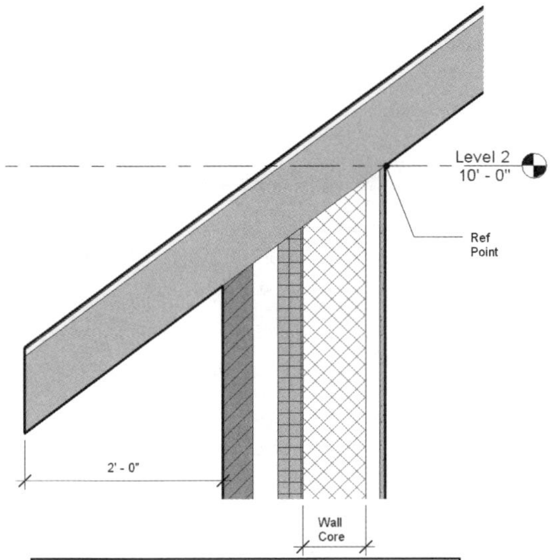

Rafter + not extended to core

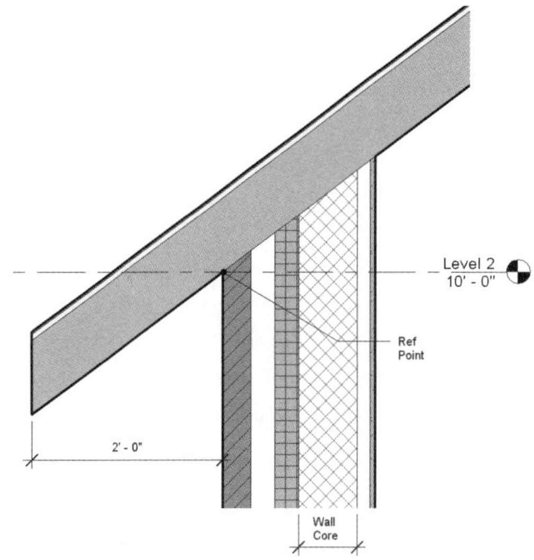

Truss + not extended to core

Revit Roof Properties under Consideration:

Extend Into Wall: (To Core) This option was *NOT highlighted* on the *Ribbon* when sketching the roof.

Rafter or Truss: This option is an *Instance Parameter* of the roof object; the example on the above left is set to *Rafter,* and the other is set to *Truss.*

Base Level: Set to *Level 2.* By associating various objects to a level, it is possible to adjust the floor elevation (i.e., *Level Datum*) and have doors, windows, floors, roofs, etc., all move vertically with that level.

Base Offset: From Level Set to *0′-0″.* This can be a positive or negative number and will remain unchanged even if the level moves.

As you can see from the previous examples, you would most often want to have *Extend to wall (to core)* selected while sketching a roof because it would not typically make sense to position the roof based on the outside face of brick or the inside face of gypsum board for commercial construction.

Even though you may prefer to have *Extend to wall (to core)* selected, you might like to have a 2′-0″ overhang relative to the face of the brick rather than the exterior face of concrete block. This can be accomplished in one of two ways:

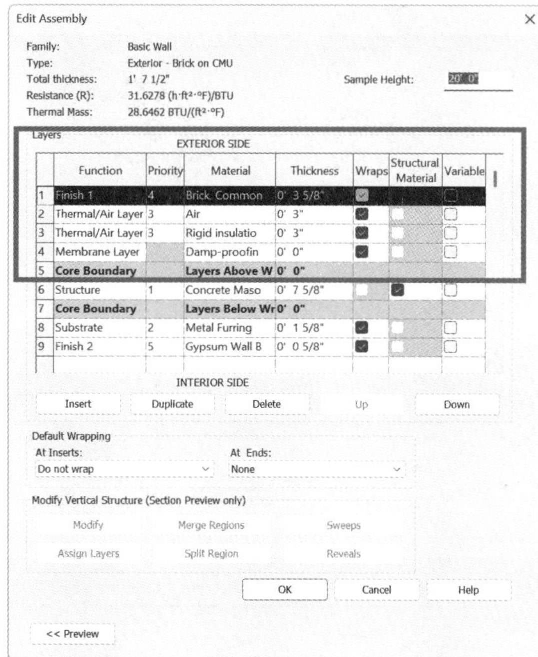

(A) You can modify the overhang while sketching the roof to include the wall thickness that occurs between the face of the wall and the face of the core: 2′-0″ + 9⅝″ = 2′-9⅝″. See the image to the right.

(B) The second option is to manually edit the sketch lines. You can add dimensions while in *Sketch* mode, select the sketch line to move, and then edit the dimension. The dimension can also be *Locked* to maintain the roof edge position relative to the wall. When you finish the sketch, the dimensions are hidden.

Energy Truss:

In addition to controlling the roof overhang, you might also want to control the roof properties to accommodate an energy truss with what is called an *energy heal*, which allows for more insulation to occur directly above the exterior wall.

To do this, you would use the *Extend into wall (to core) + Truss* option described above and then set the *Base Offset from Level* to 1′-0″ (for a 1′-0″ energy heal). See the image and the *Properties Palette* shown on the next page.

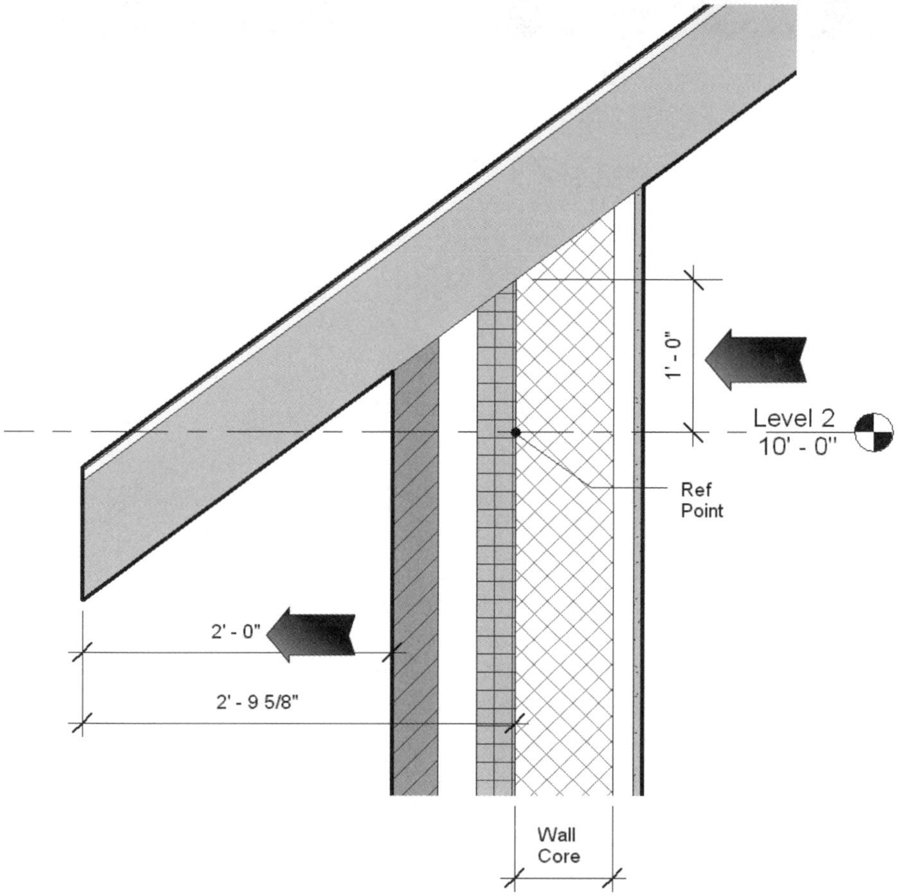

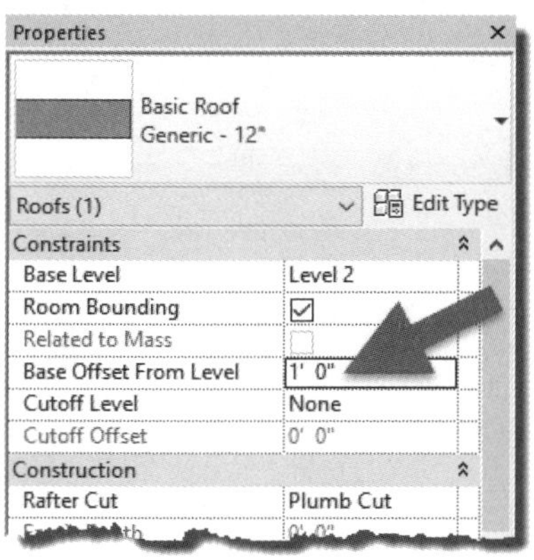

Many other properties and techniques exist for developing the roof of a project, such as the *Rafter Cut* and *Fascia Depth,* which control the fascia design. Also, you can apply a sweep to a roof edge to add a 1x fascia board around the building. These are intermediate-to-advanced concepts and will not be covered here.

This concludes the study of the *Roof* tool!

Exercise 8-2:
Gable Roof

The template file you started with already includes a Roof Plan view. You can think of this as the top plate height for your wall. This *Roof Plan* view creates a working plane for the *Roof* tool. After creating a high roof over the two-story areas, you will create a *Low Roof* view and design roofs over the one-story areas: the garage and a portion of the family room.

Create Gable Roof:

1. Open ex7-6.rvt and **Save As ex8-2.rvt**.

2. Switch to the ***Roof Plan*** view.

Your view should look like Figure 8-2.1. The walls you can see in the *Roof Plan* view were created in Lesson 5. The specified height extends into the *Roof Plan's View Range*, whereas the two walls you cannot see were created on the second floor, in Lesson 6, and the specified height does not extend up into the *Roof Plan's View Range*. This does not really matter because, as you will see in a moment, you have enough information visible to create the footprint of the roof; also, you will *Attach* the walls to the roof, just as in the previous exercises, which causes them to conform to the underside of the roof.

Because the walls do not connect, neither will the overhang lines you sketch. Before you can "finish" a roof sketch, you must have the entire perimeter of the roof drawn with line endpoints connected. Revit lets you sketch additional lines and use tools like Trim to complete the roof sketch perimeter.

3. Select the ***Roof*** tool drop-down from the *Architecture* tab.

4. Select ***Roof by Footprint*** from the drop-down menu.

5. Make sure ***Pick Walls*** is selected on the *Ribbon*.

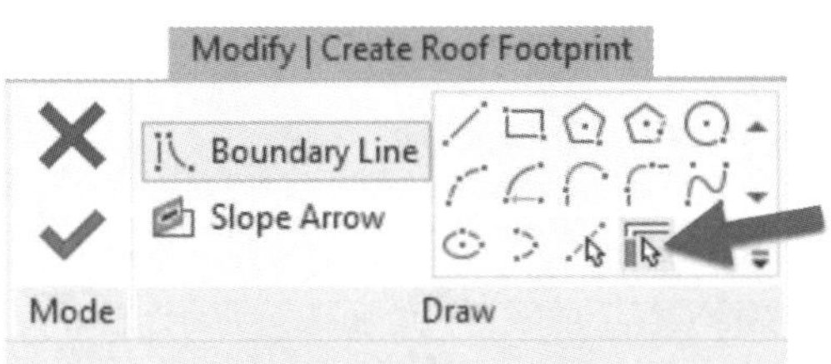

FIGURE 8-2.1 Roof Plan; initial view

First you will specify the roof overhang for the entire roof.

6. Set the *Overhang* to **1'-6"** on the *Ribbon.*

You only need to select four walls to define the extents of the gable roof you are about to create. However, the perimeter will not be closed after selecting the four walls.

7. With *Define slope* **highlighted** (i.e., active) on the *Ribbon*, select the two walls as shown in Figure 8-2.2; make sure the overhang lines are on the exterior side of the building.

   TIP: *Use the flip control icon while the line is still selected if your overhang is on the wrong side (i.e., interior).*

8. With *Defines slope* **NOT highlighted**, select the two walls as shown in Figure 8-2.2; make sure the overhang lines are on the exterior side of the building.

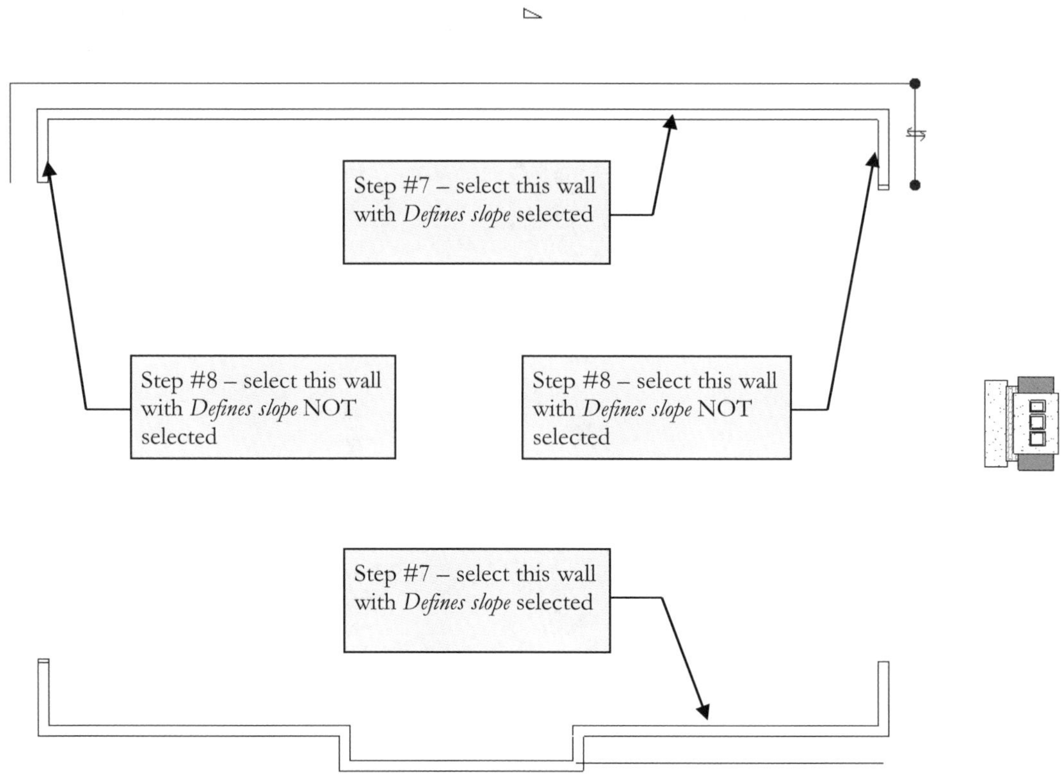

FIGURE 8-2.2 Roof Plan; four walls selected for sketching roof footprint

9. With nothing selected, change the roof pitch, or *Slope*, to **8"** on the *Properties Palette* (Figure 8-2.3).

10. Click **Apply**.

Note that the four walls, just selected, can be selected in any order. Of course, it would be easier to select all sloping edges first, then all non-sloping edges. That way, you do not have to keep toggling the *Defines slope* option on and off.

Next, you will use the *Trim* tool to close the perimeter of the roof footprint. Many of your 2D drafting skills learned early in this book can be applied to this type of *Sketch* mode.

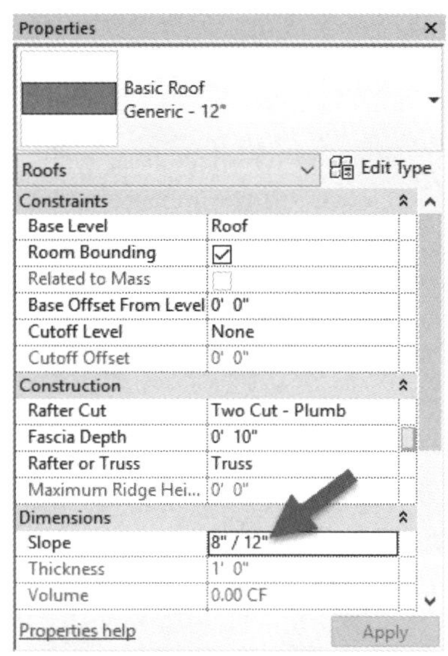

FIGURE 8-2.3 Roof Properties

Finally, notice that the roof type is set to Generic – 12, as shown in the image to the right. This can be modified similarly to walls via the *Edit Type* button.

11. While still in sketch mode, select ***Modify*** from the *Ribbon*.

12. Select the ***Trim*** icon from the contextual tab on the *Ribbon*, and then select the roof lines that are not yet connected to make them connected (Figure 8-2.4).

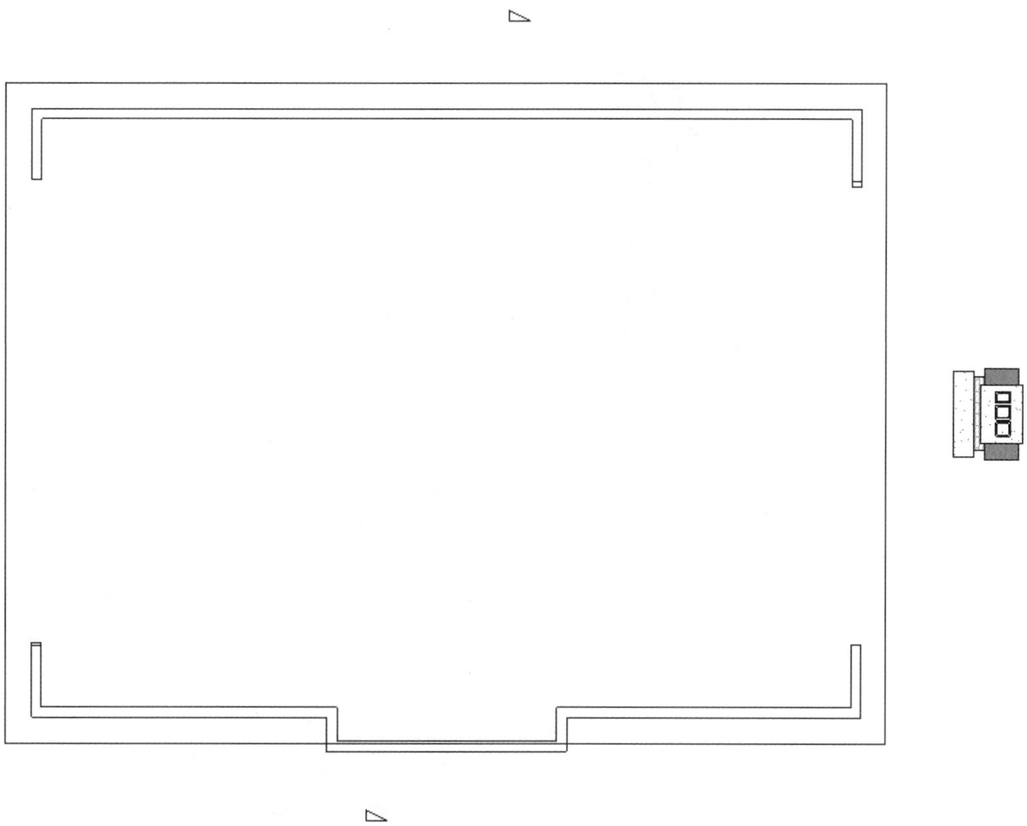

FIGURE 8-2.4 Roof Plan; entire roof perimeter defined

Now that the roof footprint is complete, you can finish the roof.

13. Select the **green checkmark** from the *Ribbon*.

14. Click **Attach** to attach the walls to the underside of the new roof (Figure 8-2.5).

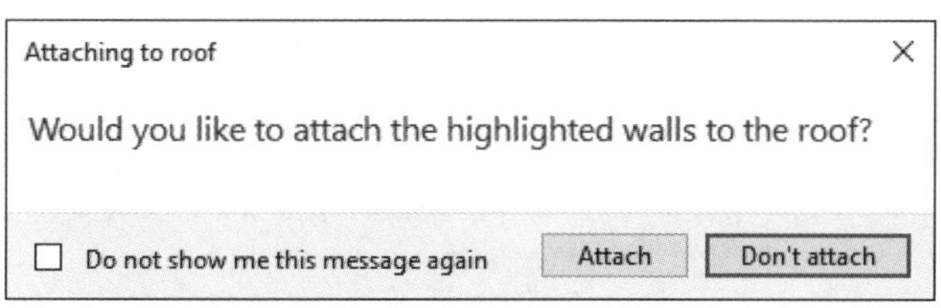

FIGURE 8-2.5 Roof Plan; attachment warning

15. Switch to your ***Default 3D*** view.

Your project should look like Figure 8-2.6. Notice that the walls that were visible in the *Roof Plan* view are now attached to the roof. The East and West walls that have not been attached can be attached manually.

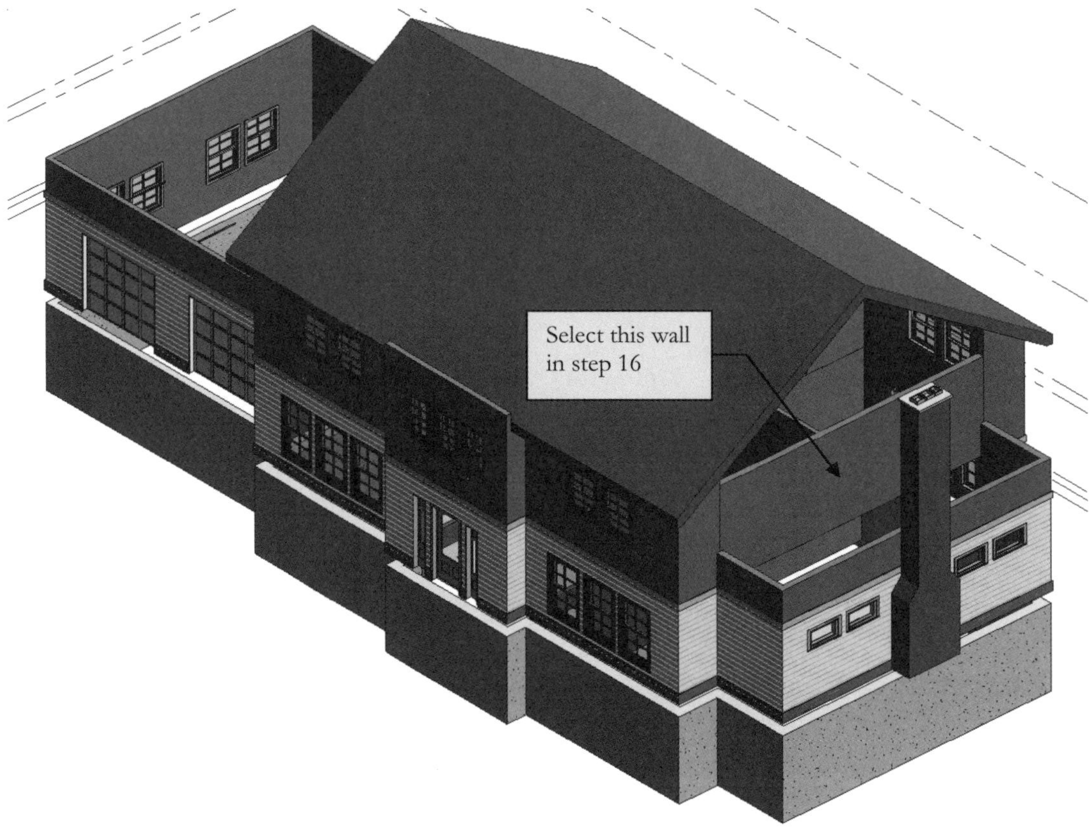

FIGURE 8-2.6 3D View; gable roof added

16. While in the 3D view, select the East wall that has not been attached to the roof yet. Notice how the wall is transparent when selected.

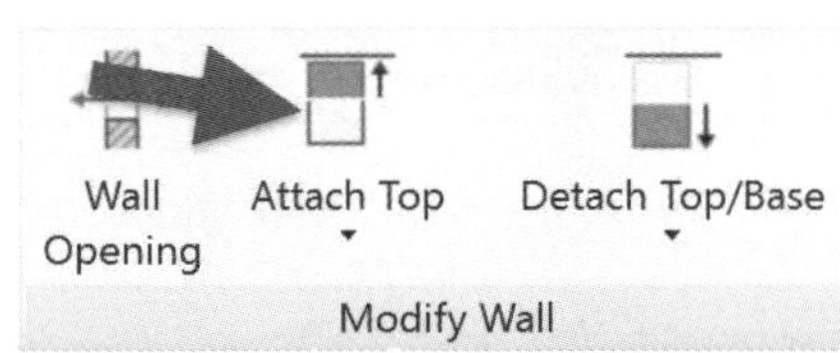

17. Select the ***Attach Top*** button from the *Ribbon*, then **select the roof** (Figure 8-2.7).

18. Repeat the previous two steps with the West wall.

TIP: *Click in the upper left corner of the Front face of the ViewCube to quickly view that side of the building (see image to the right).*

FIGURE 8-2.7 3D View; wall attached to roof

Main Entry Gable:

Next, you will draw the gable roof element over the main entry.

You can modify the existing roof to add this design feature.

19. Switch back to the ***Roof Plan*** view.
20. Select the existing **roof**, and then ***Edit Footprint*** from the *Ribbon*.
21. Select ***Pick Walls*** and then make sure the overhang is still **1'-6"** and the pitch is **8"/12"**.
22. Edit the roof sketch to look like Figure 8-2.8.

TIP: Use the Split *and* Trim *tools to modify the existing sketch.*

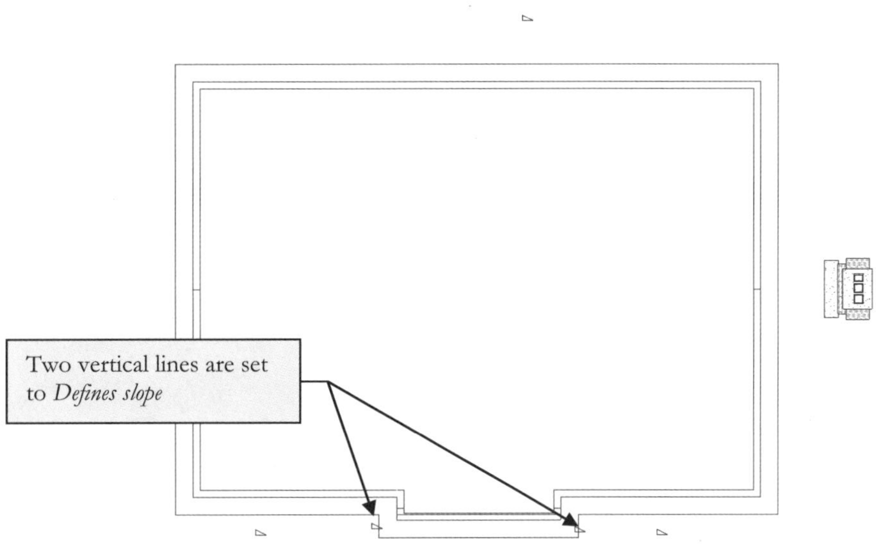

FIGURE 8-2.8 Edit roof sketch

23. Select the **green checkmark** to finish the roof.

NOTE: If you get any errors, make sure all the "defines slope" sketch lines have the same slope – select each sketch line and review its properties.

This is where the power of Revit really shines. As you can see in the *Roof Plan* view (Figure 8-2.9 below), Revit was able to interpret the sketch using the *Pitch* and *Defines slope* information to create the proper roof, complete with ridgelines and valleys.

Next, you will change the *View Range* of the *Roof* view to see the low roof, which will be added in the next exercise.

24. Select **Edit** next to *View Range* in the *Properties Palette* (make sure nothing is selected in the model first – this will make sure the *View Properties* are shown).

25. Change both *Bottom* and *View Depth* to **Unlimited**.

26. Click **OK**.

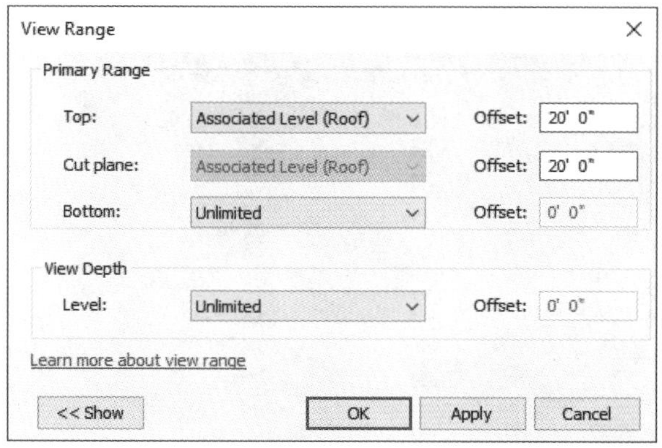

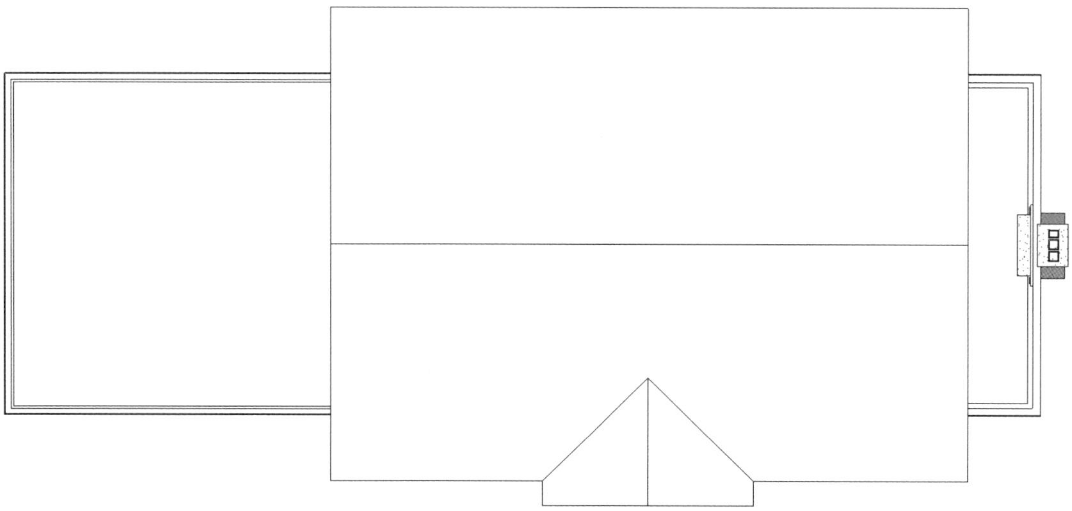

FIGURE 8-2.9 Site plan view; revised roof created

27. Switch to the ***Default 3D*** view.

When finished, your 3D view should look like Figure 8-2.10.

> **TIP:**
> Custom fascias, gutters and soffits are beyond the scope of this tutorial. However, you can take a look at the *Help* system for more information on this.
>
> After reviewing the *Help* system, try adding these techniques to your Revit project.

This entry roof element could have been drawn as a separate element. This would be useful if, for example, the fascia/eaves did not align.

FIGURE 8-2.10 3D view; Entry roof element added

28. Save your project as **Ex8-2.rvt**.

> ***TIP:*** *You have probably figured this out by now: the last view open when you close will be the current view the next time the project is opened.*

Exercise 8-3:
Low Roof Elements

In this exercise, you will add the lower roof elements, which will involve adding a new level datum for reference.

Create a New Level:

1. Open ex8-2.rvt and **Save As ex8-3.rvt.**

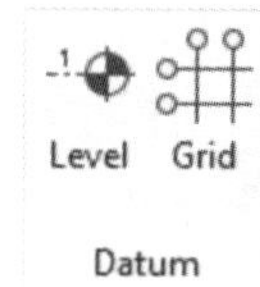

2. Open the ***South*** elevation view.

3. Click **Architecture → Datum → Level** from the *Ribbon.*

4. Draw a *Level* datum at the top of the low exterior walls, at elevation 12′-0″. Draw the level so both ends align with the other levels below and above it (Figure 8-3.1). Make sure the **Create Plan View** option is checked on the Ribbon.

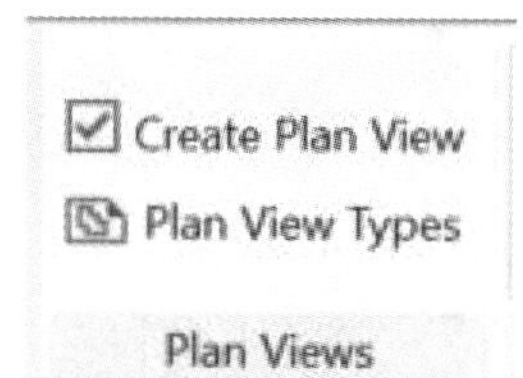

TIP: Hover your cursor over the top of the garage wall (do not click). Next, move your cursor to the left and select two points horizontally across from each other, left to right.

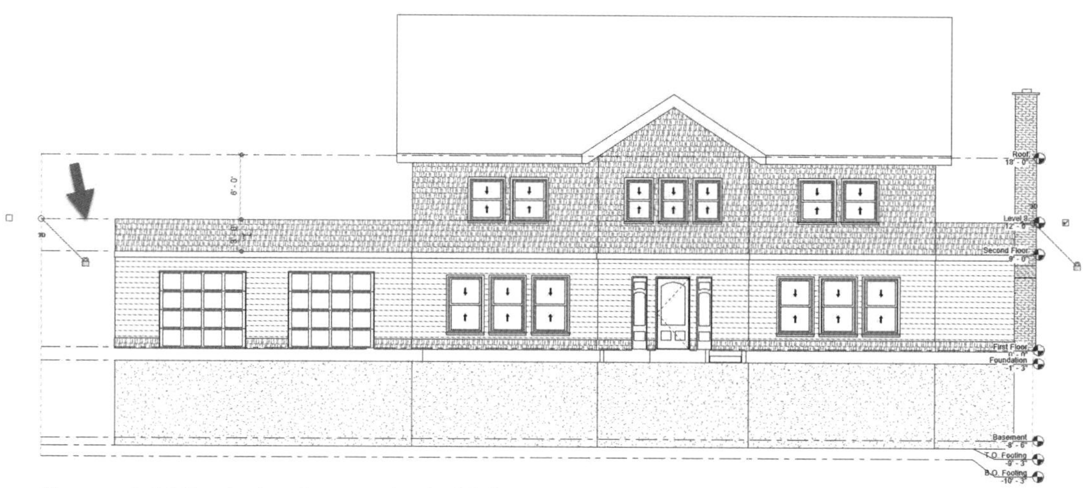

FIGURE 8-3.1 South elevation; new level added

Notice that Revit automatically names the level and creates a floor plan, reflected ceiling plan, and structural plan views with the same name (Figure 8-3.2). Next, you will rename the *Level* datum.

5. Press **Esc** or select ***Modify*** from the *Ribbon.*

6. Now select the *Level* datum you just created in the drawing window.

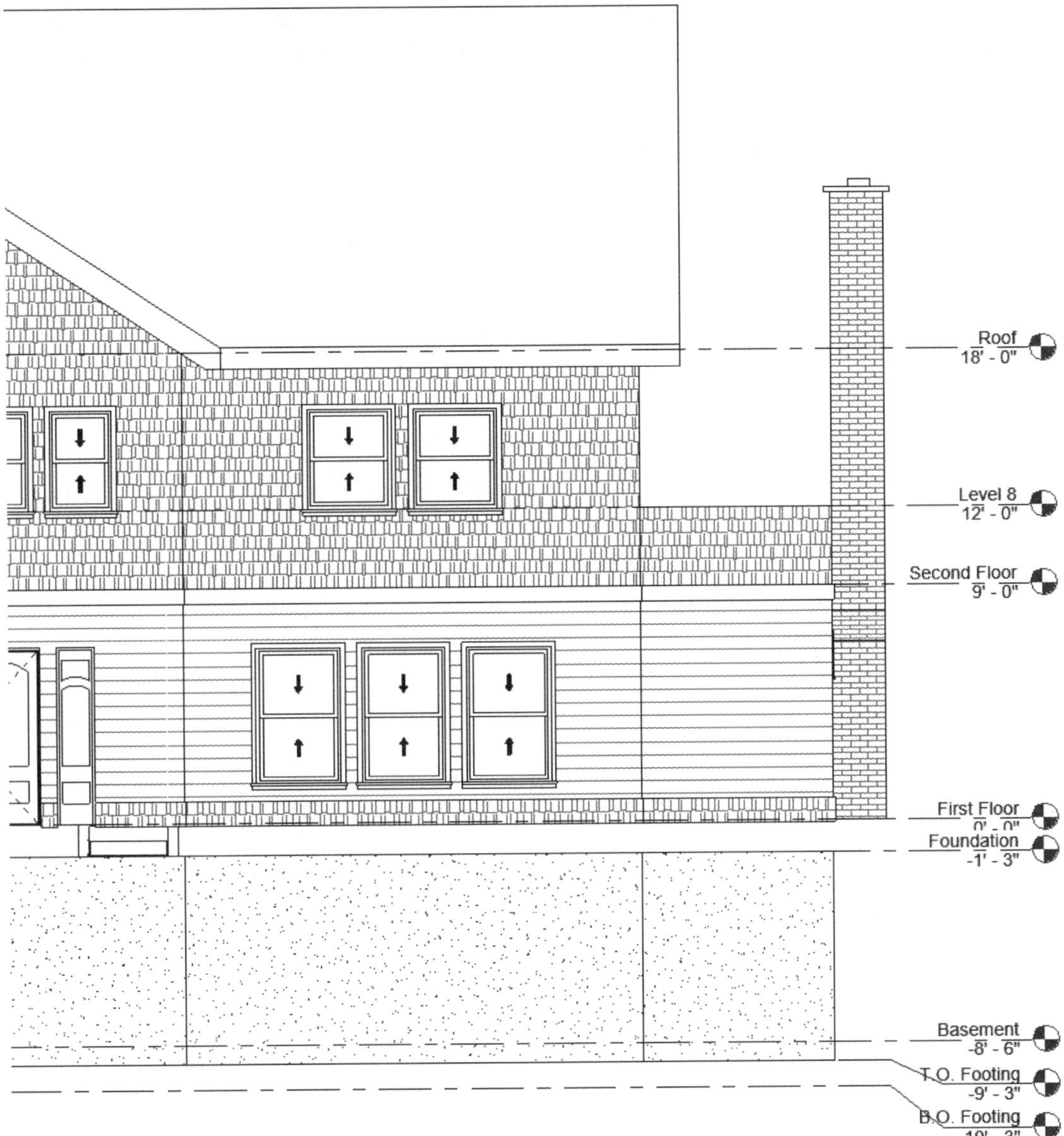

FIGURE 8-3.2 South elevation; new level added (named Level 8 in this example)

7. With the *Level* symbol selected, **drag the small circle grip** near the target symbol (see image below) to the right. This will relocate all the level targets away from the building.

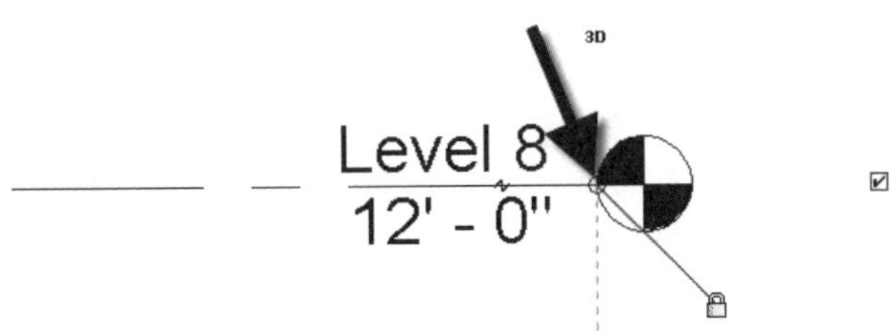

8. With the *Level* symbol still selected, click on the text to rename the level label. Press *Undo* if you accidentally click an icon and change the level position; you may need to zoom in to click the text.

9. Change the label to ***Low Roof*** (Figure 8-3.3).

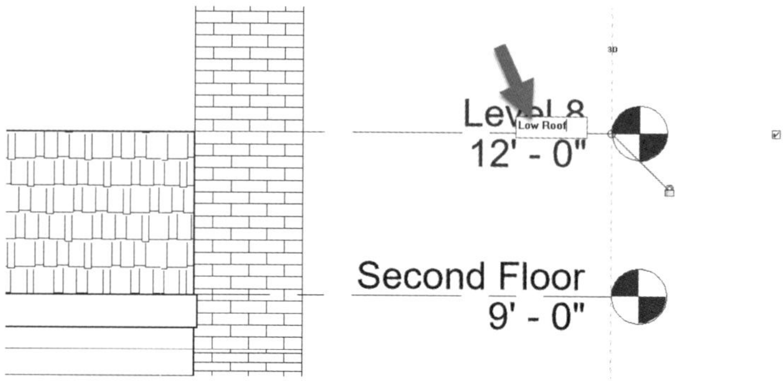

FIGURE 8-3.3 South elevation; renaming a level datum

10. Click **Yes** when prompted to rename corresponding views (Figure 8-3.4).

Notice the *Low Roof* label is now listed in the *Floor Plans* and *Ceiling Plans* sections of the *Project Browser.*

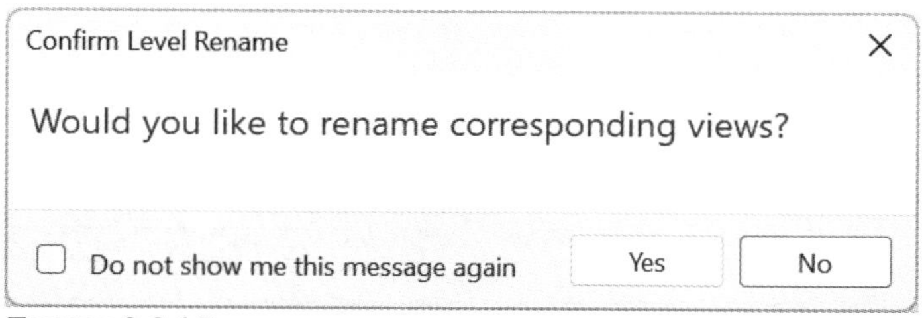

FIGURE 8-3.4 Rename prompt

Add another gable roof:

11. Open the newly created ***Low Roof*** *Floor Plan* view.

    TIP: *You may want to close the Ceiling Plan views section of the Project Browser so you don't accidentally click on them.*

12. Set *View Range* to **Unlimited** for *Bottom* & *View Depth* per step previously covered.

13. Select **Architecture → Roof →** ***Roof by footprint*** from the *Ribbon.*

14. Set the overhang to **1'-6"** on the *Ribbon.*

15. You are now prompted to select exterior walls to define the footprint. Select ONLY the three wall segments that define the *Living Room* area per **Figure 8-3.5**. Only the horizontal sketch lines should be set to '*Defines Slope*' as shown.

    REMEMBER: *Pick the exterior side of the walls.*

You will notice in Figure 8-3.5 that one section still needs to be sketched to complete the footprint or outline.

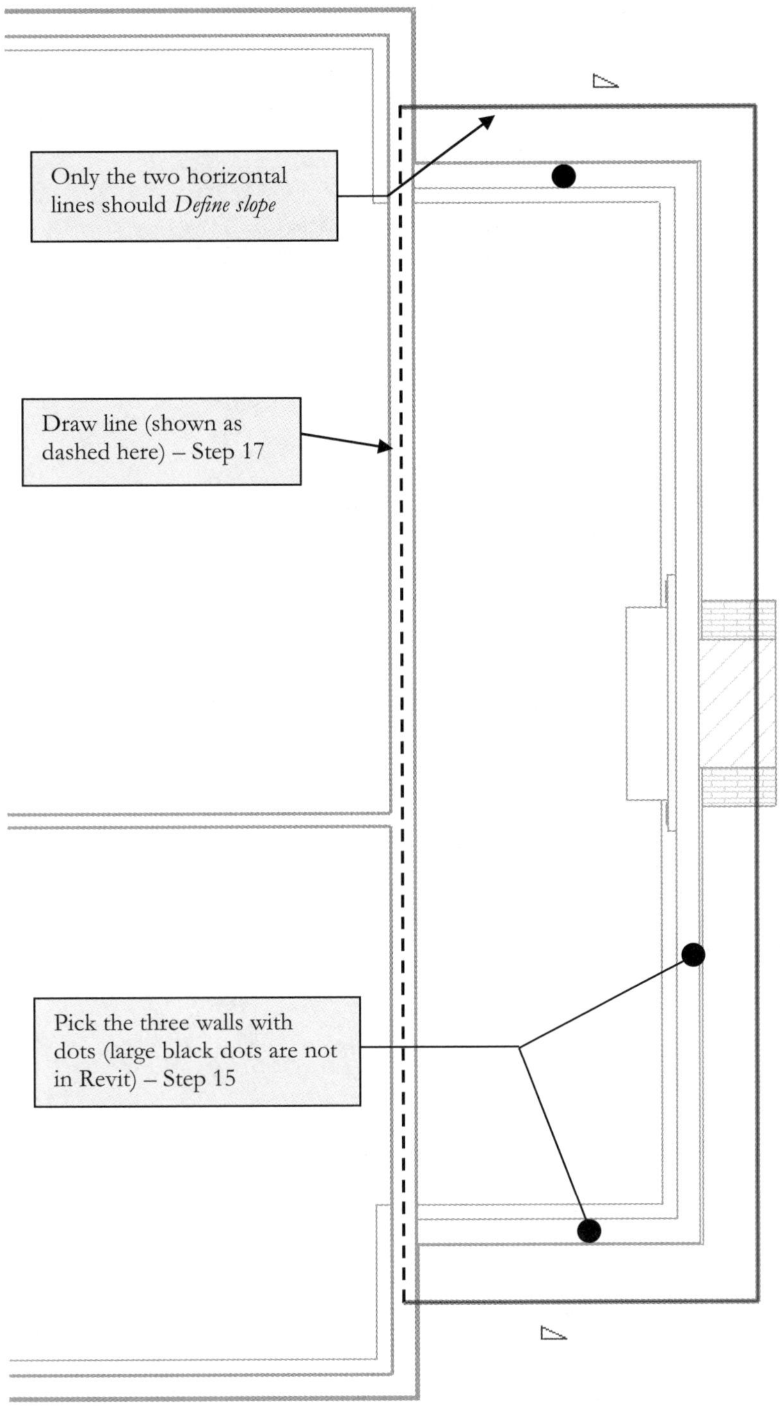

FIGURE 8-3.5 Low Roof plan view; adding roof

16. Select the ***Line*** tool from the *Ribbon* (Figure 8-3.6).

17. Draw the line to create a complete rectangle (i.e., footprint), making sure you use *Snaps* to accurately snap to the endpoints of the lines already present (Figure 8-3.5). Use *Trim* if needed. *Defines Slope* should be off here.

18. While still in sketch mode, and with nothing selected, change the *Slope* to **8″/ 12″** in the *Properties Palette.*

19. Click **Apply** in the *Properties Palette.*

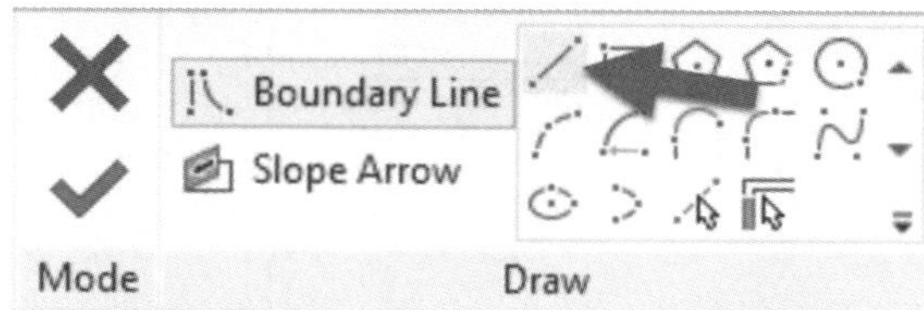

FIGURE 8-3.6 Roof sketch options

Again, this will give the roof an 8/12 pitch, meaning for every 12″ horizontally, the roof will *rise* 8″ vertically.

20. Now click the **green checkmark** from the *Ribbon* to finish the roof.

21. Click **Attach** when prompted to attach the highlighted walls to the roof (Figure 8-3.7).

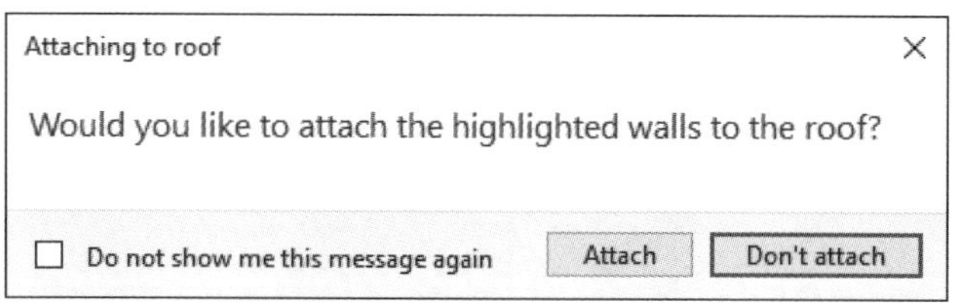

FIGURE 8-3.7 Prompt

You will now see a portion of the roof in your plan view. The cutting plane is 4′-0″ above the level, so you are seeing the roof thickness in section at 4′-0″ above the *Low Roof* level (Figure 8-3.9 on the next page).

- Switch to an elevation view to see the roof, the South elevation, shown in Figure 8-3.8.
- You can also switch to the ***Default 3D*** view to see the roof in isometric view.

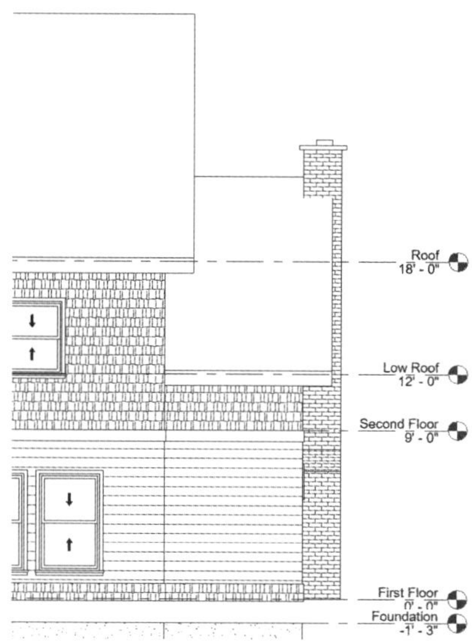

FIGURE 8-3.8 South elevation

After reviewing the roof you created, switch back to the plan view: ***Low Roof.*** You will now add a roof over the garage.

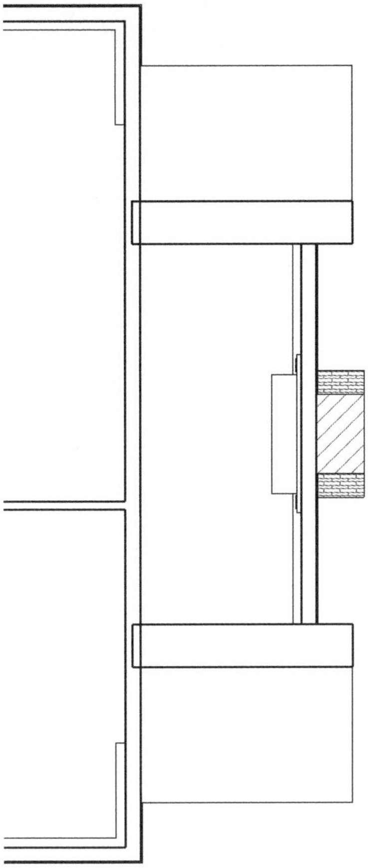

FIGURE 8-3.9 Low Roof plan view

22. **Zoom in** on the garage area.

23. Select the ***Roof*** tool and click ***Roof by Footprint***.

24. With ***Defines slope*** checked in the *Ribbon*, pick the two horizontal walls: North and South (Figure 8-3.10).

25. Unselect ***Defines slope***, then select the West wall, and use the ***Line*** tool to sketch a line to close the footprint, as shown in Figure 8-3.11. Be sure to use *Snaps* to accurately draw the enclosed area.

26. Make sure the *Slope* is set to **8"/12"** and then select the **green checkmark** from the *Ribbon* (Figure 8-3.6).

27. Click **Attach** when prompted to attach the highlighted walls to the roof (Figure 8-3.7).

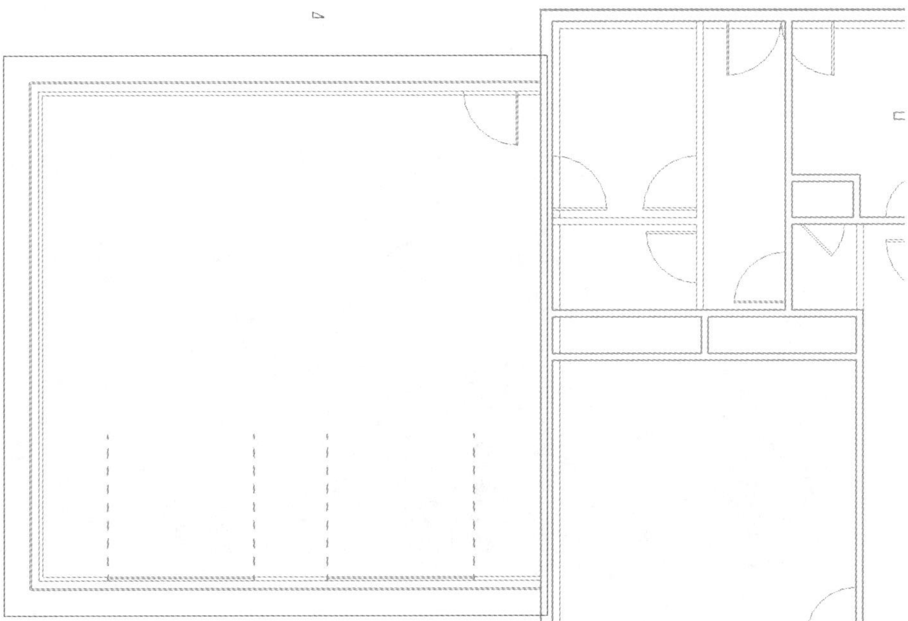

FIGURE 8-3.10 Low Roof plan view at garage

28. Switch to the ***South*** elevation view (Figure 8-3.11).

FIGURE 8-3.11 South elevation view; garage roof added

The 3D model below is shown *shaded* and has *Ambient Shadows* turned on (Figure 8-3.12).

Revit content is set up to make glass in windows and curtain walls transparent.

FIGURE 8-3.12 Shaded model

Changing to a Hip Roof:

Now that you have drawn the roof, you will see what is involved to modify the gable roof to a hip roof. In the first exercise in this Lesson, you learned how to create a hip roof from scratch. Here you will modify a previously drawn gable roof into a hip roof.

29. Switch to the ***RoofPlan*** view.

30. Click on the main roof element to select it.
    TIP: Select one of the lines at the perimeter of the roof.

31. Select ***Edit Footprint*** from the *Ribbon.*

32. Select the vertical line on the left.

33. With the left vertical line selected, check ***Defines slope*** in *Properties.*

34. Repeat these steps for the other vertical line on the right.

Your screen should look like Figure 8-3.13.

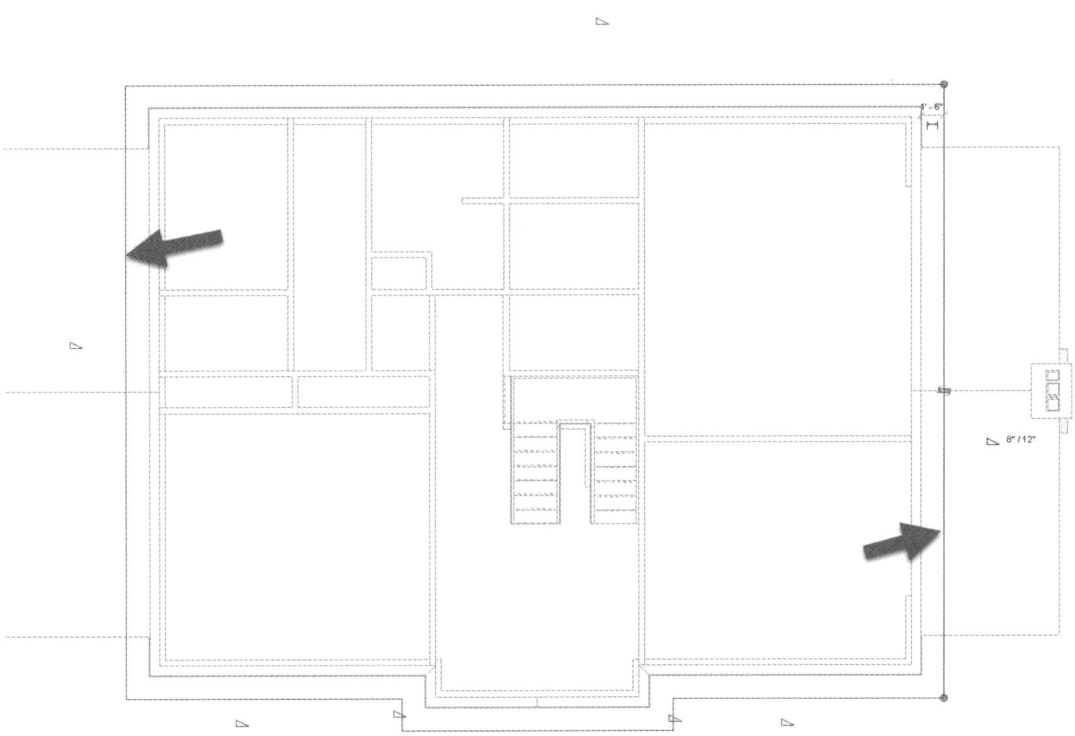

FIGURE 8-3.13 Roof Plan; vertical lines set to *Defines slope*

35. Select the **green check mark** from the *Ribbon.*

36. Switch to the ***South*** exterior elevation view.

You now have a hip roof. However, there is a little problem with the lower roofs; they do not properly intersect. This could be a problem when it rains!

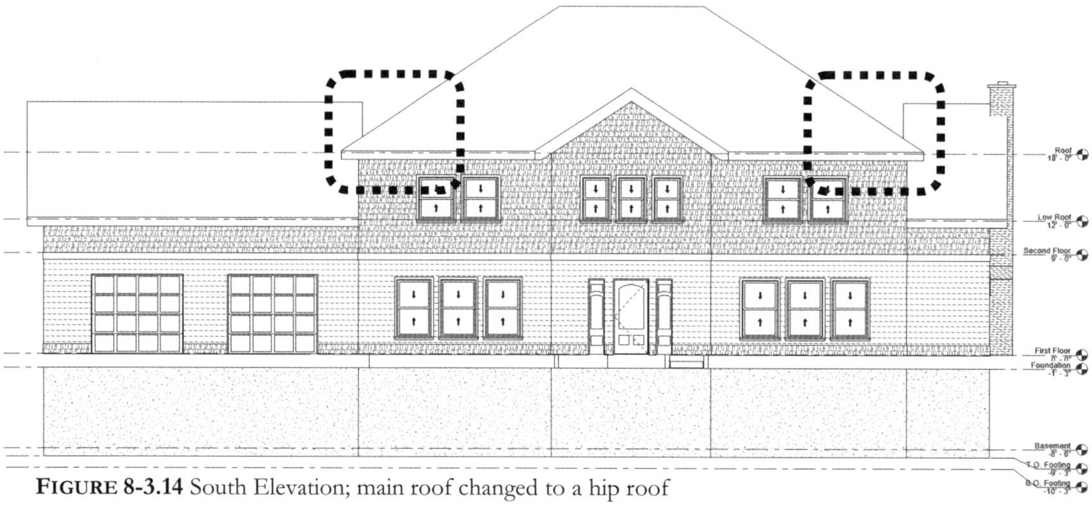

FIGURE 8-3.14 South Elevation; main roof changed to a hip roof

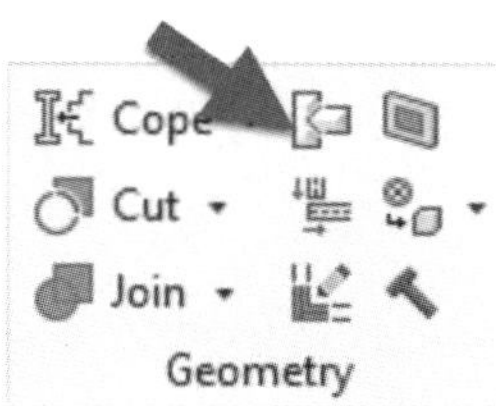

37. Switch to the ***Default 3D*** view.

38. Select **Modify → Geometry → Join/Unjoin Roof** tool from the *Ribbon.*

39. ***Join*** the lower roof over the garage to the upper roof.

TIP: Select the edge of the low roof and then select the face of the upper roof, which will be the face you wish to extend the roof to. Hover your cursor over the icon on the ribbon to see the extended tooltip for more information.

40. Now ***Join*** the low roof over the *Living Room* with the upper roof.

Your model should look similar to Figure 8-3.15.

FIGURE 8-3.15 3D view; low roofs joined to upper roof

Here you can see that the bottoms of the roofs, to be joined, do not have to align with each other.

After reviewing the two roof options, the client decides they prefer the gable option, so you will change it back. Do not simply click *Undo*; the next steps will show you how to *Unjoin* the roof.

41. Switch to the ***Roof Plan*** view.

42. Select **Modify → Geometry → Join/Unjoin Roof**.

This tool, as its name implies, allows you to both *Join* and *Unjoin* roof elements. To *Unjoin*, you simply click on a line that has been created by a *Join* and the entire *Join* will go away.

43. Select the valley line as shown in **Figure 8-3.16**.

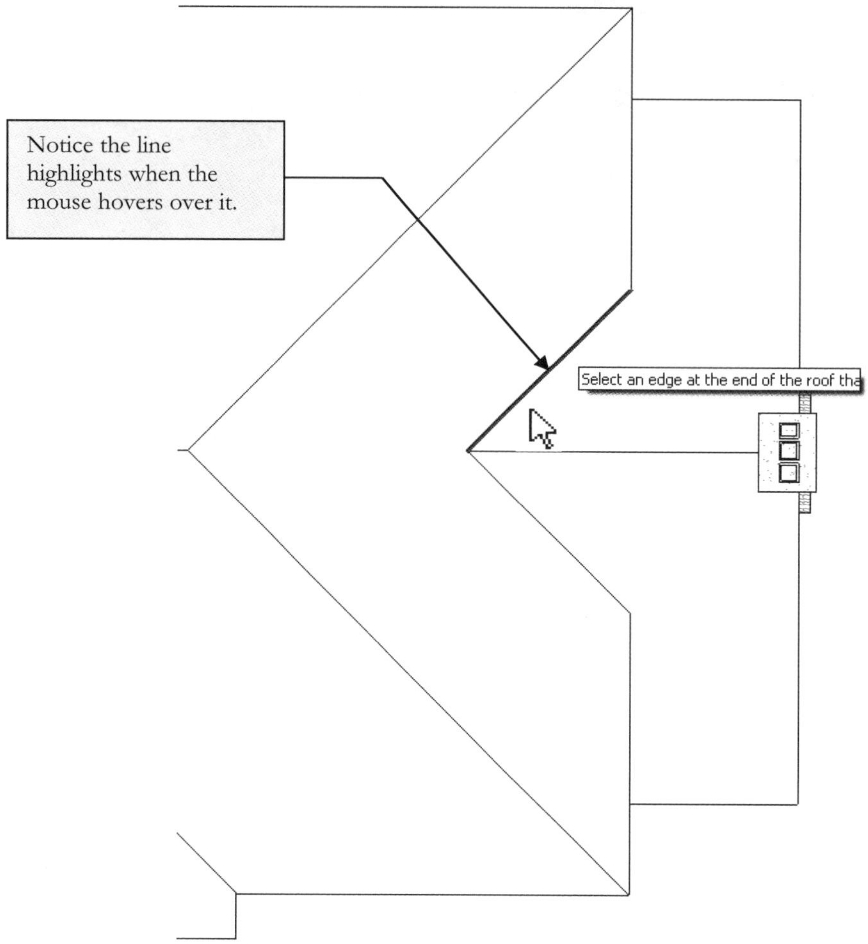

FIGURE 8-3.16 Roof plan; Unjoining the lower roof from the upper roof

As soon as you click the valley line, the roof is unjoined.

44. Repeat this process to *Unjoin* the West lower roof.

45. Change the hip roof back to a gable using the techniques previously covered (select it, edit footprint, and then deselect defines slope).

When finished, your 3D view should look like 8-3.12 again.

46. **Save** your project.

Exercise 8-4:
Skylights

This short exercise covers inserting skylights in your roof. The process is much like inserting windows. In fact, Revit lists the skylight types with the window types, so you use the *Window* tool to insert skylights into your project.

Inserting Skylights:

You will place the skylights in an elevation view.

1. Load project file **ex8-3.rvt**.
2. Switch to the ***North*** elevation view.
3. Use the ***Load Autodesk Family*** command to import the skylight family **skylight-Top-Hung** from the *Windows* section into the current project. In the *Specify Types* dialog (aka *Type Catalog*), select **24″ x 48″**.
4. Start the Window tool, pick **skylight-Top-Hung: 24″ x 48″** in the *Type Selector*.

You are now ready to place skylights in the roof. Revit will only look for roof objects when placing skylights; this is what is called a *roof-hosted family*, so you do not have to worry about a skylight ending up in a wall.

5. With ***Tag on Placement*** highlighted on the *Ribbon*, roughly place two skylights as shown in Figure 8-4.1.

   FYI: *This can be done directly in the elevation view.*

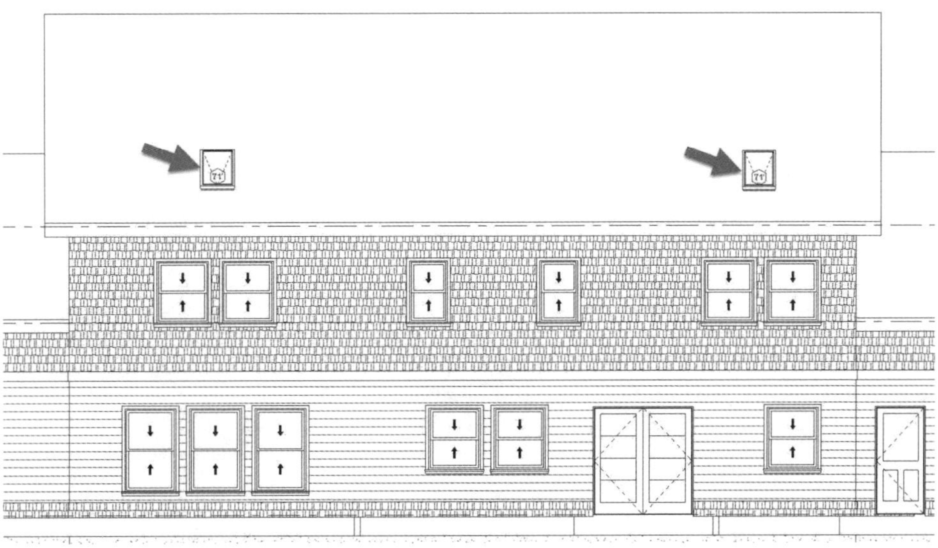

FIGURE 8-4.1 North elevation, skylights added

6. Press **Esc** or click the ***Modify*** tool to cancel the *Window* tool.

Next, align the skylights.

7. Switch to the ***East*** elevation view.

8. Select one of the visible skylights.

You should now have the skylight selected and see the reference dimensions that let you adjust the object's exact location. Occasionally, the dimension does not go to the point on the model that you are interested in referencing. Revit allows you to adjust where those temporary dimensions reference.

9. Click and drag the temporary dimension **grip** shown in Figure 8-4.2 to (wait until it snaps) the ridge of the main roof (Figure 8-4.3).

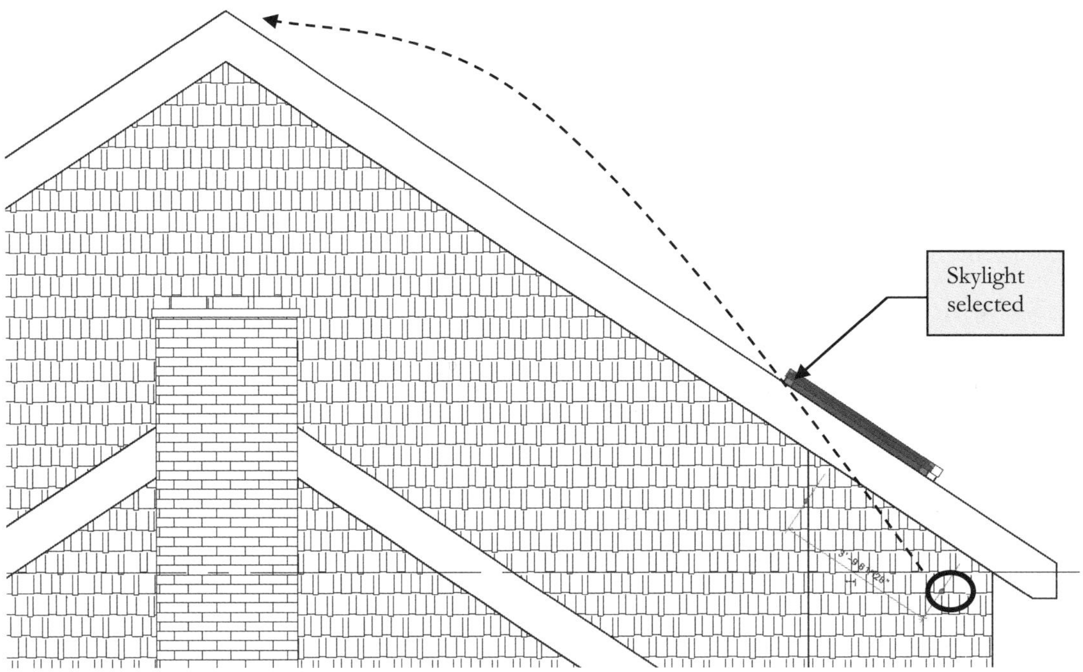

FIGURE 8-4.2 East elevation; temporary dimension shown after selecting the skylight.

10. Click the dimension text and change it to **18′-0″**.

    NOTE: *This will adjust the skylight's position relative to the ridge along the roof's face.*

11. Select the other skylight and adjust it to match the one you just revised.

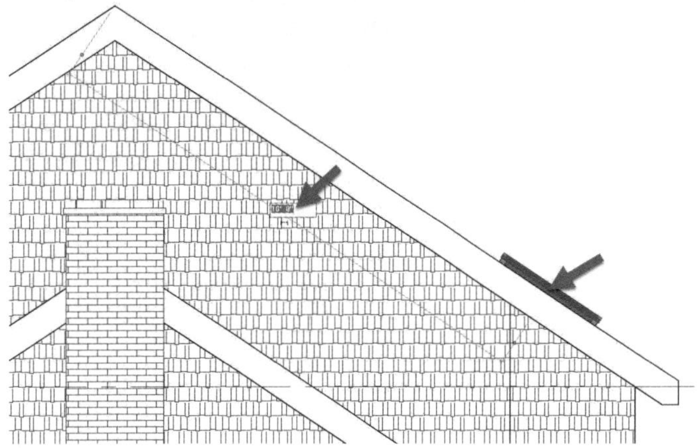

FIGURE 8-4.3 East elevation; temp dimension witness line adjusted.

Your skylights now align vertically on the roof. The same step would allow you to align the skylight horizontally.

12. Use the temporary dimensions to center the skylight over the second floor windows that are below it, on the North elevation.

13. **Zoom in** on one of the skylights.

The number may vary, which is not a problem.

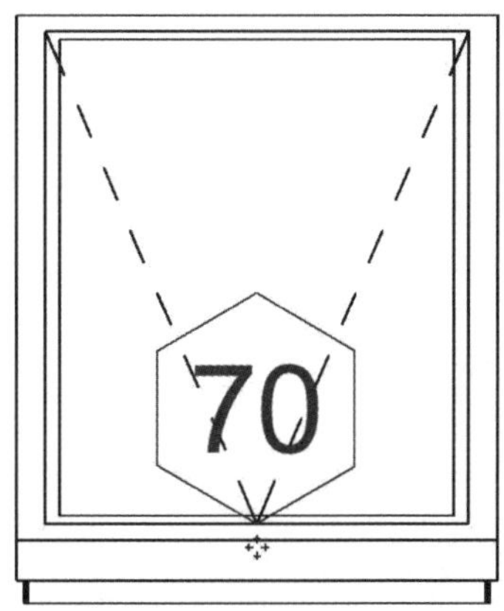

FIGURE 8-4.4 Enlarged view of skylight

14. Select the skylight's tag. You should see a symbol appear near the bottom of the tag; this is the *Move* icon (Figure 8-4.4).

15. Drag on the *Move* icon to position the skylight tag so the tag does not overlap the skylight (Figure 8-4.5).

This can be done with any tag (i.e., Door tag, Room tag, etc.).

16. Adjust the other skylight tag, which is a *Window Tag*. As you reposition these tags, you may see a reference line appear, indicating the symbol will automatically align with an adjacent symbol.

    REMEMBER: *The tag's size is determined by the View Scale setting.*

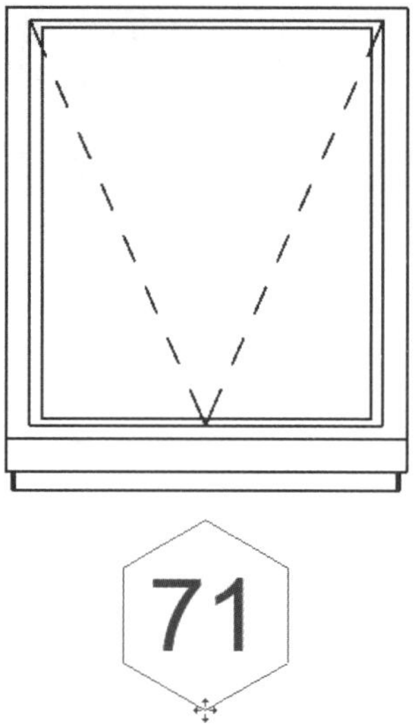

FIGURE 8-4.5 Enlarged skylight view – revised

Take a minute to look at your shaded 3D view and try orbiting the view so you can see through the skylight glass into the space below (Figure 8-4.6).

FIGURE 8-4.6 Shaded skylight view

17. **Save** as **ex8-4.rvt**.

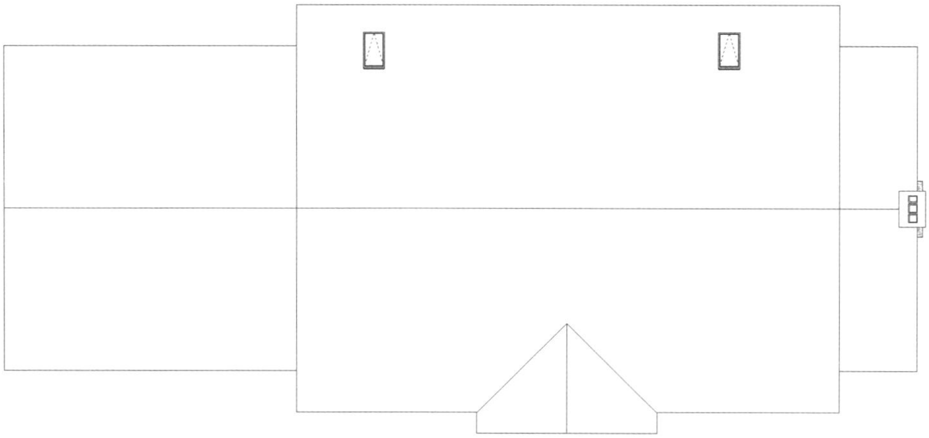

FIGURE 8-4.7 Roof plan

Self-Exam:

The following questions can be used as a way to check your knowledge of this lesson. The answers can be found at the bottom of the page.

1. You do not have to click the *green check mark* to finish a roof. (T/F)
2. The wall below the roof automatically conforms to the underside of the roof when you join the wall to the roof. (T/F)
3. The roof overhang setting is available from the *Ribbon*. (T/F)
4. To create a gable roof on a building with four walls, two of the walls should not have the ______________________ option checked.
5. Is it possible to change the reference point for a temporary dimension that is displayed while an element is selected? (Y/N)

Review Questions:

The following questions may be assigned by your instructor as a way to assess your knowledge of this section. Your instructor has the answers to the review questions.

1. When creating a roof using the "*create roof by footprint*" option, you need to create a closed perimeter. (T/F)
2. The *Defines slope* setting can be changed after the roof is finished. (T/F)
3. Skylights need to be rotated to align with the plane, or pitch, of the roof. (T/F)
4. Skylights have transparent glass in shaded views. (T/F)
5. While using the ***Roof*** tool, you can use the ___________ tool from the *Ribbon* to fill in the missing segments to close the perimeter.
6. You use the ___________ parameter to adjust the vertical position of the roof relative to the current working plane (view).
7. While using the *Roof* tool, you need to select the ___________ tool from the *Ribbon* before you can select a roofline for modification.
8. You need to use the __________________ to flip the roofline when you pick the wrong side of the wall and the overhang is shown on the inside.
9. The __________________ from the *Modify* tab (on the *Ribbon*) allows you to extend one roof element over, and into, another.
10. Changing the name of a level tag (in elevation) causes Revit to rename all the corresponding views (plan, ceiling, etc.) if you answer yes to the prompt. (T/F)

SELF-EXAM ANSWERS:
1 - F, **2** – T, **3** – T, **4** – defines slope, **5** – Y

Notes:

Lesson 9
FLOOR SYSTEMS AND REFLECTED CEILING PLANS:

In this lesson, you will learn to create floor structures and reflected ceiling plans.

Even though you currently have floor levels defined, you do not have an object that represents the mass of the floor systems. You will add floor systems with a hole for the stairs.

Ceiling systems allow you to specify the ceiling material by room and the height above the floor. Once the ceiling is added, it will appear in section views. Sections are created later in this book.

Exercise 9-1:
Floor Systems

Like other Autodesk® Revit® elements, you can select from a few predefined floor types. You can also create new floor types. In your residence, you will use a predefined floor system for the first and second floors and then create a new type for the basement and garage.

Basement Floor, Slab on Grade:

Sketching floors is a lot like sketching roofs; you can select walls to define the perimeter and draw lines to fill in the blanks, and add holes, or cut-outs, in the floor object.

1. Open ex8-4.rvt and **Save As ex9-1.rvt**.

2. Switch to the **Basement** *Floor Plan* view.

3. Select **Architecture → Build → Floor** *(just the icon, not the down-arrow).*

4. Click the **Edit Type** button on the *Properties Palette.*

5. Select **Concrete Slab – 4″** from the *Type* drop-down list near the top.

6. Click **Duplicate**.

7. Type **4″ Slab on Grade over Vapor Barrier**, then **OK**.

8. Click the **Edit** button next to the *Structure* parameter.

Here, you can change the slab thickness, but you will leave it at 4″ for the basement.

Next, you will add a vapor barrier and sand bed below the slab.

9. Insert a new layer:
    a. *Function:* **Membrane Layer**
    b. *Material:* **Vapor Retarder**
    c. *Thickness:* **0″**

NOTE: *Vapor barriers do have a thickness, of course (4mil, 6mil, etc.). However, the thickness is typically ignored on drawings. A* Membrane *is the only layer which can have no thickness; that is, a zero value.*

10. Add another layer:
    a. *Function:* **Substrate**
    b. *Priority:* **1**
    c. *Material:* **Sand** *(see **TIP** below)*
    d. *Thickness:* **4″** (Figure 9-1.1).

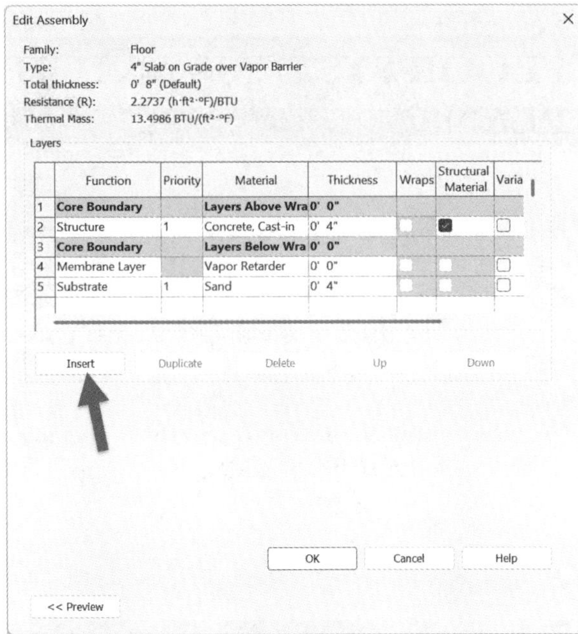

FIGURE 9-1.1 New floor system

NOTE: *The sand is sometimes placed over the vapor barrier. The sand helps to protect the vapor barrier until the rebar and concrete slab are in place. Additionally, the sand allows the concrete to cure more evenly with less chance of cupping. On the other hand, a vapor barrier directly below the slab helps prevent some floor finishes from delaminating due to moisture in the sand.*

TIP: *You can change the position of layers within a system. Simply select the row and then click the* Up *or* Down *button until positioned.*

TIP: *To load the Sand material, search for sand in the box at the top of the Material Browser (via Manage tab → Materials tool), and then double-click the Sand option in the Autodesk Library near the bottom. See Figure 9-1.2.*

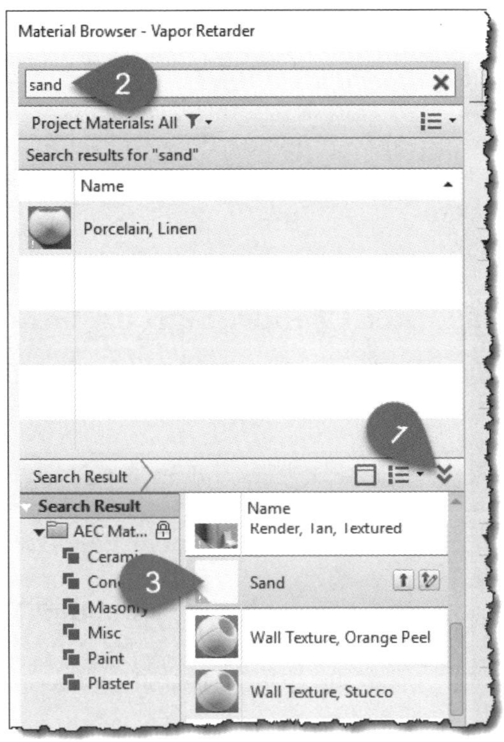

FIGURE 9-1.2 Materials Dialog

11. Click **OK** to close the open dialog boxes.

12. Select the walls in the ***Basement Plan*** as shown in Figure 9-1.3.

TIP: Select the interior side of the wall. You can use the control arrows if needed, opposite of what you did for the roof.

13. Click the **green check mark** on the *Ribbon*. 

TIP: If you get any errors, see the information in the box below.

Common Errors Finishing a Floor Sketch:

If you get an error message when trying to finish a floor sketch, it is probably due to a problem with the sketched perimeter lines. Here are two common problems:

Perimeter not closed:
You cannot finish a floor if there is a gap, large or small, in the perimeter sketch.
FIX: Sketch a line to close the loop.

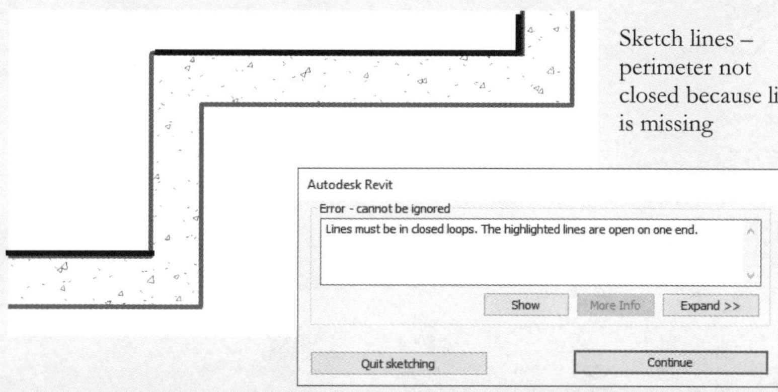

Sketch lines – perimeter not closed because line is missing

Error message after clicking finish sketch

Perimeter lines intersect:
You cannot finish a floor if any of the sketch lines intersect.
FIX: Use *Trim* to ensure all line endpoints touch.

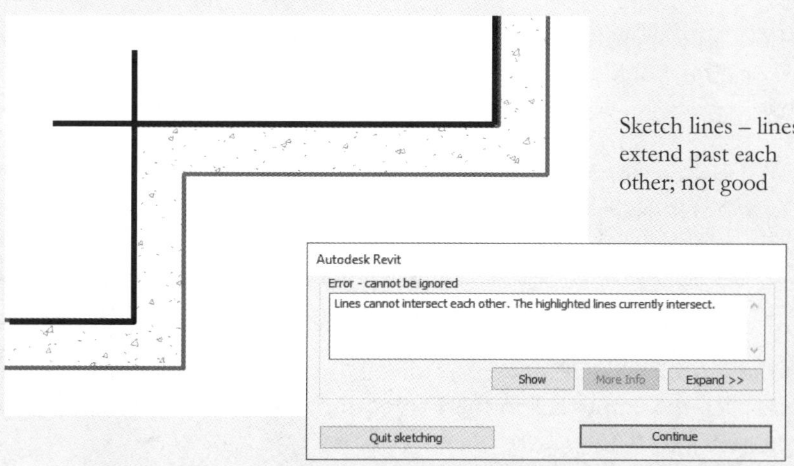

Sketch lines – lines extend past each other; not good

Error message after clicking finish sketch

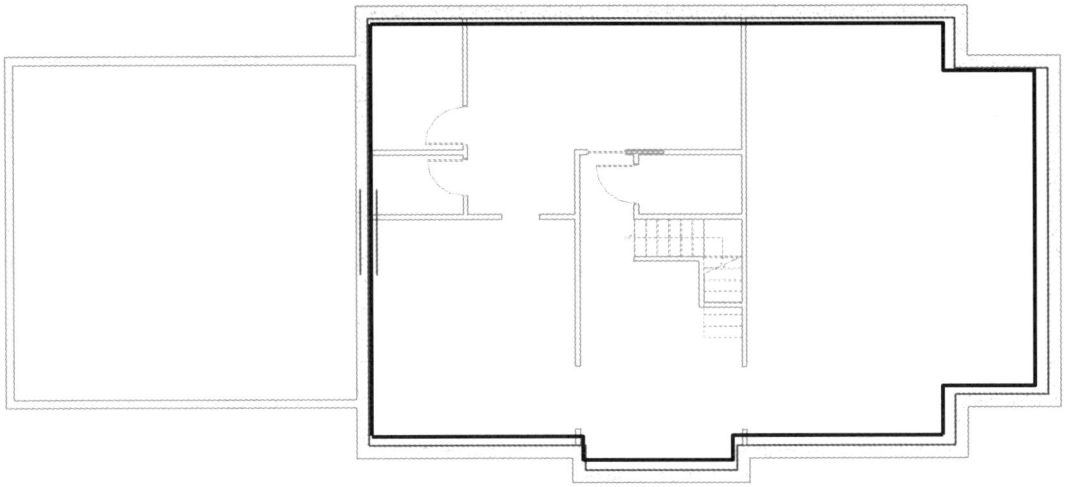

FIGURE 9-1.3 Basement floor plan; floor slab sketched

14. Click **No** when prompted to join the floor to the walls (Figure 9-1.4).

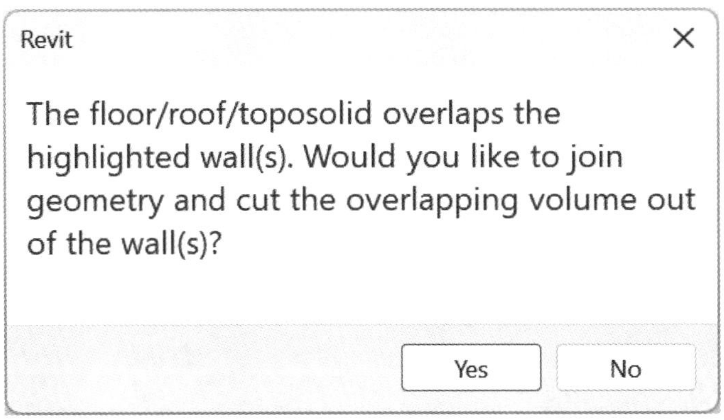

FIGURE 9-1.4 Floor creation prompt

You now have a floor at the basement level. You should see a stipple pattern representing the floor area. You would most likely want to turn that pattern off for a floor plan. You will do that next.

15. In the ***Basement*** *Floor Plan* view, type **VV**; this is the keyboard shortcut for *Visibility/Graphic Overrides.*

    TIP: You may have to click within the drawing window before typing the keyboard shortcut for Revit to recognize it.

16. In the *Visibility/Graphic Overrides* dialog, on the *Model Categories* tab and in the **Floors** row, click the empty cell in the **Projection/ Surface → Patterns** column (Figure 9-1.4).

17. With the word *Override* now showing, click the exact same location again.

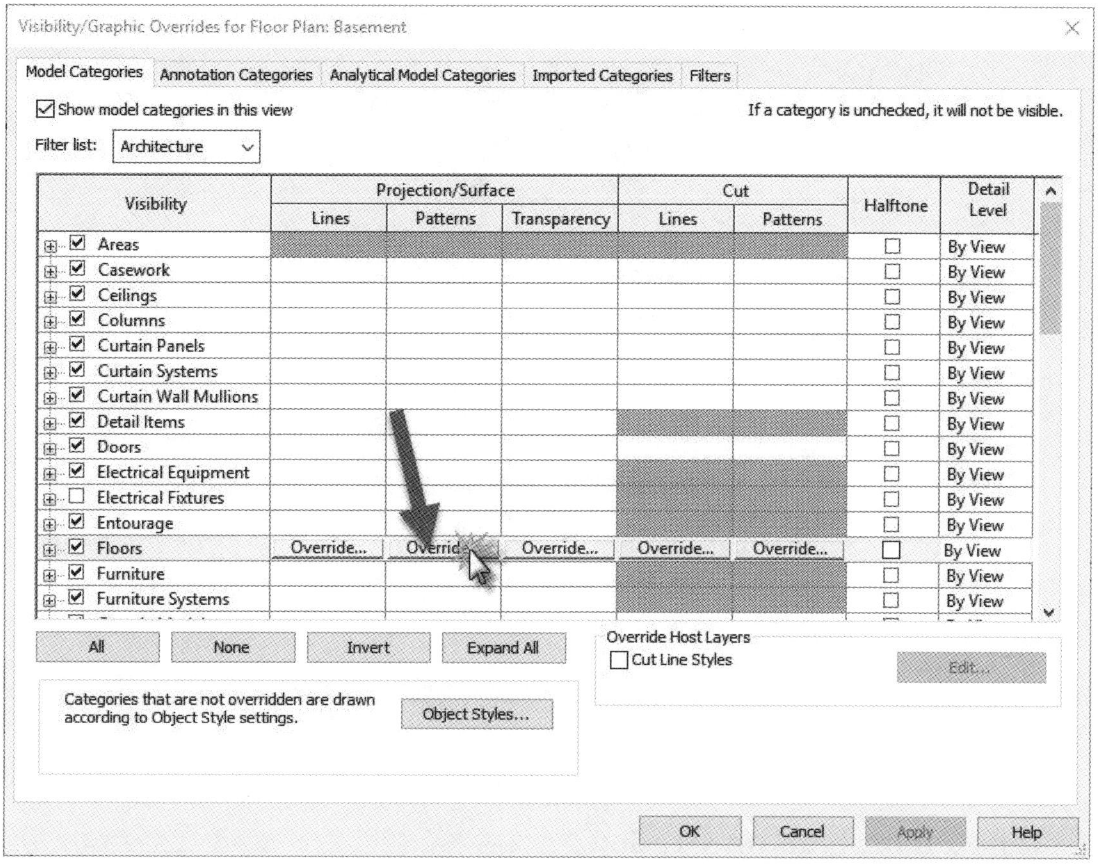

FIGURE 9-1.5 Visibility/Graphics Overrides: Editing the floor surface pattern visibility

18. Uncheck both ***Visible*** options, which will make the floor surface pattern not visible in the current view (Figure 9-1.6).

19. Click **OK** to close the dialogs.

The stipple pattern is no longer visible. The *Visibility/Graphic Overrides* dialog now indicates that the surface pattern is hidden (Figure 9-1.7). Keep in mind that this override applies only to the current view. If you create another floor using the same 4″ concrete type you just created in the Level 1 floor plan view, it would have the stipple pattern. It would even show up in another basement-level floor plan, as it is possible to create more than one view that references the same *Level Datum*.

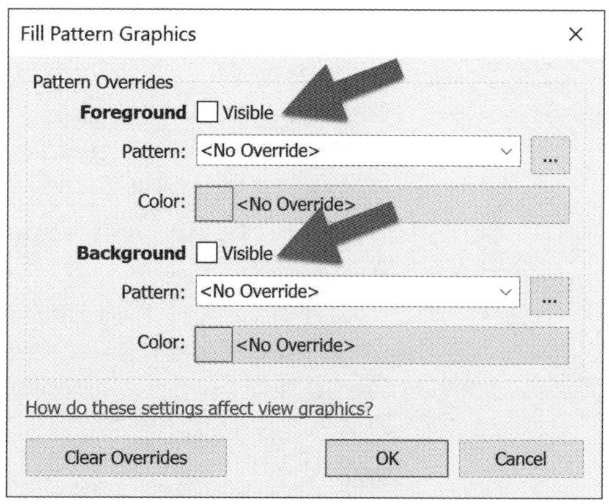

FIGURE 9-1.6 Fill Pattern Graphics

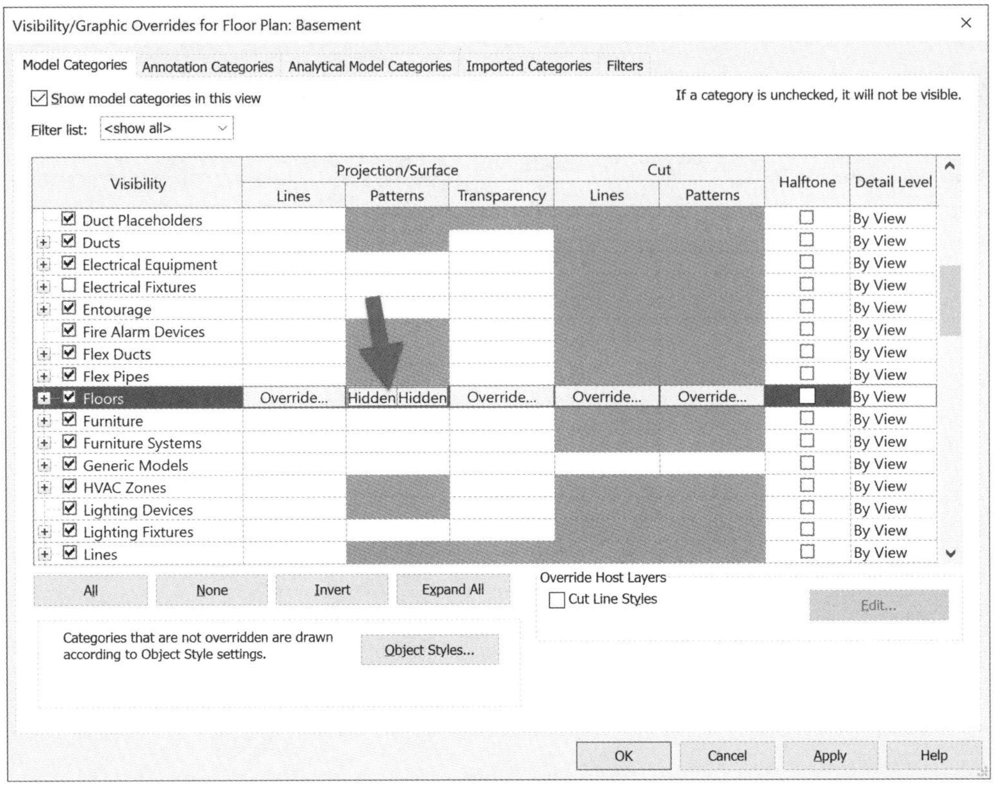

FIGURE 9-1.7 Visibility/Graphics Overrides

Garage Floor, Slab on Grade:

Now you will sketch the floor slab for the garage area. Because this floor will have vehicles parking on it, you will create a new slab type that is 6″ thick.

20. Switch to the ***First Floor*** *Plan* view.

21. Select the ***Floor*** tool.

22. Using the floor type you just created as a starting point, create a new floor type named **6″ Slab on Grade over Vapor Barrier**.

TIP: Properties Palette → Edit Type → Duplicate

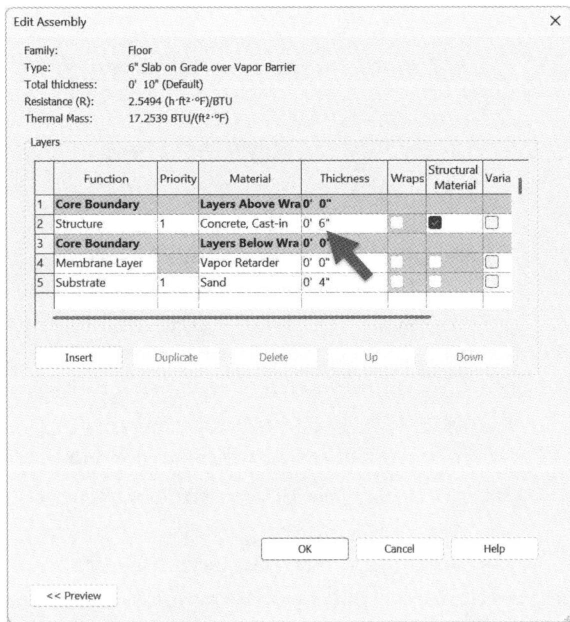

FIGURE 9-1.8 Changing the conc. slab thickness

23. Click the **Edit** button next to the *Structure* parameter.

24. Change the *Concrete* thickness from 4″ to **6″** (Figure 9-1.8).

25. Click **OK** to close the open dialog boxes.

26. With *Pick Walls* selected on the *Ribbon*, select the interior side of the four walls surrounding the garage (Figure 9-1.9).

27. Click the **green check mark** to finish the floor. Click **No** when prompted to join the wall and the floor.

You now have a floor slab in the garage area. You will notice that the floor element has a stipple pattern, even though you turned that stipple pattern off in the *Basement* view. Remember: the visibility settings are controlled by view, not project-wide, although they can be. You will turn this off later.

Notice the **Span Direction** symbol identified in the image to the right. This can be ignored for this type of floor. It is meant to define the flute direction for a metal floor/roof deck, which your residential floors will not have.

> ***FYI:*** *The Span Direction button on the Ribbon, visible while in the Floor tool, will allow you to change the span direction by picking a different sketch line.*

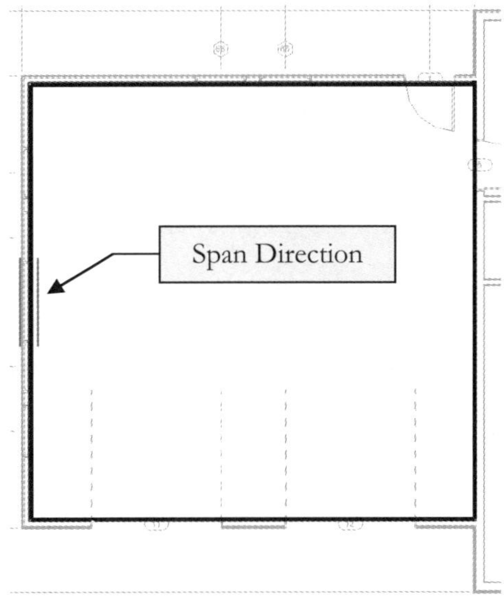

FIGURE 9-1.9 First floor: floor slab sketched

When floors are created, the top of the floor aligns with the level (see image below). Each floor plan view is associated with a level (which cannot be changed), so the view in which you create the floor determines the default level the floor references. The referenced floor level can be changed at any time. The top of the floor will stay aligned with the level even if the floor thickness is changed. However, it is possible to select the floor and change its “Height Offset From Level” parameter to change the default behavior.

Top of floor aligns with level

First Floor (Wood Joists):

28. Use the floor type *Wood Joist 10" - Wood Finish* as a starting point to create a new floor type named **Wood Joist 14" - Wood Finish**.

29. Change the *Structure* settings per the following image (Figure 9-1.10).

    FYI: This has all been covered previously.

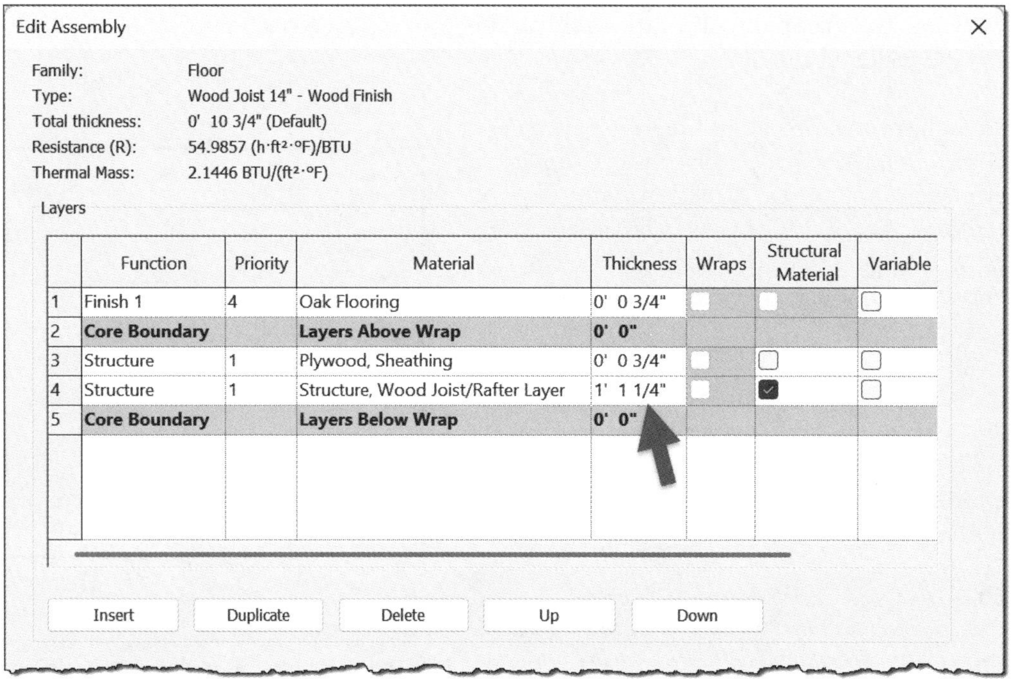

Edit Assembly

Family: Floor
Type: Wood Joist 14" - Wood Finish
Total thickness: 0' 10 3/4" (Default)
Resistance (R): 54.9857 (h·ft²·°F)/BTU
Thermal Mass: 2.1446 BTU/(ft²·°F)

Layers

	Function	Priority	Material	Thickness	Wraps	Structural Material	Variable
1	Finish 1	4	Oak Flooring	0' 0 3/4"			☐
2	**Core Boundary**		**Layers Above Wrap**	**0' 0"**			
3	Structure	1	Plywood, Sheathing	0' 0 3/4"		☐	☐
4	Structure	1	Structure, Wood Joist/Rafter Layer	1' 1 1/4"		☑	☐
5	**Core Boundary**		**Layers Below Wrap**	**0' 0"**			

Insert | Duplicate | Delete | Up | Down

FIGURE 9-1.10 Floor properties

Creating the first and second floors will be a little more involved than the basement and garage floors. This is because the upper floors require openings. For example, you need to define the stair openings. Revit makes the process very simple.

You should still be in the *Floor* tool.

30. On the *Ribbon*, check ***Extend into wall (to core)***.

    FYI: *The* Extend into wall (to core) *option will extend the slab under your wall core (wood stud and sheathing are in the core in our example) and go under the gypsum wall board. This is similar to the information presented at the end of the previous chapter.*

31. Select the exterior walls indicated in Figure 9-1.10. Select the exterior side of the wall; use the flip control arrows if needed.

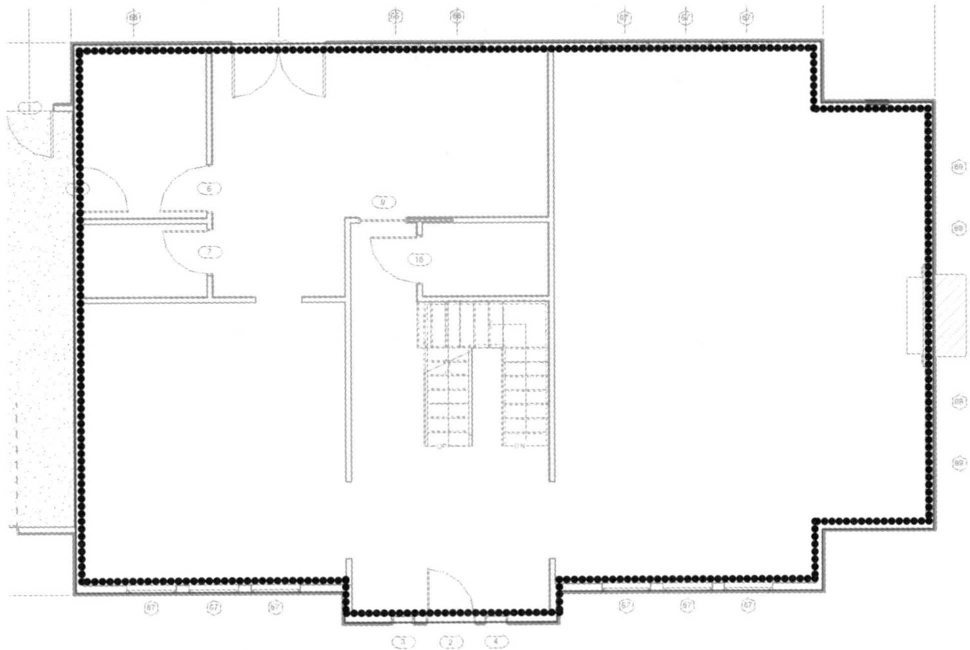

FIGURE 9-1.11 First Floor – floor system sketched

Next, you will define the hole in the floor for the stairs that lead down to the basement. You will need to use the *Lines* option from the *Draw* panel to define this area.

32. While the *Floor* tool is still active, ***Zoom In*** to the stair area.

33. Select the **Rectangle** icon on the *Ribbon*; see image below.

34. Draw a rectangle defining the stair opening; use Revit's snaps to accurately pick the points as shown in **Figure 9-1.12**.

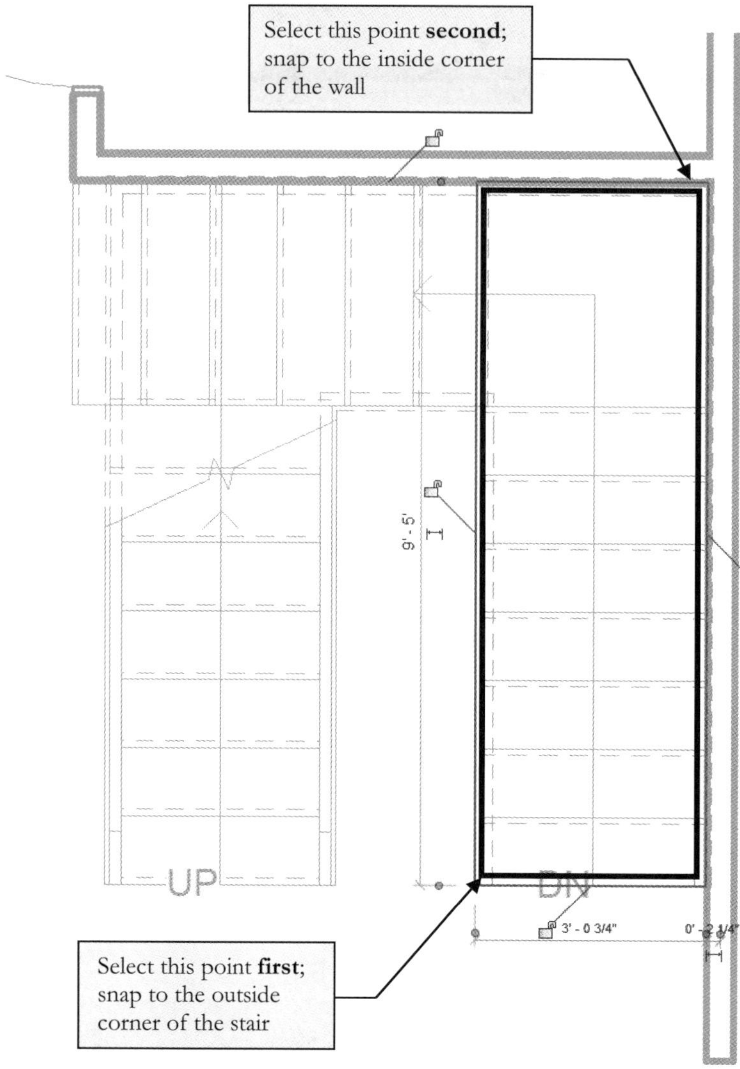

FIGURE 9-1.12 First Floor – sketching floor opening

FYI: *This floor opening has a big problem. You will see this problem when you get to the building sections exercise later in this book.*

35. Click the **green check mark** to finish the floor.

Next, you will get two prompts: one asks if you want the walls below, whose tops are set to terminate at the first floor, to attach to the new floor. The other prompt asks if you want the floor to attach to the exterior walls. You will answer **Yes** to both.

36. Click **Attach** to the prompt "*Would you like the walls that go up to this floor's level to attach to its bottom?*" (Figure 9-1.13). Also, click **OK** if prompted with a "highlighted walls are attached, but miss…" warning.

FYI: This will allow the walls to dynamically change if the floor elevation or thickness is changed.

37. Click **Yes** for the prompt to join the walls that overlap the floor system (Figure 9-1.14).

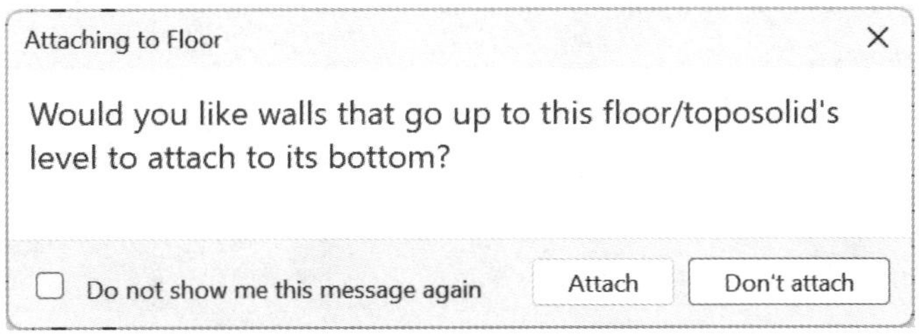

FIGURE 9-1.13 Join walls below to new floor prompt

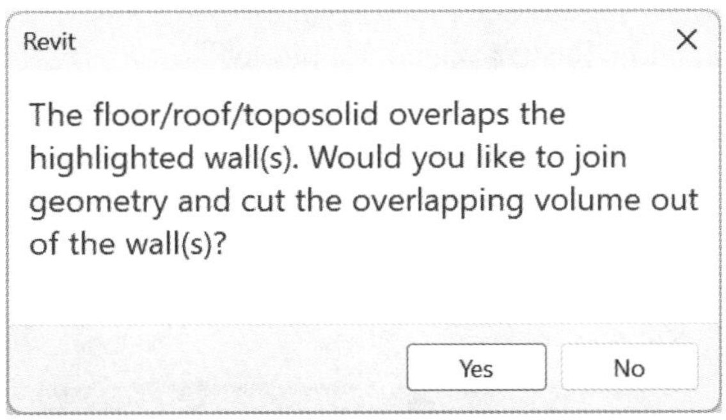

FIGURE 9-1.14 Join walls that overlap the new floor prompt

Now that the floor is placed, you should see a dense horizontal line pattern that represents the finished wood floor. This would be nice for presentation drawings, but like the basement, you will turn the floor hatch off, so the floor plan is not too cluttered.

38. Change the first floor's *Visibility* to turn off the floor pattern (Tip: type VV).

Copy/Paste the First Floor to the Second:

That completes the first floor system. Next, you will copy the floor you just created to the second floor. It would probably be easier to just create a floor from scratch, but you will get more practice editing existing elements.

39. Select the floor you just created, in the *First Floor* plan view, and select **Modify | Floors → Clipboard → Copy to Clipboard** on the *Ribbon*. See *TIP* on next page.

TIP: Selecting elements that overlap, like the exterior walls and the edge of floor system, may require the use of the Tab *key. By default, the only way to select a floor element is by picking its edge. Revit temporarily highlights elements when you move your cursor over them. But, because the floor edge may not have an "exposed" edge to select, you will have to toggle through your selection options for your current cursor location. With the cursor positioned over the edge of the floor, probably with an exterior wall highlighted, press the* Tab *key to cycle through the available options. A tooltip will display the elements. When you see* floors: floor:floor-name, *click the mouse; also watch the Status Bar.*

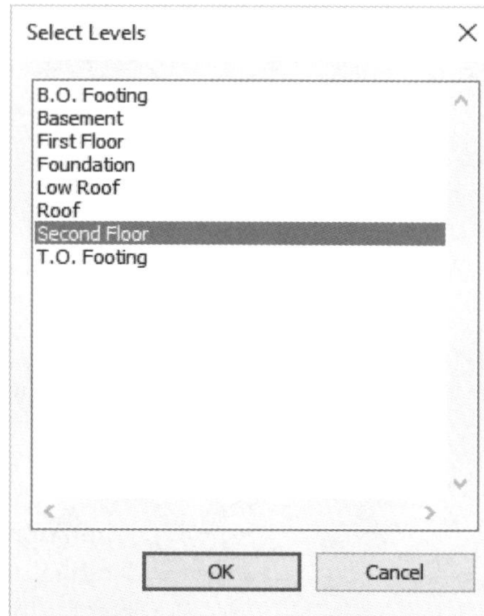

40. Pick **Modify → Clipboard → Paste → Aligned to Selected Levels**.

41. Select **Second Floor** and then **OK**.

TIP: You can press Ctrl and select more than one level.

42. Switch to the **Second Floor**.

You now have a copy of the first floor's "floor system" in the *Second Floor Plan* view (Figure 9-1.15); keep in mind that all the views are looking at a single 3D model. You will edit the sketch lines of the *Second Floor* – floor - to make the stair hole larger and remove a portion of the floor that extends past the East exterior wall.

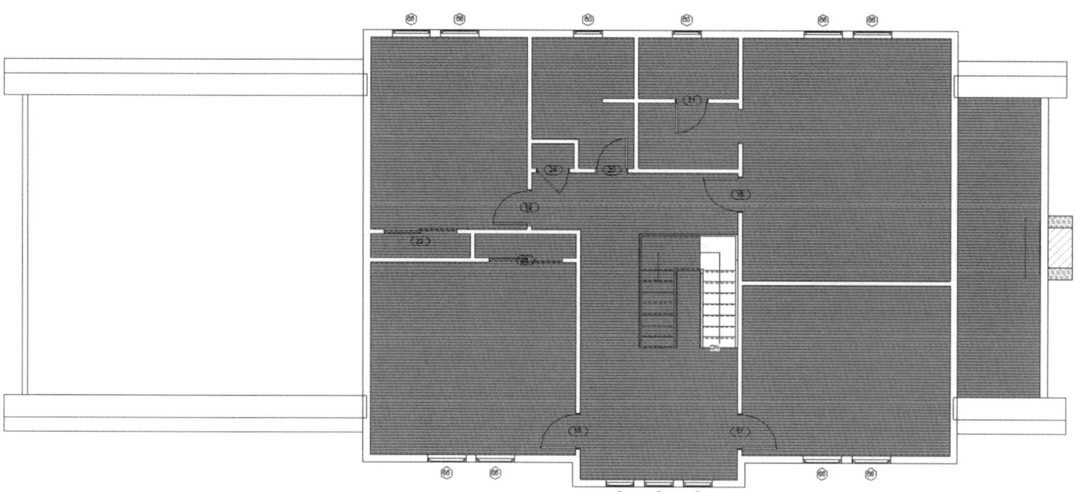

FIGURE 9-1.15 New floor added to level 2 using the paste aligned option

43. Select the floor element in the ***Second Floor Plan*** view.

TIP: The edge of the floor is "exposed" at the stair opening; this would be the easiest place to select the floor.

44. Click **Edit Boundary** from the *Ribbon*. See icon to the right.

You are now in *Sketch* mode, where you can change the perimeter and holes for the selected floor element. You can select lines and delete them, sketch new lines, and use *Trim* to modify lines.

45. Modify the lines at the far right, using *Delete* and *Trim*, so your sketch looks like Figure 9-1.16.

46. *Stair opening:* Move the West vertical line **4'-11 1/4"** farther West; the horizontal sketch lines should automatically extend, as shown in Figure 9-1.16. The overall width of the stair opening should be 8'-0"; if not, you should go back and double-check your stair dimensions with Chapter 6, page 6-25.

47. Click the **green check mark** to recreate the floor element.

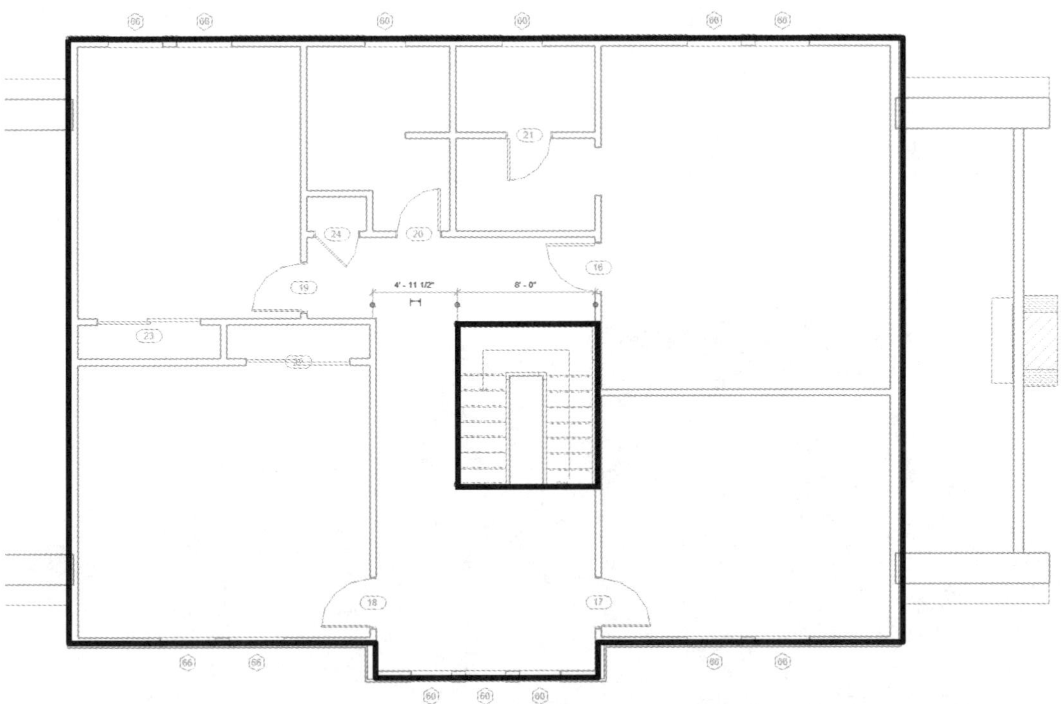

FIGURE 9-1.16 Second floor: sketch lines modified

Now that Revit is recreating the floor, it notices the walls below and at the exterior so you get the "join" prompts.

48. Click **Attach/Yes** to the two "join" prompts, if you get them.

Your ***Second Floor Plan*** view should look like Figure 9-1.17.

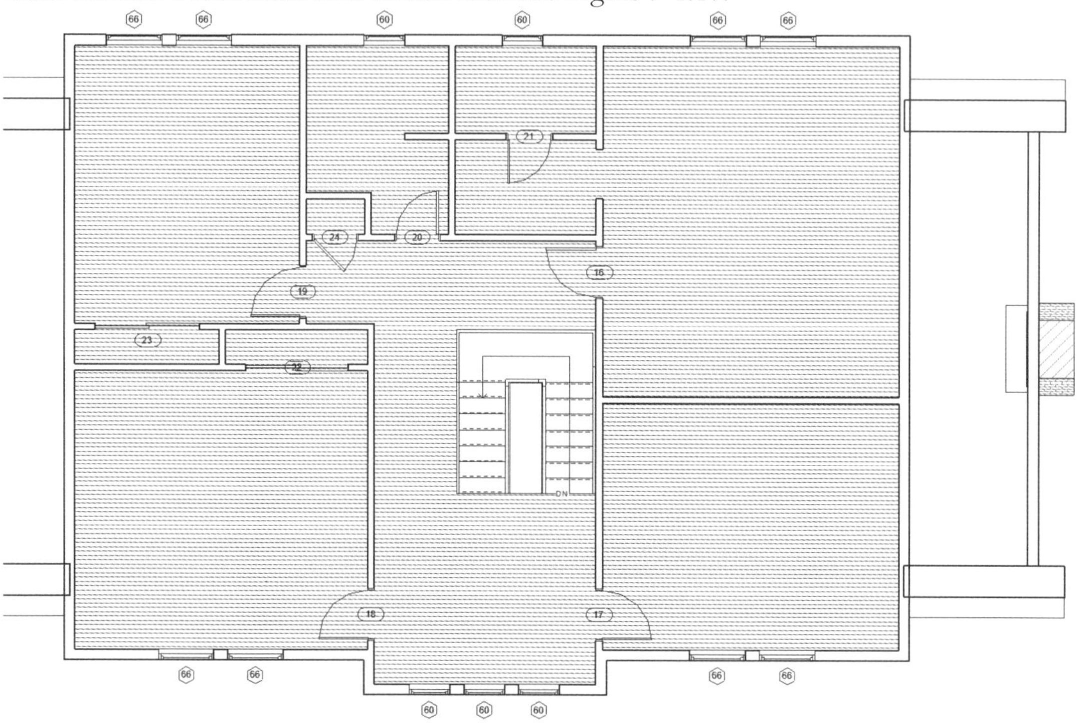

FIGURE 9-1.17 Second Floor: sketch lines modified

49. Change the second floor's *Visibility* to turn off the floor hatch.

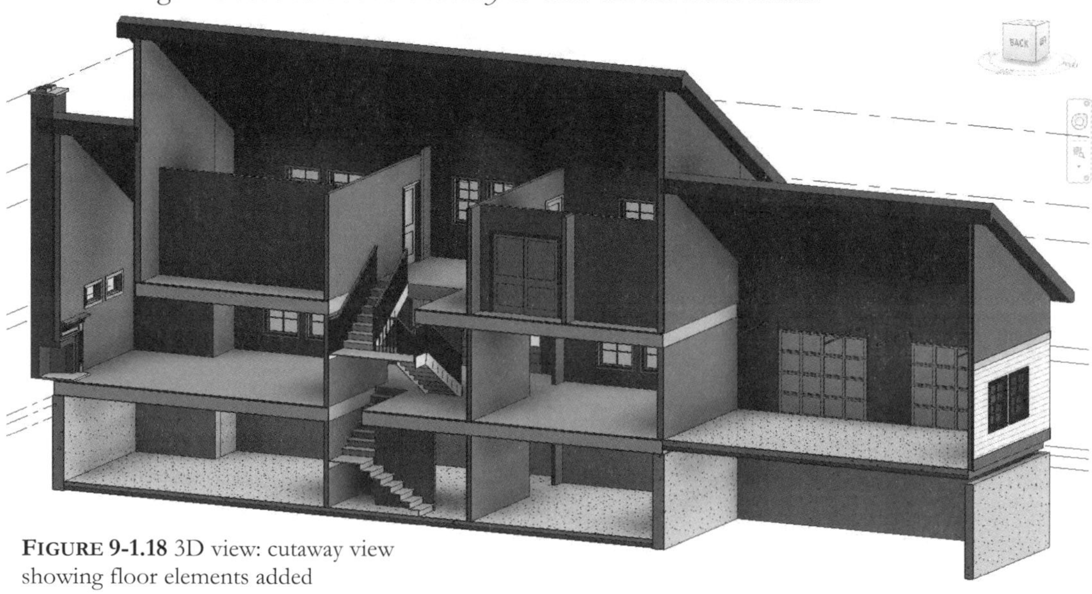

FIGURE 9-1.18 3D view: cutaway view showing floor elements added

Turning off Surface Pattern at the Source:

If you do not want a portion of your plan to show a surface pattern, you might want to remove the surface pattern associated with the floor system. That way you could leave the surface pattern setting turned on. Set the *Surface Pattern* to **None** in the *Material Editor.*

Basically, you remove the surface pattern for the *Finish* layer in a floor system.

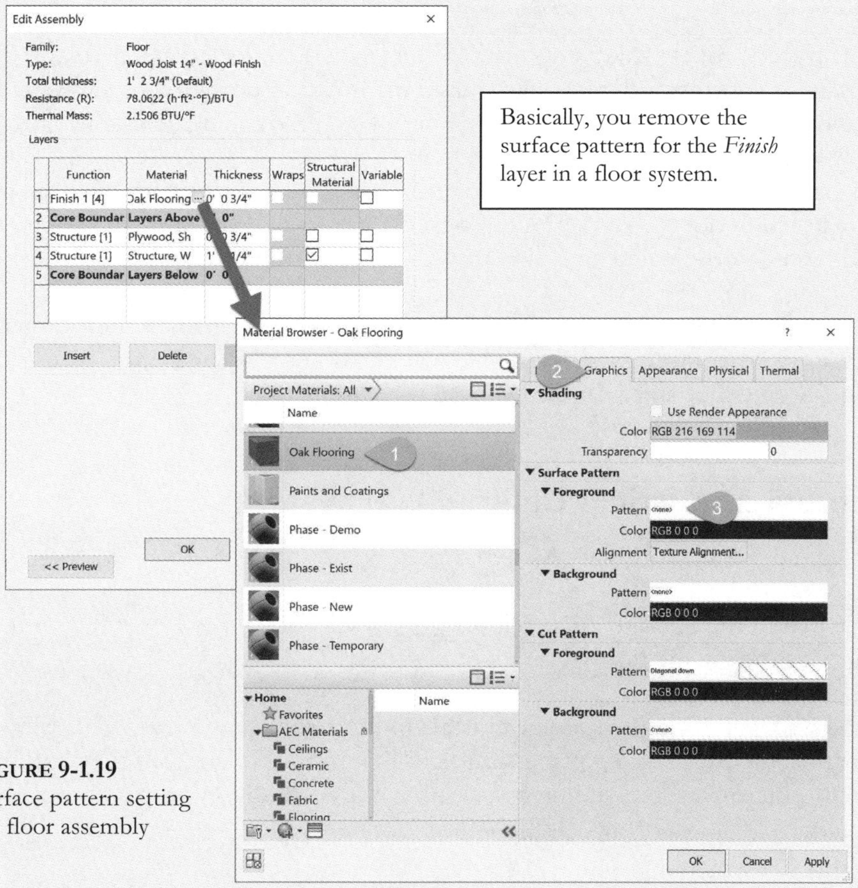

FIGURE 9-1.19
Surface pattern setting for floor assembly

50. Save your project as **ex9-1.rvt**.

Exercise 9-2:
Ceiling Systems (Susp. ACT and Gypsum Board)

This lesson will explore Revit's tools for drawing reflected ceiling plans. This will include drawing different types of ceiling systems.

Traditionally, residential projects do not typically include reflected ceiling plans. The ceilings are generally straightforward, with all required information provided in the *Room Finish Schedule* and *Sections*. However, in Revit, you will sketch the ceiling profile in the ceiling plan views, as you did for the floor systems (in their respective *floor plan* views). You want to add ceilings so they appear in sections. So, seeing as you have ceiling plans, why not include them in the construction documents set? Your design intent will be clearer, and you can ensure the lighting design is coordinated and laid out the way you want.

The use of suspended acoustical ceiling tile in residential projects is somewhat limited. However, it is occasionally used, so it will be covered here. In this lesson, you will add it to the second-floor office and a family room in the basement.

Suspended Acoustical Ceiling Tile System:

1. Open ex9-1.rvt and **Save As ex9-2.rvt**.

2. Switch to the ***Second Floor <u>Ceiling Plan</u>*** view from the *Project Browser*; ceiling plans are just below the floor plans.

Notice the doors and windows are not visible in the ceiling plan views. This is because ceiling plan views use a cutting plane similar to that in floor plans, but they look up rather than down. You can see this setting by selecting **View Range** in properties for the current view. The default value is 7′-6″. You might increase this if, for example, you had 10′-0″ ceilings and 8′-0″ tall doors. Otherwise, the doors would show because the 7′-6″ cutting plane is below the door height (Figure 9-2.1).

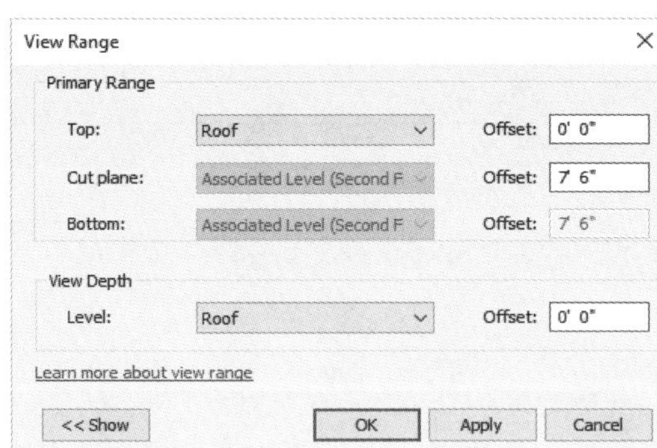

FIGURE 9-2.1 Properties: View Range settings

3. Close the *View Range* dialog box, if still open, and then select **Architecture → Build → Ceiling**.

You have four ceiling types to select from by default (Figure 9-2.2).

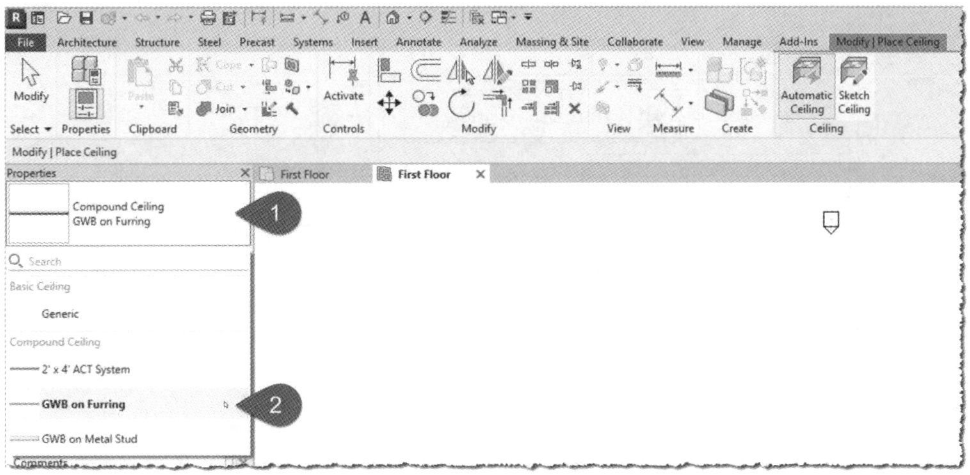

FIGURE 9-2.2 Type Selector: Ceiling: types

4. Select *Compound Ceiling:* **2′x4′ ACT System**.

Next, you will change the ceiling height. The default setting is 8′-0″ above the current level. You will change the ceiling height to 8′-4″; this will give about 6½″ of space above the ceiling to the bottom of the rafters for recessed light fixtures and any required wiring. This setting can be changed on a room-by-room basis; that is why it is an *Instance Parameter.*

5. In the *Properties Palette*, set the *Height Offset From Level* setting to **8′-4″** (Figure 9-2.3).

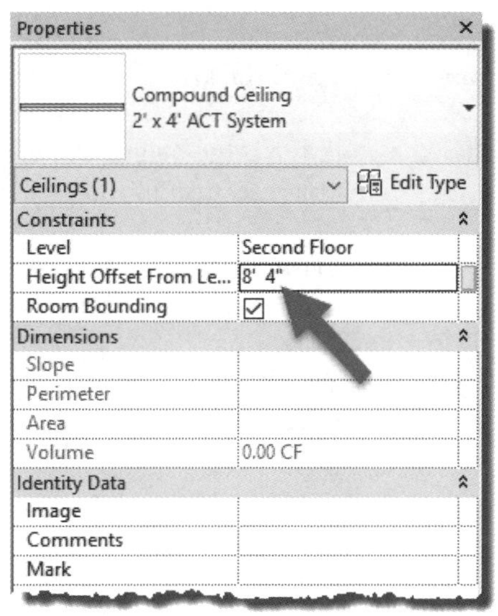

FIGURE 9-2.3 Ceiling: Properties

You are now ready to place ceiling grids. This process cannot get much easier, especially compared to 2D CAD programs.

6. Move your cursor anywhere within the office in the lower-right corner of the building. You should see the room's perimeter highlighted.

7. Pick within the room; Revit places a ceiling grid in the room (Figure 9-2.4).

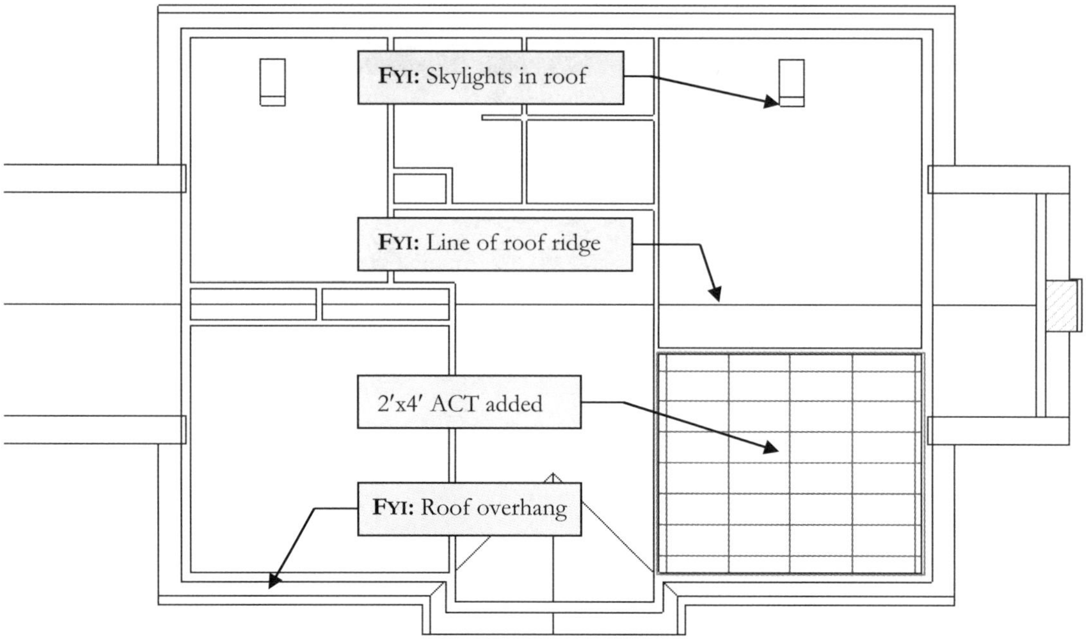

FIGURE 9-2.4: Second Floor Ceiling Plan view: 2′x4′ suspended acoustical ceiling tile added to office

You now have a 2x4 ceiling grid at 8′-4″ above the floor, the second floor in this case. Later in the book, when you get to the exercise on cutting sections, you will see the ceiling with the proper height and thickness.

Next, you will add the same ceiling system to the family room in the basement. But, you will notice the ceiling plan section in the *Project Browser* does not have a *Basement* view.

Many residential basements do not have any finished ceilings, so that view was not included in the template from which you started. Next you will create a view for this.

8. Select **View → Create → Plan Views → Reflected Ceiling Plan**.

9. Select the ***Basement*** view from this list and then click **OK** (see image to the right).

10. You are taken to the ***Basement Ceiling Plan*** view automatically.

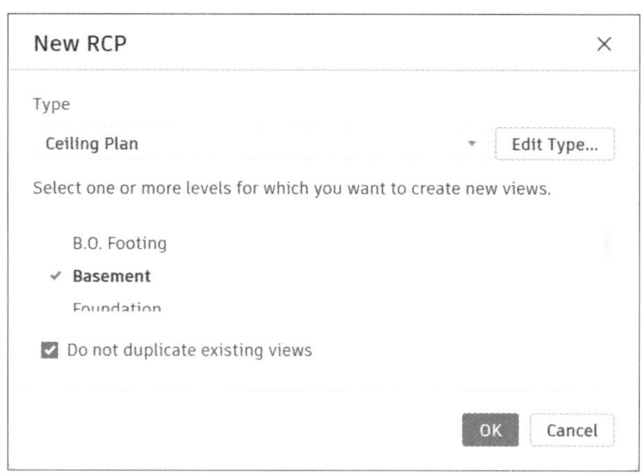

Your view should look a little funny, e.g., no walls or doors visible. You will have to adjust the *View Range* settings.

11. Click **Modify** and then set the *Cut Plane*, in *View Range*, to **6′-6″**.

You should now see the walls and doors. The doors show because the cut plane is lower than the top of the door. You will ignore that for now.

12. Use the ***Ceiling*** tool to place 2′x 4′ acoustic ceiling tile in the *Family Room*, the large room to the far East. See the following notes (Figure 9-2.5):
    a. You will probably get a symbol at the cross-hairs that indicates you cannot place a ceiling anywhere; the symbol is a circle with a slash through it. This has to do with the ceiling height.
    b. Via the *Properties Palette*, change the ceiling height to **7′-0″**.
    c. You should be able to place the ceiling system now.
    d. Revit automatically rotates and centers the ceiling grid within each room.

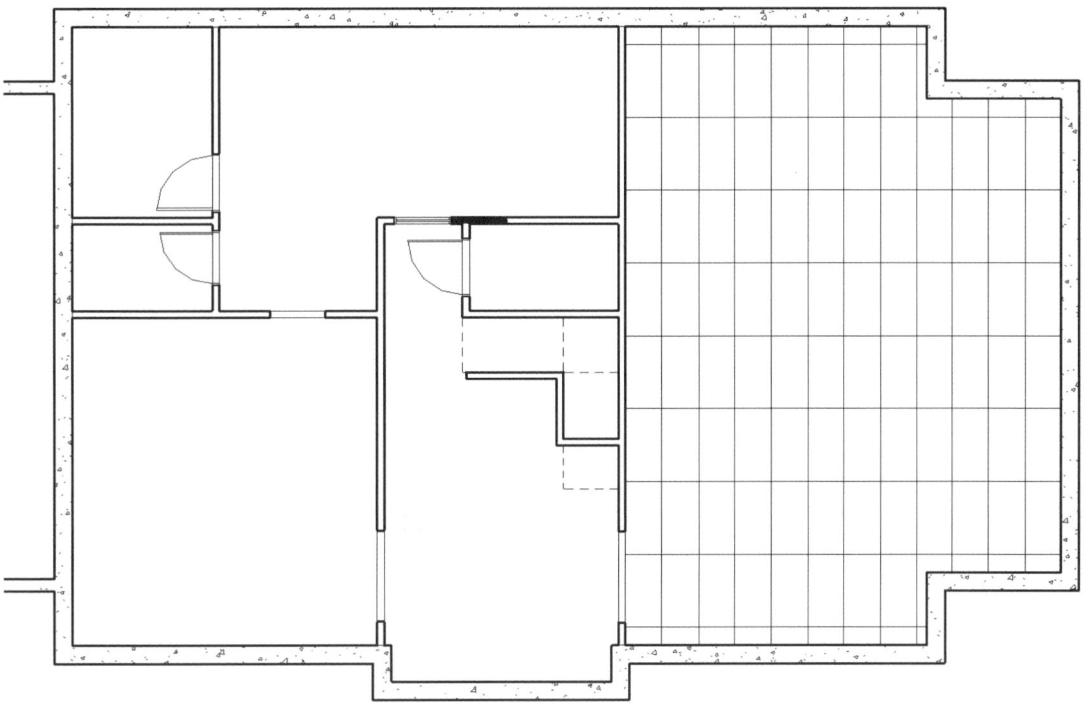

FIGURE 9-2.5: Basement Ceiling Plan view: 2′x4′ suspended acoustical ceiling tile added to Family Rm.

When you place a ceiling grid, Revit centers the grid in the room. The general rule of thumb is to avoid reducing the tile size by more than half a tile. You can see in Figure 9-2.5 that the East and West sides look OK. However, the North and South sides are small slivers. You will adjust this next.

Looking at Figure 9-2.6, you can see why it was not possible to place a ceiling until the ceiling height was lowered and why the walls did not show up; the foundation wall is only 7′-3″ above the basement floor. Thus, a floor cut plane of 7′-6″ would not show walls, and an 8′-4″ ceiling could not find walls to form a perimeter to contain it.

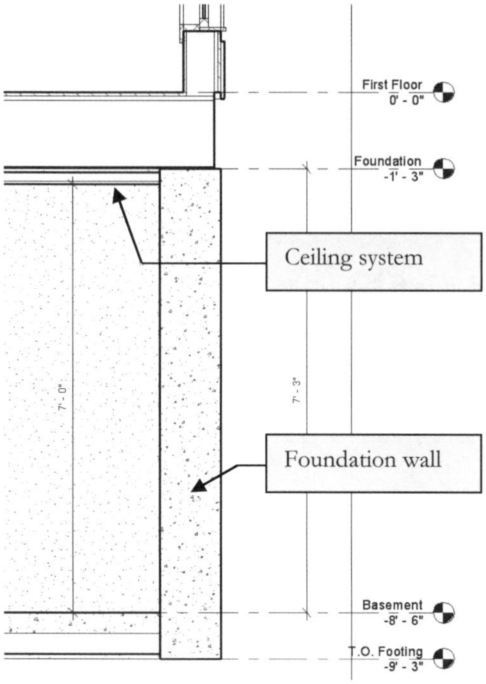

FIGURE 9-2.6
Section at basement / foundation wall

13. Select ***Modify*** from the *Ribbon.*

14. **Select** the ceiling grid. Only one line will be highlighted.

15. Use the **Move** tool to move the grid 24″ to the North (Figure 9-2.7).

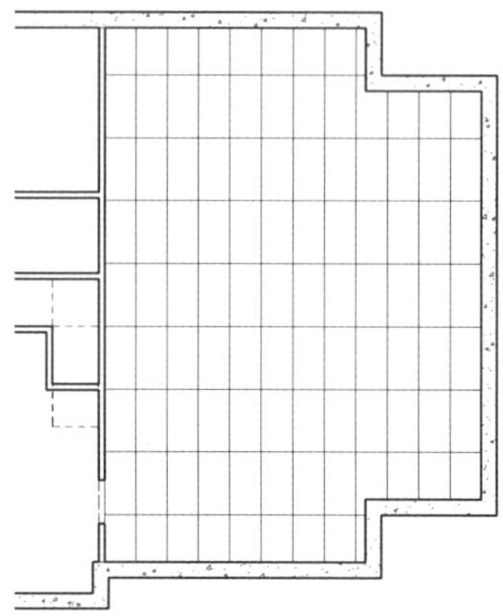

FIGURE 9-2.7
Basement: Ceiling Grid moved

Note that only the grid moved, not the ceiling perimeter.

Modifying the Suspended Acoustical Ceiling Tile System:

Making modifications to the grid is relatively easy. Next, you will adjust the ceiling height and rotate the grid.

16. In the ***Basement*** view, select the ceiling grid in the *Family Room.*

17. Within the *Properties Palette*, change the height to **7′-2″**. *(Every inch counts!)*

18. Click **Apply** to accept the new height change (or just move your cursor back into the drawing area).

19. Again, with the grid still selected, use the ***Rotate*** tool from the *Ribbon* to rotate the grid **30 degrees**.

FYI: Notice, while in the Rotate command, the <u>Center of Rotation</u> icon appears, and like in the earlier lessons, this can be dragged to a different location if needed.

TIP: *When using the Rotate tool you need to pick two points. The first point is your reference line. The second point is the number of degrees off that reference line. In this example, try picking your first point to the right as a horizontal line. Then move the cursor counter-clockwise until 30 degrees is displayed. You can also type the angle rather than clicking the second point.*

Your drawing should look similar to **Figure 9-2.8**. Notice how the perimeter of the room acts like a cropping window when you use *Move* or *Rotate* on a ceiling grid.

Deleting a Ceiling Grid:
When selecting a ceiling grid, Revit only selects one line. This does not allow you to delete the ceiling.

To delete: hover cursor over a ceiling grid line and press the TAB key until you see the ceiling perimeter highlight, then click the mouse. The entire ceiling will be selected. Press Delete.

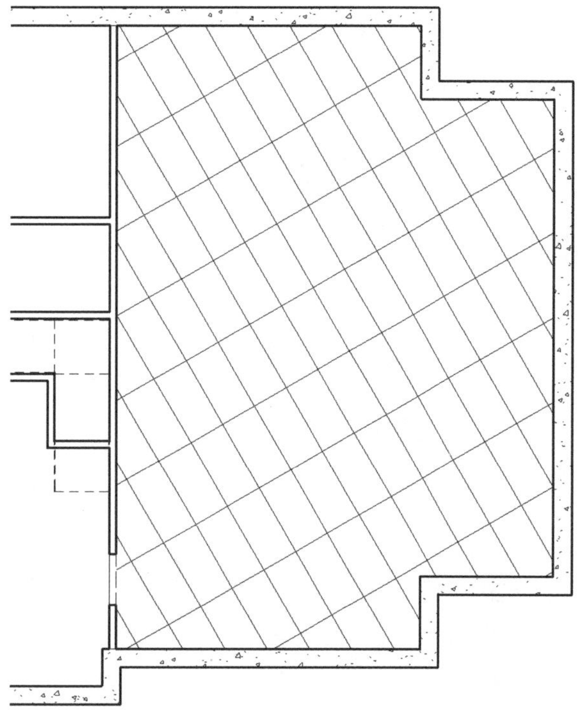

FIGURE 9-2.8 Basement: Modified Ceiling

Next, you will look at drawing gypsum board ceiling systems. The process is identical to placing the grid system. Additionally, you will create a ceiling type.

Gypsum Board Ceiling System:

You will create a new ceiling type for a gypsum board (gyp. bd.) ceiling. To better identify the areas that have a gyp. bd. ceiling, you will set the ceiling type to have a stipple pattern. This will provide a nice graphical representation for the gyp. bd. ceiling areas. The ceiling you are about to create would lean more towards a commercial application. However, it will give you a better understanding of how to create custom ceilings. You will add this ceiling to a room in the basement; assume it is being installed below HVAC ductwork, to finish the room.

20. Select **Manage → Settings → Materials**. *This is the list of materials you select from when assigning a material to each layer in a wall system, etc.*

21. Select *Gypsum Wall Board* in the name list, right-click and then select **Duplicate Material and Assets.** Enter the name **Gypsum Ceiling Board**.

22. On the Graphics tab, in the *Foreground Surface Pattern* area, pick the preview and select **Gypsum-Plaster** from the list, and then click **OK** twice (Figure 9-2.9).

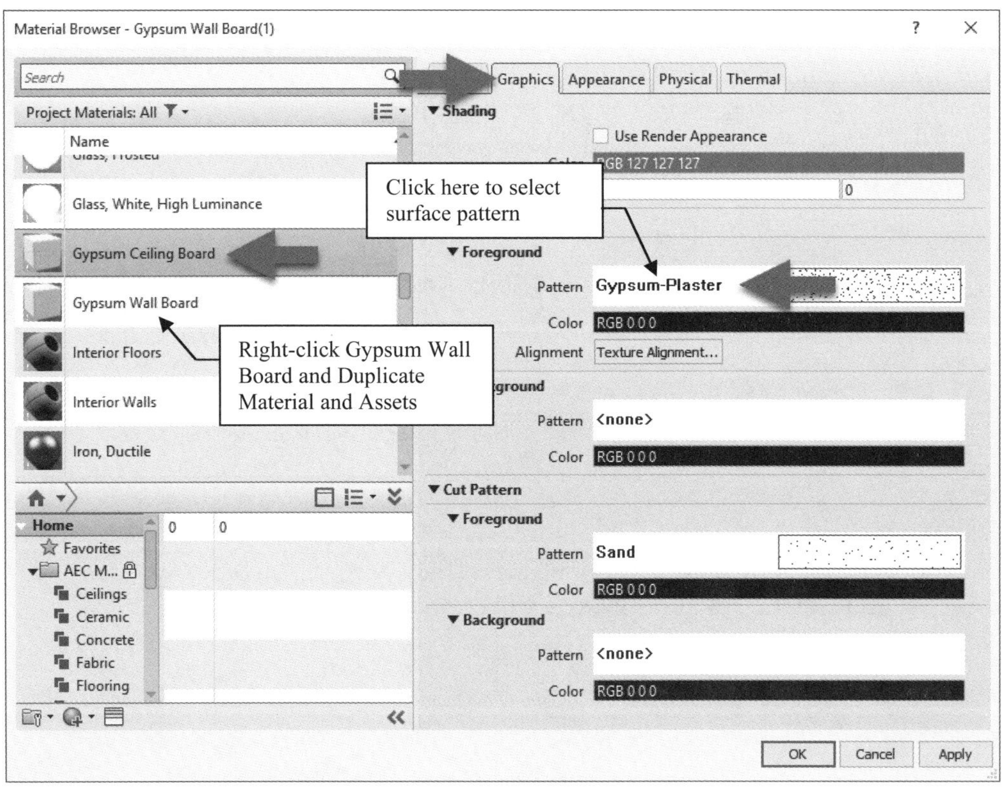

FIGURE 9-2.9 Materials dialog

The *Surface Pattern* setting is what will add the stipple pattern to the gyp. bd. ceiling areas. With this set to *none*, the ceiling has no pattern, like the basic ceiling type.

Thus, if you wanted "Carpet 1" finish to never have the stipple hatch pattern, you could change the surface pattern to none via the *Materials* dialog and not have to change each view's visibility override.

23. Select the ***Ceiling*** tool from the *Ribbon*.

24. Set the *Type Selector* to **GWB on Metal Stud**.

    FYI: You are selecting this because it is similar to the ceiling you will be creating.

25. Click the **Edit Type** button in the *Properties Palette.*

26. Click *Duplicate* and type the name **Susp GB on Metal Stud**.

27. Select **Edit** next to the *Structure* parameter.

28. Create a *Layer* and set the *Values* as follows (Figure 9-2.10):
    a. **1½" Mtl. Stud**
    b. **¾" Mtl. Stud**
    c. **Gypsum Ceiling Board** *(This is the material you created in Step 21.)*

29. Click **OK** two times.

FYI: The ceiling assembly you just created represents a typical non-residential suspended gyp. bd. ceiling system. The metal studs are perpendicular to each other and suspended by wires, similar to an ACT (acoustical ceiling tile) system.

Tip: *It is also possible to duplicate a layer, which would then only require the thickness to be modified in this example.*

You are now ready to draw a gypsum board ceiling.

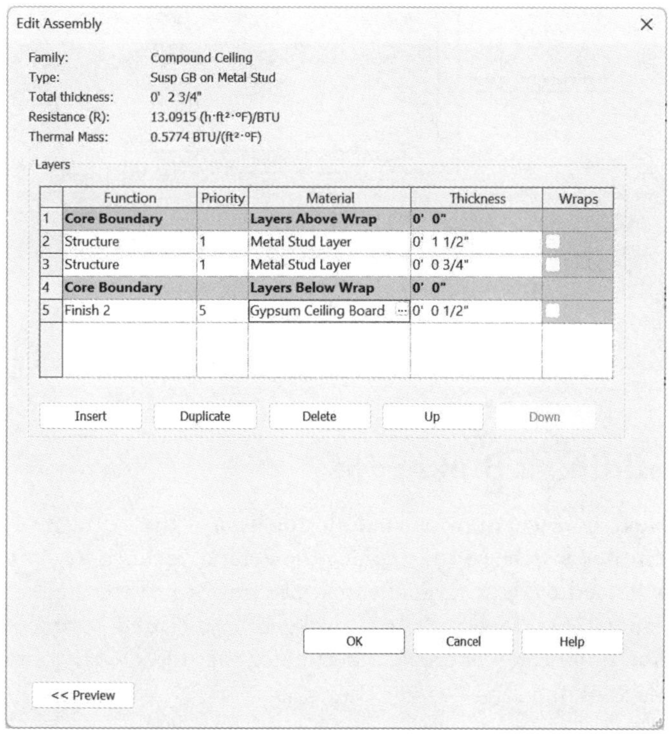

FIGURE 9-2.10 New ceiling – Edit assembly

30. Make sure **Susp GB on Metal Stud** is selected in the *Type Selector* on the *Properties Palette.*

31. Set the ceiling height to **7′-0″**.

32. Pick the lower left room as shown in **Figure 9-2.11**. If you don't see the ceiling, you may have forgotten to change the material to *Gypsum Ceiling Board* back in step 28.

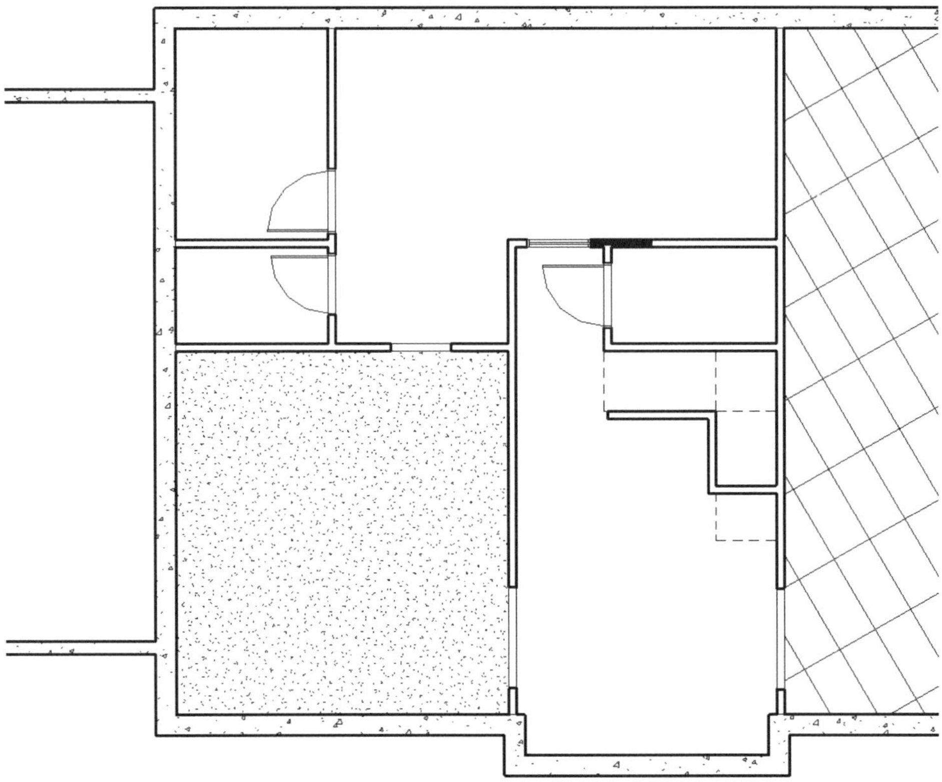

FIGURE 9-2.11 Gyp. Bd. Ceiling added

You now have a gypsum board ceiling at 7′-0″ above the basement floor slab.

Adding a Bulkhead:

Next, you will draw a ceiling in the area at the bottom of the steps. However, you cannot simply pick the room to place the ceiling because Revit would fill in the stair area. First, you will need to draw a bulkhead at the bottom of the steps. A bulkhead is a portion of wall that hangs from the floor above and creates a closed perimeter for a ceiling system to tie into. The bulkhead will create a perimeter that the *Ceiling* tool will detect for the proper ceiling placement.

33. While still in the *Basement Reflected Ceiling Plan* view, select the ***Wall*** tool.

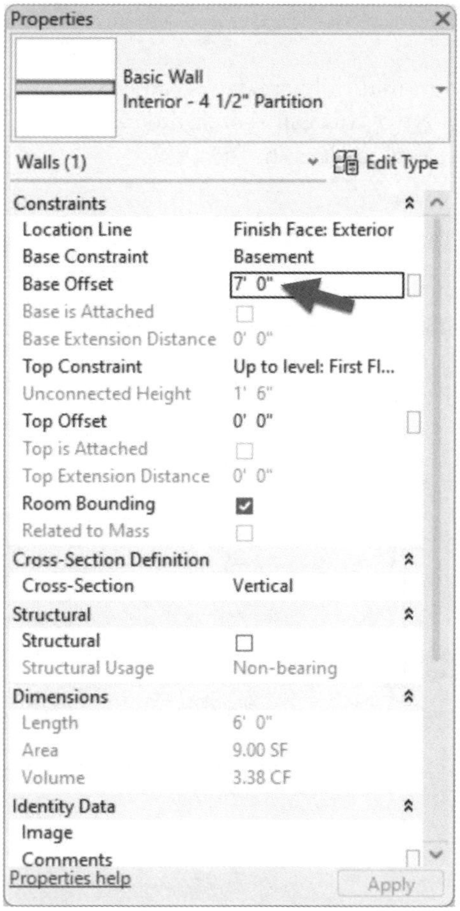

FIGURE 9-2.12 Bulkhead (wall) properties

34. Set the *Type Selector* to **Interior – 4 1/2″ Partition**.

35. In the *Properties Palette* set the *Base Offset* to **7′-0″** (Figure 9-2.12).

This will put the bottom of the wall at 7′-0″ above the current floor level, the basement in this case.

36. Set the *Top Constraint* to **Up to level: First Floor** (Figure 9-2.12).

    IMPORTANT TIP: The next time you draw a wall you will have to change the Base Offset back to 0′-0″ or your wall will be 7′-0″ off the floor; this can be hard to remember!

37. **Draw the bulkhead**; make sure you snap to the adjacent walls (Figure 9-2.13).

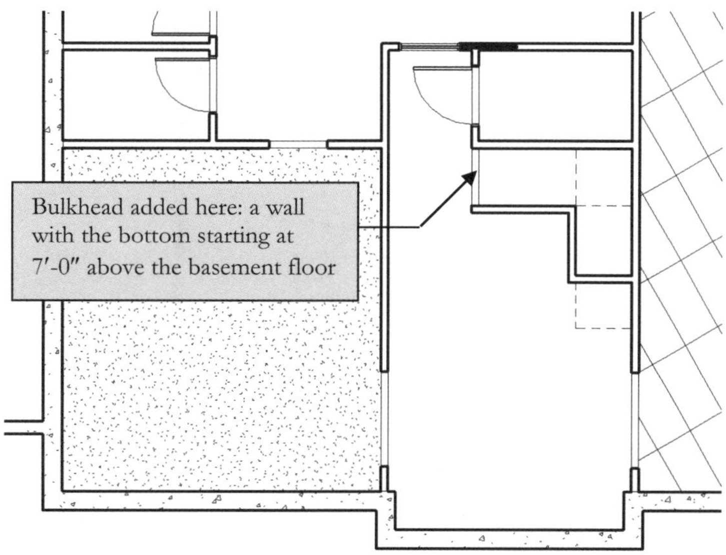

FIGURE 9-2.13 Bulkhead drawn

38. Select the ***Ceiling*** tool.

You could just pick within this room and Revit would automatically create a ceiling; however, you will look at another way to place a ceiling. Next you will sketch the perimeter of the ceiling, just like you did for the floor slabs in the previous lesson.

39. Select ***Sketch Ceiling*** from the *Ribbon*.

40. Sketch a line around the perimeter of the room using *Snaps* (Figure 9-2.14). Settings should be *Susp GB* ceiling at 7'-0".

TIP: Remember to use the Chain option.

41. Click the **green check mark** to finish the sketch.

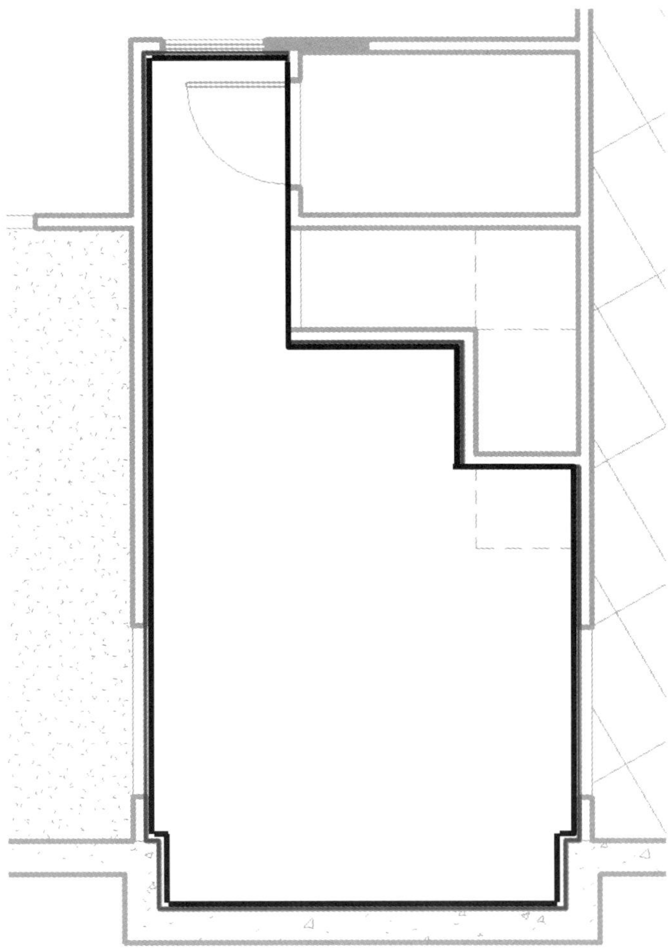

FIGURE 9-2.14 Sketching Ceiling

Your ceiling should look like Figure 9-2.15. You will see what is happening here a little better in the chapter on wall and building sections.

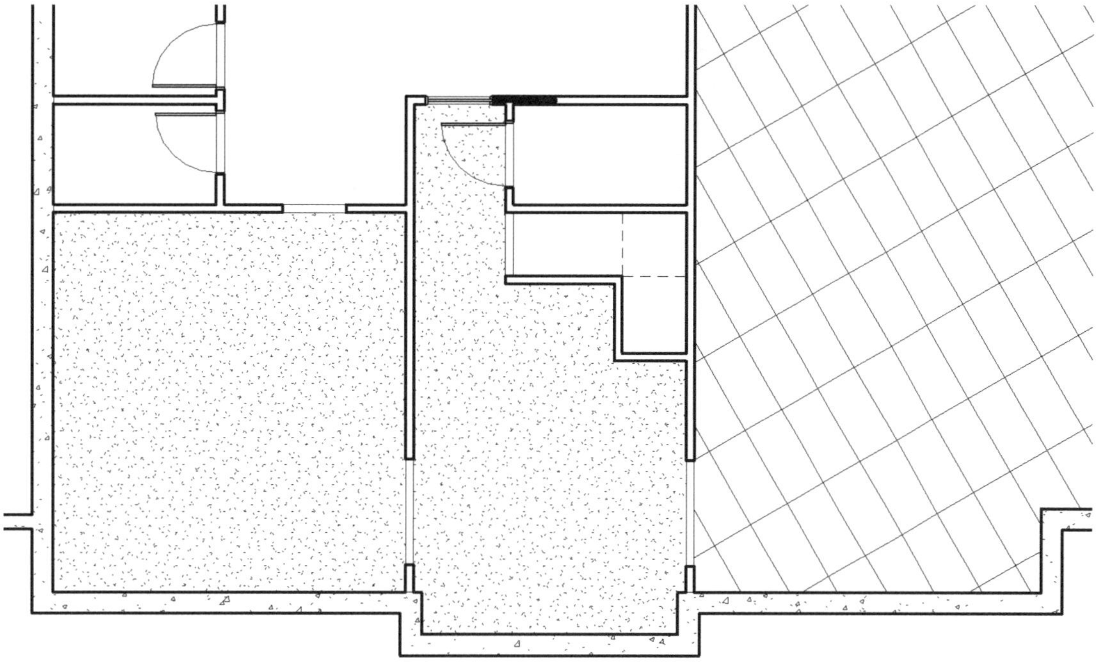

FIGURE 9-2.15 Ceiling added at bottom of steps

Modifying a Floor System to Include the Ceiling:

Next, you will modify the second floor system already in place to have gypsum board attached to the bottom of the joists. This is what is typically done in a residence, unless room is needed above the ceiling for ductwork.

42. Switch to the ***Second Floor Plan*** view (not the ceiling plan).

43. Select the floor.

    TIP: Clicking near the stair opening may be the easiest way to select the floor.

44. Via *Edit Type*, create a *Duplicate* floor from the one selected; name it **Wood Joist 14" – Wood Finish – Gyp Bd Ceiling**.

45. Edit the floor structure via *Type Properties* (Figure 9-2.16).
    a. Insert a new *Layer* at the bottom of the floor assembly
    b. Set the *Function* to **Finish 1**
    c. Priority: **4**
    d. Set the *Material* to **Gypsum Ceiling Board**
    e. Set the *Thickness* to **½"**

Why Did You Create a New Floor Type?

You needed to create a new floor type for the second floor because the first floor does not need gypsum board on the underside. When you modify a *family type*, all instances of that type are changed throughout the project. This is very powerful when you actually want to change several instances of a type. However, if you modify a type and only want the selected one to change, you are in for a big surprise when you look at the other instances of that type elsewhere in your project because they will all have changed. That is why you had to create a new floor type because that same floor type is also placed on the first floor.

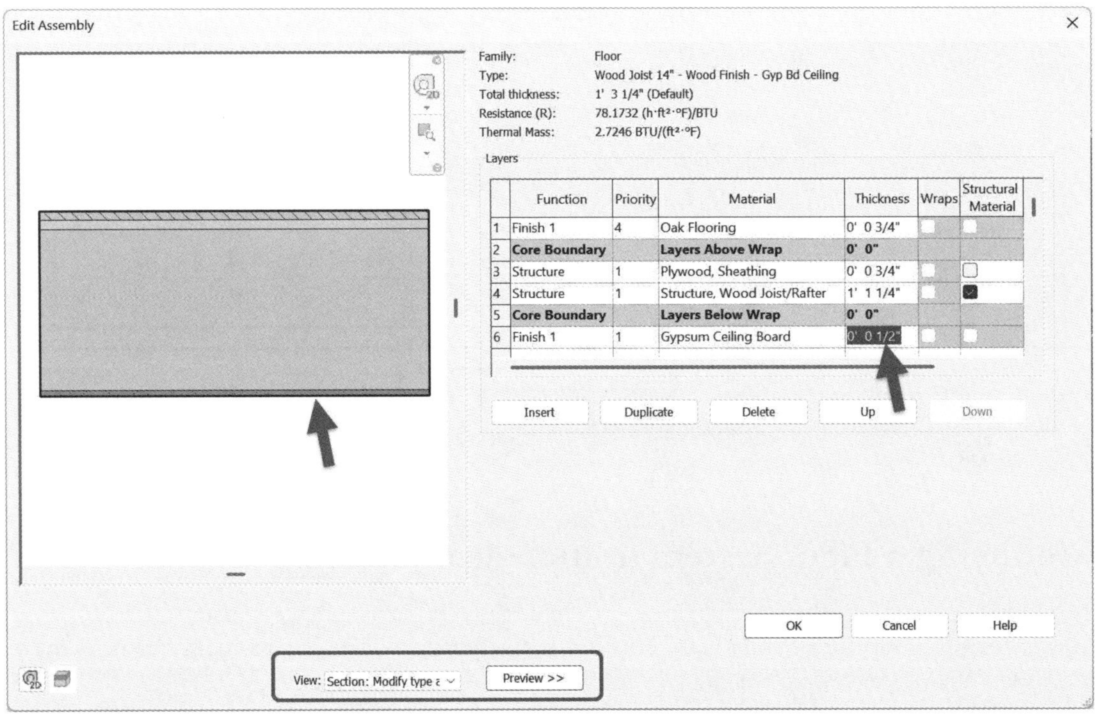

FIGURE 9-2.16 Floor system modified to include ceiling

46. Click **OK** twice to close the open dialog boxes.

Now switch to the ***First Floor Ceiling Plan*** (Figure 9-2.17) and notice that the gypsum ceiling board surface pattern is showing everywhere the floor occurs. If not, make sure the second floor system has been changed to the new type. That takes care of the ceiling for the first floor.

47. Switch to the ***Second Floor Ceiling Plan*** and add your **Susp GB on Metal Stud** at 8′-0″ high to the remaining rooms (Figure 9-2.18).

    FYI: *Once a ceiling is placed, you can select it and click* Edit Boundary *on the Ribbon. Then you can change the perimeter or add an enclosed area within the main perimeter to create a hole. This is how you would accommodate the skylights in the roof: by adding holes to the ceiling to let the light in.*

48. **Save** your project as **ex9-2.rvt**.

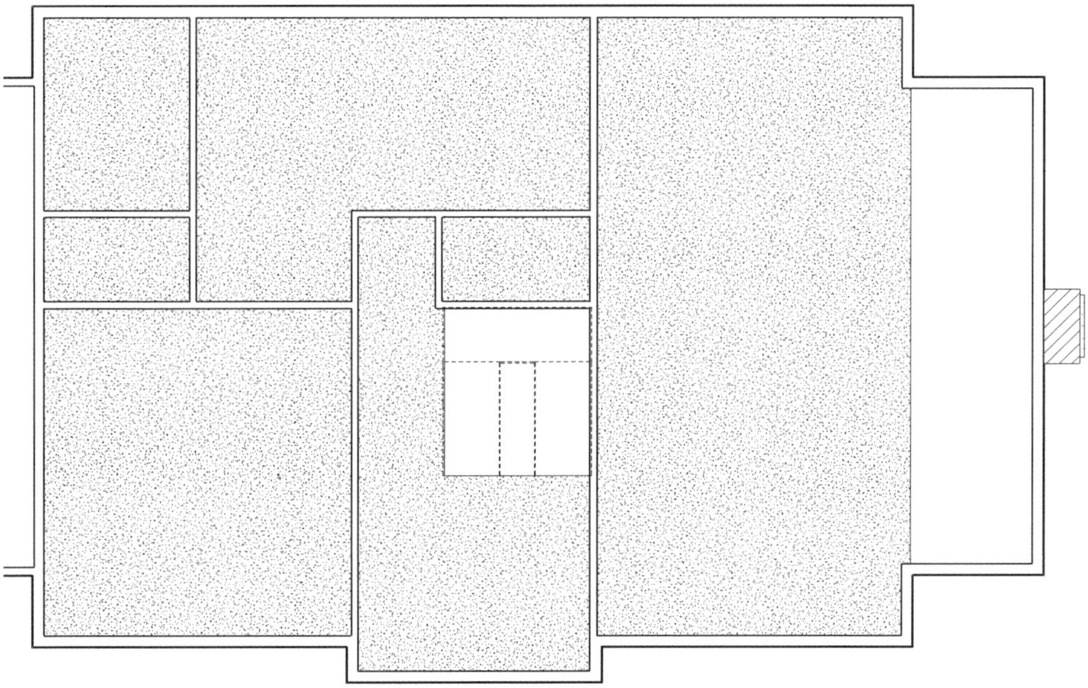

FIGURE 9-2.17 First floor ceiling plan: gypsum board added to bottom of floor structure

Real-Time Design Validation

Notice how the ceiling, which is a 3D object, covers the roof ridge line and skylights? This is very powerful because you can see all aspects of the design. If you can see ductwork in the view below, it means it was added to the model too low and needs to be raised or moved. Being able to see everything in context helps the designers validate their design solution. Also, not seeing the skylights is a problem. This means the light is being blocked by the ceiling and needs to be addressed. However, we will not be doing that in this tutorial.

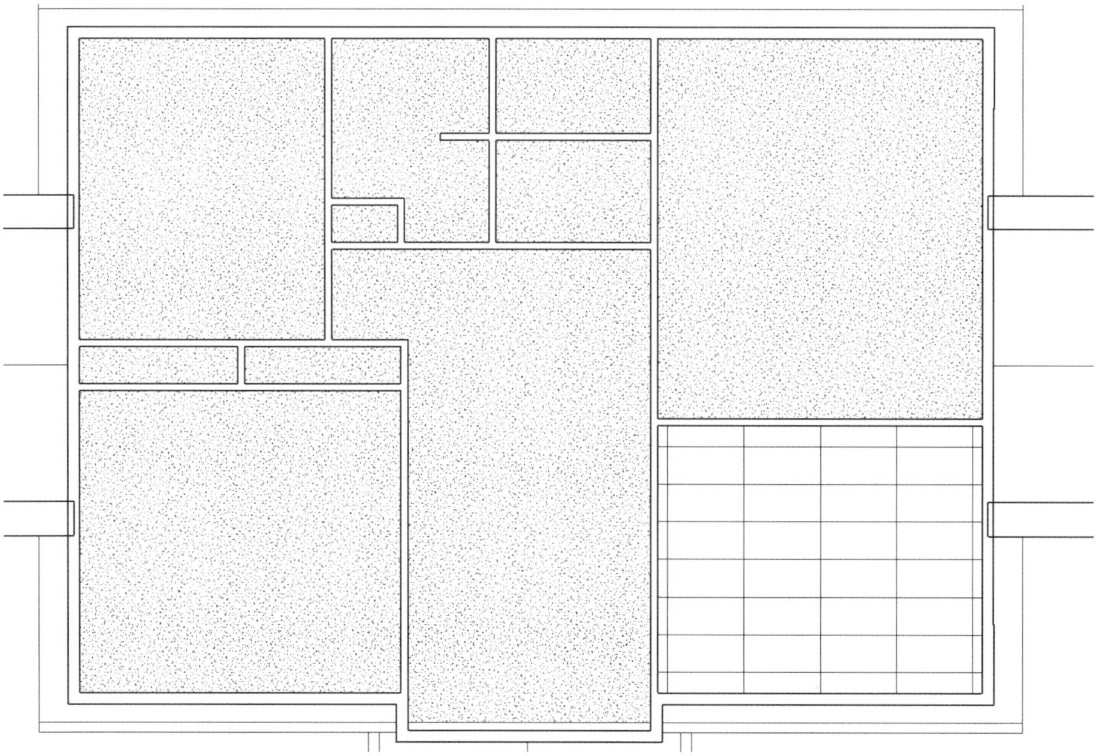

FIGURE 9-2.18 Second Floor Ceiling Plan: gypsum board ceiling system suspended at 8′-0″ AFF

Exercise 9-3:
Placing Light Fixtures

In this exercise, you will learn to load and place light fixtures in your reflected ceiling plans.

Loading Families:

Before placing fixtures, you need to load them into your project.

1. Open the **Second Floor** *Ceiling Plan,* if not already the current view.

2. Select **Insert → Load Autodesk Family** on the *Ribbon* (Figure 9-3.1).

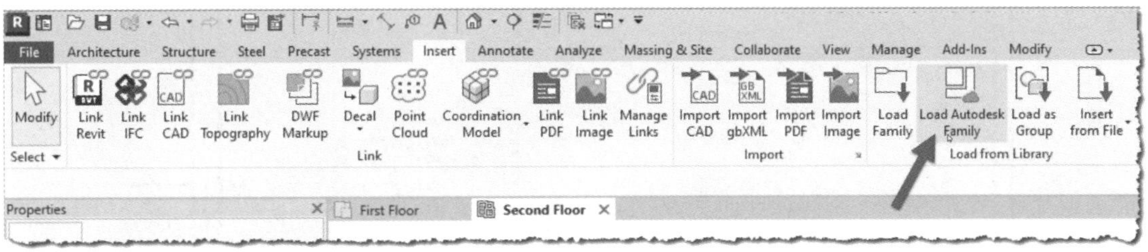

FIGURE 9-3.1 Load Autodesk Family tool on Insert tab

3. In the *Lighting\Architectural\Internal* category, select **Troffer Light - 2x4 Parabolic** and then click **Load** (Figure 9-3.2).

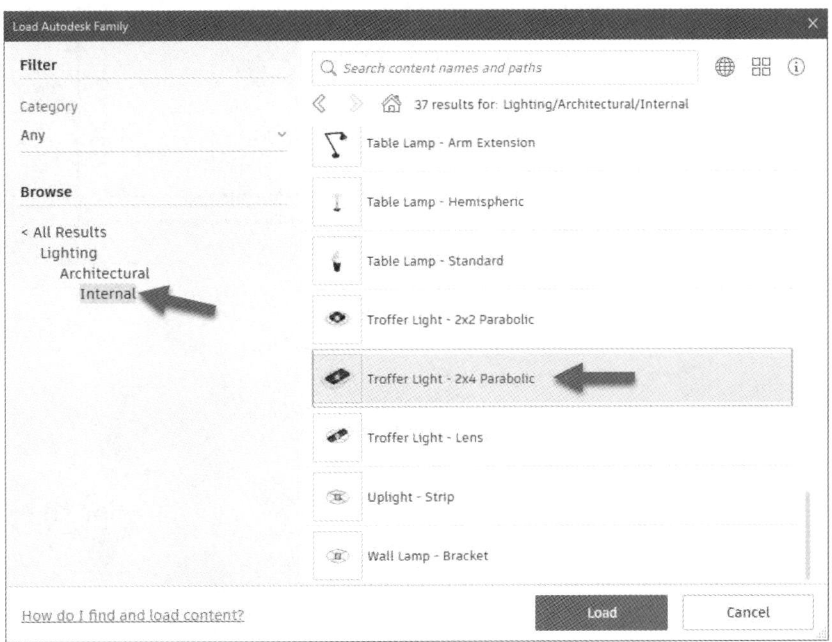

FIGURE 9-3.2 Load Autodesk Family tool

Placing Instances of Components:

You are now ready to place the fixtures in your ceiling plans.

4. Select **Lighting Fixture** from the *Systems* tab on the *Ribbon.* Pick **Troffer Light – 2′ x 4′ Parabolic: 2′x4′ (2 Lamp) – 120 V** from the *Type Selector* drop-down on the *Properties Palette.*

5. On the ***Second Floor Ceiling Plan*** view, place fixtures as shown in **Figure 9-3.3**.

   FYI: Adjust the ceiling grid position if needed.

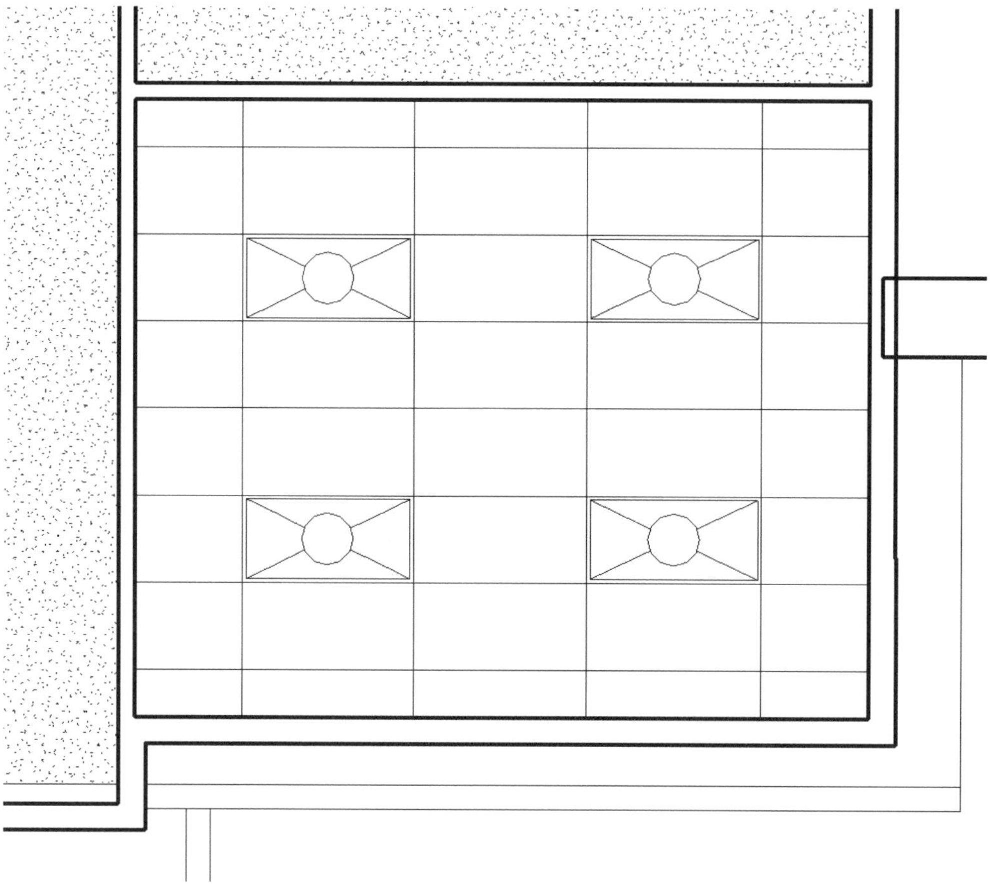

FIGURE 9-3.3 Light fixtures added to ceiling

You will need to use the Move command, or better yet, the *Align* tool, to move the fixture so it fits perfectly in the ACT grid.

6. Switch to the ***Basement Ceiling Plan*** view.

7. Now place another **2x4 light fixture** as shown in **Figure 9-3.4**.

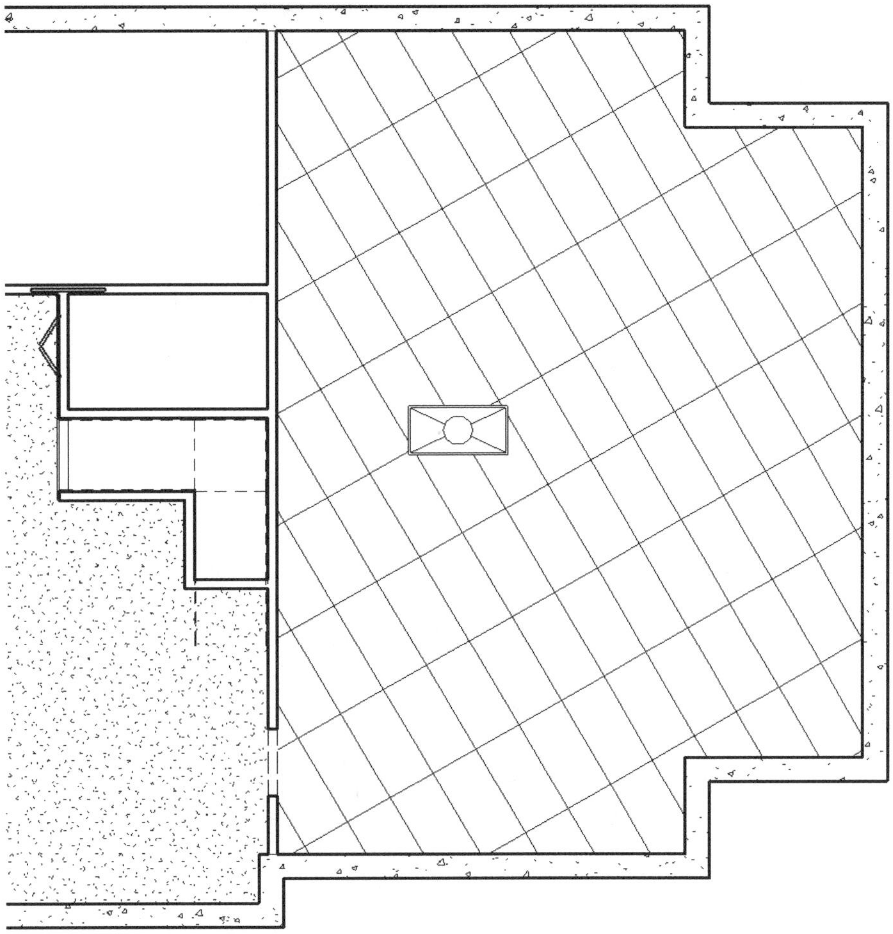

FIGURE 9-3.4 Basement ceiling plan; light fixture added

Notice the fixture does not automatically orient itself with the ceiling grid. There may be an occasion when you want this.

Also, notice the light fixture hides a portion of the ceiling grid. This is nice because the grid does not extend through a light fixture.

8. Use ***Rotate*** and ***Move*** to rotate the fixture to align with the grid (Figure 9-3.5). The *Align* tool will also work.

TIP: You can use the normal Rotate *and* Move *tools in conjunction with the Snaps.*

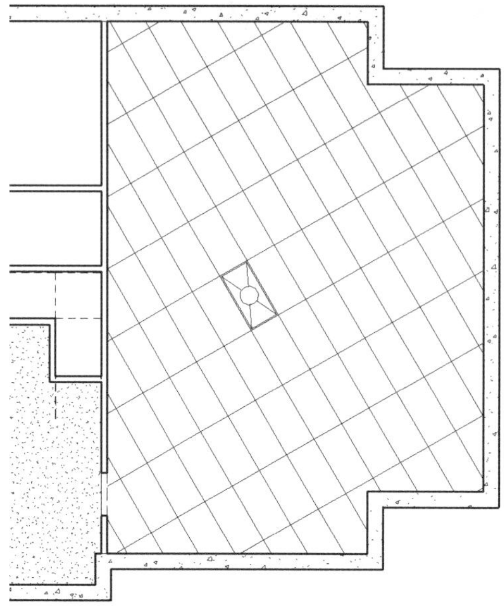

FIGURE 9-3.5 Basement Ceiling Plan; light fixture moved/rotated into place

9. Once you have one fixture rotated, it is easier to use the *Copy* tool and the *Snaps* to add rotated light fixtures. **Copy** the light fixture to match the layout in **Figure 9-3.6**. Reposition the grid as needed using the *Move* tool.

TIP: Activate Multiple *on the Ribbon when the Copy command is active.*

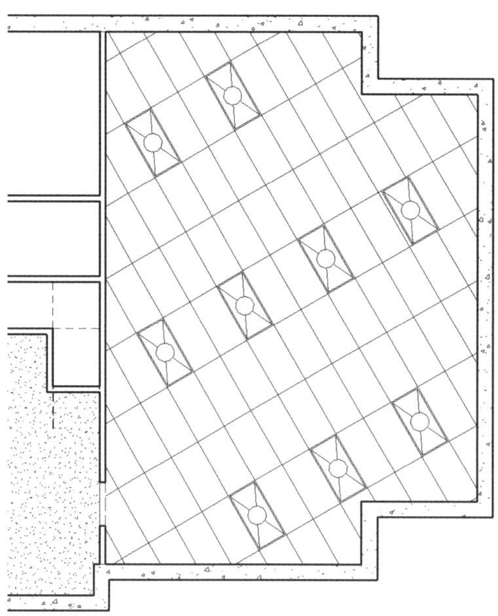

FIGURE 9-3.6 Basement Ceiling Plan; light fixture copied

10. **Save** your project as **ex9-3.rvt**.

These 2x4 light fixtures have *Rendering* settings already set up. That means the room will automatically have lights when you get to creating a photo-realistic rendering using this built-in feature!

The example image below shows a reflected ceiling plan with supply and return diffusers added. These are not used too often in residential work. They are loaded similarly to the light fixture via the component tool.

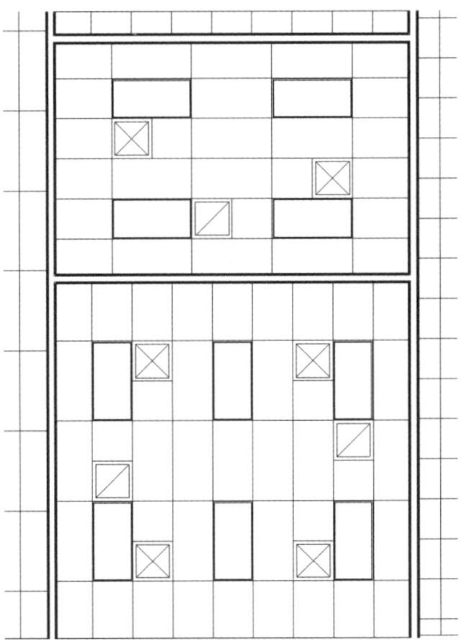

FIGURE 9-3.7 Example image; supply and return diffusers added

Reflected Ceiling Plan Symbols:

Revit provides many of the industry-standard content necessary for modeling reflected ceiling plans (RCP). As shown in Figure 9-3.7, supply air diffusers are represented by an X, and return air is represented by a diagonal line. It is typical to include an RCP symbol legend that shows each symbol and its material pattern, and lists what each represents. The *Legend* feature makes this a snap!

Component Properties

If you want to adjust the properties of a component, such as a light fixture, you can browse to it in the *Project Browser* and right-click on one of the *Types* listed. *Notice the right-click menu also has the option to select all instances of the item in the drawing.* Select *Properties.* You will see the dialog below for the 2x4 (2 lamps)-120V.

You can also click *Duplicate* and add more sizes (e.g., a 4′x4′ light fixture).

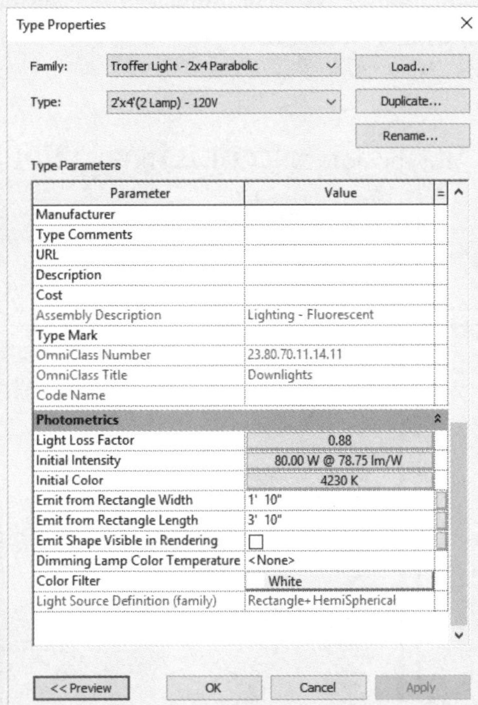

You can also select an inserted component and look at the *Properties Palette* for additional properties for that particular instance.

Exercise 9-4:
Annotations

This short section will look at adding notes to your RCP.

Adding Annotations:

1. In the ***Basement Reflected Ceiling Plan*** view, select the **Annotate → Text → Text** tool from the *Ribbon.*

2. Pick **Text: 3/32" Arial** from the *Type Selector* (Figure 9-4.1).

3. Select the **Leader** (Curved) button highlighted in **Figure 9-4.1**.

Next, you will add a note indicating that a room in the basement does not have a ceiling. First, you will draw a leader, and then Revit will allow you to type the text.

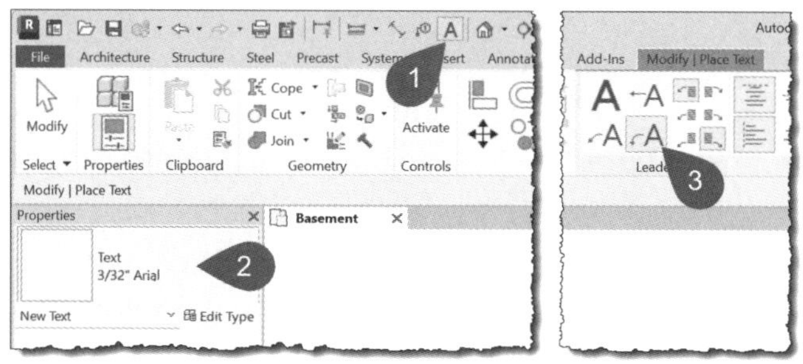

FIGURE 9-4.1 Text; Ribbon options

4. Add the note "**NO CEILING - TYPICAL**" shown in **Figure 9-4.2**.

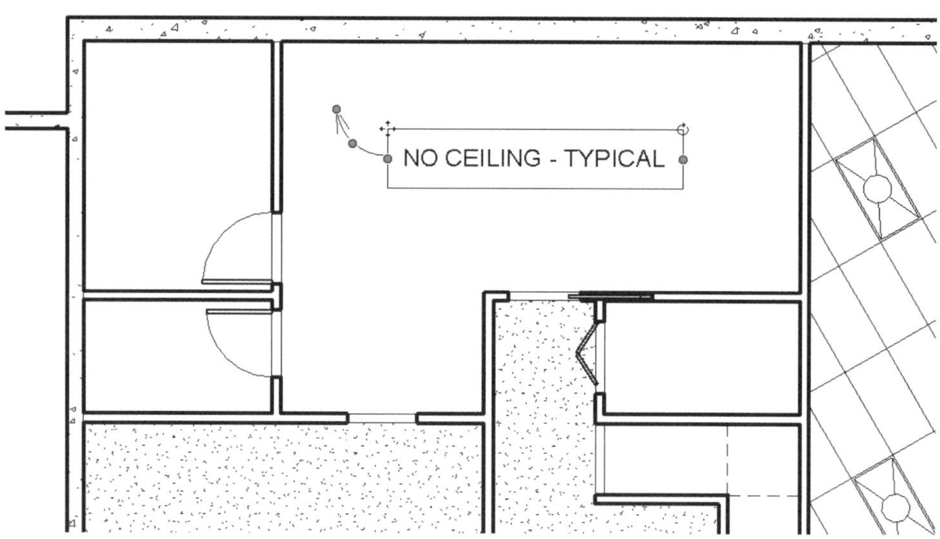

FIGURE 9-4.2 Text with Curved leader

Notice that immediately after adding the text or while it is selected, you see the *Move* icon, the *Rotate* icon, and *Grips* to edit the arrow/leader.

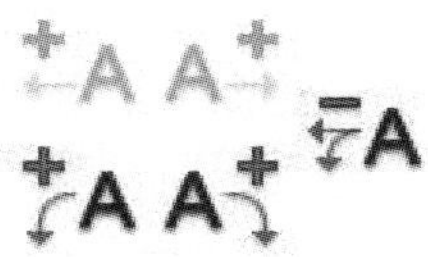

When the text is selected, you can click the "add leader" options on the *Ribbon* (shown on the left above) to add additional leaders.

Adding Text Styles to Your Project:

You can add additional text styles to your project. Some firms prefer a font with a hand-lettering look, while others prefer something like Arial. These preferences can be saved in the template file to ensure consistency and availability (assuming the font is installed on each computer). Next, you will add a new style to your Revit project.

5. Click on the ***Text*** tool.

6. Next, click **Edit Type** in the *Properties Palette.*

7. Select **Duplicate** and enter **1/4″ OUTLINE TEXT** (Figure 9-4.3).

8. Next, make the following adjustments to the *Type Properties* (Figure 9-4.4).
    a. Text Font: **Swis721 BdOul BT**
    b. Text Size: **¼″**

NOTE: You can use any Windows True-Type font. If you do not have this font, select another that best matches (Figure 9-4.5).

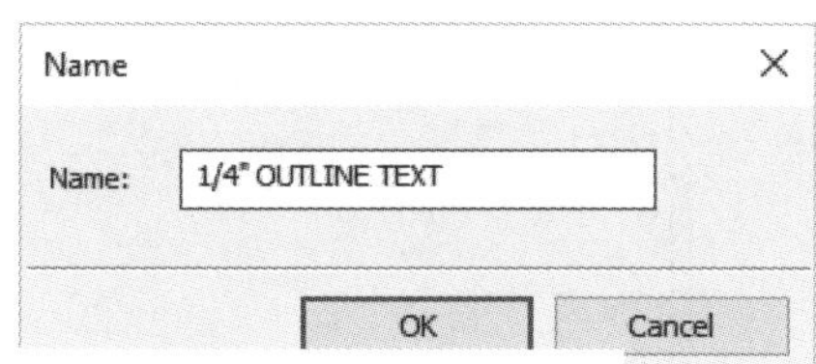

FIGURE 9-4.3 New text name

The text size you entered in Step 8 is the size of the text when printed. Revit automatically scales the text in each view, based on the *View Scale* setting. For example, if you add 3/32 text to a ⅛ floor plan view, the text will be 9″ tall. If you add text to a ¼″ plan view, the text will be 4½″ tall. When both the ¼″ and ⅛″ plan views are placed on a sheet, the text for each is 3/32″ tall. Here is what happens: adding text to the ¼″ plan causes the 3/32″ text to be scaled up 48 times, and when the plan view is placed on a *Sheet,* the entire view, including the text, is scaled down 1/48 times; thus, the text makes a full loop back to being 3/32″ tall.

If you change the *View Scale* of the drawing, the text size will automatically change, so the text is always the correct size when printing. It is best to set the drawing to the correct scale first, as changing the *View Scale* can require a lot of work, repositioning resized text that may overlap something or be too big for a room.

9. Select **OK** to close the open dialog.

You should now have the new text style available in the *Element Type Selector* on the *Ribbon*.

10. Use the new text style to create the text shown below (Figure 9-4.5).

    TIP: *Select the text only option on the Ribbon – i.e., No Leader.*

When typing text, you simply click somewhere in the view to complete the text string; pressing *Enter* just adds more lines.

11. Save as **ex9-4.rvt**.

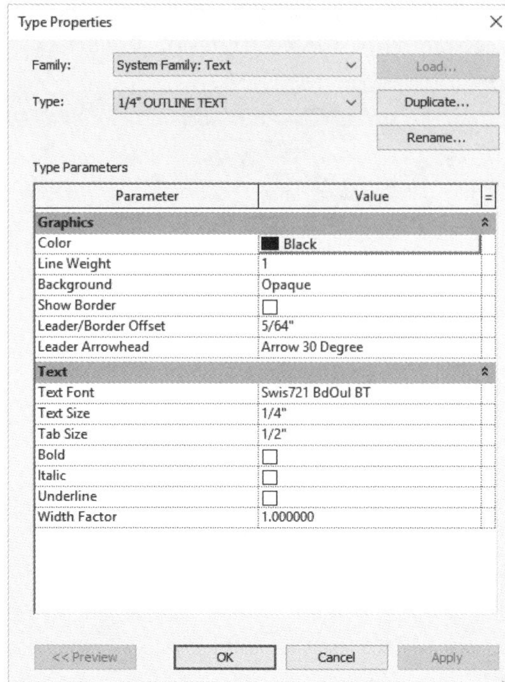

FIGURE 9-4.4 New text properties

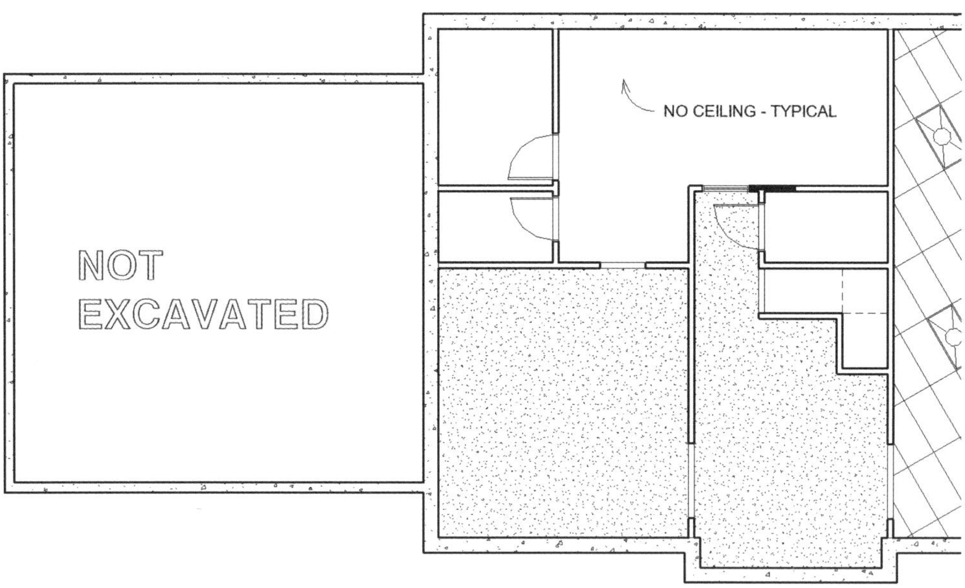

FIGURE 9-4.5 New text style added

Self-Exam:

The following questions can be used as a way to check your knowledge of this lesson. The answers can be found at the bottom of the page.

1. You must pick walls to define floor areas. (T/F)
2. Use the Ctrl key to cycle through the selection options. (T/F)
3. When you add a floor element in plan view, the floor does not show up right away in the other views, i.e., 3D, Sections, etc. (T/F)
4. You use the ________________ feature if you need to add a new product, like exterior plaster, so you can add it to wall types and other systems.
5. You have ______ different types of leader options with the *Text* tool (not including the 6 leader location icons).

Review Questions:

The following questions may be assigned by your instructor as a way to assess your knowledge of this section. Your instructor has the answers to the review questions.

1. It is not possible to create new text styles. (T/F)
2. You can add additional light fixture sizes to the family as required. (T/F)
3. The light fixtures automatically turn to align with the ceiling grid. (T/F)
4. You can adjust the ceiling height room by room. (T/F)
5. Revit allows you to model bulkheads by adjusting the bottom position of the wall. (T/F)
6. You can use any Windows True Type font in Revit. (T/F)
7. Use the ____________________ tool if the ceiling grid needs to be at an angle.
8. Use the ____________________ tool to adjust the ceiling grid location if a ceiling tile is less than half its normal size.
9. Use the ________________________ tool to adjust whether an element's surface pattern is displayed (i.e., the stipple for the gypsum board ceiling).
10. What is the current size of your project (after completing exercise 9-4)?

    __________________________ MB.

SELF-EXAM ANSWERS:
1 – F, **2** – F, **3** – F, **4** – Material, **5** – 4

Notes:

Lesson 10
ELEVATIONS:

This lesson will cover interior and exterior elevations. The default template you started with already has the four main exterior elevations set up. You will investigate how Autodesk® Revit® generates elevations and the role the elevation tag plays in that process.

Exercise 10-1:
Creating and Viewing Exterior Elevations

Here, you will look at setting up an exterior elevation and how to control various options.

Setting up an Exterior Elevation:

Even though you already have the main exterior elevations set, you will go through the steps to set one up. Many projects have more than four exterior elevations, so all exterior surfaces are elevated.

1. Open your project, ex9-4.rvt, and **Save As ex10-1.rvt**.

2. Switch to your ***First Floor*** plan view.

3. Select **View → Create → Elevation** *(not the down-arrow)*.

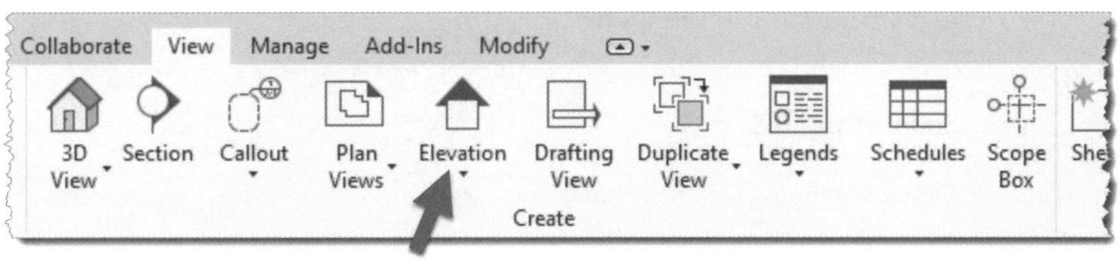

4. Make sure the *Type Selector* is set to *Elevation:* **Building Elevation** and then place the elevation tag in plan view as shown in Figure 10-1.1.

   NOTE: As you move the cursor around the screen, before clicking to place it, the Elevation Tag automatically turns to point at the building.

You now have an elevation added to the *Project Browser* in the *Elevations* section. **The first thing you should do after placing an elevation is rename it**; the default name is not very descriptive. These generic names would get very confusing on larger projects with dozens of views and several people working in the model.

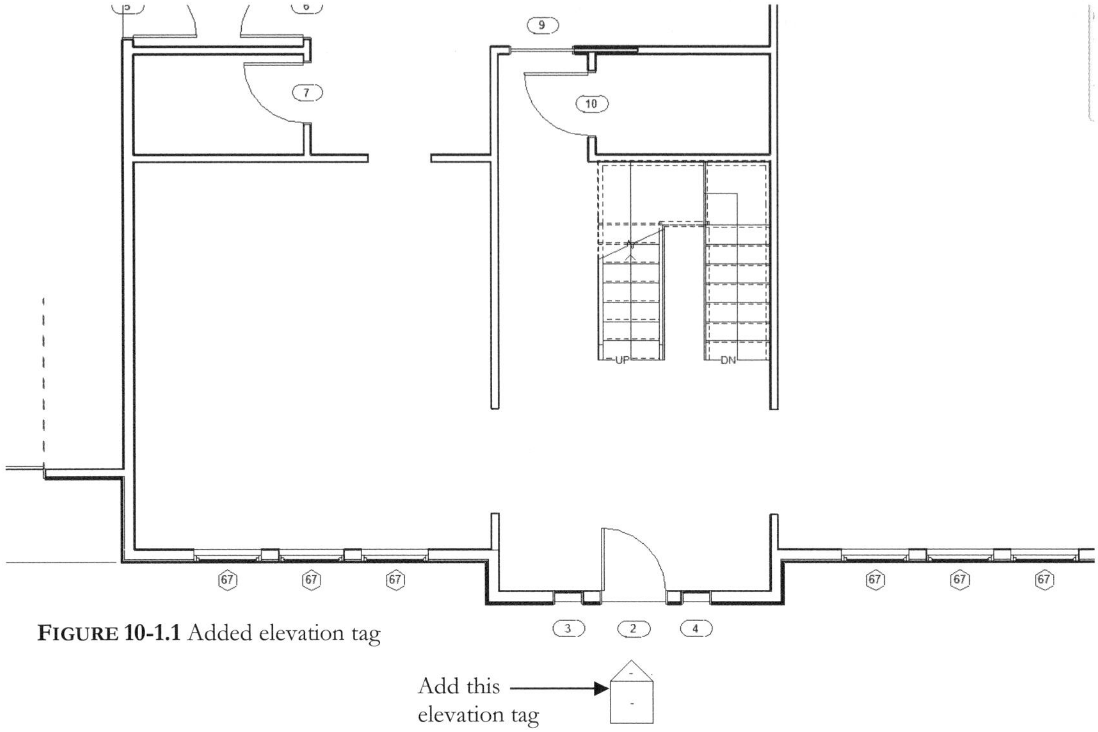

FIGURE 10-1.1 Added elevation tag

After placing an elevation tag, you should rename the elevation view in the project browser.

5. **Right-click** on the new view name, in the *Project Browser*, and select **Rename** (Figure 10-1.2).

6. Type: **South – Main Entry**.

The name should be descriptive so you can tell where the elevation is just by the name in the *Project Browser.*

7. Double-click on **South –Main Entry** in the *Project Browser.*

The elevation may not look correct right away (Figure 10-1.3). You will adjust this in the next step. Notice, though, that an elevation was created simply by placing an *Elevation Tag* in plan view.

8. Switch back to the ***First Floor Plan*** view.

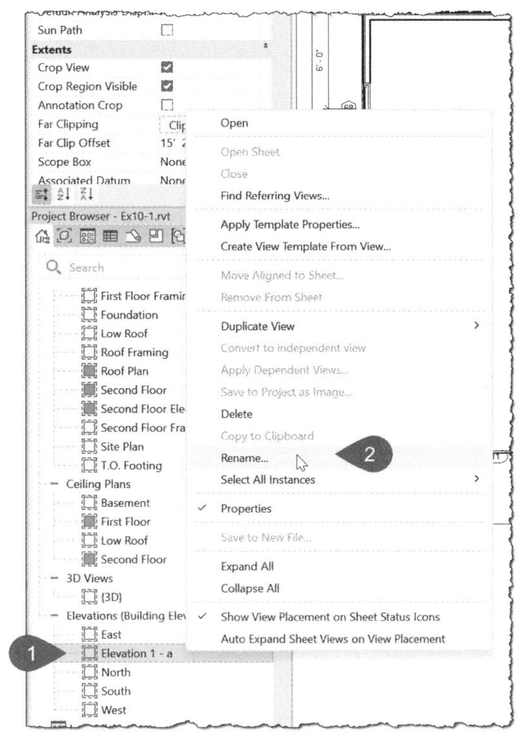

FIGURE 10-1.2 Renaming new view

FIGURE 10-1.3 Initial elevation view

Next, you will study the options associated with the elevation tag. This, in part, controls what is seen in the elevation.

9. The elevation tag has two parts: the pointing triangle and the square center. Each part will highlight as you move the cursor over it. **Select the square center part.**

You should now see the symbol shown on the right.

View direction boxes:
The checked box indicates the direction the elevation tag is looking. You can check or uncheck the other boxes. Do NOT do that at this time. Each checked box adds another view name to the *Project Browser*.

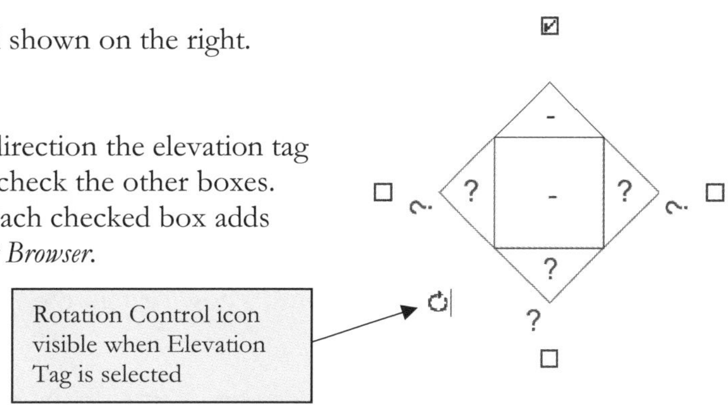

Rotation Control:
Clicking and dragging on this allows you to view a wall at right angles to it in plan, for example.

> **Interior Elevations:**
> When adding an interior elevation tag to the floor plan, you should select *Interior Elevation* from the *Type Selector*. This will use a different symbol to help distinguish the interior tags from the exterior tags in the plan views. Also, the interior and exterior views are separated in the *Project Browser*, making it easier to manage views as the project continues to develop.

10. Press the **ESC** key to unselect the elevation tag.

11. Select the "pointing" portion of the elevation tag.

Your elevation tag should look similar to Figure 10-1.4.

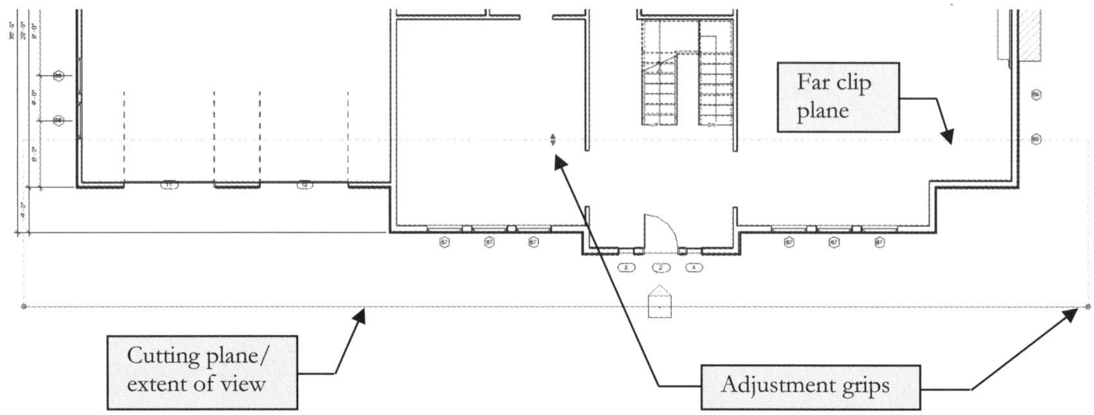

FIGURE 10-1.4 Selected elevation tag

The elevation tag, as selected in Figure 10-1.4, has several features for controlling how the elevation looks. Here is a quick explanation:

- **Cutting plane/extent of view line:** This controls how much of the 3D model is elevated from left to right (i.e., the width of the elevation).
- **Far clip plane:** This controls how far into the 3D model the elevation view can see.
- **Adjustment grips:** You can drag this with the mouse to control the features mentioned above.

Next, you will take a look at the new elevation's *View Properties*. You can do this in one of the following ways:

a. Select the "pointing" portion of the elevation tag (which should currently be selected based on the previous step).

b. Select the view label (South – Main Entry in this example) in the *Project Browser.*

c. Open the view and look at the *Properties Palette* while nothing in the model is selected.

You have several options in the *Properties Palette* (Figure 10-1.5). Notice the three options with check boxes next to them; these control the following:

- **Crop View**: This crops the width and height of the view in elevation.
  Adjusting the width of the cropping window in elevation also adjusts the "extent of view" control in plan view.

- **Crop Region Visible**: This displays a rectangle in the elevation view indicating the extent of the cropping window, described above.
  When selected in elevation view, the rectangle can be adjusted with the adjustment grips.

- **Far Clipping**: If this is turned off, Revit will draw everything visible in the 3D model, *within the "extent of view."*

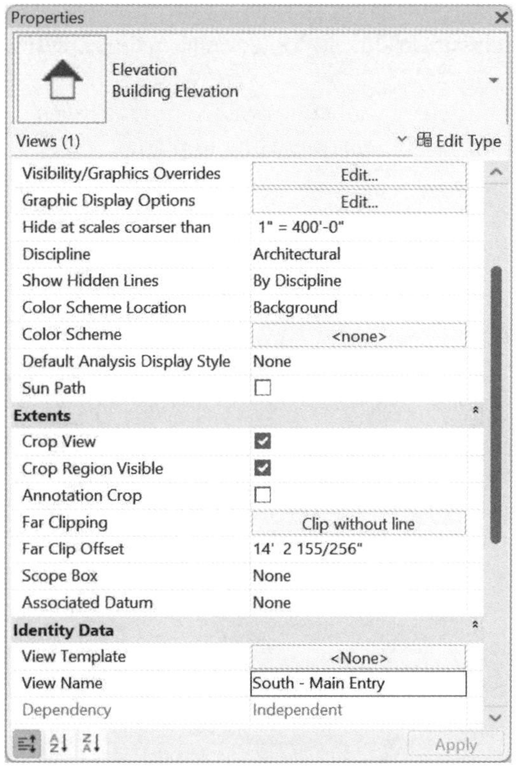

FIGURE 10-1.5 South – Main Entry view properties

You will manipulate some of these controls next.

12. With the elevation tag still selected (as in Figure 10-1.4), drag the "cutting plane/ extent of view" line up **into** the main entry as shown in Figure 10-1.6.

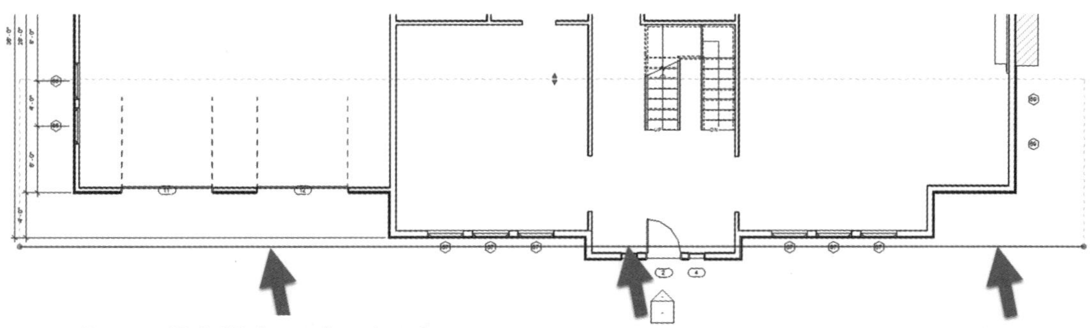

FIGURE 10-1.6 Relocated cutting plane

13. Now switch to the elevation view ***South – Main Entry***. Adjust the **Crop Region** so the entire roof is visible; click the *Crop Region* to select it and drag the top grip upward. ***FYI:*** The roof's ridge line will not be visible yet.

Your elevation should look similar to Figure 10-1.7.

The main entry wall and roof are now displayed in section because of the location of the elevation tag's *cutting plane* line in plan.

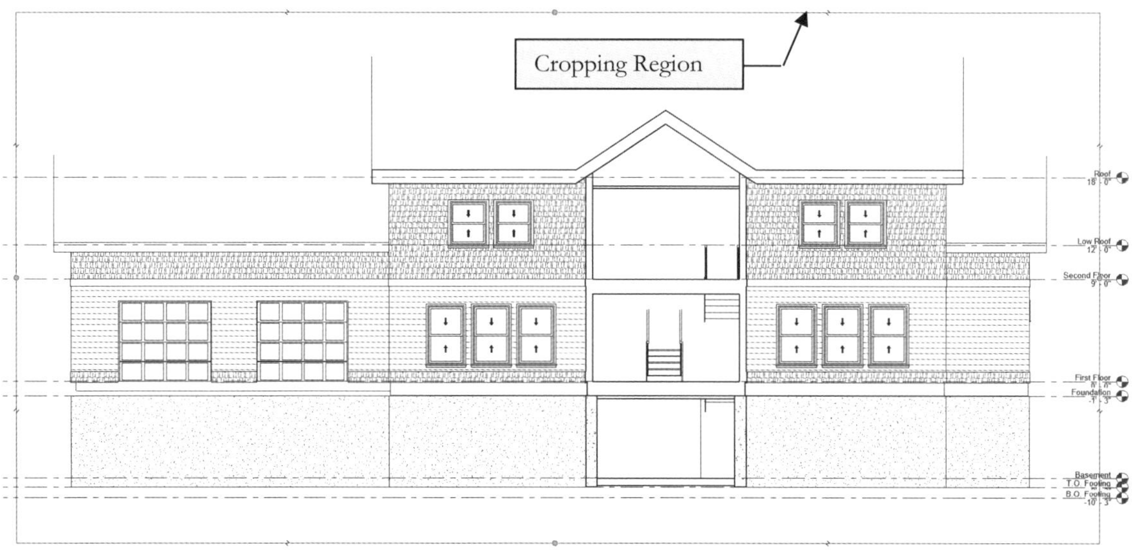

FIGURE 10-1.7 Elevation with cutting plane thru front entry

Notice that the roof is not fully visible. This is not related to the cropping window shown in Figure 10-1.7. Rather, it is related to the *Far Clip Plane* set in the plan view.

14. Adjust the *Far Clip Plane* in the ***First Floor*** *Plan* view so that the entire roof shows in the ***South – Main Entry*** view.

   TIP: *Click on the grip and drag the* Far Clip Plane *North until it is past the ridge line, which is at the middle of the building. You may need to adjust the crop region again.*

Now, when you switch back to the ***South – Main Entry*** elevation view, you should see the entire roof.

Next, you will adjust the elevation tag to set up a detail elevation for the main entry area.

15. In the ***First Floor Plan*** view, adjust the elevation tag to show only the main entry wall (Figure 10-1.8).
    - The cutting plane/extent of view line is moved South so it is outside of the building footprint.
    - Use the left and right grips to shorten the same line.

16. Switch to the ***South – Main Entry*** view to see the "detail" elevation you are setting up (Figure 10-1.9).

17. Set the ***View Scale*** to **½" = 1'-0"** on the *View Control Bar* at the bottom of the screen.

Notice how the *Level Datum* tags have changed to a smaller size. *Undo* and try it again if you missed it. You did notice the levels were automatically added, right?

18. Click the ***Hide Crop Region*** icon on the *View Control Bar* to make the *Crop Region* disappear.

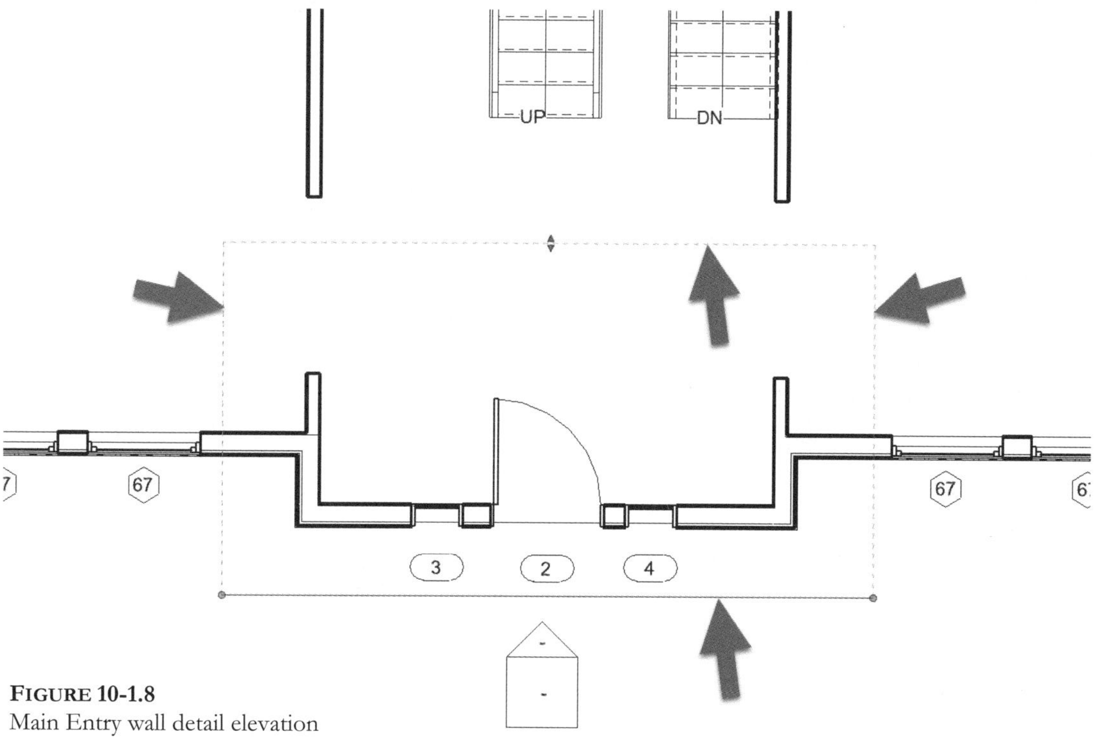

FIGURE 10-1.8
Main Entry wall detail elevation

Once you modify the view constraints in plan view (Figure 10-1.8) and you switch to the new elevation view, you can click on the *crop region* and use the grips to make the view wider. You might want to do this to make sure the roof overhang shows. Note that the Crop Region must be visible to make these edits.

When you drag the *crop region* to the right, the *Level Datum* tags move so they do not overlap the elevation. This is another example of Revit taking the busy work out of designing a residence!

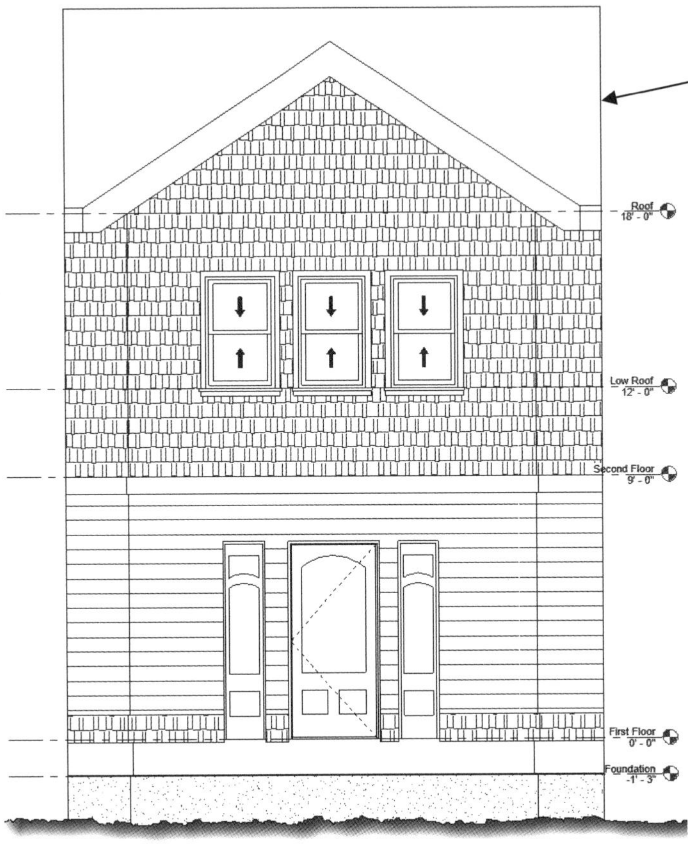

Crop region; visibility should be turned off in Step 18.

DETAIL ELEVATION:
A detail elevation like this might be used to dimension various items like the mail box, sign, special siding/ trim, etc. The scale would typically be larger than the full South elevation so you can fit more notes and dimensions.

This view might be placed on a sheet with the other elevations or any sheet where you can find room.

FIGURE 10-1.9 Main Entry wall detail elevation

Many designers like to change the line weight around portions of the building that protrude out from the main elevation. This helps the builder and the client read the drawings more easily. However, Revit does not do this automatically. It can be done manually using the **Linework** tool on the *Modify* tab. When the tool is active, you can select a line style from the *Ribbon*, then click lines in the model to override their default settings. These lines will adjust as the model is changed. Selecting **<by category>** for a line style, then clicking an overridden line, will set it back to its original state. Give it a try!

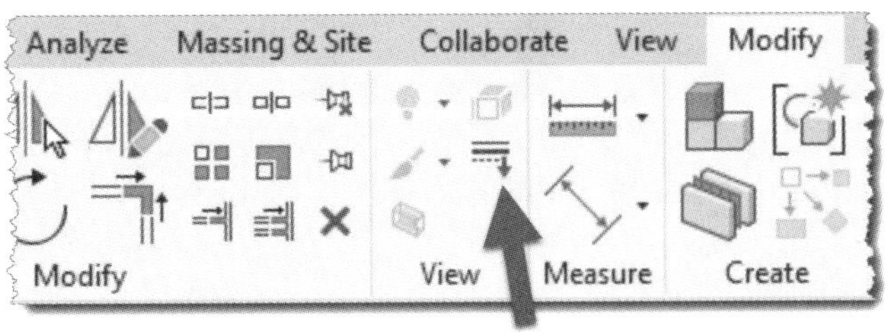

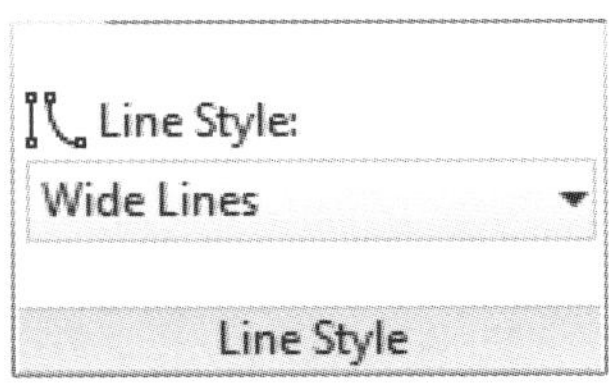

19. **Save** your project as **ex10-1.rvt**.

Exercise 10-2:
Modifying the Project Model: Exterior Elevations

The purpose of this exercise is to demonstrate that changes can be made anywhere, and all other drawings are automatically updated.

Modify an Exterior Elevation:

1. Open ex10-1.rvt and **Save As ex10-2**.

2. Open the ***West*** exterior elevation view. Adjust the start and end locations of the *Level Datum* lines to be closer to the edge of the building (Figure 10-2.1).

3. Using the **Ctrl** key, select the two double-hung windows on the right, two of the four windows in the garage wall.

You will delete the two selected windows and move the remaining two windows to the center of the wall.

4. Press the **Delete** key to erase the selected windows.

5. Select the remaining two windows and use the ***Move*** tool to approximately center them on the wall/roof ridge, keeping the vertical alignment unchanged (Figure 10-2.1). The next page will discuss how to center them more precisely.

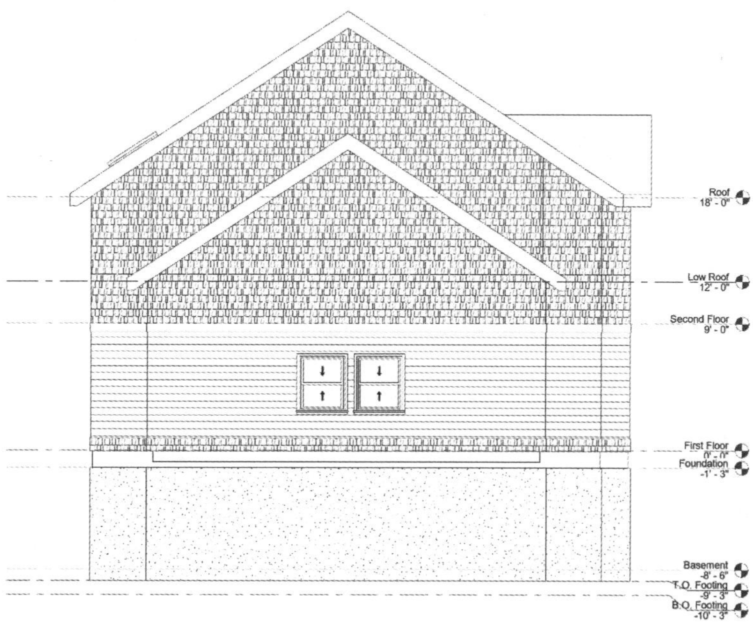

FIGURE 10-2.1 Modifying windows on the West elevation

Now you will switch to the *First Floor Plan* view to see your changes.

6. Switch to the ***First Floor*** plan view and zoom in on the garage area (Figure 10-2.2). Adjust the window position per the information mentioned below.

Notice how the windows in plan have changed to match the modifications you just made to the exterior elevations? This only makes sense, seeing as both the floor plan and the exterior elevation are projected 2D views of the same 3D model. Both views are directly manipulating the 3D model.

Also, notice that even the dimensions are adjusted! Revit is all about reducing drafting time and maximizing design time. Step 5 had you approximately locate the windows; now you can select the windows in plan and type the exact dimension you want; 12′-0″ centers them on the building.

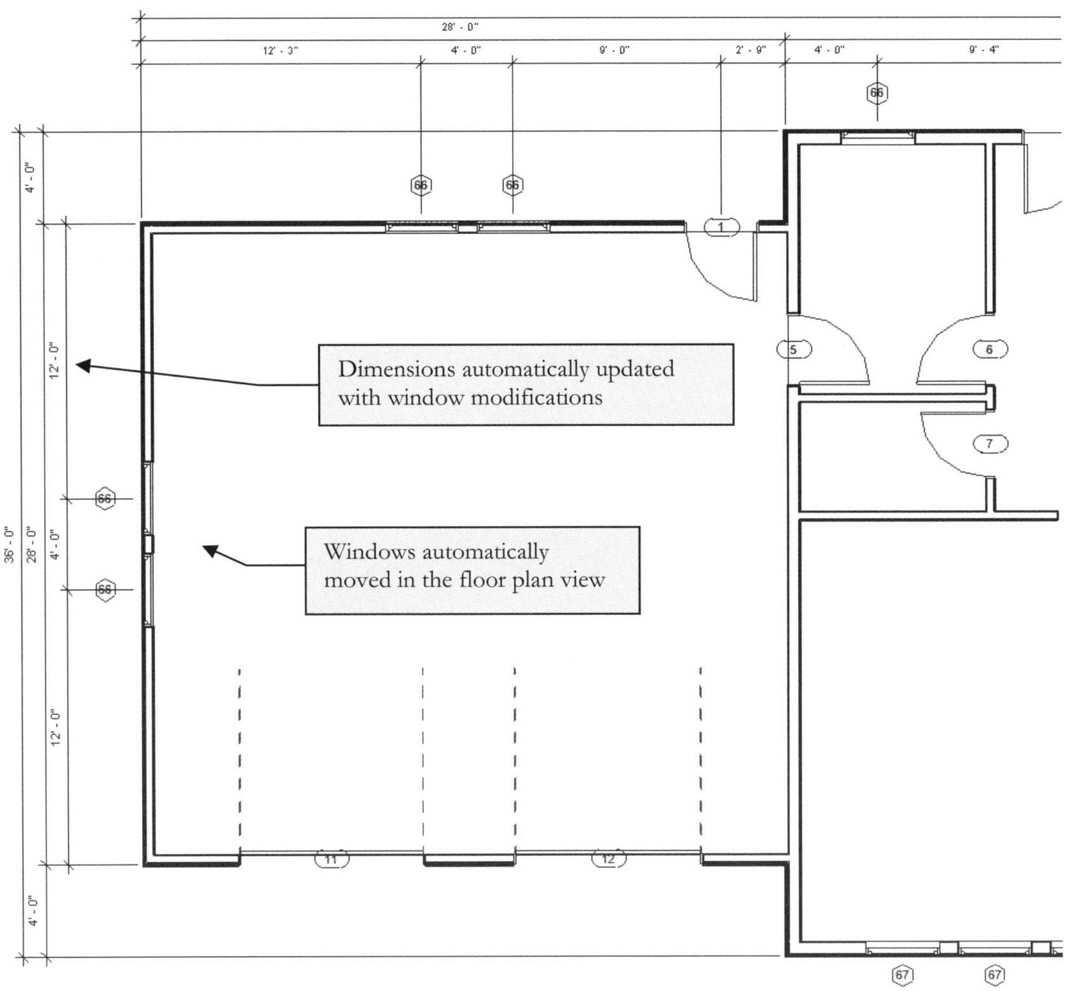

FIGURE 10-2.2 Changes automatically made to the floor plan

Next, you will insert a window in elevation. This will demonstrate, first, that you can actually add a window in elevation, not just in a plan view, and second, that the other views are automatically updated.

7. Switch to the ***North*** exterior elevation view.

8. Select the ***Window*** tool from the *Architecture* tab.

9. From the *Type Selector*, choose Window-*Double-Hung* : **38"x46"**.

Notice that, with the window selected for placement, you have the usual dimensions, which help you place the window accurately. As you move the window around, you should see a dashed horizontal cyan colored line indicating the default sill height, although you can deviate from this in elevation views.

10. Place a window approximately as shown in **Figure 10-2.3**.

    TIP: *The window should be about centered between the existing windows.*

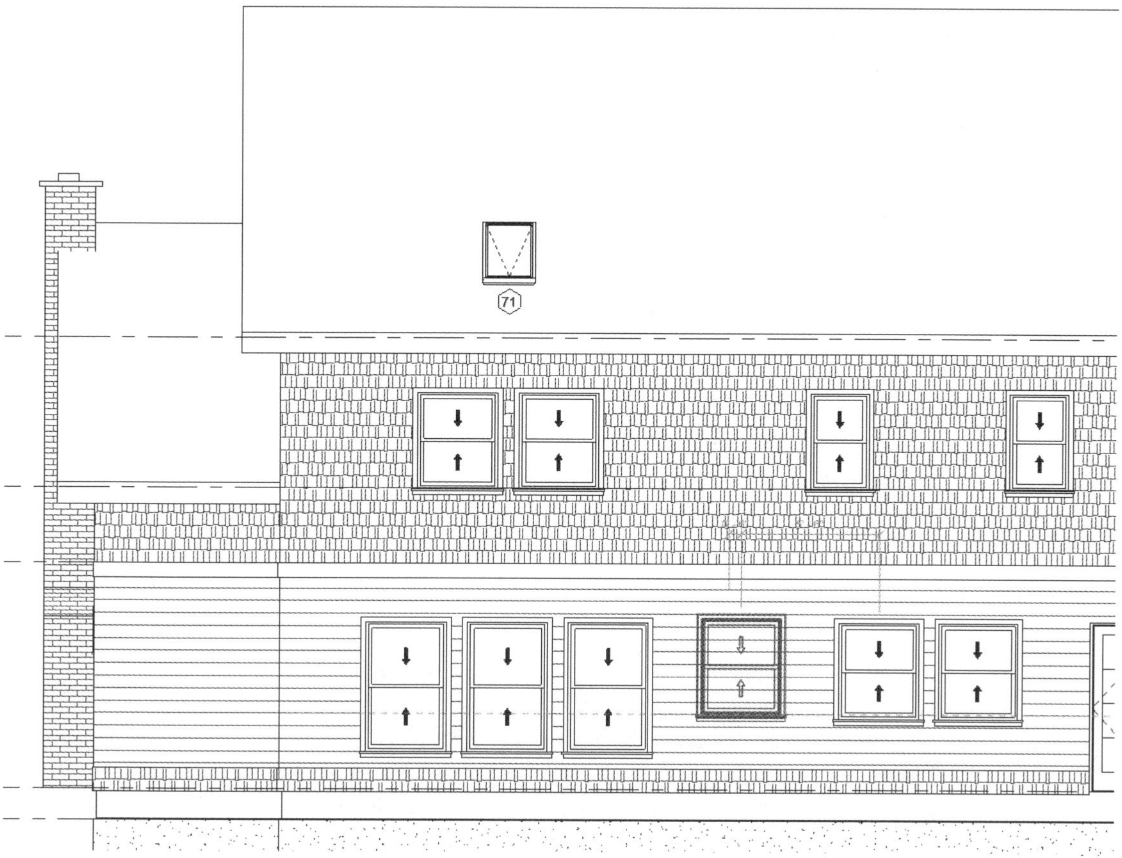

FIGURE 10-2.3 Placing a window on the North elevation

If you laid out the interior walls as described in Lesson 5, you should get a warning message when inserting the window. This is because the interior wall between the kitchen and the living room conflicts with the exterior window. Revit is programmed to see that conflict and bring it to your attention. You can ignore this error because it is possible to build a wall up to the center of a window; some Revit errors you cannot ignore because they will have a negative impact on Revit's functionality.

11. Click the "X" in the upper-right corner to ignore the wall/window conflict warning (Figure 10-2.4).

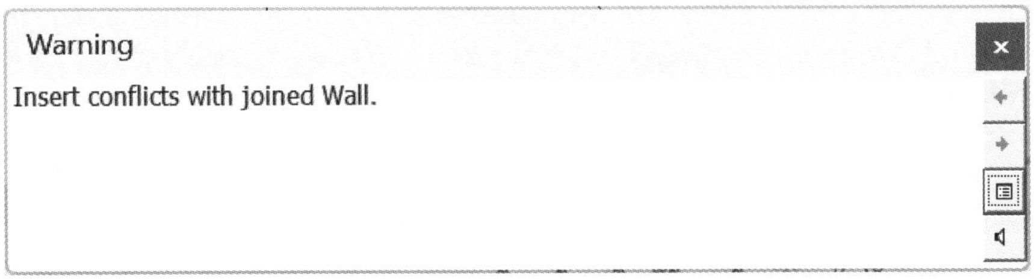

FIGURE 10-2.4 Conflict warning

12. Switch to the ***First Floor*** plan view to see the problem (Figure 10-2.5).

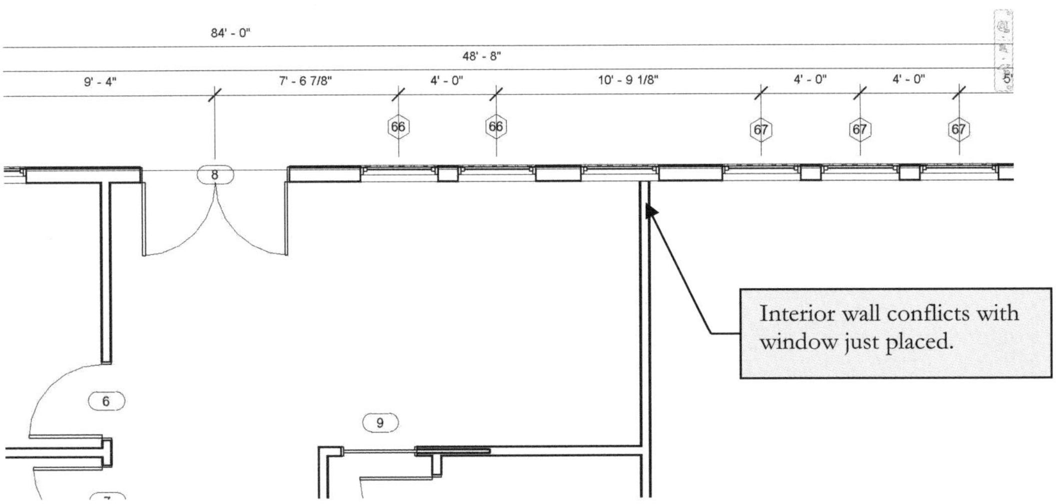

FIGURE 10-2.5 First Floor – kitchen area

13. While in plan view, select the new window and **Delete** it.

Why did the window location dimensions update in Figure 10-2.2 and not in Figure 10-2.5? The first had dimensions associated with the windows and the latter did not. When you dimension something in Revit, the witness lines "remember" what they are dimensioning to and move with that element. Also, notice how the window was tagged in elevation view, but not in plan view like the previously placed windows? The tag is only added in the view the element was placed in but can be manually tagged in any view (even multiple times).

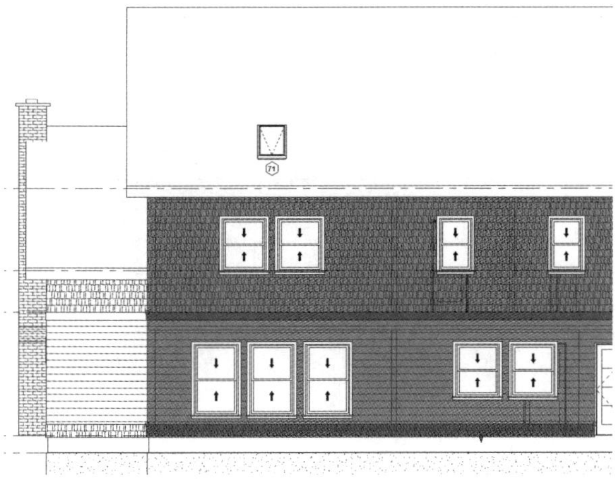

FIGURE 10-2.6 Transparent selections

TIP: When working in the exterior elevation view, you can quickly see where the interior walls are simply by selecting the exterior wall (Figure 10-2.6).

Whenever something is selected, it turns blue and becomes transparent. Thus, the things behind the element are temporarily visible.

Adding Shutters to the North Elevation:

Next you will add shutters to the North elevation. You will need to load a family from the content provided with this book.

14. Switch back to the ***North*** elevation view and notice that the new window is gone, per your plan change.
15. Switch to the ***Insert*** tab on the *Ribbon*.
16. Using *Load Family*, load **shutter (high-res)** from the provided online files. See the inside front cover of this book for instructions.
17. With the ***Component*** tool active and **Shutter (high-res): 18″ x 48″** selected in the *Type Selector*, place a shutter in elevation as shown in Figure 10-2.7 (upper-left window on North Elevation).

    TIP: If the shutter does not land in the correct spot, select it and use the arrow keys (on the keyboard) to nudge it into place, or use the Align tool per the tip below.

18. Use the same technique to place the remaining shutters shown in **Figure 10-2.8**.
19. Add shutters to the South elevation per **Figure 10-2.9**.

TIP: USING THE ALIGN TOOL
Don't forget about the Align *tool. Simply drop your shutter somewhere near the window and use the* Align *tool to move it into place. After placing the shutter, click* Align, *select the edge of the window, then select the edge of the shutter to move it into place. If the window moves, you picked in the wrong order – click* Undo *and try again. Also, immediately after you use* Align, *you can click the* Padlock *to maintain a parametric relationship, meaning if the window moves, even in a plan view, the shutters will move with it!*

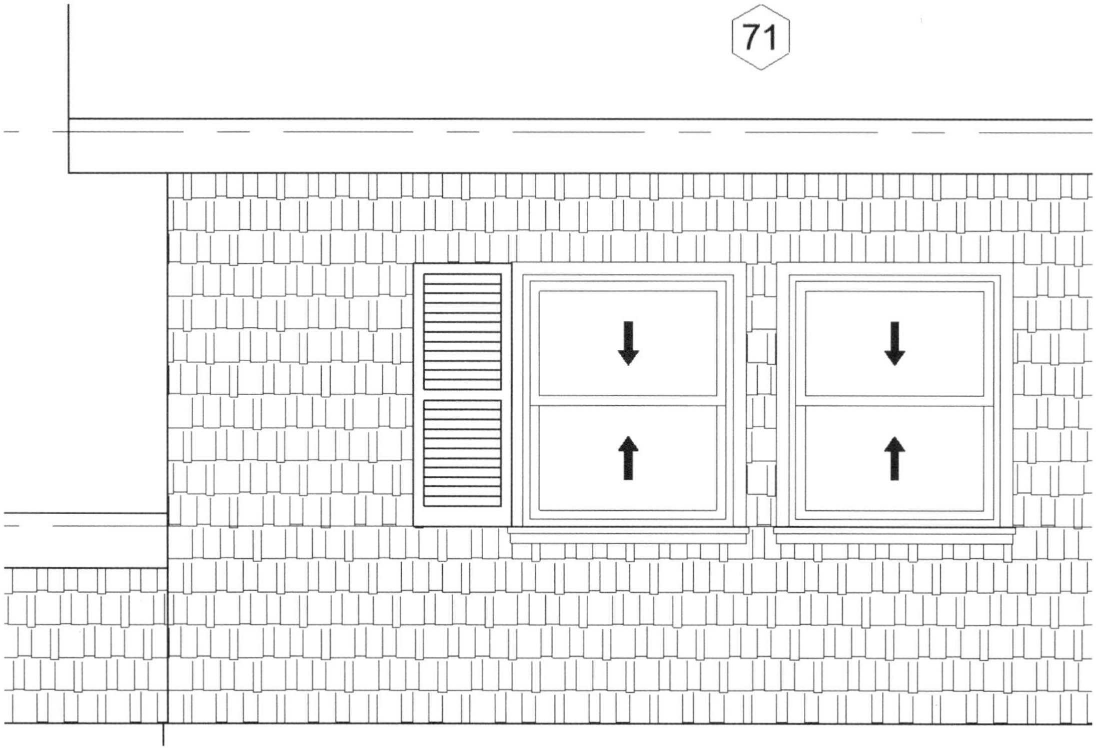

FIGURE 10-2.7 Placing a shutter on the North elevation

The shutter element has been configured so it can only be placed on a wall (this is called a *wall-hosted family*). If you move the cursor over a door or window, you get the (⃠) symbol, meaning it cannot be placed there.

FIGURE 10-2.8 (8) Shutters added to the North elevation

FIGURE 10-2.9 (4) Shutters added to the South elevation

20. **Save** your Project as ex10-2.rvt.

REMINDER: ENTERING DIMENSIONS IN REVIT

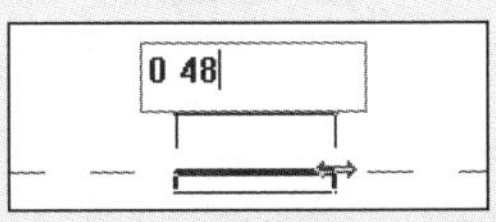

As your experience with Revit grows, you will want to learn some shortcuts for using the program. One shortcut is how you enter dimensions when drawing. You probably already know, maybe by accident, that if you enter only one number (e.g., 48) and press Enter, Revit interprets it as feet (e.g., 48′-0″). So, if you want to enter 48″, you may be typing 0′-48″ or 48″. Both work, but having to press the Shift key to get the inch symbol takes a little longer.

Here are some options for entering dimensions:

0 48	*Revit reads this as 48″ (zero space forty-eight)*
48	*Revit reads this as 48′-0″*
5.5	*Revit reads this as 5′-6″*
0 5.5	*Revit reads this as 5 ½″*
2 0 1/4	*Revit reads this as 2′-0¼″ (two space zero space fraction)*

Exercise 10-3:
Creating and Viewing Interior Elevations

Creating interior elevations is very much like exterior elevations. In fact, you use the same tool. The main difference is that you are placing the elevation tag inside the building, rather than on the exterior.

Adding an Interior Elevation Tag:

1. Open project ex10-2.rvt and **Save As ex10-3.rvt.**

2. Switch to the ***First Floor*** plan view.

3. Select the ***Elevation*** tool from the *View* tab.

In the next step you will place an elevation tag. Before clicking to place the tag, try moving it around to see how Revit automatically turns the tag to point at the closest wall.

4. Select *Elevation:* **Interior Elevation** and then place an elevation tag, looking East, or to the right, in the living room area (Figures 10-3.1a and b).

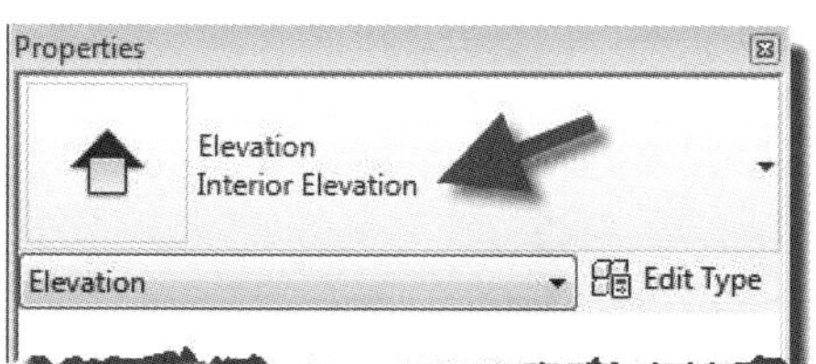

FIGURE 10-3.1A Element Type Selector

REMEMBER: The first thing you should do after adding an Elevation Tag *is to give it an appropriate name in the* Project Browser *list.*

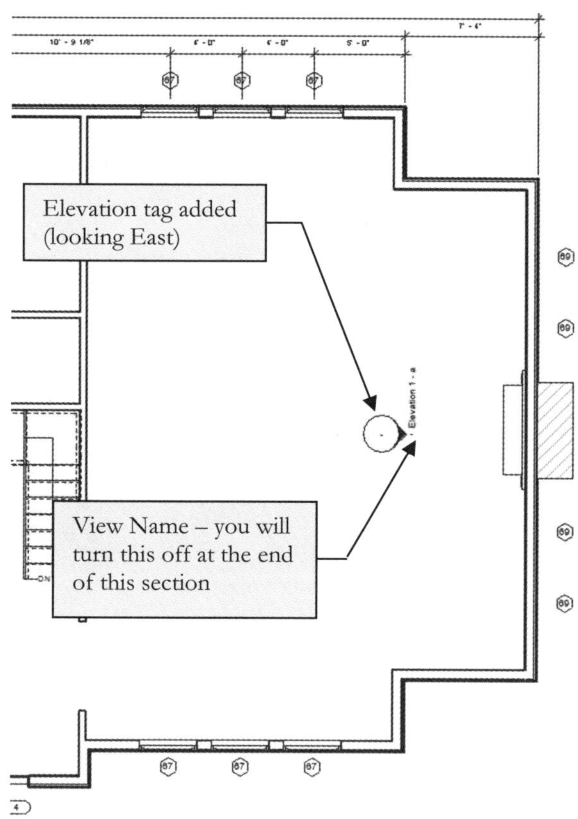

FIGURE 10-3.1B First floor: Elev tag added in Living Rm

5. Change the name of the new elevation to **Living Room – East** in the *Project Browser.*

6. Switch to the ***Living Room – East*** view.

    TIP: Try double-clicking on the elevation tag, the pointing portion.

Initially, your elevation should look like Figure 10-3.2; if not, you will adjust it momentarily, so do not worry. *Notice how Revit automatically controls line weights for things in sections versus elevations.*

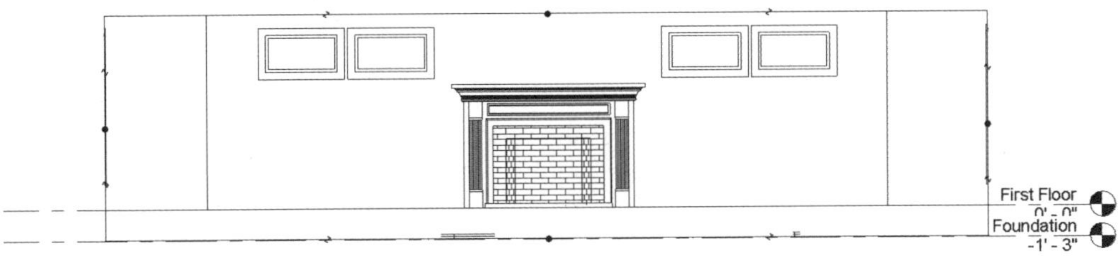

FIGURE 10-3.2 Living Room - East, initial view

7. Switch back to the ***First Floor Plan*** view.

8. Pick the "pointing" portion of the elevation tag, so you see the view options (Figure 10-3.3).

You should compare the two drawings on this page (Figures 10-3.2 and 10-3.3) to see how the control lines in the plan view dictate what is generated and visible in the elevation view for both width and depth.

Revit automatically found the left and right walls, the floor and ceiling in the elevation view.

Notice the *Far Clip Plane* is also acceptable. If you cannot see the fireplace in the elevation view, that means the *Far Clip Plane* needs to be moved farther to the right.

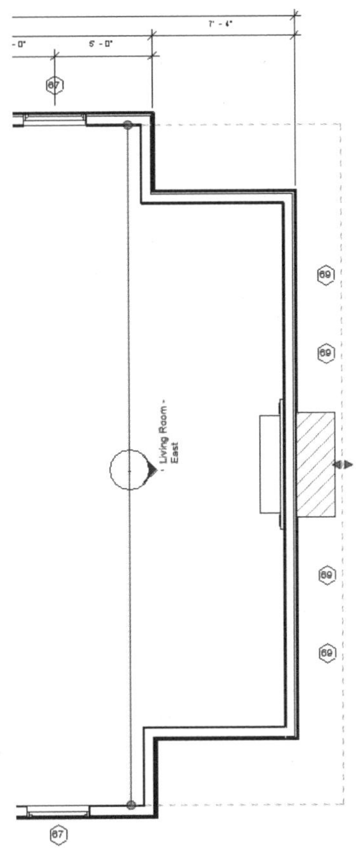

FIGURE 10-3.3 Elevation tag selected

FYI: *The elevation tags are used to reference the sheet and drawing number so the client or contractor can find the desired elevation quickly while looking at the floor plans. This will be covered in a later lesson. It is interesting to know, however, that Revit automatically does this, fills in the elevation tag when the elevation is placed on a sheet and will update it if the elevation is moved.*

9. Switch back to the ***Living Room - East*** view.

Just to try adjusting the *crop region* to see various results, you will extend the top upward to see the second floor.

10. Select the *cropping region* and drag the top middle grip upward, to increase the view size vertically (Figure 10-3.4).

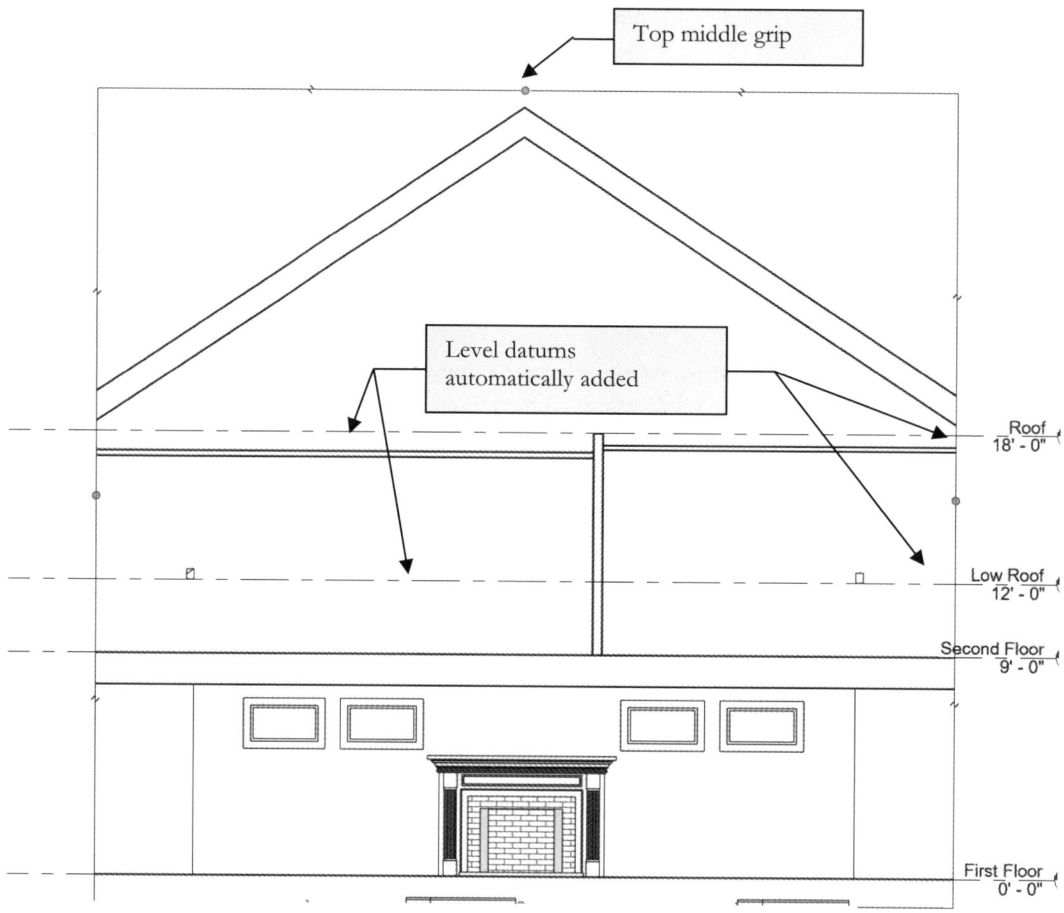

FIGURE 10-3.4 Living Room - East elevation: crop region selected and modified

Here you get a sneak peek at the "sections" portion of this book. Notice that additional level datums were automatically added as the view grew to include more vertical information (e.g., second floor, roof).

11. Now select **Undo** to return to the previous view state (Figure 10-3.2).

As you probably noticed, the interior elevation shows the *Foundation* level datum below the *First Floor* level datum. The *Foundation* level datum is not necessary in this view, so you will remove it from this view.

> **IMPORTANT:** You cannot simply delete the level datum, as it will actually delete all related views from the entire project (i.e., floor and ceiling plan views). This will delete any model elements hosted by that level (walls, doors, windows), as well as any tags, notes, and dimensions in that view.

To remove a level datum, you select it and tell Revit to hide it in the current view. You will do this next.

12. Click on the horizontal line portion of the ***First Floor*** level datum.

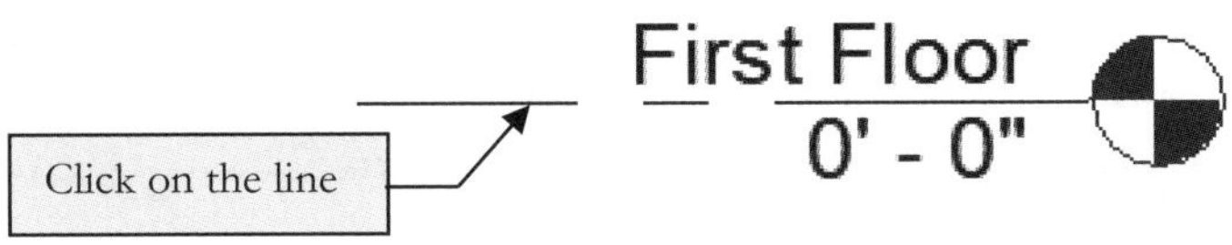

13. Right-click and select **Hide in View → Elements** from the pop-up menu.

    TIP: Selecting Category *would make all level datum elements disappear from the current view.*

14. Adjust the bottom of the ***crop region*** to align with the *First Floor* level (horizontal line).

15. On the *View Control Bar*, make sure the ***View Scale*** is set to **¼"=1'-0"**.

Your elevation should look like Figure 10-3.5.

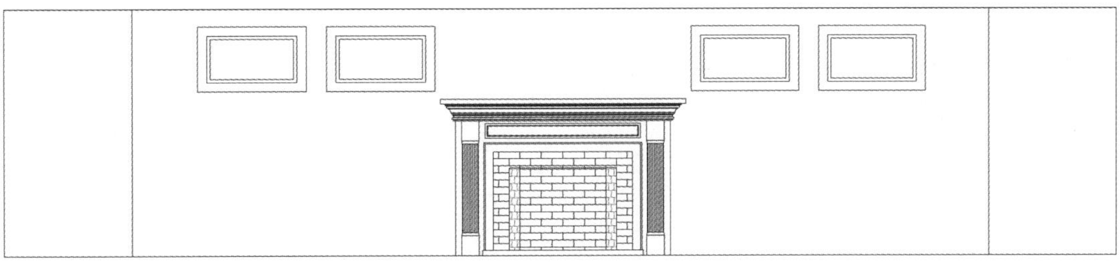

FIGURE 10-3.5 Living Room - East Elevation

You can leave the *crop region* on to help define the elevation's perimeter. You can also turn it off; however, some lines that are directly under the *crop region* might disappear. You could use the *Detail Line* tool to manually define the perimeter using a heavy line.

TIP: If perimeter lines disappear when you print interior elevations, try unchecking Hide Crop Regions *in the Print dialog, and turn off the ones you don't want to see.*

Turning off the View Name on the Elevation Tag:

The interior elevation tag currently has the view name showing (in plan view). You will turn this off as it is not required on the construction drawings.

16. Select **Manage → Settings → Additional Settings** (down-arrow)**→ Annotations → Elevation Tags**

17. Set the *Type* to **½" Circle** (Figure 10-3.6).

18. Select **Elevation Mark Body_Circle: Filled Arrow** from the *Elevation Mark* drop-down list (Figure 10-3.6).

19. Click **OK** to close the dialog box.

The view name is no longer shown in the *elevation tags* in the floor plan view.

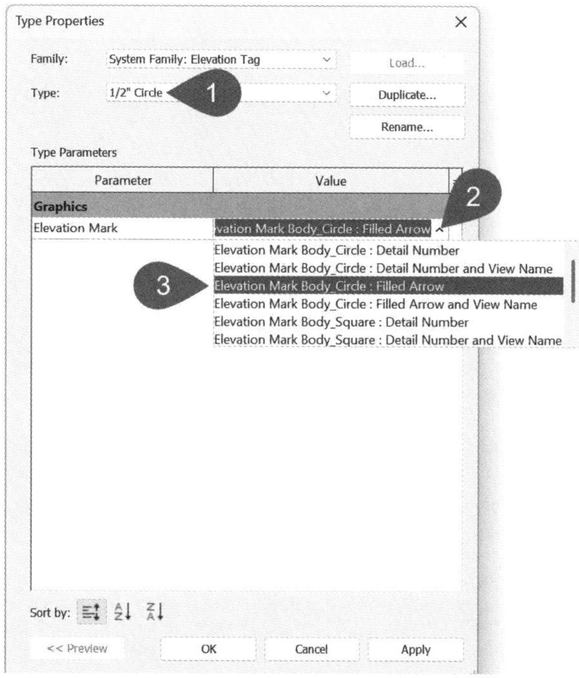

FIGURE 10-3.6 Adjusting the interior elevation tag

FYI: If you right-click on an elevation view name in the Project Browser, you will notice you can Duplicate *the view (via Duplicate View → Duplicate). This is similar to how a floor plan is duplicated with one major variation: when an elevation view is duplicated, Revit actually just copies another elevation tag on top of the one being duplicated in the plan view. This is because each elevation view requires its own elevation tag. If two views could exist based on one elevation tag, then Revit would not know how to fill in the drawing number and sheet number if both views are placed on a sheet.*

Adding Annotation:

Now you will add a note and dimensions to the interior elevation view.

20. Add the (2) dimensions and (1) text (3/32″ text style) with leader shown in Figure 10-3.7.

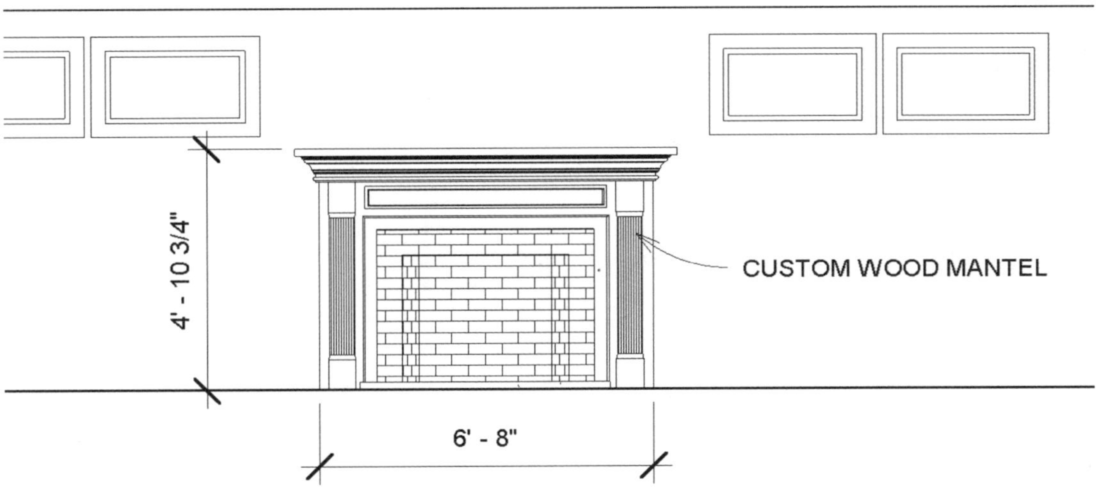

FIGURE 10-3.7 Living Room - East elevation: annotation added

It is possible to add *Detail Lines* to this view to represent baseboard or other details, such as wall bracing. This is often done for finer details that are not modeled. This approach improves model performance but will not appear in sections or renderings.

21. On the *View Control Bar*, set the ***View Scale*** to **½″=1′-0″**.

Notice the text and dimensions automatically resize to match the new scale. When space permits, most residential interior elevations are ½″ = 1′-0″.

22. Save your project as **ex10-3.rvt**.

Exercise 10-4:
Modifying the Project Model: Interior Elevations

This short exercise, similar to Exercise 10-2, will look at an example of Revit's parametric change engine. All drawings are generated from one 3D model.

Modify the Interior Elevations:

1. Open ex10-3.rvt and **Save As ex10-4.rvt**.
2. Open the ***Living Room - East*** elevation view.

You will move the windows and add an exterior door.

3. Select both of the windows on the right, using the **Ctrl** key to select multiple objects at one time.
4. Use the ***Move*** tool to move the windows 6″ to the right, i.e. South.
5. Repeat the previous steps to *Move* the other two windows 6″ towards the left, i.e. North.
6. In the *Living Room - East* elevation view, use the ***Door*** tool to place a **Door-Exterior-Single-Entry-Half Flat Glass-Wood_Clad: 36″ x 80″** door in the wall to the far left (North). See Figure 10-4.1.

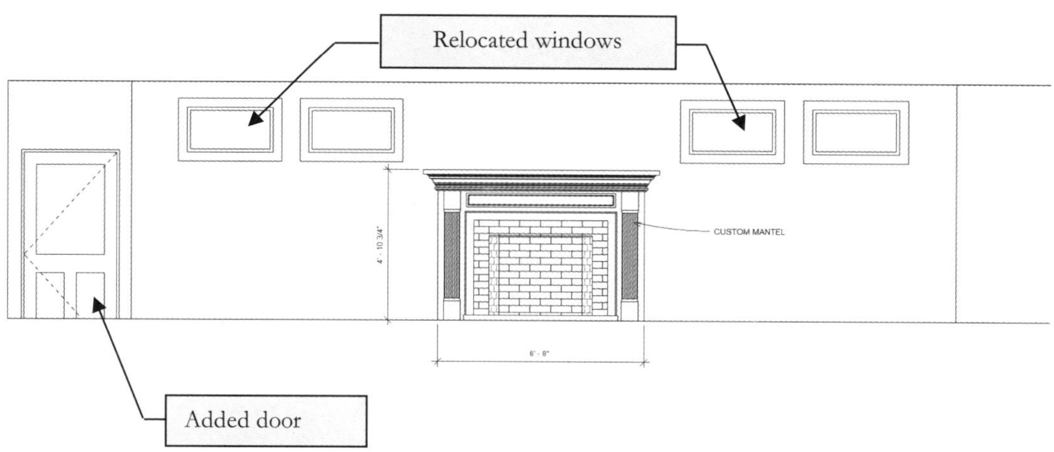

FIGURE 10-4.1 Living Room - East - modified

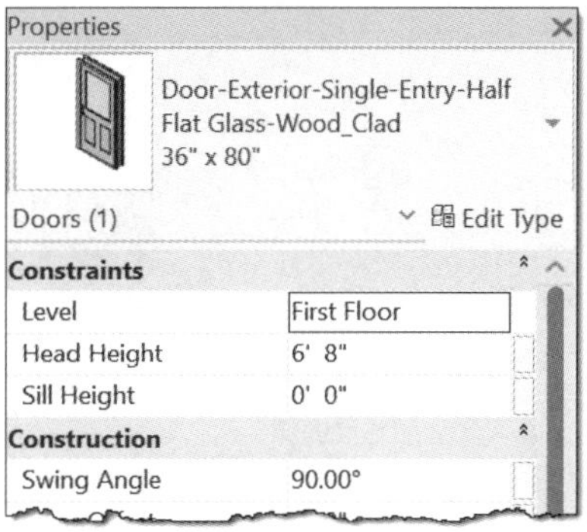

You moved the windows out from the mantel, so they provide a little more space between them. Revit allows you to design in all views!

You may notice, in Figure 10-4.1, that the door bottom is below the floor level; this is a problem only if your cursor was near the bottom of the wall when you clicked. You will fix it next.

7. Select the new door in the *Living Room – East* view.

8. In *Properties*, change the **level** from *Foundation* to ***First Floor*** if needed.

The vertical door position should now look correct (Figure 10-4.2).

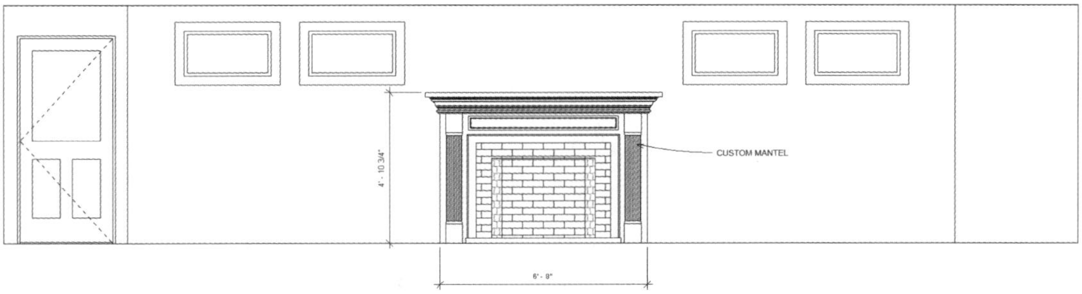

FIGURE 10-4.2 Living Room - East elevation: door height adjusted

Notice that, back in the Properties Palette for the new door, there's a setting called *Sill Height.* This setting allows you to move the door vertically, relative to the specified level. For example, you might have a second-floor door that opens onto a low roof, but the door needs to be 1′-0″ above the second floor for this door to work correctly (roof insulation, flashing, etc.). You simply select the door and adjust its *Sill Height* to 1′-0″, with the level set to *Second Floor* via the *Properties Palette.*

Now it is time to see the changes to the plan views.

9. Switch to the ***First Floor Plan*** view (Figure 10-4.3).

When placing a door in elevation, you may have to switch to plan view to verify the door swing is the way you want it. You can control the door swing in elevation: right-click and select “flip hand” or “flip facing.”

In elevation, you can adjust many things this way. Some examples are ceiling height, interior and exterior windows, wall locations, perpendicular to the current view, etc.

Notice that the door does not have a door tag like the other doors in the plan view. This is because the door was not placed in this view. You will learn how to add this tag later.

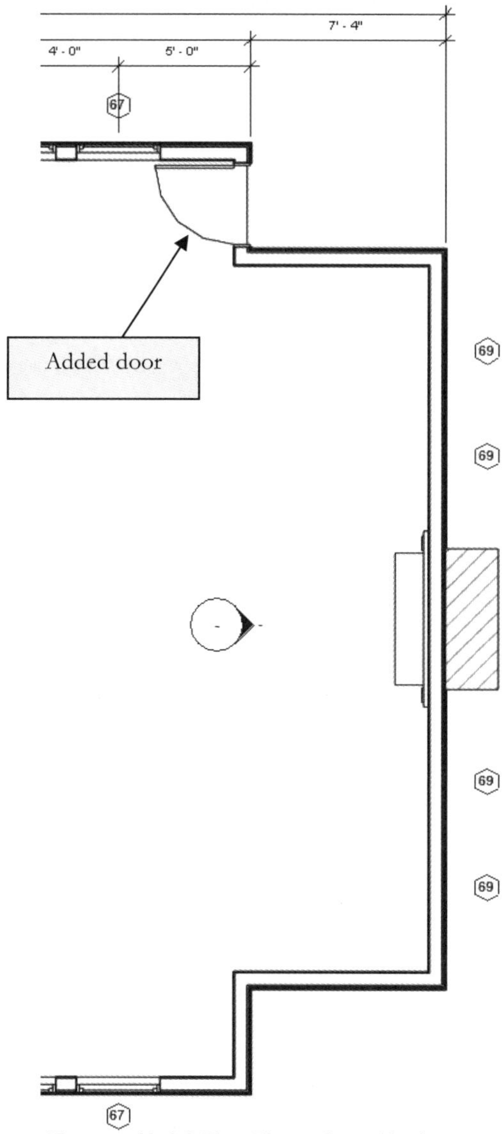

FIGURE 10-4.3 First Floor plan with changes

10. Save your project as **ex10-4**.

Exercise 10-5:
Design Options

This exercise will look at a feature called *Design Options.* This feature allows you to present two or more options for a portion of your design without saving a copy of your project or maintaining more than one project until the preferred design option is selected.

Design Options Overview:

A Revit project can have several design option studies at any given time; you might have an (A) entry porch options study, (B) a kitchen options study, and a (C) master bedroom furniture layout options study in a project. Each of these studies can have several design options. For example, the entry porch study might have three options: 1. flat roof, 2. shed roof, and 3. shed roof with a dormer-type embellishment.

A particular study of an area within your project is called a *Design Option Set*, and the designs associated with a Design Option Set are called Options. Both the *Design Option Set* and the *Options* can be named (see the examples below, on the next page).

One of the *Options* in a *Design Option Set* is designated as the Primary option (the others are called Secondary Options); this is the option shown by default in all new and existing views. However, you can adjust a view's visibility to display a different option. Typically, you would duplicate a view, adjust its visibility, and rename it so each option is at your fingertips.

When you and/or the owner select the preferred design, set that *Option* to *Primary*. Finally, you select the Accept Primary tool, which deletes the *Secondary Options* and the *Design Option Set*, leaving the *Primary Option* as part of the main building model.

Design Option Set

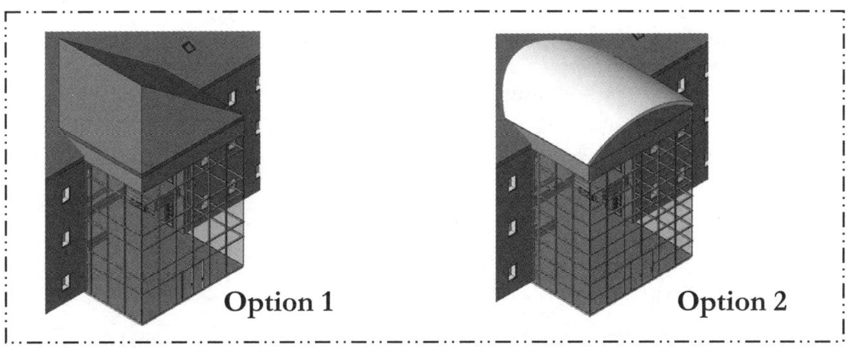

The following images (Figures 10-5.1a and b) provide an overview of the *Design Options* dialog box and *Status Bar* tools. See Step 2 to access this dialog.

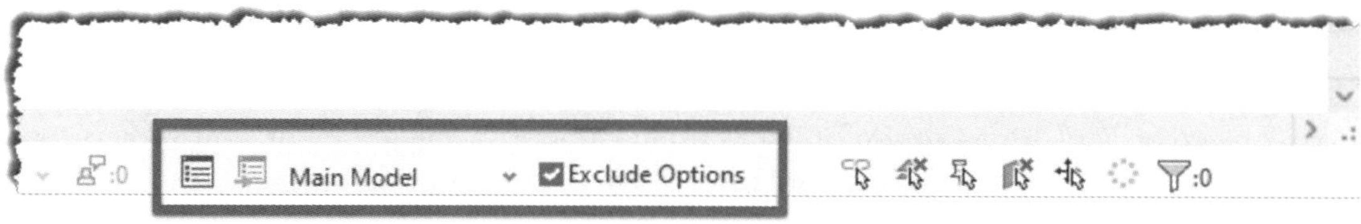

FIGURE 10-5.1A
Status Bar; Design Options tools

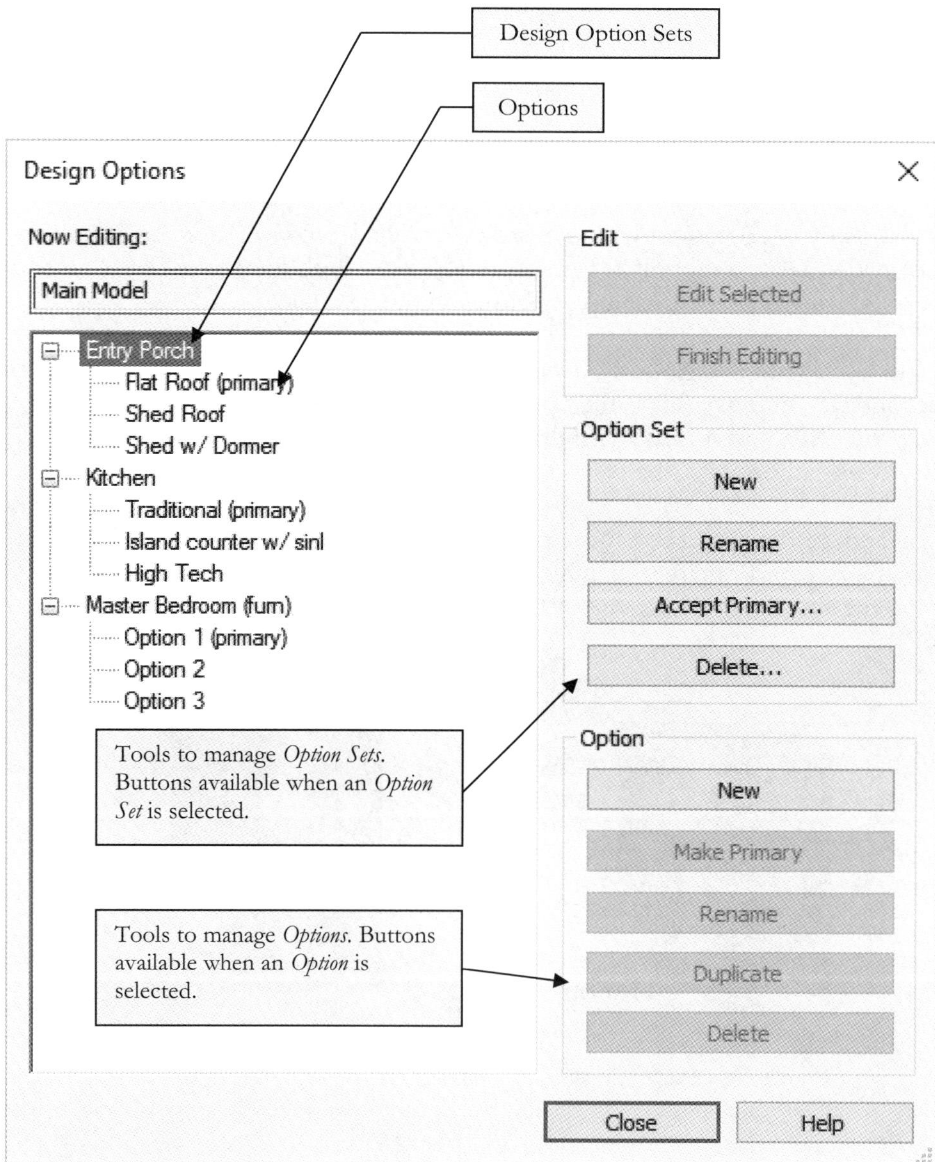

FIGURE 10-5.1B Design Options Dialog

Notes about the *Design Options* dialog box:

Edit buttons:

You can edit a *Design Option* by selecting an *Option* (in the window area on the left) and then clicking the **Edit Selected** button. Next, you add, move, and delete elements in that *Design Option.*

When you finish editing a Design Option, reopen the *Design Options* dialog and click the **Finish Editing** button.

If you are currently in an *Option Editing* mode, the *Now Editing* area in the *Design Options* dialog displays the *Option* name being modified, otherwise it displays *Main Model.*

Option Set buttons:

The **New** button is always available. You can quickly set up several *Option Sets.* Each time you create a new *Option Set,* Revit automatically creates a *Primary Option* named *Option 1.*

The other buttons are only available when an *Option Set* label is highlighted (i.e., selected) in the window list on the left.

The **Accept Primary** button makes the Primary Option of the selected set part of the building model and deletes the set and its secondary options. This is a way of "cleaning house" by getting rid of unnecessary information, which helps to better manage the project and keeps the file size down.

Option buttons:

These buttons are only available when an *Option* (primary or secondary) is selected within an *Option Set.* You can quickly set up several *Options* without having to add any content (e.g., walls, components) to them immediately.

The **Make Primary** button allows you to change the status of a *Secondary Option* to *Primary.* As previously mentioned, the *Primary Option* is the one shown by default in existing and new views. You can only have one *Primary* option in an *Option Set.*

The **Duplicate** button copies all the elements in the selected Option into a new Option, making the file larger because you are technically adding content to the project. You can then use the copied elements (e.g., walls, furniture, etc.) as a starting point for the next design option. This is handy if the various options are similar.

Now you will put this introductory knowledge to use!

Setting up a Design Option Set:

In this exercise, you will create two *Design Option Sets*: one for the Main Entry Roof and another for the windows above the Entry Door. You will create an alternate roof and window design for your project.

You could just create one *Design Option Set* with two design options. However, by placing the roof options in one *Option Set* and the windows in another, you actually get four design options in total; you can mix and match the roof and window options.

Setting up Design Options in Your Project:

First, you will set up the *Option Sets* and *Options*.

1. Open ex10-4.rvt and **Save As ex10-5.rvt**.

2. Click the **Design Options** icon on the *Status Bar* .

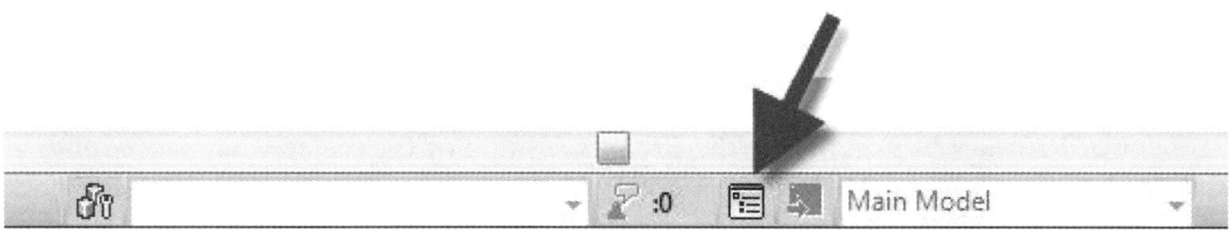

You are now in the *Design Options* dialog box (Figure 10-5.2). Your dialog will look like this one, basically empty:

3. In the *Option Set* area, click **New**.

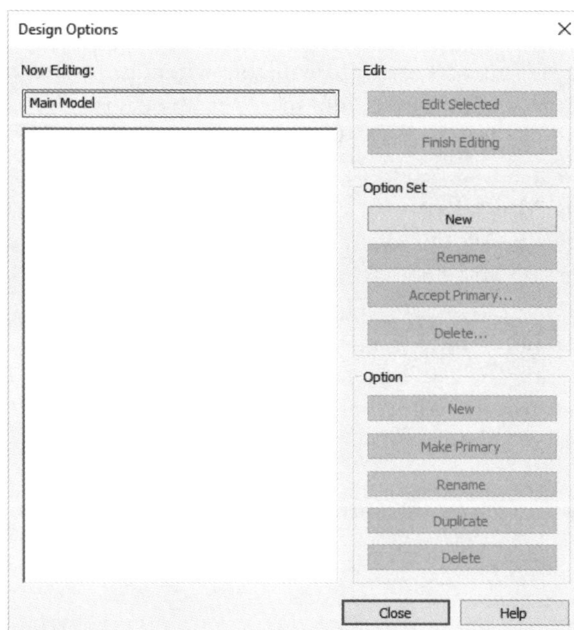

FIGURE 10-5.2 Design Options Dialog; initial view

Notice that an *Option Set* named *Option Set 1* has been created. Revit also automatically created the *Primary Option* named *Option 1* (Figure 10-5.3). Next, you will rename the *Option Set* to something that is easier to recognize.

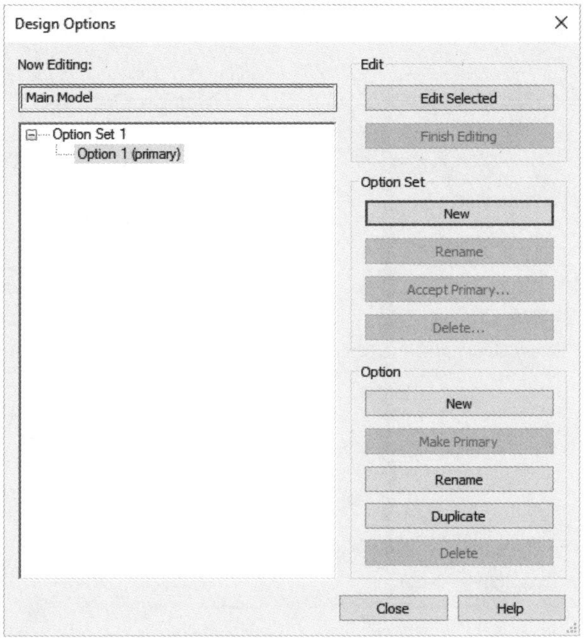

FIGURE 10-5.3 Design Options dialog; new option set created

4. Select the *Option Set* currently named *Option Set 1* and then click the **Rename** button in the *Option Set* area.

   WARNING! *Be sure you are not renaming the* Option *but rather the* Option Set.

5. In the *Rename* dialog type **Entry Windows** (Figure 10-5.4).

6. Click **OK** to rename.

Giving the *Option Set* a name that is easy to recognize makes it easier to manage the various options later, especially if you have several.

Next, you will create a *Secondary Option* for the *Entry Windows* option set.

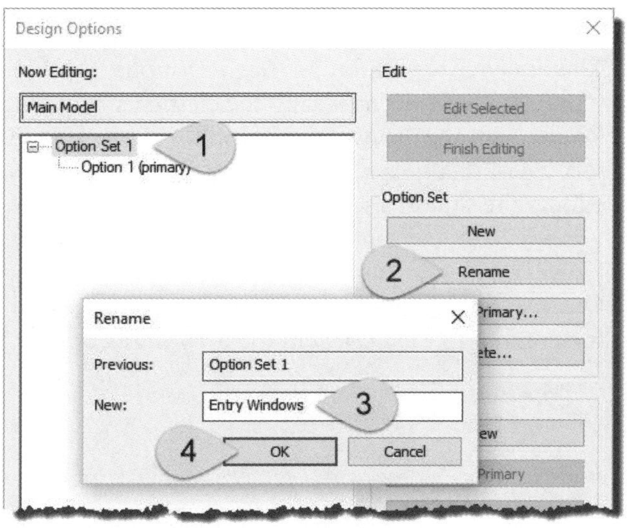

FIGURE 10-5.4 Rename Option Set dialog

7. With the *Entry Windows* option set selected, click **New** in the *Option* area (Figure 10-5.5).

Notice a secondary *Option* was created and automatically named *Option 2*. If you have descriptive names for the options in a set, use them. In this example, you can leave them as they are.

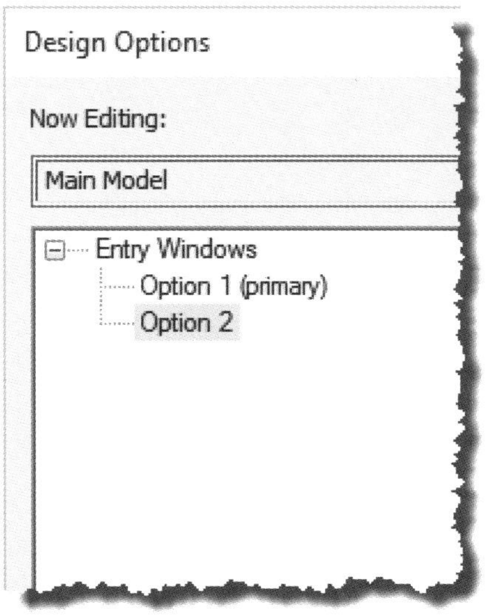

FIGURE 10-5.5
Design Options dialog; secondary option created

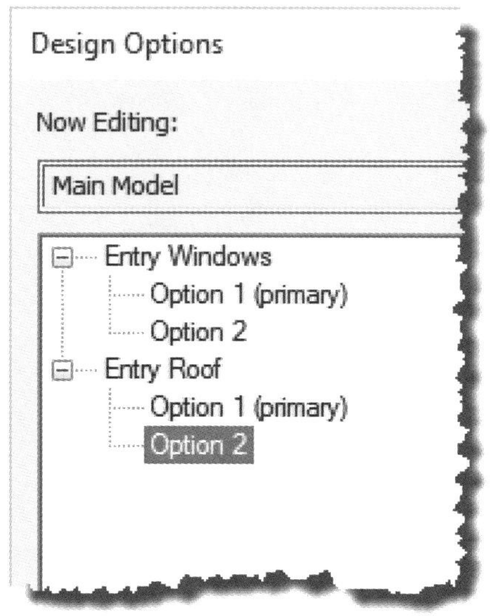

FIGURE 10-5.6
Design Options dialog

8. Create an *Option Set* for the roof (Figure 10-5.6):
   a. Name the set ***Entry Roof***
   b. Create a secondary option

The basic idea behind the Design Options feature is that you set up the Option Set and Options, then start modeling the elements related to the current *Option*. So, you select the *Option* from the drop-down list on the *Status Bar*, make the additions and modifications relative to that *Design Option*, and finally switch the drop-down back to *Main Model* to finish editing the option and then be able to make changes in the main model.

However, in your case, you want to move some content that has already been drawn to *Option 1*. Revit has a feature that lets you move content to a Design Option Set, which copies the content to the *Options* in the *Set* you select.

Entry Windows Design Option:

You are now ready to set up the different design options.

9. Close the *Design Options* dialog and switch to the ***3D*** view; adjust the view so you are looking at the main entry (South elevation).

Unfortunately, you cannot just select the windows and add them to a *Design Option Set* because they are hosted elements that require a wall to be inserted in. Therefore, you will also add the entry walls and door to the *Design Option Set*.

10. **Select** the three walls at the main entry, three windows and main entry door/sidelights; orbit as required.

11. Click the **Add to Set** icon on the *Status Bar*.

12. Select *Entry Windows* from the dialog drop-down and then click **OK** (Figure 10-5.7).

The selected items are now in both *Option 1* and *Option 2* under the option set *Entry Windows* because both options were selected in the previous dialog, Figure 10-5.7.

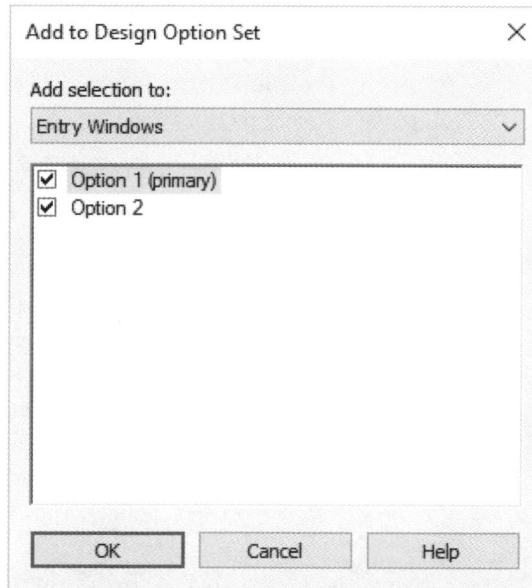

FIGURE 10-5.7 Add to Design Option Set Dialog

From this point forward, you can only modify the entry windows, door, and walls when in *Option 1* or *Option 2 Edit* mode. In this case, the tables are turned: you cannot edit the main building model because *Active Only* is checked on the *Status Bar*.

13. In the ***Design Options*** drop-down list, on the *Status Bar*, select ***Entry Windows: Option 2*** as shown in the image below.

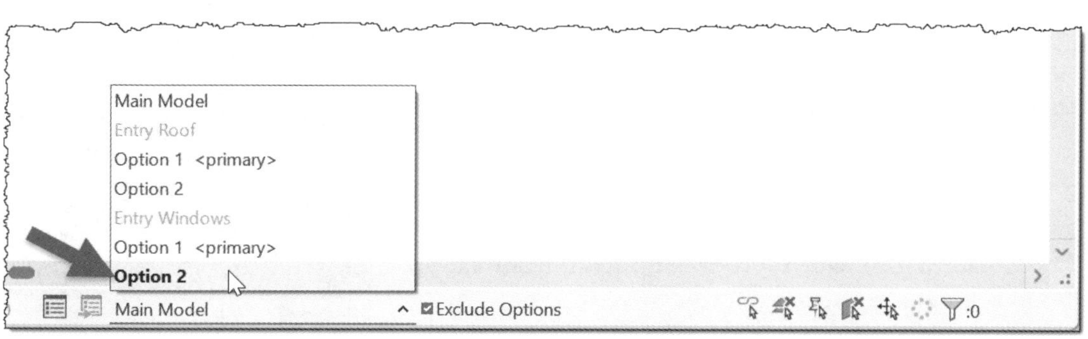

Now you should notice that the main building model is slightly grey and not editable; it is not editable because *Active Only* is selected on the *Status Bar.* All hosted elements for the wall were also moved into the *Design Option,* specifically, three windows and a door. You will change the windows per Figure 10-5.8.

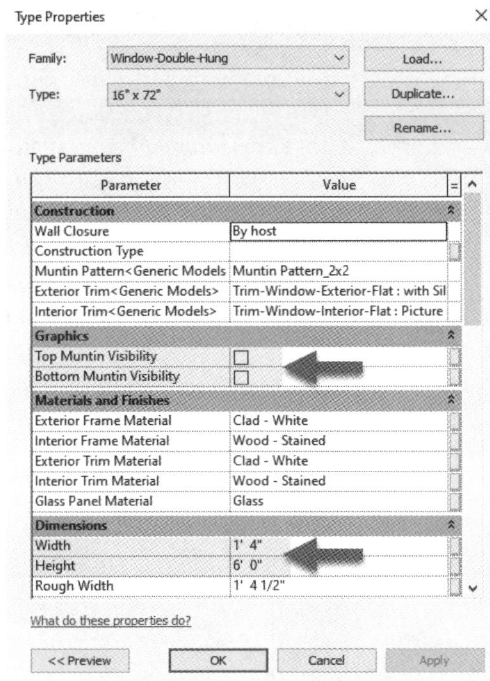

14. Zoom in on the main entry, particularly the second-floor window area in your ***3D*** view.

15. Select the three windows <u>above</u> the main entry door and make a new type called **Window-Double-Hung: 16″ x 72″** per these steps (see image to right):

    a. Select any type in *Type Selector*
    b. Click **Edit Type**
    c. Select **Duplicate**
    d. New name: **16" x 72"**
    e. Change *Width* parameter: **1'-4"**
    f. Change *Height* parameter: **6'-0"**
    g. *Top Muntin Visibility*: **uncheck**
    h. *Bottom Muntin Visibility*: **uncheck**

16. Adjust the window head (i.e., top) to **7′-0″** via the *Properties Palette* for the selected windows.

17. Change the *Design Options* drop-down list, on the *Status Bar*, back to ***Main Model***.

It now appears like all your changes disappeared, right? Well, if you recall from the introduction to this exercise, the *Primary Option* is displayed by default for all new and existing views. So, when you finished editing *Entry Windows: Option 2* the *3D* view switched back to the *Primary Option*, which is currently set to *Option 1* (Fig. 10-5.6).

Next, you will create a new view and adjust its *Visibility* to display *Option 2* of the *Entry Windows* options set.

First, you will create a duplicate copy of the *3D* view.

18. In the *Project Browser*, under *3D Views*, right-click on the **{3D}** label.

19. Select **Duplicate View → Duplicate** from the pop-up menu.

You now have a copy of the *3D* view named *{3D} Copy 1*.

FIGURE 10-5.8
3D View: second floor windows modified

20. **Rename** the new 3D view to ***Entry Windows Option 2***.

21. Switch to your new view, if needed.

22. Select **View → Graphics → Visibility/Graphics** (or type **VV**).

23. Click on the **Design Options** tab at the top of the dialog.

24. Change the *Design Option* parameter for *Entry Windows* to ***Option 2*** (Figure 10-5.9).

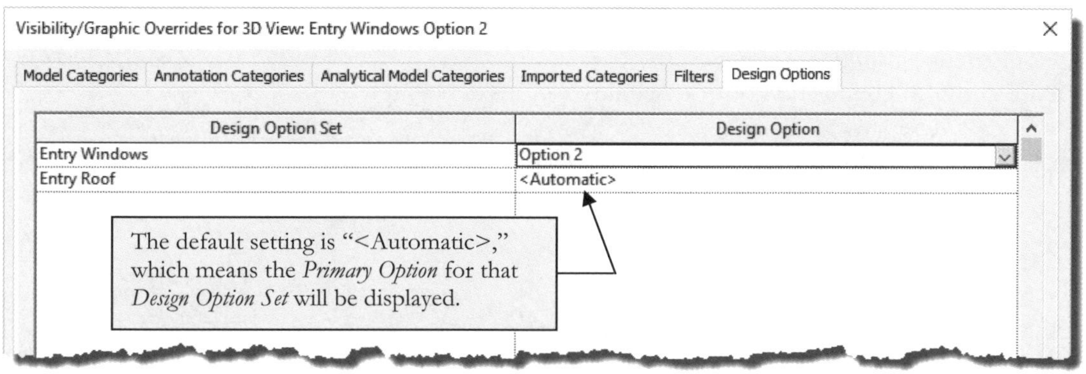

FIGURE 10-5.9 Visibility/Graphic Overrides dialog: modified Entry Windows design option visibility

25. Click **OK** to close the dialog.

Now, with the *Default 3D* view and the *Entry Windows: Option 2* view, you can quickly switch between design options. Both views could be placed side by side on the same sheet and printed out for a design critique.

Entry Roof Design Option:

Now you will add an option for a roof over the entry door.

26. Select *Entry Roof:* ***Option 2*** from the *Design Options* drop-down list on the *Status Bar.*

You will add a roof shortly.

27. Switch to the **South** elevation view.

28. Zoom in to the area below the entry windows, just above the front door.

Next, you will create an *in-place family* to represent a curved roof option over the entry area. Basically, you will create a solid by specifying a depth, then draw a profile of the curved roof using lines.

29. Click **Architecture → Build → Component (down-arrow) → Model In-Place**.

You are immediately prompted to select a *Family Category*. This allows Revit to understand how other elements should interact with the object(s) you are about to create and control visibility.

30. Select **Roofs** from the *Family Category* list (Figure 10-5.10).

31. Click **OK**.

You are now prompted to provide a name for the new *in-place family*.

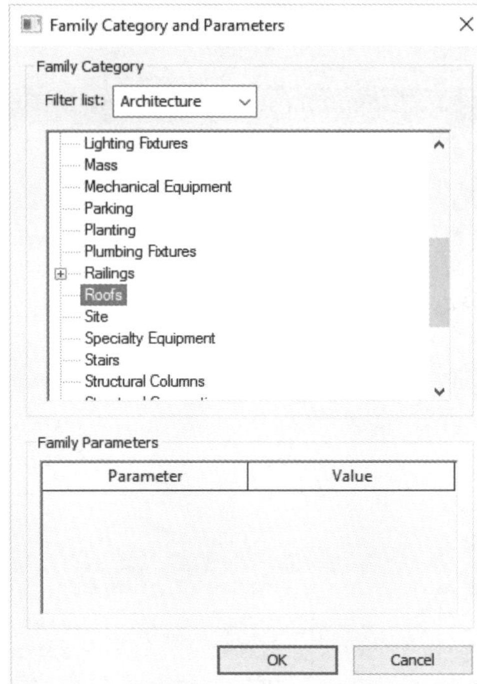

FIGURE 10-5.10 Family Category and Parameters dialog

32. For the family *Name*, type **Entry Roof** (Figure 10-5.11).

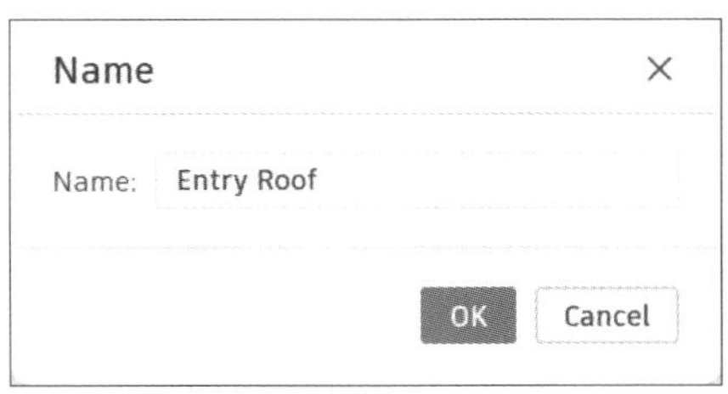

FIGURE 10-5.11 Family name prompt

You are now in a mode where you draw the *Entry Roof*. Notice that the *Ribbon* has special buttons on the Architecture tab that provide the tools needed to create a family. You are continuously in the *Model In-Place* mode until you select *Finish Model* (green check mark) or *Quit Model* (red x) from the *Ribbon*.

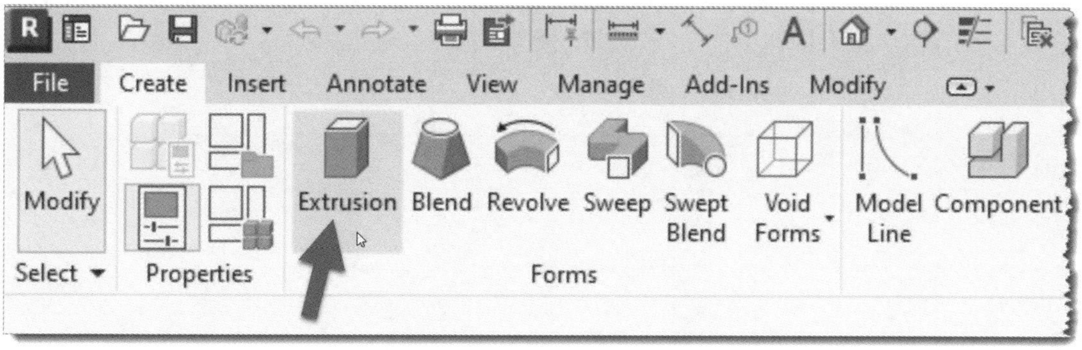

FIGURE 10-5.12 Form Ribbon; select Extrude

You will now select the type of solid you wish to create.

33. Select **Create → Forms → Extrusion.**

Finally, you are prompted to select a plane in which to start drawing the profile of the solid to be extruded. Even though the view is a 2D representation of a 3D model, Revit needs to know where you want the 3D solid created so it can show it in other views (both 2D and 3D). You will select the entry wall as a reference surface to establish a working plane.

34. Select **Pick a Plane** and click **OK** (Figure 10-5.13).

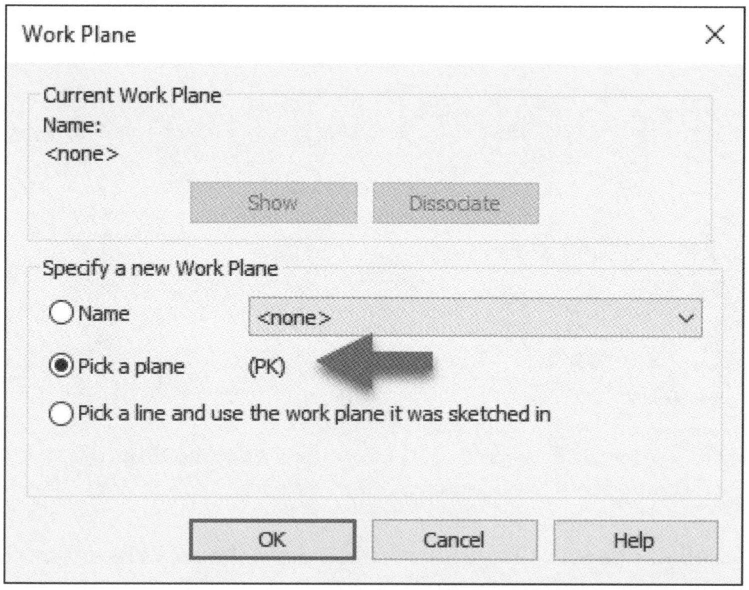

FIGURE 10-5.13 Work Plane dialog; select Pick a Plane

35. Move the cursor near the edge of the entry wall and then click to select it.

TIP: If needed, click the Tab *key until a heavy line appears around the perimeter of the wall. Then click the mouse to select (Figure 10-5.14). Do not hold down the Tab key.*

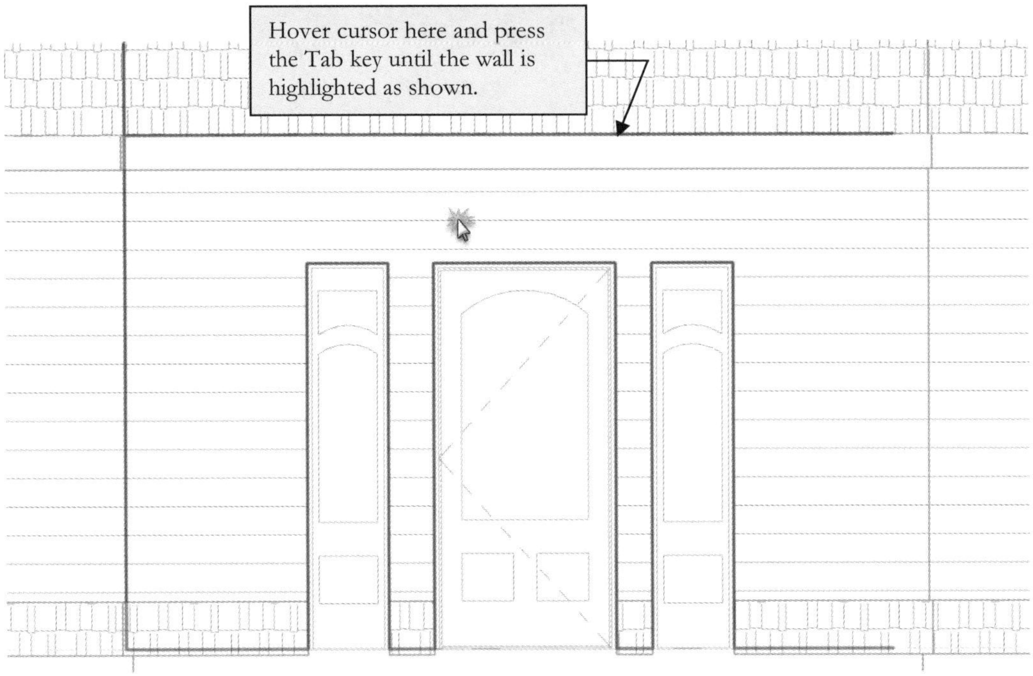

FIGURE 10-5.14 South Elevation; select wall to establish work plane

Next, you will draw an arc to specify the bottom edge of the curved roof design option. Notice the *Ribbon* changed again to display tools for drawing an extruded solid.

36. On the *Ribbon*, enter **2'-0"** for the ***Depth*** (see image below).

    FYI: *A negative number for the depth would cause the solid to project in towards the building from the work plane.*

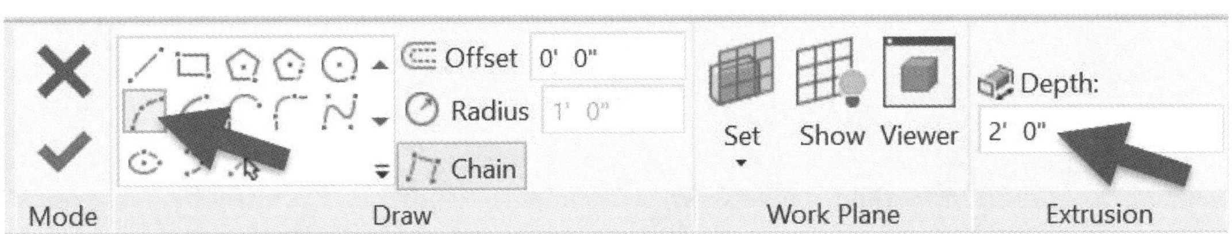

37. Click the **Start – End – Radius Arc** icon from the *Draw* panel on the contextual tab: *Modify | Create Extrusion* (see image above).

38. Pick the three points shown in Figure 10-5.15 to draw the arc. The angle is not critical; get as close as possible. The ends of the arc are approximately straight up from the edge of the entry door side lights below.

    TIP: *Try typing* SO *before clicking the third point to temporarily turn off the Snaps for one pick (SO = Snap Off).*

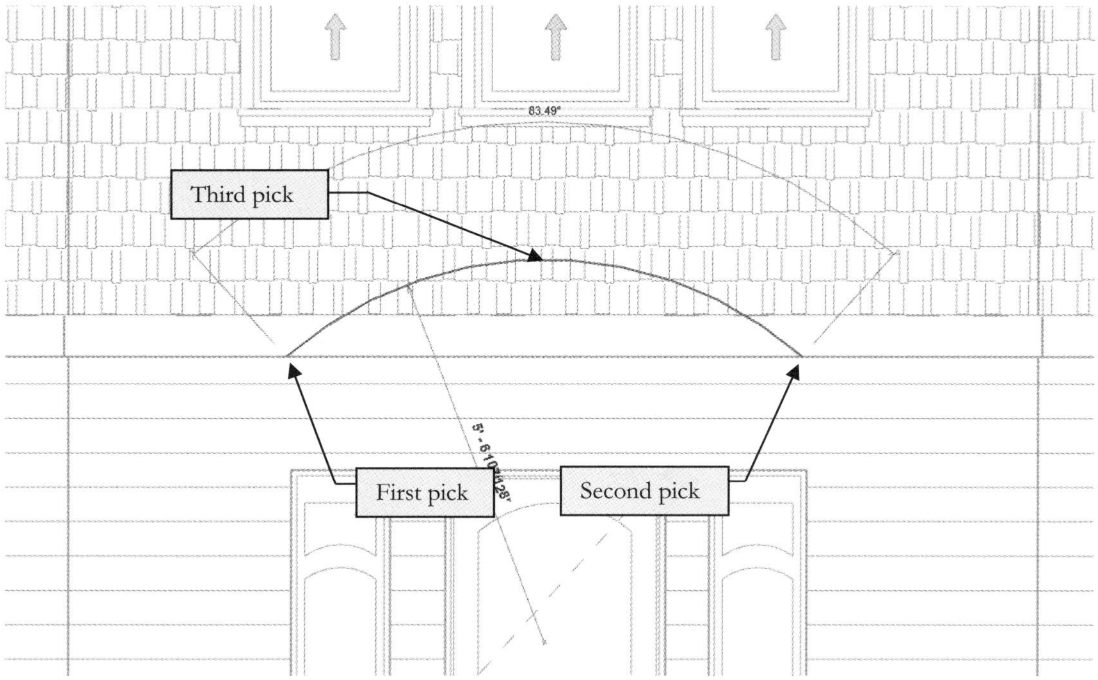

FIGURE 10-5.15 South Elevation; drawing arc to define roof

Now you will draw another arc 7¼″ above the previous one.

39. Press **Esc** and then use the *Start-End-Radius Arc* draw tool again, enter **0 7.25** for the *Offset* on the *Ribbon.*

40. Draw another **Arc** picking the exact same three points; be sure to snap to the endpoints and midpoint of the previous arc (Figure 10-5.15).

Notice that an arc is drawn offset 7¼″ from the points you picked. If you pick the first two points in the other direction, the arc would be offset in the other direction, downward in this case.

Next, you will draw two short lines to connect the endpoints of the two arcs. This will create a closed area, which is required before finishing the sketch. Think of it this way: you need to completely define at least two dimensions before Revit can create the third.

41. Click the "straight line" icon on the *Draw* panel (see image to right); this will switch you from drawing arcs back to straight line segments. Set the *Offset* back to **0″**.

42. Zoom in and sketch a short line on each end of the arc as shown in Figure 10-5.16; be sure to use your *Endpoint* snaps (type SE).

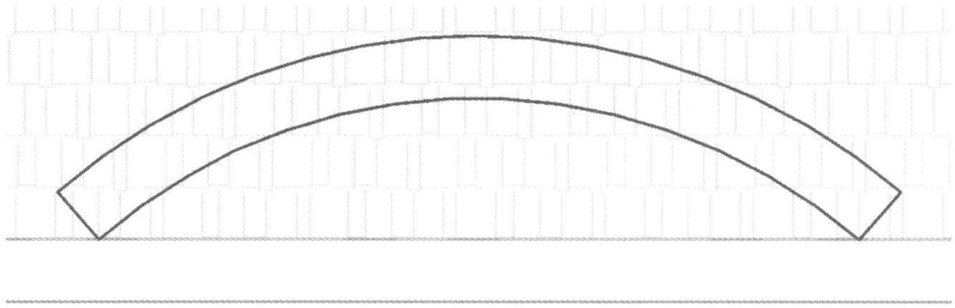

FIGURE 10-5.16 South elevation; two arcs and two short lines define roof profile

43. Click the **green checkmark** from the *Ribbon*. 

TIP: If you get any warnings, it may be because one or more of the profile's corners do not form a perfect intersection; zoom in to see them, then use the Trim tool to close the corners. Delete any stray lines.

You are still in the *Model In-Place Family* mode. Before you finish, you will apply a material to the roof element.

44. Click the new roof to select it, if needed.

45. In the *Properties Palette*, click in the *Material* value field and then click the "…" icon that appears.

The *Materials* dialog opens.

46. Select **Roofing, Metal** from the list of predefined *Materials* (i.e., the AEC Materials library). See Fig 10-5.17.

FYI: Notice the Appearance asset material is set to anodized aluminum with a dark bronze color for Metal – Roofing.

47. Click **OK** to close the *Materials* dialog. 

You are now ready to finish the family.

48. From the *Ribbon* click **Finish Model**.

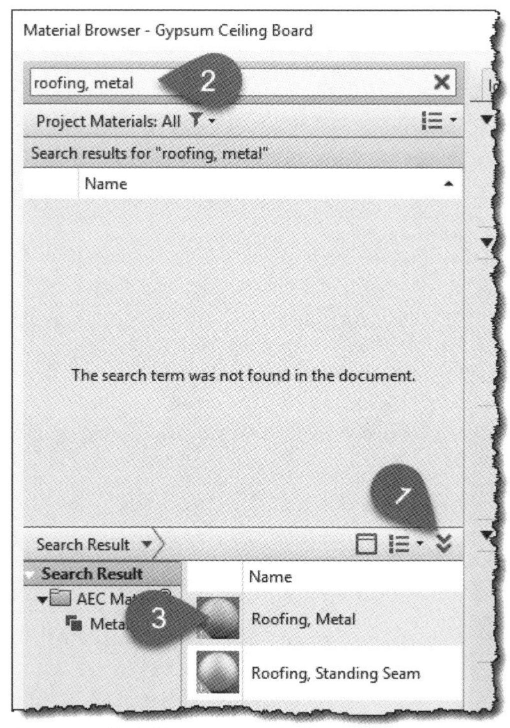

FIGURE 10-5.17 Materials dialog
Step one, in the image, toggles the visibility of the external Autodesk material library. You need to see this library in order to load materials from it into your model.

Next you will move the roof down a little. At this point, the only "mode" you are in is for editing the *Entry Roof: Option 2*.

49. Click on the roof to select it.

50. Use the arrow keys on the keyboard to nudge the roof element down until it looks similar to Figure 10-5.18.

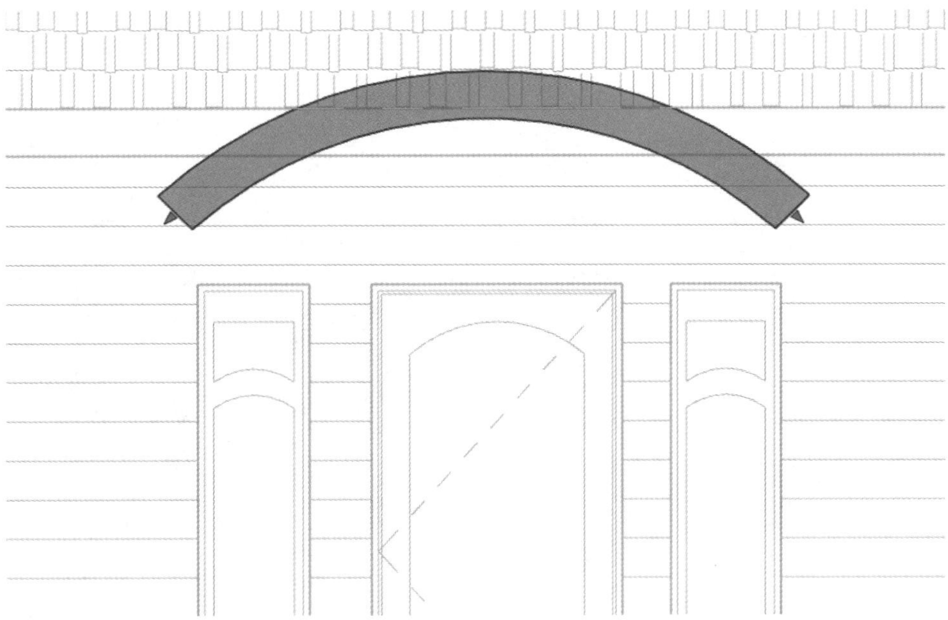

FIGURE 10-5.18 South elevation; roof element moved to a lower position

Notice the arrow grips at each end of the roof element when it is selected? Clicking one of these grips allows you to extend that solid perpendicular to the arrow. Try it; just *Undo* (Ctrl+Z) when you are done experimenting. It works better on rectilinear objects.

You are now ready to finish editing the current design option for now.

51. Set the *Design Options* drop-down back to ***Main Model***.

As before, the option you were just working on was not the *Primary Option* in the *Entry Roof* design set, so the current view reverted to *Entry Roof: Option 1*, which is the primary view.

You will create a 3D view that has *Option 2* set to be visible for both the *Entry Window* option set and the *Entry Roof* option set.

52. Right-click on the ***Default 3D*** view and click **Duplicate View → Duplicate**.

53. Rename the duplicated view to **Entry – Option 2**.

54. Switch to the new view (*Entry – Option 2*); you should already be in that view.

55. Click **Visibility/Graphics** from the *View* tab (or type **VV**).

56. On the *Design Options* tab, set <u>both</u> *Option Sets* to ***Option 2*** in the *Design Option* column.

57. Click **OK** to close the dialog.

FIGURE 10-5.19 Entry – Option 2 view with shadows on

You can now see a 3D view of your new entry roof option. The previous image has shadows turned on. This can provide a very dramatic result with almost no extra effort. The shadows can be useful while designing; however, you will probably have them turned off most of the time just to maintain system performance.

To turn on shadows, you simply click the *Shadows* toggle icon on the *View Control Bar* at the bottom of the screen.

Because the new entry roof element is a roof in Revit, you can attach walls to it, meaning a wall top would conform to the underside of the curved roof.

Another entry roof option might be a more traditional shed-type porch roof like the one shown above. You might try adding this roof to the *Option 1* placeholder. Simply sketch a roof by footprint, with only the South edge set to *Defines slope*.

58. **Save** your project as **ex10-5.rvt**.

TIP: *The Design Options feature can also be used to manage alternates, where both the base bid and the alternate(s) need to be drawn.*

Self-Exam:

The following questions can be used as a way to check your knowledge of this lesson. The answers can be found at the bottom of the page.

1. The plan is updated automatically when an elevation is modified but not the other way around. (T/F)
2. You can use the *Elevation* tool to place both interior and exterior elevations. (T/F)
3. You can rename elevation views to better manage them. (T/F)
4. You have to resize the level datums and annotations after changing a view's scale. (T/F)
5. How do you enter 5½″ without entering the foot or inch symbol? ____________

Review Questions:

The following questions may be assigned by your instructor as a way to assess your knowledge of this section. Your instructor has the answers to the review questions.

1. The visibility of the *crop region* can be controlled. (T/F)
2. You **have to** manually adjust the lineweights in the elevations. (T/F)
3. As you move the cursor around the building, during placement, the elevation tag turns to point at the building. (T/F)
4. There is only one part of the elevation tag that can be selected. (T/F)
5. You cannot adjust the "extent of view" using the *crop region*. (T/F)
6. What is the first thing you should do after placing an elevation tag?

   ____

7. Although they make the drawing look very interesting, using

   the __________________ feature can cause Revit to run extremely slow.
8. With the elevation tag selected, you can use the ______________________ icon to adjust the tag orientation to look at an angled wall.
9. You need to adjust the ______________________ to see objects, in elevation, that are a distance back from the main elevation.
10. What feature allows you to develop different ideas? ______________________

SELF-EXAM ANSWERS:
1 – F, **2** – T, **3** – T, **4** – F, **5** – 0 5.5

Lesson 11
SECTIONS:

Sections are an important documentation tool in a set of architectural drawings. They help the builder understand vertical relationships. Architectural sections can occasionally contradict other drawings, such as mechanical or structural drawings. One example is a beam shown on the section that is smaller than what the structural drawings call for; this creates a problem in the field when the duct does not fit in the ceiling space. The ceiling is lowered and/or the duct is reduced in size, ultimately compromising the design to some degree.

Autodesk® Revit® significantly helps to avoid these types of conflicts. Sections, like plans and elevations, are generated from the 3D model. Thus, it is virtually impossible to have a conflict between the architectural drawings. Many structural, mechanical, and electrical engineers also use Revit for even greater coordination, helping eliminate conflicts and redundancy in drawings.

Exercise 11-1:
Specify Section Cutting Plane in Plan View

Similar to elevation tags, placing the section "graphic" in a plan view actually generates the section view. You will learn how to do this now.

Placing Section Marks:

1. Open ex10-5.rvt and **Save As ex11-1.rvt**.

2. Switch to the ***First Floor*** plan view.

3. Select **View → Create → Section.**

TIP: You may also select the Section icon from the Quick Access Toolbar, which would be more convenient.

4. Draw a **Section** mark as shown in Figure 11-1.1. Start on the left side in this case. Use the *Move* tool if needed to accurately adjust the section after insertion. The section line should go through the stair landings (Figure 11-1.1).

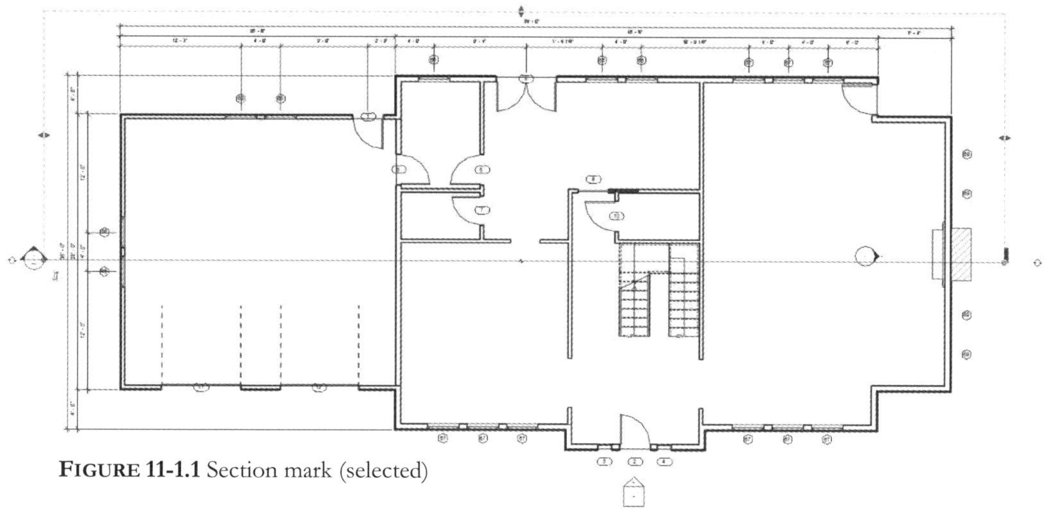

FIGURE 11-1.1 Section mark (selected)

Figure 11-1 shows the section selected. The section tag features are very similar to the elevation tags covered in the previous lesson. You can adjust the depth of view (far clip plane) and the section width using the *Adjustment Grips.*

You can see that the *Far Clip Plane* location in the plan view is out past the building perimeter; this means you will see everything (Figure 11-1.1). Anything passing through the section line is in section; everything else you see is in elevation (Revit calls it "projection"). Also, you can see the roof is shown in section exactly where the section line is shown in plan. Figure 11-1.2 also shows the *crop region.*

The *Section* tool is almost exactly like the *Elevation* tool.

FIGURE 11-1.2 Longitudinal section view

Notice in the *Project Browser* that a new category has been created: *Sections (building Section)*. If you expand this category, you will see the new section view listed; it is called *Section 1*. You should always rename any new view right after creating it. This will help with navigation and when it comes time to place views on sheets for printing.

5. Rename the section view *Section 1* to ***Longitudinal Section***.

6. Switch to the new section view, ***Longitudinal Section***.

   TIP: Double-click on the section bubble head to open that view. The section needs to be unselected first; double-click on the blue part.

7. In the *Properties Palette*, with nothing selected in the model, change the *View Properties* so the *Detail Level* is set to **Medium**.

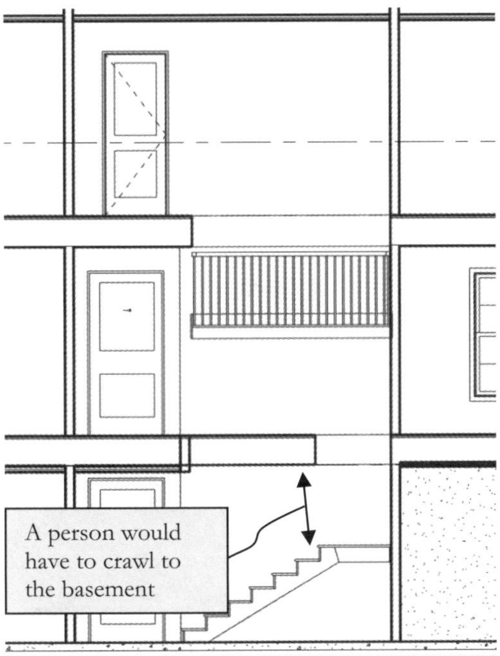

FIGURE 11-1.3 Section view – zoomed in

Notice how the walls change to show more detail. You can also set this on the *View Control Bar* at the bottom-left of the screen.

8. **Zoom in** on the portion of the section near the stairs.

You should notice an added level of detail in the section view.

You may also notice a big problem, as first mentioned on page 9-10: in Figure 11-1.3, the stairs to the basement are obstructed by the first floor system. You will fix this soon.

The image below lists the additional terms for the section graphics in the plan view, compared to elevation tags.

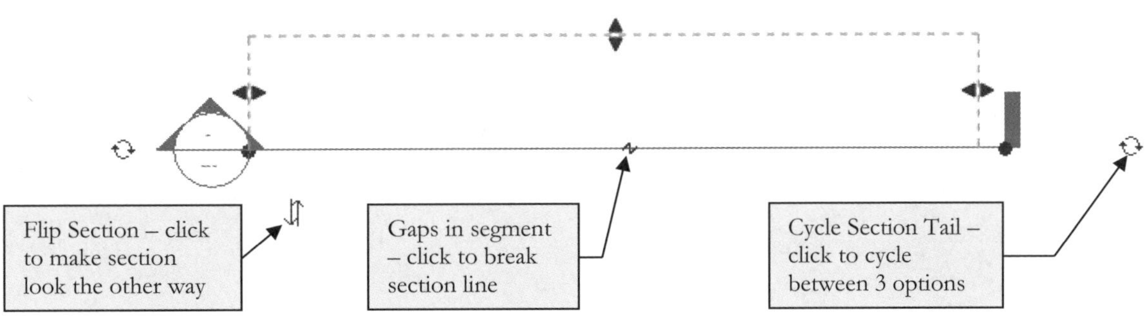

9. Create another **section** in the *First Floor* plan view as shown in **Figure 11-1.4**.

   TIP: *You can use the control arrows to make the section look the other direction.*

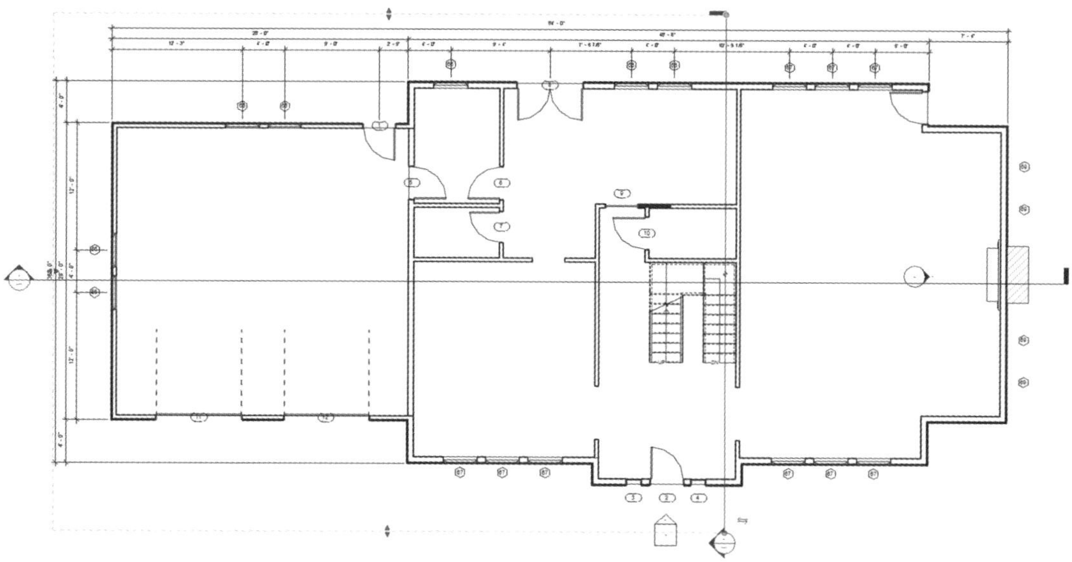

FIGURE 11-1.4 Plan view; Section tag (selected)

10. Rename the new section view to ***Cross Section 1*** in the *Project Browser.*

11. Switch to the ***Cross Section 1*** view.

12. Set the *Detail Level* to ***Medium*** and turn off the ***crop region*** visibility via the *View Control Bar* (Figure 11-1.5).

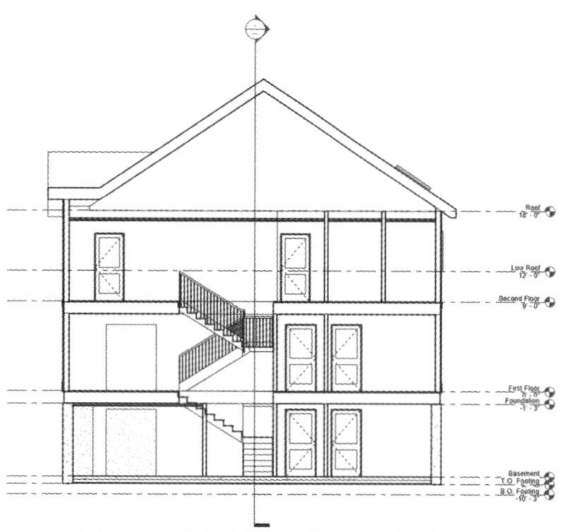

FIGURE 11-1.5 Cross Section 1 view

Revit automatically displays lines as heavier for elements in section than for elements beyond the cutting plane and shown in elevation (aka projection).

Also, with the *Detail Level* set to *Medium*, the walls and floors are hatched to represent the material in section (when a material is selected for a layer within the wall structure definition via type properties). In this example, notice the foundation walls have a fill pattern for concrete shown in section.

Notice that the *Longitudinal Section* mark is automatically displayed in the *Cross Section 1* view. If you switch to the *Longitudinal Section* view, you will see the *Cross Section 1* mark. Keeping with Revit's philosophy of changing everything anywhere, you can select the section mark in the other section view and adjust its various properties, like its *Far Clip Plane.*

FYI: In any view that has a section mark *in it, you can double-click on the round reference bubble to quickly switch to that section view. However, the section cannot be selected.*

Modifying the First Floor Stair Opening:

Next, you will fix the problem with the stair opening in the first floor system. Basically, you will switch to the *First Floor Plan* view and select the floor. Then click Edit Boundary on the *Ribbon*, and modify the sketch to enlarge the stair opening.

13. Switch to the ***First Floor*** plan view.

14. Select the floor; use *Tab* if required to highlight the floor element for selection.

    TIP: You can also toggle on Select Element by Face on the Status Bar and select the floor anywhere within its boundary.

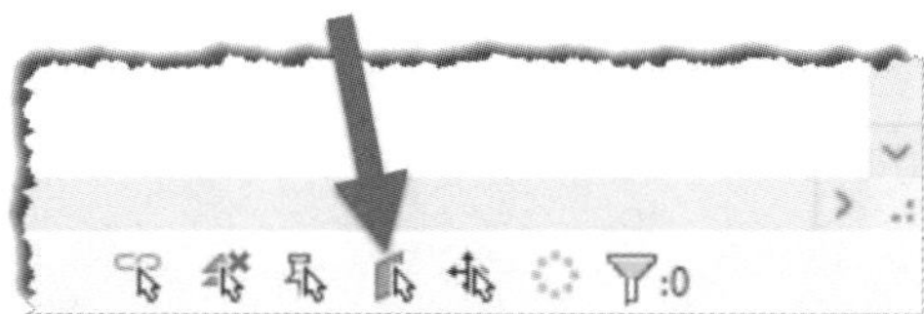

15. Click **Edit Boundary** on the *Ribbon* (see image below).

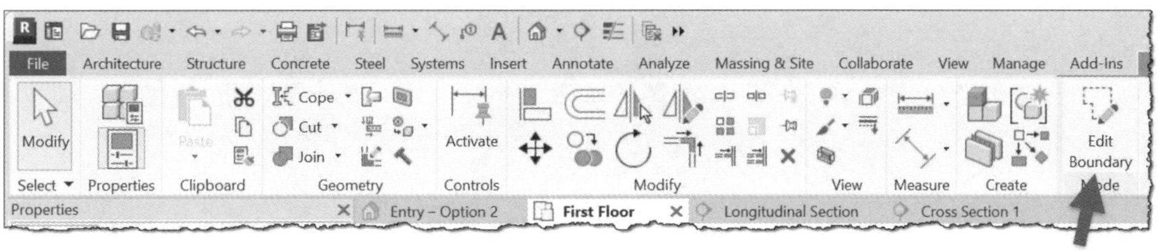

The floor is now back in sketch mode, as it was when it was first created.

16. Use the *Line* and *Edit* tools, such as *Split* and *Trim*, to modify the sketch of the floor opening as shown in Figure 11-1.6.

17. Click the **green check mark** and choose **Don't Attach** to the *attach walls* prompt.

18. Switch back to the ***Longitudinal Section*** view.

Notice the stair no longer has a problem (Figure 11-1.7).

19. **Save** your project as **ex11-1.rvt**.

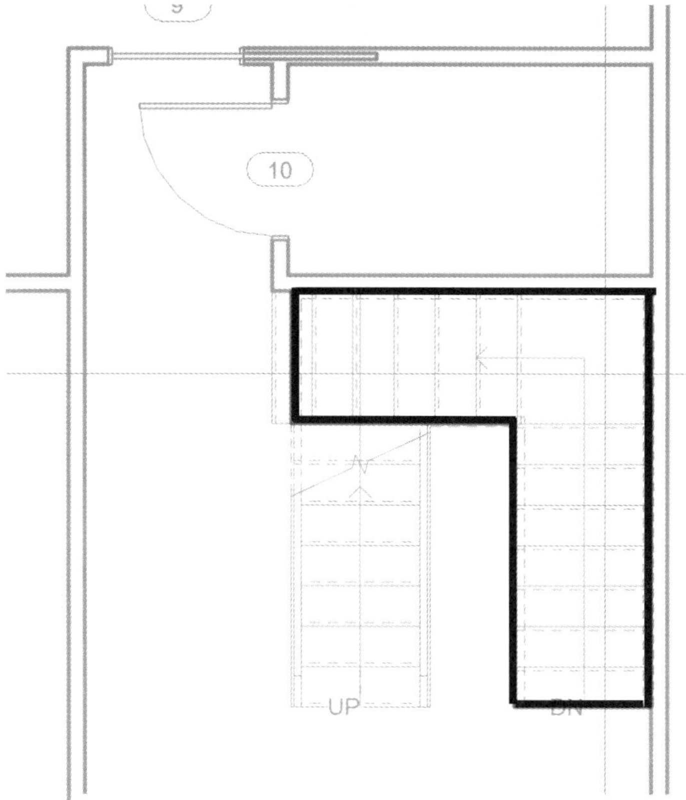

FIGURE 11-1.6 Plan view – Floor, sketch edit

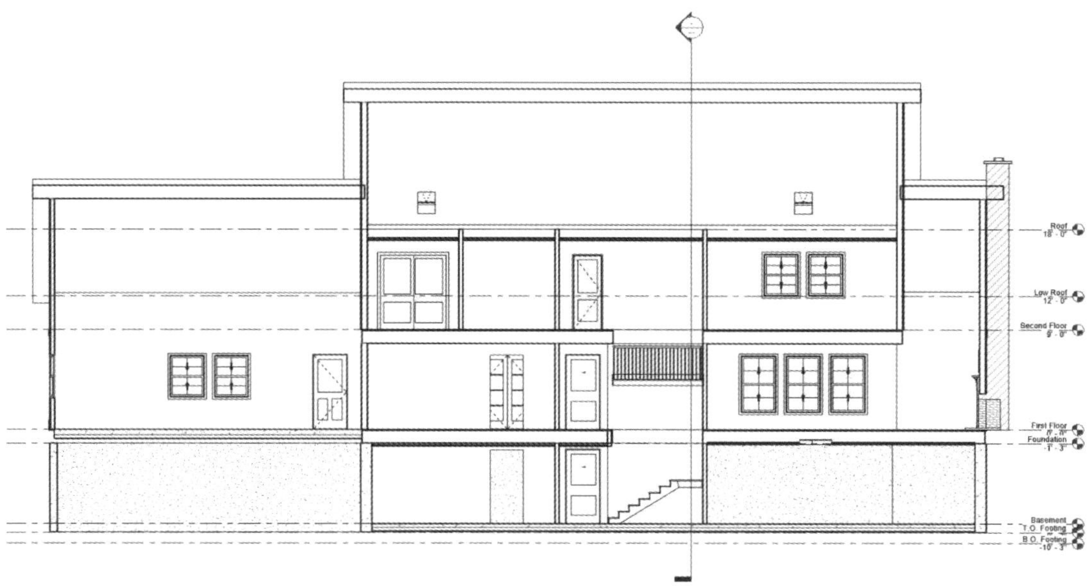

FIGURE 11-1.7 Longitudinal view – First floor element modified

Exercise 11-2:
Modifying the Project Model in Section View

Again, similar to elevation views, you can modify the project model in section view. This includes adjusting door locations and ceiling heights.

Modifying Doors in Section View:

In this section you will move a door and delete a door in section view.

1. Open ex11-1.rvt and **Save As ex11-2.rvt**.

2. Open ***Cross Section 1*** view.

Looking back to Figure 11-1.5, you should notice the wall below the basement stair still extends up through the stair. You will move the wall over in the section view and then note that the adjacent wall and ceilings all automatically adjust in other views.

3. Use the ***Align*** tool to make the wall align with the edge of the floor opening (Figure 11-2.1).

   TIP: *Pick the edge of the floor first and then the face of the wall to align with the selected edge.*

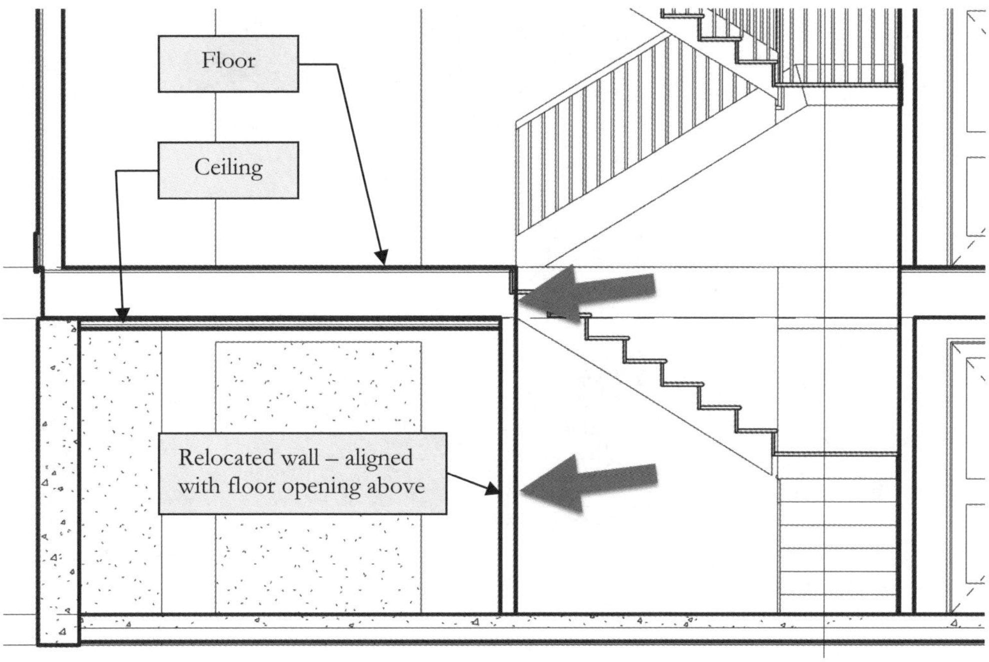

FIGURE 11-2.1 Cross Section 1 view; wall below stair moved

4. Switch to the ***Basement*** ceiling plan view.

Notice the wall below the stair moved South and the ceiling automatically adjusted as well (Figure 11-2.2).

As long as a wall that defines the ceiling perimeter is not deleted or shortened so that the ceiling perimeter is no longer defined, Revit will automatically update the ceiling. If the perimeter does become undefined, you may have to edit it manually. **Avoid deleting objects** just to redraw them, because "hosted" elements, such as lights, switches, and dimensions, will become un-hosted.

A cutaway 3D view of the current state of the model is shown below (Figure 11-2.3).

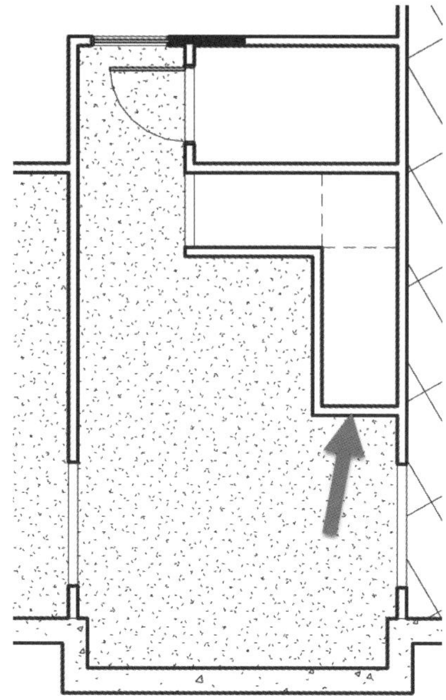

FIGURE 11-2.2 Basement Floor Plan view; notice changes

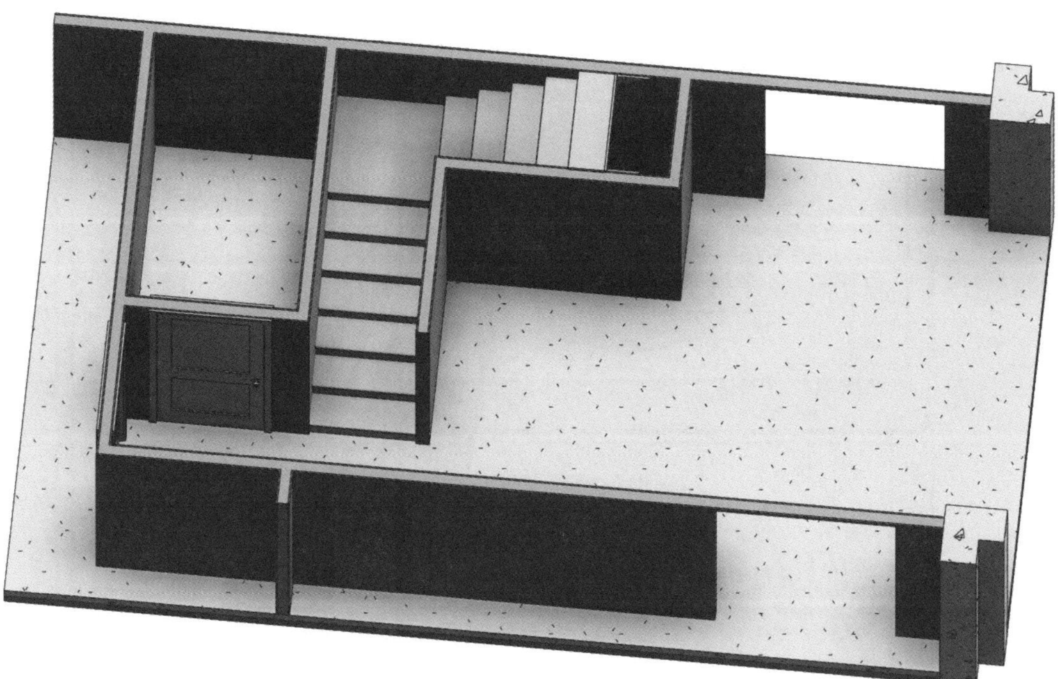

FIGURE 11-2.3 Cutaway view of current state of model in basement

Next, you will adjust the ceiling height via your *Longitudinal Section* view.

5. Switch to ***Longitudinal Section*** view.

6. At the basement level, select the suspended acoustical ceiling tile system in the *Family Room* (lower right room).

Notice that while a ceiling is selected in a section view, a temporary dimension appears. This dimension allows you to directly change the ceiling height.

FYI: *The dimension may be overlapping a wall.*

7. Change the ceiling height to **6′-8″** using the temporary dimension. If required, adjust the witness lines to go from the top of the basement floor slab to the bottom of the ceiling.

Now, as you can see in the section view (Figure 11-2.4), the ceiling has lowered and there is more room for the recessed light fixtures shown; notice the lights lowered automatically.

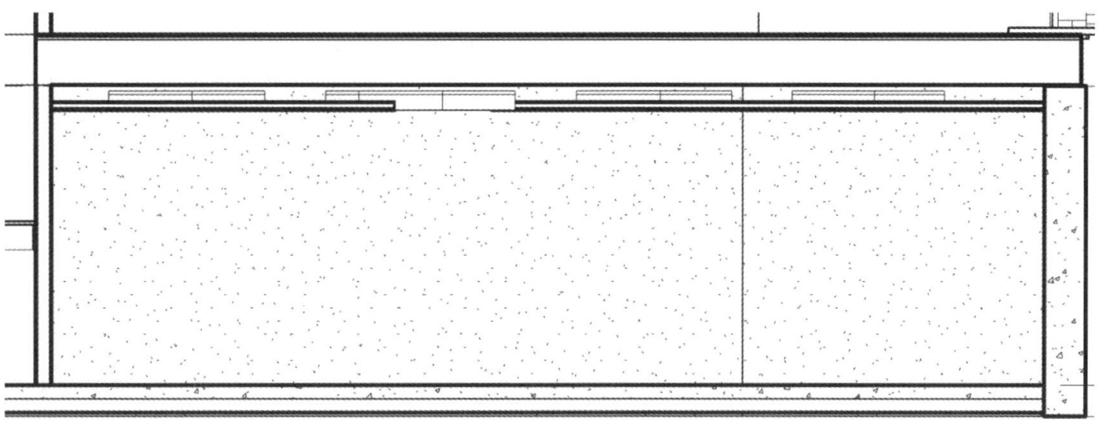

FIGURE 11-2.4 Cross Section 1 view; ceiling height modified

Adding the Strip Footing Below the Foundation Wall:

A strip footing, in Revit, can be just a wall type set up as concrete. The width of the "wall" is set to be the width of your footing, as is the height. Revit provides a predefined wall and plan view in the residential template, making the process very easy.

8. Switch to the plan view called ***T.O. Footing***.

   FYI: *T.O. means "Top Of," i.e., "Top Of Footing."*

9. Select the ***Wall*** tool and then select *Basic Wall:* ***24" Footing*** from the *Type Selector.*

10. Set the *Location Line* to **Wall Centerline** and make sure the *Depth* is set to **B.O. Footing** (B.O. means Bottom of Footing) on the *Ribbon* (Figure 11-2.5).

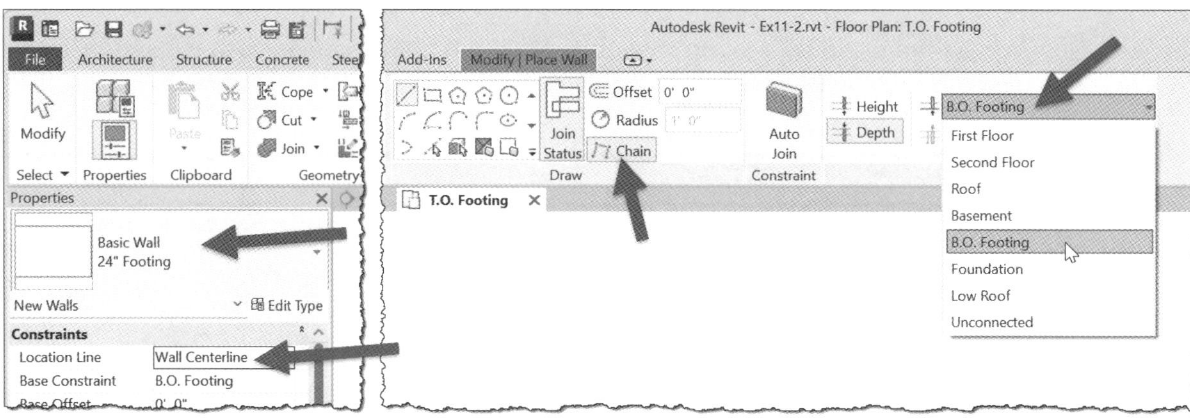

FIGURE 11-2.5 Foundation wall settings

11. Select **Chain** on the *Ribbon.*

12. Start picking the intersection of wall centerlines, working around the perimeter of the building; also, add a footing below the wall between the garage and the house. You want the 24" footing to be centered on the foundation wall (Figure 11-2.6).

    TIP: *Setting the Location Line to Wall Centerline is for the wall you are about to draw. Revit will automatically "snap" to the centers of previously drawn walls. Hover your cursor over the center of the wall until you see a dashed magenta/purple reference line, letting you know you are snapped to the center of the wall, and then move your cursor towards the end of that wall/purple reference line and click.*

After drawing the footings, you will notice the interior side of the footing will disappear because it is below the basement floor slab; it is visible in the garage area because it is unexcavated.

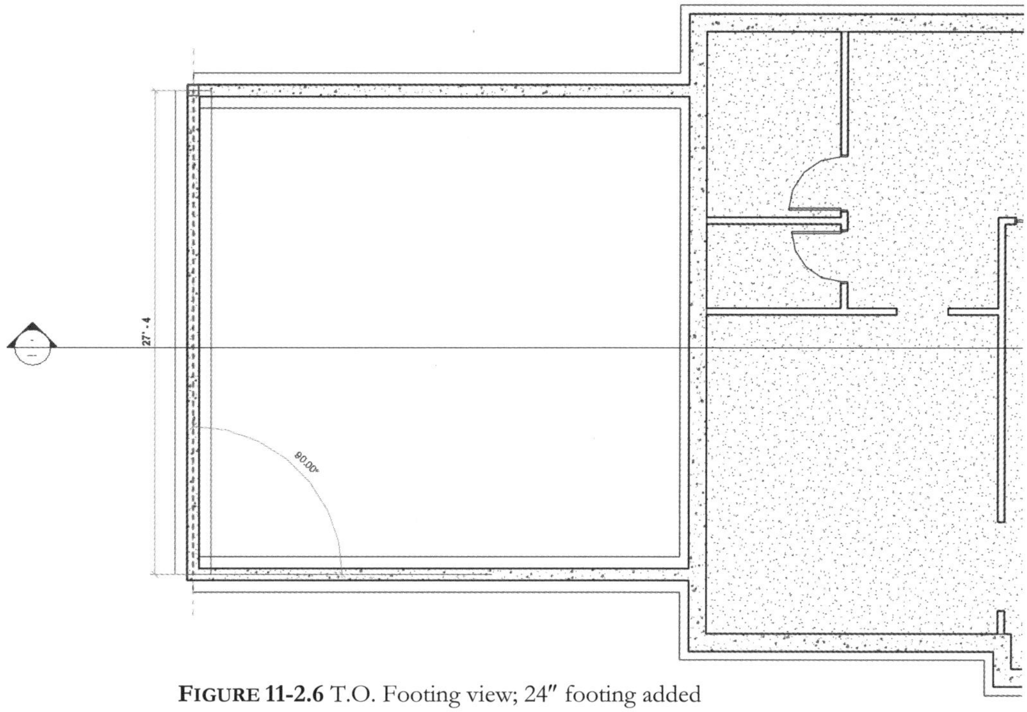

FIGURE 11-2.6 T.O. Footing view; 24″ footing added

13. Switch back to the section view ***Cross Section 1***.

As you can see (Figure 11-2.7), the footings have been added.

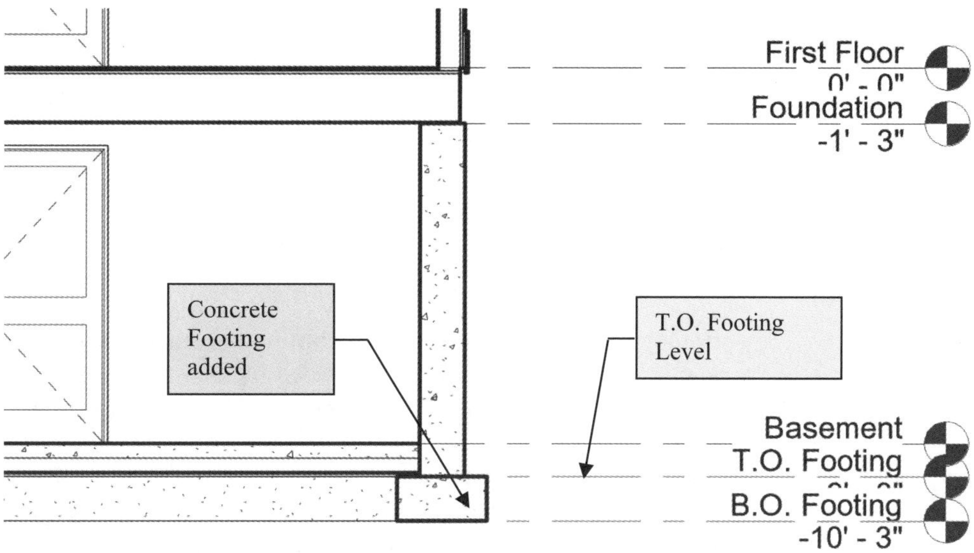

FIGURE 11-2.7 Cross Section 1 view (modified)

If you look at the properties for the *24″ footing* wall type, you can see how the wall was created relative to the *T.O. Footing* view in which you drew it.

Notice the *Base* and *Top Constraints* are selected. The *Base Constraint* is set to *B.O. Footing*, and the *Top Constraint* is set to *Up to level: T.O. Footing.* Also, notice that the Unconnected Height is grayed out, meaning you cannot change this setting, which makes sense since you have dynamically defined both the top and bottom of the wall.

The distance between the two levels is 1′-0″, so the footing is 1′-0″ high.

In *Cross Section 1* view, try clicking on the *B.O. Footing* text (i.e., the -10′-3″ text) and change it to -11′-3″ and notice the footing size will automatically change (see image to the right).

If you try this, make sure you *UNDO* so that when you finish this exercise, your footing is only 1′-0″ thick.

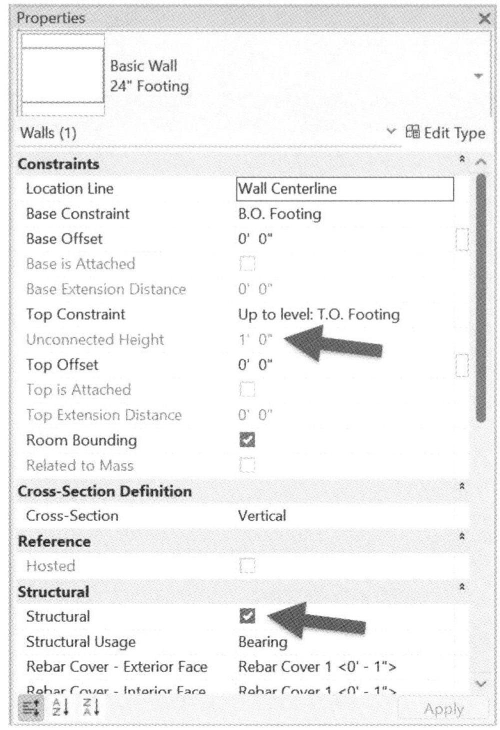

FIGURE 11-2.8 Properties for 24″ Footing wall

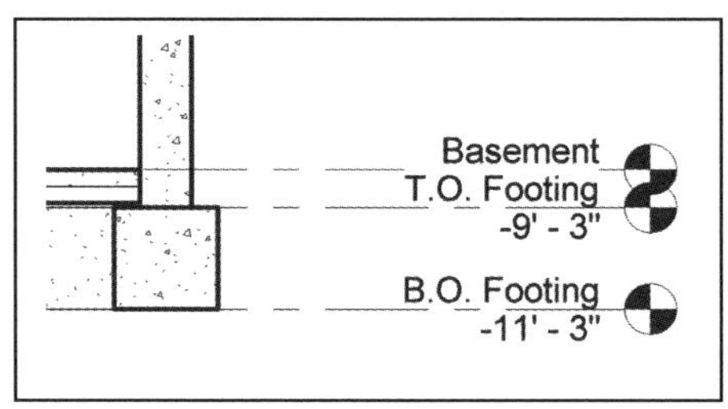

Adding the Strip Footing Using the Foundation Tool on the Structure tab:

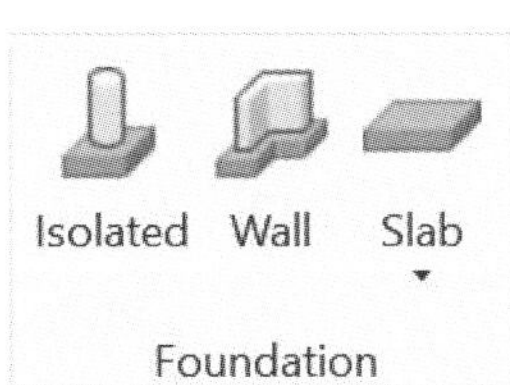

Revit offers another tool to add continuous strip footings below your foundation wall. On the *Foundation* panel (on the *Structure* tab) you can select the ***Wall Foundation*** tool. Then you simply select foundation walls and Revit automatically places a footing, centered, and directly under the wall. If you want to try this option, you can delete a portion of footing and use the *Structure* tool to replace it. If you try this, make sure you *Undo* before proceeding.

Modifying the Footing Linework in Plan View:

Revit has predefined settings for line styles and line weights. Most of the time, Revit software developers have selected settings satisfactory to most designers, which is great because it saves a lot of time. However, you will occasionally want to tweak these prescribed settings. As mentioned in the previous chapter, Revit makes this easy with the ***Linework*** tool on the *Modify* tab. Basically, you select the *Linework* icon, select the desired setting from the *Type Selector* (e.g., lineweight or line style), and then select the lines to change. This change only applies to the current view.

You will try this next, switching the footing lines to dashed.

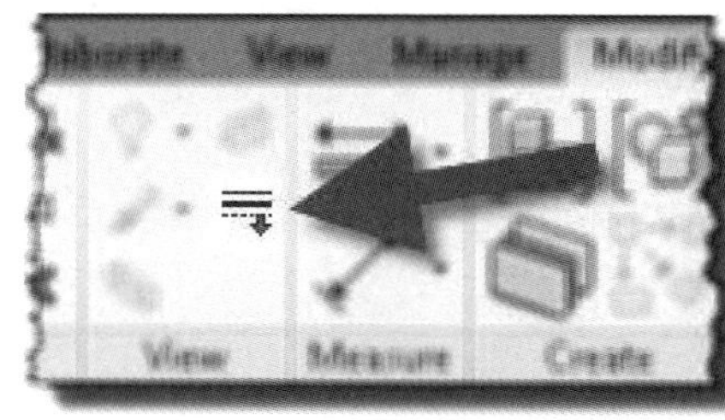

14. Switch back to the ***T.O. Footing*** view.

15. Select **Modify → View → Linework**.

16. Select **Hidden** from the *Line Style Panel* on the *Ribbon* (Figure 11-2.9).

17. Click all the visible footing lines. Click Ctrl+Z if you pick another line by accident; that will *Undo* the previous pick.

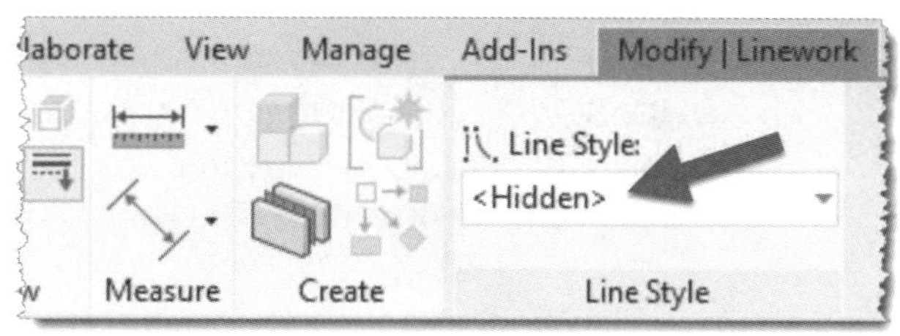

FIGURE 11-2.9 Linework icon selected

The footing lines are now the hidden line style (i.e., dashed) in the current view (Figure 11-2.10).

18. Save your project as **ex11-2.rvt**.

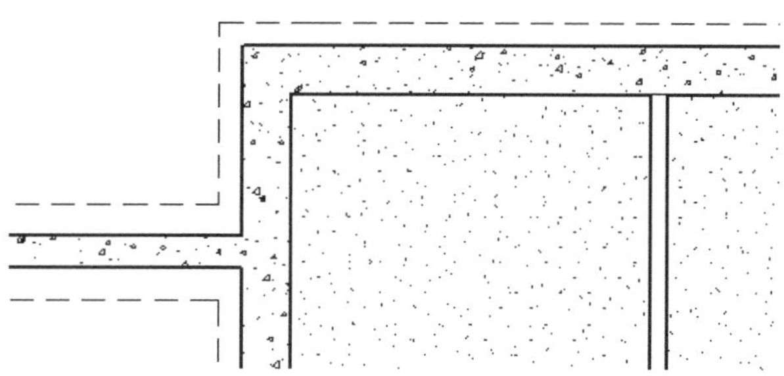

FIGURE 11-2.10 Footing lines dashed

*FYI: The Linework tool will work on most lines generated by the model that are visible in a view. In the above example, the **Filter** feature in Revit might be more appropriate, as you can set up a view to dash all walls with the word "footing" in their name. This is just one example of how Filter can be used. This will affect both current and future walls visible in the current view. This filter can then be applied to other views if desired.*

Stepped Footings:

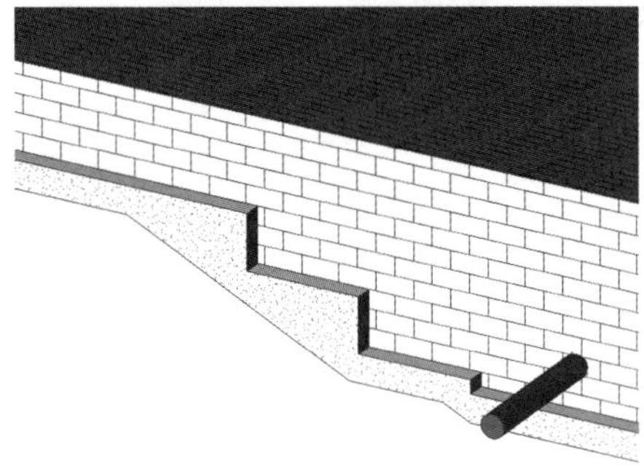

Foundation walls and footings often need to step on sloped sites and around utilities. This is a little more work to set up in Revit, but it is still very doable. You will not actually do this at this time, but the concept will be covered here to get you started in the right direction when you need to implement this type of design.

Basically, you *Split* the footings at the step locations and adjust the vertical position of each section of footing.

You do not need to split the foundation wall; you will see why in a moment.

- In elevation or plan view, use the ***Split*** tool to break the footings up where each step needs to occur.
- Modify the *Base* and *Top Constraints* for each wall as required to ensure they are in the correct vertical positions (Figure 11-2.11).

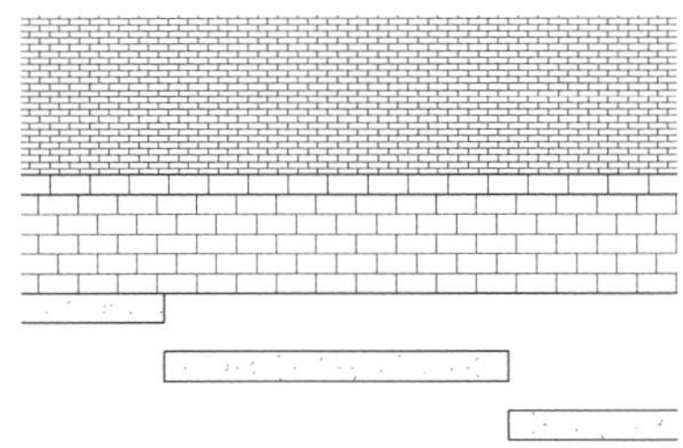

FIGURE 11-2.11
Footing Split and heights adjusted

- In an elevation or section view, select the foundation wall and pick the **Edit Profile** button on the *Ribbon.*
- Use the ***Lines*** tool, on the *Ribbon*, and any of the edit tools (*Split*, *Trim*, *Mirror*, etc.) to redefine the perimeter of the wall in elevation. Modify the bottom magenta sketch line to follow the tops of the footings. Click **Finish Edit Mode** (i.e., green checkmark) when done (Figure 11-2.12).

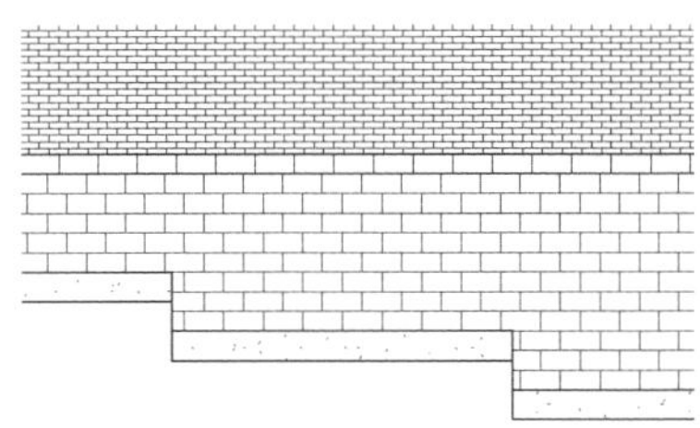

FIGURE 11-2.12
Foundation wall modified (via Edit Profile)

- Using the same technique as for the footing "wall" (i.e., *Edit Profile*), you can edit the profile of the footings, so they appear correctly in elevation making sure the adjacent edges touch.
- When you **Finish Edit Mode** on the footings, you should see the footings join together and appear monolithic. If not, you can use the ***Join Geometry*** tool unless the edges do not touch perfectly, in which case you need to use *Edit Profile* again and fix the problem.

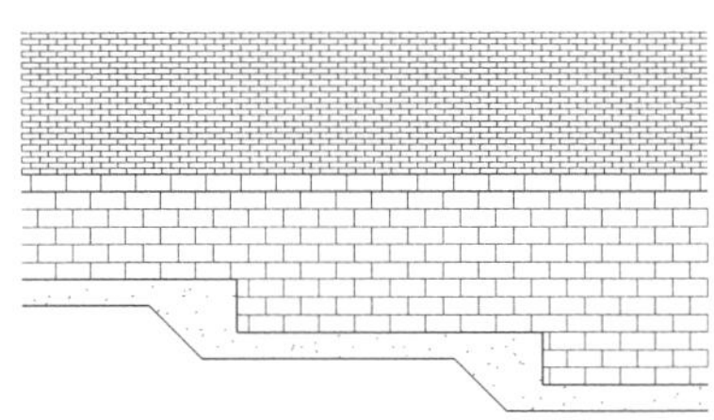

FIGURE 11-2.13
Footing "wall" modified (via Edit Profile)

Exercise 11-3:
Wall Sections

So far in this lesson, you have drawn building sections. Building sections are typically 1/8″ or 1/4″ scale and contain minimal detail and annotations. Wall sections are drawn at a larger scale and have much more detail. You will look at setting up wall sections next.

Setting up the Wall Section View:

1. Open ex11-2 and **Save As ex11-3.rvt**.

2. Switch to the ***Cross Section 1*** view.

3. From the *View* tab on the *Ribbon*, click the rectangular ***Callout*** tool and then select *Section:* **Wall Section** from the *Type Selector*.

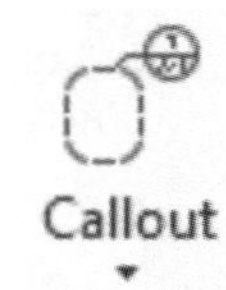

4. Place a **Callout** as shown in Figure 11-3.1.

   TIP: Pick in the upper left and then in the lower right to place the Callout tag; do not click-n-drag.

   TIP: You can use the control grips *for the Callout tag to move the reference bubble if desired; for example, move it away from notes/dimensions.*

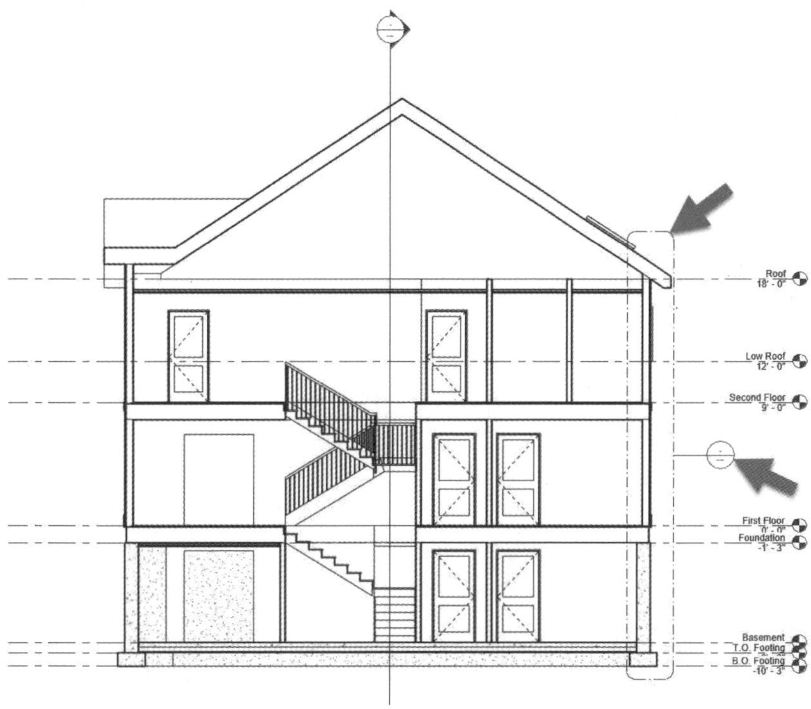

FIGURE 11-3.1 Cross Section 1 view with Callout added

Notice that a view was added in the *Sections (Wall Section)* category of the *Project Browser*. Because *Callouts* are detail references to a section view, it is a good idea to keep the new callout view name similar to the name of the section.

Additionally, *Callouts* differ from section views in that the callout is not referenced in every related view. This example is typical in that the building sections are referenced from the plans, and wall sections are referenced from the building sections. The floor plans can get pretty messy if you try to add too much information.

5. Double-click on the reference bubble portion of the *Callout* tag to open the ***Cross Section 1 – Callout 1*** view (Figure 11-3.2).

Notice, down on the *View Control Bar*, that the scale is set to ½″ = 1′-0″. This affects the elevation tags, text, datums and any annotation you add.

6. On the *View Control Bar* set:
   a) *View Scale* to **¾″ = 1′-0″**
   b) *Detail Level* to **Fine.**

Notice the level datum's size changed.

If you zoom in on a portion of the *Callout* view, you can see the detail added to the view. The wall's interior lines are added, and the materials in section are hatched (see Figure 11-3.4, at the second floor line).

You can use the *Detail Lines* tool to add more detailed information to the drawing. For example, you could show the truss, wall base, and flashing. Walls can be configured to have wall bases, which are set up as sweeps.

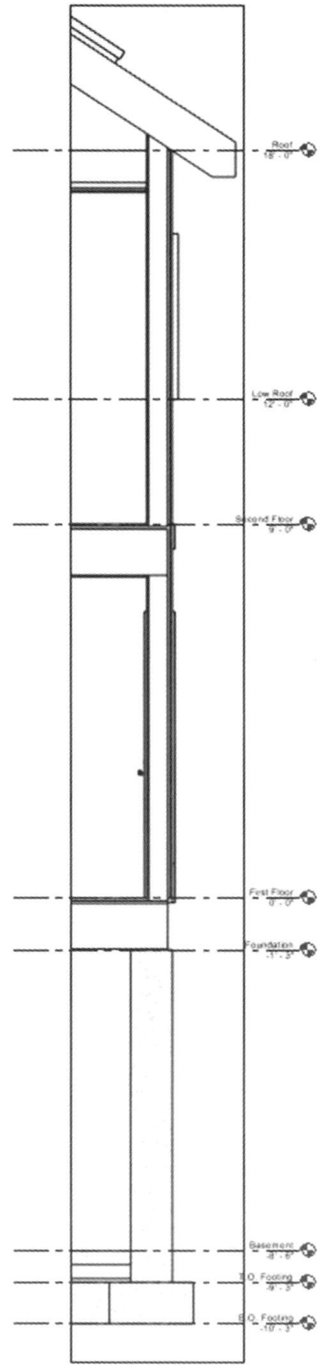

FIGURE 11-3.2 Callout of Cross Section 1

As before, you can turn off and adjust the *crop region*. If you set the *Detail Level* to **Coarse**, you get just an outline of your structure. The *Coarse* setting is more appropriate for building sections than wall sections. Figure 11-3.3 is an example of the *Coarse* setting.

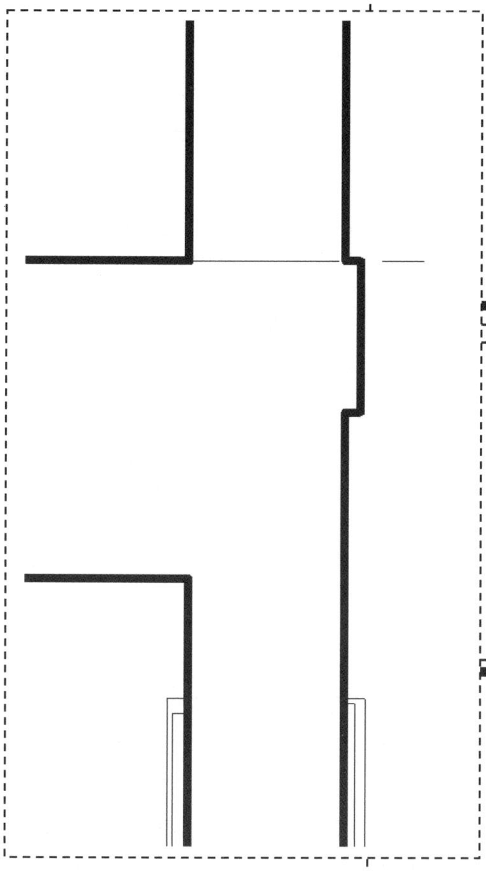

FIGURE 11-3.3 Callout view (zoomed in); detail level: Coarse

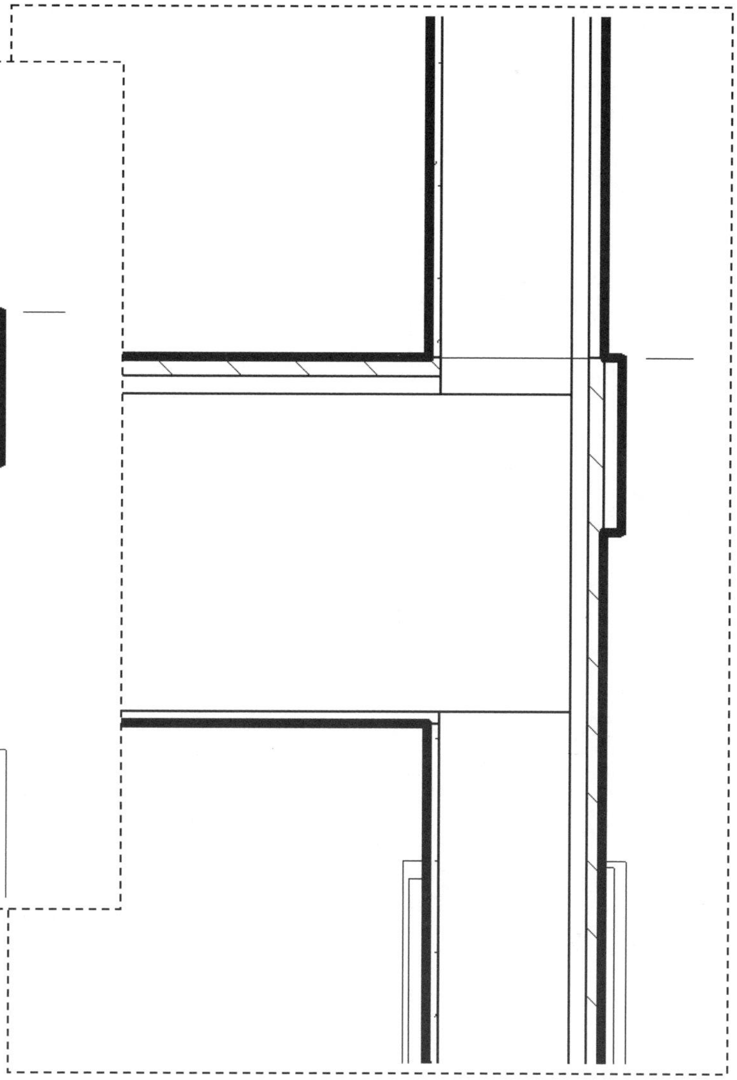

FIGURE 11-3.4 Callout view (zoomed in); detail level: Fine

Refining the Walls:

Now that the residence is more developed, you will modify various wall properties to better reflect what they would be in the real world. Both the main building walls and the garage need a little attention.

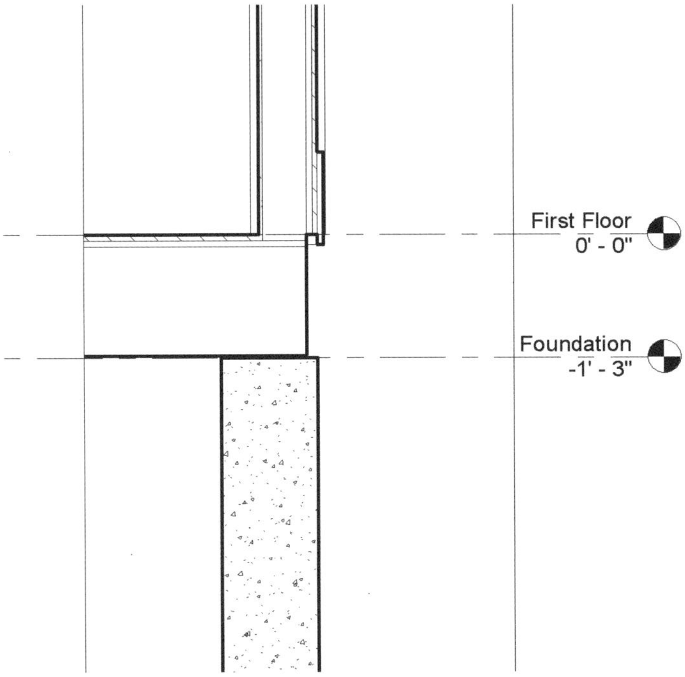

In the larger-scale wall section, you can see a few problems that need to be addressed.

A – The siding and sheathing need to extend down and over the edge of the flooring.

B – The top of the foundation wall needs to be modified to accommodate a 2x plate for the floor joists to bear on and attach to.

FIGURE 11-3.5 First floor condition in Wall Section view

7. In the wall section view, *Callout of Cross Section 1*, click to select the ***Foundation*** datum and then click to select the elevation text **-1′-3″** and change it to **-1′-4 ½″**.

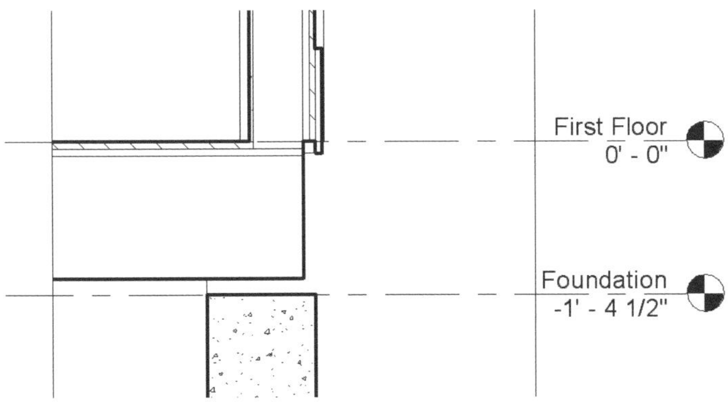

You have now provided space for a continuous 2x board (which is 1 ½″ high). This board will be added later.

Note that **all** of the foundation walls in the model have been changed by this one modification!

FIGURE 11-3.6 Top of foundation wall modified

Next, you will adjust the sheathing and siding. Revit provides a way in which specific "layers" (i.e., the sheathing and siding in this example) can extend down farther than the rest of the wall (i.e., the wood studs and gypsum board). You will modify your exterior walls, except at the garage, so that the sheathing and siding extend down to the top of the foundation wall. To do this you need to make one change within the wall type.

8. In the wall section view, select the exterior wall *Basic Wall:* **Exterior - Wood Shingle over Wood Siding on Wood Stud**.

9. Select **Edit Type** on the *Properties Palette* and then click **Edit** next to the *Structure* parameter.

10. Make sure the preview pane is displayed by clicking the **Preview** button in the lower left.

11. Below the preview pane, set the *View* to **Section: Modify type attributes** so the wall is shown in section (Figure 11-3.7).

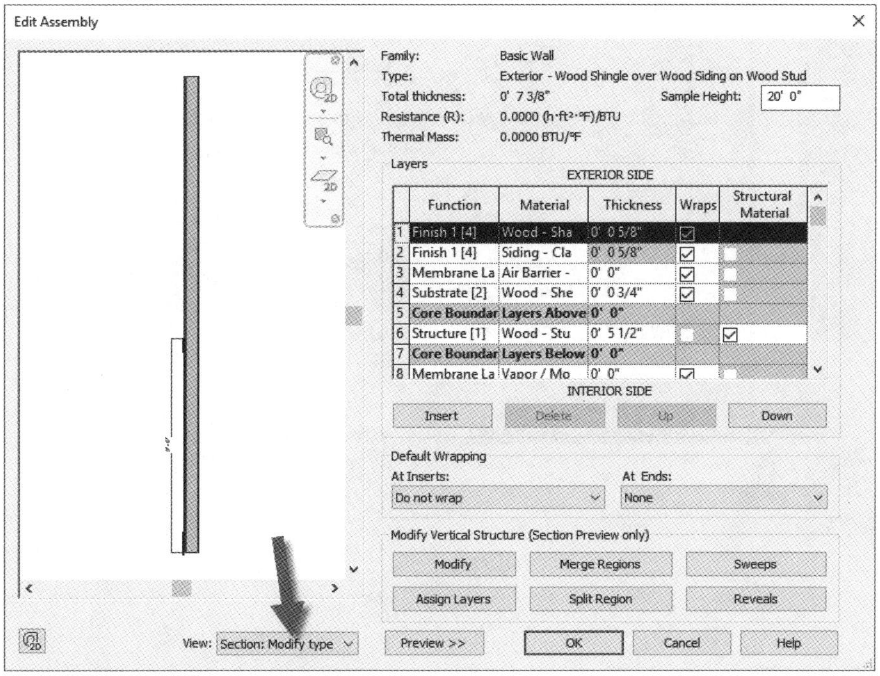

FIGURE 11-3.7 Wall structure – edit assembly

Next, you will zoom in on the bottom of the wall in the preview pane and unlock the bottom edge of the siding and sheathing layers. This will allow the unlocked material to extend up or down apart from the bottom location of the wall.

12. Click in the preview pane to make sure it is active, and then scroll the wheel on your mouse to zoom in on the bottom of the wall; you can also press the wheel button while moving the mouse to pan.

13. Click the **Modify** button (Figure 11-3.8).

14. Click the bottom edge of the siding "layer" (Figure 11-3.8).

Be sure you have the bottom edge of the siding layer selected. You should see a padlock symbol above it. Next you will click that symbol to unlock it. As soon as you make this change you will have a new parameter associated with that wall type named *Base Extension Distance*, which is an *Instance Parameter*, allowing you to change this value on a wall-by-wall basis. Entering a positive number moves the sheathing and siding up that distance from the bottom of the wall and a negative number moves it down.

15. Click the padlock symbol so it is shown in the **unlocked** position.

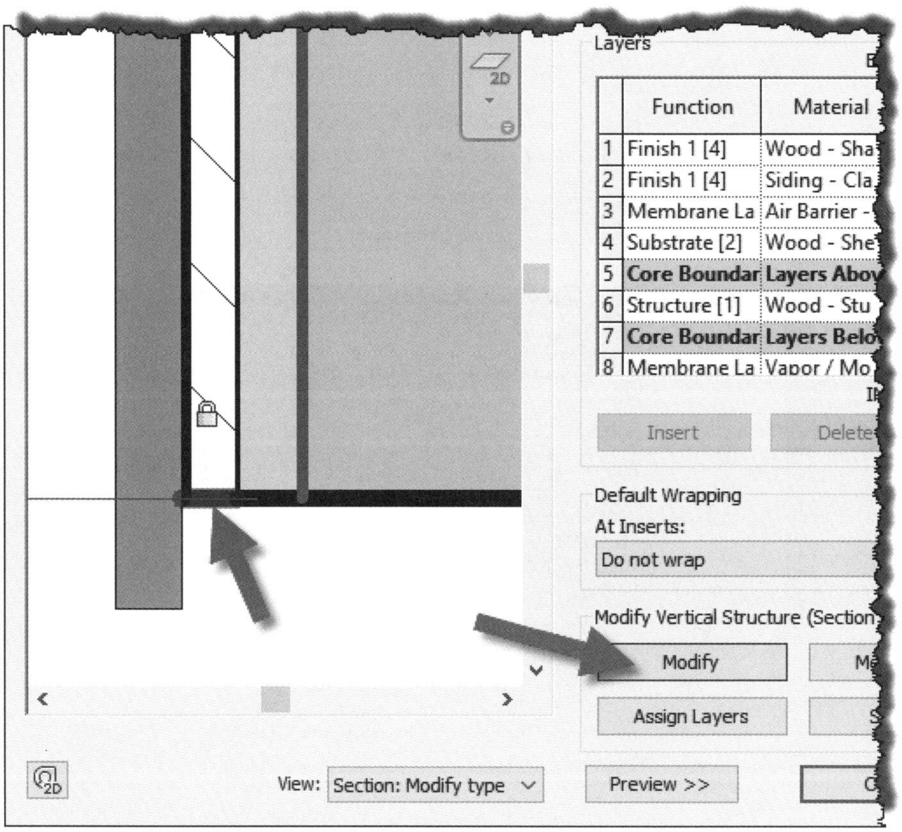

FIGURE 11-3.8 Enabling base extension for selected wall type

You will repeat the previous two steps for the sheathing layer as well.

16. Click on the bottom edge of the sheathing layer.

17. Click the padlock symbol to unlock it.

    ***FYI:** Only one contiguous group of layers can be set up to move up and down like this. Contiguous means the layers have to touch each other.*

18. Click **OK** to close the open dialog boxes.

19. Switch to the ***First Floor Plan*** view.

In the next step you will select all the exterior walls except the three at the garage. In order to select the three walls at the front entry, you will need to uncheck an option on the *Status Bar*; you will do this next.

20. Uncheck **Exclude Options** on the *Status Bar* (lower right).

21. Hover your cursor over one of the exterior walls to highlight it, but do not click, and then press the **Tab** key, which will highlight all the exterior walls. Click to select the highlighted walls.

    ***FYI:** Alternately you can simply hold down the Ctrl key and individually pick each wall.*

22. Press the **Shift** key and select the <u>four</u> garage walls, one at a time while holding the Shift key down, to un-select them (if they are selected).

23. With all the exterior walls selected, except the <u>four</u> garage walls, draw your attention to the ***Properties Palette***.

24. Set the *Base Extension Distance* to **-1′-4″**. Do not forget to add the negative sign at the beginning. See Figure 11-3.9.

This will make the sheathing and siding extend down 1′-4″ below the bottom of the wall.

FIGURE 11-3.9 Base Extension Distance

25. Switch back to ***Callout of Cross Section 1*** to see the modified wall (Figure 11-3.10).

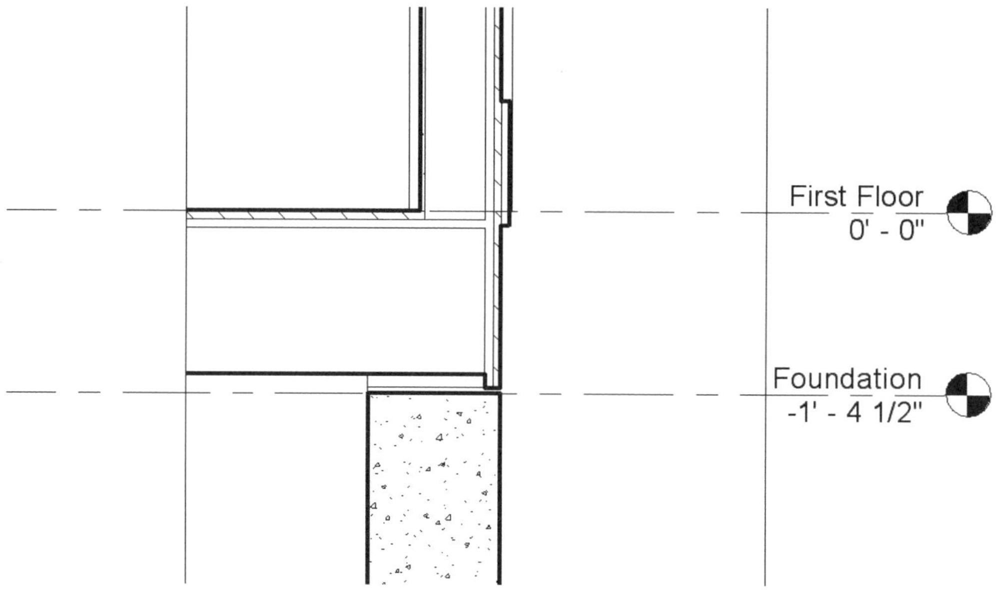

FIGURE 11-3.10 Results of 'Base Extension Distance' modification

26. Switch back to plan view and enter edit mode ***Entry Windows – Option 2***, via the *Status Bar*, so you can make the same change to the three entry walls located in the second design option for the entry windows. Refer to previous sections for more information on editing *Design Options*. Switch back to **Main Model** when done.

Wall Section at Garage:

Next, you will set up a wall section view at the garage wall.

27. Switch to the ***Longitudinal Section***.

28. Add a "wall section" type **Callout** at the garage wall (Figure 11-3.11).

29. Rename the new view to ***Garage Wall Section***.

30. **Open** the *Garage Wall Section* view.

As you can see, the top of the foundation wall is not correct for the garage area. The foundation wall typically comes up to the top of the floor slab or 8-16″ above that. You will make this change next.

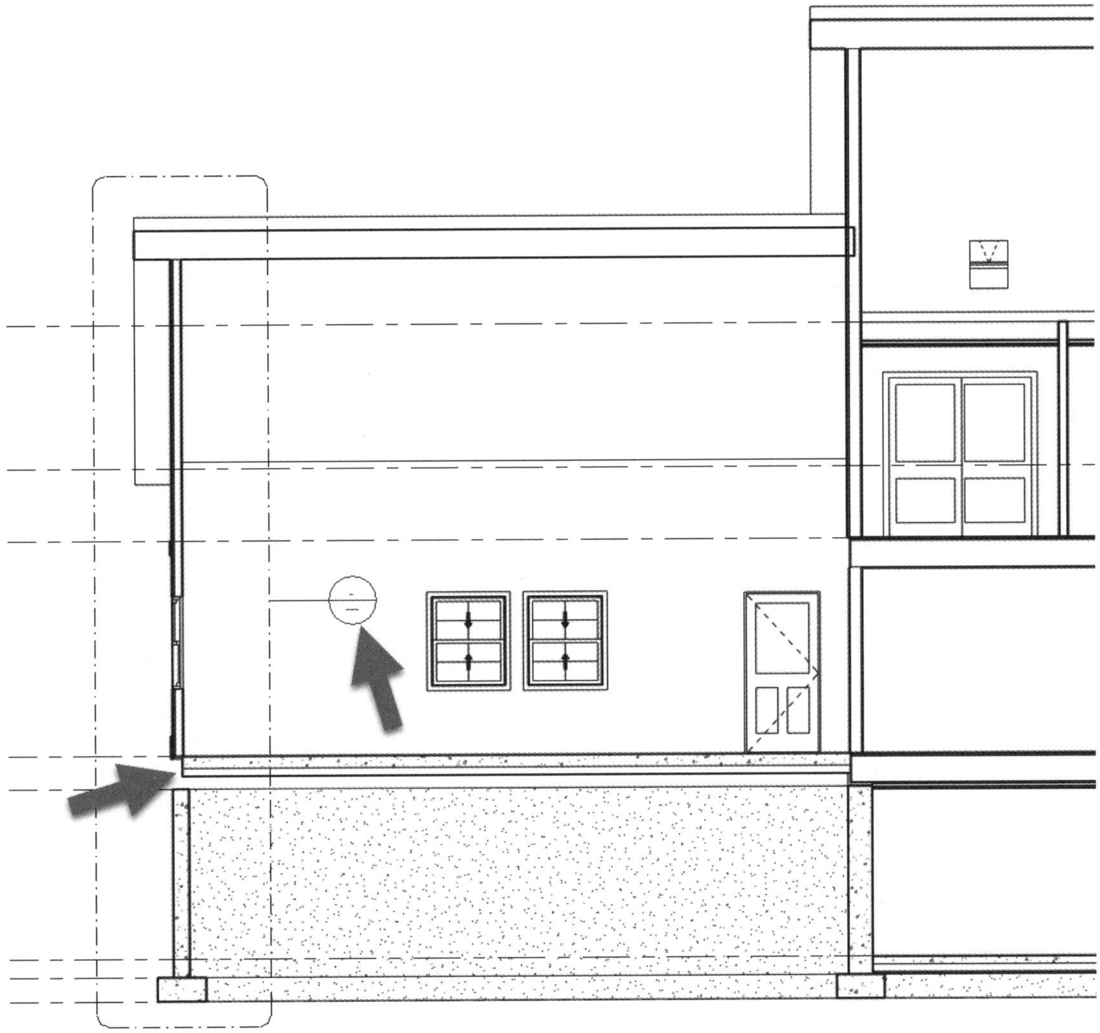

FIGURE 11-3.11 Callout added to longitudinal section

31. Switch to the ***Basement Floor Plan*** and select the <u>three</u> exterior foundation (8" concrete) walls at the garage.

32. In *Properties Palette*, set the *Top Constraint* to **Up to level: First Floor**.

33. Switch back to the ***Garage Wall Section*** view.

As shown in the figure below, the foundation wall and floor slab overlap. You will fix this.

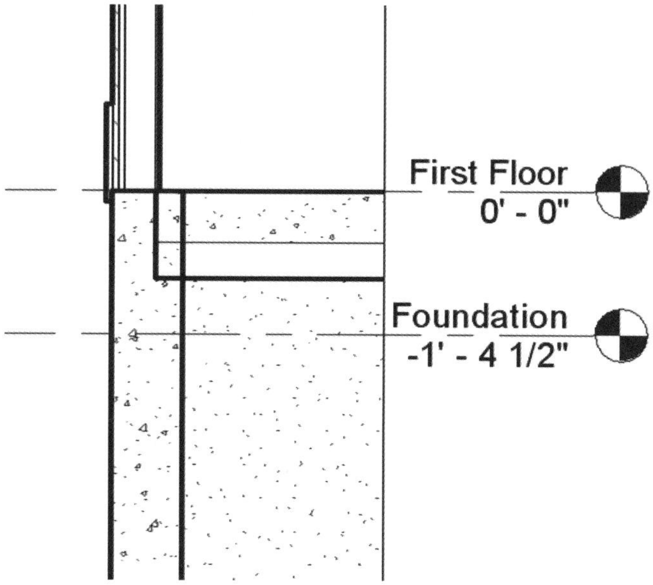

FIGURE 11-3.12
Garage Wall Section – edge of slab condition

34. Click **Modify → Geometry → Join**.

35. Select the foundation wall and then the floor slab.

Your wall section should now look like Figure 11-3.13. You can use the *Linework* tool to edit line styles or weights if desired.

36. **Save** your project as **ex11-3.rvt**.

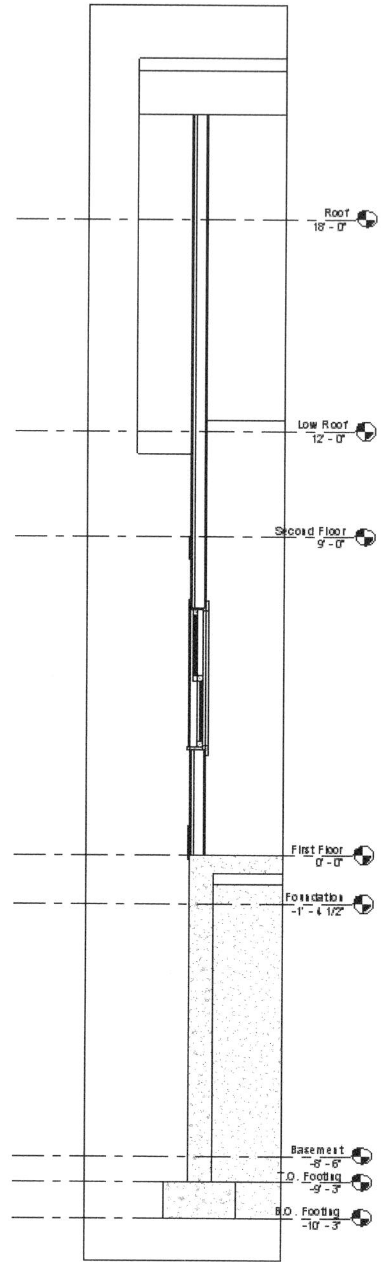

FIGURE 11-3.13
Garage Wall Section

***TIP:** The wall section in Figure 11-3.13 shows two level datums that are not required in this view (Low Roof and Foundation). You cannot delete them, but you can select them; right-click and then pick* Hide in View → Elements *from the pop-up menu. Click* Reveal Elements *on the View Control Bar to see them again.*

Exercise 11-4:
Annotation and Detail Components

This exercise will explore adding notes, dimensions and detail components to your wall section.

Add Notes and Dimensions to Callout of Cross Section 1:

1. Open ex11-3.rvt and *Save As* **ex11-4.rvt**.
2. Switch to ***Cross Section 1 – Callout 1*** view.
3. Click the ***Hide Crop Region*** icon on the *View Control Bar*.
4. Add the three dimensions as shown in **Figure 11-4.1**.

TIP: Revit lets you dimension to the window opening even though you are not cutting directly through a window in the current view. However, switching temporarily from Hidden to Wireframe can help.

These dimensions are primarily for the carpenters framing the stud wall. Typically, when a window opening is dimensioned in wood stud framing, the dimension has the suffix R.O. This stands for Rough Opening, clearly representing that the dimension identifies an opening in the wall. You will add the suffix next.

5. Select the dimension at the window opening.
6. Click directly on the blue dimension text (i.e., 3′-10″).
7. Type **R.O.** in the *Suffix* field and then click **OK**.

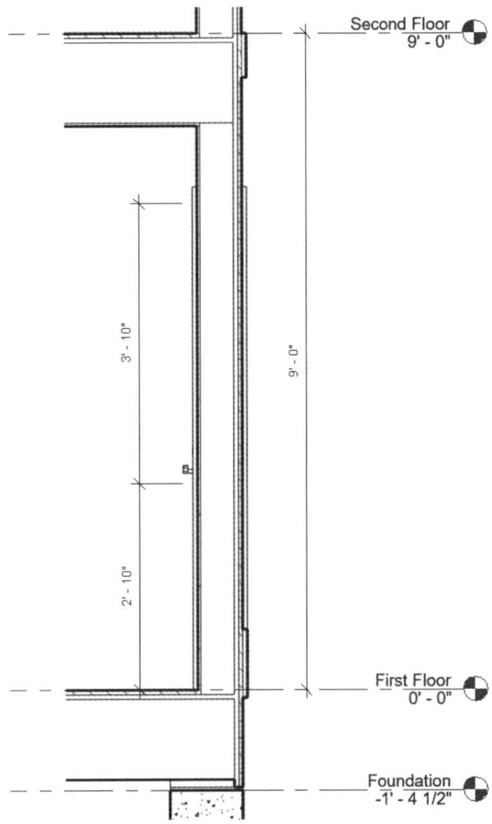

FIGURE 11-4.1 Added dimensions

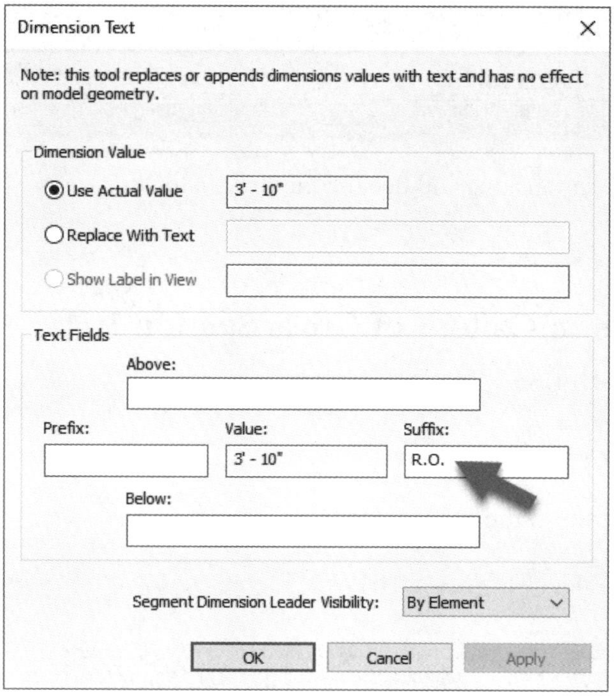

FIGURE 11-4.2 Selected dimension properties

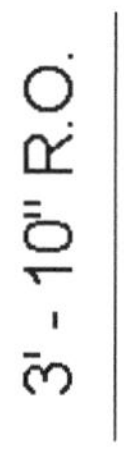

FIGURE 11-4.3 Dimension with suffix

Figure 11-4.3 shows the dimension with the added suffix.

8. Use the same process to add the text "WINDOW BEYOND" in the *Below* field (Figure 11-4.4).

This added text will persist even if the dimension length value is changed as a result of model edits.

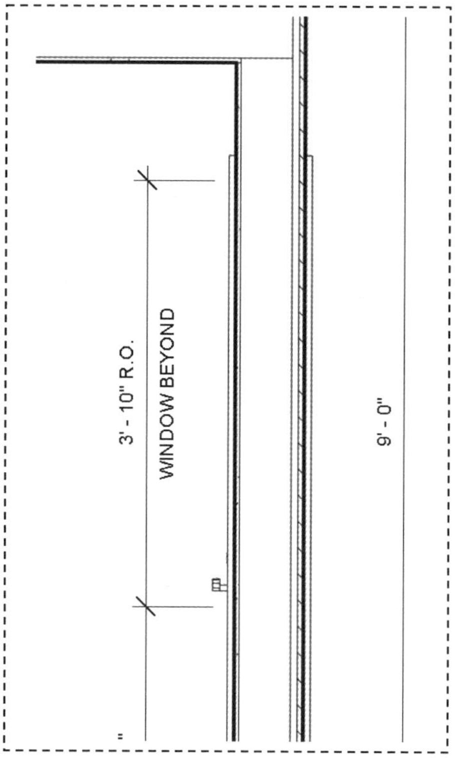

FIGURE 11-4.4 Text added below dimension

9. Turn the *crop region* back on for a moment.

10. Select the ***crop region***.

Notice the dashed line that shows around the *crop region*? It has its own set of positioning grips. This dashed lined area allows you to control the visibility of various elements in the current view, such as text. You will adjust the right-hand side to accommodate more text and notes.

11. Drag the control grips for the vertical dashed line on the right as per **Figure 11-4.5**.

12. Turn the *crop region* off.

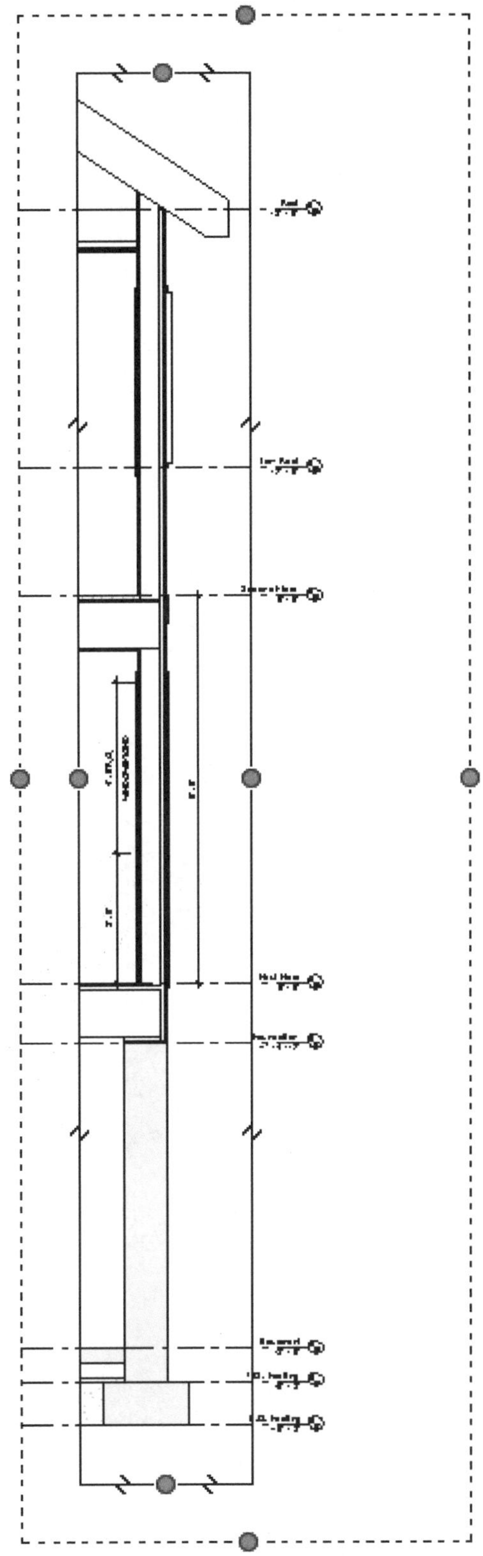

FIGURE 11-4.5 Crop Region Edits

13. Add the notes with leaders shown in Figure 11-4.6 (See Step 14); the text *Type* should be 3/32" Arial.

    TIP: *Select the Text tool and then one of the leader icons on the Ribbon (see image to the right).*

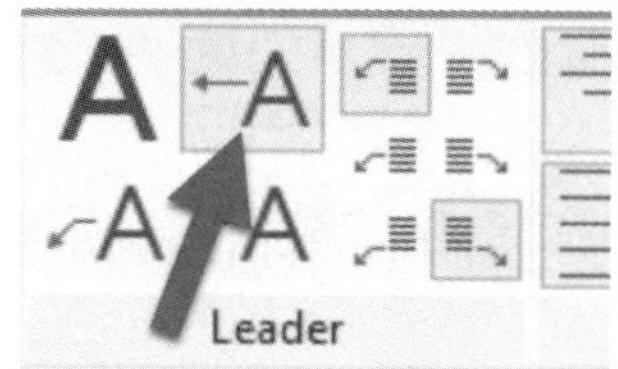

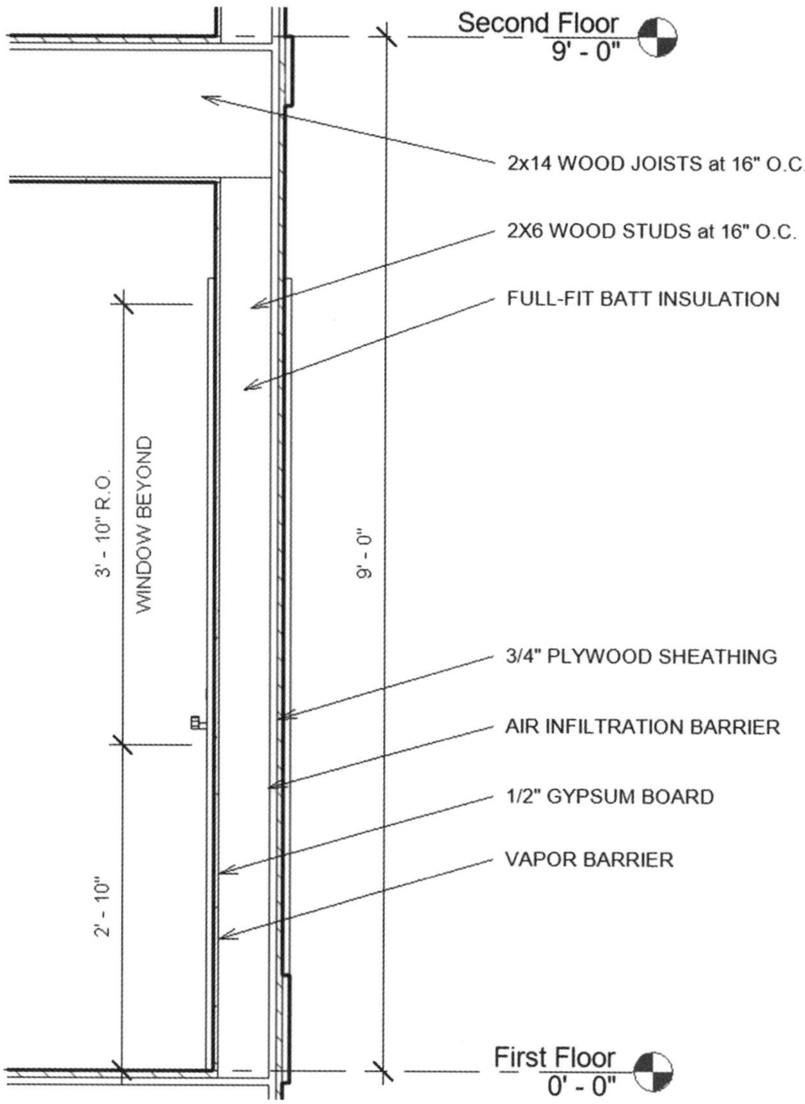

FIGURE 11-4.6 Notes added to wall section

14. The text style should be set to **3/32" Arial**; it may still be set to the last text style you used in this book: ¼" Outline Text.

15. Select the text and use the grips and the justification buttons to make the text look like **Figure 11-4.6**.

Adding Detail Components:

Revit provides a way to quickly add common 2D detail elements, such as dimensional lumber in section, anchor bolts, and wall base profiles, to "embellish" your sections. These are just a few loaded with your template file (Figure 11-4.7); many others can be created or downloaded from the internet.

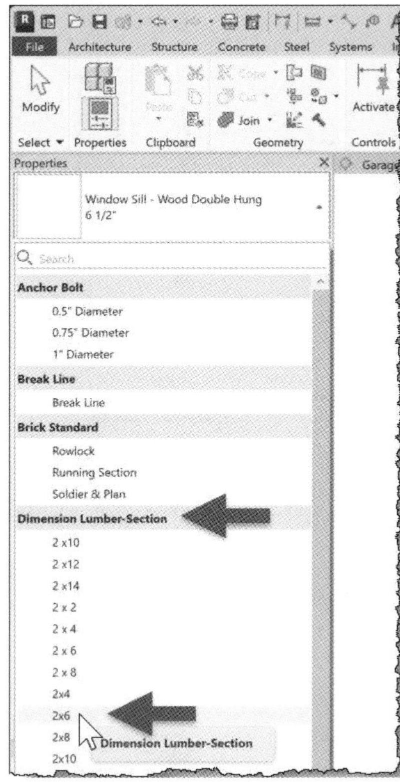

FIGURE 11-4.7
Detail Components; Type Selector open

Next, you will add just a few *Detail Components* to gain a basic understanding of how this feature is used.

You will add a 2x6 sill plate and a double top plate. You will also add the batt insulation symbol in the stud cavity.

16. Select **Annotate → Detail → Component → Detail Component**.

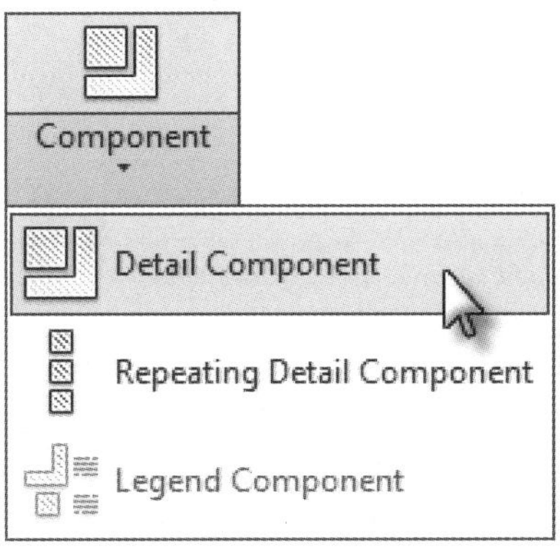

17. From the *Type Selector*, pick *Dimension Lumber-Section* **2 x 6**.

18. Add the sill plates as shown in Figure 11-4.8.

TIP: *When placing the 2x6, you will need to press the spacebar to* Rotate*, and then* Move *to properly position the element. The sill plate should be directly on the ¾" wood sheathing. Note that the horizontal line that extends through the sill plate is the level datum.*

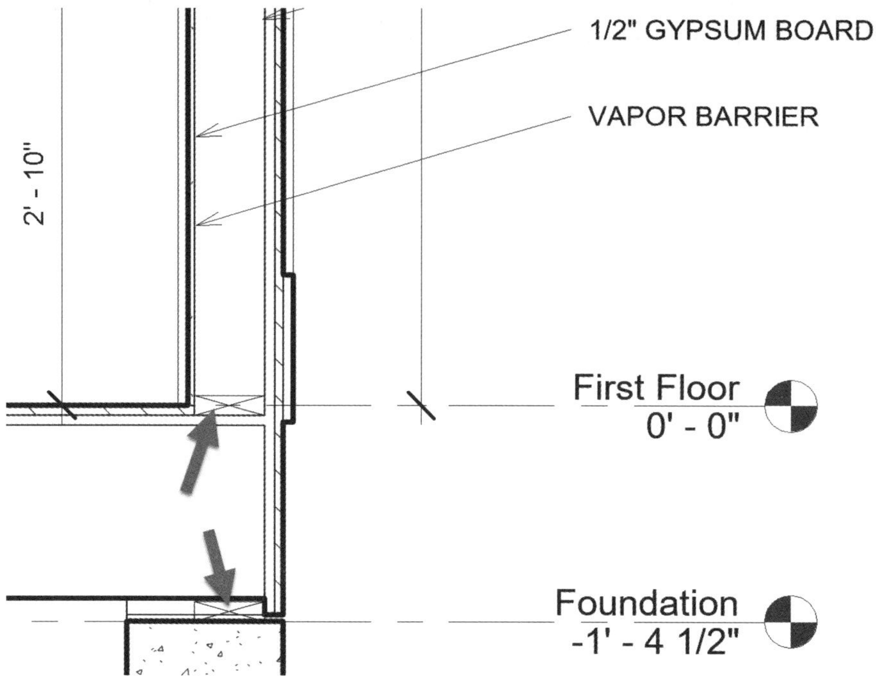

FIGURE 11-4.8 Cross Section 1 – Callout 1 view; 2 x 6 sill plates added

Detail Components can be copied after you place one in the view. This eliminates the need to rotate the stud in this example.

19. Use **Copy** and **Snaps** to add the double top plate (Figure11-4.9).

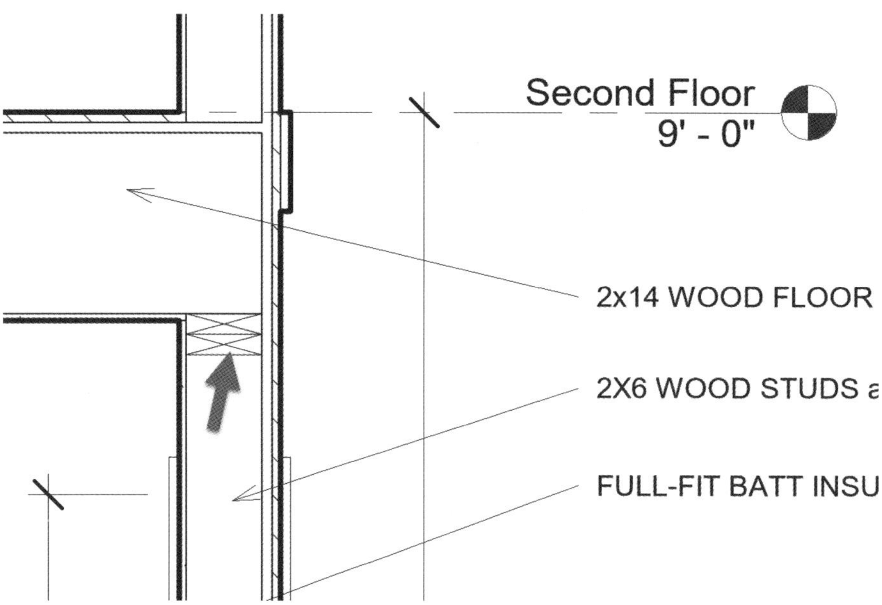

FIGURE 11-4.9 Cross Section 1 – Callout 1 view; 2 x 6 dbl. top plate added

Next, you will add the batt insulation.

20. Select **Annotate → Detail → Insulation**.

21. Pick the midpoint of the sill plate and the top plate to draw a line that represents the center of the batt insulation symbol; you can pick in either direction (Figure 11-4.10).

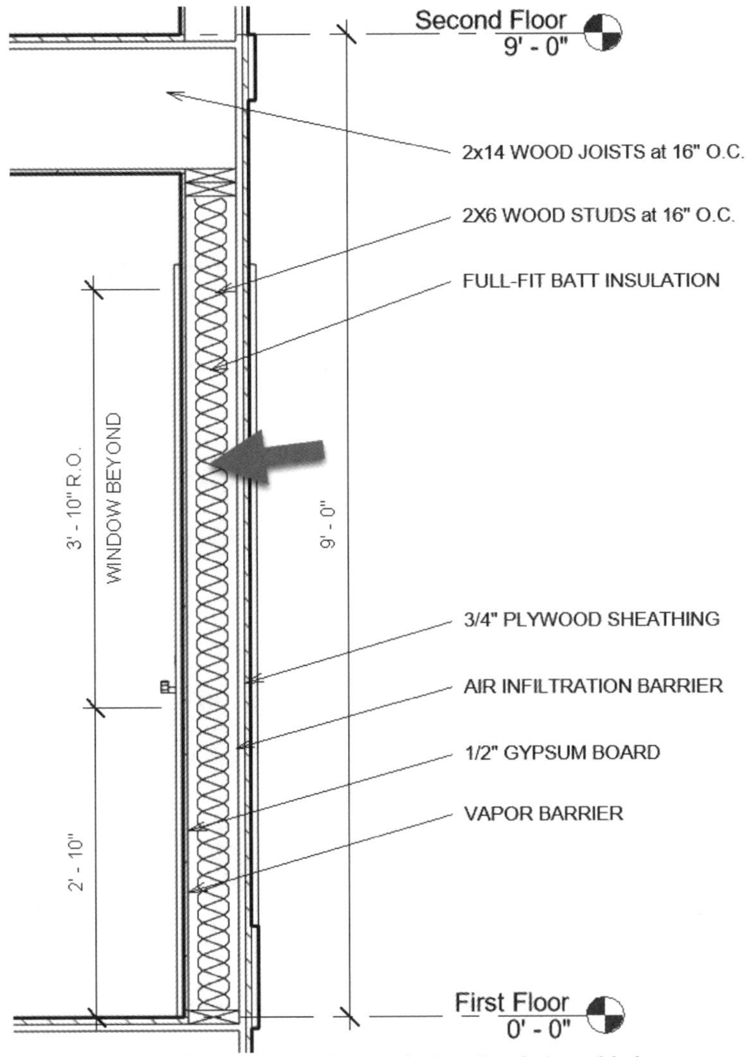

FIGURE 11-4.10 Callout of Cross Section 1 view; Insulation added

Next, you will adjust the insulation width to fit the stud cavity (i.e., 5½″ wide).

22. Click **Modify** and then click to select the insulation just drawn.

23. In the *Properties Pallet*, adjust the **Insulation Width** to **5½″** (Figure 11-4.11).

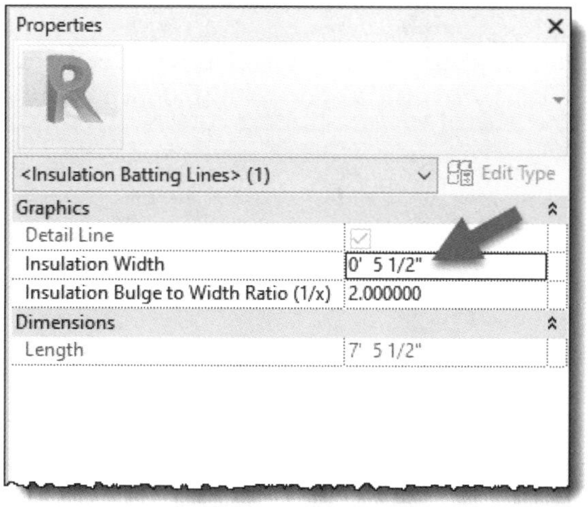

FIGURE 11-4.11 Insulation properties

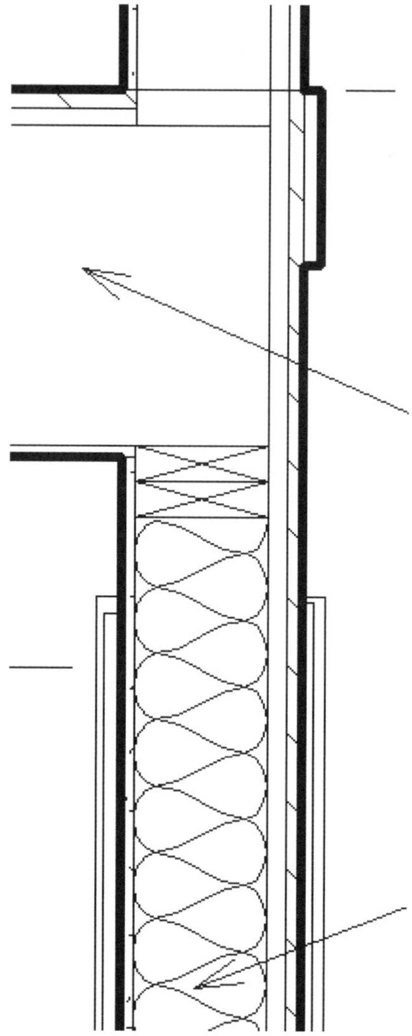

FIGURE 11-4.12
Insulation width changed

The tools we just used are on the Annotate tab of the Ribbon because they are 2D graphics that only appear in the current view.

Drawing some elements rather than modeling them three-dimensionally can save time and system resources. A file could get very large if you tried to model everything. Of course, every time you skip drawing in 3D, you increase the chance of error. It takes a little experience to know when to model and when not to model.

FYI: Architectural text is typically all uppercase.

Loading Additional Detail Components:

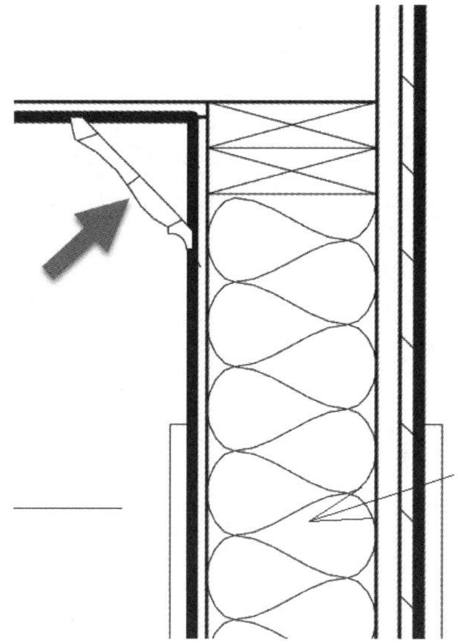

In addition to the *Detail Components* that are preloaded with the template file you started with, you can load more from the online Revit content library.

24. Click **Insert → Load Autodesk Family**.

25. Select **Detail Items** from the list on the left.

26. Browse to *Wood* and *Plastic\Architectural Woodwork\Wood Trim.*

27. Click the file named ***Crown Molding-Section*** and then click **Load**.

You now have access to the newly imported crown molding component. Take a minute to observe some of the other *Detail Components* that may be loaded into the project; for example, in the *Metals\Structural Steel Framing* folder, you can load a steel beam family that contains all the standard shapes as types (Figure 11-4.13).

28. Add the *Crown Molding* (3/4" x 5 7/8") to the intersection between the wall and the ceiling using the ***Component*** tool on the *Annotate* tab (not the *Architecture* tab).

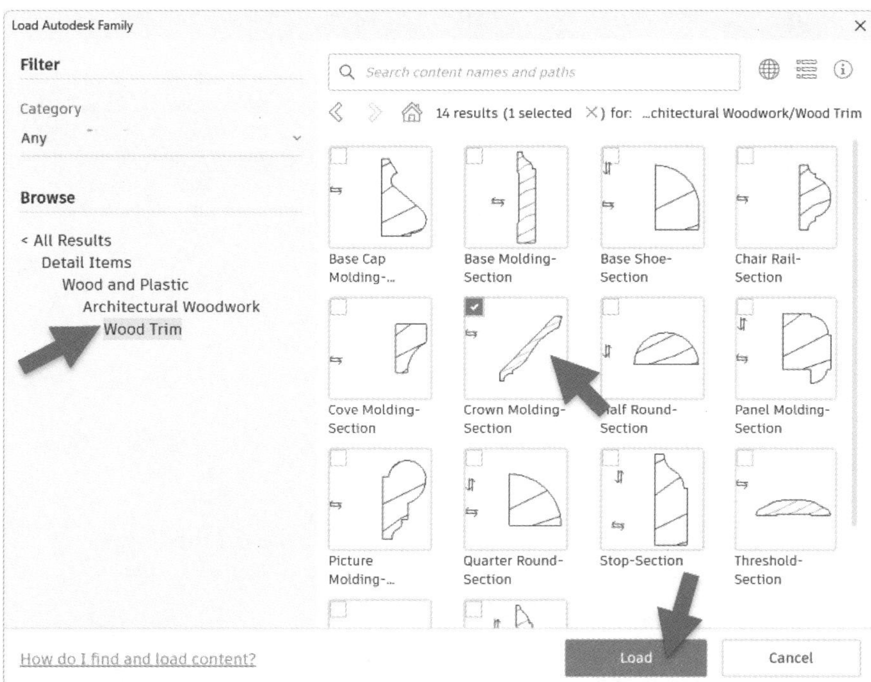

FIGURE 11-4.13 Load Detail Component dialog, Crown Molding-Section selected

Using Repeating Details:

Many details and sections have components that occur multiple times, one right after another. Some examples are brick, siding and floor joists in section. Revit provides a tool, called *Repeating Details*, which can basically copy any *Detail Component* the required number of times to fill the space between two pick points you select with the mouse. The spacing of the *Detail Component* being copied has to be predefined when setting up the *Repeating Detail* style.

29. Click **Annotate → Detail → Component → Repeating Detail**.

30. From the *Type Selector*, select *Repeating Detail:* **Lap Siding 6″**.

For now, you will draw the siding off to one side just to test this feature. Make sure you are within the *crop window* area or you will not see the results.

31. Pick two points similar to those shown in Figure 11-4.14.

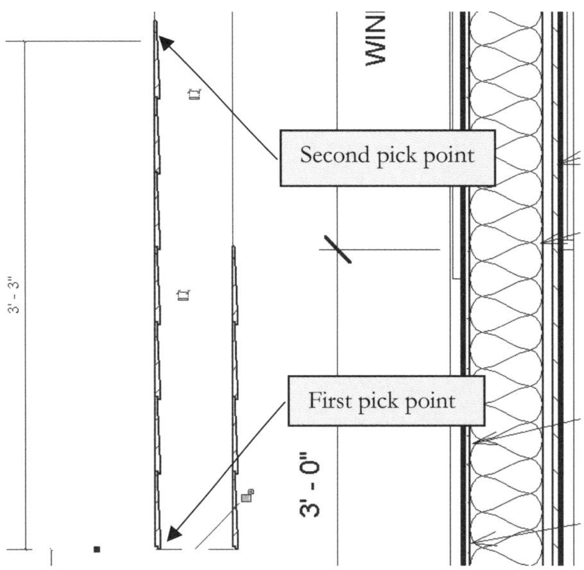

The example to the left shows two *Repeating Details* added. You can adjust them via the grips or the temporary dimensions.

FIGURE 11-4.14 Repeating Detail added: lap siding

32. Try adjusting the length of the siding by selecting it and clicking on the dimension text.

33. **Delete** the *Lap Siding* repeating detail.

34. **Save** your project as **11-4.rvt**.

Self-Exam:

The following questions can be used as a way to check your knowledge of this lesson. The answers can be found at the bottom of the page.

1. The controls for the section mark, when selected, are similar to the controls for the elevation tag. (T/F)

2. *Detail Components* added in this lesson were 3D. (T/F)

3. The footings drawn in this lesson were a Revit wall type. (T/F)

4. The *crop region* is represented by a rectangle in the section view. (T/F)

5. Use the _________ tool to reference a larger section off a building section.

Review Questions:

The following questions may be assigned by your instructor as a way to assess your knowledge of this section. Your instructor has the answers to the review questions.

1. The visibility of the *crop region* can be controlled. (T/F)

2. It is not possible to draw a leader without placing text. (T/F)

3. When a section mark is added to a view, all the other related views automatically get a section mark added to them. (T/F)

4. It is possible to modify elements such as doors, windows and ceilings in section views. (T/F)

5. You cannot adjust the "depth of view" using the *crop window*. (T/F)

6. What is the first thing you should do after placing a section mark?

   ____

7. If the text appears to be excessively large in a section view, the view's

   ____________________________ is probably set incorrectly.

8. The abbreviation R.O. stands for ______________________________.

9. Describe what happens when you double-click on the section bubble:

   ___________________________________.

10. Revit provides _____ different leader options within the *Text* command, not including the leader location options.

SELF-EXAM ANSWERS:
1 – T, **2** – F, **3** – T, **4** – T, **5** - callout

Notes:

Lesson 12
INTERIOR DESIGN:

This lesson explores some interior design elements of a floor plan, such as toilet room layouts and kitchen cabinets. Additionally, you will look at placing furniture and guardrails into your project.

Exercise 12-1:
Bathroom Layouts

Bathroom layouts involve placing toilets, tubs, and sinks. You will start with the half bath on the first floor.

1. Open ex11-4.rvt and **Save As ex12-1.rvt.**

The template you started with has everything you need to design and model this room. You will create the layout shown in Figure 12-1.1.

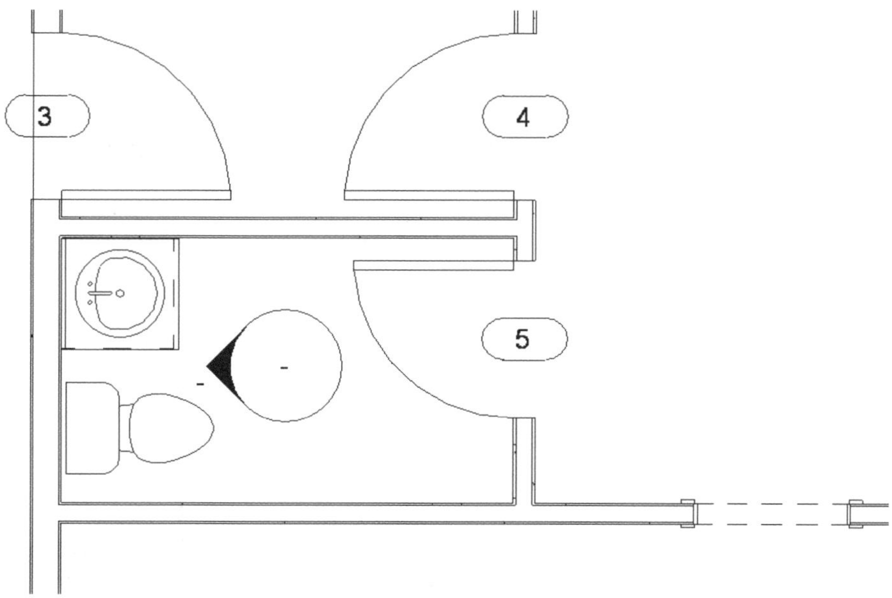

FIGURE 12-1.1 First Floor plan view: half bath layout

2. Switch to ***First Floor*** plan view (not the ceiling plan view) and zoom in on the half bath next to the garage, North of the dining room.

The first step will be to place the toilet.

3. With the *Component* tool selected on the *Architecture* tab, pick **Toilet-Domestic-3D** from the *Type Selector.*

4. **Place** the toilet in the middle of the room and then *Move* and *Rotate* into place utilizing *Snaps* (Figure 12-1.2).

   TIP: *Press the spacebar to rotate the toilet before placing it.*

The toilet is 1″ out from the wall, which is typical for floor–mounted tank–type toilets.

The overlapping letters, C and L, are the symbol for "centerline." This means that the middle of the toilet is 1′-4″ from the wall. Actually, if you were to add this dimension, Autodesk® Revit® would automatically add this symbol if the *Centerline Symbol* parameter is enabled in the dimension's properties!

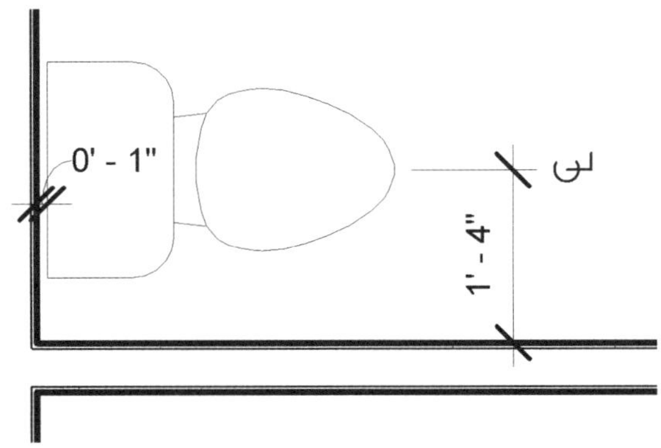

FIGURE 12-1.2 Toilet location

If you want to ensure the 1′-4″ dimension never changes, add the dimension shown, then click the padlock symbol to lock it. Then, anytime the wall moves, the toilet will move with it. If you want the constraint but do not want the dimension, you can delete the dimension, and Revit will ask you if you want to maintain the constraint after the dimension is deleted.

Next, you will add the sink. This consists of three separate components: a base cabinet, a countertop, and a sink, which is similar to what you would have in the "real-world." First, you will add the base cabinet.

5. Place a <u>*Vanity Cabinet-Double Door Sink Unit:*</u> **24″** using the *Component* tool (Figure 12-1.3).

   TIP: *Use the spacebar to rotate.*

   TIP: *It is hard to tell which side of the cabinet is the front in plan view; the side the cursor is attached to is the back. If you add it incorrectly, you will see the problem when you set up the interior elevation.*

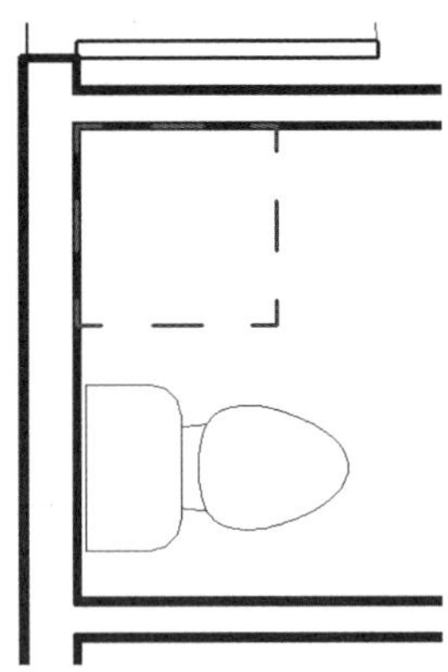

FIGURE 12-1.3 Vanity base cabinet added

Next, you will add the countertop. Revit has one that already has a hole in it for the sink. You will have to adjust the length to fit your cabinet.

6. Using the *Component* tool, place the *Vanity Counter Top w Round Sink Hole:* **24″** depth in the middle of the room.

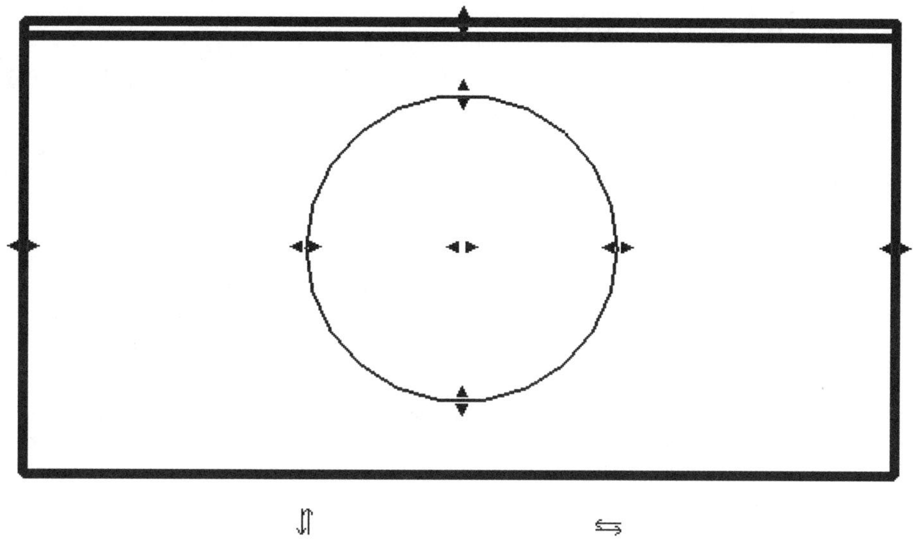

FIGURE 12-1.4 Vanity counter top temporarily placed in middle of room

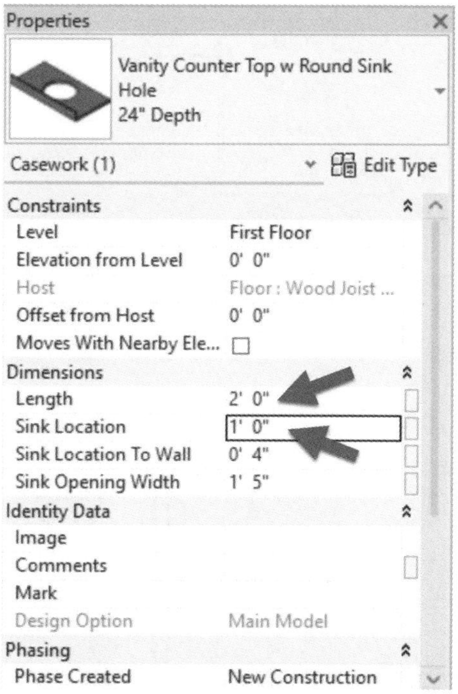

FIGURE 12-1.5 Vanity counter top properties

You will notice that the counter top is 48″ long; you will change this to 24″ in a moment. When selected, you see several arrow-grips which allow you to graphically adjust the size of the selected element.

7. With the countertop selected, note the ***Properties Palette*** options.

8. Change the *Length* to **2′-0″** and the *Sink Location* to **1′-0″** (Figure 12-1.5).

9. Click **Apply**, or just move your cursor back into the drawing window.

The countertop is now the correct size for your base cabinet.

10. Use ***Move*** and ***Rotate*** to position the countertop over the vanity base cabinet; use **Snaps** for accuracy.

11. Again, using the *Component* tool, add *Sink Vanity-Round:* **19″ x 19″**. Press the spacebar to rotate the sink 90 degrees and then visually place the sink in the center of the hole in the countertop.

Your plan should now look like Figure 12-1.1, less the elevation tag, which you will add next.

Interior Elevation View:

Next, you will set up an interior elevation view for the half bath. You will also add a mirror above the sink in elevation view. As you can see, the tasks in this book build on previously learned material; refer back to previous chapters for a refresher. Using these features multiple times will help you to become more efficient and to better understand the tools.

12. Place an **Elevation** tag, with the *Type Selector* set to **Interior Elevation**, looking towards the "wet" wall, the wall with fixtures on it (Figure 12-1.6).

    FYI: *A "wet" wall is any wall that has plumbing fixtures on it and piping behind it.*

    TIP: *When placing the Elevation Tag, Revit turns the pointer to look at the closest wall, so you will have to place the tag close to the West wall (overlapping the plumbing fixtures) and then move the tag back as a separate step.*

13. Rename the new view to **1/2 Bath** in the *Project Browser.*

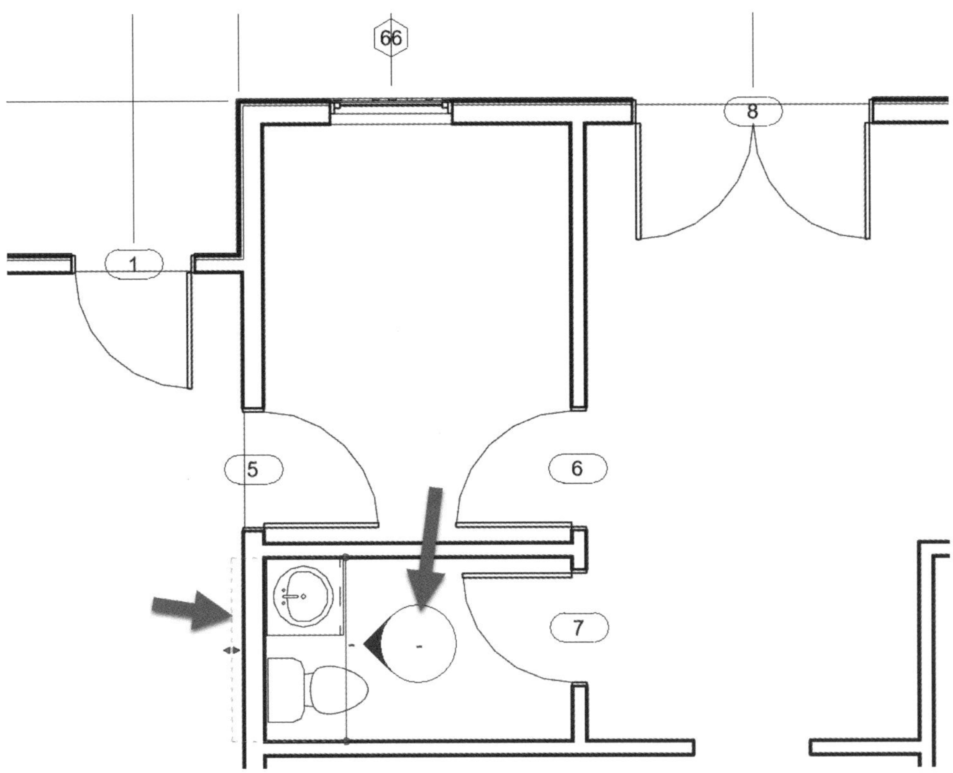

FIGURE 12-1.6 Elevation tag added and adjusted

14. Switch to the new view; click the *crop region* and drag the bottom up so the floor system does not show. Your view should look like Figure 12-1.7.

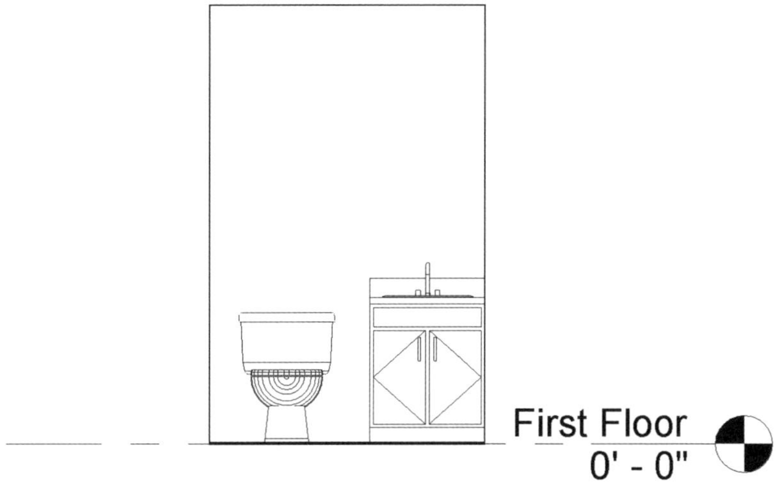

FIGURE 12-1.7 ½ Bath elevation

15. Change the *View Scale* to **½" = 1'-0"**.

16. Use Load Autodesk Family to download the family named **Mirror-Ellipse.rfa**.

17. Using the **Competent** tool, set the *Type Selector* to *Mirror-Ellipse:* **18" x 36"**.

18. While in the ***1/2 Bath*** elevation view, place the mirror as shown in Figure 12-1.8.

19. Add the notes and dimensions shown in Figure 12-1.8.

TIP: As you are drawing the leaders, Revit will help you align your pick points vertically so the leaders and notes align; just watch for the dashed vertical reference line before picking your points.

20. Using the same techniques just covered, lay out the two second floor bathrooms per **Figure 12-1.9**; use the tub loaded with the template.

    a. Make the larger vanity cabinet and countertop 4'-0" wide.

    b. Adjust the interior walls to fit the tub exactly, if needed.

    c. Remember to add a mirror above the sink.

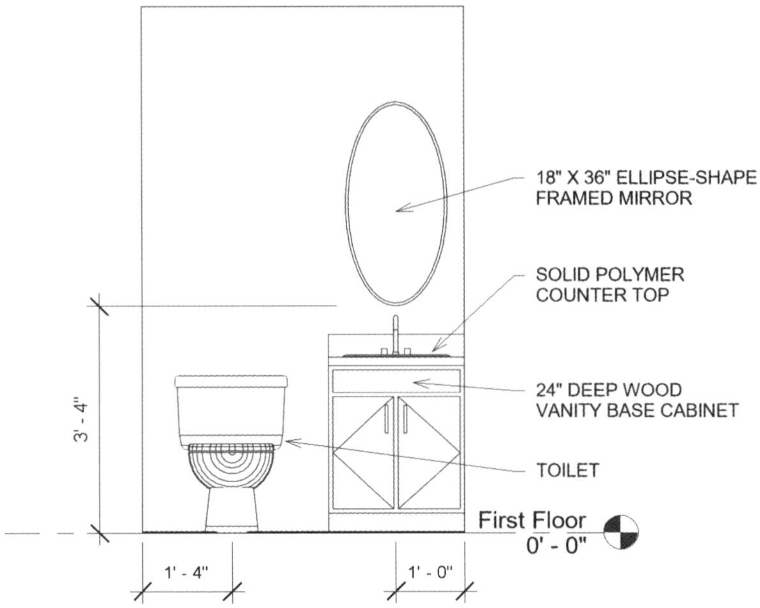

FIGURE 12-1.8 Interior elevation with mirror and notes added

FYI: *Keep in mind that many of the families that come with Revit, or any program for that matter, are not necessarily drawn or reviewed by an architect. The point is that the default values, such as mounting heights, may not meet ADA, national, state, or local codes. Items such as accessible mirrors have a maximum height off the floor to the reflective surface that Revit's standard components may not comply with. However, as you apply local codes to these families, you can reuse them in the future.*

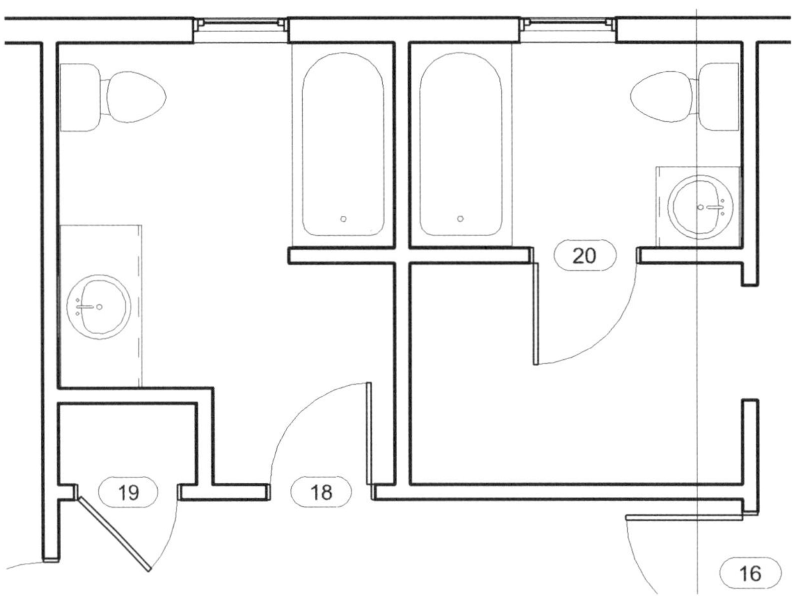

FIGURE 12-1.9 Second Floor Bath Rooms

21. **Save** your project as **ex12-1.rvt**.

Exercise 12-2:
Kitchen Layout

In this exercise, you will look at adding kitchen cabinets and appliances to your project. As usual, Revit provides several predefined families that can be placed in the project.

Placing Cabinets:

You will add base cabinets and appliances first.

1. Open ex12-1.rvt and **Save As ex12-2.rvt.**

2. Switch to the ***First Floor*** plan view and zoom into the kitchen.

   FYI: As with other families (i.e., doors and windows), Revit loads several Types *to represent the most valuable and useful sizes available. Cabinets typically come in 3″ increments, with different types (e.g., single- or double-door units) having maximum and minimum sizes.*

3. With the ***Component*** tool selected, place the families, cabinets, **and appliances**, as shown in Figure 12-2.1; use *Snaps* for accuracy. Remember that the cursor is at the back of the cabinet when placing the component.

   FYI: Many of the specified families are already loaded into your project from the residential template you started with; the others can be loaded manually from the Revit-provided online content library via Insert → Load Autodesk Families.

4. Select one of the base cabinets and click **Edit Type** from the *Properties Palette.*

Notice the height is 2′-10½″ which, when combined with a 1½″ standard countertop, gives you a 3′-0″ surface.

Next, you will add the countertops to the base cabinets. You will place three separate countertop elements (Figure 12-2.2). You will adjust the lengths of the countertops to fit the cabinets below.

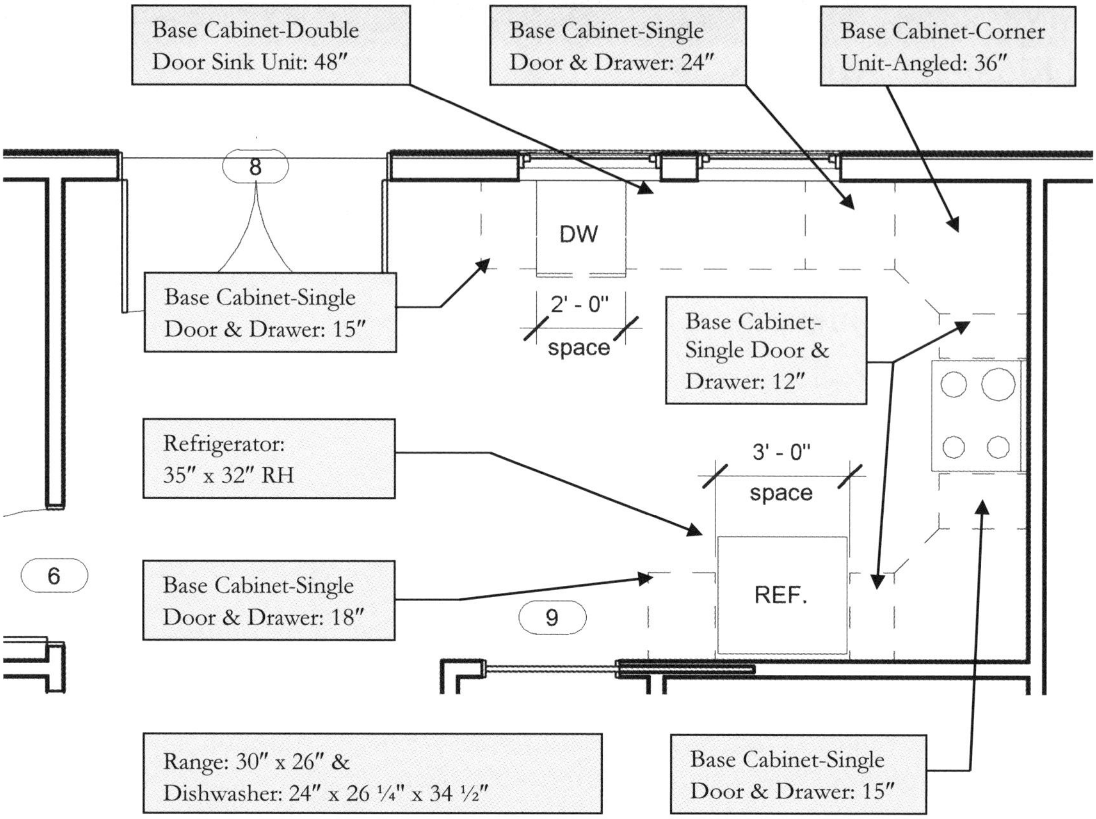

FIGURE 12-2.1 First Floor Plan View: base cabinets added to kitchen

5. Per the steps listed below, add the **countertops** shown in Figure 12-2.2, using *Snaps* to accurately place them.

   a. Load the families not currently loaded in your project from the *Casework* section of the online content provided with Revit.

   b. Place the bottom-right corner unit (use *Move*, *Mirror* and *Snaps*) and then, with the unit selected, drag one of the end grips back to align with the edge of the cabinet below.

   c. Load and place the other corner unit with the sink hole.
      i. Adjust the edge locations (use *Properties* for accuracy)
      ii. Adjust sink hole via *Properties Palette*: *Sink Location*: **5′-4″**

   d. Add the two straight countertops as shown.

   e. Verify the *Height* is **3′-0″** via *Properties*; this is driven by a **Type Property**, not the *Instant Parameter* called *Offset*.

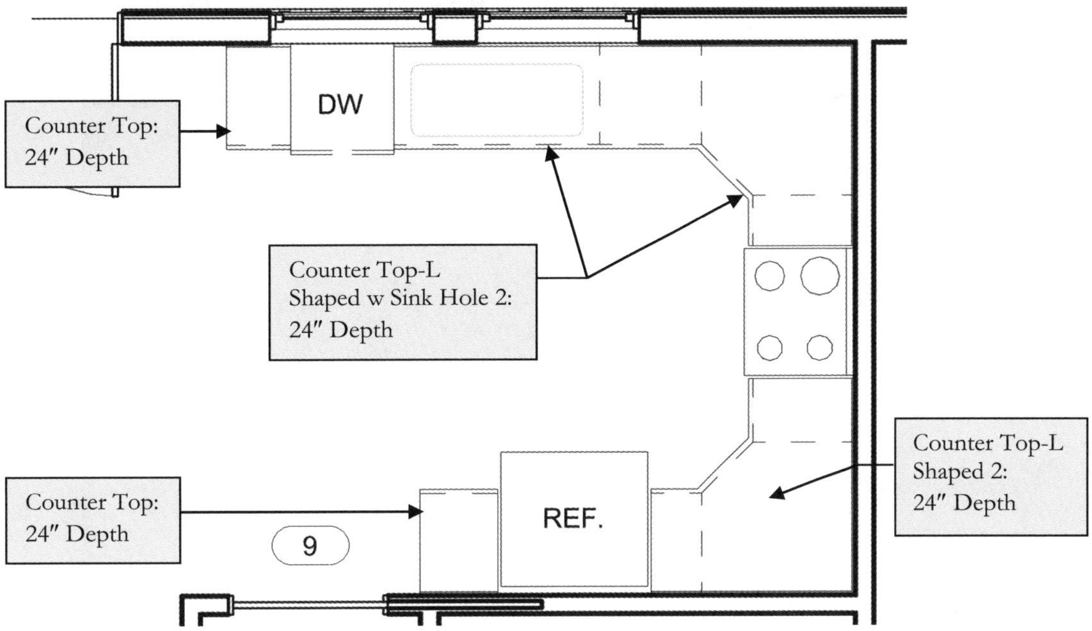

FIGURE 12-2.2 First Floor Plan View: countertops added

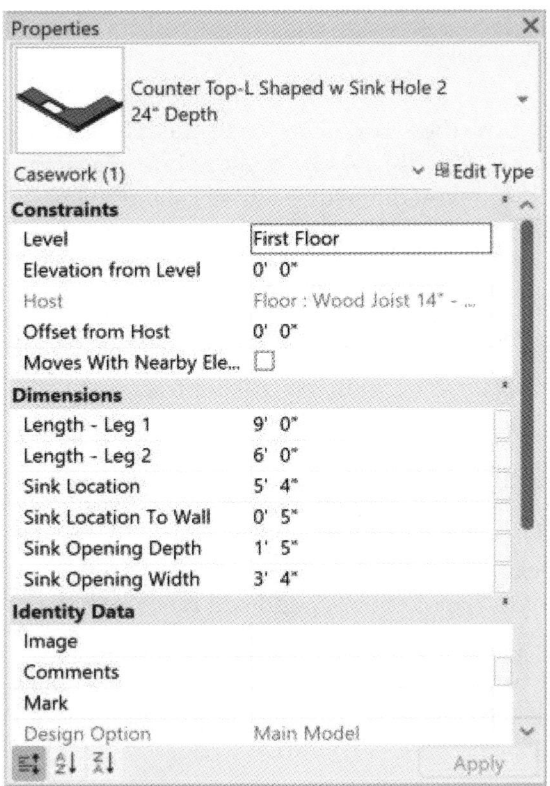

FIGURE 12-2.3 Properties for Counter Top with Sink Hole: 24″ Depth

6. Select the countertop with the sink hole and go to the ***Properties Palette***.

7. Change the following (Figure 12-2.3):
   a. Sink Location to Wall: **5″**
   b. Sink Opening Depth: **1′-5″**
   c. Sink Opening Width: **3′-4″**

TIP: *Some settings are per instance (i.e., the settings in the palette to the left) and others are per type (i.e., clicking the* Edit Type *button –* Type Parameters*); the Instant Parameters only affect the selected item. So, if you place another instance of this family in the basement, the sink can be in a different location.*

8. Using the *Component* tool, add **Sink Kitchen-Double: 42″ x 21″** to your project – centered on the sink hole (Figure 12-2.4).

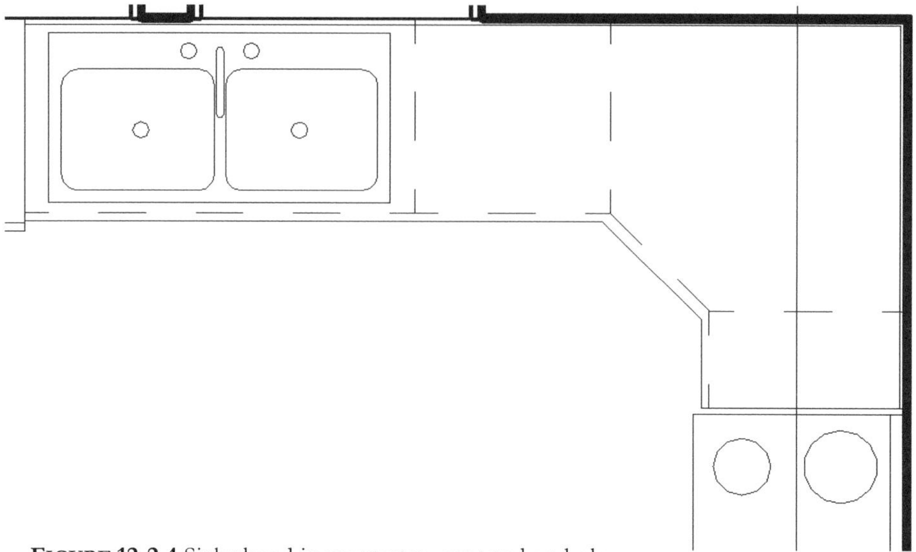

FIGURE 12-2.4 Sink placed in countertop, centered on hole

Placing Wall Cabinets:

Next, you will add a couple of wall cabinets to see how they work. They are similar to adding base cabinets, except they depend on walls (i.e., they are wall-hosted). You can only place an upper cabinet on a wall, not in the middle of a room as you did with the base cabinets. The base cabinets are set up to sit on the floor, and the upper cabinets are assigned a height above the floor, on the wall, via *Properties*.

9. Using the ***Component*** tool, add the upper cabinets as shown in **Figure 12-2.5**:

   a. Move the cursor close to a wall until you see the cabinet, which means Revit found a wall.

   b. Center the upper cabinet above the range, leaving an equal space on each side of the cabinet; these spaces will get a filler that matches the cabinets.

   c. The numbers (which represent the cabinet width) and graphic Xs in the cabinets are for clarity of this step only; you do not need to add these items.

   d. Use both single and double upper cabinets as necessary.

   e. If you have trouble adding the uppers at the pocket door location, add them to the right and move them into place.

   f. At the corners, use the *Upper Cabinet-Corner Unit-Wall* family.

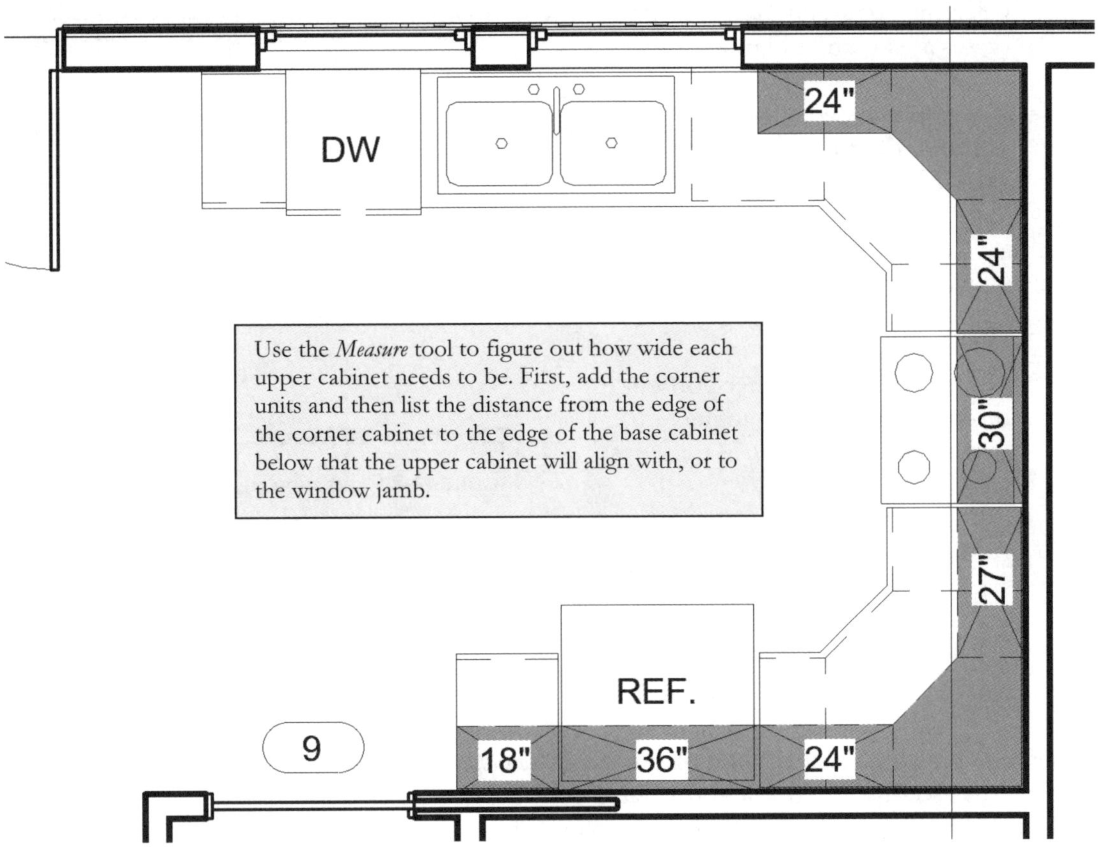

FIGURE 12-2.5 First Floor plan view: upper cabinets added (shade and Xs added for clarity in this image)

The heights of the cabinets will be adjusted in the interior elevation view.

FYI: *Wall cabinets are typically dashed in plan because they are above the* floor plan cut plane.

Creating the Interior Elevations:

10. Add an interior **Elevation Tag** as shown in Figure 12-2.6.

    TIP: *Make sure you select* Interior Elevation *from the Type Selector.*

11. Rename the new elevation view to ***Kitchen (east)***.

12. Select the **circle** portion of the symbol; the symbol should look like Figure 12-2.7 when selected correctly.

13. Click the *North* and *South* check-boxes as shown in Figure 12-2.7.

14. **Rename** the two new views to ***Kitchen (north)*** and ***Kitchen (south)***.

The single elevation tag in plan view is associated with the three kitchen elevation views.

15. Double-click the pointer portion of the elevation tag pointing towards the East to open that view.

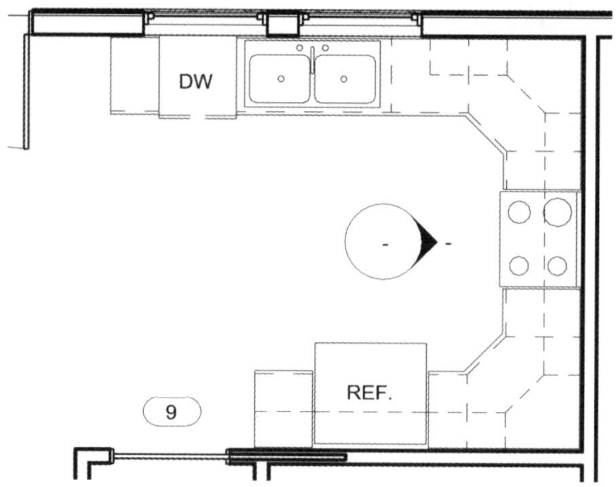

FIGURE 12-2.6 Elevation tag added to kitchen

16. Adjust the ***crop region*** so the floor system is not visible.

17. Set the *View Scale* to **½" = 1'-0"**; your interior elevation view should look like **Figure 12-2.8**.

Depending on where, exactly, you placed the *Elevation Tag*, you may see the side of the refrigerator or a section through it, as in Figure 12-2.8. In this case, you will want to adjust the view so you see the cabinets beyond, which is more important to show. You will switch back to the plan view and adjust the views settings.

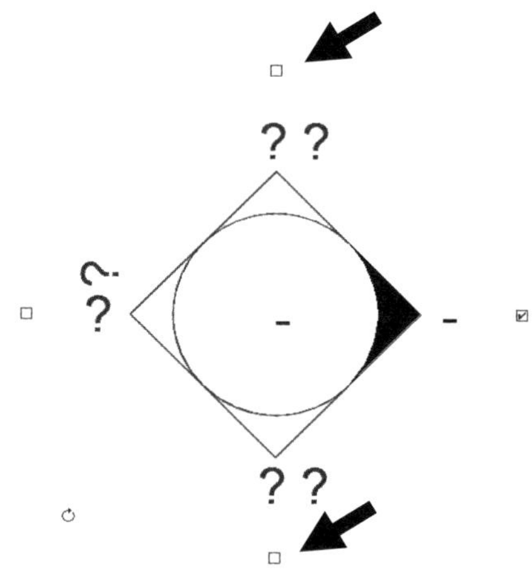

FIGURE 12-2.7 Elevation tag selected

18. Switch back to the ***First Floor*** plan view.

19. Click to select the *East view's* pointer portion of the elevation tag so you see the *Extent of View/Far Clip Plane* lines.

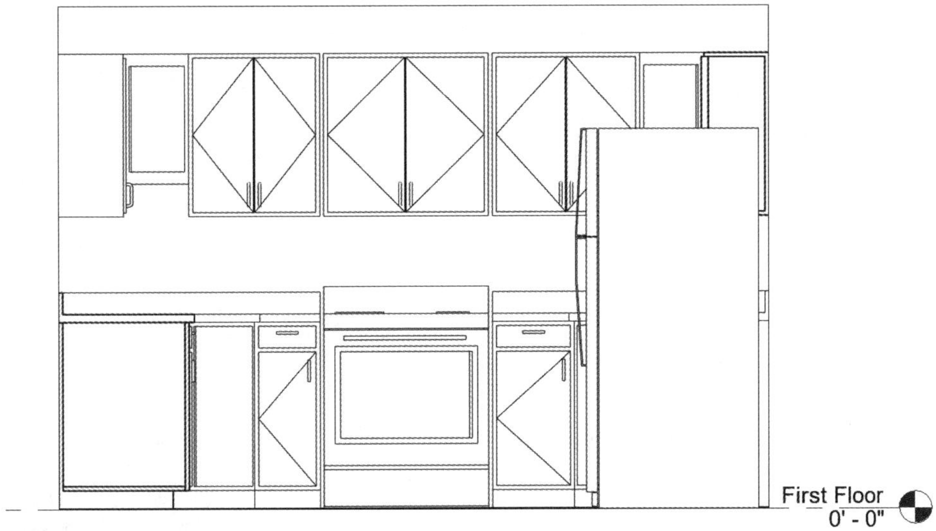

FIGURE 12-2.8 Kitchen (east); initial view

20. Click and drag to adjust the location of the *Extent of View* line as shown in Figure 12-2.9; also, adjust the *Far Clip Plane* to be in the wall as shown.

Notice the *Extent of View/Cut Plane* line has been moved to the east of the refrigerator, and the *Far Clip Plane* is in the middle of the wall.

21. Switch back to the ***Kitchen (east)*** view and note the changes (Figure 12-2.10).

You will modify one more thing in this view before moving on. The height of the wall cabinets needs a little work (Figure 12-2.10); the corner wall cabinets are too short and the cabinet over the range is too tall. You can adjust these in either the plan or elevation view. You will adjust them in the elevation view so you can immediately see the changes.

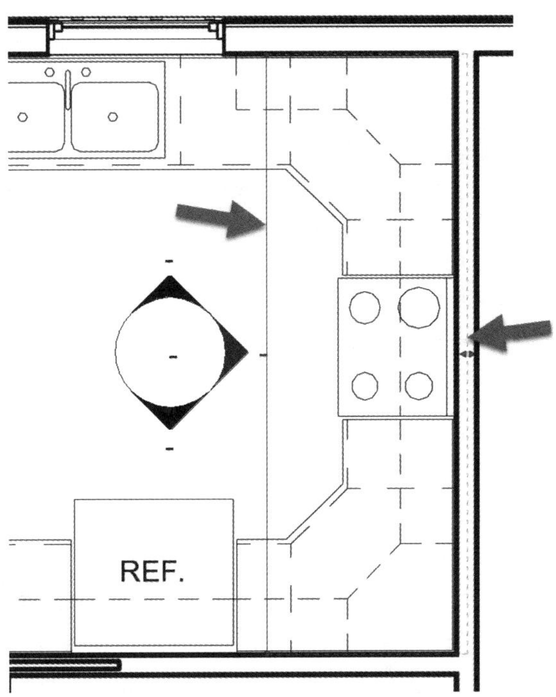

FIGURE 12-2.9 First Floor; elev. tag selected

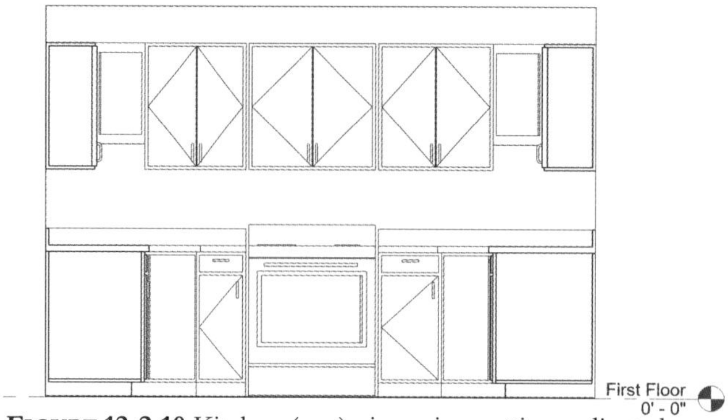

FIGURE 12-2.10 Kitchen (east) view; view settings adjusted

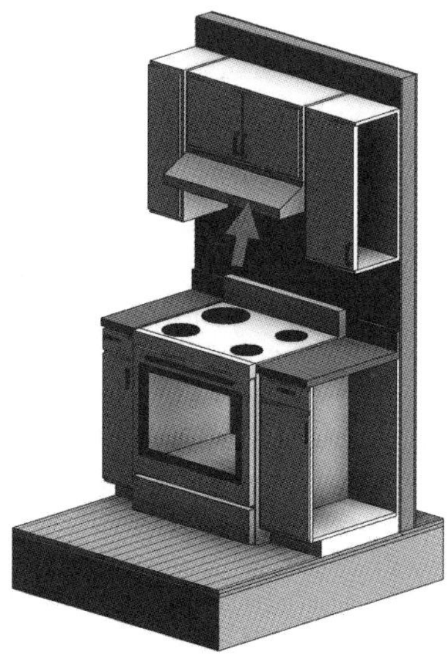

22. Select both **corner** upper cabinets and change their *Height* to **2′-6″** [Type Property] and the *Elevation from Level* to **4′-6″** (2′-6″ + 4′-6″ = 7′-0″ to top) [Instance Property]. Make these changes via the *Properties Palette* and *Type Properties.*

23. Select the upper cabinet above the range and change its height to **15″** and the elevation so the top stays at 7′-0″.

24. Load the **Range Hood** family provided with this book. *Tip:* place in plan view with temporary elevation of -2'-0" and then adjust in elevation.

Your elevation should now look like Figure 12-2.11. Notice that the cabinets on the right and left, which are actually in section, have heavier lines than the cabinets that are in elevation (aka projection). Again, Revit saves time by assuming the industry standard. However, you can use the *Linework* tool to change this if you so desire!

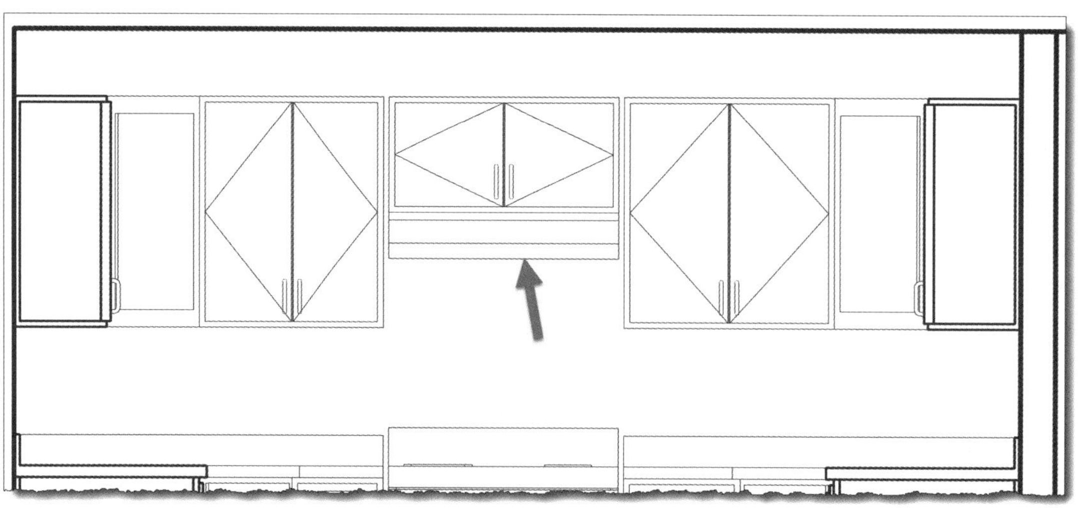

FIGURE 12-2.11 Kitchen (east) view; view settings adjusted

You will add notes and dimensions to the elevation.

25. Add the notes and dimensions per **Figure 12-2.12**.

26. Select the ***Linework*** tool from the *Modify* tab and set the *Line Style* (on the *Ribbon*) to **Wide lines**. Select the perimeter lines so they stand out more.

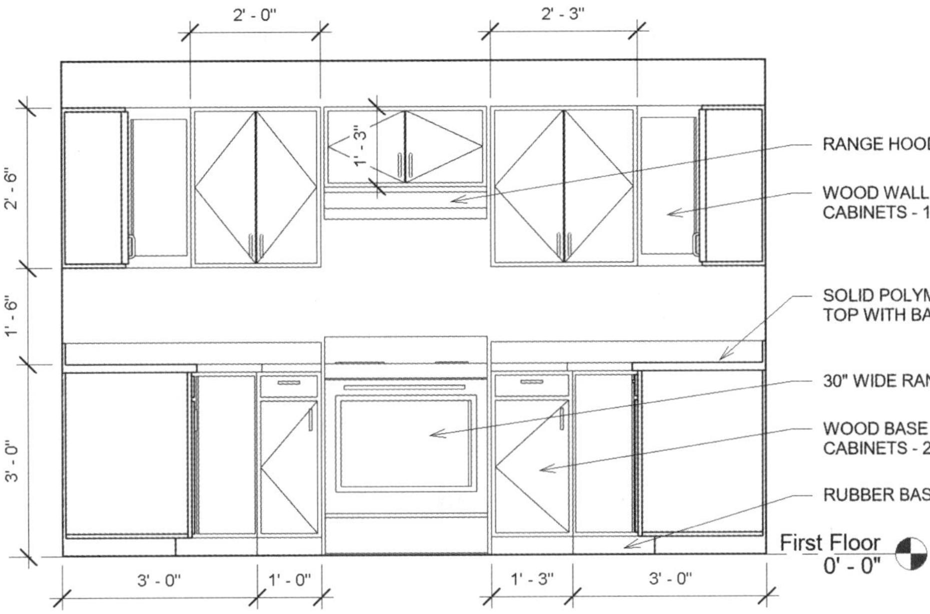

FIGURE 12-2.12 Interior elevation with annotations

That is it for the East elevation! Next, you will take a quick look at the other two elevations you set up in the kitchen.

27. Switch to the ***Kitchen (north)*** view.

28. Adjust the *crop region* and the perimeter lines per the previous elevation (Figure 12-2.13).

29. Change the *View Scale* to **½" = 1'-0"**.

You will notice right away that the windows conflict with the cabinets, the sink cabinet is not tall enough, and the countertop does not extend over the dishwasher. Both of these required changes can be made in either the plan or the elevation; again, you will make changes in the elevation view so you can see the results.

First, you will fix the windows. An error like this could easily be overlooked using a traditional CAD program because the exterior elevation and the interior elevations are separate/independent drawing files; so you could fix the height of the windows in the interior elevation, but forget to change the exterior elevation, where the windows are specified and ordered from. In Revit, it is not even possible to have one window be two different sizes in the same project file.

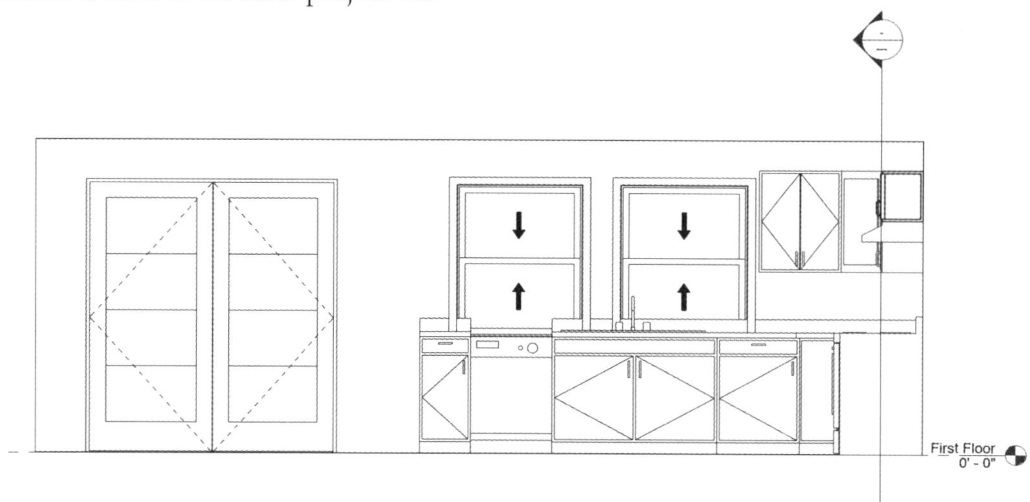

FIGURE 12-2.13 Kitchen (north); initial view

30. Select the **Base Cabinet-Double Door Sink Unit** cabinet and adjust its height, via *Edit Type*, to match the other base cabinets; **2' 10 1/2"**.

31. Select the *Section* line, right-click, and pick **Hide in View → Elements**. You do not need to see that section mark here.

32. Select the two windows in the ***Kitchen (north)*** view.

33. Via *Properties*, create a new window *Type*, via *Edit Type → Duplicate*, named <u>*Window-Double-Hung:*</u> **38″ x 38″**:
    a. Set the *Height* to **3′-2″** – *Type Parameter*
    b. Click **OK** and then adjust the sill height for the selected windows to **3′-6″**.

Now the windows do not conflict with the countertop's backsplash. Next, you will adjust the countertop.

34. In the ***Kitchen (north)*** view, zoom in on the dishwasher area.

35. Select the **Counter Top** over the **15″** wide base cabinet, to the left of the dishwasher, and press the **Delete** key to erase it.

36. Using the ***Align*** tool, select the left-edge of the 15″ wide base cabinet and then select the left edge of the remaining countertop. The countertop should now align with the edge of the cabinets.

FYI: *You must pick these items in the specified order.*

Your modified *Kitchen (north)* should look like Figure 12-2.14.

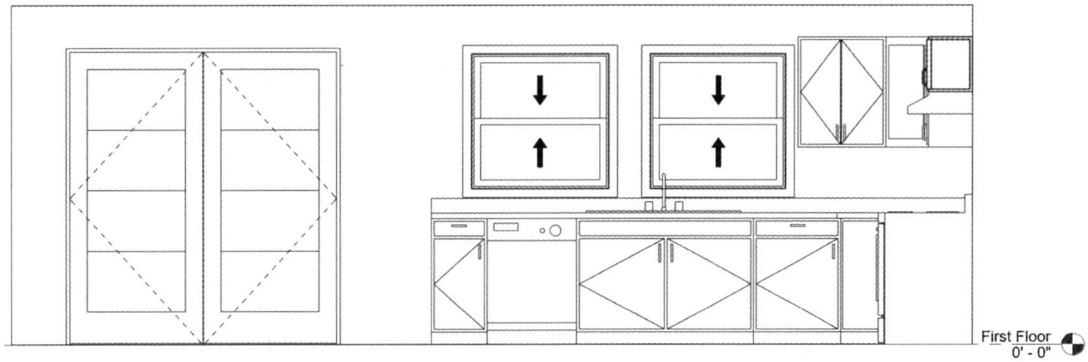

FIGURE 12-2.14 Kitchen (north); modified view

37. Open ***Kitchen (south)***.

38. Modify the ***crop region*** and the perimeter linework.

If you cannot see the refrigerator doors, you would now realize that the refrigerator was inserted backwards (Figure 12-2.15). You will fix this now.

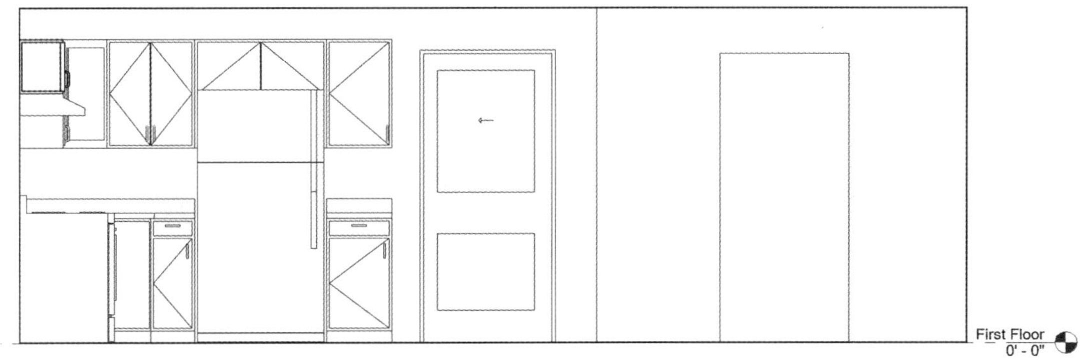

FIGURE 12-2.15 Kitchen (south); initial view

39. Set the scale to **½" = 1'-0"** and ***Hide*** the building section mark.

40. If needed, ***Rotate*** the refrigerator (in plan view) 180 degrees (if required – the door handles should be visible if facing the correct way). Also, move the *Range Hood* against the wall if not properly positioned in this view.

41. Modify the upper cabinet above the refrigerator to be **12"** tall, with the top at **7'-0"**.

TIP: If this cabinet were used anywhere else in the project, you would have had to make a duplicate before changing the height; otherwise, all the cabinets would have changed as well, because it is a Type Parameter you are changing, not an Instance Parameter.

Often, you have a portion of a wall with little on it, so it is not worth elevating. In the ***Kitchen (south)*** view, you will crop a portion of the wall on the right.

42. Click the ***crop region*** and drag the right side of the *crop region* rectangle towards the left so only the portion of elevation shown in Figure 12-2.16 is visible.

Your ***Kitchen (south)*** view should now look like Figure 12-2.16.

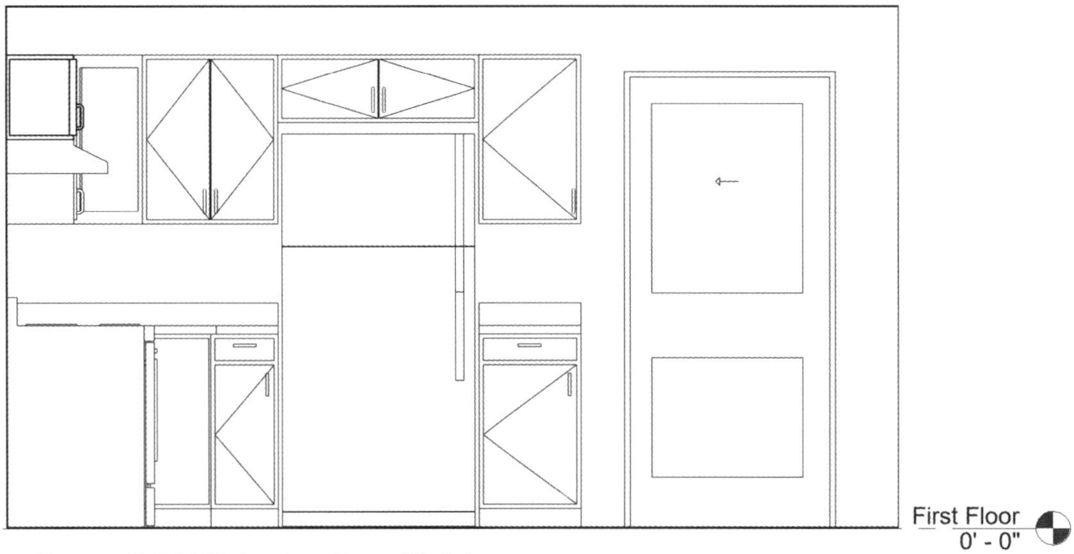

FIGURE 12-2.16 Kitchen (south); modified view

The last thing you will adjust are the lines in the cabinet elevations that indicate the swing of the cabinet door; these lines are typically dashed lines.

There are two ways to accomplish this. One way will only affect the current view (View → *Visibility/Graphics*), and the other will affect the entire project (Manage → *Settings* → *Object Styles*). You want this change applied everywhere, so you should implement it using the latter method.

43. Select **Manage → Settings → Object Styles**.

44. On the *Model Objects* tab, click the plus symbol next to **Casework** in the *Category* column (Figure 12-2.17).

45. Change the **Line Pattern** for *Elevation Swing* to **Hidden 1/8"** (Figure 12-2.17).

46. Click **OK** to see the results in the three kitchen elevations.

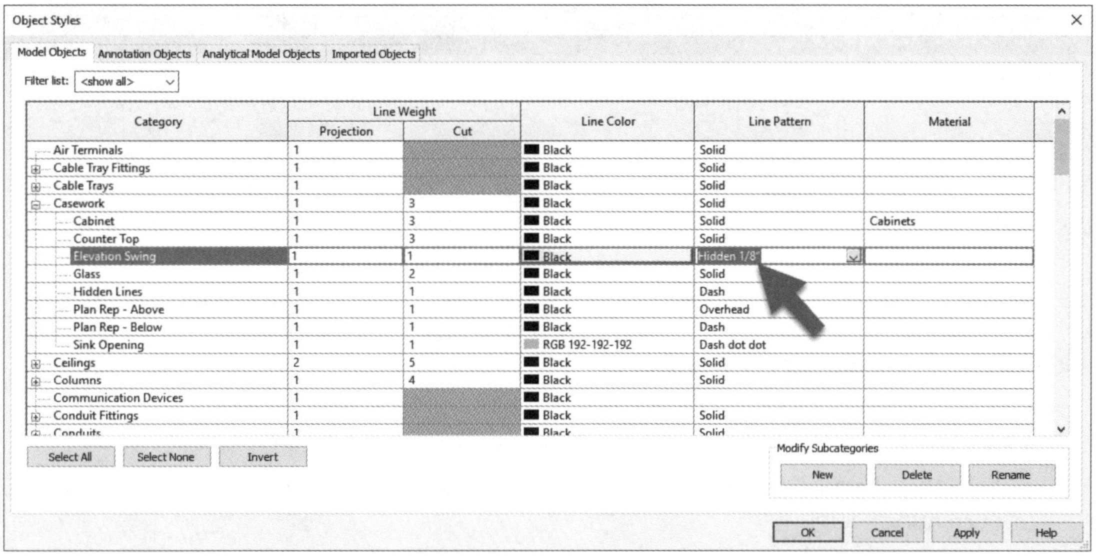

FIGURE 12-2.17 Object Styles dialog box; controls project wide graphics settings

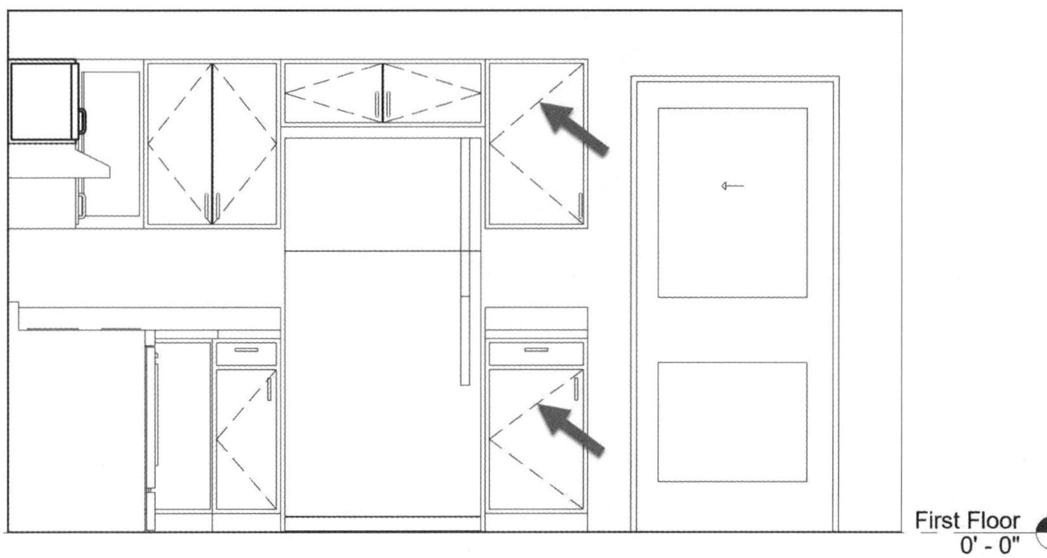

That is it for the kitchen! With a little practice, you could design a kitchen in very short order.

47. **Save** your project as **ex12-2.rvt**.

TIP: *The North American Architectural Woodwork Standards (https://www.naaws-committee.com/) provides Revit families for most industry-standard cabinets. You can download the cabinets from their website via the 'Cabinet Design Series' page. You can even print a small flyer with an image of each cabinet available for download.*

Exercise 12-3:
Furniture

This lesson will cover the steps for laying out furniture. The processes are identical to those previously covered for toilets and cabinets. First, you will start with the office on the second floor.

Loading Necessary Families:

1. Open ex12-2.rvt and **Save As ex12-3.rvt**.

2. Select the **Load Family** tool, on the *Insert* tab, and load the following items into the current project:

   Autodesk Files *(via Load Autodesk Family)*

   a. **Furniture_System-Standing_Desk-L_with_Square_End-Corner_Angled: 72"x72"x24"** (Furniture System\Standing Desks)
   b. **Chair-Executive** (Furniture\Seating)
   c. **Sofa-Pensi** (Furniture\Seating)
   d. **Table-Round** (Furniture\Tables)

   Provided Files *(see inside front cover of this book)*

   e. **Copier-Floor**

TIP: You can set the View mode for the Open dialog box that appears when loading local content from your computer. One option is Thumbnail *mode, which displays a small thumbnail for each file in the current folder. Press Ctrl + spin your mouse wheel to adjust the preview size. This makes it easier to see the many symbols and drawings that are available for insertion.*

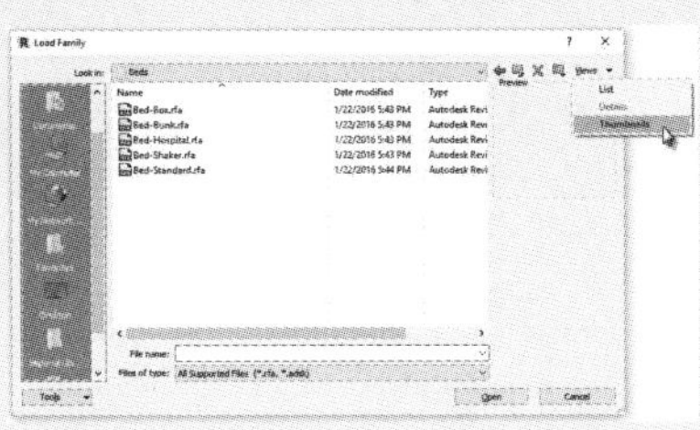

Above: View set to List mode

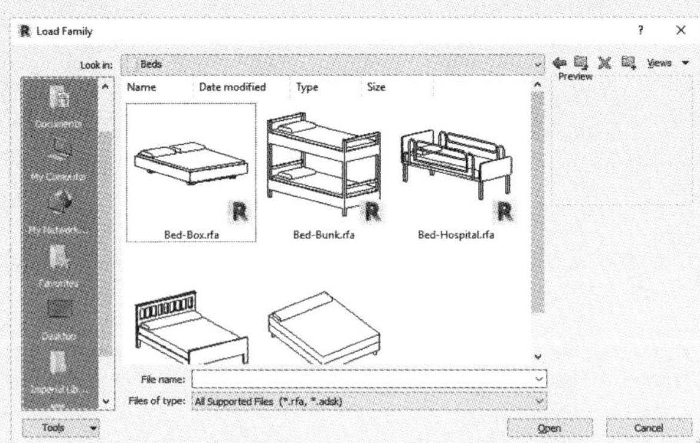

Right: View set to Thumbnail mode

Designing the Office Furniture Layout:

3. Switch to the ***Second Floor*** plan view.

4. Using the **Component** tool, place the furniture as shown in Figure 12-3.1.

TIP: Use Snaps to assure accuracy; use Rotate and Mirror as required.

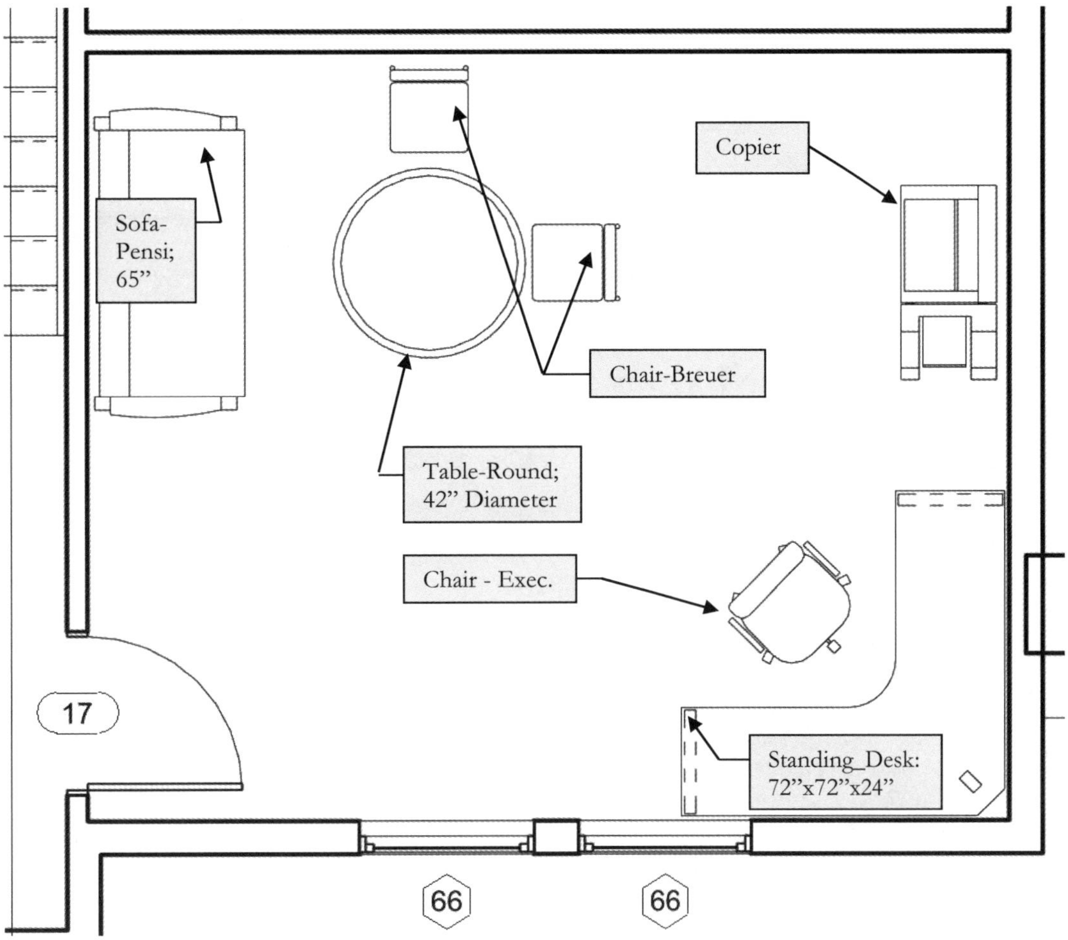

FIGURE 12-3.1 Second Floor – Office furniture layout

Look at the type properties for the Standing Desk to see the *Height* parameter, which controls the height of the surface above the current floor. For this family, it is an instance parameter as the height can vary.

You may want to browse through the component library and online for miscellaneous residential furniture. You can add dining room tables and chairs, bookshelves, a washer and dryer, etc. If you are working on this in a classroom, your instructor may require you to complete this suggested step. An example of a few items placed is shown in Figure 12-3.2.

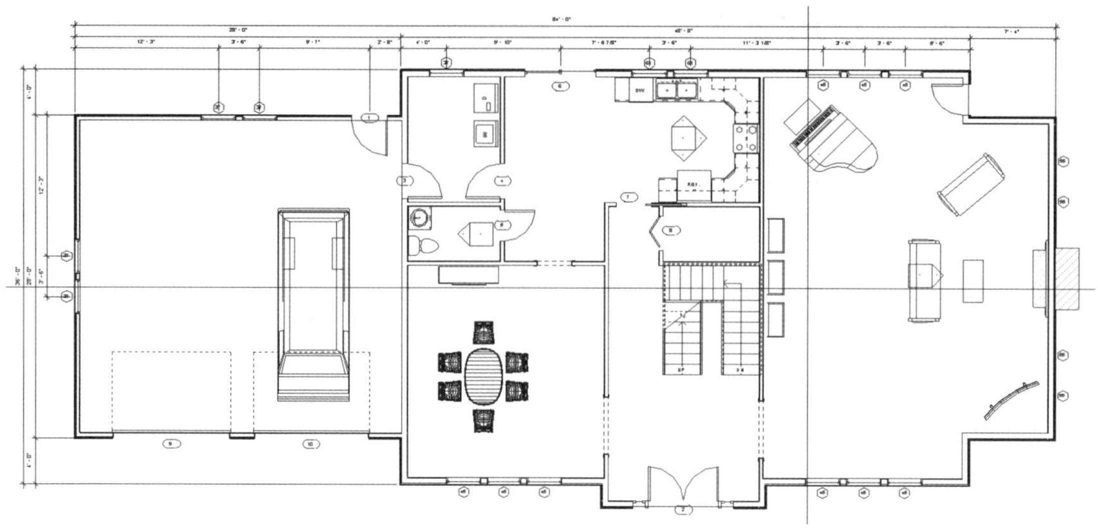

FIGURE 12-3.2 First Floor; one possible furniture layout

3D View of Office Layout:

Next, you will view a 3D model of your office area. This involves adjusting the visibility of the roof and skylights.

5. Switch to the ***Default 3D*** view via the *QAT*.

6. Adjust the 3D view using orbit (see tip below) and zoom to look at the roof area above the second-floor home office.

   TIP: While pressing the Shift key, also press the wheel button on the mouse and drag the mouse around to "orbit" the model without selecting any icons or commands first. Also, selecting an object in the view makes the model pivot about the selected object.

7. Type **VV** to access the *Visibility/Graphics Overrides* dialog box. Remember, these settings are only for the current view.

8. Uncheck the *Ceilings* and the *Roofs* category then click **OK**.

The ceilings and roof should not be visible now. However, you should still see the light fixtures floating in space. You will make those disappear next.

9. Select one of the 2′ x 4′ light fixtures floating above the office.

10. Click the ***Temporary Hide/Isolate*** tool from the *View Control Bar.*

You should see the menu shown in **Figure 12-3.3** show up next to the *Hide/Isolate* icon. This allows you to isolate an element, so it is the only thing on the screen. Or you can hide it, so the element is temporarily not visible.

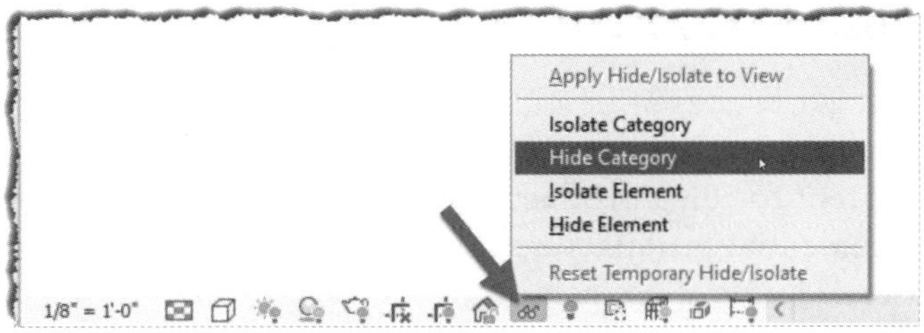

FIGURE 12-3.3 Hide/Isolate pop-up menu

11. Click **Hide Category** in the menu (Figure 12-3.3).

    FYI: *Picking category rather than element makes all the lights temporarily hidden.*

12. For more practice orbiting, adjust your ***3D*** view to look similar to **Figure 12-3.4**; try looking at the room from other angles as well.

You will now restore the original visibility settings for the ***3D*** view. Notice that the Hide/Isolate icon now has a colored background, indicating that something in the project is temporarily hidden from view.

13. Click the *Hide/Isolate* icon and then select ***Reset Temporary Hide/Isolate*** from the pop-up menu.

14. Reset the ***3D*** view's visibility settings so the ceilings and roof are visible (type VV).

15. Click the *Home* icon via the ***ViewCube*** to reset the view (Figure 12-3.5).

16. **Save** your project as **ex12-3.rvt**.

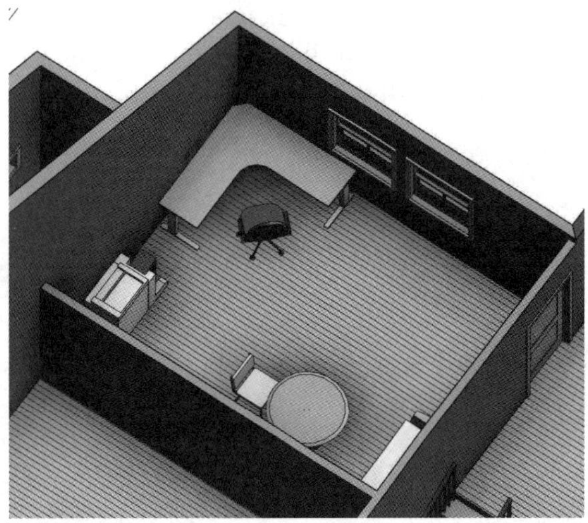

FIGURE 12-3.4 3D view with ceiling/roof/lights hidden

Online Content:

A few websites offer additional content for use in Revit; some is free, and some is not. Many product manufacturers provide Revit content for their products. This makes it easier for designers to include that manufacturer's product in their projects, both in virtual and real projects.

FIGURE 12-3.5 Home icon next to ViewCube; Home icon is only visible when cursor is over ViewCube.

Here are just a few examples of sites one might download Revit content from:

- www.revitcity.com *(free content provided by other users)*
- www.turbosquid.com *(buy, sell, and trade other user's content)*
- www.arcat.com, www.revit-content.com, bimobject.com,

You should occasionally search the internet to see if additional content becomes available. You can do an internet search for "revit content"; make sure to include the quotation marks. Rendering content, such as that offered by www.archvision.com, will be covered in Chapter 14.

Also, be sure to check out the residential appliances (Autodesk content). The image below shows a few examples rendered with Enscape (www.enscape3d.com). This author previously wrote this post when this content first came out:
https://bimchapters.blogspot.com/2017/07/revit-20181-new-content-part-1.html

Exercise 12-4:
Adding Guardrails

This lesson will cover the steps for laying out guardrails. The steps are simple; you select your style and draw its path.

Adding a Guardrail to the Second Floor Stair Area:

1. Open ex12-3.rvt and **Save As ex12-4.rvt.**
2. Switch to the **Second Floor** plan view.

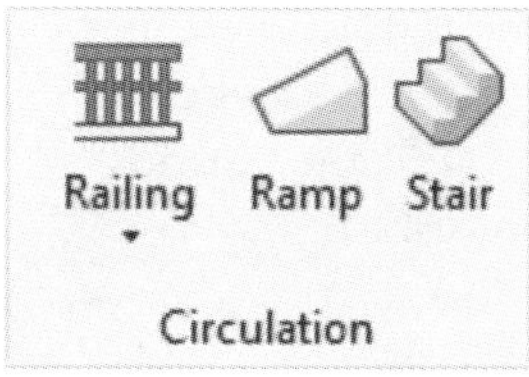

3. Select **Architecture → Circulation → Railing → Sketch Path.**
4. **Zoom** into the stair area.

At this point you will draw a line representing the path of the guardrail. The railing is offset to one side of the line, similar to walls. However, you do not have the *Location Line* option as you do with the *Wall* tool, so you have to draw the railing in a certain direction to get the railing to be on the floor and not hovering in space just beyond the floor edge.

5. Draw a line along the edge of the floor as shown in **Figure 12-4.1**.

   TIP: Select Chain *on the Ribbon to draw the railing with fewer picks.*

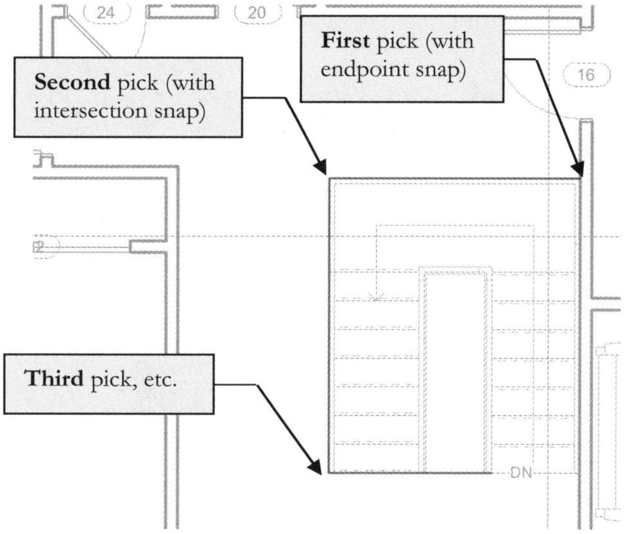

FIGURE 12-4.1 Second Floor: adding a guardrail

6. Click the **green checkmark** from the *Ribbon* to finish the railing.

The railing has now been drawn. In the next step you will switch to a 3D view and see how to quickly change the railing style. This will also involve changing the height of the railing. Most building codes require the railing height be 42″ when the drop to the adjacent surface is more than 30″; this is called a guardrail.

7. Switch to the ***3D*** view.

8. Hide the ceilings and roof as previously reviewed (***Tip:*** *Temp. Hide/Isolate*), and then zoom into the railing just added to the second floor. Notice the railing style shown in Figure 12-4.2.

9. Select the railing. You may have to use the *Tab* key to cycle through the various selection options.

10. With the railing selected, select the other railing types available in the *Type Selector* on the *Properties Palette.* When finished, make sure *Railing:* **Handrail – Rectangular** is selected.

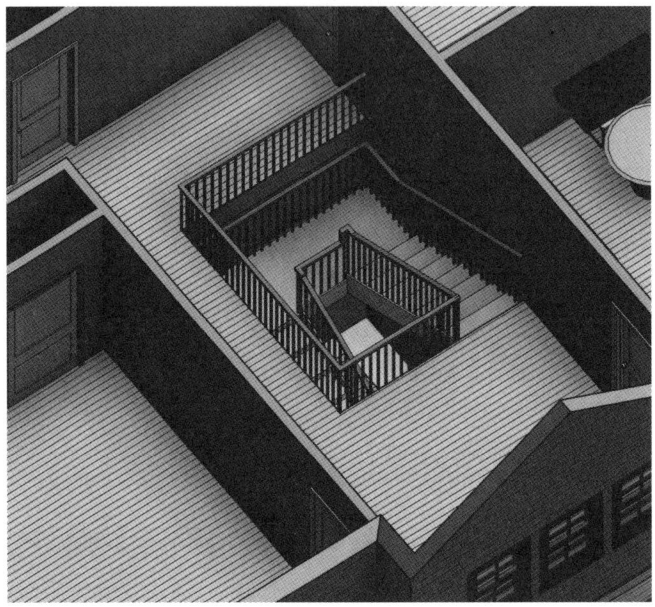

FIGURE 12-4.2 Added railing – 3D view

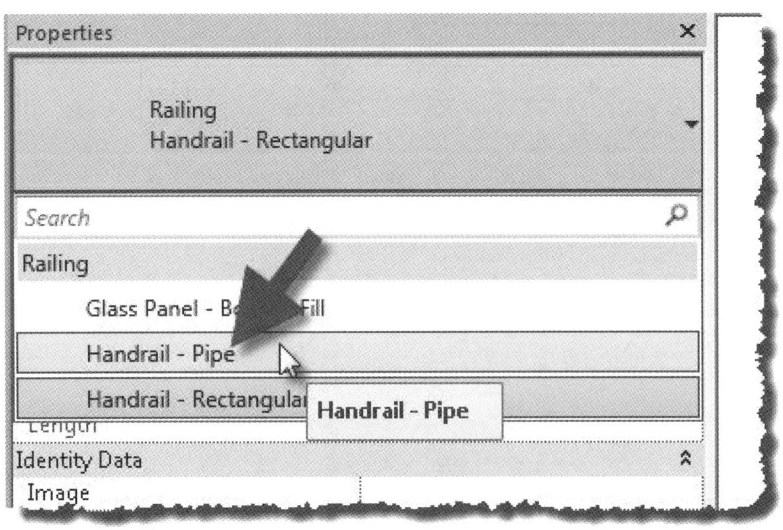

Modify Railing via the *Properties Palette*

When the alternate style was selected, your railing should have appeared as shown in Figure 12-4.3. Even the stairs' railing could be changed with a similar step. This style is too contemporary for this design, so you will not use it at this time.

FYI: You can change the height via Type Properties.

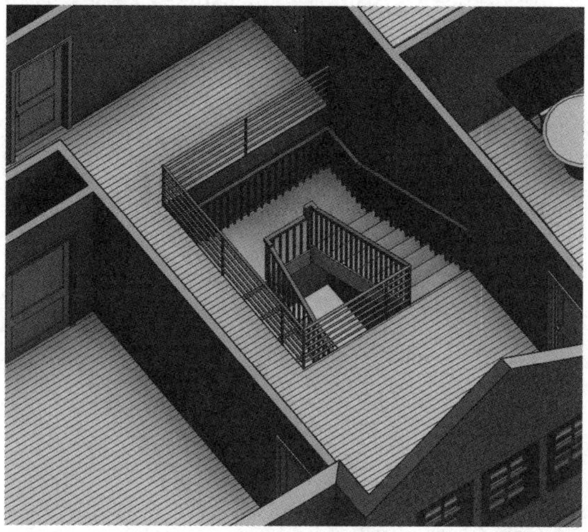

FIGURE 12-4.3 Railing with alternate style

Editing the Sketch Lines for the Stair Railing:

You will notice, in the image above (Figure 12-4.3), that a portion of the railing added with the stair is not required along the wall. You will edit the railing sketch lines to remove this conflict.

11. Switch to the ***First Floor Plan*** view.
12. Select the outer railing for the upper stair; use the *Tab* key to cycle through your selection options.
13. Click the **Edit Path** button on the *Modify | Railings* tab.
14. Delete the sketch lines on the north and east walls, shown dashed in Figure 12-4.4.

FYI: The railing added with the stair is simply a separate railing element that was automatically added with the stair.

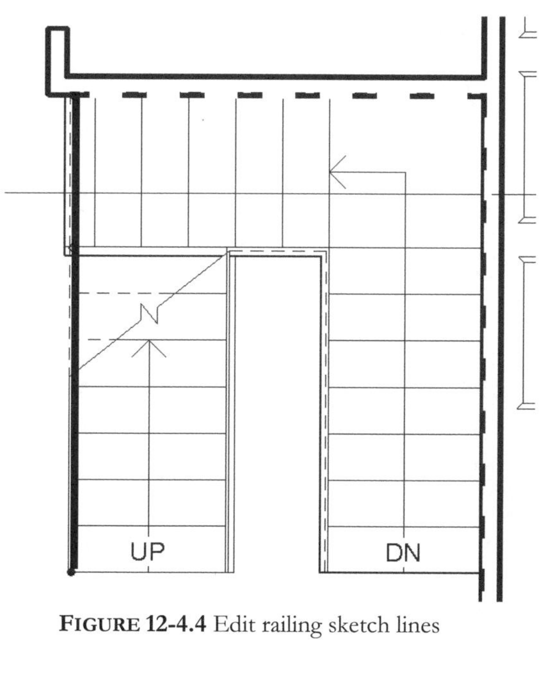

FIGURE 12-4.4 Edit railing sketch lines

15. Select the **green check mark** on the *Design Bar* when finished.

16. Reset the 3D view so the roof and ceiling elements are visible.

Switching back to the ***3D*** view, you notice the railing along the walls is gone (compare 12-4.3 and Figure 12-4.5). Revit is consistent in how the various 3D components are defined and edited using 2D sketch linework. This consistency helps reduce the learning curve.

FIGURE 12-4.5 Railing conflict resolved

The *Railing* tool can be used to create fairly complex railings. The image below shows the interface for setting up the baluster placement (Figure 12-4.6). This kind of advanced control is beyond the scope of this textbook.

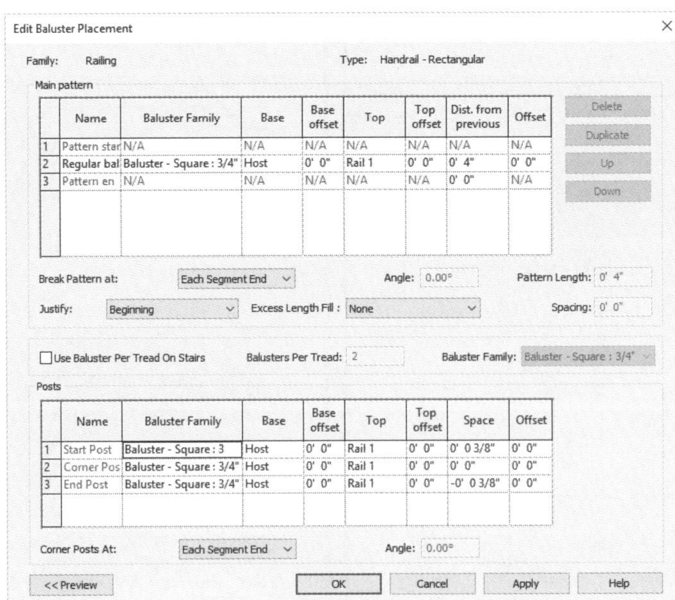

FIGURE 12-4.6 Dialog to control baluster and newel post placement

Make sure to examine the stair and railing sample file provided by Autodesk.

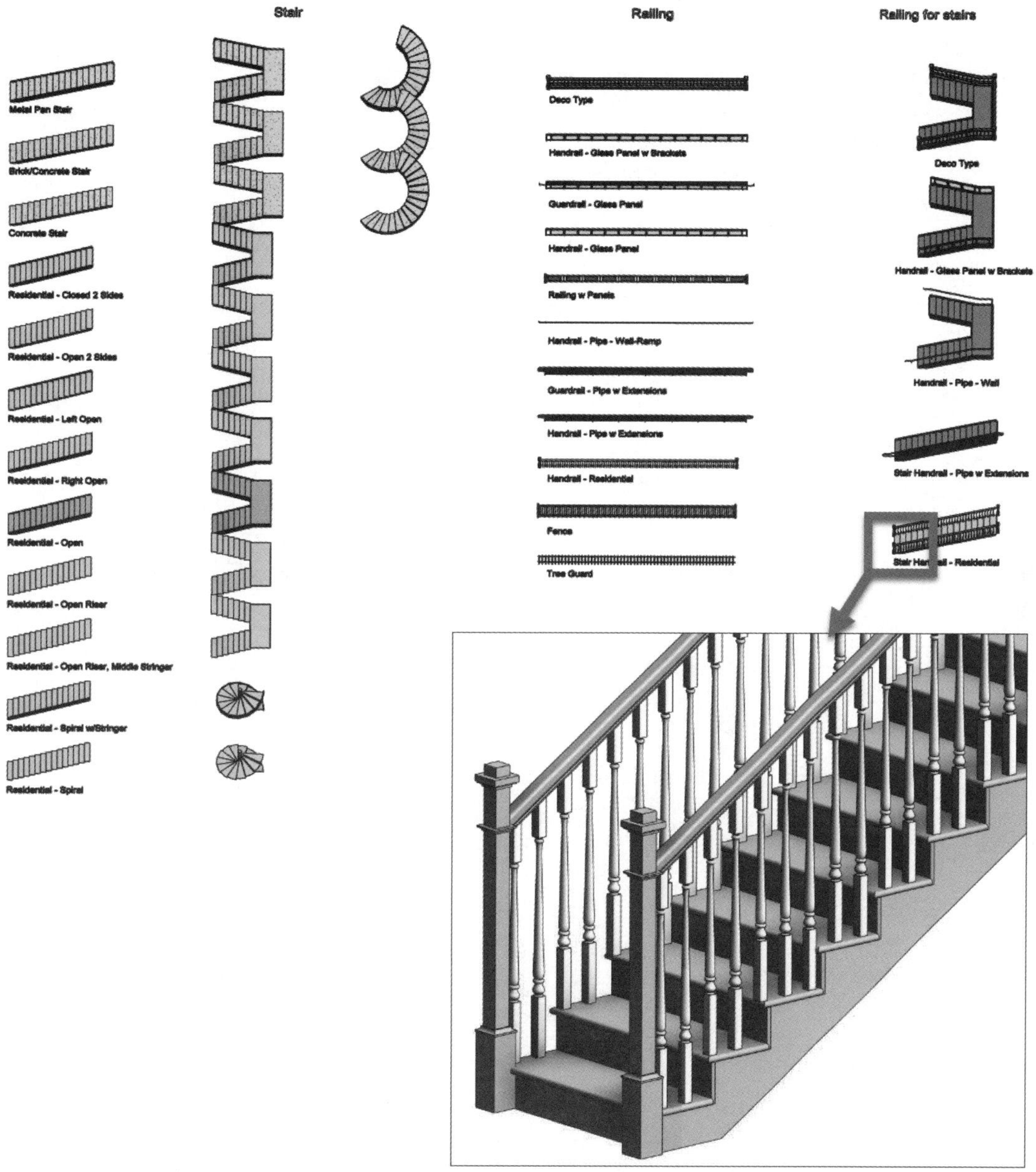

Learn more in this blog post:
https://bimchapters.blogspot.com/2018/12/new-revit-2019-sample-file-stair-and.html

You can *Copy/Paste* a railing style from this drawing into one of your project files. Then you select your railing and pick the newly imported one from the *Type Selector*. This process was done to achieve the image below (Figure 12-4.8). Notice the traditional balusters and newel post.

17. **Save** your project as **ex12-4.rvt**.

Self-Exam:

The following questions can be used as a way to check your knowledge of this lesson. The answers can be found at the bottom of the page.

1. The bathroom fixtures are preloaded in the template file. (T/F)

2. You do not need to be connected to the internet when you want to download content provided with this book. (T/F)

3. Revit content may not always be in compliance with local codes. (T/F)

4. You can use *Crop Region* to crop a portion of wall that is blank. (T/F)

5. Click the _______________tool to modify the path of a railing.

Review Questions:

The following questions may be assigned by your instructor as a way to assess your knowledge of this section. Your instructor has the answers to the review questions.

1. Revit provides several different styles of vanity cabinets for placement. (T/F)

2. Revit automatically adds a rail to every stair. (T/F)

3. It is not possible to draw dimensions on an interior elevation view. (T/F)

4. Cabinets typically come in 2″ increments. (T/F)

5. Base cabinets automatically have a countertop on them. (T/F)

6. When you create a hole in a floor, Revit automatically adds a railing. (T/F)

7. You can use the __________________________ to control element visibility.

8. What is the current size of your Revit Project? ________________________

9. What should you use to assure accuracy when placing cabinets? __________

10. You use the ___________________ tool to make various components temporarily invisible.

SELF-EXAM ANSWERS:
1 – T, **2** – F, **3** – T, **4** – T, **5** – Edit Path

Lesson 13
SCHEDULES:

You will continue studying the powerful features of Autodesk® Revit®. The ability to create parametric schedules is very useful; for example, you can delete a door number on a schedule, and Revit will delete the corresponding door from the plan.

Exercise 13-1:
Room and Door Tags

This exercise will show you how to add room tags and door tags to your plans. As you insert doors, Revit can automatically add tags to them. However, if you copy or mirror a door, or add one in elevation, you may lose the tag and have to add it again.

Adding Rooms and Room Tags:

You will add a *Room* object, which will also add a *Room Tag* to the current view, to each room on your first floor plan. A *Room* object is not visible by default. It is an object which is used to calculate area, volume, and store information about the room (i.e., the I in BIM… **B**uilding **I**nformation **M**odeling).

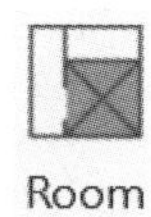

1. In the **First Floor** view, select **Architecture → Room & Area → Room.**

Placing a *Room* is similar to placing a ceiling in the reflected ceiling plan: as you move your cursor over a room, its perimeter highlights. When the room you want to place a *Room* element in is highlighted, click to place it there. You are actually placing a *Room* and a *Room Tag.*

2. Place your cursor within the *Entry* area and place a *Room* (Figure 13-1.1). Make sure *"Tag on placement"* is highlighted on the *Ribbon.*

   a. Press the Esc key to cancel the room command.

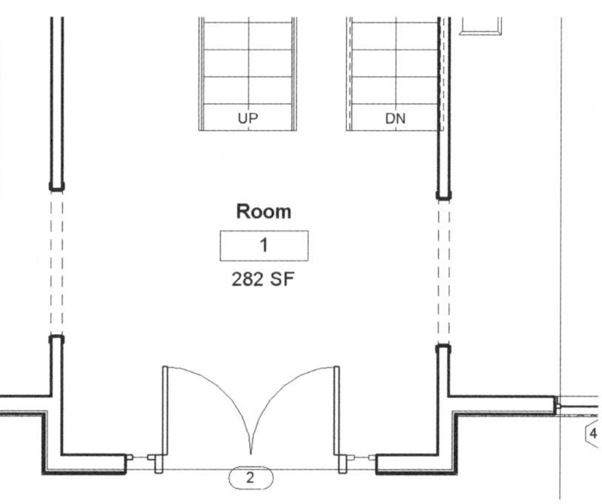

FIGURE 13-1.1 Room & Room Tag added to entry

By default, Autodesk Revit will simply label the space 'Room' and number it '1.' You will change these to something different.

The wall openings may let the Room element extend into adjacent rooms as shown in Figure 13-1.2a below. Next, you will correct this problem with a special line used to contain rooms when there is no wall, or at an opening in a wall.

3. Add **Room Separator** lines within each opening pointed out below (Figure 13-1.2a).

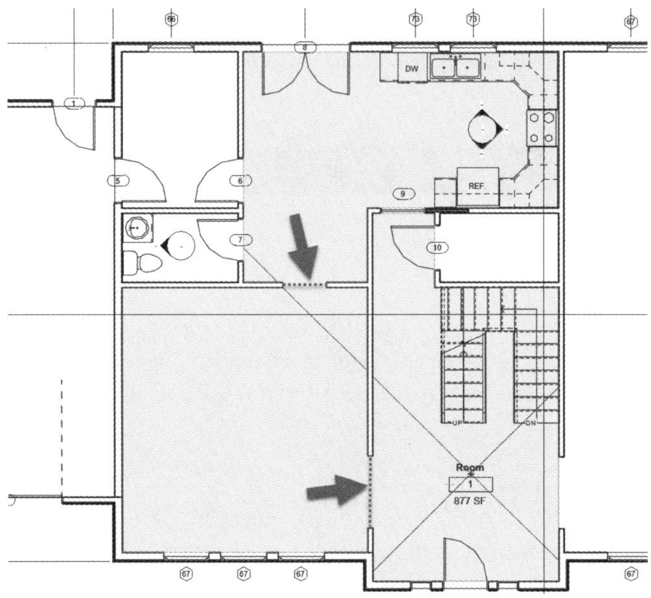

FIGURE 13-1.2A Room tags – First Floor

The room element is now confined to the entry area, as shown in Figure 13-1.2b.

4. Click on the ***Room Tag*** you just placed to select it.

5. Now, click on the room name label to change it; enter **ENTRY** (all caps).

6. Now click on the room number to change it; enter **100** (Figure 13-1.2b).

Now that the entry room is confined properly, the remaining first floor rooms can be placed.

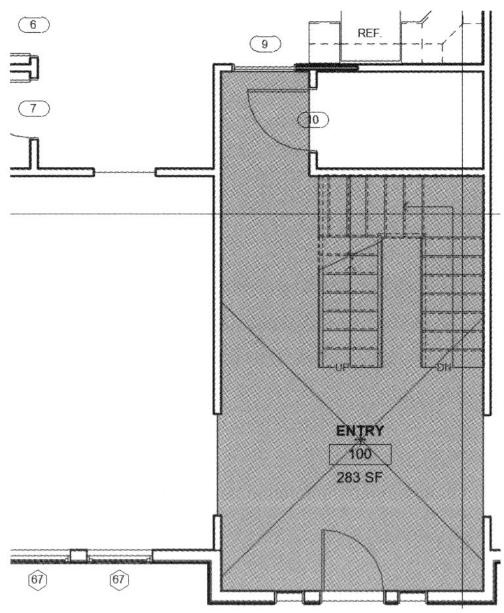

FIGURE 13-1.2B Room confined to entry

7. Add *Rooms/Room Tags* for each room on the first floor, incrementing each room number by 1 (Figure 13-1.3). Be sure to change the room names as well.

TIP: During placement, pressing the spacebar will toggle the tag between horizontal and vertical orientation.

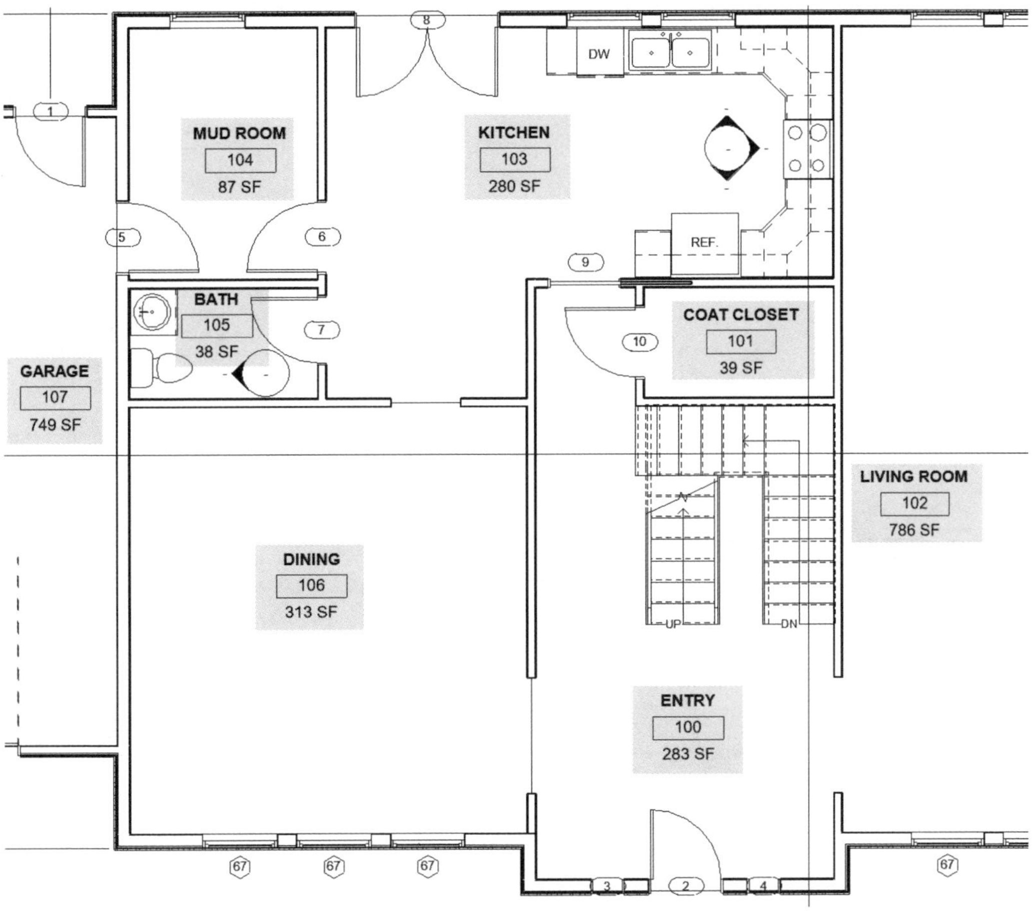

FIGURE 13-1.3 First Floor Room added – highlighted in this image for clarity

Second and Basement Floors:

8. Add *Rooms/Room Tags* to the *Second Floor*. The numbering should start with 200; place the first room, and then change the number to 200. This will make the remaining rooms the correct number. Add the *Room Separator* as pointed out. Do **not** change the room names (Figure 13-1.4).

9. Add *Rooms/Tags* to the *Basement Floor Plan*. The numbering should start with 1; **do** change the room names (Figure 13-1.5). Add the *Room Separator* lines as pointed out.

FYI: Room tags *can also be added to your building sections, as the* Room *element will now be there! When the Room element already exists, in plan or section, you use the* Room Tag *tool, not the* Room *command.*

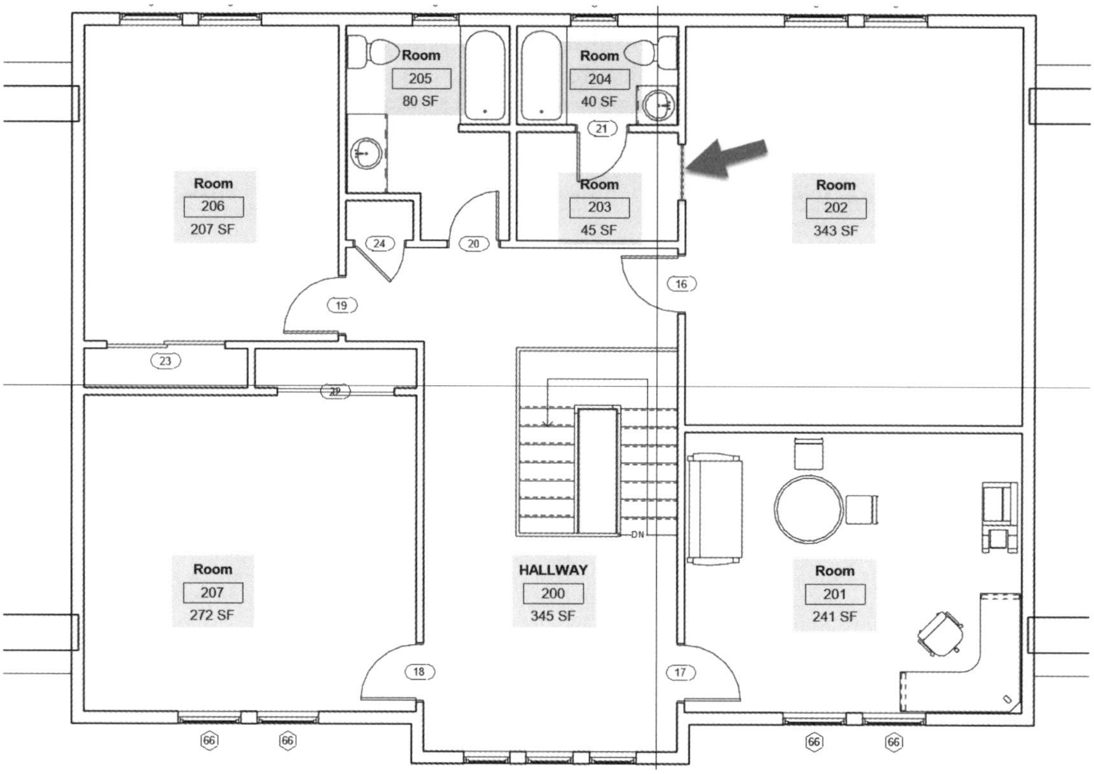

FIGURE 13-1.4 Second Floor – Room /Room tags

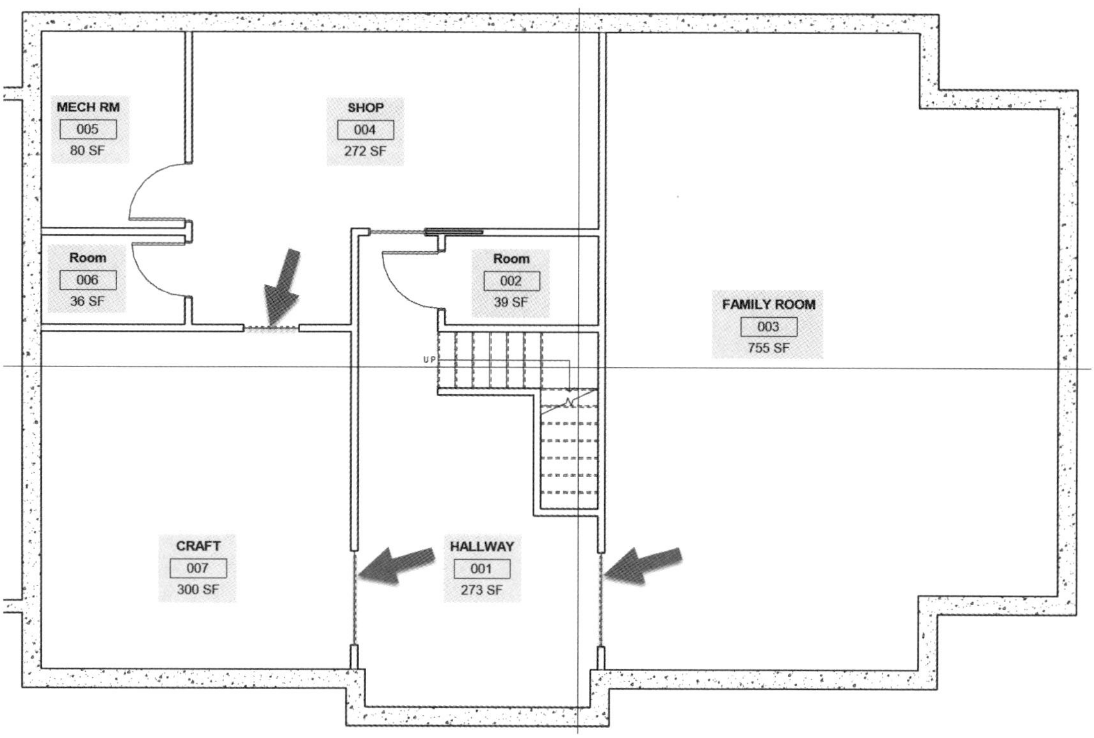

FIGURE 13-1.5 Basement – Room tags

Adding Door Tags:

Next, you will add *Door Tags* to any doors that are missing them. Additionally, you will adjust the door numbers to correspond to the room numbers.

Revit numbers the doors in the order they are placed into the drawing. This would make it difficult to locate a door by its door number if door number 1 were on the first floor and door number 2 were on the second floor, etc. Typically, a door number matches the room number it swings into. For example, if a door swings into a room numbered 104, the door number would also be 104. If the room had two doors, they would be numbered 104A and 104B.

10. Switch to **First Floor** plan view.

11. Select **Annotate → Tag → Tag By Category** from the *Ribbon* (Figure 13-1.6).

    TIP: *This tool can also be selected from the Quick Access Toolbar or by typing TG.*

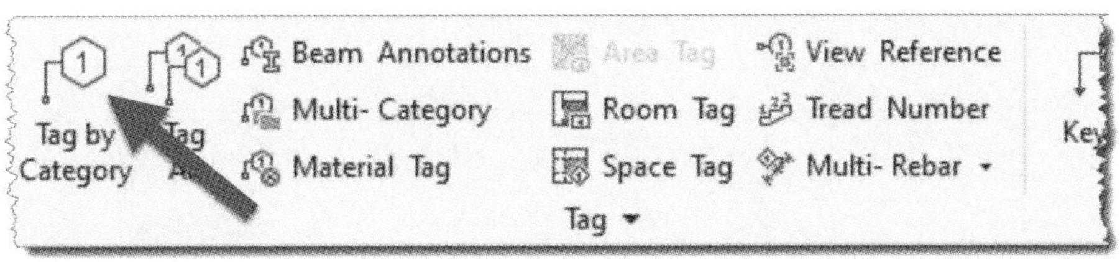

FIGURE 13-1.6 Annotate tab

Notice, as you move your cursor around the screen, Revit displays a tag for any element that can have a tag when the cursor is over it. This includes walls, doors, windows, and related items. When you click the mouse, is when Revit actually places a tag.

12. **Unselect** the ***Leader Line*** option on the *Ribbon.*

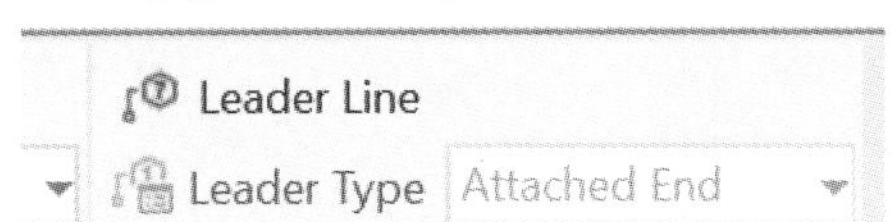

13. Place a ***Door Tag*** for each door that does not have a tag; do this for each level.

    TIP: *Press the spacebar to* Rotate *before clicking to place the tag.*

    TIP: *These should mainly be the doors in the Basement, and the one added in elevation in the Living Room.*

14. **Renumber** all the *Door Tags* to correspond to the room they open into; do this for each level. Figure 13-1.7 shows the first floor, and Figure 13-1.8 shows the second floor. **Also, reposition door tags that overlap any other lines.**

    REMEMBER: *Click* Modify, *select the* Tag, *and then click on the number to edit it.*

TIP – TAG ALL *(Figure 13-1.6): This tool allows you to quickly tag all the elements of a selected category (e.g., doors) at one time. After selecting the tool, choose a category from the list and specify whether you want a leader. When you click* OK, *Revit tags all the untagged doors in that view. This helps to avoid not tagging a door. However, all doors will appear in the schedule, whether they are tagged or not.*

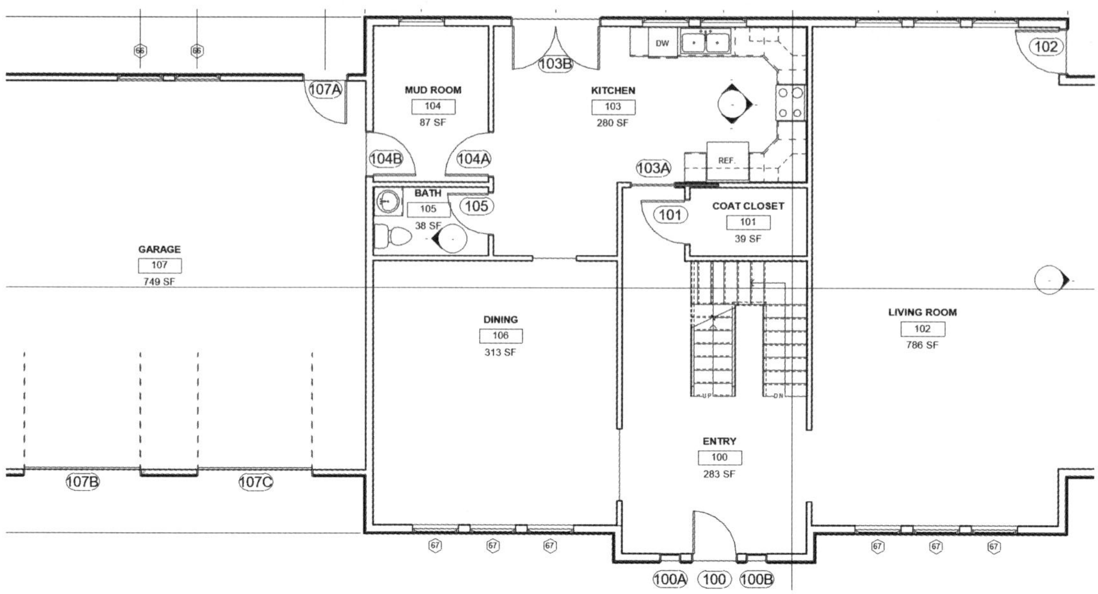

FIGURE 13-1.7 First Floor; door tags (tags enlarged for printing)

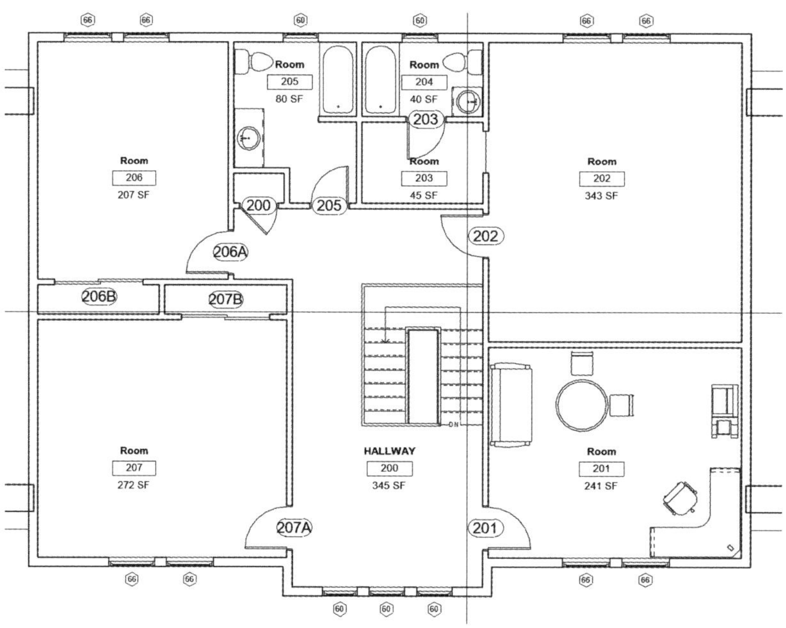

FIGURE 13-1.8 Second Floor; door tags (tags enlarged for printing)

TIP: *The wall Instance Parameter in the Properties Palette must be set to "room bounding" for the Room tool to consider a wall as part of the perimeter within a particular room; this is the default setting. For example, you could set a closet wall so it was not "room bounding," so Revit would ignore it when creating the Room, thus adding the closet square footage to the room total.*

15. **Save** your project as **ex13-1.rvt**.

Exercise 13-2:
Generate a Door Schedule

This exercise will look at creating a door schedule based on the information currently available in the building model (i.e., the *Room* and *Door* elements). The tags report only information stored within the element they tag, so you can delete a tag at any time without losing information. The tag can then be added later if required; tags are view-specific.

Create a Door Schedule View:

A door schedule is simply another view of the building information model (BIM). However, this view displays numerical data rather than graphical data. Just like in a graphical view, if you change the view, it updates all related views. For example, if you delete a door from the schedule, it is removed from the plans and elevations.

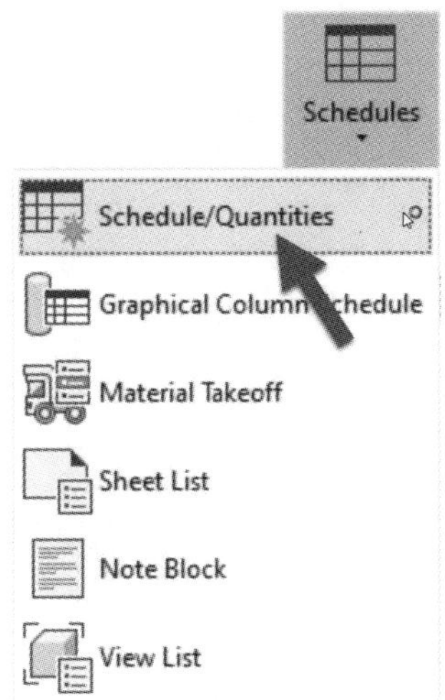

1. Open ex13-1.rvt and **Save As ex13-2.rvt.**

2. Select **View → Create → Schedules → Schedules/Quantities**.

3. Select ***Doors*** under *Category* and then click **OK** (Figure 13-2.1).

FYI: *The template you started with already has a door schedule set up and ready to use, so the first door you added was already scheduled. However, you will go through the steps to set up a schedule so you understand how one is created. It is possible to have more than one door schedule, and each can report different information stored within the doors.*

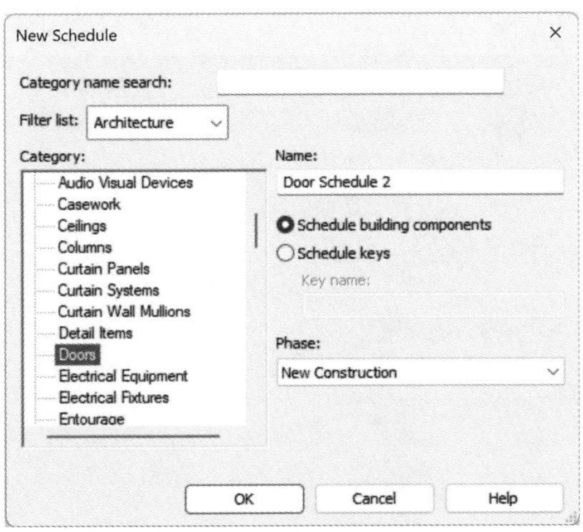

FIGURE 13-2.1 New Schedule dialog

You should now be in the *Schedule Properties* dialog, where you specify what information is displayed in the schedule, how it is sorted, and the text format.

4. On the ***Fields*** tab, *Add* the information you want displayed in the schedule. Select the following (Figure 13-2.2):
   a. Mark
   b. Width
   c. Height
   d. Frame Material
   e. Frame Type
   f. Fire Rating

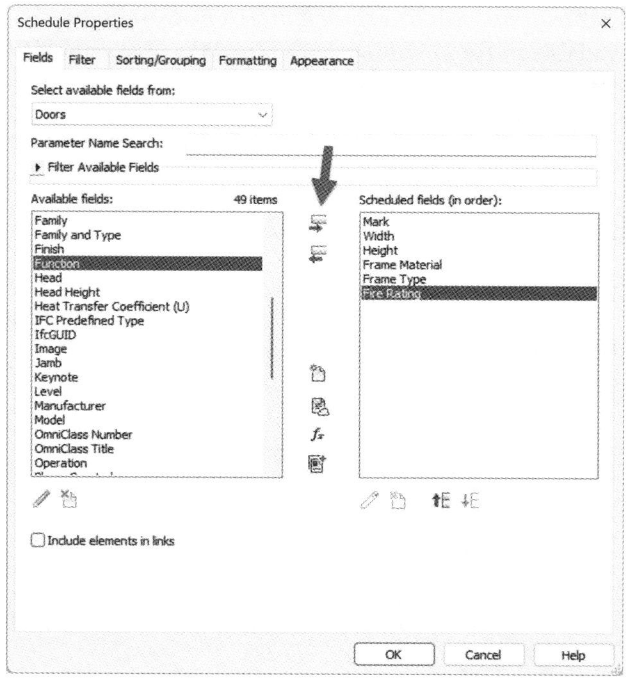

FIGURE 13-2.2 Schedule Properties; Fields tab

As noted in the dialog, the fields added to the list on the right are in the order they will be in the schedule view. Use the *Move Parameter Up* and *Move Parameter Down* buttons to adjust the order if necessary.

5. Do **NOT** click OK. You need to adjust one more thing.

   TIP: *If you accidentally clicked* OK, *click the* Edit *button next to the Fields parameter in the Properties Palette.*

6. On the ***Sorting/Grouping*** tab, set the schedule to be sorted by the **Mark** (i.e., door number) in *Ascending* order (Figure 13-2.3).

TIP: *The* Formatting *and* Appearance *tabs allow you to adjust how the schedule looks. Some of the formatting is not displayed until the schedule is placed on a sheet.*

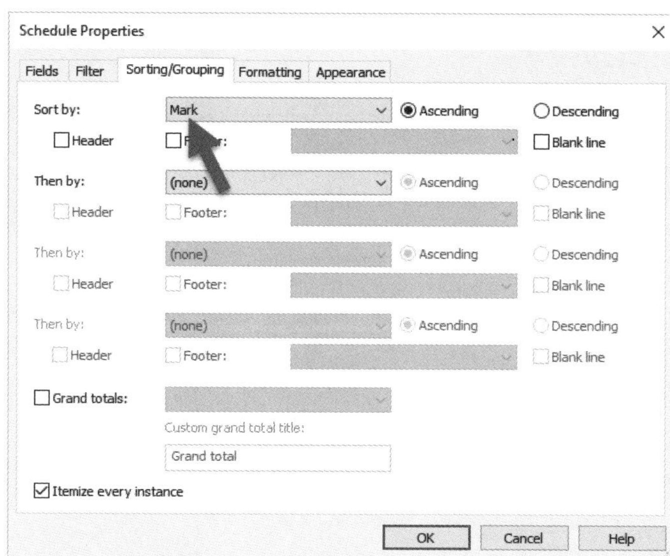

FIGURE 13-2.3 Schedule Properties; Sorting tab

7. Click the **OK** button to generate the schedule view.

You should now have a schedule similar to Figure 13-2.4.

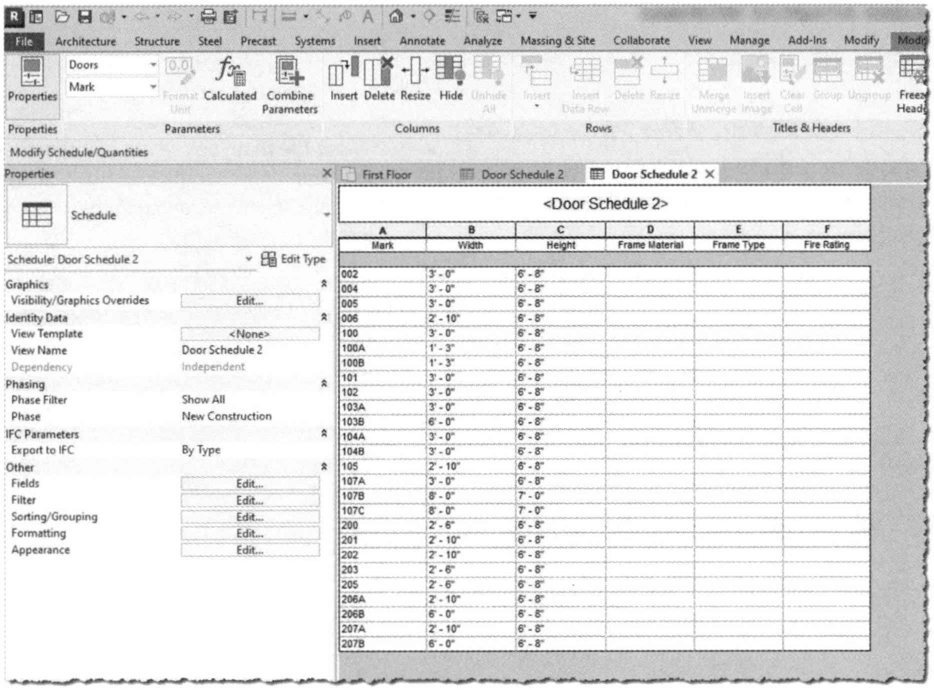

FIGURE 13-2.4 Door schedule view

Next, you will see how deleting a door number from the schedule deletes the door from the plan.

8. Switch to the ***Door Schedule 2*** view, under *Schedules/Quantities* in the *Project Browser*, if you are not already there.

Next, you will delete door *102* from the ***Door Schedule*** view; this was the door you added in an interior elevation, the exterior door in the *Living Room*.

9. Click in the cell with the number **102**.

10. Now click the **Delete** [Rows] button from the *Ribbon* (Figure 13-2.5).

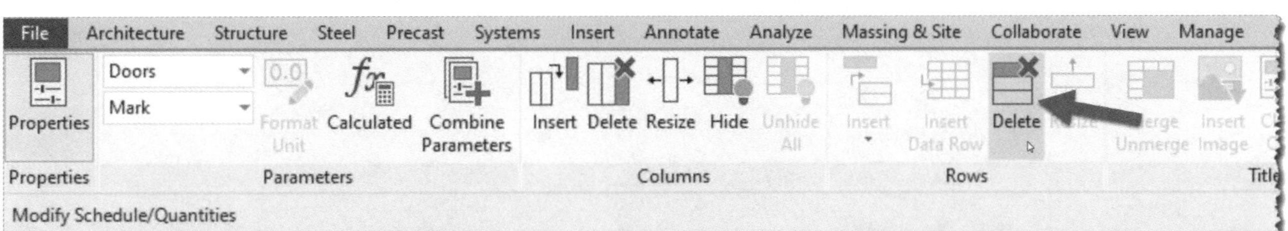

FIGURE 13-2.5 Ribbon panel for the door schedule view

You will get an alert. Revit is telling you that the actual door will be deleted from the project model (Figure 13-2.6).

11. Click **OK** to delete the door (Figure 13-2.6).

12. Switch back to the ***First Floor*** view and notice that door 102 and its tag have been deleted from the project model (Figure 13-2.7).

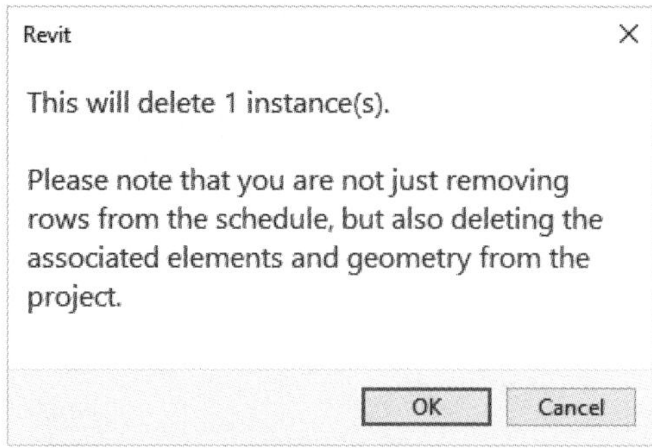

FIGURE 13-2.6 Revit alert message

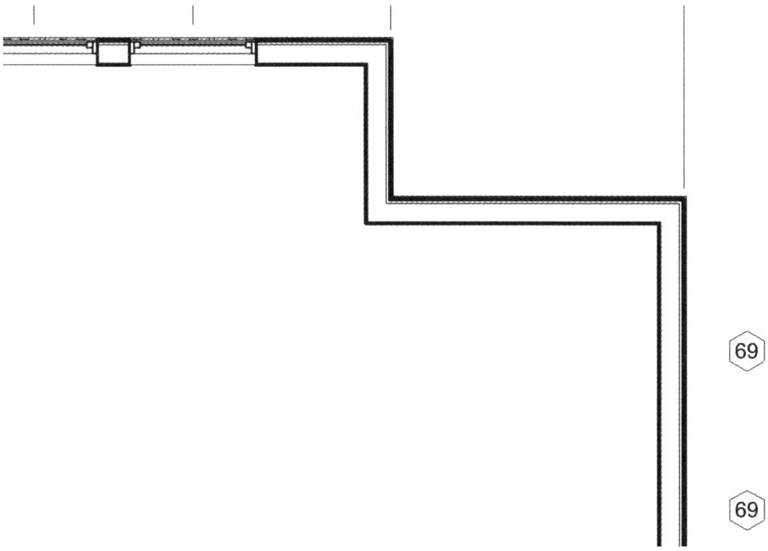

FIGURE 13-2.7 First Floor plan view; door 102 has been removed

13. **Save** your project as **ex13-2.rvt.**

TIP: *You can also change the door number in the schedule and even the size; however, changing the size actually changes the door's Type Property, which affects all door instances of that type.*

Exercise 13-3:
Generate a Room Finish Schedule

In this exercise, you will create a room finish schedule. The process is similar to the previous exercise.

Create a Room Finish Schedule:

1. Open ex13-2.rvt and **Save As ex13-3.rvt**.
2. Select **View → Create → Schedules → Schedule/Quantities**.
3. Select **Rooms** under *Category* and then click **OK** (Figure 13-3.1).

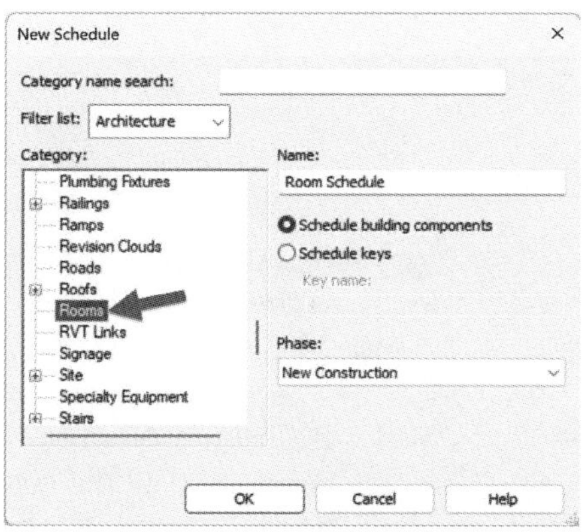

FIGURE 13-3.1 New Schedule dialog

4. In the ***Fields*** tab of the *Schedule Properties* dialog, add the following fields to be scheduled (Figure 13-3.2):
   a. Number
   b. Name
   c. Base Finish
   d. Floor Finish
   e. Wall Finish
   f. Ceiling Finish
   g. Area

Area is not typically listed on a room finish schedule. However, you will add it to your schedule to see the various options Revit allows.

5. On the ***Sorting/Grouping*** tab, set the schedule to be sorted by the **Number** field.
6. On the ***Appearance*** tab, set the *Title text* to **1/8" Arial** (Figure 13-3.3).

   TIP: *it is possible to create a new text style that is set to bold or with a different font and then use it here.*

7. Select **OK** to generate the ***Room Schedule*** view.

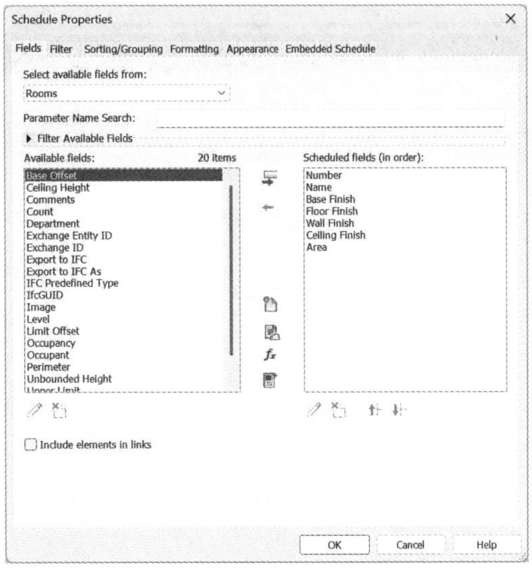

FIGURE 13-3.2
Schedule Properties - Fields

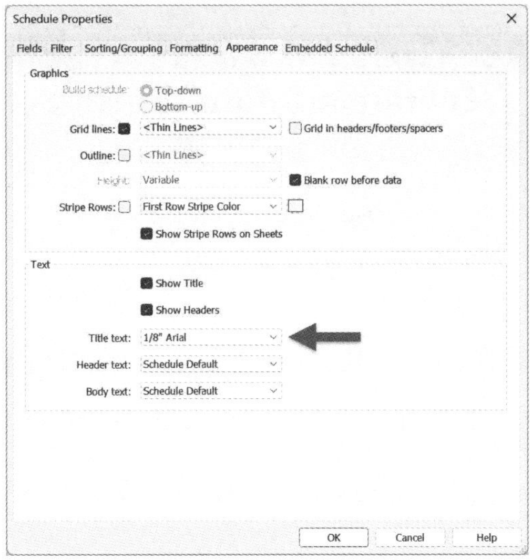

FIGURE 13-3.3
Schedule Properties - Appearance

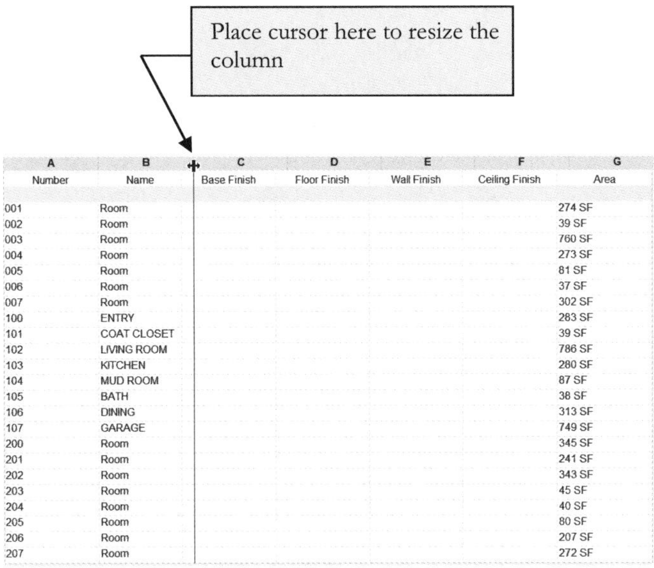

A	B	C	D	E	F	G
Number	Name	Base Finish	Floor Finish	Wall Finish	Ceiling Finish	Area
001	Room					274 SF
002	Room					39 SF
003	Room					760 SF
004	Room					273 SF
005	Room					81 SF
006	Room					37 SF
007	Room					302 SF
100	ENTRY					283 SF
101	COAT CLOSET					39 SF
102	LIVING ROOM					786 SF
103	KITCHEN					280 SF
104	MUD ROOM					87 SF
105	BATH					38 SF
106	DINING					313 SF
107	GARAGE					749 SF
200	Room					345 SF
201	Room					241 SF
202	Room					343 SF
203	Room					45 SF
204	Room					40 SF
205	Room					80 SF
206	Room					207 SF
207	Room					272 SF

FIGURE 13-3.4 Room Schedule view

Your schedule should look similar to the one to the left (Figure 13-3.4).

8. Resize the ***Name*** column so all the room names are visible. Place the cursor between *Name* and *Base Finish* and drag to the right until all the names are visible.

FYI: *If you right-click on a column, you can select to hide it. Why add a column if you are just going to hide it? Well, for Revit to do calculations on data, the required parameters must be "in" the schedule, not just the project.*

Modifying and Populating a Room Schedule:

Like the door schedule, the room schedule is a tabular view of the building model, so you can change the room name or number on the schedule or in the plans.

9. In the ***Room Schedule*** view, change the name for room **201** (which happens to be in the lower right corner of floor plan) to **OFFICE**.

   TIP: Click on the current room name and then click on the down-arrow that appears. This gives you a list of all the existing names in the current schedule; otherwise, you can type a new name.

10. Switch to the ***Second Floor*** plan view to see the updated *Room Tag*.

You can quickly enter finish information to several rooms at one time. You will do this next.

11. In the ***Second Floor*** plan view, select the **Rooms** (not the *Room Tags*) for all bedrooms (three total); move the cursor near the *Room Tag* until you see the room highlight with an "X" (Figure 13-3.5).

   REMEMBER: Hold the Ctrl key down to select multiple objects.

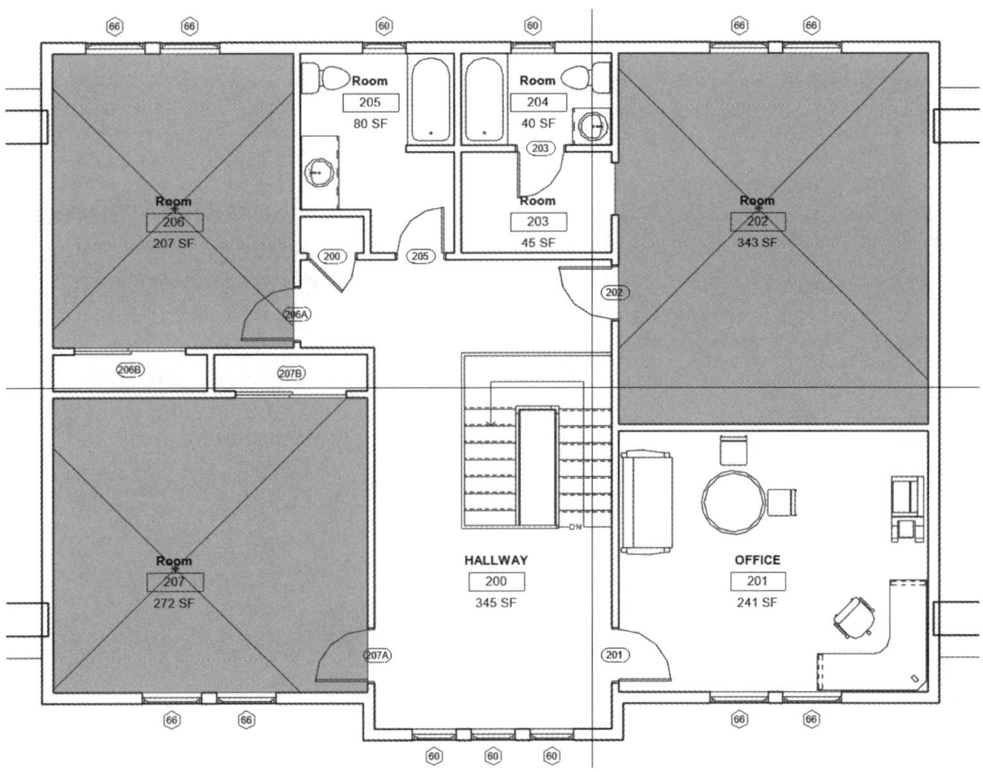

FIGURE 13-3.5 Second Floor Plan – Rooms selected

The parameters listed here are the same as the *Fields* available for display in the *Room Schedule.* When more than one room is selected, and the parameter value differs (e.g., different names), the value field says "<varies>". Otherwise, the values are displayed for the selected room. Next, enter the values for the finishes.

12. In the *Properties Palette*, change the *Name* field; enter **BEDROOM**.

13. Enter the following for the finishes (Figure 13-3.6):
    a. *Base Finish:* **WOOD**
    b. *Ceiling Finish:* **GB** *(Gb = gypsum board)*
    c. *Wall Finish:* **PAINT-1**
    d. *Floor Finish:* **CARPET-1**

FIGURE 13-3.6 Properties for three selected rooms

14. Click **Apply**.

15. Switch back to the ***Room Schedule*** view to see the automatic updates (Figure 13-3.7).

You can also enter data directly into the *Room Schedule* view, but only one room at a time.

Hopefully, in the future, Revit will be able to enter the finishes based on the wall's *Material* settings, as well as floor and ceiling types previously created in the project!

TIP: *To add or adjust fields and formatting, click one of the* ***edit*** *buttons in the Properties Palette. This gives you the same options that were available when you created the schedule.*

<Room Schedule>						
A	B	C	D	E	F	G
Number	Name	Base Finish	Floor Finish	Wall Finish	Ceiling Finish	Area
001	Room					274 SF
002	Room					39 SF
003	Room					760 SF
004	Room					273 SF
005	Room					81 SF
006	Room					37 SF
007	Room					302 SF
100	ENTRY					283 SF
101	COAT CLOSET					39 SF
102	LIVING ROOM					786 SF
103	KITCHEN					280 SF
104	MUD ROOM					87 SF
105	BATH					38 SF
106	DINING					313 SF
107	GARAGE					749 SF
200	Room					345 SF
201	OFFICE					241 SF
202	BEDROOM	WOOD	CARPET-1	PAINT-1	GB	343 SF
203	Room					45 SF
204	Room					40 SF
205	Room					80 SF
206	BEDROOM	WOOD	CARPET-1	PAINT-1	GB	207 SF
207	BEDROOM	WOOD	CARPET-1	PAINT-1	GB	272 SF

FIGURE 13-3.7 Room Schedule; new data added

If you have trouble finding a room in the *Floor Plan* view, you can click the room number in the *Schedule* view and then click the **Highlight in Model** button on the *Ribbon.*

16. **Save** your project as **ex13-3.rvt**.

FYI: *When the* Room Tag *is selected, not the Room element, you can change its type from the Type Selector. The other option available, by default, is one without the square footage listed below the room number. For the cubic footage to show up, the* Area and Volumes Computations *dialog must be set to calculate volumes – see image to right.*

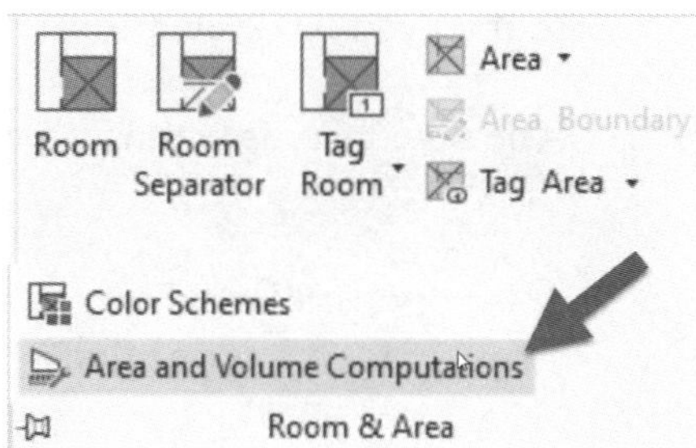

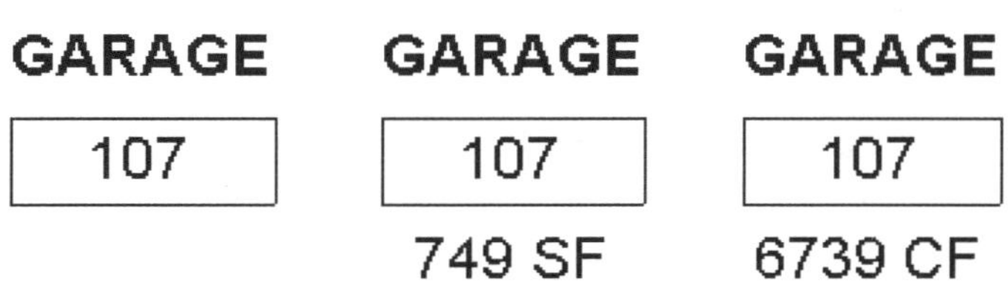

FIGURE 13-3.8 Room Tag options in current project

Self-Exam:

The following questions can be used as a way to check your knowledge of this lesson. The answers can be found at the bottom of the page.

1. Doors are automatically numbered based on the room number. (T/F)
2. The area for a room is calculated when a *Room*, and tag, is placed. (T/F)
3. Revit can tag all the doors not currently tagged on a given level with the *Tag All* tool. (T/F)
4. You can add or remove various fields in a door or room schedule. (T/F)
5. Click Delete on the *Ribbon* to delete a door from a schedule. (T/F)

Review Questions:

The following questions may be assigned by your instructor as a way to assess your knowledge of this section. Your instructor has the answers to the review questions.

1. You can add a door tag with a leader. (T/F)
2. You can add a fire rating by selecting a door, then *Properties Palette.* (T/F)
3. A door can be deleted from the door schedule. (T/F)
4. The schedule formatting only shows up when you place the schedule on a sheet. (T/F)
5. It is not possible to add the finish information (i.e., base finish, wall finish) to multiple rooms at one time. (T/F)
6. To modify the schedule view, click Edit in the *Properties Palette.* (T/F)
7. Use the ______________ palette to adjust the various fields associated with each Room in a plan view.
8. Most door schedules are sorted by the _____________ field.
9. You can select a different *Room Tag* via the *Type Selector.* (T/F)
10. A schedule is just another way of looking at the building information model, a tabular view of the project database. (T/F)

SELF-EXAM ANSWERS:
1 – F, **2** – T, **3** – T, **4** – T, **5** – T

Lesson 14
Site Tools and Photo-Realistic Rendering:

You will take a look at the site design tools and the photo-realistic rendering abilities of Autodesk® Revit®. Revit uses a rendering technology called **Autodesk Raytracer®**.

Exercise 14-1:
Site Tools

This exercise will give the reader a quick overview of the site tools available in Revit. The site tools are not intended to be an advanced site development package. Autodesk has other programs, much more capable of developing complex sites, such as AutoCAD Civil 3D. These programs are used by professional Civil Engineers and Surveyors. Contours, or surface tin, generated by advanced civil CAD programs can be used to create a Toposolid object in Revit.

In this lesson, you will create a topography object from scratch rather than using imported CAD geometry; you will also add a driveway and sidewalk.

Once the topography object (the topography object, or element, is 3D geometry that represents part *or* all of the site) is created, the grade line will automatically show up in building and wall sections, exterior elevations, and site plans. The sections even have the earth pattern filled in below the grade line.

As with other Revit elements, you can select the object after it is created and set various properties for it, such as surface material, phase, etc. One can also return to *Sketch* mode to refine or correct the surface; this is done in the same way most other sketched objects are edited: by selecting the item and clicking *Edit Sketch* on the *Ribbon*.

Overview of Site Tools on the Ribbon:

Below is a brief description of what the site tools are used for. After this short review, you will try a few of these tools on your residence project.

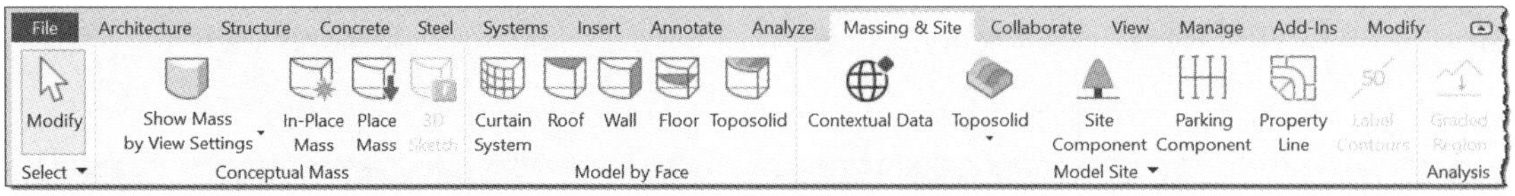

Contextual Data: Imports 3D data from trusted sources, such as ground surfaces and property lines, which can also be used for analysis in Forma (Revit is a Forma-connected client).

Toposolid: Creates a 3D surface of the ground by picking points, specifying the elevation of each point picked, or by using linework within a linked AutoCAD drawing that were created at the proper elevations.

The following commands are only visible when a Toposolid is selected:

Sub-Divide: Allows an area to be defined within a previously drawn toposolid; the result is an area within the toposolid that can have a material different from the toposolid itself. The sub-division is still part of the toposolid and will move with it when relocated. If a subregion is selected and deleted, the original surface and properties for that area are revealed.

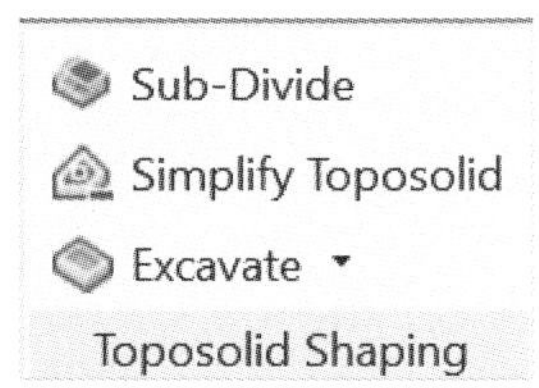

Simplify Toposolid: Reduce the number of points used to define the surface to improve system performance.

Excavate: Use floor and roof elements to define areas of a toposolid to cut away.

Site Component: Items like benches, dumpsters, etc., that are placed directly on the toposolid at the correct elevation at the point picked.

Parking Component: This is a parking stall layout that can be copied around to quickly lay out parking lots. Several types can be loaded, which specify both size and angle.

Property Line: Creates property lines in plan views only.

Label Contours: Adds an elevation label to the selected contours.

FYI: Contours are automatically generated from the toposolid.

Graded Region: This tool is used to edit the grade of a toposolid that represents the existing site conditions, and the designer wants to use Revit to design the new site conditions. This tool is generally intended for use only once; when used, it copies the existing site conditions to a new phase and sets the existing site for demolition in the new construction phase. The newly copied site object can then be modified for the new site conditions.

Site Settings:

Each Toposolid element created in a Revit model has its own *Contour Display* settings.

The ***Contour Display*** dialog is accessed via the Type Properties of a selected Toposolid element.

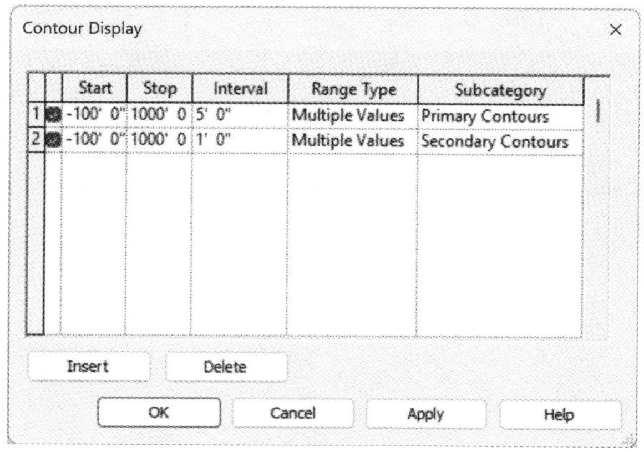

This dialog controls if the contours are displayed when the *toposolid* is visible, via the check box, and at what interval. If the *Interval* is set to 1′-0″ you will see contour lines that follow the ground's surface, and each line represents a vertical elevation change of 1′-0″ from the adjacent contour line. The contour lines alone do not tell you what direction the surface slopes in a plan view; this is why *Contour Labels* are important.

The default settings show primary and secondary contour lines. The **primary contour** lines occur every 5' vertically, in place of the **secondary contour** line in the same location. This is mainly a graphical setting that makes every fifth contour a thicker/darker line.

<u>Smooth Shading</u>: Used to improve the visual quality of a toposolid on-screen when using shaded, consistent colors, textures, and realistic visual styles.

The ***Smooth Shading*** toggle is accessed from the down *arrow* next to the *Model Site* panel title.

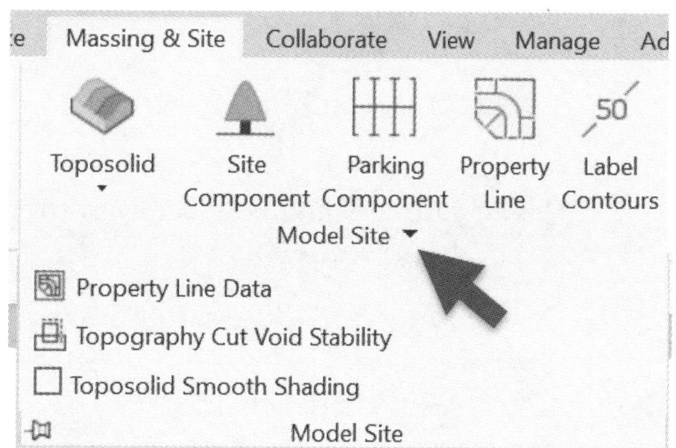

<u>Topography Cut Void Stability</u>: This command can be used if there are problems cutting a toposolid with a void element.

<u>Property Line Data</u>: This dialog controls how angles and lengths are displayed for information describing property lines.

The ***Property Line Data*** dialog is accessed from the down *arrow* next to the *Model Site* panel title.

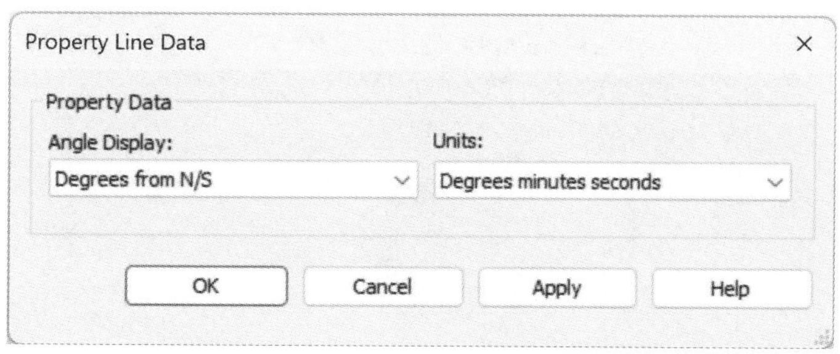

Creating Topography in Revit

1. Open your Revit project ex13-3.rvt and **Save As ex14-1.rvt**.
2. Switch to the ***Site Plan*** view via the *Project Browser.*

Here, you will basically see what appears to be a roof plan view of your project (Figure 14-1.1). This view has visibility set so you see the project from above, and the various site categories are enabled so they are automatically visible once created. Next, you will take a quick look at the *View Range* for this view so you understand how things are set up.

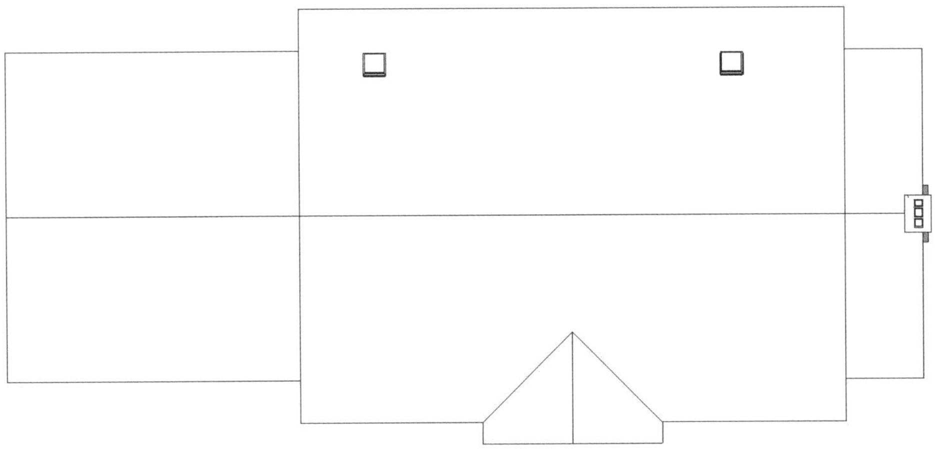

FIGURE 14-1.1 Initial Site Plan view

3. Make sure nothing is selected in the view so you have access to the view properties in the *Properties Palette.*
4. In the *Properties Palette*, scroll down if necessary, and select **Edit** next to *View Range.*

Here you can see the site is being viewed from 200′ above the first floor level, so your building or roof would have to be taller than that before it would be cut like a floor plan. The *View Depth* could be a problem here: on a steep site, the entire site will be visible if any part of it falls within the specified *View Range.* However, items completely below the *View Range* will not be visible.

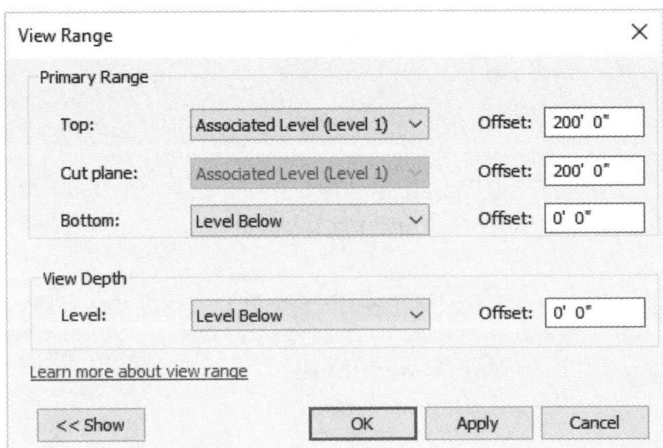

5. In the *View Depth* section, set the **Level** to **B.O. Footing**.

This change will ensure everything shows up on a steeper site, as you will now be looking deeper into the model.

6. Click **OK** to close the open dialog.

When creating the topography, you will want to be able to see the exterior walls so you can pick points on those walls to define the grade at the building. At the moment, the roof obscures the view of the exterior walls. Next, you will modify the view so the roof elements are transparent and dashed, revealing the building's perimeter while still indicating where the roof overhangs are.

7. Select one of the roof objects in the *Site Plan* view.
8. Right-click and select **Override Graphics in View → By Category** (Figure 14-1.2).

FYI: As the menu name implies, the graphics will only be modified in the current view. Also, by selecting "By Category" *rather than* "By Element" *you will be modifying all roof elements, not just the selected one.*

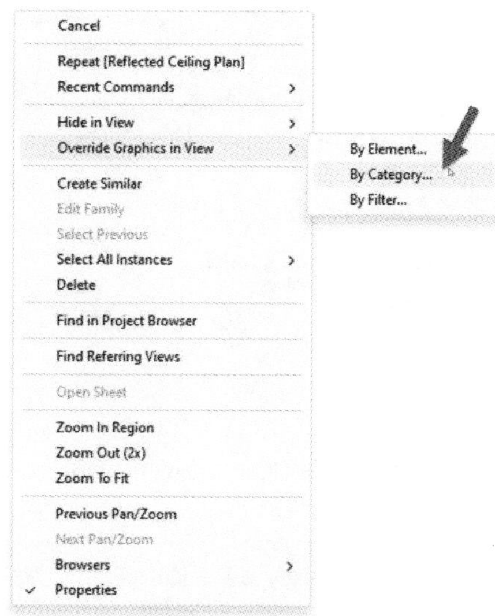

FIGURE 14-1.2 Graphics override by view

9. Click the **Open the Visibility Graphics dialog…** button and make the changes shown in Figure 14-1.3:
   a. Set the *Projection* lines for "Roofs" to **Dash 3/32"**.
   b. Set the *Transparency* to **50%**.

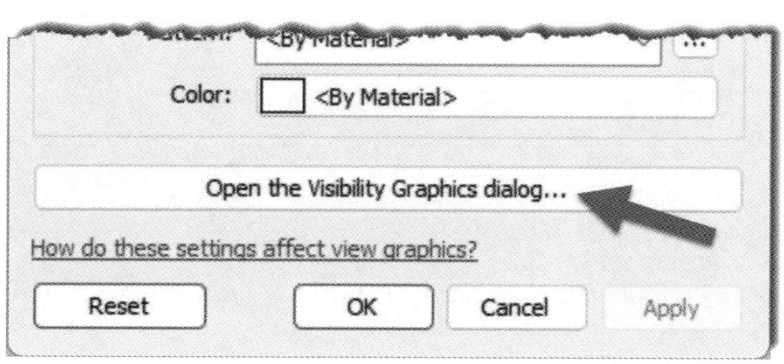

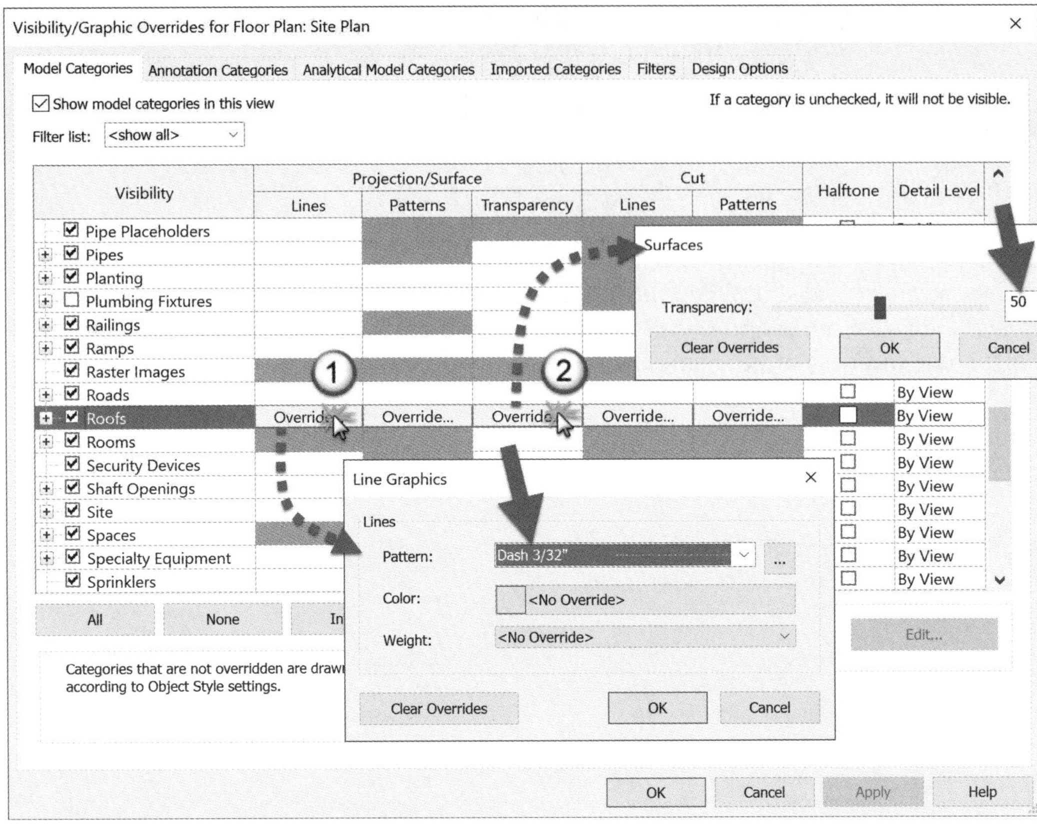

FIGURE 14-1.3 Graphics override by view

Your *Site Plan* should now look similar to Figure 14-1.4.

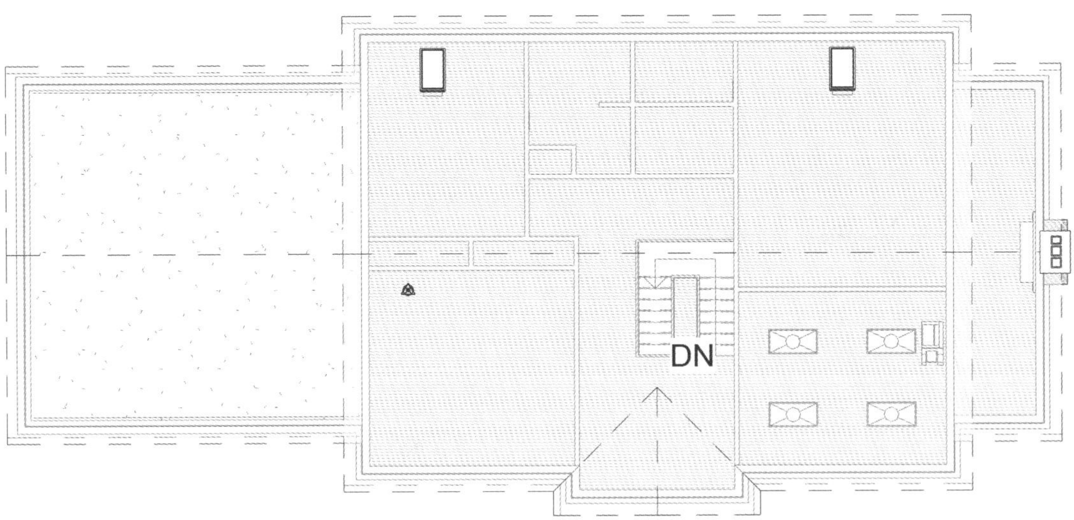

FIGURE 14-1.4 Site plan with dashed roof

Next, you will make the floating skylights hidden in the *Site Plan* view as well. In addition to controlling the graphics by view, you can also control object visibility by view via the right-click menu. You will do this next to hide the skylights.

10. Select one of the skylights and then right-click (Figure 14-1.5).

11. From the pop-up menu, select **Hide in view → Elements**.

12. Repeat the previous two steps to hide the other skylight.

TIP: The only way to see these skylights again, in this view, is to click the Reveal Hidden Elements icon at the bottom of the screen (the lightbulb icon).

The skylights are now hidden; however, the hole in the roof is still visible.

TIP: You could use the Linework tool set to <Invisible Lines> to hide the opening if needed.

You are now ready to create the site object.

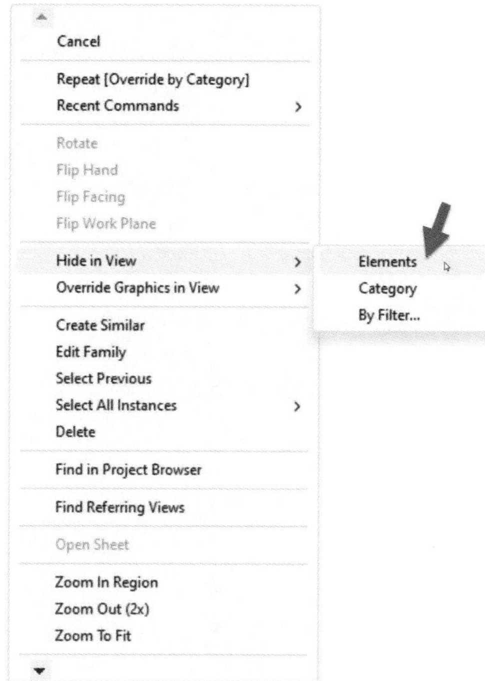

FIGURE 14-1.5
Right-click with skylight selected

13. Select **Massing & Site → Model Site → Toposolid** from the *Ribbon.*

14. Select the Rectangle option and sketch the perimeter approximately as shown in the following image; the exact size does not matter.

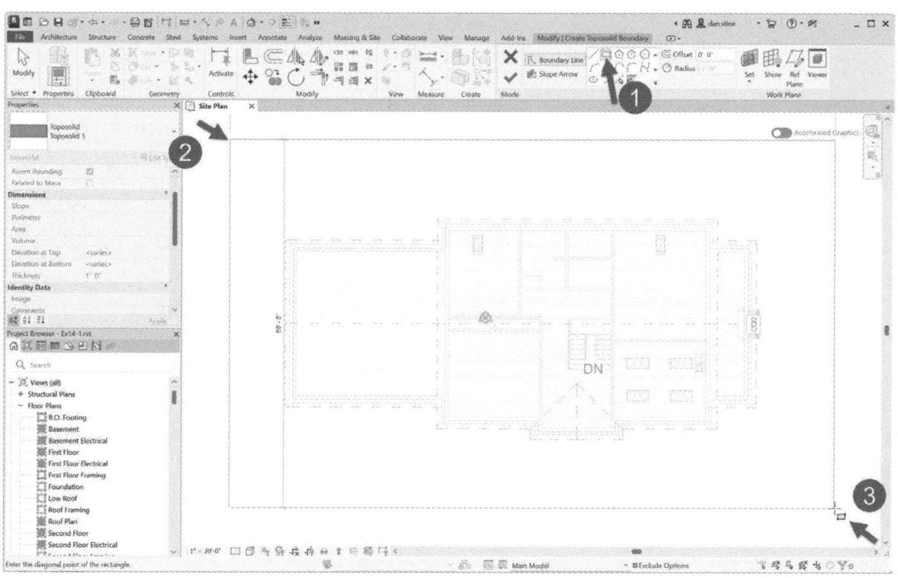

FIGURE 14-1.6 Sketching Toposolid boundary line

Next, you will finish the sketch, which will result in a perfectly flat ground plane. The sub-elements of the Toposolid are then modified, which allows points to be added at specific elevations. Each point added warps the surface, making it conform to the existing and/or proposed ground.

15. Click the **green checkmark** to finish the Toposolid sketch.

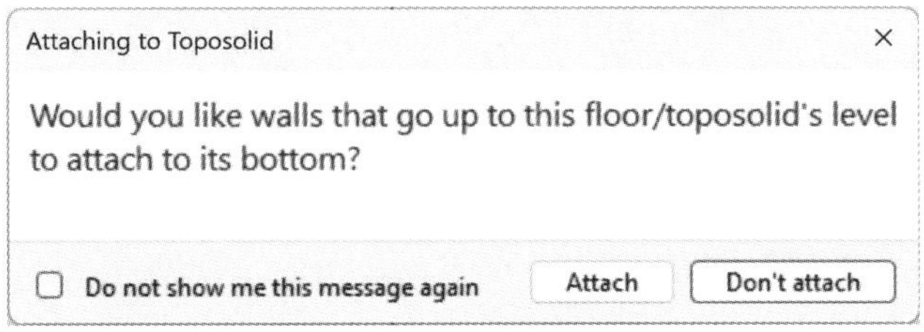

16. Click **Don't Attach** when prompted to attach walls below.

Currently, the ground plane aligns with the first floor because that is the level associated with the site plan view. In the next steps, the Toposolid will be lowered, and points will be added to define the ground at various locations around the building's perimeter.

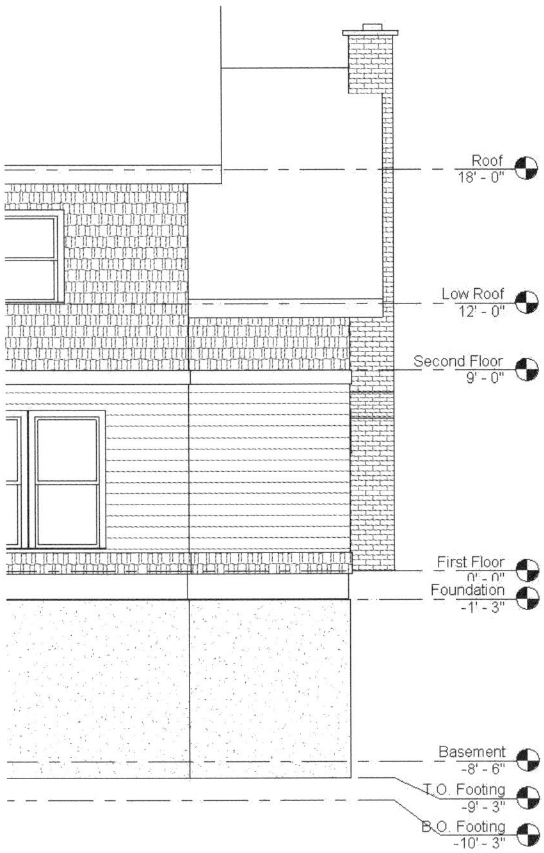

FIGURE 14-1.7 Partial South Elevation

For reference, before moving the toposolid and adding points, review the image to the left (Figure 14-1.7) and the comments below.

The elevation you enter for each point should relate to the *Level* datums set up in your project. For example, look at your *South Exterior* elevation (Figure 14-1.7). Recall that the first floor is set to 0′-0″ and the top of the foundation is set to -1′-3″ (notice the minus sign).

As you can see in the *South Elevation*, the only place you would want to add Points at an elevation of 0′-0″ would be at the garage doors. Everywhere else should be at about -1′-6″ so the grade does not rise higher than the top of the foundation wall and come into contact with any wood.

17. With the Toposolid selected, edit the Structure via Type Properties, making the following edits (Fig. 14-1.8):
    a. Material: **Earth**
    b. Thickness: **10'-0"**
    c. **OK** to overlap warning

18. With the Toposolid selected in the Site Plan view, edit the **Height Offset From Level** to **-2'-6"** in the Properties palette.

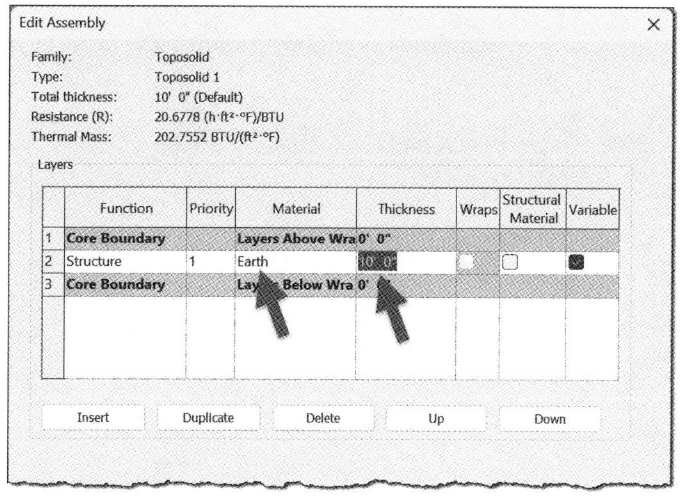

FIGURE 14-1.8 Toposolid edit assembly adjustments

19. With the Toposolid still selected, click **Add Point** (Figure 14-1.9).

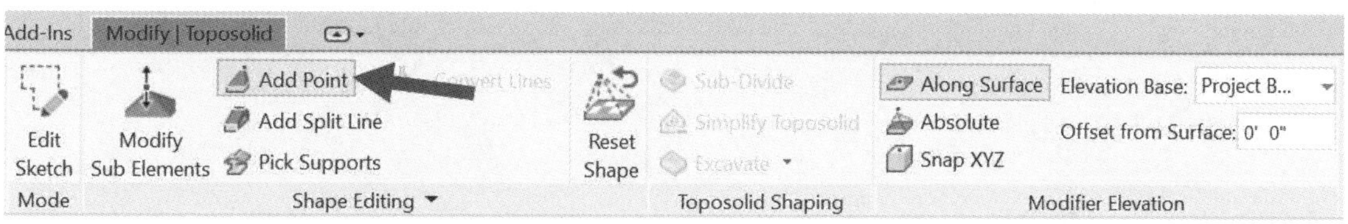

FIGURE 14-1.9 Adding points to toposolid

20. Pick the two points shown in Figure 14-1.10.

TIP: You should be able to Snap *to the edge of the garage doors even though you cannot see them. Points can also be copied.*

After placing each point, they need to be selected so the elevation can be modified.

21. While the Toposolid is still selected, and *Add Point* is active, click the **Modify Sub Elements** button on the Ribbon.

22. Click on each of the points just placed and edit the value to **0'-0"**, one at a time (Figure 14-1.11).

Tip: *If you accidentally unselect the toposolid, click it again, and click Modify Sub Elements.*

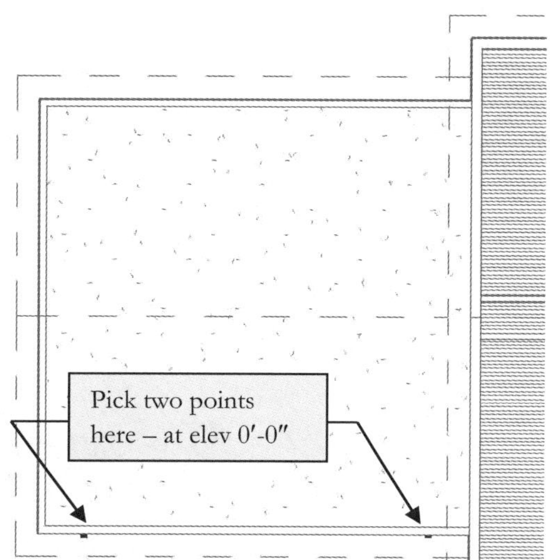

FIGURE 14-1.10 Partial site plan view

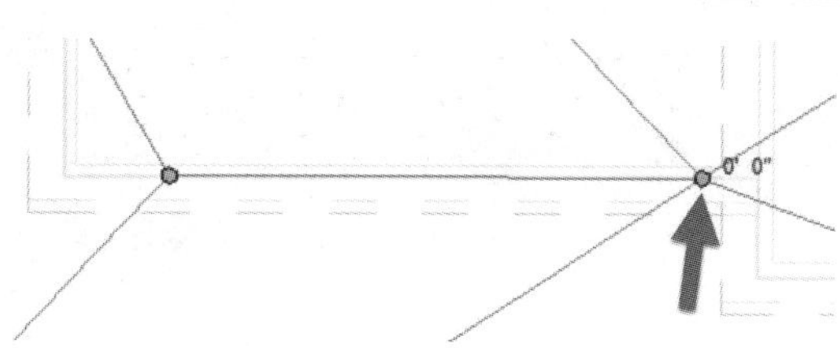

FIGURE 14-1.11 Edit point elevation

23. Add additional points with their elevation set to **-1′-6″** (do not forget the minus sign) per Figure 14-1.12.

FYI: *The elevations selected will generally provide a positive slope away from the building; this will be visible in elevations and sections.*

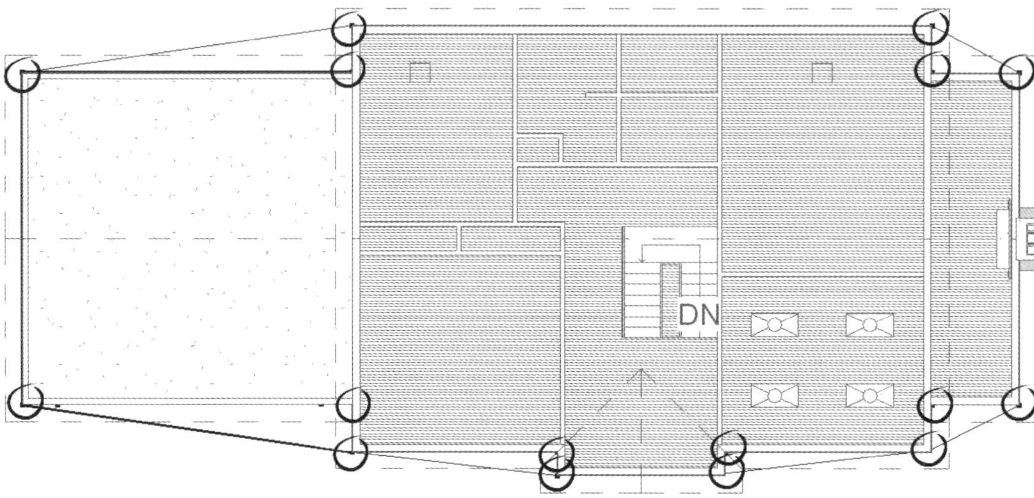

FIGURE 14-1.12 Site plan view – 16 points to be selected (elev -1′-6″)

24. Click the Modify button on the Ribbon to complete the Toposolid edits.

Revit has now modified the toposolid based on the points you specified. The more points you add, the more refined and accurate the surface will be. Ideally, you would use the *Toposolid* tool to create a surface from a surveyor's points file or contour lines drawn in an AutoCAD file; Revit can automatically generate surfaces from these sources. This process is beyond the scope of this tutorial. See Revit's *Help System* for more information.

25. Switch to the ***3D*** view to see your new ground surface (Figure 14-1.13). ***TIP:*** Type **VV** and turn on the *Roof* category if needed.

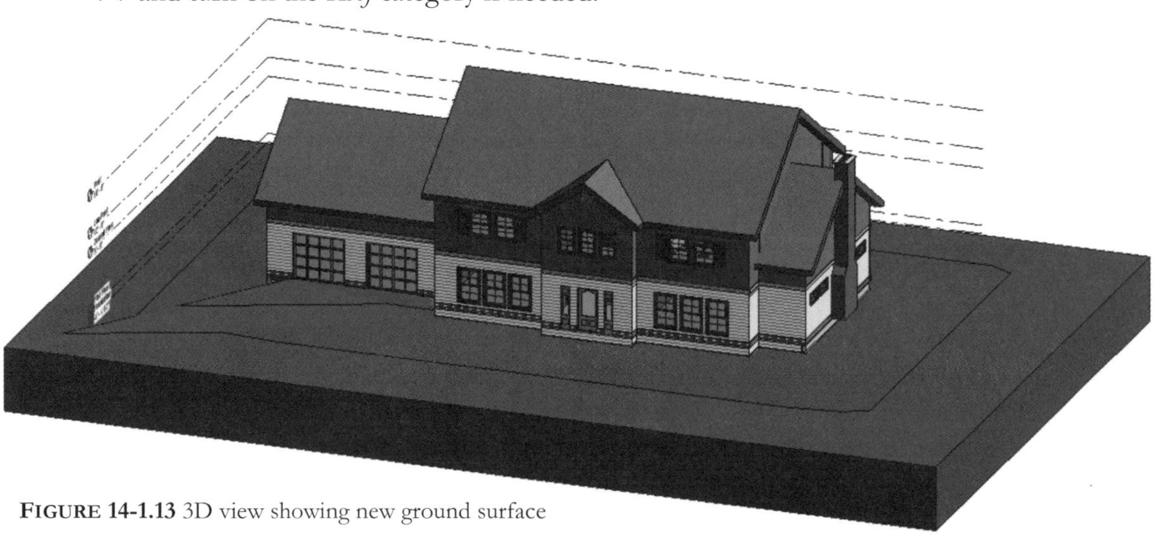

FIGURE 14-1.13 3D view showing new ground surface

Unfortunately, the toposolid object cannot distinguish between the inside and the outside of the building. So if you were to cut a section through the building, you would see the earth poche, or fill pattern, both inside and outside the building (Figure 14-1.14a).

Therefore, you will need to create an ***In-place Mass*** element that will cut an area out of the ground (Figure 14-1.14b).

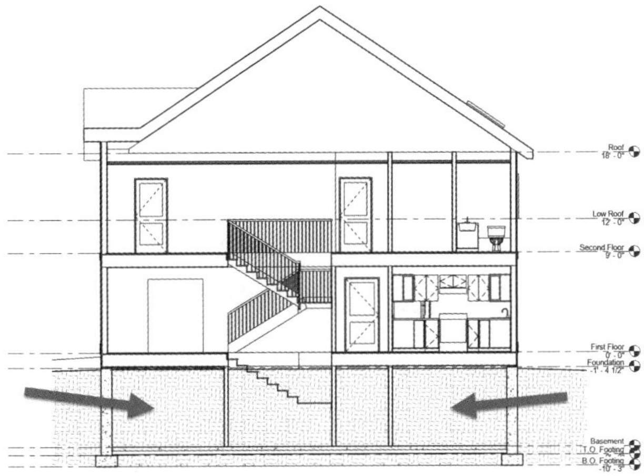

FIGURE 14-1.14A Section BEFORE in-place mass is added

FIGURE 14-1.14B Section AFTER in-place mass is added

26. Switch to the ***Basement Floor Plan*** so you can see the foundation walls which will be used to define the perimeter of the In-place Mass.

27. Select **Massing & Site → Conceptual Mass → In-Place Mass**.

28. Click **Close** to the "Show Mass Enabled" prompt.

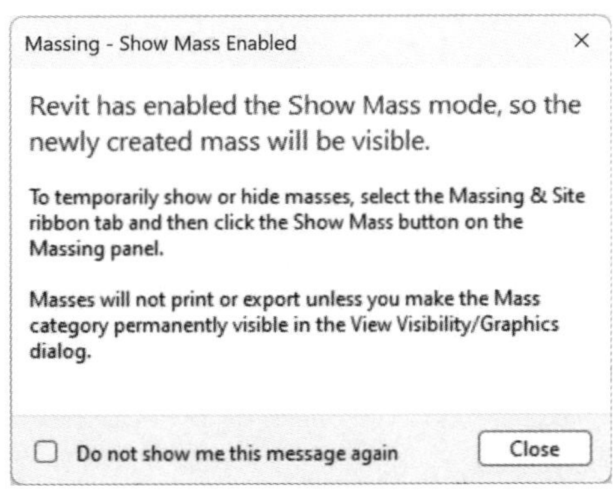

Note that the Mass category is turned off by default in all views. When using a Mass tool, the Mass category is made visible even though the category may be turned off in some views.

29. Name the In-Place Mass **Basement Void** (Figure 14-1.15).

30. Select the **Line** option on the Ribbon (Figure 14-1.16).

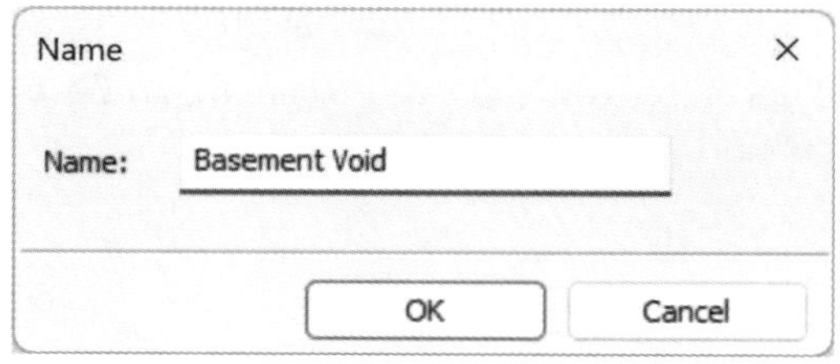

FIGURE 14-1.15 Name in-place mass

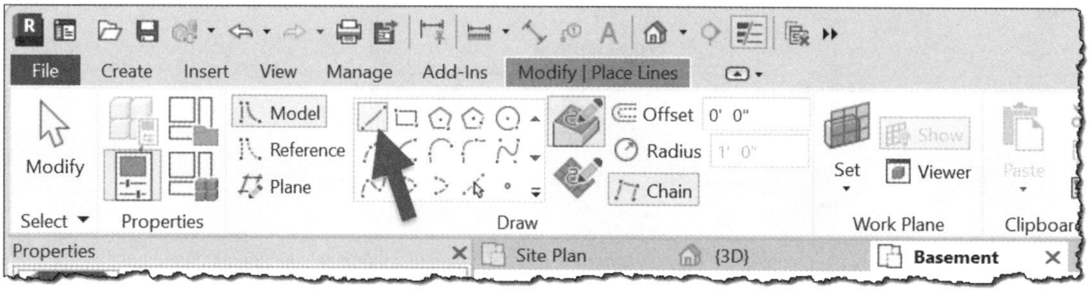

FIGURE 14-1.16 Select the line segment option

31. Snapping to the foundation wall corners, sketch lines around the exterior side of the foundation walls, except at the garage (Figure 14-1.17).

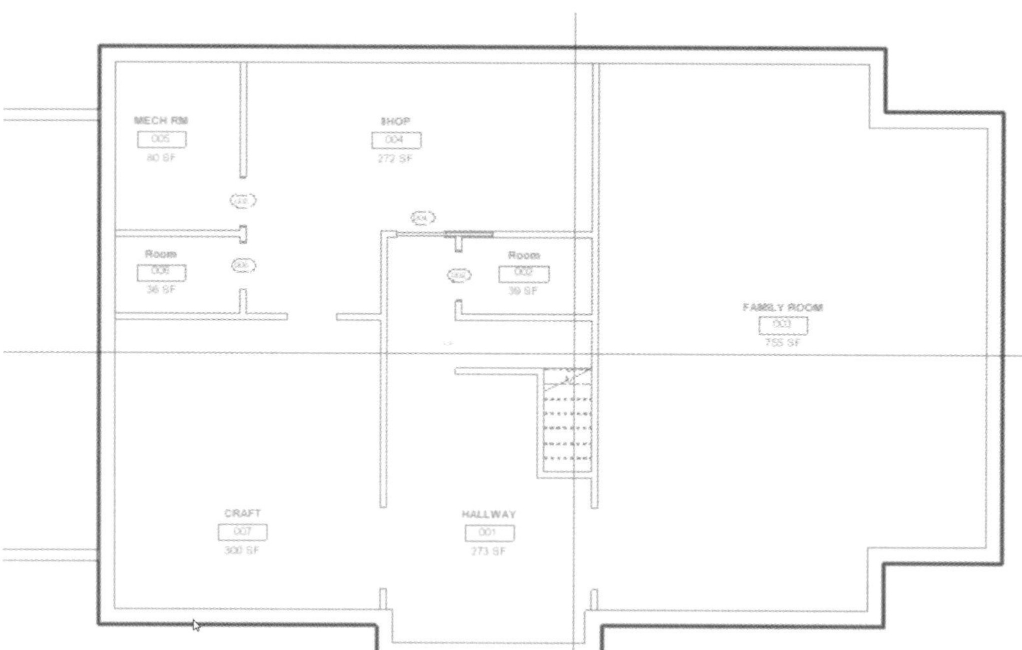

FIGURE 14-1.17 In-Place sketch lines on exterior side of basement foundation walls

32. Select the enclosed perimeter line just created – a single click should select the entire outline.

33. With the perimeter sketch selected, click **Create Form → Void Form** on the Ribbon as shown to the right.

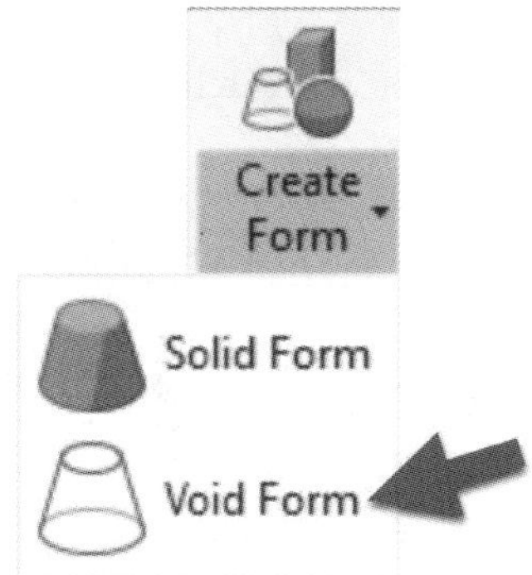

34. Switch to the south elevation view and drag the top grip down to align with the First Floor level (Figure 14-1.18).

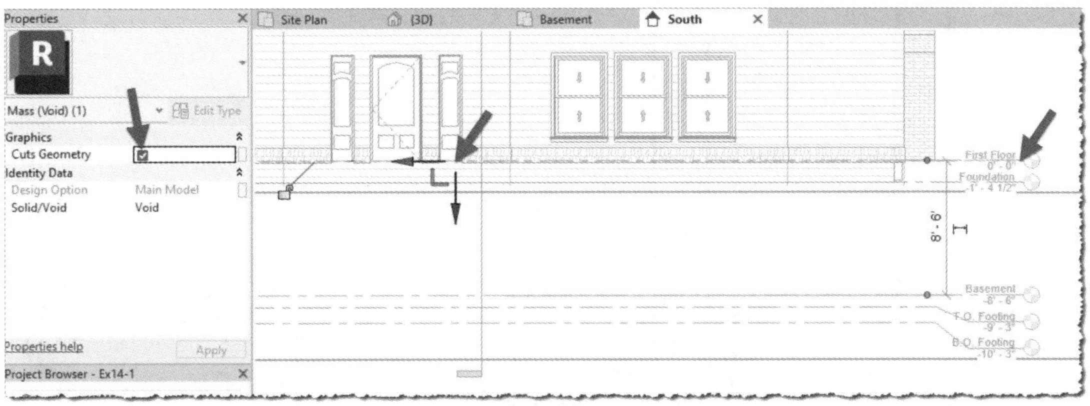

FIGURE 14-1.18 Top of mass void adjust to align with first floor level

Before the In-Place Mass can be finished, it must cut something; otherwise, an error will occur. This step can be tricky as the Mass void element can be difficult to select.

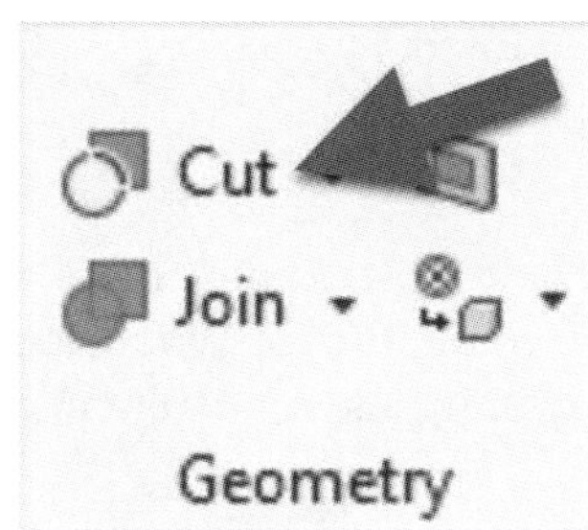

35. Switch to the default 3D View and select the **Modify → Cut** from the Ribbon.

36. Select the Mass Void and then the Toposolid.

37. Click the **green checkmark** to finish the toposolid.

The ground is now cut out of the basement, but the floors and walls overlap the ground (Figure 14-1.19a). To resolve this, the Cut command is needed at each element. This only has to be done once between the element and the toposolid and then will look correct in all views (Figure 14-1.19b).

Tip: Another option that is quicker but offers less control it to select the Toposolid and use the **Excavate** sub-command on the Ribbon… this will allow you to pick the basement floor, which will cut the toposolid, removing the earth from the basement area.

38. Switch to the Cross Section view, and select **Modify → Cut** from the Ribbon.

39. Select the toposolid and then the foundation wall. Repeat this step for each element in which the earth pattern is showing.

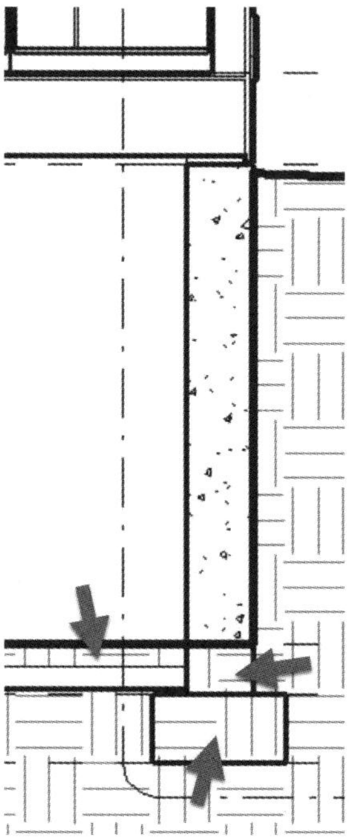

FIGURE 14-1.19A

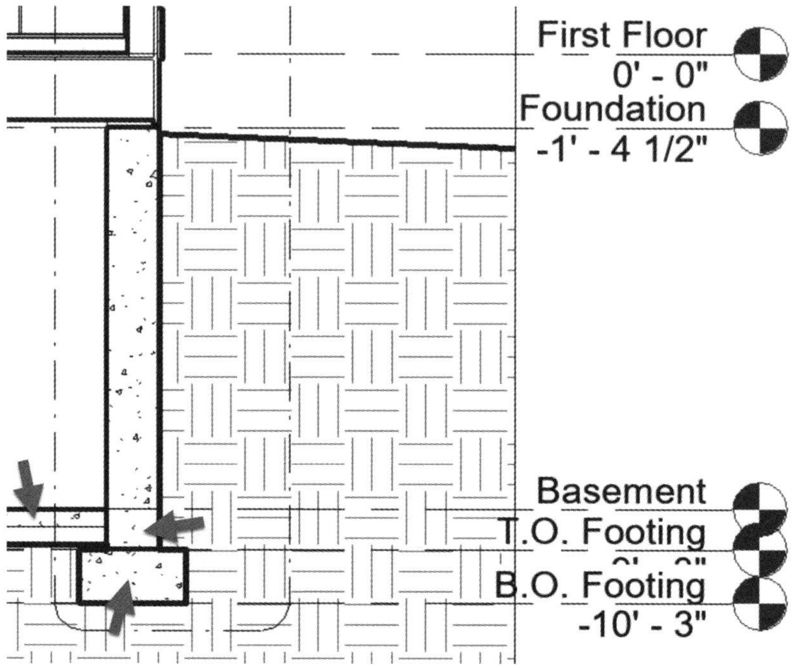

FIGURE 14-1.19B Before and after cutting geometry

The toposolid now has a cut out of the basement. The 3D view below was created by selecting the toposolid and using the Temporary Hide/Isolate tool to Isolate the selected element, the toposolid in this case.

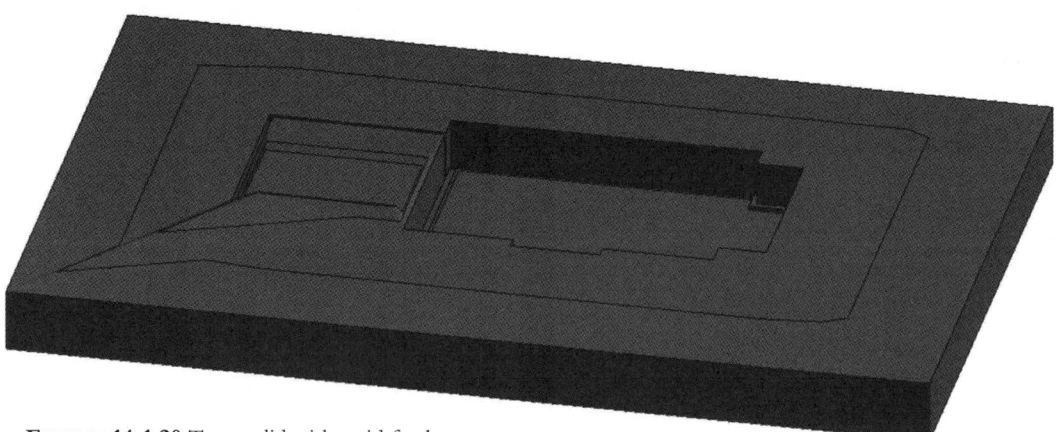

FIGURE 14-1.20 Toposolid with void for basement

If you had a basement with multiple levels, maybe a tuck-under garage at the basement level that dropped 8″ levels below the rest of the basement, you would need to create multiple in-place mass elements to cut the ground down by different amounts.

Next, you will quickly create a driveway and sidewalk to wrap up this lesson.

You can use the *Sub-Division* tool to create the driveway and sidewalks. The *Sub-Division* tool defines an area that is still part of the main site object.

40. Switch back to the ***Site Plan*** view.

41. Select the Toposolid and then click the ***Sub-Divide*** tool and sketch the lines for the driveway (see Figure 14-1.14).

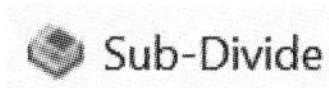

42. Click the **green check mark** on the *Ribbon* to finish the subregion.

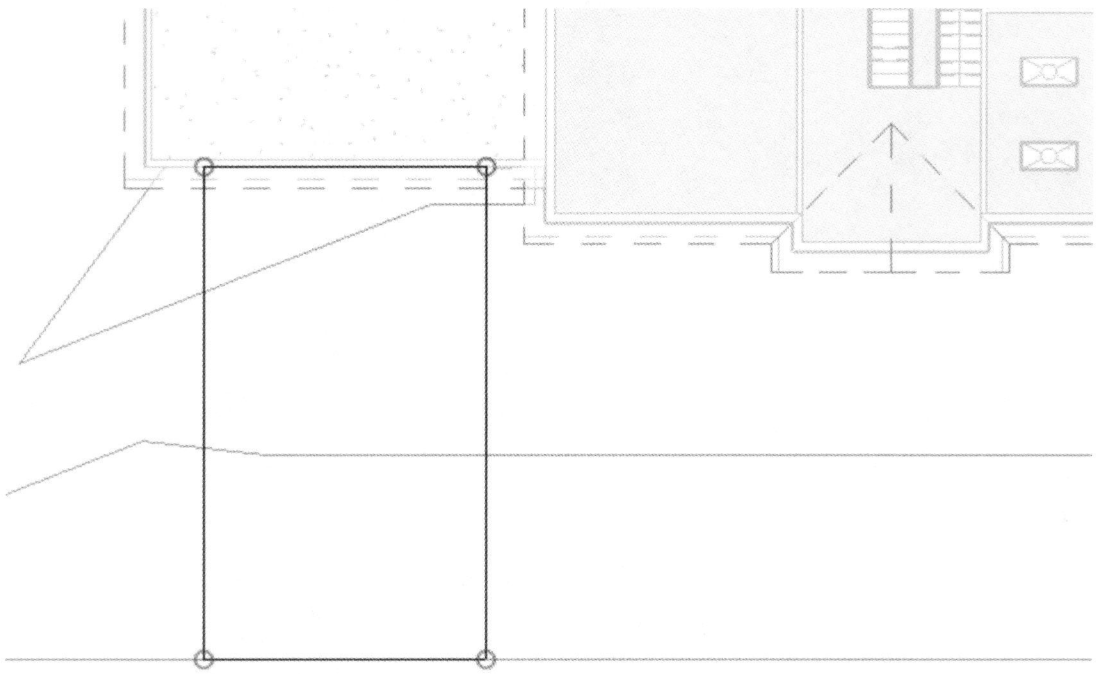

FIGURE 14-1.21 Partial site plan – closed sketch lines for sub-divsion

43. Switch to ***3D*** view to see your driveway (Figure 14-1.15). Notice the 2D lines sketched in the *Site Plan* view have been projected down onto the surface of the 3D site object!

Notice that the driveway is too thick and the material needs to be applied (Figure 14-1.22). You will learn how to change this in a moment. Also, observe that the grade slopes up at the garage doors because the two points on either side of the doors are at elevation 0′-0″.

44. Select the driveway element and adjust the *Sub-Divide Offset* to **0'-1"** in Properties (Figure 14-1.22). *Tip:* The height can also be a negative value to create a recess.

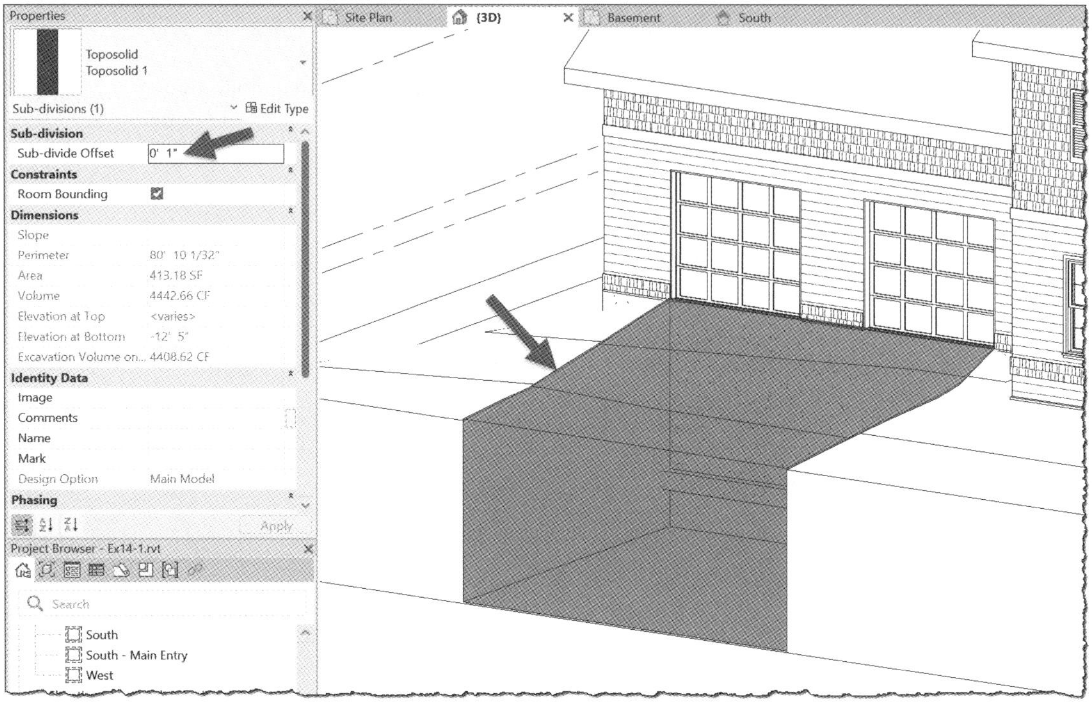

FIGURE 14-1.22 Driveway added

45. Use techniques previously covered, and add a sidewalk as shown in Figure 14-1.23 below. You can also add a stair up to the front door (Figure 14-1.26).

FIGURE 14-1.23 3D view with driveway and sidewalk added

46. In the ***Default 3D*** view, select the *driveway* sub-division.

47. Click **Edit Type** in *Properties* and **Duplicate** the type; name it "Driveway".

Layers

	Function	Priority	Material	Thickness	Wraps	Structural Material	Vari
1	**Core Boundary**		**Layers Above Wrap**	**0' 0"**			
2	Structure	1	Asphalt, Pavement, Dark Grey	0' 5"	☐	☐	☑
3	**Core Boundary**		**Layers Below Wrap**	**0' 0"**			

Insert Duplicate Delete Up Down

FIGURE 14-1.24 New Toposolid for driveway

Load materials as needed from the Autodesk library within the *Material Browser.* (Tip: search for them.)

48. **Edit** the *Structure* as shown in Fig. 14-1.24.

49. Make a new Toposolid named "Sidewalk" with material **Concrete, Cast-in-Place, Gray**, and apply it to the sidewalk.

Layers

	Function	Priority	Material	Thickness	Wraps	Structural Material	Variable
1	**Core Boundary**		**Layers Above Wra**	**0' 0"**			
2	Structure	1	Grass	0' 0 1/2"	☐	☐	☐
3	Structure	1	Earth	10' 0"	☐	☐	☑
4	**Core Boundary**		**Layers Below Wra**	**0' 0"**			

Insert Duplicate Delete Up Down

FIGURE 14-1.25 New Toposolid for driveway

50. Edit **Toposolid 1** as shown in Figure 14-1.25. Edit the Grass material so *Use Render Appearance* is checked on the *Graphics* tab, within the *Material Browse.*

51. Make sure the *Visual Style* for your ***3D*** view is set to **Shaded, Consistent Colors, or Realistic** so you can see a presentation version of the materials.

TIP: Set via the View Control Bar at the bottom of the Drawing Window.

That concludes this overview of the site tools provided within Revit.

FIGURE 14-1.26 Stair, railing and model text added

Exercise 14-2:
Creating an Exterior Rendering

The first thing you will do is set up a view. You will use the *Camera* tool to do this. This becomes a saved view that can be opened at any time from the *Project Browser.* Several cameras can be added to a project.

Creating a Camera View:

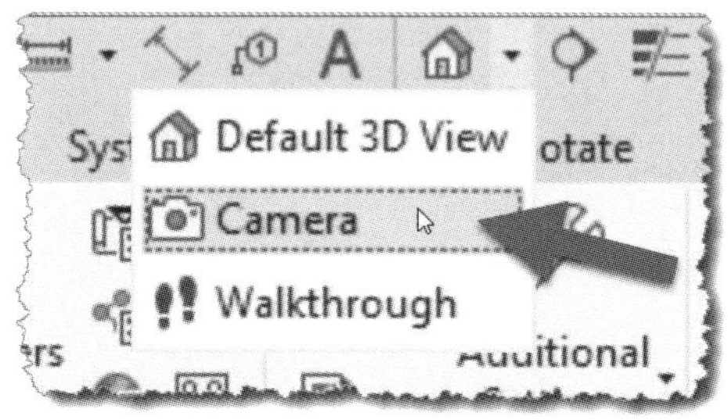

1. Open the **First Floor** plan view and **Zoom to Fit** so that you can see the entire plan (or type ZF).

2. On the *QAT*, select the down-arrow next to the 3D view and then select **Camera.** See the image to the right.

3. Click the mouse in the lower right corner of the screen to indicate the camera eye location (Figure 14-2.1).

   NOTE: *Before you click, Revit tells you on the Status Bar it first wants the eye location, and you can set the eye level on the Ribbon.*

4. Next, click near the entry door (Figure 14-2.1).

Revit will automatically open a view window for the new camera. Take a minute to look at the view and make a mental note of what you see and do not see in the view (Figure 14-2.2).

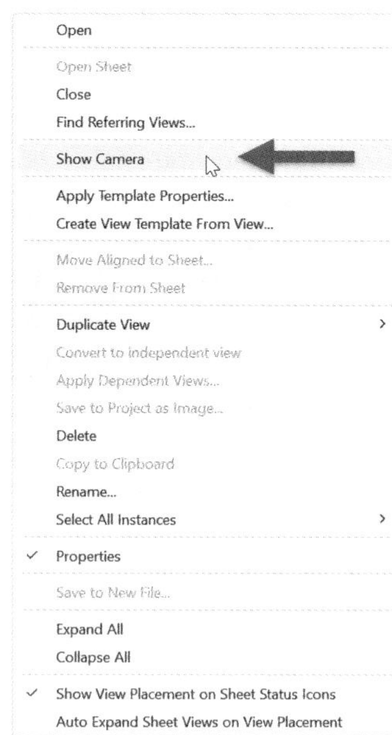

5. Switch back to the **First Floor** plan view.

6. Adjust the camera, using its grips, to look similar to Figure 14-2.3.

   TIP: *If the camera is not visible in plan view, right-click on the 3D view name in the Project Browser (3D View 1) and select Show Camera (see image to the right); do all this while still in the first floor plan view.*

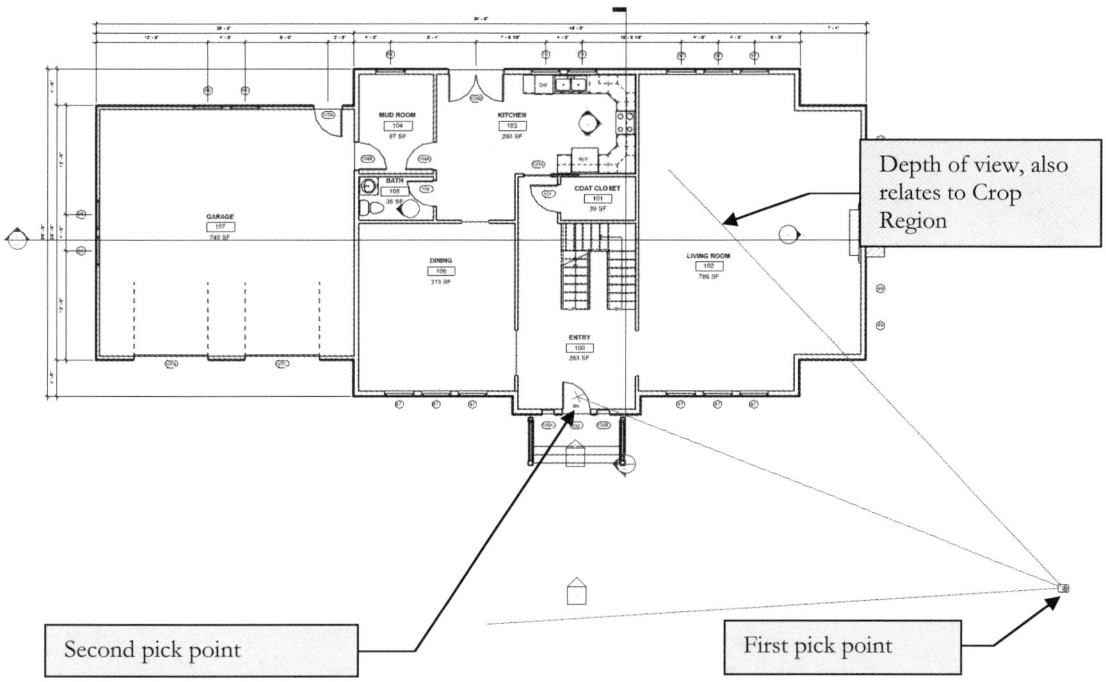

FIGURE 14-2.1 Placing a Camera in plan view

FIGURE 14-2.2 Initial Camera view

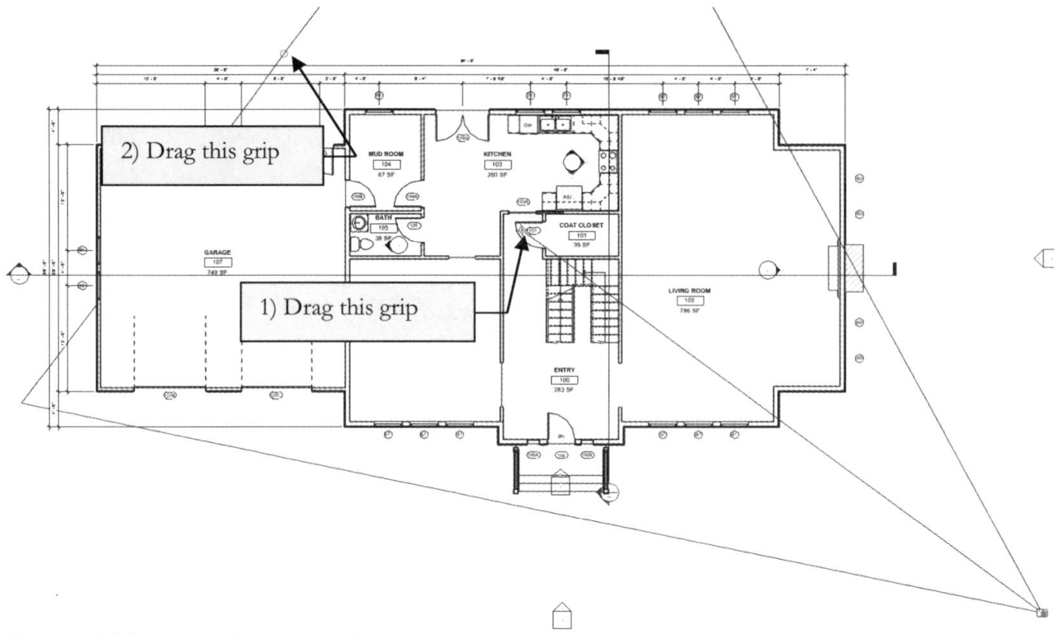

FIGURE 14-2.3 Revised camera – plan

7. Now switch to **3D View 1** and adjust the **Crop Region** to look similar to **Figure 14-2.4**.

   FYI: You may need to adjust the Camera location back in the plan view as well.

This will be the view you render later in this exercise.

FIGURE 14-2.4 Revised camera – 3d View 1

Assigning Materials to Elements:

Materials use repeatable and seamless images to represent the materials your building will be constructed with.

Typically, materials are added during modeling. For example, when you create a material using the *Materials* command on the *Manage tab*, you can assign it to elements in the model at that time. Of course, you can go back and add or change it later. Next, you will change the material assigned for the brick chimney.

8. Switch to **First Floor** plan view.

9. Select the fireplace, not the mantel.

10. Click **Edit Type** on the *Properties Palette.*

11. Click on the *Exterior Material* value; notice the material selected for the exterior finish is **Masonry – Brick** (Figure 14-2.5).

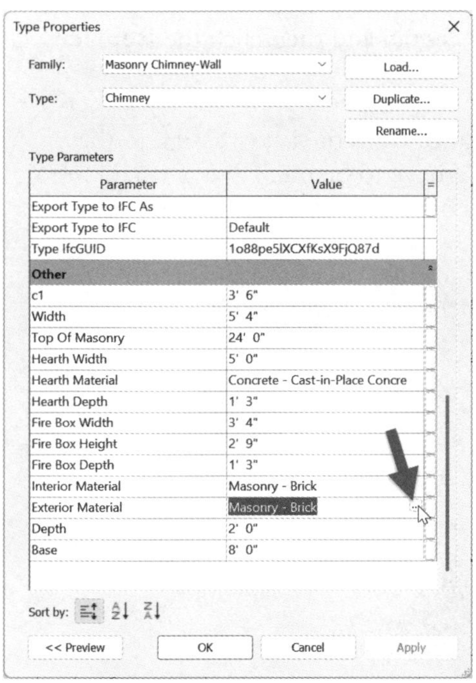

FIGURE 14-2.5 Chimney properties

12. Click the icon to the right of the label **Masonry – Brick**.

Now you will take a look at the definition of the material *Masonry – Brick*.

FYI: *From the* Manage *tab you can also select* ***Materials****.*

You are now in the *Material Browser* dialog. You should notice that a material is already selected on the left. Next, you will select a different brick material.

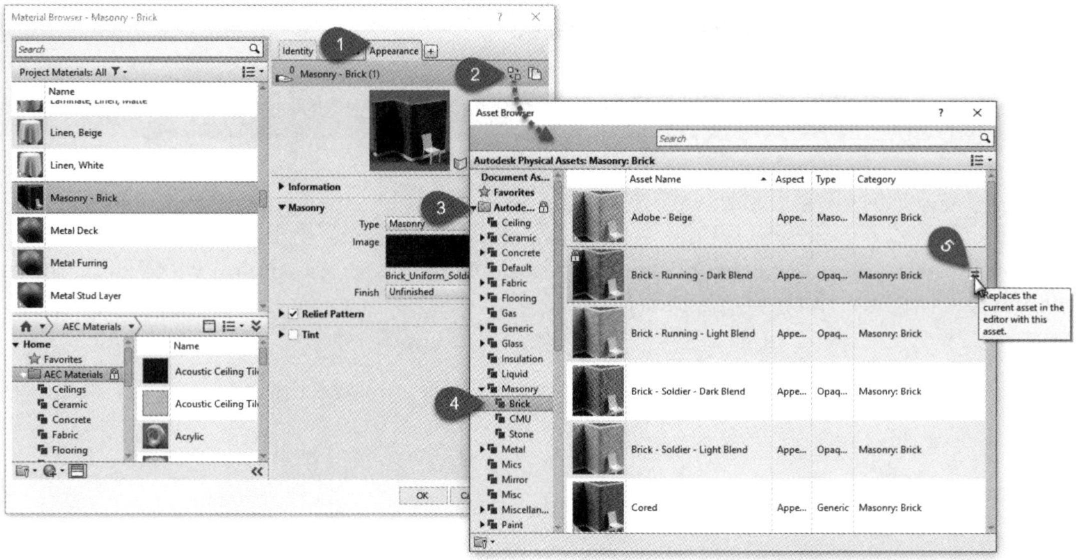

FIGURE 14-2.6 Materials Browser dialog

13. In the *Material Browser* dialog, select the *Appearance* tab and then click the **Replace this asset** link (Steps 1 and 2, Figure 14-2.6).

You can browse the thumbnails and select any appearance from the list to assign to the *Masonry – Brick* material in Revit. The material does not have to be brick, but it would be confusing if something else were assigned to the material named *Masonry – Brick*.

14. Select the *Appearance Library* category and then *Masonry\Brick* (Steps 3 and 4), locate the **Brick - Running – Dark Blend** and then click the Replace link (Step 5) (Figure 14-2.6).

Notice the material preview is now updated.

15. Click **OK** to close the *Material Browser* and *Properties* dialog boxes.

Now, when you render any object (wall, ceiling, etc.) that has the material "Masonry – Brick" associated with it, it will have the 'dark blend' brick on it.

If you need more than one brick color, you simply create/duplicate a new material in the *Material Browser* dialog and assign that material to another element.

Project Location:

A first step in setting up a rendering is to specify the location of the project on the Earth. This is important for accurate daylight studies.

16. Select **Manage → Project Location → Location**.
17. In the *Project Address* field, enter **Duluth, MN**.
    a. You may also enter your location if you wish.
    b. It is also possible to enter the project's street address.
18. Press **Enter**.

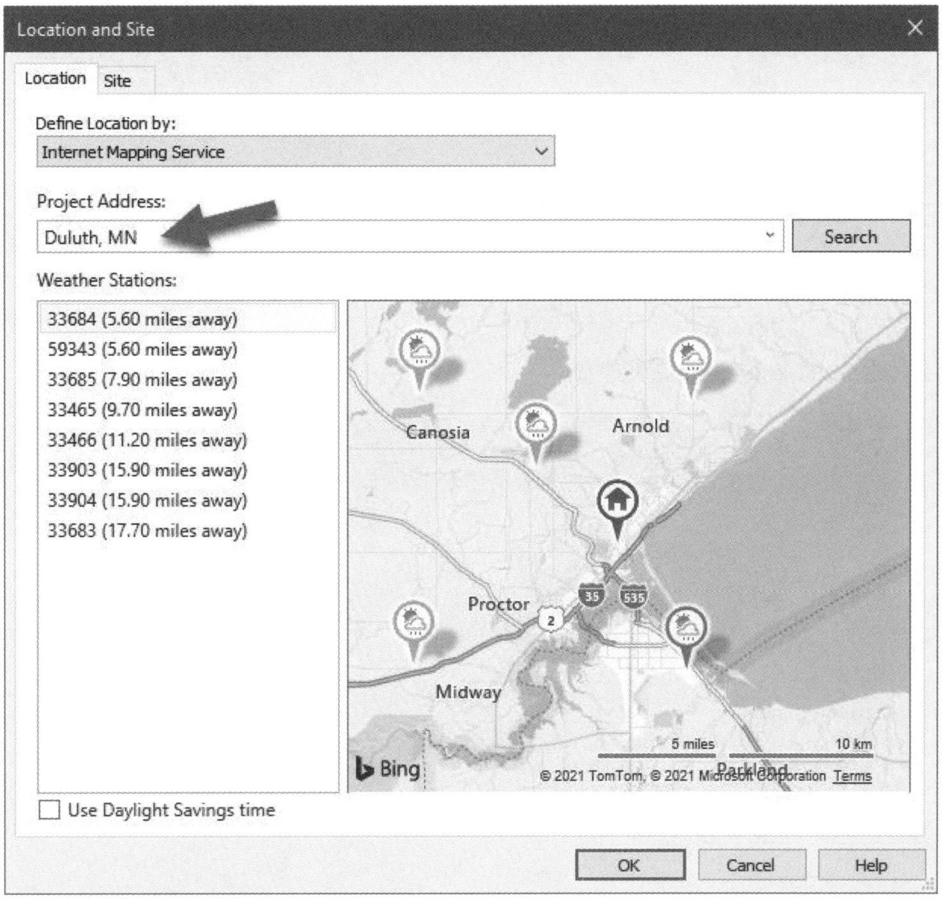

FIGURE 14-2.7 Location Weather and Site dialog

You should now see an internet-based map of your project location, complete with longitude and latitude (Figure 14-2.7).

19. Click **OK**.

Sun Settings:

Another step in preparing a rendering is to define the sun settings. You will explore the available options.

20. Select **Manage → Settings → Additional Settings** (*drop-down list icon*) → **Sun Settings**.

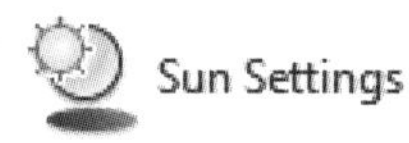

21. Make the following changes (Figure 14-2.8):
    a. Solar Study: **Still**
    b. Select **Summer Solstice** on the left.
    c. **Uncheck** *Ground Plane at Level.*
    d. Change the year to the current year.

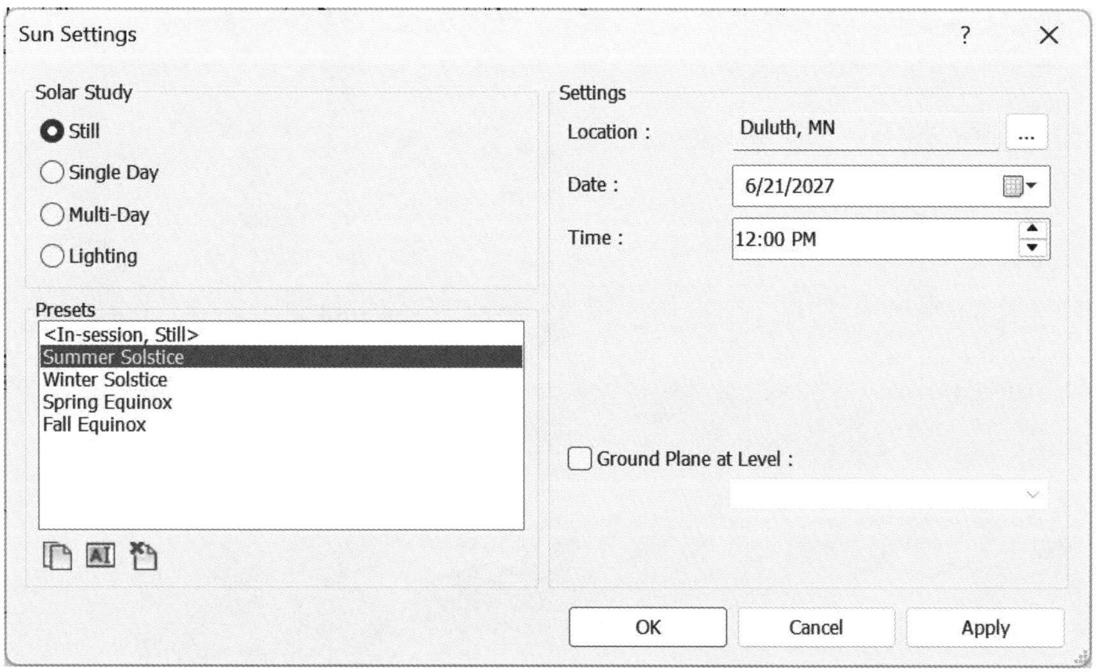

FIGURE 14-2.8 Sun Settings dialog

22. Click **OK** to close the dialog.

Setting Up the Environment:

You have limited options for setting up the building's environment. If you need more control than what is provided directly in Revit, you will need to use another program like Autodesk 3DS Max or Chaos Enscape, which is designed to work with Revit and can create extremely high-quality renderings and animations.

23. Switch to your camera view: **3D View 1**.

24. Select the **Show Rendering Dialog** icon on the *View Control Bar*; it looks like a teapot (Figure 14-2.9).

FIGURE 14-2.9 Render dialog icon

FYI: This icon is only visible when in a 3D view, which is the same with the Navigation Wheel *and* ViewCube.

The *Rendering* dialog box is now open (Figure 14-2.10). This dialog box allows you to control the environmental settings you are about to explore and actually create the rendering.

FIGURE 14-2.10 Rendering dialog

25. In the *Lighting* section, click the down-arrow next to *Scheme* to see the options; select **Exterior: Sun and Artificial** (Figure 14-2.11).

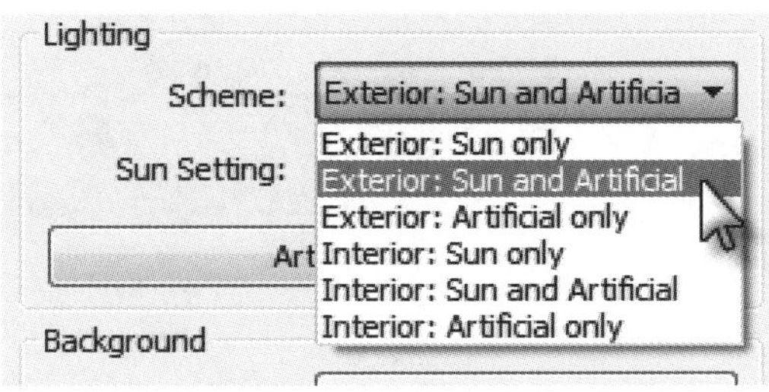

FIGURE 14-2.11 Lighting options

The lighting options are very simple choices: is the rendering an interior or exterior rendering, and is the light source *Sun*, *Artificial*, or both? You may have artificial lights, that is, light fixtures like the ones you placed in the office, but you still only desire a rendering based solely on the light provided by the sun.

26. Also in the *Lighting* section, set the *Sun* to **Still** and **Summer Solstice**.

FYI: In the Sun Settings dialog box, Revit lets you set up various "scenes" which control time of day. Two examples might be:

- *Daytime, summer*
- *Nighttime, winter*

Looking back at Figure 14-2.8, you would click *Duplicate* and provide a name. This name would then be available from the *Sun* drop-down list in the *Render* dialog box.

27. Click on the **Artificial Lighting** button.

You will now see a dialog similar to the one shown to the right (Figure 14-2.12). You will see several 2x4 light fixtures. The light fixtures relate to the fixtures you inserted in the reflected ceiling plans. It is very convenient that you can place lights in the ceiling plan and have them ready to render whenever you need to (i.e., render and cast light into the scene!). Here you can group lights together so you can control which ones are on (e.g., exterior and interior lights).

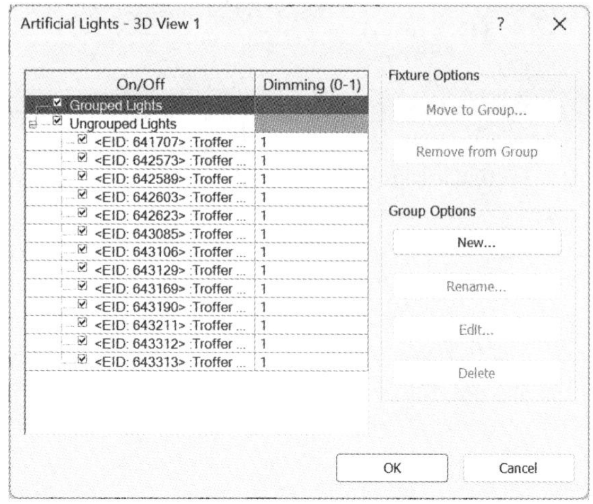

FIGURE 14-2.12 Scene Lighting dialog

28. Click **Cancel** to close the *Artificial Lighting* dialog.

29. Click the down-arrow next to *Style* in the *Background* area (Figure 14-2.13).

    a. Notice the options; click **Sky: Few Clouds** to keep that option selected.

30. Click the "**X**" to close the Rendering dialog box for now. Your settings will be saved.

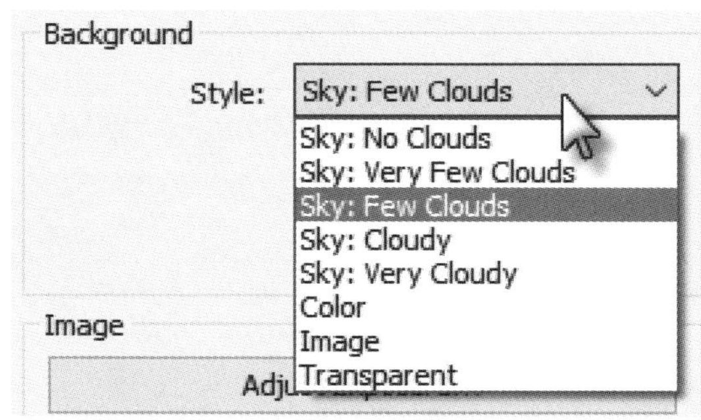

FIGURE 14-2.13 Background options

Notice that for the background, one option is Image. This allows you to specify a photograph of the site or one similar. It can prove difficult getting the perspective just right, but the end results can look as if you took a picture of the completed building.

Next, you will place a few trees into your rendering. You will adjust their exact location so they are near the edge of the framed rendering, so as not to cover too much of the building.

31. Switch to the **Site Plan** plan view and select **Component** from the *Architecture* tab.

32. Pick **RPC Tree – Red Maple - 30'** from the *Type Selector* on the *Properties Palette.*

FYI: If the tree is not listed in the Type Selector, click Load Autodesk Family and load the RPC Tree - Deciduous *tree family from the* Plantings *folder.*

33. Place four trees as shown in **Figure 14-2.14**; you will make one smaller in a moment.

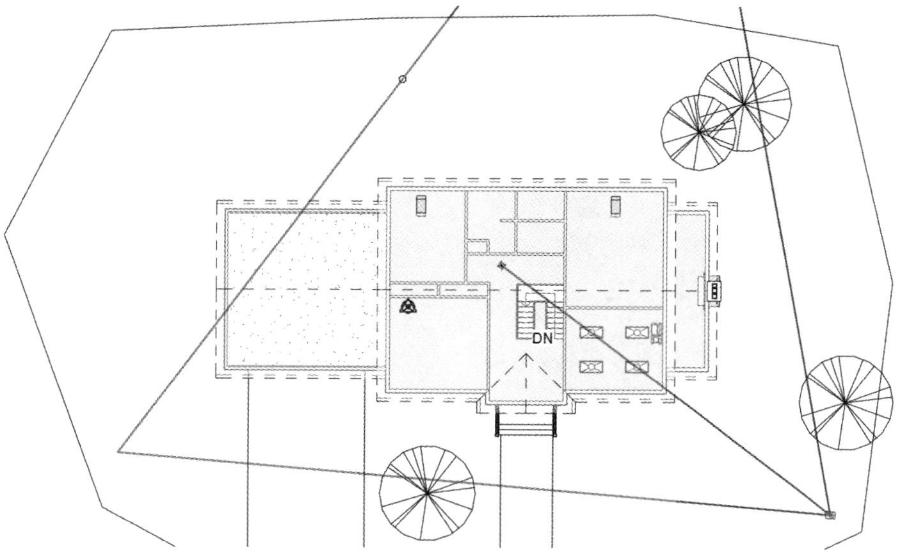

FIGURE 14-2.14 Site plan with trees added

34. Adjust the trees in plan view, reviewing the effects in the *3D View 1* view, so your 3D view is similar to Figure 14-2.15.

    TIP: Adjust the crop region if required.

35. In the **First Floor** plan view, select the tree that is shown smaller in **Figure 14-24.**

36. Click **Edit Type** on the *Properties Palette.*

37. Click **Duplicate** and enter the name **Red Maple - 24'**.

38. Change the *Height* to **24'** (it is currently 30'), and then click **OK** to close the open dialog boxes. See image to the right.

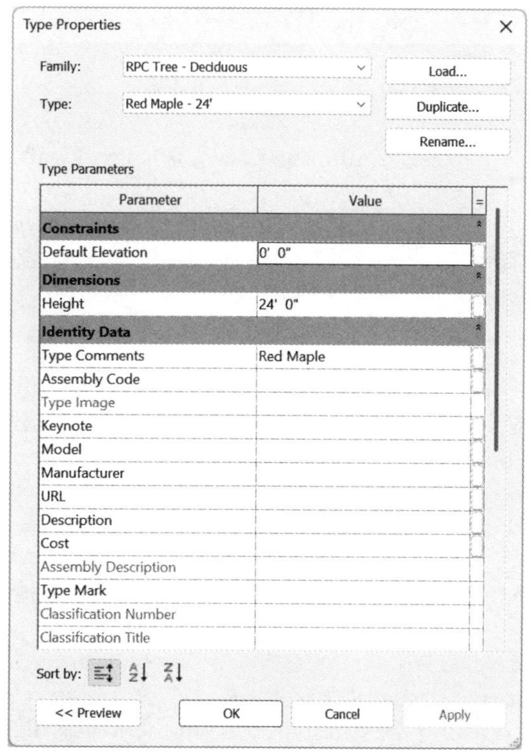

The previous three steps allow you to have a little more variety in the trees being placed. Otherwise they would all be the same height, which is not very natural.

FIGURE 14-2.15 3D View 1 – with trees

39. Open the **3D View 1** camera view.

40. Open the *Rendering* dialog.

41. Make sure the *Quality* is set to **Draft**.

FYI: The time to process the rendering increases significantly as the quality level and resolution are raised.

42. Click **Render** from the *Rendering* dialog box.

You will see the following progress bar while Revit is processing the rendering (Figure 14-2.16).

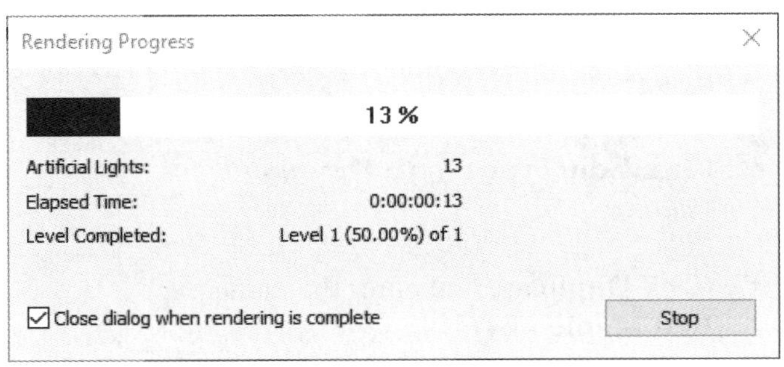

FIGURE 14-2.16 Rendering progress

After a few minutes, depending on your computer's speed, you should have a rendered image similar to Figure 14-2.17 on the next page. You can improve image quality by adjusting the quality setting in the *Render* dialog. However, these higher settings require substantially more time to render. The last step before saving the Revit project file is to save the rendered image to a file.

FYI: *Each time you make changes to the model that are visible from that view, you will have to re-render the view to get an updated image. Depending on exactly how your view was set up, you may be able to see light from one of the light fixtures in the second floor office or see the stair and railing through the window. In Revit, you can set glazing in windows to be transparent. Renderings with artificial lighting can take a lot longer to render.*

FIGURE 14-2.17 Rendered view – low resolution draft setting

43. From the *Rendering* dialog select **Export**.

    FYI: *The 'Save to Project' button saves the image within the Revit Project for placement on Sheets; this is convenient but does make the project size larger so you should delete the old ones when they are not needed anymore!*

44. Select a *location* and provide a *file name.*

45. Set the *Save As* type to **JPEG**.

46. Click **Save**.

The image file you just saved can now be inserted into MS Word or Adobe Photoshop for editing, or it can be emailed to your client. It can also be enhanced with AI, using tools like Chaos Veras, OpenAI ChatGPT, or Google Nano Banana.

Design Options can also be rendered:

You can render your design options alongside the primary options. As mentioned before, you can copy a view and change its visibility settings to show specific design options, or you can just change the settings for the current view. You will do that next.

47. In the **3D View 1** view, adjust the **View Properties** so the curved entry roof and taller entry windows are visible. Refer back to the *Design Options* section if necessary – page 10-25 (Tip: VV and adjust the Design Options tab).

48. **Render** the image, adjusting these settings:

    a. Quality: **Medium**
    b. Output Settings: **Printer @ 300dpi**
    c. Lighting: **Exterior: Sun only**

49. **Save** your project as **ex14-2.rvt**.

Notice the large tree casting shadows on the ground and its reflections in the windows when the angle and lighting are right. Remember, the angle and location of the shadows depend on the time, date, and location on Earth; if you change those settings, the shadows will change accordingly. You also need to set true North for the given site! This can be done via **Manage → Project Location → Rotate True North**.

The image to the right was generated using **Google's Nano Banana**. The lower-quality Revit rendering was provided along with a text prompt. It often takes a few attempts to get the desired results, and even then, it might be necessary to use Photoshop. But the future of rendering is AI.

FIGURE 14-2.18 Rendered view with design options adjusted

FIGURE 14-2.19 Rendering enhanced using Google Nano Banana

As you can imagine, an image like this could really "sell" your design to the client. Revit makes the process of getting to this point much easier than legacy CAD programs and techniques used prior to Revit.

Exercise 14-3:
Rendering an Isometric in Section

This exercise will introduce you to a 3D view tool called *Section Box*. This tool is not necessarily related to renderings, but combining the two features can produce dynamic results.

Setting up the 3D View:

1. Open file ex14-2.rvt and **Save As ex14-3.rvt**.

2. Switch to the **Default 3D** view via the icon on the *QAT (not the 3D View 1 from Exercise 14-2)*.

3. Make sure nothing is selected so the *Properties Palette* shows the current view's properties. If something is selected, you can still see the current view's properties by selecting **3D View: {3D}** from the drop-down list below the *Type Selector*.

4. Activate the **Section Box** parameter and then click **Apply**.

You should see a box appear around your building, similar to Figure 14-3.1. When selected, you can adjust the size of the box with its grips. Anything outside the box is not visible. This is a great way to study a particular area of your building while in an isometric view. You will experiment with this feature next.

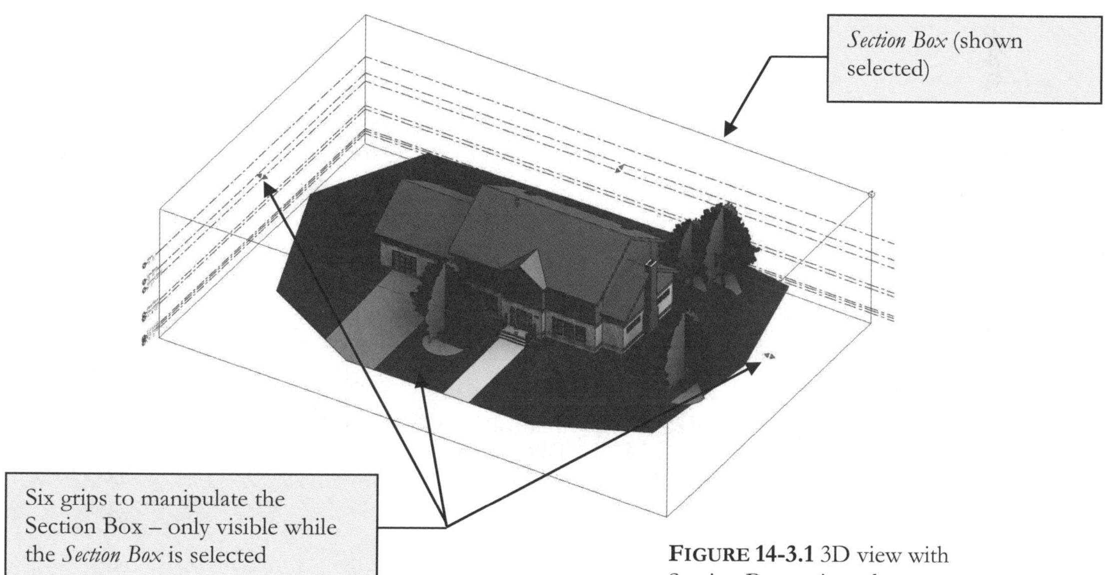

FIGURE 14-3.1 3D view with Section Box activated

5. To practice using the **Section Box**, drag the grips around until your view resembles Figure 14-3.2.

TIP: This may require the ViewCube tool as well, or hold Shift + drag the Wheel button on the mouse.

   a. Click and drag the grip from the top downward.

   b. Click and drag the grip for the East (right) face toward the West (left).

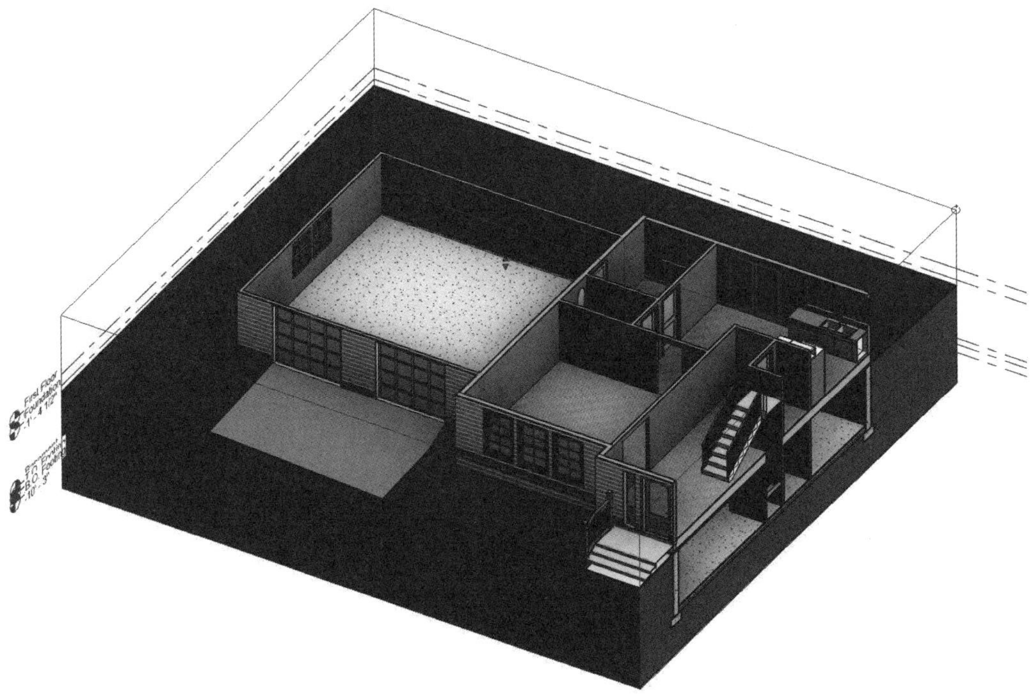

FIGURE 14-3.2 3D view with adjusted Section Box

Did you notice the grips look different? One grip looks like two arrows rather than a small square. You can still click on any part of the grip and drag it, but you can also single-click on one of the arrows to slightly adjust the section box in the direction the arrow points. This is similar to the nudge feature, when an element is selected, and you use the arrow keys to move it just a little bit.

This creates a very interesting view of the First Floor plan. What client would have trouble understanding this illustration?

6. Now readjust the **Section Box** to look similar to **Figure 14-3.3**.

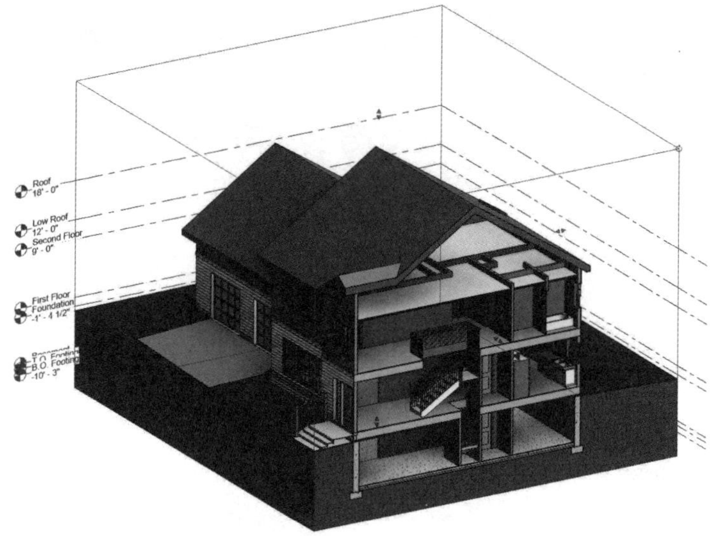

FIGURE 14-3.3 3D view

7. On the View Control bar, select the Sun icon and then pick **Sun Settings** and change the following *Sun* settings (Figure 14-3.4): ***TIP:*** *Set* Solar Study *to* Still *first and then click any* ***named*** *preset.*

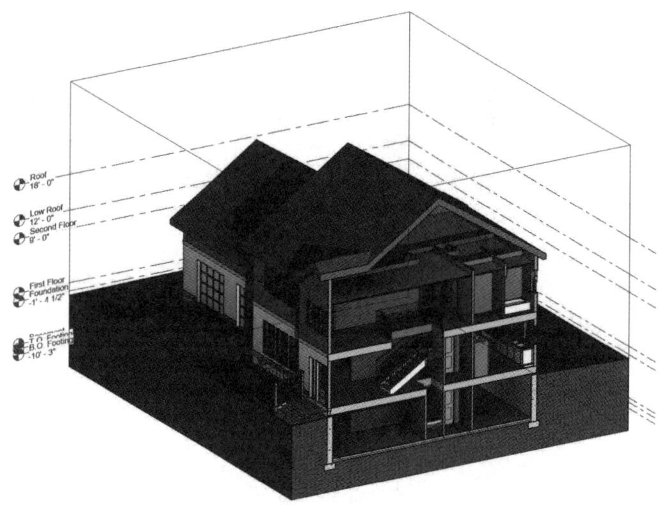

   a. New name: **28 February 8am** (via Duplicate)
   b. Month: **2** (February)
   c. Day: **28**
   d. Time: **8:00am**

FYI: *Do not forget, without doing any rendering in Revit, you can turn on the shadows in any view. You can even turn on shadows in your 2D exterior elevation view (see below) for a great effect with little effort!*

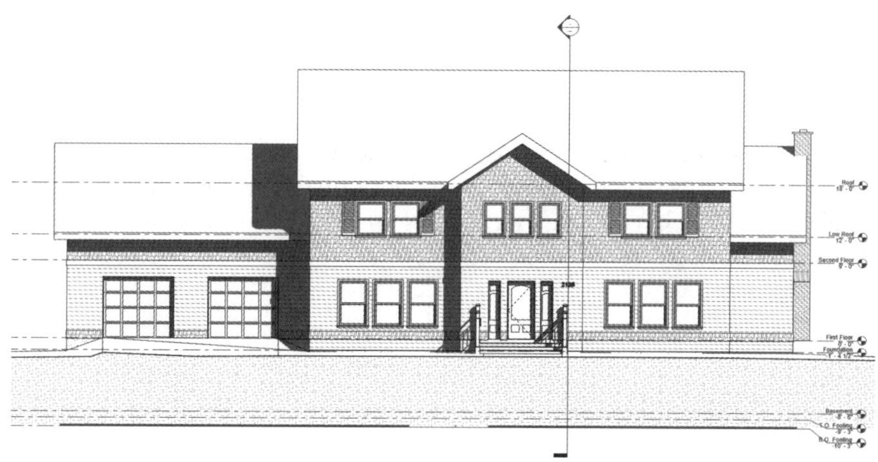

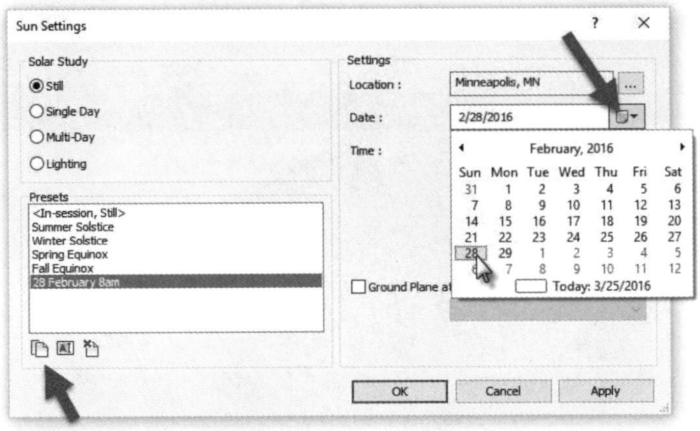

FIGURE 14-3.4 Modified Sun Settings

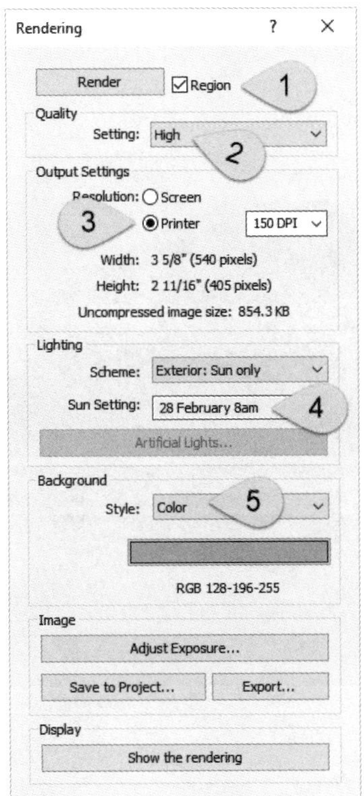

8. Select the **Render** icon, select the *Scheme*: **Exterior: Sun only**, and then set *Sun Setting* to **28 February 8am**.

9. Set the options as shown in the image to the left, including setting the *Background Style* to **Color**.

10. Select the **Region** option and then adjust the "render region crop" that appears in the view to indicate the area to be rendered.

TIP: This tool is nice for checking a material before rendering the entire building, which takes longer.

11. Click the **Render** button.

The image will take a few minutes to render, depending on your computer's speed. When finished, it should look similar to **Figure 14-3.5**. The image looks much better on the screen or printed in color.

As mentioned previously, you can increase the rendering quality settings to achieve much better results, though it will take longer. Also, higher-quality images can be printed larger without pixilation. If you have time, try changing the Quality to Best and the Resolution to 300dpi. Note the difference in the time to complete.

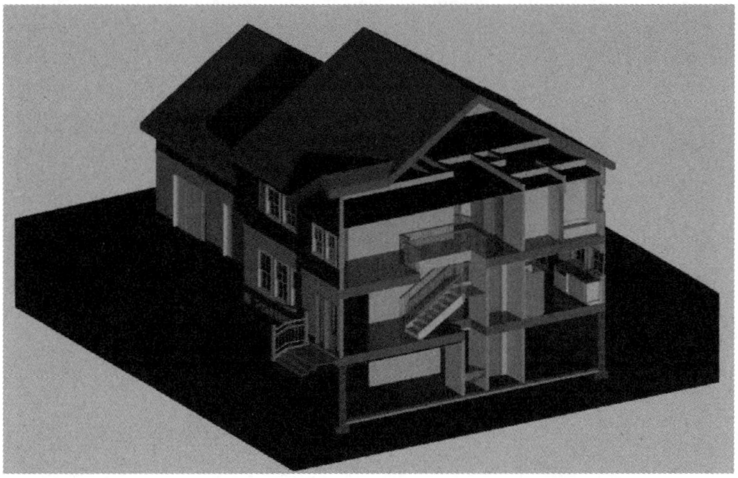

FIGURE 14-3.5 Rendered isometric view - draft settings selected

Adjusting an Element's Material:

As previously mentioned, most elements already have a material assigned to them. This is great because it lets you quickly render your project to get preliminary images. However, they usually need adjustment. You will do this next.

12. In the *Render* dialog, click the *Show Model* button at the bottom; the rendered view disappears. Close the *Render* dialog.

13. Select one of the cabinets in the kitchen.

14. Click the **Edit Type** button in the *Properties Palette.*

Notice the Cabinet Material parameter is set to **<By Category>** (Figure 14-3.6). You could change the material here for just the selected cabinet type; however, by setting a material to be *By Category* you can quickly change the material for all the cabinets at one time, without having to select every cabinet.

Sun Path

It is possible to turn on the feature called Sun Path. This shows the path of the sun over a day and a year. This is accessed from the View Control Bar while in a 3D view.

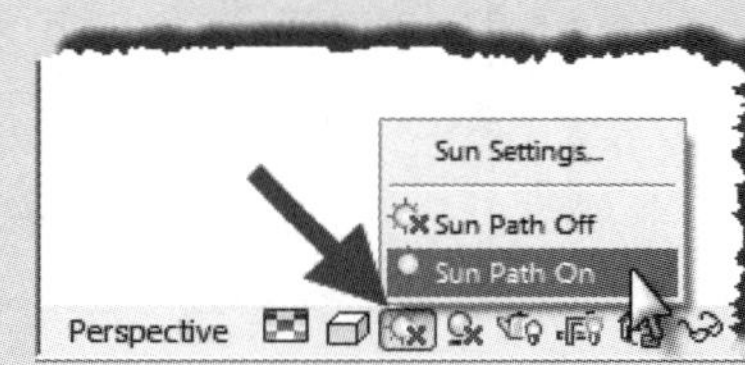

Once on, you can click and drag the sun along its daily or yearly path!

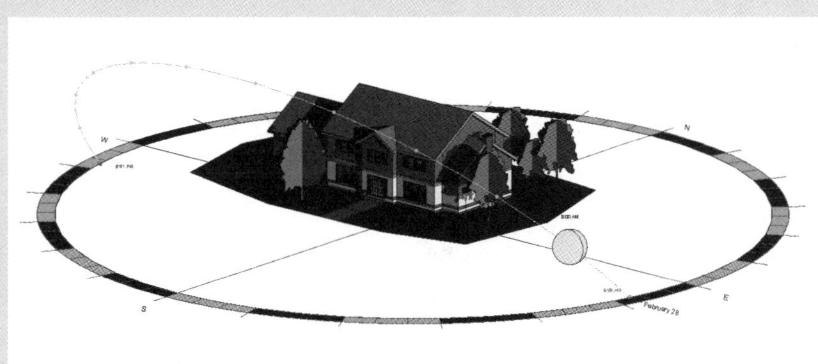

15. **Close** the *Type Properties* dialog.

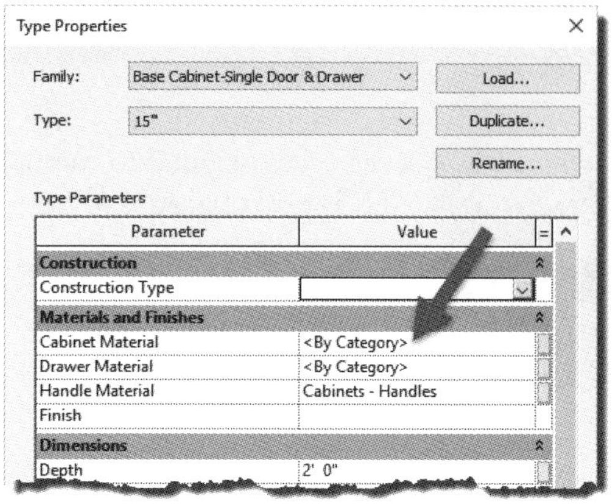

FIGURE 14-3.6 Cabinet properties

The next step will open the dialog box which controls color, line weight, line pattern and material, for both hatching and rendering representations. This is for the entire project, with the exception of any overrides added per view via VV.

16. Select **Manage → Settings → Object Styles**.

17. Expand the **Casework** category (Figure 14-3.7).

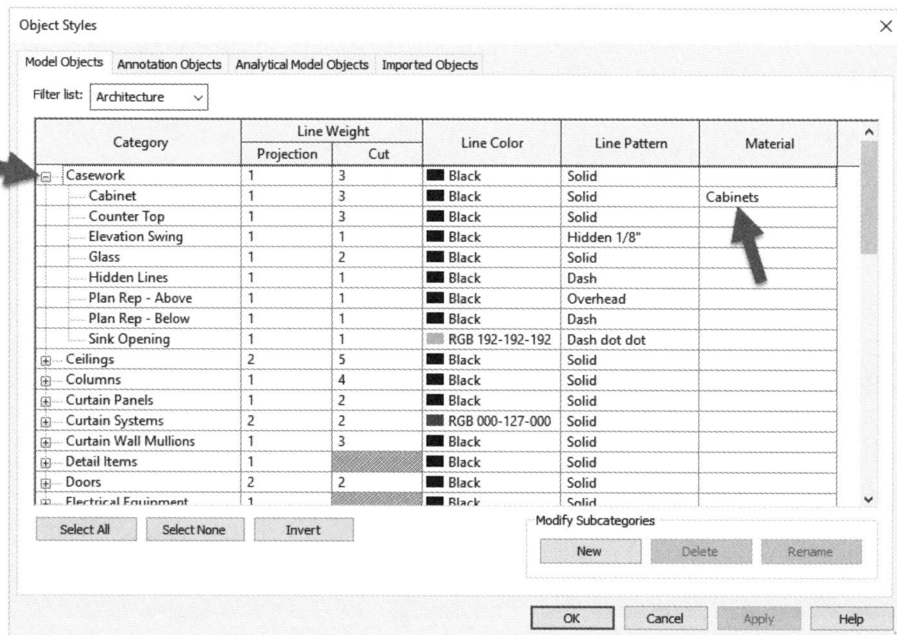

FIGURE 14-3.7 Object Styles dialog

The *Cabinet* subcategory has a material assigned to it called **Cabinets**.

18. Click on **Cabinets** in the *Material* column, and then click the "**…**" button that appears to the right.

You are now in the *Material Browser* dialog box, where you can create and edit *Materials*.

19. Open the *Asset Browser* by clicking the **Replace this asset** link on *Appearance* tab as previously covered (Figure 14-3.8).

20. Change the *Appearance* material to **Cherry - Semigloss** (Figure 14-3.8).

    TIP: Select the category label Wood *under Appearance Library first.*

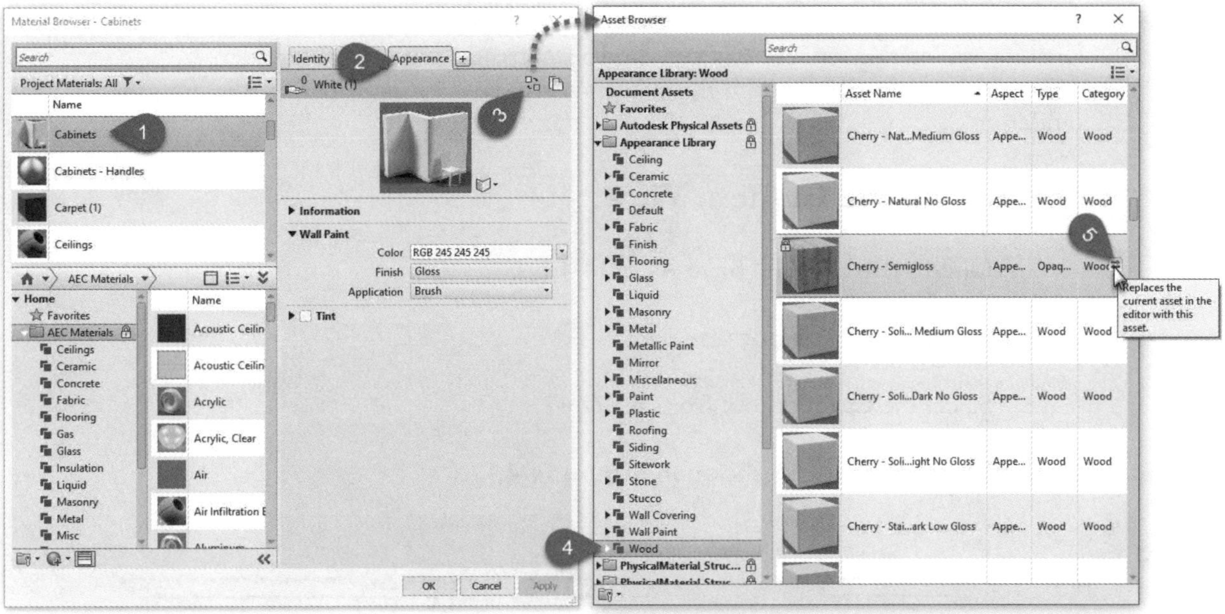

FIGURE 14-3.8 Material dialog – with *Asset Browser* open

21. Click **OK** to close the open dialog boxes.

22. You can now re-render the 3D view and see the results.

23. **Save** your project as ex **14-3.rvt**.

    TIP: While in the 3D view with the Section Box active, you can zoom in to an area, just like you can in other views, and render that enlarged area (just check the "Region" option in the Render dialog). Similarly, you can change the material for the countertop, faucet, dishwasher, etc.

Exercise 14-4:
Creating an Interior Rendering

Creating an interior rendering is very similar to creating an exterior rendering. This exercise will walk through the steps involved in creating a high-quality interior rendering.

Setting Up the Camera View:

1. Open ex14-3.rvt and **Save As ex14-4.rvt**.
2. Open the **First Floor** plan view.
3. Select the **Camera** tool from the *QAT*.
4. Place the *Camera* as shown in **Figure 14-4.1**.

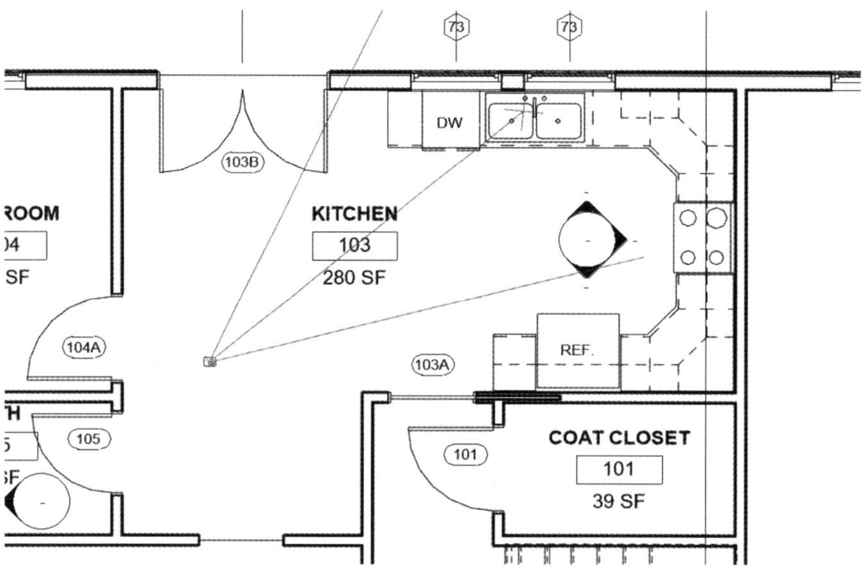

FIGURE 14-4.1 Camera placed – Kitchen

Revit uses default heights for the camera and the target (shown on the Ribbon during camera creation). These heights are based on the current level's floor elevation plus the eye height of an average-height person in the USA. These reference points can be edited via the camera properties.

Revit will automatically open the newly generated camera view. Your view should look similar to **Figure 14-4.2**.

FIGURE 14-4.2 Initial interior camera view

5. Using the **Crop Region** rectangle, modify the view to look like **Figure 14-4.3**; select it and then drag the grips.

6. Uncheck **Far Clip Active** in the *Properties Palette*. Copy the two trees in the back of the house into a position so they can be seen through the window over the sink.

   TIP: *You will have to switch to plan view to adjust the camera's depth of view to see the trees.* REMINDER*: If the camera does not show in plan view, right-click on the camera view label in the Project Browser, while in plan view, and select* Show Camera. *You may need to switch between the plan and camera views several times to adjust the trees so they are visible through the windows.*

7. Switch back to **First Floor** plan to see the revised *Camera* view positions.

Notice the field of view triangle is wider based on the changes to the **Crop Region** in the camera view (Figure 14-4.4).

FIGURE 14-4.3 Modified interior camera

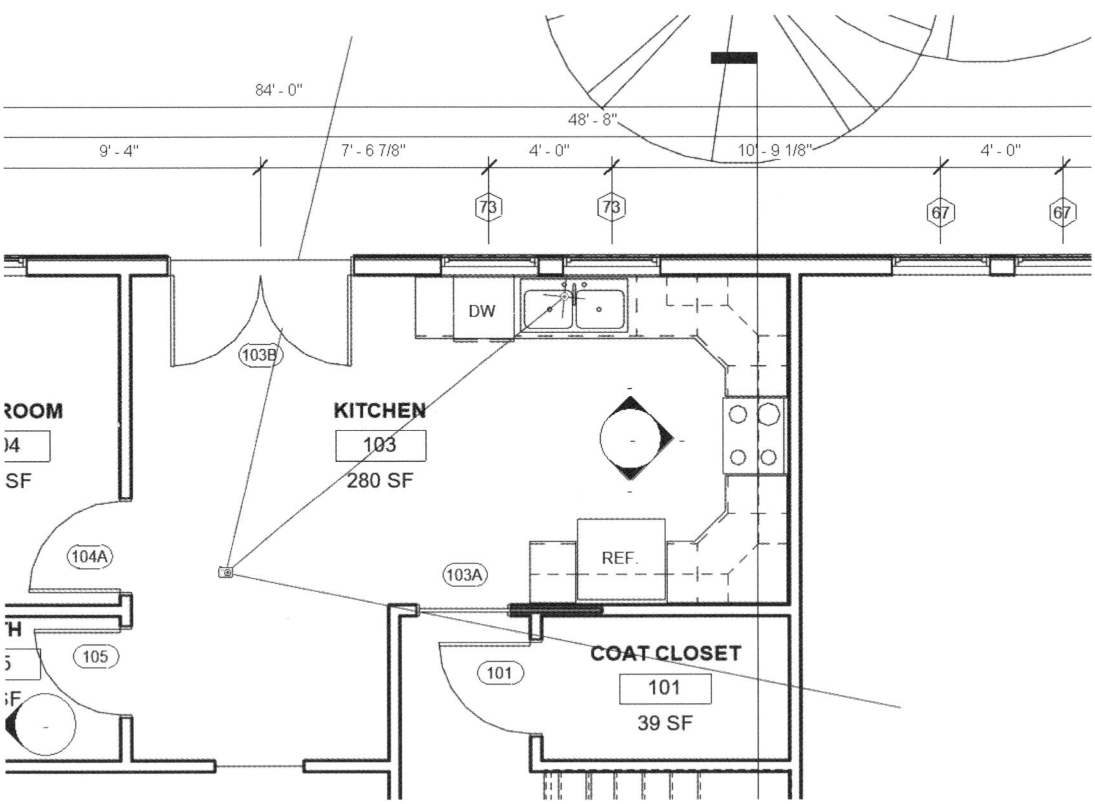

FIGURE 14-4.4 Modified camera – First Floor

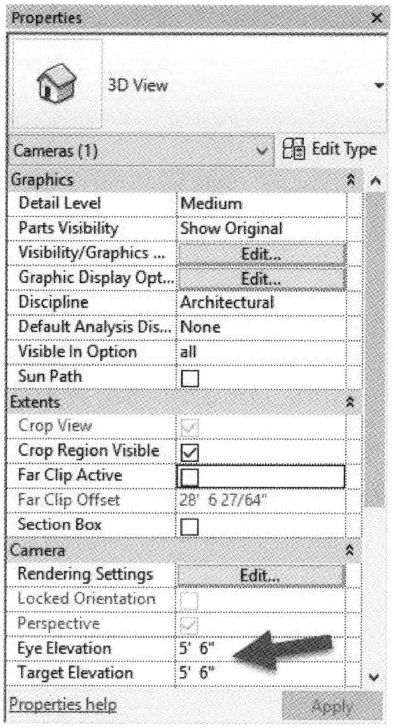

FIGURE 14-4.5 Camera properties

8. Select the *Camera.*

9. Make sure the **Eye Elevation** is **5′-6″** (Figure 14-4.5).

Notice the other camera settings; these are the properties of the 3D view itself. Changing the *Target Elevation* would cause the camera to look up at the ceiling or down at the floor, depending on the value entered.

10. Click **Apply** if any changes were needed.

The vertical lines are distorted due to the wide field of view, crop region. This is similar to what a camera with a 10-15mm lens would get in the finished building.

Creating the Rendering:

Next, you will render the interior kitchen view.

11. In the interior camera view, create a new item in *Sun Settings* dialog as shown below (Figure 14-4.6).

    Name: **Kitchen**
    Azimuth: **302.00**
    Altitude: **34.00**

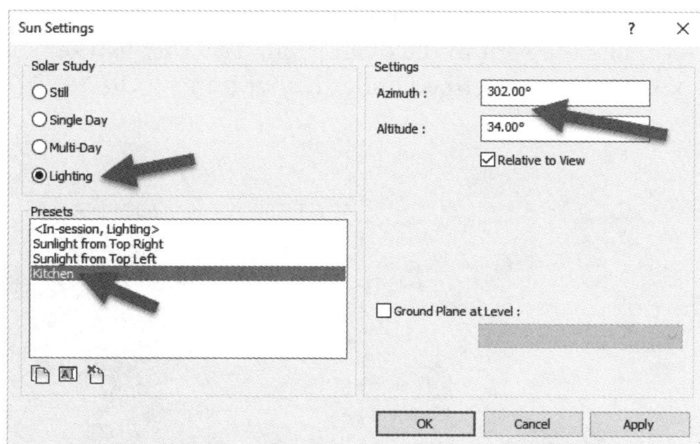

FIGURE 14-4.6 Sun Settings

You just created a "fake" sun angle to improve the rendering for presentation purposes. This may be useful if the exact north is not known or the designer wants to leverage a little artistic freedom.

12. Select **Show Rendering Dialog** from the *View Control Bar.*

13. Settings should be **Medium** *quality and* **150 dpi**.

14. Set the *Scheme* to **Interior: Sun only**; be sure to select "interior:" as it makes a big difference.

15. Click **Render** to begin the rendering process.

This will take several minutes depending on the speed of your computer. When finished, the view should look similar to **Figure 14-4.7**.

16. Click **Export** from the *Rendering* dialog box to save the image to a file on your hard drive. Name the file **Kitchen.jpg** (jpeg file format).

You can now open the *Kitchen.jpg* file in Adobe Photoshop or insert it into an MS Word type program, or equivalent, to manipulate or print.

To toggle back to the normal hidden view, select **Show the Model** from the *Rendering* dialog box.

There are many things you can do to make the rendering look even better. You can add interior light fixtures and props (e.g., pictures on the wall, items on the countertop, and lawn furniture in the yard). Once you add interior lights, you can adjust the Sun Setting to nighttime and then render a night scene.

> ***TIP:** Setting the Output to Printer rather than Screen allows you to generate a higher resolution image. Thus, between the Quality setting and the Output setting you can create an extremely high-quality rendering, but it might take hours if not days to process!*

Revit also gives you the ability to set a material to be self-illuminating. This will allow you to make a button on the dishwasher look like it is lit up or, if applied to the glass on the range door, like the light in the oven is on! You can also set a lamp shade to glow when a light source has been defined under it so it looks more realistic.

FIGURE 14-4.7 Rendered view

You can quickly add another camera view to look at the other half of the kitchen. The ability to stretch the *Crop Region* allows you to create interesting views like the one below, which is really more like a panoramic view than a traditional camera view (Figure 14-4.8).

FIGURE 14-4.8 Another rendered view

17. **Save** your project as **14-4.rvt**.

Realistic Display Setting:

In addition to *Shade* and *Hidden Line* display settings, you can also select *Realistic*. This will show the *Render Appearance* materials on your building without the need to do a full rendering. However, the shadows and shaded areas are not nearly as realistic as a full rendering.

This is a great way to get an idea of how the materials look, but you will find it best to minimize its use, as Revit will run much slower.

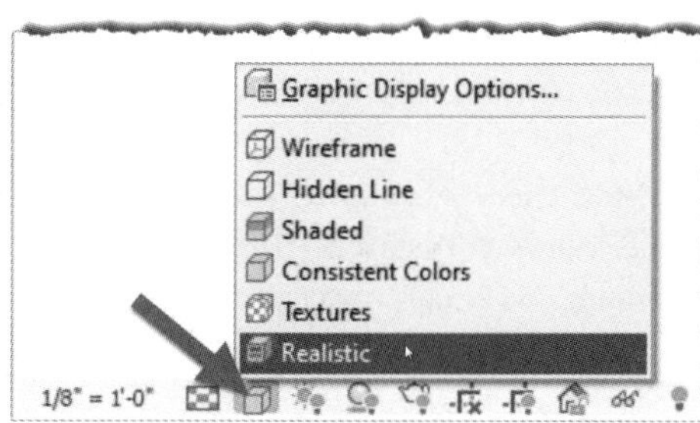

Duplicating a Material:

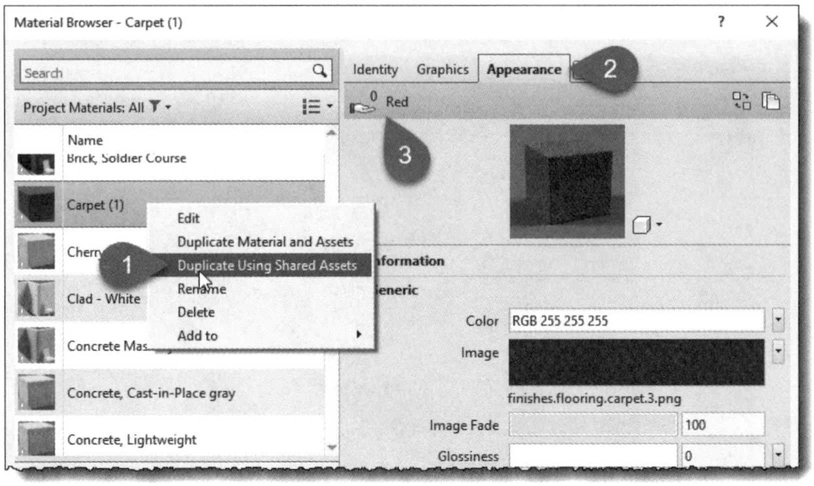

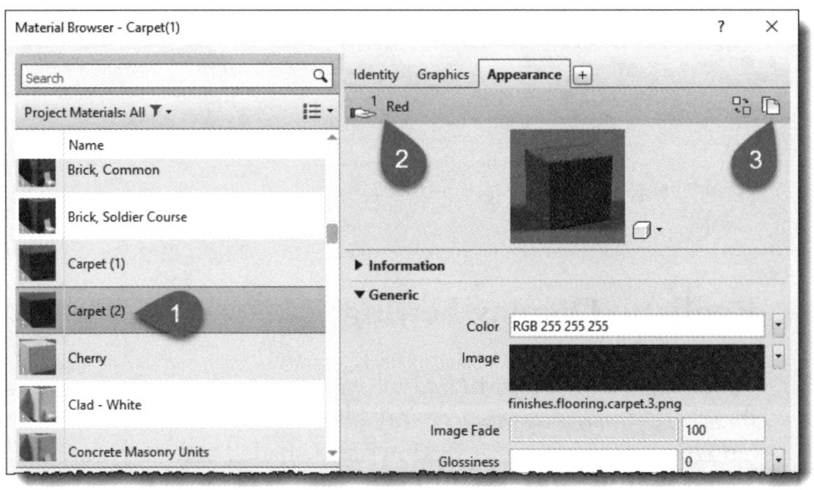

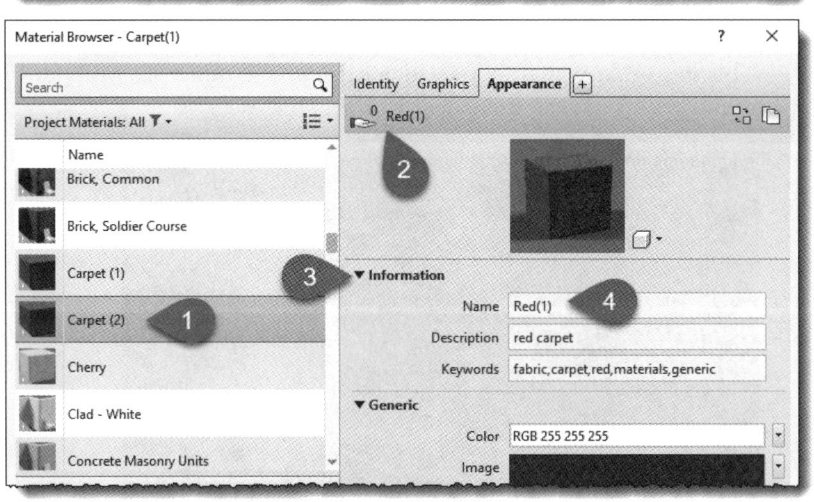

It is important to know how to properly duplicate a *Material* in your model so you do not unintentionally affect another *Material.* The information on this page is mainly for reference and does not need to be done in your model.

If a material is duplicated using the **Duplicate using Shared Assets** option, the **Appearance Asset** will be associated to the new *Material* AND the *Material* you copied it from! For example, in the image below, we will right-click on Carpet (1) and duplicate it. Before we duplicate it, notice the *Appearance Asset* named "RED" is not shared (arrow #3 in the image below).

Once you have duplicated a *Material*, notice the two carpet materials in this example; now, indicate they both share the same *Appearance Asset.* Changing one will affect the other. Click the **Duplicate this asset** icon in the upper right (second image).

Once the *Appearance Asset* has been duplicated (third image), you can expand the information section and rename the asset. You can now make changes to this material without affecting other materials.

Exercise 14-5:
Adding People to the Rendering

Revit provides a few free RPC people to add to your renderings; RPC stands for Rich Photorealistic Content. These are files from a third-party company that provides 3D content for use in renderings (http://www.archvision.com). You can buy additional content in groupings, such as college students or per item. In addition to people, they also offer items such as cars, plants, trees, and office equipment.

Loading Content into the Current Project

1. Open ex14-4.rvt and **Save As 14-5.rvt**.
2. Switch to the **First Floor** plan view.
3. Click the **Load Autodesk Family** button on the *Ribbon.*
4. Search for **RPC** and select both the **RPC Female** and **RPC Male** files, and click **Load** to import them into your project.
5. Select the **Component** tool from the *Architecture* tab.
6. Place one **Male** and one **Female**, specified via the *Type Selector*, as shown in **Figure 14-5.1**.

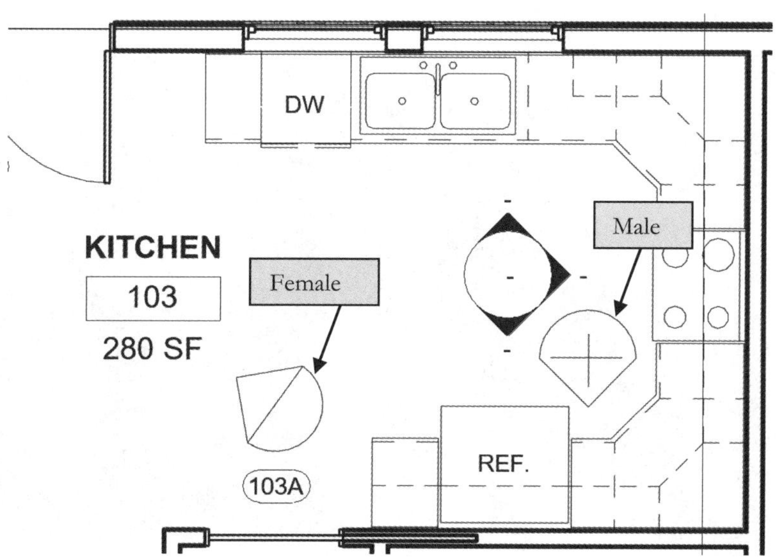

FIGURE 14-5.1 Kitchen – RPC people added

The line in the circle (Figure 14-5.1) represents the direction a person is looking. You simply *Rotate* the object to make adjustments. The image below shows the RPC people that can be placed in your project. **Notice the two families each have multiple types.**

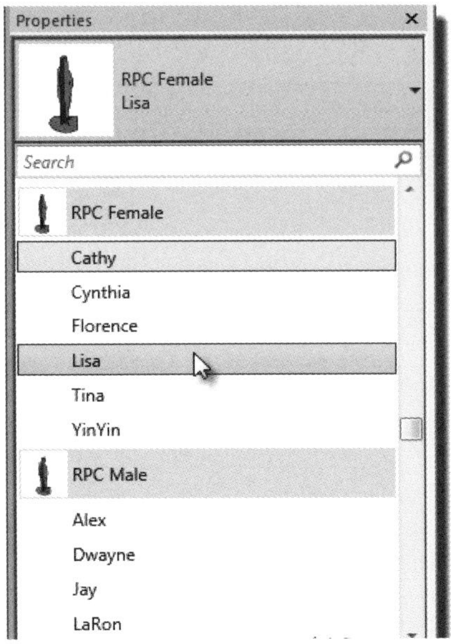

FIGURE 14-5.2
Type Selector – Properties Palette

7. Switch to your interior kitchen camera view.

8. Set the *Quality* setting to **Medium**.

9. Set the *Sun Setting* to **Kitchen**.

10. Click **Render**.

Additional RPC content can be purchased from ArchVision via their website: www.archvision.com. They have a yearly subscription option which provides hundreds of trees, cars and people to add to your renderings.

Your rendering should now have people in it and look similar to **Figure 14-5.4**. Notice how the people cast shadows; remember the only light source is the sunlight coming through the two windows and the glass door. If you want to change the people, simply select them and pick from the *Type Selector*.

Adding people and other "props" gives your model a sense of scale and makes it look a little more realistic. After all, architecture is for people. These elements can be viewed from any angle. Try a new camera view from another angle to see how the people adjust to match the view and perspective; see Figure 14-5.3, front of the female model versus the side view below.

FIGURE 14-5.3 Interior kitchen view with people added

FIGURE 14-5.4 Interior kitchen view with people added

11. **Save** your project as **ex14-5.rvt**.

Enscape (low cost for students)
There is an add-in for Revit called **Enscape**, a real-time rendering environment that can also be used for videos, VR, and Google Cardboard. This add-in is offered to students at a reduced cost. Check it out at www.enscape3d.com. This add-in comes with a large asset library, as shown to the right.

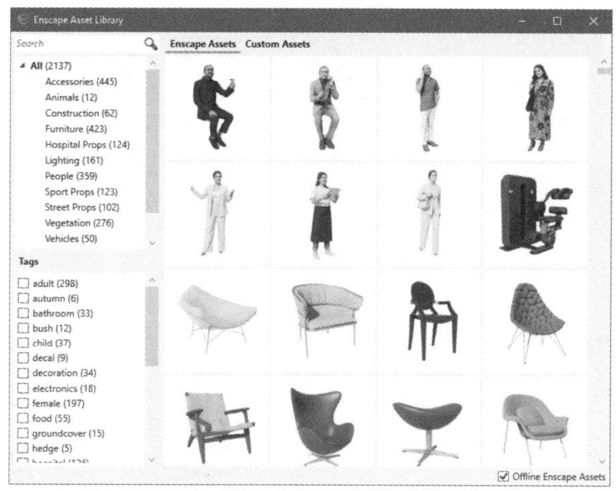

Other rendering tools include Twinmotion, D5, and even ChatGPT or Nano Banana (upload an image, even a shaded view can work well and produce good results).

Sketchy Lines

Be sure to check out the **Sketchy Lines** options available via View Properties → **Graphic Display Options**. Tip: Also turn on **Smooth lines with anti-aliasing** when using the *Sketchy Lines* feature.

Self-Exam:

The following questions can be used as a way to check your knowledge of this lesson. The answers can be found at the bottom of the page.

1. Creating a camera adds a view to the *Project Browser* list. (T/F)
2. Rendering materials are defined in Revit's *Materials* dialog box. (T/F)
3. After inserting a light fixture, you need to adjust several settings before rendering to get light from the fixture. (T/F)
4. You can adjust the season, which affects how the trees are rendered. (T/F)
5. Use the ______________ tool to hide a large portion of the model.

Review Questions:

The following questions may be assigned by your instructor as a way to assess your knowledge of this section. Your instructor has the answers to the review questions.

1. Draft renderings can be printed very large with no pixilation. (T/F)
2. You cannot get accurate lighting based on day/month/location. (T/F)
3. Adding components, i.e. families, to your project does not make the project file bigger. (T/F)
4. Creating photo-realistic renderings can take a significant amount of time for your computer to process. (T/F)
5. The RPC people can only be viewed from one angle. (T/F)
6. The RPC components do not cast shadows. (T/F)
7. Adjust the ___________________ to make more of a perspective view visible.
8. You use the _____________ tool to load and insert RPC people.
9. You can adjust the Eye Elevation of the camera via the camera's ______________________.
10. What is the file size of (completed) Exercise 14-5? _________________ MB

SELF-EXAM ANSWERS:
1 – T, **2** – T, **3** – F, **4** – F, **5** – Section Box

Notes:

Lesson 15
Construction Documents Set:

This lesson will look at bringing everything you have drawn thus far together onto sheets. The sheets, once set up, are ready for plotting. Basically, you place the various views you have created on sheets. The scale for each view is based on the scale you set when drawing that view, so it's important to set it correctly because it affects text and symbol sizes. When finished setting up the sheets, you will have a set of drawings ready to print individually or all at once.

Exercise 15-1:
Setting up a Sheet

Creating a Sheet View:

1. Open ex14-5.rvt and **Save As** 15-1.rvt.

2. Select **View → Sheet Composition → Sheet**.

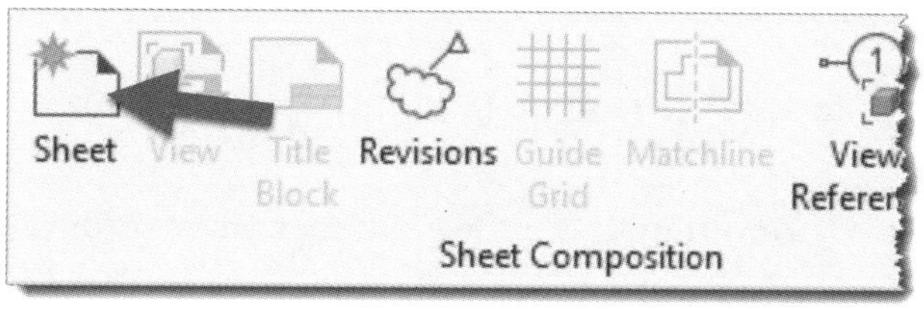

Next, Autodesk® Revit® will prompt you for a *Titleblock* to use. The template file you started with has two *titleblock families* to choose from: 11 x 17 and 22 x 34 (Figure 15-1.1).

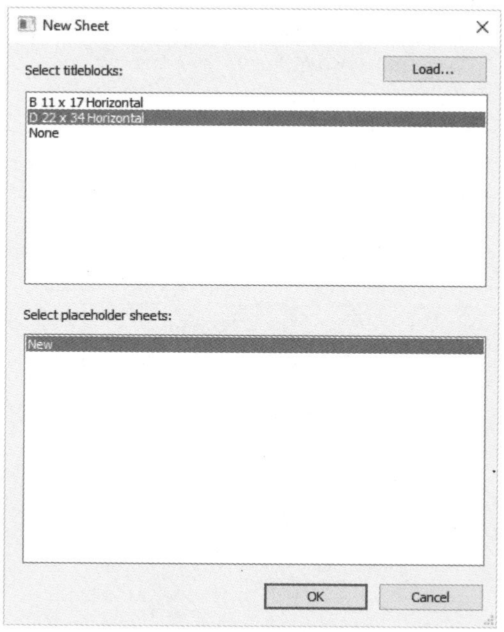

FIGURE 15-1.1 Select a Titleblock

3. Select the **D 22x34 Horizontal** titleblock and click **OK**.

That's it; you have created a new sheet that is ready to have views and/or schedules placed on it!

NOTE: A new view shows up in the Project Browser under the heading Sheets. *Once you get an entire CD set ready, this list can be very long.*

Autodesk Revit also lets you create placeholder sheets, which allow you to add sheets to the sheet index without the need to have a sheet show up in the *Project Browser*. This is helpful if a consultant, such as a food service designer, is not using Revit. This feature allows you to add those sheets to the sheet index. Placeholder sheets can only be added in the sheet list schedule by using the *New Row* tool on the *Ribbon*. Once a placeholder sheet exists, it can be turned into a real sheet by selecting from the lower list in the dialog to the left.

FIGURE 15-1.2 Initial Titleblock view

4. **Zoom in** to the sheet number area (lower right corner).

5. Adjust the text to look similar to **Figure 15-1.3**. Click on the text and edit it; make sure *Modify* is selected first.

TIP: Select the title block, hover the cursor over the text you wish to edit, and then click. Notice some of the fields are filled in based on the project setup you did earlier in the book (chapter 5)—project name and number, for example.

Notice the time and date stamp. This helps to remember when a sheet was plotted, especially if you forget to update the date before printing.

FIGURE 15-1.3 Revised Titleblock data

6. **Zoom out** so you can see the entire sheet (type ZF).

7. With the sheet fully visible, click and drag the **Living Room - East** view, under *Elevations (Interior elevations)*, from the *Project Browser* onto the sheet view. Let go of the mouse button once it is within the drawing window; do not click yet.

You will see a box that represents the extents of the view you are placing on the current sheet. If the box is larger than the sheet, this means the *View Scale* is to a scale that is too large. You would need to open the view and adjust the *View Scale*.

8. Move the *Viewport* around until the box is in the upper-right corner of the sheet (this can be repositioned later at any time) and click to place.

Your view should look similar to **Figure 15-1.4**.

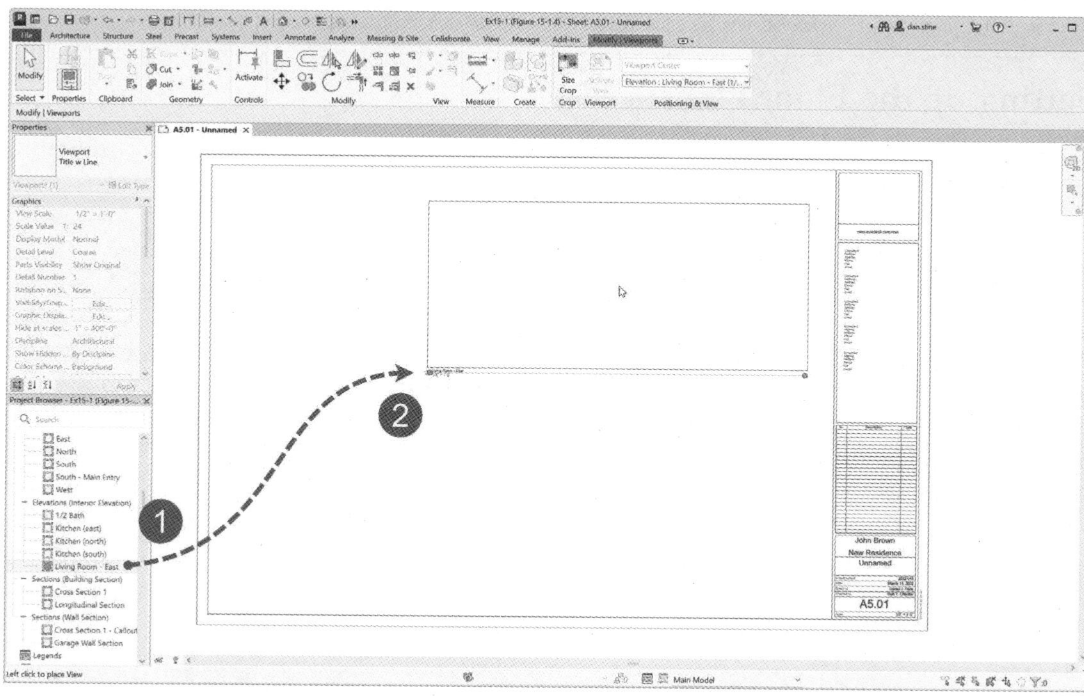

FIGURE 15-1.4 Sheet with Living Room view placed on it

9. Click the mouse in a white area, not on any lines, to deselect the *Living Room - East* view. Notice the extents box goes away.

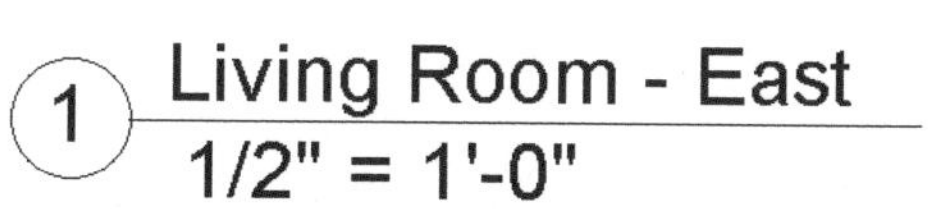

FIGURE 15-1.5 Drawing title

10. **Zoom in** on the lower left corner to view the drawing identification symbol that Revit automatically added (Figure 15-1.5).

NOTE: Each drawing placed on a sheet automatically gets a number, starting with one. The next drawing you add will be number two. Also, notice that the icon next to the view name in the Project Browser is filled, indicating the view is placed on a sheet (views can only be placed on one sheet due to automatic numbering/ coordination).

The view name, from the *Project Browser*, is listed as the drawing title. This is another reason to rename the elevation and section views as you create them. Also, notice that the drawing scale is listed. Again, this comes from the *View Scale* setting for the *Living Room - East* view.

As you can see, if you add furniture to the living room, it shows up; normally, this is turned off in interior elevation views. You can turn these off using the same technique covered later in this chapter for the trees in the exterior elevations.

> **Duplicate Sheet Numbers:** Revit allows a sheet number to exist only once per project. It is possible to create a **Sheet Collection**, which can have the same sheet number repeated once (per collection). This would, for example, allow more than one project to be worked on in the same Revit model, such as a hospital.

Setting up the Floor Plans:

Setting up floor plans is easy; actually, they are already set up from the template you started with.

11. From the *Sheets* section in the *Project Browser*, double-click on the sheet named **A1 – First Floor Plan** to open it.

As you can see, the floor plan is already set up on a sheet. Again, a few things can be turned off (i.e., trees, RPC People) per the techniques covered next. You would also want to move the exterior elevation tags closer to the building so they are within the title block if they are not already.

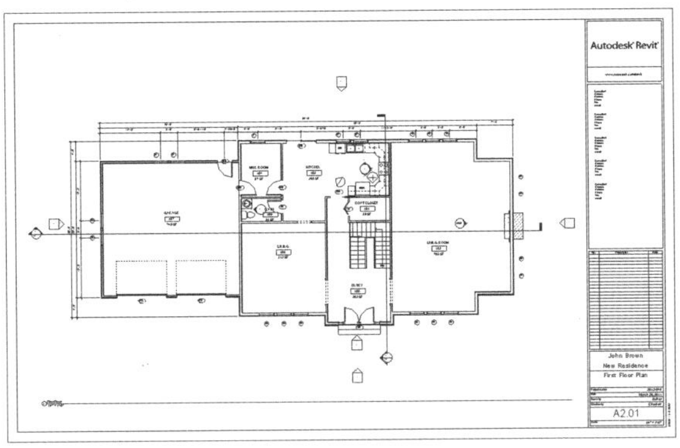

12. Adjust the location of the plan view on the sheet if needed. Click and drag to move it.

13. Change the sheet number to **A2.01**, and then close the First Floor Plan, *Sheet.*

Setting up the Exterior Elevations:

Next you will set up the exterior elevations. Again, the sheets are already set up, but the views have not been placed on the sheets like the floor plans have.

14. Open Sheet **A6 – Elevations** and drag the ***South*** elevation view onto the sheet. Place the drawing near the bottom and centered on the sheet.

Your drawing should look similar to Figure 15-1.6.

FIGURE 15-1.6 South exterior elevation

Next, you will turn off the trees in the *South* view. Normally, you would turn them off in all views. However, you will only turn them off in the *South* view to show that you can control visibility per view on a sheet.

15. In the sheet view, click on the *South* exterior elevation view to select it; the outer extents rectangle is called the *viewport* (Figure 15-1.6).

16. Now **right-click** and select **Activate View** from the pop-up menu. ***TIP:*** *You can also double-click within the view to activate it.*

At this point, you are in the viewport and can make changes to the project model to control visibility, which is what you will do next.

17. Turn on **View Cropping** and **Show Crop Region** on the *View Control Bar*; adjust the crop region to minimize the space needed by the view on the sheet. When finished, hide the crop region.

18. Make sure nothing is selected. With nothing selected in the view, the *Properties Palette* displays the activated view's properties, as if you were in the view rather than the sheet.

19. Click the **Edit** button next to *Visibility/Graphics Overrides*. ***TIP:*** Or type VV.

20. In the *Visibility* dialog, **uncheck Planting**.

21. Close the open dialog box.

22. Right-click anywhere in the drawing area and select **Deactivate View** from the pop-up menu. ***TIP:*** *Double-clicking outside of view will also deactivate the view.*

Now the trees are turned off for the *South* elevation; if you had another elevation view on the same sheet, the trees would still be visible in that view.

23. Add the ***North*** elevation to the **A7 – Elevations** *Sheet.*

    TIP: *You may need to switch to the North view and turn on the* Crop *and* Crop Display *icons on the View Control Bar to make the area placed on the sheet smaller so it will fit; when finished, turn off* Crop Display *but leave* Crop View *turned on. Or use the Activate View option just covered.*

Now you will stop for a moment and notice that Revit is automatically referencing the drawings as you place them on sheets.

24. Switch to ***First Floor*** (Figure 15-1.7).

Notice in Figure 15-1.7 that the number A6 represents the sheet number that the drawing can be found on. The number one (1) is the drawing number to look for on sheet A6. The empty tag is the enlarged elevation view you set up earlier in the book; it has not been placed on a sheet yet, so it is not filled in.

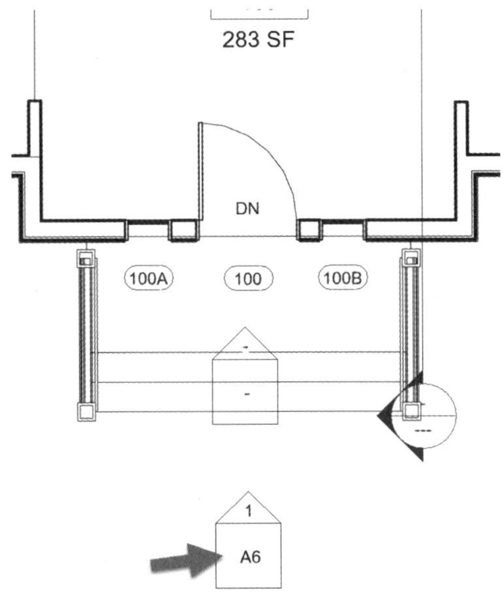

FIGURE 15-1.7 First Floor – elevation tag filled-in

Setting up Sections:

25. Open *Sheet* **A8 – Building Sections** and place *Cross Section 1.*

26. Open *Sheet* **A9 – Building Sections** and place the *Longitudinal Section* view on the *Sheet.*

27. Switch to *First Floor* plan view and zoom into the area shown in Figure 15-1.9.

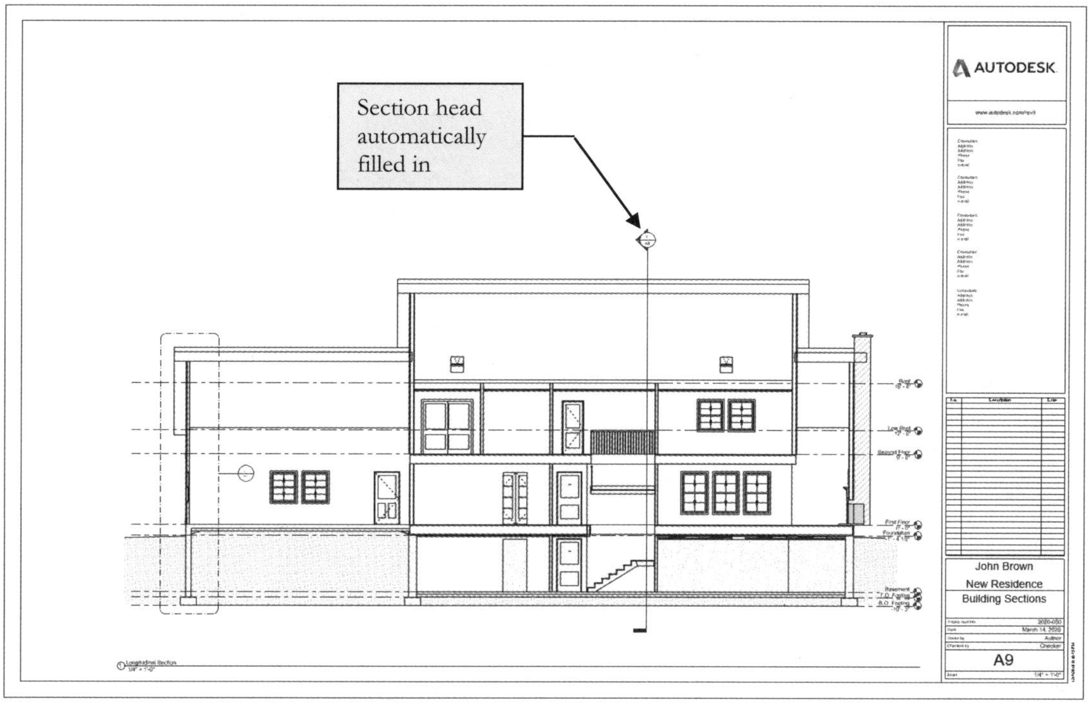

FIGURE 15-1.8 A9 – Building Sections sheet

Notice, again, that the reference bubbles are automatically filled in when the referenced view is placed on a sheet. If the drawing is moved to another sheet, the reference bubbles are automatically updated.

You can also see in Figure 15-1.8 that the reference bubbles on the building sections are filled in.

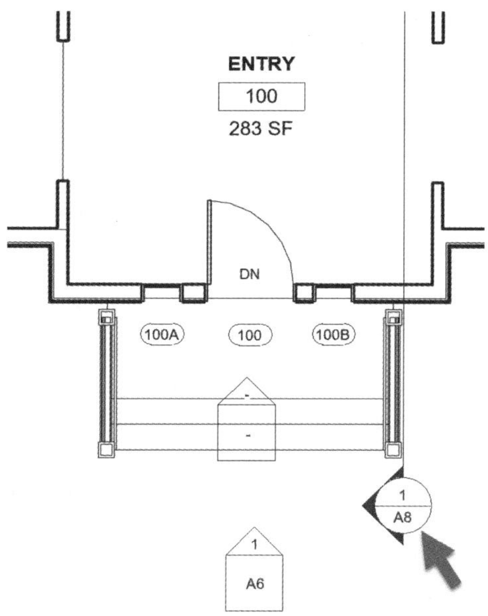

FIGURE 15-1.9 First Floor – Section ref's filled in

Set up the Remaining Sheets:

Next, you set up sheets for the remaining views that haven't yet been placed on a sheet, except for the 3D views.

28. Add the remaining views to the appropriate sheets; if one does not exist, you can create a new sheet.

> **Question:** On a large project with hundreds of views, how do I know for sure if I have placed every view on a sheet?
>
> **Answer:** In addition to the Project Browser icons (filled = the view is on a sheet), Revit has a feature called *Browser Organization* that can hide all the views that have been placed on a sheet. You will try this next.

Take a general look at the *Project Browser* to see how many views are listed.

29. Select **View → Windows → User Interface** *(drop-down)* **→ Browser Organization.**

30. On the *Views* tab, click the checkbox next to **not on sheets** (Figure 15-1.10).

31. Click **OK**.

32. Notice the list in the *Project Browser* is now smaller (Figure 15-1.11).

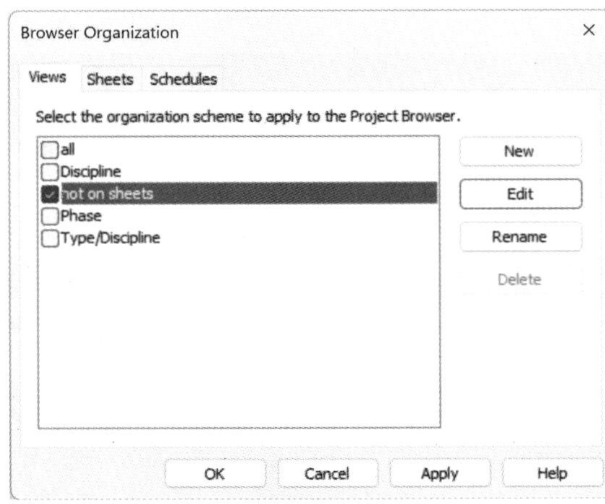

FIGURE 15-1.10 Browser Organization dialog

The *Project Browser* now only shows drawing views that have not been placed onto a sheet. Of course, you could have a few views that do not need to be placed on a sheet, but this feature will help eliminate errors. Also notice the label at the top: *Views (not on sheets)*; this tells you what mode or filter the *Project Browser* is in.

Next you will reset the *Project Browser.*

33. Open *Browser Organization* again and check the box next to **all** and click **OK** to close the dialog box.

TIP: You can also select the title Views *at the top of the Project Browser and toggle between filter types via the Type Selector.*

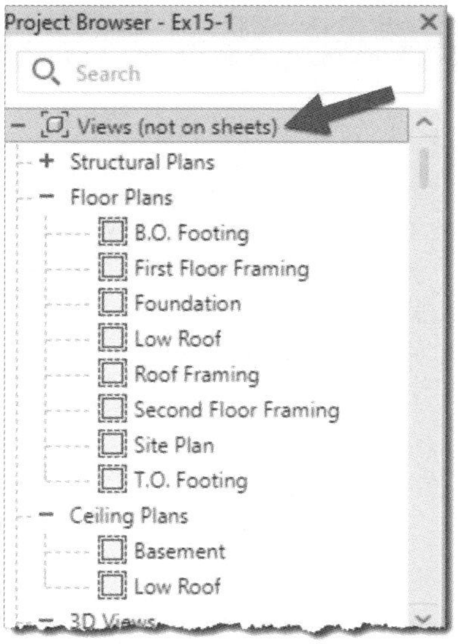

FIGURE 15-1.11 Project Browser

Sheets with Design Options:

Finally, you will set up a sheet to show the two *Design Options*.

34. Create a *Sheet* named ***Entry Options*** and number it **A100**.

35. Place both *Entry – Option 2* 3D views on the new sheet and change the scale to **⅛″ = 1′-0″**.

    TIP: Select the placed view and change the scale in the Properties Palette.

36. **Save** your project as **ex15-1.rvt**.

Each 3D view has its *Visibility* modified to show the desired *Design Options*. When a view is placed on a sheet, those settings are preserved.

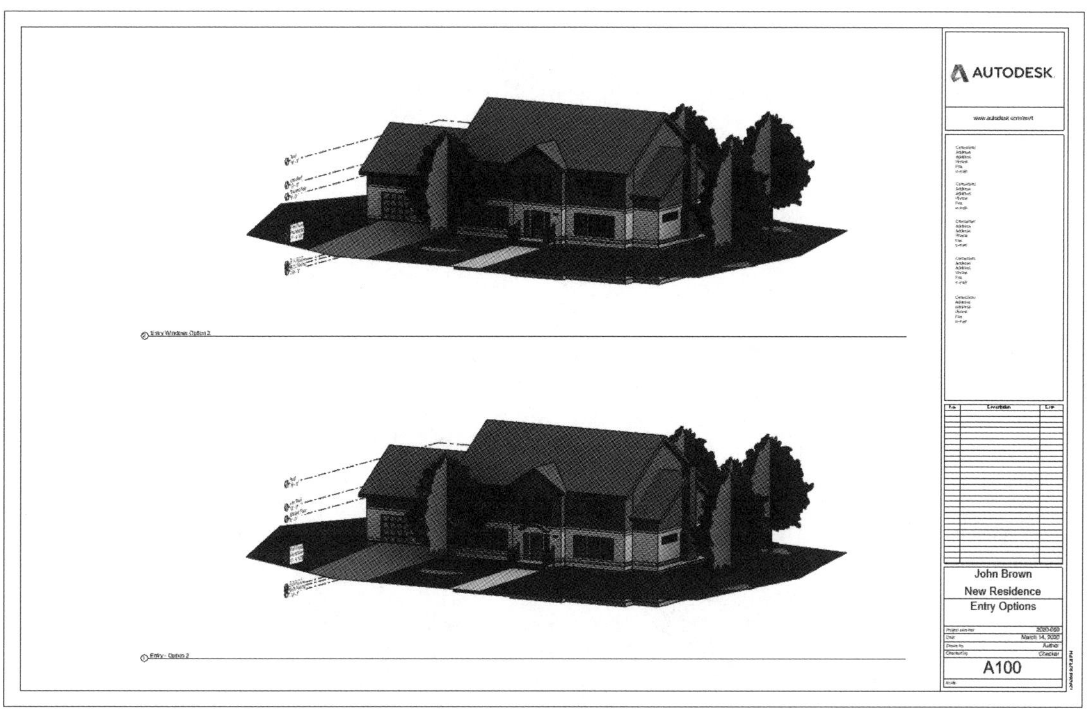

FIGURE 15-1.12 Entry Options Sheet; two views with Design Options added

Exercise 15-2:
Sheet Index

Revit can automatically create a Sheet List (or sheet index). This feature uses the same schedule creation interface previously covered. Whenever a sheet is added or removed from the project, this *Sheet List* will automatically update. You can even use the *Sheet List* to make changes to the sheet. For example, if you noticed a few sheets were not all uppercase, you could change them in the *Sheet List,* and the sheets themselves would update as they represent the same information. You will study this feature now.

Creating a Sheet List View

1. Open ex15-1.rvt and **Save As** ex15-2.

2. Select **View → Create → Schedules** *(down-arrow)* **→ Sheet List**.

You are now in the *Sheet List Properties* dialog box. Here you specify which fields you want in the sheet index and how to sort the list (Figure 15-2.1).

3. Add **Sheet Number** and **Sheet Name** to the right (click *Add* →).

4. Click **OK**.

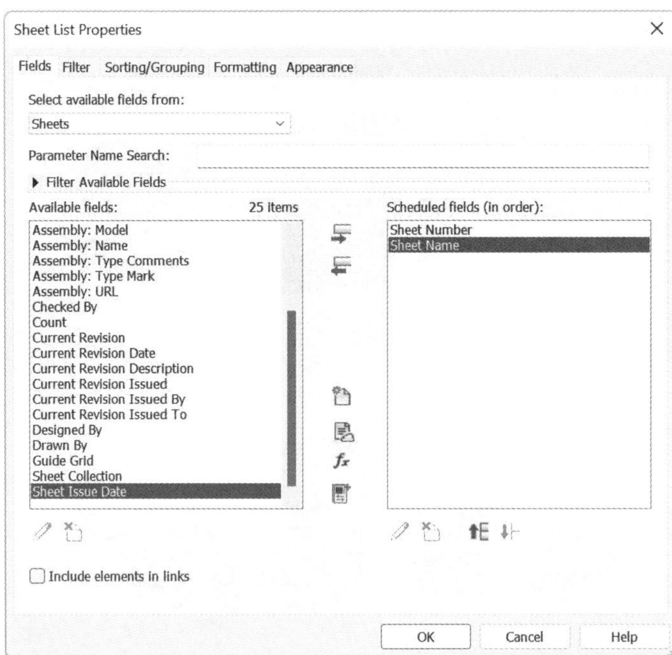

FIGURE 15-2.1 Sheet List Properties Dialog; sheet number and name added

Now you should notice that the *Sheet Names* are cut off because the column is not wide enough (Figure 15-2.2). You will adjust this next.

5. Move your cursor over the right edge of the *Sheet List* table and click-and-drag to the right until you can see the entire name (Figure 15-2.2).

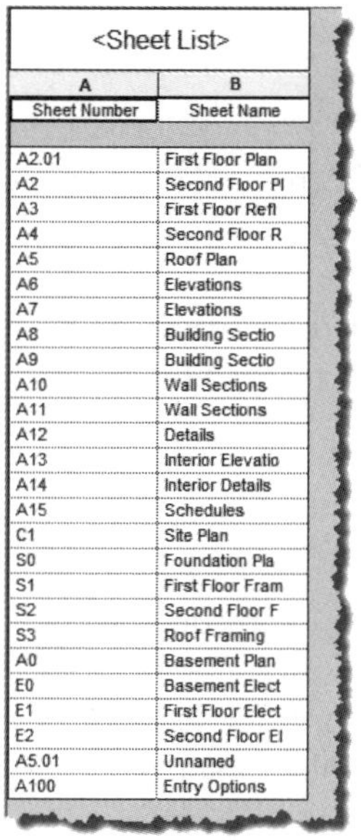

<Sheet List>	
A	B
Sheet Number	Sheet Name
A2.01	First Floor Plan
A2	Second Floor Pl
A3	First Floor Refl
A4	Second Floor R
A5	Roof Plan
A6	Elevations
A7	Elevations
A8	Building Sectio
A9	Building Sectio
A10	Wall Sections
A11	Wall Sections
A12	Details
A13	Interior Elevatio
A14	Interior Details
A15	Schedules
C1	Site Plan
S0	Foundation Pla
S1	First Floor Fram
S2	Second Floor F
S3	Roof Framing
A0	Basement Plan
E0	Basement Elect
E1	First Floor Elect
E2	Second Floor El
A5.01	Unnamed
A100	Entry Options

FIGURE 15-2.2 Sheet List view; notice sheet names are cut off in right column

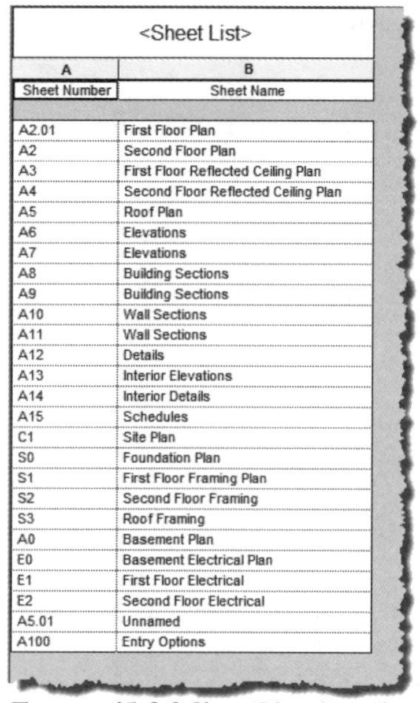

<Sheet List>	
A	B
Sheet Number	Sheet Name
A2.01	First Floor Plan
A2	Second Floor Plan
A3	First Floor Reflected Ceiling Plan
A4	Second Floor Reflected Ceiling Plan
A5	Roof Plan
A6	Elevations
A7	Elevations
A8	Building Sections
A9	Building Sections
A10	Wall Sections
A11	Wall Sections
A12	Details
A13	Interior Elevations
A14	Interior Details
A15	Schedules
C1	Site Plan
S0	Foundation Plan
S1	First Floor Framing Plan
S2	Second Floor Framing
S3	Roof Framing
A0	Basement Plan
E0	Basement Electrical Plan
E1	First Floor Electrical
E2	Second Floor Electrical
A5.01	Unnamed
A100	Entry Options

FIGURE 15-2.3 Sheet List view; sheet names are now visible

Adjusting Which Sheets Show Up in the List:

Looking at the *Sheet List* (Figure 15-2.3), you decide to remove the *Entry design options* sheet (i.e., sheet A100) from the list as it is not part of the construction document set.

As with other schedules, this is live data which is directly connected to the model. If you change a sheet number here, the number will change throughout the project. If you delete a number (i.e., a row), Revit will delete the sheet from the project.

You will look at the option that lets you remove a sheet from the list without deleting it.

6. Right-click on sheet **A100** in the sheet list and select **Delete Row**. You will NOT actually delete this sheet, so do not click **OK**.

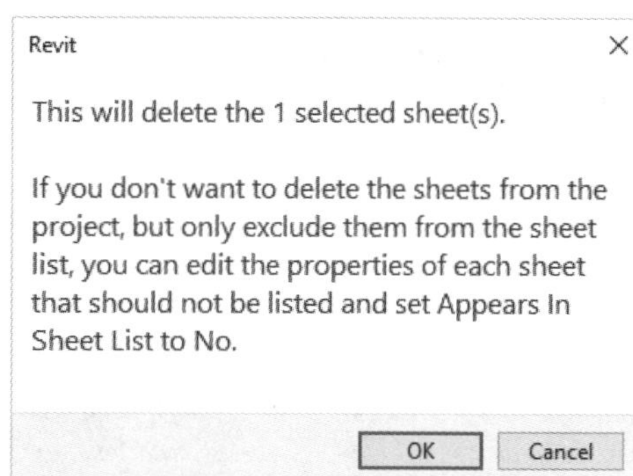

You will get a warning that the sheet will be deleted and what to do if you only want to remove it from the *Sheet List*.

7. Click **Cancel**.

8. Select *Sheet* **A100 – Entry Options** in the *Project Browser.*

9. In the P*roperties Palette*, uncheck **Appears In Sheet List** (Figure 15-2.4) and then click **Apply**.

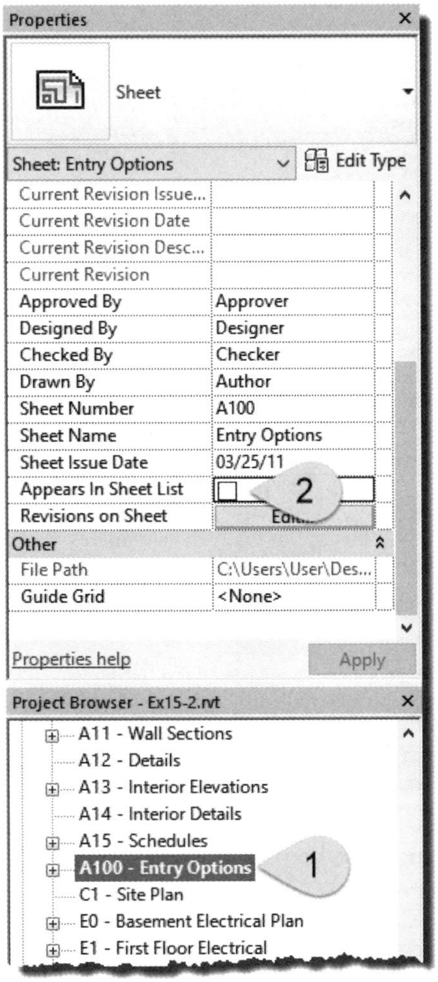

FIGURE 15-2.4 Properties for sheet A100

Notice the *Sheet* was removed from the *Sheet List* view, but is still in the project.

10. In the *Sheet List*, right-click on sheet **A13 Interior Elevations** and select **Delete** (Row) from the menu.

11. Click **OK**.

Not only was the sheet removed from the *Sheet List*, it was also deleted from the project. However, any views placed on a sheet are not deleted from the project. Next, you will renumber a sheet via the *Sheet List*.

12. Click in the cell with the sheet number **A5.01** and change the number to read **A13**.

Now an existing sheet has been renumbered and so have all the detail, elevation and section bubbles that point to this sheet.

13. In the *Properties Palette*, click the **Edit…** button next to **Sorting/Grouping**.

14. Set *Sort By* to **Sheet Number**.

15. Click **OK** to close the open dialog box.

Now the sheets should be sorted correctly, including the sheet you just renumbered.

TIP: You can create a custom parameter and sort the sheets based on the information entered there. This allows you to place the sheets in any order you wish. Usually, the "C" (i.e., civil) sheets are before the "A" (i.e., architectural) sheets. So, for example, all the "C" sheets could have the value "02" entered in the custom parameter, and the "A" sheets could all have the value "03" entered. Then, in sorting and grouping, you would sort by your custom parameter and then by sheet number. You can create the custom parameter on the Fields *tab in the* Sheet List *schedule (Figure 15-2.1) by clicking the* Add Parameter *button.*

Setting up a Title Sheet:

Now you will create a title sheet to place your sheet index on.

16. Create a new sheet:
    a. *Number:* **T1**
    b. *Name:* **Title Sheet**

17. From the *Schedules/Quantities* category of the *Project Browser*, place the view named ***Sheet List*** on the *Title Sheet* via drag-and-drop.

18. With the schedule selected on the sheet, drag the column grips so each row is only one line (Figure 15-2.5).

19. Create a new text style named **1" Arial**, and adjust the settings accordingly.

    TIP: Select the Text *tool, click* Edit Type, *and then* Duplicate.

Sheet List	
Sheet Number	Sheet Name
A2.01	First Floor Plan
A2	Second Floor Plan
A3	First Floor Reflected Ceiling Plan
A4	Second Floor Reflected Ceiling Plan
A5	Roof Plan
A6	Elevations
A7	Elevations
A8	Building Sections
A9	Building Sections
A10	Wall Sections
A11	Wall Sections
A12	Details
A13	Interior Elevations
A14	Interior Details
A15	Schedules
C1	Site Plan
S0	Foundation Plan
S1	First Floor Framing Plan
S2	Second Floor Framing
S3	Roof Framing
A0	Basement Plan
E0	Basement Electrical Plan
E1	First Floor Electrical
E2	Second Floor Electrical
A5.01	Unnamed
A100	Entry Options

FIGURE 15-2.5 Adjusting column width

20. Add large text across the top of the sheet that reads "NEW RESIDENCE FOR JOHN BROWN" (Figure 15-2.6).

Next, you will place one of your rendered images that you saved to file, which is a raster image. If you have not created a raster image, you should refer back to Lesson 14 and create one now. Otherwise, you can use any PNG or JPG file on your hard drive if necessary.

If you used the *Save to Project* feature, you can simply drag one of the images listed under *Renderings* from the *Project Browser*. The interior kitchen rendering was added to the title sheet using this method. Here you can see Revit has added a *Drawing Title* tag beneath the image, which would allow you to reference this image from another location.

21. Select **Insert → Import → Import Image**.

22. Browse to your JPG or PNG raster image file, select it and click **Open** to place the Image.

23. Click on your *Title Sheet* to locate the image; use the corner grips to resize the image.

Your sheet should look similar to Figure 15-2.6.

FIGURE 15-2.6 Sheet View: Title Sheet with drawing list, text and image added

24. Select **Insert → Link → Manage Links, Images (**tab).

You are now in the *Manage Links* dialog which gives you a little information about the image (although not a link) and allows you to delete it from the project (Figure 15-2.7).

***FYI:** You can delete a view from a Sheet without deleting the view from the project. Also, you can only place a view on one sheet; you would have to duplicate the view in order to have that view repeated.*

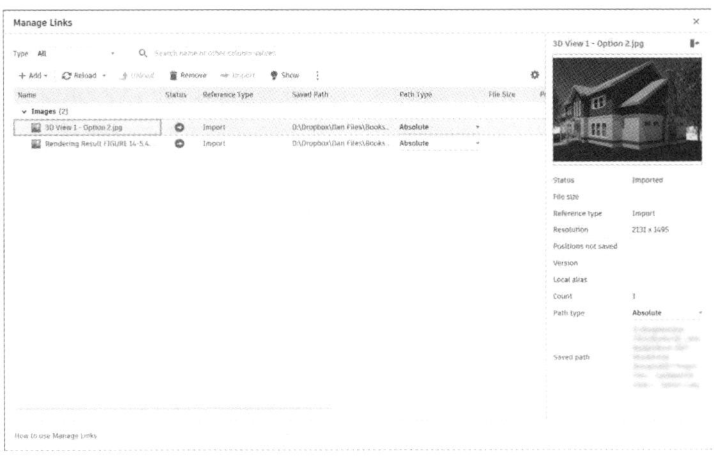

FIGURE 15-2.7 Manage Links dialog

***TIP:** You can use the standard modification tools on raster images (e.g., Move, Copy, Rotate, and Resize). You can also control the draw order to make sure your leaders pointing at the image show up.*

25. Close the ***Manage Images*** dialog.

Exporting a 3D DWFx File:

The *3D DWFx* file is an easy way to share your project file with others without the need to give them your editable Revit file or the need for the recipient to have Revit installed.

> ***NOTE:** You can download Revit from Autodesk's website and run it in* viewer mode. *It's free – full Revit with no save functionality.*

The 3D DWFx file is much smaller in file size than the original Revit file. Also, *Autodesk Design Review* is a free DWF viewer that can be downloaded from www.autodesk.com.

26. Switch to your ***Default 3D*** view and disable the *Section Box* if it is still active.

You must be in a 3D view for the 3D DWF feature to work. If you are not in a 3D view, you will get 2D DWF files:

27. Select **File Tab → Export → DWF.**

28. Click the **Next** button in the lower right (Figure 15-2.8); specify a file name and location for the DWF file and then click **Save**.

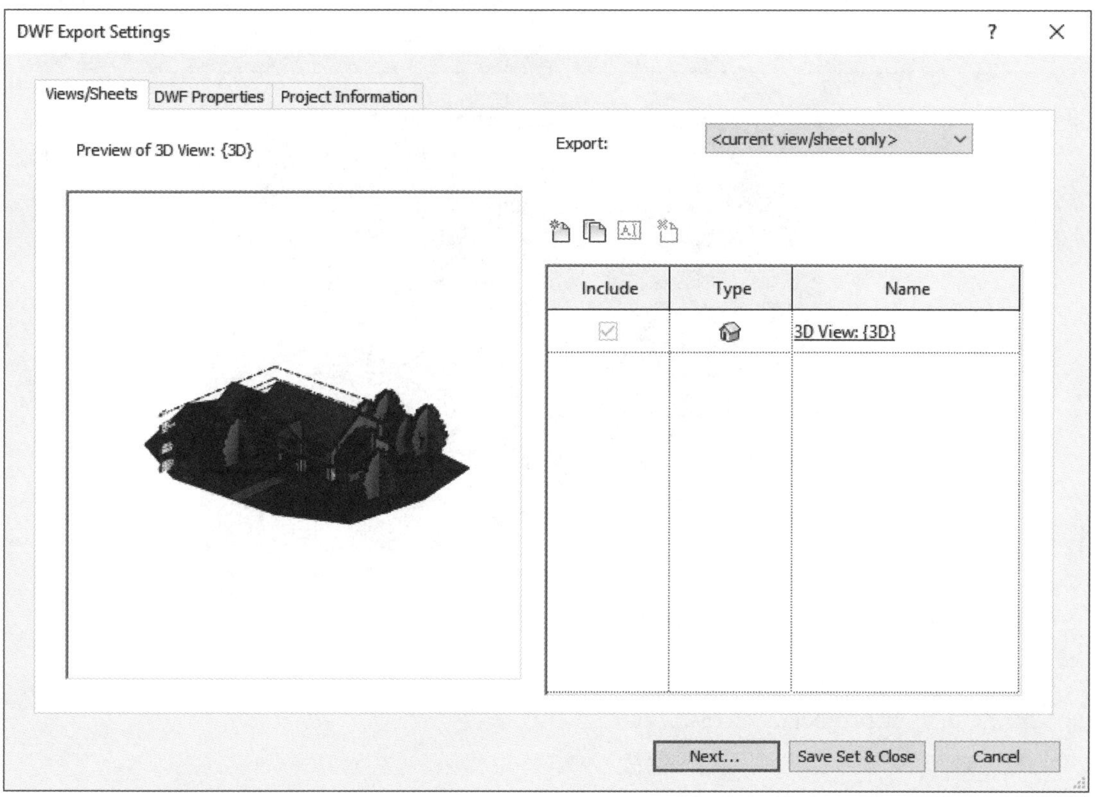

FIGURE 15-2.8 DWF export options

That's all you need to do to create the file. Now you can email it to the client or a product representative to get a cost estimate on windows, for example.

The 3D DWF file is about 2mb, whereas the Revit project file is 13 MB. Your file sizes will vary slightly based on factors like the number of families loaded. In many cases, networks and servers are set up so they cannot receive large files via email, so the 3D DWF is very useful.

The DWF viewer can be downloaded from http://usa.autodesk.com/design-review/. Once installed, you can access it from *Start* → *All Programs* → *Autodesk* → *Autodesk Design Review 2017*. You can zoom, orbit, and select objects. Notice the information displayed on the left when the front door is selected (see image below). Also, notice that under the *Windows* heading, the sizes and quantities are listed.

> **TIP:** *Autodesk Design Review 2017 is a free download from Autodesk. This is their full-featured DWF viewer and markup utility!*

This DWF file can also be used in conjunction with **Autodesk Quantity Takeoff** to develop cost estimates for your project. See Autodesk's website for more information.

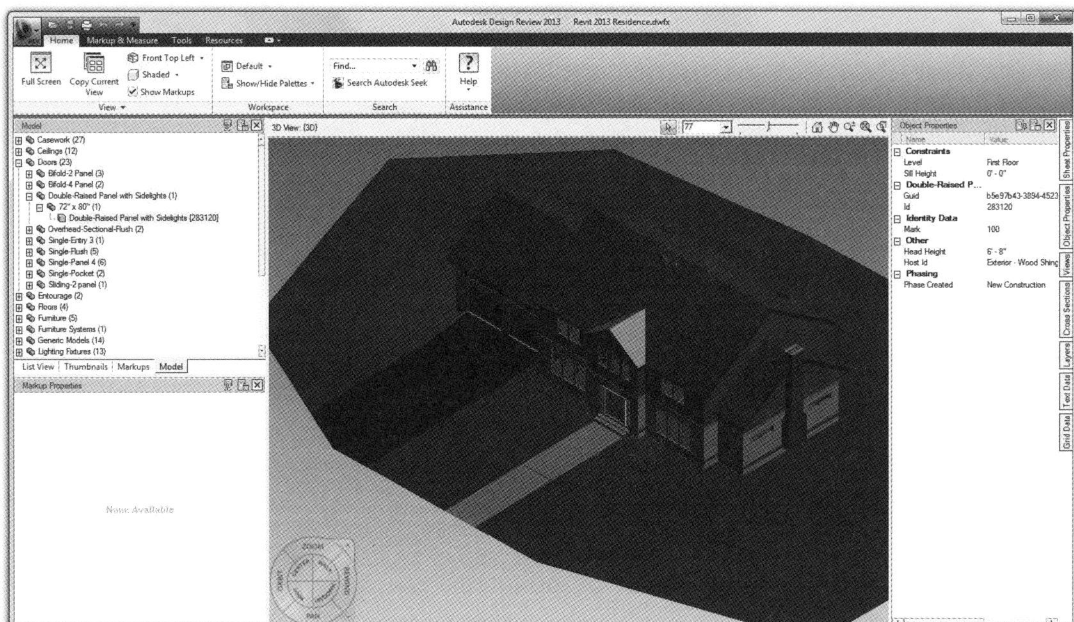

FIGURE 15-2.9 3D DWF in Autodesk Design Review

29. **Save** your project as **ex15-2.rvt**.

Exercise 15-3:
Printing a Set of Drawings

Revit has the ability to print an entire set of drawings, in addition to printing individual sheets. You will study this now.

Printing a Set of Drawings:

1. **Open ex15-2.rvt**.

2. Select **File Tab → Print → Print**.

3. In the *Print Range* area, click the option **Selected views/sheets** (Figure 15-3.1).

4. Click the **Select…** button within the *Print Range* area.

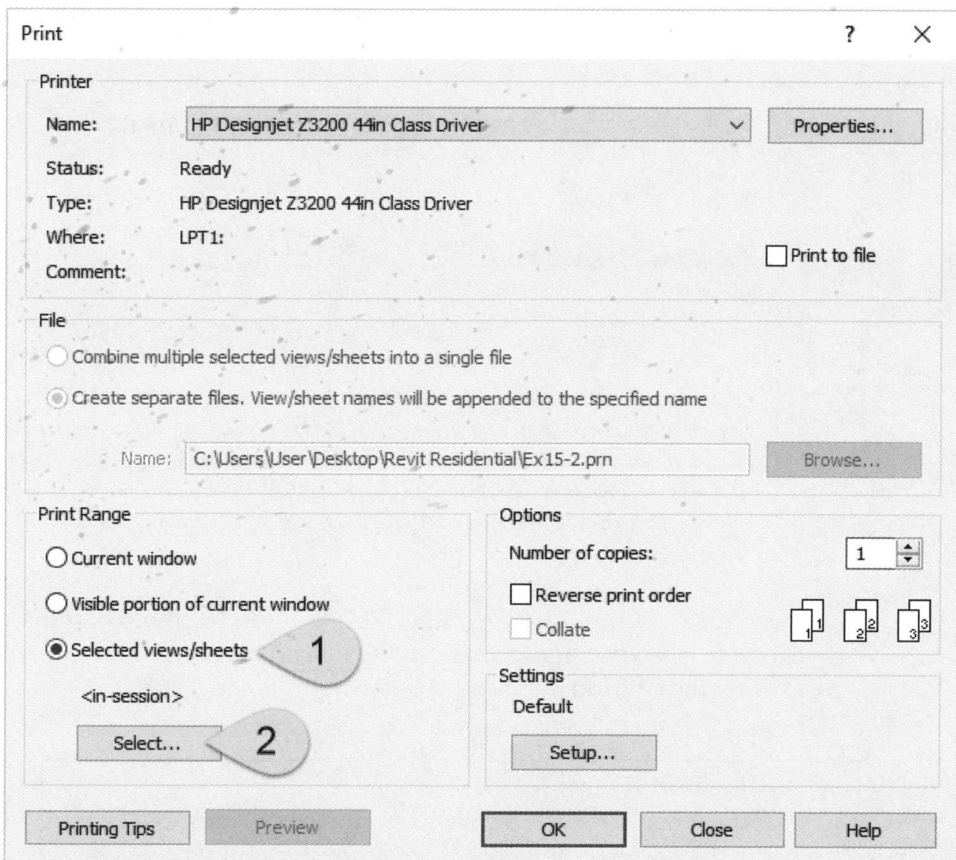

FIGURE 15-3.1 Print dialog box

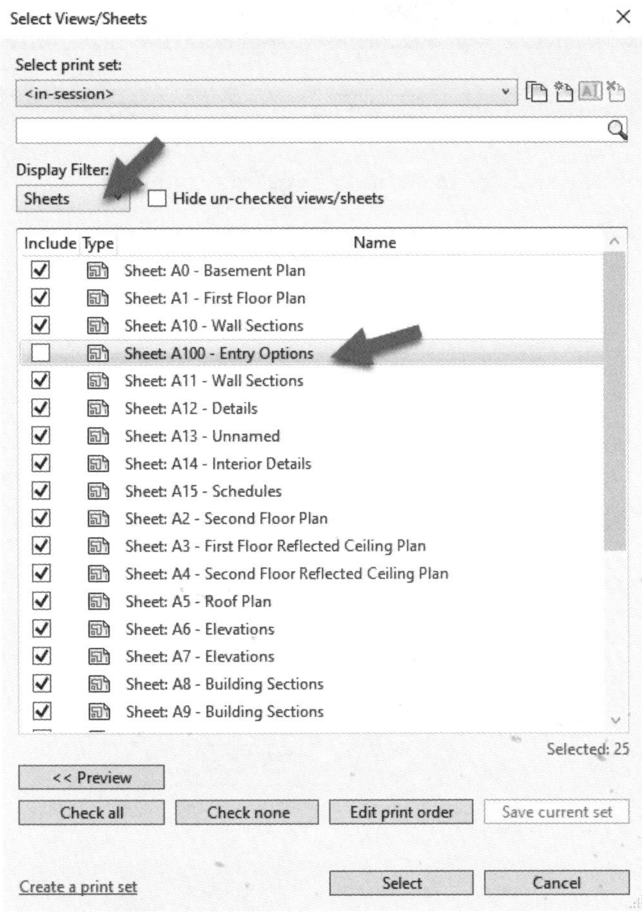

FIGURE 15-3.2 Set tool for printing

You should now see a listing of all *Views* and *Sheets* (Figure 15-3.2).

Notice at the top you can filter to just list sheets (not 2D or 3D views). Because you are printing a set of drawings you will want to see only the sheets.

5. **Uncheck** the **Views** option.

The list is now limited to just *Sheets* that have been set up in your project.

6. Select all the drawing sheets except **A100**.

7. Click **Select** to close the ***View/ Sheet Set*** dialog.

8. IF YOU ACTUALLY WANT TO PRINT A FULL SET OF DRAWINGS, you can do so now by clicking OK. Otherwise click **Cancel**.

9. You do not need to save the file.

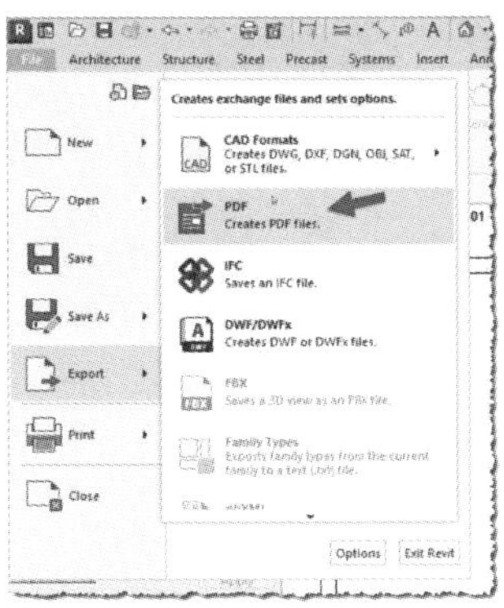

FYI: Once you have selected the sheets to be plotted and click OK, you are prompted to save the list. This will save the list of selected drawings to a name you choose. Then, the next time you need to print those sheets you can select the name from the drop-down list at the top (Figure 15-3.2). On very large projects (e.g., 20 floor plan sheets) you could have a Plans list saved, a Laboratory Interior Elevations list saved, etc.

Autodesk can export to PDF. This tool can be found on the File tab, as shown in the image to the right. This is often the preferred format to send clients.

> **Autodesk User Certification Exam**
> Be sure to check out Appendix A for an overview of the official Autodesk User Certification Exam and the available study book and software, sold separately, from SDC Publications and this author.
>
> Successfully passing this exam is a great addition to your resume and could help set you apart and help you land a great job. People who pass the official exam receive a certificate signed by the CEO of Autodesk, the makers of Revit.

Self-Exam:

The following questions can be used as a way to check your knowledge of this lesson. The answers can be found at the bottom of the page.

1. You have to manually fill in the reference bubbles after setting up the sheets. (T/F)
2. You cannot control the visibility of objects per *viewport.* (T/F)
3. It is possible to see a listing of only the views that have not been placed on a sheet via the *Project Browser.* (T/F)
4. You only have to enter your name on one titleblock, not all. (T/F)
5. Use the ______________ tool to create another drawing sheet.

Review Questions:

The following questions may be assigned by your instructor as a way to assess your knowledge of this section. Your instructor has the answers to the review questions.

1. You need to use a special tool from the *Ribbon* to edit text in the titleblock. (T/F)
2. The template you started with has two titleblocks to choose from. (T/F)
3. You only have to enter the project name on one sheet, not all. (T/F)
4. The scale of a drawing placed on a sheet is determined by the scale set in that view's *Properties.* (T/F)
5. You can save a list of drawing sheets to be plotted. (T/F)
6. Use the __________________ tool to edit the model from a sheet view.
7. The reference bubbles will not automatically update if a drawing is moved to another sheet. (T/F)
8. On new sheets, the sheet number on the titleblock will increase by one from the previous sheet number. (T/F)
9. DWF files can consist of an entire set of drawings which a client/owner can view with a free download, similar to Adobe PDF files. (T/F)
10. It is not possible to remove a sheet from the *Sheet List* without deleting that sheet from the project. (T/F)

SELF-EXAM ANSWERS:
1 – F, **2** – F, **3** – T, **4** – F, **5** – Sheet

Notes:

INDEX

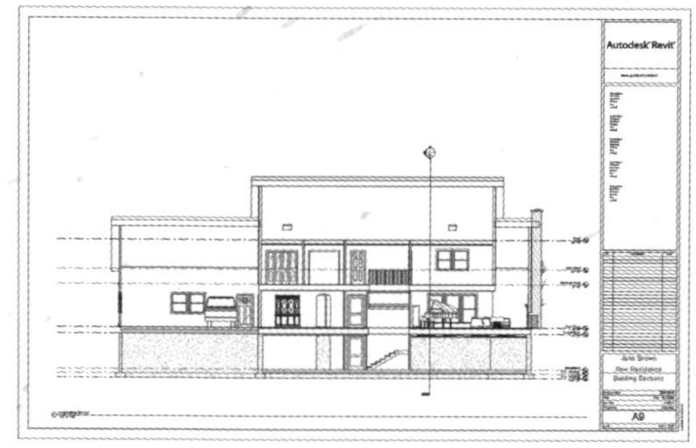

Sections *Sample image from page 15-7*

Renderings *Sample image from page 14-44*

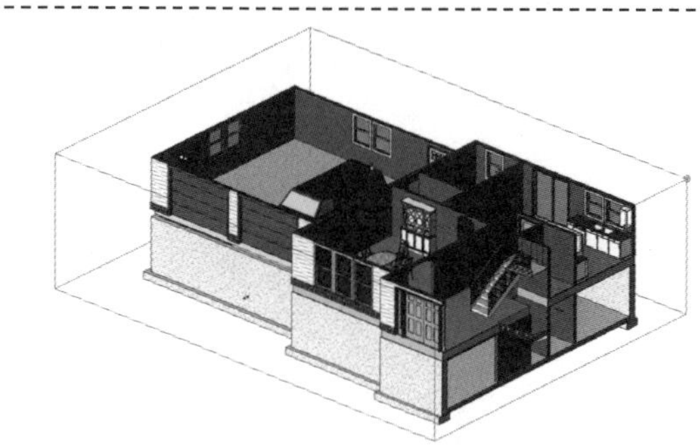

3D Views *Sample image from page 14-29*

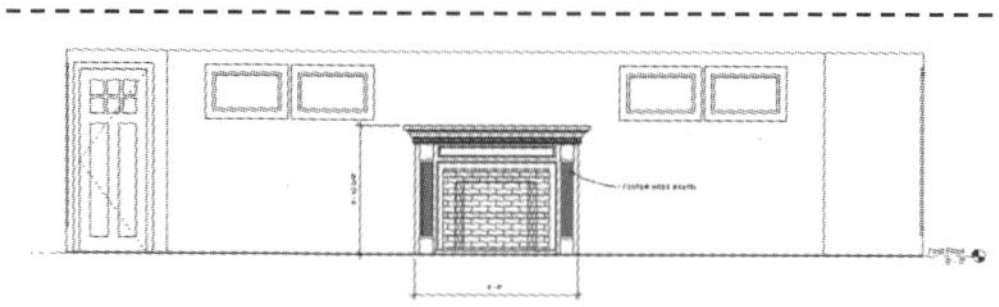

Interior Elevations *Sample image from page 10-23*

Notes:

Autodesk User Certification Exam
Be sure to check out Appendix A for an overview of the official Autodesk User Certification Exam and the available study book and software, sold separately, from SDC Publications and this author.

Successfully passing this exam is a great addition to your resume and could help set you apart and help you land a great a job. People who pass the official exam receive a certificate signed by the CEO of Autodesk, the makers of Revit.